Foods
THAT
Harm
Foods
THAT
Heal

READER'S DIGEST

FOODS
THAT
HARM
FOODS
THAT
HEAL

AN A-Z GUIDE TO SAFE AND HEALTHY EATING

 Reader's Digest

The Reader's Digest Association (Canada) Ltd., Montreal

Address any comments about
Foods That Harm, Foods That Heal to
Editor, General Books, c/o Customer Service,
Reader's Digest, 215 Redfern Ave.,
Westmount, Quebec H3Z 2V9.
Website address: http://www.readersdigest.ca

To order additional copies of
Foods That Harm, Foods That Heal,
call 1–888–459–5555.

Canadian Cataloguing in Publication Data
Main entry under title: Foods that harm, foods that heal
Includes index.
  ISBN 0-88850-536-1
  1. Dietetics. 2. Health—Nutritional aspects. 3. Nutrition.
I. Reader's Digest Association (Canada).
TX355.F65 1997   615.8'54   C96-900159-2

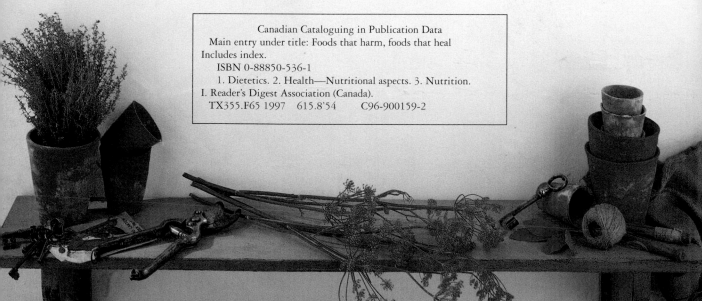

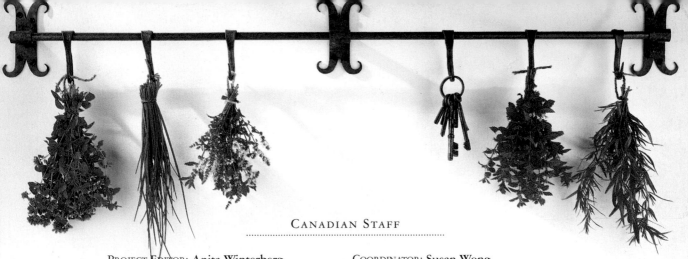

CANADIAN STAFF

PROJECT EDITOR: **Anita Winterberg**
DESIGNER: **Andrée Payette**
COPY EDITOR: **Gilles Humbert**
PICTURE RESEARCHER: **Rachel Irwin**
PRODUCTION MANAGER: **Holger Lorenzen**

COORDINATOR: **Susan Wong**
ART DIRECTOR: **John McGuffie**
EDITORIAL DIRECTOR, BOOKS AND
   HOME ENTERTAINMENT: **Deirdre Gilbert**
CONSULTANT: **Joseph A. Schwarcz, Ph.D.**

U.S. STAFF

PROJECT EDITOR: **Suzanne E. Weiss**
PROJECT ART EDITOR: **Marisa Gentile Raffio**
EDITOR: **Theresa Lane**

EDITORIAL ASSISTANT: **Vita Gardner**
SENIOR ASSOCIATE ART EDITOR: **Todd Victor**
ASSOCIATE ART EDITOR: **Bruce R. McKillip**

CONTRIBUTORS

EDITORIAL DIRECTOR/PRODUCER
Genell J. Subak-Sharpe, M.S.

MEDICAL CONSULTANTS
Morton D. Bogdonoff, M.D.
  Professor of Medicine
  New York Hospital–Cornell Medical Center
Karen Levine, R.D.
  Staff Dietitian
  Harlem Hospital Center

WRITERS/EDITORS
Arlyn Apollo
Diana Benzaia
Jean Callahan
Mikola De Roo
Nicole Freeland
Emily Paulsen
Rosemary Perkins
Ann Forer Stockton

TECHNICAL SUPPORT
Debra Rabinowitz
Dushan G. Lukic
Carl Li

INDEXER
Rose Bernal
Joseph Marchetti

RESEARCHERS
Helene MacLean
Sarah Subak-Sharpe

COPY EDITORS
Gina Grant
Diana Marsh
Joseph Marchetti
Judy Yelon

PHOTOGRAPHERS
Karl Adamson
Colin Cooke
Gus Filgate
Vernon Morgan
Carol Sharpe
Jon Stewart

FOOD STYLISTS
Nir Adar
Karen Temple

ILLUSTRATORS
Julia Bigg
Diek Bonson
Glynn Boyd Harte
Clare Melinsky
Francis Scappatricci
Lesli Sternberg
Sam Thompson
Charlotte Wess

NOTE TO READERS:

The information in this book should not be
substituted for, or used to alter, medical therapy
without your doctor's advice. For a specific health problem,
consult your physician for guidance.

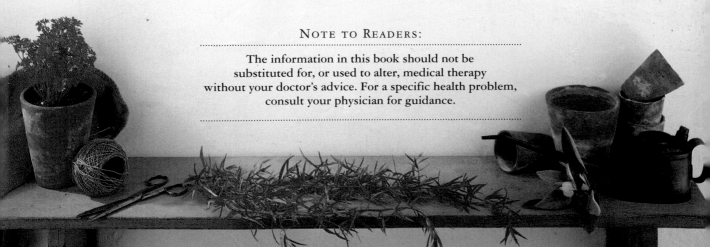

ABOUT THIS BOOK

More than ever, people are realizing that what they eat does make a difference, not only in the way they look and feel but also in the length and quality of their lives. But if you are like most people, you are confused by the often conflicting headlines and sound bites proclaiming that what was "in" yesterday is "out" today. Are eggs again on the "safe" list? Are organic foods really more nutritious than conventionally grown ones? Can eating lots of fruits and vegetables really lower your risk of cancer? These are but a few of the questions answered in clear, understandable terms in FOODS THAT HARM, FOODS THAT HEAL.

In preparing this book, a team of medical experts has sifted through thousands of scientific studies and reports in order to separate the hype and myths from the facts. Impartial, up-to-date, and supported by scientific evidence, FOODS THAT HARM, FOODS THAT HEAL stresses that if you follow the basic tenets of variety, moderation, and balance and plan your daily diet in accordance with Health Canada's Food Guide Rainbow, you'll find you can partake of almost every food without worry or guilt. You'll also learn how you can use foods to lower your risk of many common diseases, and what you should eat if you fall ill.

Following a simple A-to-Z format, FOODS THAT HARM, FOODS THAT HEAL provides invaluable information about foods, nutrients, and dozens of common diseases. There are special features on eating during the different life stages, from infancy to old age, as well as such timely issues as genetically altered foods, irradiation, pesticides, and pollution.

You can tell at a glance the major nutrients in foods, their benefits, and drawbacks. In general, a food described as an excellent source of a vitamin or mineral will supply all or most of the Recommended Nutrient Intake (RNI) of that particular nutrient. Such terms as "good"

and "useful" indicate lesser, but still valuable, amounts; consult the text for more specific amounts and percentages. Cross-references, printed in small capital letters, guide you to related entries. A glossary defines unfamiliar or technical terms; there is also a listing of useful organizations that can provide further information and resources.

Throughout, there is one important underlying message: Eating healthful foods need not be complicated or dull; it can be a pleasurable experience, made even more so by knowledge and understanding.

—Joe Schwarcz, Ph.D.

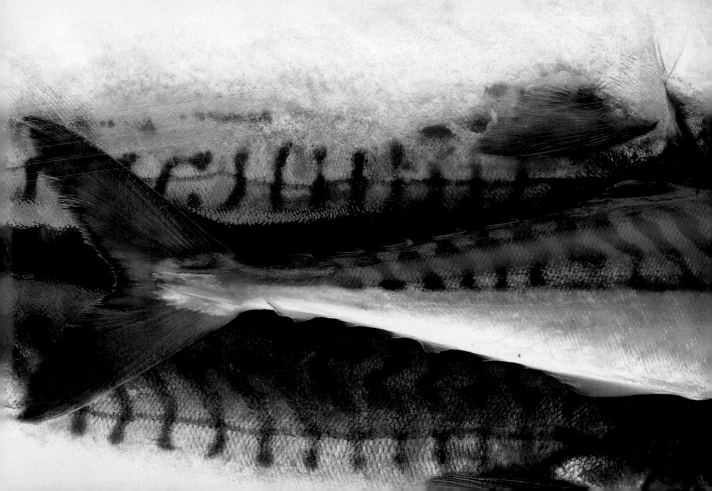

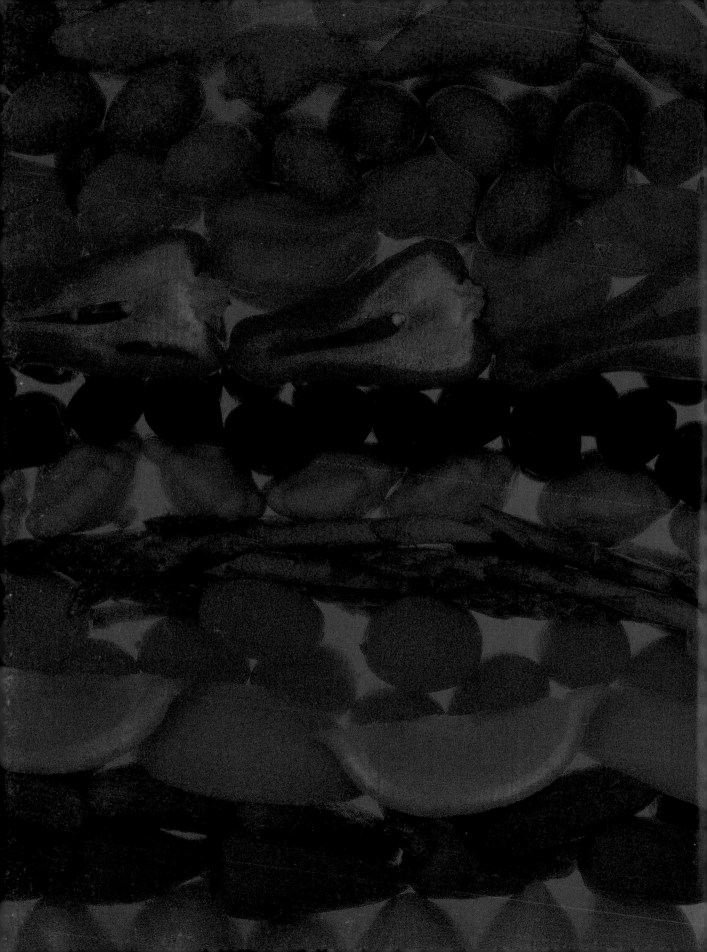

ACNE

EAT PLENTY OF
- *Fresh fruits and vegetables for vitamins A and C.*
- *Whole grains and cereals for B vitamins and zinc.*
- *Lean meat, poultry, and fish for zinc.*

AVOID
- *Kelp supplements.*
- *Iodized salt.*
- *High doses of B vitamins.*

Almost everyone experiences an occasional flare-up of acne—usually just a few blackheads and pimples, less often deep, scarring cysts. Although acne can occur at any age, it is most prevalent during adolescence, afflicting 85 percent of all teenagers to varying degrees.

Dermatologists stress that diet and other lifestyle factors, including cleanliness and sexual activity, do not cause acne. Still, parents and even some teen magazines keep the diet myth alive by insisting that eating chocolate, French fries, sweets, and other high-fat, sugary teen favorites can lead to acne. In rare instances, sensitivity to a food may exacerbate existing acne, but it is unlikely that any food actually causes it. (An exception is kelp, a seaweed sold as a dietary supplement or a salt substitute; it can cause severe cystic acne. Iodized salt can also provoke an acne flare-up.)

Hormones are responsible for most cases of acne. The surge of androgens (male sex hormones) that occurs during puberty prompts the skin's oil (sebaceous) glands to enlarge and increases the production of sebum, the oily substance that lubricates the skin. Boys are more severely affected by acne than girls. Still, even adult women find that acne flares up in periods of hormonal change, such as before menstruation, during pregnancy, or at the time of menopause.

Androgens also stimulate the growth of body hair and cause increased shedding of the cells that line follicles, the skin cavities from which hair grows. This cellular debris then clogs pores and blocks the flow of sebum; the resulting swollen glands form a whitehead, or closed comedo. If part of the pore remains open, the sebum exposed to oxygen darkens and becomes a blackhead; any inflammation will result in a pus-filled pimple. Cystic acne, the most severe form, develops when the blocked glands become infected by bacteria that normally inhabit the skin.

Because severe acne tends to run in families, heredity is suspected of playing a role in causing it. A number of medications can also cause acne; major offenders include steroids and other hormonal agents, iodine preparations, lithium, anticonvulsants, and drugs used to treat tuberculosis. The use of oily makeup can further clog pores and worsen acne; exposure to industrial oils and chemicals, such as naphthalenes and biphenyls, can cause acne too.

Stress often triggers a flare-up of acne, most likely by altering hormone levels. In turn, hormonal changes can stimulate food cravings, especially for chocolates and other sweets. Consequently, the acne sufferer may erroneously attribute the acne to gorging on chocolates or sweets, rather than stress, the real culprit for both.

DIET AND SKIN HEALTH

Clear, glowing skin reflects overall good health. This requires not only a balanced diet but also regular exercise, adequate sleep, and avoiding such detrimental habits as smoking and excessive exposure of the skin to sun. Vitamins A and C are essential for building and maintaining healthy skin; a daily diet that provides five or more servings of fresh vegetables and fruits (at least one citrus) will provide adequate amounts of these nutrients. B vitamins are thought to regulate sebum production; whole-grain cereals and breads, dried beans and other legumes, and lean meats are excellent sources of these vitamins. These foods also provide good amounts of zinc, a mineral that some studies link to skin health.

Some teenagers attempt to self-treat acne with high-dose vitamin and mineral supplements, an approach that can actually worsen the condition. Recent studies show that high doses of vitamins B_1, B_6, and B_{12} can trigger acne, and high doses of vitamin A can cause dry, flaking skin and hair loss.

ACNE TREATMENTS

Once or twice a day, gently wash the skin with a mild, nonmedicated unscented soap, rinse with cool water, and pat dry. Avoid scrubbing or using abrasive pads or grains—these irritate the skin and can even worsen acne. If the skin is very oily, wipe it gently with a cotton ball soaked in witch hazel. Use water-based, unscented cosmetics.

Most persistent mild to moderate acne can usually be controlled with nonprescription drugs, such as 2.5- or 5-percent strength benzoyl peroxide gel, lotion, or ointment. Start with a nightly application, and after a week add a morning application. Improvement should occur within 3 weeks; if not, try a stronger 10-percent solution.

A dermatologist may prescribe tretinoin, a topical medication derived from vitamin A; an antibiotic, in either topical or pill form, may also be tried. Isotretinoin (Accutane), a potent oral drug, is reserved for severe cystic acne.

ADDITIVES: HELPFUL OR HARMFUL?

For centuries, people have enhanced their foods with various flavorings, preservatives, and dyes. Still, consumers worry that some of the food additives in use today may be harmful.

Few foods reach today's supermarkets free of additives, substances that do not occur naturally in a food. These include preservatives to prevent spoilage; emulsifiers to prevent water and fat from separating; thickeners; vitamins and minerals, either to replace nutrients lost in processing or to increase nutritional value; sugar, artificial sweeteners, salt, and other flavorings to improve taste; and dyes to make everything from oranges to soft drinks more visually appealing.

In all, Canadian food processors may use any of about 2,800 additives. Although many people question the safety of these additives, there is little evidence that they constitute a major health risk for most people. In fact, thanks to some of these additives, Canadians enjoy history's safest and most abundant assortment of foods.

The most common food additives are sugar, corn syrup, other sweeteners, and salt; they are used both to enhance flavor and to retard spoilage. Many other additives offer their own unique health benefits; these include calcium, as well as ascorbic acid (vitamin C),

HIDDEN EXTRAS.
Accidental additives, such as pesticides and the hormones fed to some farm animals, make their way into our food.

BENEFITS
- *Prevent spoilage and rancidity.*
- *Enhance flavor and appearance.*
- *Boost nutritional content.*

DRAWBACKS
- *Susceptible people may suffer allergic or adverse reactions.*
- *Some can exacerbate medical conditions.*

---

vitamin E, and other ANTIOXIDANTS that prevent fats from turning rancid and also may protect against cancer, heart disease, and other diseases.

More problematic, at least to the public, are substances with strange chemical names like sodium stearyl fumarate (an additive to improve the texture and handling properties of baked goods)

and dioctyl sodium sulfosuccinate (an emulsifier and flavor enhancer in processed foods). These substances are considered harmless, but consumers who don't understand why such chemical compounds are added to foods are understandably wary.

THE QUESTIONABLE FEW

The majority of food additives are without a doubt safe, but there are exceptions, and every now and then, one is removed from the market. The fact that some dyes, such as Red # 2, are allowed in Canada but are banned in the U.S. demonstrates that in some cases, "safety" is open to interpretation. On the other hand, controversial actions have

COMMON FOOD ADDITIVES

Consumer concerns over food additives often stem from misinformation or confusion over long chemical names.

All new additives receive federal government approval; older additives are presumed to be generally safe.

TYPE OF ADDITIVE	FOUND IN	FUNCTION
PRESERVATIVES		
Antimicrobials		
Benzoic acid and benzoates	Soft drinks, beer, fruit products, margarine, acidic foods.	Extend shelf life and protect food from fungi and bacteria.
Nitrites and nitrates	Processed meats, such as sausages, hot dogs, bacon, ham, and lunch meats. Smoked fish.	Extend shelf life and protect food from fungi and bacteria; preserve color in meats and dried fruits.
Sulfites	Dried fruits, shredded coconut, fruit-based pie fillings, relishes.	Extend shelf life and protect food from fungi and bacteria.
Antioxidants		
Ascorbic acid (vitamin C) and ascorbates	Fruit products (juices, jams, and canned fruits), acidic foods, and fatty foods that become rancid.	Ascorbates prevent fruit juices from turning brown and fatty foods from becoming rancid. They also improve baking quality in wheat.
BHA or BHT	Fatty foods that can turn rancid, such as baked products, cereals, potato chips, and fats and oils.	Prevents fatty foods from turning rancid when exposed to oxygen.
Tocopherols (vitamin E)	Oils and shortenings.	Prevent rancidity in fats and other damage to food due to exposure to oxygen.

COLORINGS		
Beta carotene	Many processed foods, especially sweets and products marketed for children, soft drinks, baked goods, and confectionery items, such as frosting, jams, and margarine. Also used in bologna and other processed meats as well as to color the skins of oranges and certain other fruits.	Make food look more appetizing by meeting people's food color expectations; for example, turning cherry Jell-O red.
Caramel		
Carrot oil		
Citrus red # 1		
Dehydrated beets		
FD&C colors: Blue # 1, 2; Red # 2; Yellow # 5, 6		

FLAVOR ENHANCERS		
Dioctyl sodium-sulfosuccinate	Mixes, processed foods.	Improve the flavor of many canned or processed foods.
Disodium guanylate	Canned meats, meat-based foods.	
Hydrolyzed vegetable protein	Mixes, stock, processed meats.	
Monosodium glutamate (MSG)	Chinese food, dry mixes, stock cubes, and canned, processed, and frozen meats.	Heightens taste perception so that foods seem to taste better.

EMULSIFIERS, STABILIZERS, AND THICKENERS		
Carrageenan	Sauces, soups, breads, baked goods, frozen desserts, ice cream, low-fat and artificial cream cheese, condiments, jams, jellies, chocolate, puddings, and milk shakes.	Improve texture and consistency of processed foods by increasing smoothness, creaminess, and volume. Hold in moisture and prevent separation of oil and water. Excessive pectin can result in bloating.
Cellulose		
Glycerol		
Guar gum		
Gum arabic		
Lecithin		
Pectins		

MONOSODIUM GLUTAMATE

Used as a flavor enhancer, monosodium glutamate (MSG) is a common ingredient in Oriental cooking. It tastes salty and slightly bitter, but does not actually change the flavor of food. Instead, it acts on the tongue to heighten the perception of certain tastes and minimize others. Thus, it masks the unpleasant taste of fermented or slightly spoiled foods and brings out other more agreeable flavors.

MSG occurs naturally in dried seaweed; more commonly, it is made from wheat or corn gluten or the liquid waste of sugar-beet refining. In susceptible people, MSG may trigger headaches, various idiosyncratic reactions, or a flare-up of CELIAC DISEASE symptoms.

fueled worries about complete groups of additives in some instances. The case of artificial sweeteners is a prime example. Cyclamates were banned in the U.S. in 1969, when a group of researchers reported an apparent increased incidence of cancer in rats fed large amounts of the sweetener. Canadian authorities were not convinced that this study showed a risk for humans, and Canada, and at least 40 other countries, allows the use of cyclamates. Saccharin, on the other hand, is allowed as an additive in the U.S.; in Canada, however, it may be sold only as a tabletop sweetener. The issue, once again, is possible carcinogenicity based on studies of rats fed massive amounts of saccharin, but humans have been using saccharin for over a hundred years with no ill effects. Aspartame was approved despite concerns over its potential problems for people with phenylketonuria, a rare hereditary metabolic disorder. Some studies also suggest that in isolated cases aspartame can trigger seizures or headaches, but the vast majority use it without obvious problems.

ACCIDENTAL ADDITIVES

Some 10,000 substances make their way into food during growing, processing, and packaging; some of these accidental additives can pose more of a health threat than preservatives and other direct additives. Some foods, for example, contain traces of pesticides sprayed on crops or applied to the soil. Environmental POLLUTANTS in foods, such as PCBs, mercury, and lead, are harmful when ingested in large quantities.

Sometimes allergic reactions that are blamed on foods or intentional additives are actually triggered by an unintended additive. For example, a person who has never had a food allergy may inexplicably develop hives or a rash after drinking milk. In some cases, allergists have traced the symptoms to penicillin rather than to the milk itself. How does this antibiotic get into milk? Mastitis, a common problem in cows, is treated with penicillin injected directly into the udder. The resulting small amounts of penicillin in the milk would not be harmful for most people, only to those who are allergic to the drug.

A PRUDENT APPROACH

Even though the benefits of most food additives outweigh any potential risks, prudence and moderation should prevail in their use, and some can be avoided entirely. A person concerned about food dyes, for example, usually can buy natural items, such as undyed oranges, which may have a mottled, pale yellow or green-tinged skin. The natural fruit may not be as pretty as the color-treated, but it will taste as good or perhaps even better, because it has ripened longer on the tree.

Some additives pose problems for people with certain medical conditions. Anyone with high blood pressure or any condition that mandates a low-salt diet should check the labels on all processed foods for various forms of sodium, all of which contain salt. Similarly, people trying to reduce sugar intake should look for lactose and other ingredients ending in "ose"; these are forms of sugar. Those with an inherited tendency to store excessive iron, a condition called hemochromatosis, should avoid iron-enriched breads, cereals, and other products. Sulfites used to preserve the color of dried fruits, frozen French fries, and sauerkraut can trigger an asthma attack in susceptible people.

Some additives amount to overkill; this is especially true of highly fortified cereals. It's unrealistic to expect a bowl of cereal to provide 100 percent of the Recommended Nutrient Intake (RNI) for a dozen or more vitamins and minerals; a high-fiber, whole-grain cereal is just as healthful. Calcium is now added to orange juice, bread, and a variety of other foods. These products may be fine for someone who shuns milk and other foods naturally high in calcium, but may actually be harmful to people who suffer from rare conditions such as milk-alkali syndrome, characterized by too much calcium in the blood.

Remember, too, that preserved foods have more additives than their fresh counterparts. Fresh meat, poultry, and fish do not contain the nitrates and other preservatives found in smoked or processed meats.

AGING AND DIET

*As you get older, your body's energy needs drop; at the
same time, demands for some nutrients increase. New studies
indicate some of these can slow the aging process.*

While aging is inevitable, many of the degenerative changes that prevail among the elderly are not if preventive steps are taken. Recent medical research confirms that good nutrition can prevent or at least slow such debilitating conditions as osteoporosis, diabetes, and heart disease. In fact, one report estimates that one-third to one-half of the health problems of people over the age of 65 are related to diet. In contrast, various studies of Mormons, Seventh-Day Adventists, and Trappist monks—all people who follow a vegetarian diet and engage in a prudent lifestyle—show that they enjoy increased life expectancy.

On the whole, the elderly are the most poorly nourished group of all North Americans. There are many reasons for this: A person's appetite and the senses of taste and smell decline with age, making food considerably less appealing. Many older people experience difficulty chewing; in addition, heartburn, constipation, lactose intolerance, and other digestive problems increase with age and contribute to poor nutrition. The loss of a partner, or difficulty in shopping or preparing meals, may result in a person subsisting on tea, toast, sweets, canned soups, and other convenience foods that provide little nutrition.

A number of older people living on a fixed income usually cannot afford such nutritious foods as fresh fruits, vegetables, fish, and meat. Also, some of them fall victim to nutrition quackery or engage in misguided self-treatment with high-dose vitamins and minerals. None of these problems are insoluble, but finding solutions to them may take a bit of effort (see Practical Tips, p.15).

CHANGING NEEDS

A person's body composition changes with age, as muscle mass decreases, often due to disuse, and fatty tissue increases. Because metabolism slows down, fewer calories are required; experts estimate that the average person should consume 10 percent fewer calories for every decade after the age of 50. Therefore, a 50-year-old who needs 1,800 calories a day will require 1,440 at age 70, and perhaps even fewer if he is sedentary. People who

AN APPETITE FOR LIVING. *A meal is always more enjoyable when shared with friends. Try to eat a balanced diet, whatever your age.*

BASIC DIETARY RECOMMENDATIONS

The National Institute on Aging in the United States recommends that an older person's daily diet include the minimum number of servings outlined below. Sugar, salt, and fats should be used sparingly; alcohol should be consumed only in moderation, defined as one drink a day for women and two for men.

FOOD GROUP	PROVIDES
STARCHES (COMPLEX CARBOHYDRATES)	
At least 5 servings: Whole grains, breads, and cereals; brown rice, kasha, millet, and other grains; dried beans, peas, lentils, and other legumes; potatoes, pasta, and other starchy foods.	Thiamine, riboflavin, niacin, folate, B_6 and other B vitamins; fiber; and complete protein when grains and legumes are combined.
VEGETABLES AND FRUITS	
At least 5 servings: Fresh vegetables and fruits, including dark green leafy vegetables, such as broccoli, cabbage, kale, and spinach; yellow vegetables, such as carrots and squash; citrus fruits, berries, tomatoes, bananas, and other fruits.	Vitamins C and A, beta carotene, riboflavin, folate, various minerals, and fiber. These are needed to prevent deficiency disorders and may protect against cancer.
HIGH-PROTEIN FOODS	
At least 2 servings: Lean beef, lamb, chicken and other poultry; fish and other seafood; eggs, tofu, and a combination of grains and legumes.	Thiamine, riboflavin, niacin, and vitamins E, B_6, and B_{12}; iron, zinc, and other minerals. Canned sardines and salmon with bones provide calcium.
DAIRY PRODUCTS	
At least 2 servings: Low-fat milk, cheese, yogurt, and other milk products. (Choose lactose-reduced milk and yogurt if you have trouble digesting regular milk; see INTOLERANCE.)	Protein, calcium, vitamins A and D. Needed to prevent the loss of bone minerals that frequently occurs with increasing age.

fail to cut back on food intake are likely to gain weight, increasing the risk of heart disease, diabetes, and osteoarthritis.

With increasing age, the body is less efficient in absorbing and using some nutrients; osteoporosis and other medical conditions common among older people also change nutritional needs. Consequently, an older person is likely to need extra amounts of the following essential nutrients:

Calcium to prevent osteoporosis and maintain healthy bones.

Vitamin D, which the body needs in order to absorb the calcium.

Vitamin B_{12} to build red blood cells and maintain healthy nerves.

Vitamin E to help protect against heart disease.

Zinc to help compensate for lowered immunity due to aging.

Potassium, especially in the presence of high blood pressure or the use of diuretic drugs.

Fiber to prevent constipation.

A LITTLE VARIETY.
A balanced diet that contains a wide assortment of fresh foods will usually provide all the vitamins, minerals, and energy that an older person needs to maintain optimal health and vitality.

Some doctors recommend a daily vitamin and mineral supplement to ensure that an older person takes in 100 percent of the Recommended Nutrient Intakes (RNIs). Others feel this is unnecessary if the person eats a varied diet (see Basic Dietary Recommendations, facing page). In any event, high-dose supplements should be avoided unless recommended by a physician or dietitian, as they can lead to nutritional imbalances. For example, zinc supplements can interfere with the body's use of folic acid; iron can inhibit proper calcium and zinc absorption; vitamin A overdose can even cause death.

PRACTICAL TIPS

• Plan meals for regular times during the day rather than snacking.
• Strive to make meals pleasurable, even if you're eating alone. Set the table or prepare an attractive tray. Turn on your favorite music to improve your mood.
• If you dislike eating alone, organize regular potluck meals with friends and neighbors. Or consider joining an organization that provides an opportunity to dine with others.
• Select foods that provide contrasts in color, texture, and flavor. Avoid adding salt to improve flavor; instead, use herbs and spices. A sprinkling of nutmeg or cinnamon can compensate for a diminished sense of taste.
• A small glass of wine or beer with a meal aids digestion and adds to eating pleasure. But don't substitute alcohol for food, and check with your doctor to make sure that it does not interact with any medications you might be taking.
• Make sure you drink six to eight glasses of water, juice, or other nonalcoholic fluid a day. Older people often experience decreased thirst or they reduce fluid intake because of bladder-control problems. This can contribute to constipation and kidney problems

and increase the risk of dehydration in hot weather.
• If you have trouble chewing, there's no need to resort to a bland liquid diet, which can lead to constipation and perhaps even malnutrition. Instead, prepare fish or ground meat and purée vegetables, soups, and other nutritious foods.
• Take daily walks or engage in other

Case Study

Joe, a 71-year-old retired accountant, had never paid much attention to shopping and cooking—his wife had always taken care of those chores. When his wife died, Joe found mealtimes increasingly trying. He didn't like to eat alone in restaurants, although now and then he'd go on an excursion to pick up a sandwich from the neighborhood deli. Joe tried frozen TV dinners a few times but rarely enjoyed the way they tasted. About the only time he had a real meal was when friends invited him to eat with them. Otherwise, Joe's diet consisted of cold cereal and canned beans or soup.

Over several months, Joe came down with a number of colds. He often felt tired and listless, feelings that he attributed to lingering sadness and loneliness after his wife's death.

When Joe's sister, Elsa, came to visit for a few days, she was appalled by his diet and emotional state. "You're not getting any vegetables or fruits," she admonished him. "No wonder you feel run-down and catch one cold after another!" Still, she realized that nagging would not

get Joe out of his doldrums; he needed motivation and guidance.

Elsa found that the local Seniors Center had a daily lunch program; even better, she learned the center also offered a cooking course. Elsa finally convinced Joe to check out the latter.

Happily, the cooking class turned out to be exactly what Joe needed. He enjoyed learning to make interesting meals, and a trip to the supermarket gave Joe insight into buying fresh produce. Some fellow students were also without partners, and they began to cook and eat together.

At the urging of the class instructor, Joe helped organize weekly home cooking sessions, in which class members took turns playing host. Between sessions, Joe practiced his new food shopping and preparation skills. As he later confided to his sister, the cooking classes helped change his life. Joe not only found new friends and an enjoyable hobby, but he also began to pay more attention to eating a balanced, healthful diet.

exercise, but first consult your doctor for an appropriate routine. Exercise not only preserves muscle strength but also improves appetite and mood.
• If you're on a tight budget, organize a shopping co-op with others in a similar situation. Buying larger quantities is more economical; share with others, or divide the food into smaller portions and freeze them for future use.

AIDS AND HIV INFECTION

CONSUME PLENTY OF
- *Meat, liver, eggs, milk, and other high-calorie, high-protein foods to prevent weight and muscle loss.*
- *Pasta and other starchy foods, cooked vegetables, pasteurized juices, and canned or stewed fruits for essential vitamins and minerals.*

CUT DOWN ON
- *Fatty foods and whole-grain products if they cause diarrhea.*
- *Coffee, tea, and other caffeinated drinks that can cause diarrhea and reduce absorption of some nutrients.*

AVOID
- *Raw or undercooked foods, especially shellfish, eggs, and rare or uncooked processed meats.*
- *Alcohol, which can worsen diarrhea and interact with AIDS medications.*

There is still no cure for AIDS (acquired immune deficiency syndrome), nor is there a special diet for people infected with HIV, the human immunodeficiency virus that causes the disease. But good nutrition can help prevent or delay weight loss and other AIDS complications. Doctors often advise HIV-positive patients to consult a qualified clinical dietitian, preferably while still healthy, to learn about sound nutrition.

Asymptomatic HIV-infected individuals should follow the same dietary practices recommended for healthy people, but with added precautions. Because the HIV organism attacks the immune system, it makes a person more vulnerable to infections, including FOOD POISONING from salmonella, shigella, campylobacter, and other bacteria. Such food-borne infections occur more frequently and are more severe in people with reduced immunity.

AIDS is a wasting disease, and death is often due to starvation rather than to other HIV complications. An AIDS patient should eat as much as possible and, unless markedly obese, not worry about gaining a few pounds. The extra weight can be critical in seeing a patient through a crisis when he can't eat.

Unfortunately, maintaining good nutrition is complicated by the ways in which AIDS affects the digestive system. It reduces absorption of nutrients, especially folate, riboflavin, thiamine, and vitamins B_6 and B_{12}; it often causes intractable DIARRHEA, which causes further nutritional loss; and it increases the risk of intestinal infections. Many AIDS patients also suffer appetite loss and bouts of nausea, either from the disease or from medications.

If rapid weight loss occurs, the patient may require artificial (hyperalimentation) feeding; this is generally administered through a gastric feeding tube inserted into the stomach or an intravenous line that pumps predigested nutrients into the bloodstream. Some AIDS specialists advise starting artificial feeding even before there is rapid weight loss, especially if nutrients are not being absorbed properly.

FOOD SAFETY

Anyone who is HIV-positive, or a person who prepares food for an AIDS patient, must pay special attention to food safety. Eggs should be boiled for at least 7 minutes or cooked until hard; meat and fish should be cooked until well done, with an internal temperature of 165°F (74°C) to 212°F (100°C). Raw oysters and other shellfish, sushi, steak tartare, rare hamburgers and roast beef as well as homemade mayonnaise and ice cream made with raw eggs must be avoided. Commercial mayonnaise and hard ice cream and sherbet are safe.

Fruits and vegetables are not as likely to cause problems as animal products. Even so, they should be washed carefully in soapy water and rinsed thoroughly. Many doctors advise following the same precautions as when traveling abroad; eat only cooked vegetables, and eat fruits that are peeled, stewed, or canned. Others feel that salads and some raw fruits and vegetables are safe but warn that these may be difficult for an AIDS patient to digest.

USE OF SUPPLEMENTS

Nutritionists generally recommend that HIV-positive people take a multiple vitamin and mineral pill to prevent nutritional deficiencies; however, supplements with more than 100 percent of the Recommended Nutrient Intakes (RNIs) should be used only if prescribed by a doctor. Many patients self-treat with high-dose supplements, a course that can lead to serious problems. High doses of vitamin C, for example, can worsen diarrhea.

Some self-help groups advocate taking high doses of zinc and selenium to bolster the immune system. There is no proof that supplements of these nutrients protect against AIDS-related infections; in fact, studies show that taking 200mg to 300mg of zinc a day for 6 weeks actually lowers immunity. Excessive selenium can also cause nausea, vomiting, and diarrhea.

Another dangerous dietary approach entails following a macrobiotic regimen, especially one that is restricted to brown rice and a few vegetables. Such a diet can actually worsen AIDS, because it fails to provide adequate nutrition; additionally, the excessive fiber can exacerbate diarrhea.

Herbal medicine is a popular self-care approach, though there is no evidence for its efficacy. Caution is needed as some herbal preparations contain substances that can cause serious side effects or interact with medications. Check with a doctor before taking any herbal or other preparation or engaging in self-treatment or alternative medicine.

ALCOHOL

BENEFITS

- *Moderate consumption cuts heart-attack risk by raising HDL cholesterol.*
- *In small amounts, it can improve appetite and aid digestion.*
- *May foster a happy mood.*

DRAWBACKS

- *Can provoke mood swings, aggression, and hangovers.*
- *Interacts with many medications.*
- *Over time, moderate to high intake increases the risk of cancers, stroke, heart and liver disease, and dementia.*

People have used alcohol in one form or another since prehistoric times. While alcohol is drunk for its mood-altering effects, in the past it was also used as an anesthetic, tonic, and disinfectant. Even today, alcohol is an ingredient in many over-the-counter medications.

Ethyl alcohol (ethanol), the main active ingredient of alcoholic beverages, is made by yeast fermentation of starch or sugar. Almost any sweet or starchy food—potatoes, grains, honey, grapes and other fruits, even dandelions—can be turned into alcohol.

Unlike most foods, alcohol is not digested; instead, 95 percent of it is absorbed into the bloodstream from the stomach and small intestine within an hour after ingestion. (The other 5 percent is eliminated through the kidneys, lungs, or skin.) The liver breaks down, or metabolizes, alcohol; the time this takes depends upon whether the alcohol is ingested with food and upon the person's sex, weight, body type, and tolerance level, which increases with time and use. On average, however, it takes the liver 3 to 5 hours to completely metabolize an ounce of alcohol.

Although the effect is the same over time, distilled liquors, such as whiskey and gin, have a more immediate impact than wines or beers, and all alcohol is

WHAT'S IN A DRINK

Alcohol contains 7 calories per gram, compared with 4 calories per gram of protein or carbohydrate and 9 calories per gram of fat. Some wines provide small amounts of iron and potassium, and beer contains niacin, vitamin B$_6$, chromium, and phosphorus. To benefit from the nutrients in these beverages, you would have to consume much more than the recommended limit of two drinks per day for a man or one for a woman. Each beverage listed below provides about ½ ounce of ethanol, the usual definition of a drink.

ITEM	ALCOHOL VOLUME	SERVING SIZE (OZ)	CALORIES
MIXED DRINKS WITH DISTILLED SPIRITS			
Bloody Mary	12%	5	116
Daiquiri	28%	2	111
Gin and tonic	9%	7.5	171
Manhattan	37%	2	128
Martini	38%	2.5	156
Piña colada	12%	4.5	262
Screwdriver	8%	7	174
Tequila sunrise	14%	5.5	189
Tom Collins	9%	7.5	121
Whiskey sour (using bottled mix)	17%	3.5	160
WINE AND WINE-RELATED PRODUCTS			
Regular wines	10%–14%	4	85
Sweet white wine	10%–14%	4	100
Light wines	6%–10%	5	65
Wine coolers (fruit juice, carbonated water, white wine, sugar)	3.5%–6%	12	220
Port	19%	4	158
Sherry	19%	3	125
ORDINARY BEER			
Regular	3%–5%	12	150
Light	3%–5%	12	100
STRONGER BREWED BEVERAGES			
Ales, porters, stouts, and malt liquors	5%–8%	12	150

COMPARISON OF UNIT MEASURES

½ oz ethanol = 1½ oz of 80-proof liquor = 4 oz or 5 oz of wine = 12 oz of beer

absorbed more quickly when mixed with a carbonated beverage, such as club soda. Once in the bloodstream, alcohol reaches the brain in minutes. At first it acts as a stimulant, producing euphoria. This soon gives way to central nervous system depression and feelings of numbness, and finally to sleep or unconsciousness. Rapid ingestion of a large amount of alcohol can be fatal.

The term *proof* indicates alcohol concentrations; in Canada, proof is twice the alcohol content. Thus, a 90-proof liquor is 45 percent alcohol.

ALCOHOL AND CHOLESTEROL

Studies have found that drinking small amounts of alcohol, especially red wine, lowers the risk of a heart attack, presumably by reducing the detrimental effects of elevated blood cholesterol and by preventing clot formation. The mechanisms are unclear, but some researchers note that red wines contain BIOFLAVONOIDS (as do white wines in smaller amounts), a type of antioxidant. These substances protect cells from the damage that normally occurs when the body uses oxygen; they may also fortify LDL (low-density lipoprotein) cholesterol against oxidation (it's believed that oxidation of LDLs causes coronary arteries and other blood vessels to clog).

Other studies show that one or two drinks a day (see What's in a Drink, p.17) may increase the levels of protective HDL (high-density lipoprotein) cholesterol. But doctors note that even this amount of alcohol raises the risk of high blood pressure, stroke, liver disease, and certain cancers. They also suggest safer options; eating grapes, for example, provides even more bioflavonoids than wine, and aspirin is more effective in preventing clots.

ALCOHOL'S ADVERSE EFFECTS

Overconsumption of alcohol invariably results in a hangover; just how much is necessary to produce that misery de-

DID YOU KNOW?

• The hops that give beer its somewhat distinctive bitterness and aroma come from a vine that is a relative of cannabis.

• A cold shower, strong coffee, and similar folk remedies are of no value in helping a person sober up.

• Large amounts of alcohol lower sexual performance in men. Alcohol reduces levels of testosterone, the male sex hormone, while increasing estrogen levels, which can lead to impotence, shrunken testicles, and male breast growth.

pends on the biochemical individuality of the consumer, and the type of drink consumed. Symptoms may include thirst, headache, diarrhea, gastrointestinal upset, nausea, and irritability. Because of alcohol's diuretic effect, a person is likely to wake up feeling dehydrated; drinking water before going to bed may reduce these effects. The severity of a hangover is partially influenced by congeners, by-products of the fermentation process that contribute to the taste and aroma of an alcoholic beverage. The more congeners in a drink, the more severe a hangover may be. Brandy has the greatest number of congeners, followed by red wine, rum, whiskey, white wine, gin, and vodka.

Other, more serious effects of alcohol include the following:

Brain and nerves. Alcohol reduces blood flow to the brain and is also toxic to brain cells. Long-term overindulgence results in memory loss, nerve damage, and even dementia.

Liver. Because this organ metabolizes alcohol, it is vulnerable to damage, including a fatty liver, alcoholic hepatitis, and eventually scarring, or cirrhosis.

Heart. Even small amounts of alcohol may provoke cardiac arrhythmias. Long-term use of alcohol increases the risk of high blood pressure and heart

disease, especially cardiomyopathy, an enlargement and weakening of the heart muscle.

Digestive system. Alcohol raises the stomach's output of hydrochloric acid, which can worsen an ulcer. It also relaxes the sphincter between the esophagus and the stomach, resulting in heartburn from a backflow of acid.

EFFECTS ON NUTRITION

Small amounts of alcohol can stimulate appetite and aid digestion; overindulgence quickly erases the benefits. Even a weekend of heavy drinking causes a buildup of fatty cells in the liver. While this organ has remarkable recuperative powers, continued use can lead to permanent liver damage and problems in metabolizing glucose and various vitamins and minerals. These nutritional deficiencies can lead to other more serious conditions, such as anemia, nerve damage, and mental problems.

Long-term alcohol use often results in excessive weight gain, even though the person may consume less food. This is because alcohol is high in calories (see What's in a Drink, p.17) and is often consumed with fatty, high-calorie foods like salted peanuts and potato chips.

ALCOHOLISM

EAT PLENTY OF
• *Seafood, lean pork, and enriched cereals and breads for extra thiamine.*
• *Dark green leafy vegetables, oranges and other fresh fruits, poultry, and enriched cereals and breads for folate.*
• *Legumes, pasta, and other starchy foods for carbohydrate.*

AVOID
• *Alcohol in any form.*

In general, alcoholism is defined as chronic drinking that interferes with one's personal, family, or professional life. While an occasional drink is not likely to be harmful, it's important to recognize that alcohol is easily abused.

Factors that are thought to foster alcoholism include a genetic predisposition, learned behavior, and childhood experiences, including abuse. Progression of the disease varies from one person to another. For some, it develops as soon as they begin to drink; for most people, however, it progresses slowly from periodic social drinking to more frequent indulgence until finally the person is addicted.

Some alcoholics are binge drinkers and can go for weeks or even months without alcohol. But once they have a drink, they are unable to stop until they are incapacitated or pass out. Although these drinkers have difficulty maintaining sobriety, they are unlikely to suffer severe withdrawal symptoms when they abstain. In other cases, abstinence of 12 to 24 hours will produce withdrawal symptoms, such as sweating, irritability, nausea, vomiting, and weakness. More severe symptoms develop in 2 to 4 days and may include delirium tremens (DTs), a condition marked by fever and delirium.

EFFECTS OF ALCOHOLISM

Chronic overuse of alcohol takes a heavy psychological and physical toll. Alcoholics often do not appear to be intoxicated, but their ability to work and go about daily activities becomes increasingly impaired. They are very susceptible to depression, mood changes, and even violent behavior. Their suicide rate is higher than that of the general population. Alcoholics tend to be heavy smokers and may misuse other drugs, such as tranquilizers. On average, alcoholism shortens life expectancy, not only from suicide but also because it

HIGH AND LOW SPIRITS. *While alcohol can lift the spirits, too much can lead to depression and even aggression.*

raises the risk of other life-threatening diseases, including cancer of the pancreas, liver, and esophagus. Women who drink heavily while pregnant may have a baby with fetal alcohol syndrome, a constellation of birth defects, including mental retardation.

NUTRITIONAL EFFECTS

Alcoholism can lead to malnutrition, not only because chronic drinkers tend to have poor diets, but also because alcohol alters digestion and metabolism of most nutrients. Severe thiamine deficiency (marked by muscle cramps and wasting, nausea, appetite loss, nerve disorders, and depression) is extremely common, as are deficiencies of folate, riboflavin, vitamin B_6, and selenium. Disturbance of vitamin A metabolism can result in night blindness. Because many alcoholics suffer deficiency of vitamin D, which metabolizes calcium, they are at risk of bone fractures and osteoporosis. Impaired liver and pancreatic function may result in faulty fat digestion.

Since alcohol stimulates insulin production, glucose metabolism speeds up and can result in low blood sugar. In addition, alcoholics are often overweight, due to the calories in alcohol.

Once an alcoholic stops drinking, the nutritional problems are tackled one by one. Supplements are prescribed to treat deficiencies. A diet addresses underlying problems; for example, an overweight person needs a diet that reverses nutritional deficiencies without additional weight gain. If there is liver damage, protein intake must be monitored to prevent further liver problems.

MAINTAINING SOBRIETY

Abstinence, the only real treatment for alcoholism, is difficult to achieve and maintain. Withdrawal may require medical supervision and a stay in a hospital or clinic setting. Afterwards, support groups are critical. These groups, such as Alcoholics Anonymous, can usually be found listed in the local Yellow Pages.

ALLERGIC REACTIONS TO FOODS

Scores of the ordinarily harmless substances in foods,
the air, and objects we touch can provoke symptoms ranging
from a runny nose and hives to fatal anaphylaxis.

Allergies occur when our immune system overreacts to minute amounts of foreign substances. Approximately one in four North Americans—or some 70 million people—suffer from allergies. Of these, food allergies make up only a small percentage. Far more common are allergic reactions to pollen and other inhaled substances, medications, and substances that are absorbed into the skin.

Doctors do not completely understand why so many people have allergies, though heredity is instrumental. If both parents have allergies, their children will almost always follow suit, although the symptoms and allergens may be quite different. Food allergies in infants and children, however, tend to lessen as they grow, and the problem may disappear by adulthood.

Allergies basically develop in stages. When the immune system first encounters an allergen (or antigen)—a substance that it mistakenly perceives as a harmful foreign invader—it signals specialized cells to manufacture antibodies, or immunoglobulins, against it. The person will not experience an allergic reaction in that initial exposure; however, if the substance again enters the body, the antibodies programmed to mount an attack against it will go into action. In some instances, the response will not produce symptoms; but the stage will have been set. At some future date, an antigen-antibody reaction may provoke cells in the immune system to release large amounts of histamines and other chemicals that are responsible for an allergic response. When this happens, symptoms can range from something as mild as a sneeze or runny nose to an extremely serious reaction, such as sudden death.

COMMON SYMPTOMS

The most common symptoms of food allergies are nausea, vomiting, diarrhea, constipation, indigestion, headaches, skin rashes or hives, itching, shortness of breath (including asthma attacks), and, in severe cases, widespread swelling of the skin and mucous membranes. Swelling in the mouth or throat is potentially fatal because it can block the airways to the lungs. In the most severe cases, anaphylactic shock—a life-threatening collapse of the respiratory and circulatory system—may develop.

The allergen usually provokes the same symptoms each time, but many factors affect their intensity, including stress, how much of the offending food was eaten, how it was prepared, and whether it was eaten with other foods. Some people can tolerate small amounts of an offending food; others are so hypersensitive that they react to even a minute trace.

Most allergic reactions arise quickly, usually within a few minutes or up

to 2 hours after the allergen enters the body. In unusual cases, however, the reaction may be delayed for up to 48 hours, making it more difficult to identify the allergen.

PINPOINTING ALLERGENS

Some allergens are easily identified because characteristic symptoms will develop immediately after eating the offending food. In other instances, it may be necessary to keep a carefully documented diary of the time and content of all meals and snacks and the appearance and timing of any subsequent symptoms. After a week or two, a pattern may emerge. If so, eliminate the suspected food from the diet for at least a week, and then try it again. If symptoms develop only in the latter part of this experiment, chances are you have identified the offending food.

In more complicated cases, allergy tests may be required. The most common are skin tests; food extracts are placed on the skin, which is then scratched or pricked, allowing the penetration of a small amount of the extract. Development of a hive or itchy swelling usually indicates an allergic response. In some cases, a doctor may order a RAST (radioallergosorbent test) blood study in which small amounts of the patient's blood are mixed with food extracts and then analyzed for signs of antibody action. This test is more expensive than skin tests but may be safer for hypersensitive people, who may have a severe reaction to the skin test.

Still other tests may involve a medically supervised elimination diet and challenge tests. In one variation, the patient is put on a hypoallergenic diet of foods that are unlikely to cause allergies—for example, lamb, rice, carrots, sweet potatoes, and pears—for 7 to 10 days, at which time all allergic symptoms should completely disappear. (If they don't, a reaction to something other than food should be

COMMON FOOD ALLERGENS AND THEIR SYMPTOMS

Almost any food can provoke an allergic reaction. The following, listed in descending order with the most likely to occur at top, are the most common.

FOOD TYPES	PROBLEM FOODS	SYMPTOMS
Milk and milk products	Dairy products, such as milk, cheeses, yogurt, cream, ice cream, cream soups, and certain baked goods and desserts.	Constipation, diarrhea, and vomiting are most common; less frequent are rashes, hives, and breathing problems.
Eggs (especially egg whites)	Cakes, mousses, ice cream, sherbets, and other desserts; mayonnaise, salad dressings, French toast, waffles, and pancakes.	Rashes or hives, swelling, and intestinal upsets. Can trigger asthma attacks and eczema in some people.
Fish	Fresh, canned, smoked or pickled fish, fish-liver oils, caviar, foods containing fish, such as bisques, broths, and stews.	Rashes or hives, and perhaps red itchy eyes or a runny nose. Can trigger asthma attacks, diarrhea, and, rarely, anaphylaxis.
Shellfish	Crustaceans, such as shrimp, crab, lobster, and crayfish; mollusks, such as clams, oysters, and scallops; and seafood dishes.	Nausea, prolonged intestinal upsets, migraines, skin rashes, and swelling; possible anaphylaxis.
Wheat and wheat products	Cereals, bread or bread-related products, dry soup mixes, cakes, pasta, gravies, dumplings, products containing flour; beer and ale.	Diarrhea and other intestinal upsets, migraine headaches, and eczema.
Corn	Foods with corn as a vegetable, such as vegetable soup; baby foods (with cornstarch), baking mixes, processed meats, corn oils, margarine, salad dressings, MSG, and baked goods.	Rashes or hives, breathing problems, diarrhea and other intestinal upsets.
Nuts and peanuts	Candy and baked goods with pecans, walnuts, almonds, cashews, hazelnuts, pistachios, and peanuts; oils from nuts.	Intestinal upsets and breathing problems; possible anaphylaxis, usually when nuts are a hidden ingredient.
Fruits	Citrus fruits; in pollen-allergic persons, usually melons and other fruits with seeds.	Facial rash or hives, and itching or tingling sensations in the mouth.
Chocolate	Candy bars, baked goods, and other products containing cocoa or chocolate. (Testing often shows allergies are due to milk, nuts, or other ingredients added to chocolate.)	Rashes or hives; if milk or nuts are the real culprit, reactions may be more severe.

suspected.) The doctor then administers small amounts of food or food extracts, usually in capsule form, to see if an allergic response occurs.

Warning: Some people put themselves on highly restricted diets without proper medical consultation. This can result in serious nutritional deficiencies; it is best to consult a doctor.

LIVING WITH ALLERGIES

Once the offending allergens have been identified, eliminating those foods from the diet should solve the problem. But this can be more complicated than it sounds. Some of the most common food allergens, such as milk, eggs, wheat, and corn, are hidden ingredients in many processed foods (see Common Food Allergens and Their Symptoms, p.21). When you shop, scrutinize all food labels carefully. Also, many foods are chemically related; thus, a person allergic to lemons may also be allergic to oranges and other citrus fruits. In some cases, the real culprit may be a contaminant or an accidental additive in food. For example, some people who are allergic to orange juice and other citrus juices may actually be able to tolerate the peeled fruits themselves, since it is limonene, the oil in citrus peels, that often produces the allergic reaction. Some people only experience food allergy symptoms if they consume the offending food just before exercising.

Eating out can pose a few problems. When invited to someone's home, let your host know in advance if you are allergic to specific foods. Or ask about the menu; if it presents problems, offer to bring a substitute dish for yourself. Usually, however, it's sufficient to make inquiries upon arrival and then quietly decline the problem dishes.

In restaurants, ask servers about food ingredients before ordering. If they are unable to answer your questions, ask that they be directed to the chef. In order to avoid potential allergens, some people will have to select simple, ungarnished dishes, such as unseasoned broiled fish, a baked potato, and steamed vegetables. Or call the restaurant ahead of time to request that food be specially prepared.

TREATING EMERGENCIES

If you have had—or your doctor believes you are susceptible to—severe hives, asthma attacks, or anaphylactic reactions, you should always wear a medical identification pendant or carry

RISK-FREE FOODS. *Experts believe that some foods, including those pictured below, seldom if ever set off allergic reactions.*

emergency medical information in your wallet or purse. Your doctor may also recommend that you carry antihistamine medication or an easy-to-inject form of epinephrine (Adrenalin) to use in case of breathing problems or another severe allergic reaction.

A DIFFERENT PROBLEM

Many people mistakenly assume they have food allergies when, in fact, the problem is INTOLERANCE. The symptoms may be similar, but an allergic reaction is mediated through the immune system, whereas food intolerance originates in the gastrointestinal system and entails an inability to digest or absorb certain substances.

One of the most common types is lactose intolerance, in which a person lacks an enzyme (lactase) needed to digest milk sugar. The degree of lactose intolerance varies in different people. In severe cases even a tiny amount of milk sugar may provoke symptoms—generally abdominal pain and bloating, diarrhea, and flatulence. However, lactose-reduced dairy products are available, as are tablets that can be taken before eating; these have the enzyme that makes digesting dairy products possible. In contrast, a person who is allergic to milk will still have symptoms after ingesting even lactose-free milk products.

ALZHEIMER'S DISEASE

EAT PLENTY OF

- *Eggs, liver, soybeans and soy products, whole grains, brewer's yeast, and wheat germ—all reasonably good sources of lecithin and choline.*

AVOID

- *Zinc supplements, which may hasten the onset of symptoms.*
- *Alcohol, which can worsen memory loss and dementia.*

Alzheimer's disease is the leading cause of dementia in people over the age of 65, affecting some 300,000 Canadians. There are no specific diagnostic tests for Alzheimer's, but before arriving at a diagnosis, tests are needed to rule out a stroke, a brain tumor, nutritional deficiencies, thyroid disorders, syphilis, and other possible causes of dementia.

The cause of Alzheimer's disease remains unknown, but researchers theorize that chromosomal and genetic factors are responsible for many cases. The increased incidence of Alzheimer's among people with Down's syndrome, which is caused by a chromosomal abnormality, seems to support this theory. Researchers have discovered a genetic marker, a type of lipoprotein that can be detected by blood tests, that identifies people likely to develop the disease.

In addition, hormonal factors are under study. Women are afflicted more often than men; some recent studies indicate that estrogen replacement may protect against Alzheimer's. Thyroid disorders are also linked to an increased risk of the disease. The long-term use of nonsteroidal anti-inflammatory drugs (NSAIDs) has been linked with a reduced incidence of the disease.

There have been other intriguing leads, but researchers have been unable to pinpoint any specific dietary factors that increase the risk of or help to prevent Alzheimer's disease. Over the years, some research has implicated aluminum, which has been found in the abnormal tangles of brain cells in some Alzheimer's patients. However, extensive studies have failed to prove that aluminum actually causes the disease, and most experts now discount it as a factor. Still, some people believe it is prudent to avoid taking antacids with large amounts of aluminum or using cookware that allows the metal to leach into food. Concern has also been raised about the aluminum content of drinking water in areas where aluminum compounds are used as flocculating agents in municipal water treatment.

DIET AND ALZHEIMER'S

Researchers now think that a buildup of zinc may be a more relevant factor than aluminum; laboratory experiments show that zinc can transform the protein in brain cells into abnormal tangles indistinguishable from those of Alzheimer's. Other studies indicate that taking high-dose zinc supplements may hasten the progression of memory loss and other manifestations of the disease.

People with Alzheimer's disease have abnormally low levels of choline acetyltransferase, an enzyme necessary to make acetylcholine, a brain chemical believed to be instrumental in learning and memory. Also, the brain cells most affected by Alzheimer's are those that normally respond to acetylcholine. In addition, tacrine (Cognex), a new drug that appears to improve the memory of some Alzheimer's patients, increases levels of acetylcholine. Some nutrition researchers theorize that supplements or foods high in lecithin or choline (the major component of acetylcholine) can also slow the progression of Alzheimer's by raising acetylcholine production. So far, studies have failed to document its value, but some nutritionists feel that foods high in lecithin and choline may

FOODS THAT MAY SLOW ALZHEIMER'S

Eggs are a good dietary source of choline—a component of lecithin. They are also a good source of protein, iron, vitamin B$_{12}$, and other B vitamins.

Soybeans and other soy products are rich in choline and provide protein, carbohydrate, calcium, and fiber.

Wheat germ and whole grains supply choline, carbohydrate, vitamin E, B vitamins, and numerous minerals.

help forestall Alzheimer's symptoms and will certainly do no harm; these include egg yolks, organ meats, soy products, wheat germ, and whole grains.

As Alzheimer's disease progresses, its victims may forget to eat or may limit their diets to sweets or other favorite foods. These patients should be persuaded to eat nutritionally balanced meals. They may even need to be spoon-fed if they have difficulty feeding themselves. A multivitamin supplement may also be advisable; however, high-dose supplements should not be administered unless specifically recommended by a physician. Contrary to media reports, there is no proof that high doses of vitamin E benefit Alzheimer's patients.

Even in small amounts, alcohol destroys brain cells, a loss that a healthy person can tolerate but one that can accelerate the progression of Alzheimer's disease. Alcohol interacts with antidepressants, sedatives, and other medications prescribed for Alzheimer's patients. It's a good idea to withhold all alcohol from persons with the disease.

ANEMIA

EAT PLENTY OF

- Organ meats, beef and other meats, poultry, fish, and egg yolks for iron and vitamin B_{12}.
- Dried beans and peas, tofu and other soy products, dates, raisins, dried apricots, and blackstrap molasses—all good plant sources of iron.
- Iron-enriched breads and cereals.
- Citrus fruits and other good sources of vitamin C, which increase the body's iron absorption.
- Green leafy vegetables for folate.

CUT DOWN ON

- Bran, spinach, and rhubarb, which hinder iron absorption.
- Zinc and calcium supplements, antacids, coffee, and tea, which also reduce iron absorption.

AVOID

- Iron supplements, unless prescribed by a physician.

Anemia is the umbrella term for a variety of disorders that are characterized by the inability of red blood cells to carry sufficient oxygen. This may be due to an abnormality in the shape or composition of the cells or a deficiency in their number. One of the common abnormalities is a low level of hemoglobin, the iron- and protein-based red pigment in blood that carries oxygen from the lungs to all body cells. Symptoms of anemia, therefore, reflect oxygen starvation. In mild anemia, this may include general weakness, pallor, fatigue, and brittle, spoon-shaped nails. More severe cases are marked by shortness of breath, fainting, and cardiac arrhythmias.

IRON-DEFICIENCY ANEMIA

In Canada the most common type of anemia is due to iron deficiency, which is usually caused by massive or chronic

Case Study

After weeks of feeling tired and short of breath, Roy, a retired librarian, went for a checkup. Blood studies showed that Roy was anemic, and a stool test indicated hidden intestinal bleeding was the likely cause. Roy's doctor sent him for a colonoscopy, which revealed a suspicious growth in the uppermost segment of the bowel. A biopsy confirmed that the growth was cancerous.

In preparation for colon surgery 3 weeks later, the doctor prescribed iron pills to help build up Roy's hemoglobin levels. The surgeon removed the diseased segment of Roy's colon and rejoined the healthy portions. The cancer was in an early stage, so bowel function returned to normal within 10 days. Because he was still anemic, Roy was instructed to take iron pills for another 3 months and to eat a diet of iron-rich foods.

blood loss. Surgery patients, accident victims, or people with a bleeding ulcer or intestinal cancer often have iron-deficiency anemia. In fact, a blood test that shows iron deficiency often prompts a physician to investigate the possibility of colon cancer. Women with heavy menstrual periods, especially adolescents, are at risk.

Dietary iron deficiency is relatively uncommon in Canada because the typical diet—high in meat and iron-enriched breads and cereal—usually provides more than enough iron for most people. Some exceptions, however, are infants and young children who drink mostly milk; pregnant women because they need extra iron for their developing fetus and their own expanded blood volume. Vegetarians, too, may become iron deficient; as may people with inflammatory disorders.

OTHER TYPES OF ANEMIA

Hemolytic anemia occurs when red blood cells are destroyed more rapidly than normal. The cause may be hereditary or one of a variety of diseases, including leukemia and other cancers, abnormal spleen function, autoimmune disorders, and severe hypertension.

Pernicious, or megaloblastic, anemia is caused by a deficiency of vitamin B_{12}, which is necessary to make red blood cells. This deficiency can result from a vegetarian diet that eschews all animal products, but the most common cause is an intestinal disorder that prevents absorption of the vitamin.

Deficiency of folate, another B vitamin, can also cause anemia in pregnant women (who need extra folate for the developing fetus), in alcoholics, and in elderly people.

Relatively rare types of anemia include thalassemia, an inherited disorder, and aplastic anemia, which may be caused by infection, exposure to toxic chemicals or radiation, or a genetic disorder.

HOW MUCH IRON DO YOU NEED?

The human body recycles iron to make new red blood cells. Even so, the body loses an average of 1mg for men and 1.5mg for women during their reproductive years. The body absorbs only a small percentage of dietary iron, so the Recommended Nutrient Intakes (RNIs) call for consuming more than what is lost: 9mg a day for adult men and post-menopausal women, 13mg for women under 50 and for pregnant women, with an additional 5mg during the second trimester, and an additional 10mg during the third trimester.

Those who have nutrition-related anemias can benefit from a session with a registered dietitian or a qualified nutritionist to help structure a more healthful diet. The best sources of iron are animal prod-ucts—meat, fish, poultry, and egg yolks. The body absorbs much more of the heme iron found in these foods than the nonheme iron from plant sources, such as green leafy vegetables, dried fruits, soy and other legumes, and iron-enriched breads and cereals. Combining iron-rich foods with citrus or other fruits and vegetables high in vitamin C increases iron absorption; conversely, antacids and bran bind with iron and prevent the body from using it.

Cooking tomatoes and other acidic foods in iron pots can add large amounts of iron to food. For example, 4 ounces of tomato sauce provides 0.7mg of iron; cooking it in an iron pot adds 5mg. Foods cooked in ironware may be discolored, but the taste is unaffected.

ANOREXIA NERVOSA

TAKE
- *At least a small amount of a variety of nutritious foods.*
- *Multivitamin pills and calorie-enriched liquid supplements if approved by a doctor.*

AVOID
- *Coffee, diet soft drinks, and low-calorie diet foods.*
- *Appetite suppressants, diuretics, and laxatives.*

The self-starvation that is a hallmark of anorexia nervosa is caused by a complex psychiatric disorder that afflicts between 1 and 2 percent of Canadians, mostly adolescent girls or, less commonly, young women. (Only about 5 percent of anorexics are males; they are often weight-conscious adolescent boys who are dancers or athletes.)

The cause of anorexia—a medical term for appetite loss—is unknown. Researchers believe that a combination of hormonal, social, and psychological factors are responsible. The disease often begins in adolescence, a time of tremendous hormonal and psychological change. Convinced that she is too fat, regardless of how much she weighs, the girl begins obsessive dieting. Some girls adopt a very restricted diet. Others become overly preoccupied with food, often planning and preparing elaborate meals that they then refuse to eat. And when the anorexic does eat, she may resort to self-induced vomiting or laxative abuse to avoid gaining weight. Many anorexics also exercise obsessively, often for several hours a day.

As the disease progresses, menstruation ceases and nutritional deficiencies develop. Many anorexics try to hide their thinness by wearing oversized clothes; physical indications of anorexia include fatigue, nervousness or hyperactivity, dry skin, hair loss, and intolerance to cold. More serious consequences include cardiac arrhythmias, loss of bone mass, kidney failure, and in about 15 percent of cases, death.

TREATMENT STRATEGIES

Anorexia often requires intensive long-term treatment, preferably by a team experienced with eating disorders: a doctor to treat starvation-induced medical problems, a psychiatrist, and a dietitian. Family members can also benefit from counseling.

Anorexics tend to be defensive about their eating habits and resistant to treatment. Most anorexics are treated on an outpatient basis, but in severe cases, hospitalization and intravenous nutritional therapy are necessary.

The biggest hurdle is to help the anorexic overcome her abnormal fear of food and distorted self-image of being fat. Counseling is directed to uncovering the source of these fears.

In the beginning, the patient is offered small portions of nutritious and easily digestible foods, perhaps eggs, custards, soups, and milk shakes. Portion sizes and the variety of foods are increased gradually to achieve a steady weight gain. This does not require huge amounts of food; instead, doctors strive for a varied diet that provides adequate protein for rebuilding lost lean tissue, carbohydrate for energy, and a moderate amount of fat for extra calories. Extra calcium and a multivitamin pill may also be given.

Because an anorexic is skilled at deceiving others about her eating and relapses are common, close monitoring may be necessary to make sure that she is really eating. But avoid making food a constant source of attention and conflict; group therapy can be more helpful than parental nagging.

ANTIOXIDANTS: SORTING THROUGH FACTS AND HYPE

Since oxygen is essential for life, it's ironic that its use by the body sets the stage for aging and many diseases. The good news is that antioxidants in foods seem to stave off these effects.

Similar to the oxygen requirements of a burning fire, every cell in your body needs a steady supply of oxygen to derive energy from digested food. But consuming oxygen comes with a price; it also releases free radicals, unstable molecules that can damage healthy cells as they careen through the body. Free radicals are highly reactive because they contain an unpaired electron in search of a mate. As soon as these radicals are formed, they search for molecules with which they can react, or oxidize. Oxidation in this sense refers to a process by which a molecule loses electrons.

Although all healthy cells produce small amounts of free radicals, excessive bombardment by these molecules damages cellular DNA and other genetic material. However, human cells have protective enzymes that repair 99 percent of oxidative damage. But oxygen metabolism is not the only source of oxidative damage; it can come from X-rays, ultraviolet rays, radon, tobacco smoke, and other environmental pollutants. The cumulative effect can cause irreversible cellular changes, or mutations, that can result in cancer and other diseases.

The body's immune system seeks out and destroys these mutated cells, in much the same way as it eliminates invading bacteria and other foreign organisms; this mechanism lessens with age, however. The body becomes more vulnerable to free-radical damage, and the incidence of degenerative disorders increases. Consequences range from harmless pigmented skin patches to more serious disorders, such as cataracts, cancer, and a host of degenerative diseases.

BENEFITS
- *Protect against cancer, heart disease, cataracts, and other degenerative diseases.*
- *May slow the aging process.*
- *Prevent the spoilage of oils and processed foods.*

DRAWBACKS
- *May have detrimental effects if taken as high-dose supplements.*

Antioxidants are molecules that combine with free radicals, rendering them harmless. The major antioxidants are vitamins C and E; beta carotene, which the body converts to vitamin A; and selenium. BIOFLAVONOIDS, substances found in citrus fruits, grapes, and other fresh fruits and vegetables, have antioxidant properties, as do some other phyto-

ANTIOXIDANT PANTRY. *Fresh fruits and vegetables, fatty fish, nuts, legumes, and various vegetable oils are rich sources of antioxidants.*

chemicals, that is, substances which are found in plants.

Numerous studies show a reduced incidence of cancer and heart attacks in people who eat plenty of fruits, vegetables, and whole-grain products—the best food sources of antioxidants. Recent research indicates that antioxidants such as vitamin E may prevent heart disease by hindering the oxidation of LDLs (low-density lipoproteins), the harmful cholesterol. Unoxidized LDLs are relatively benign, but after oxidation they promote ATHEROSCLEROSIS, the development of artery-clogging plaque. Oxidation also facilitates the uptake of LDLs into artery walls; a process that may be blocked by beta carotene.

Less is known about how antioxidants hinder cancer; researchers theorize that prevention of DNA damage is a factor. Recent studies indicate that vitamin C may protect against skin cancer and melanoma.

ANTIOXIDANT PILLS

Doctors discourage taking high-dose antioxidant supplements. When taken in large amounts, some nutrients that are normally antioxidants may have the opposite effect and actually increase oxidation. For example, when taken by someone who has large iron reserves, high doses of vitamin C become pro-oxidant. Similarly, recent studies failed to find any benefit from high-dose beta carotene supplements and even suggested that they could lead to an increased risk of lung cancer in smokers.

Supplements exceeding the RNIs should be taken only under medical supervision. High doses of vitamin E, for example, can interfere with blood clotting and increase the risk of a bleeding emergency. Even so, supplements may be prescribed for some heart patients, because it is impossible to get protective amounts (200mg to 400mg a day) from diet alone.

PROTECTIVE PLANT CHEMICALS

Because plants are also susceptible to disease, they have developed their own protective substances, called phytochemicals (from phyton, *the Greek term for plant). Mounting research shows that many phytochemicals also protect humans against cancer and other diseases.*

PHYTO-CHEMICAL	FUNCTIONS	SOURCES
Allylic sulfides	May stimulate production of protective enzymes.	Garlic, onions
Bioflavonoids	Antioxidant; inhibit cancer-promoting hormones.	Most fresh fruits and vegetables
Catechins (tannins)	Antioxidant.	Berries, green tea
Curcumin	Protects against tobacco-induced carcinogens.	Turmeric, cumin
Genistein	Inhibits tumor growth.	Soybeans
Indoles	Inhibit estrogen, which stimulates some cancers; induce protective enzymes.	Broccoli, cabbage, cauliflower, mustard greens
Isoflavones	Block estrogen uptake by cancer cells.	Beans, peanuts and other legumes, peas
Isothiocyanates	Induce production of protective enzymes.	Horseradish, mustard, radishes
Lignans	Inhibit estrogen and block prostaglandins.	Flaxseed, walnuts
Lycopene	Antioxidant; may protect against prostate cancer.	Pink grapefruit, tomatoes, watermelon
Monoterpenes	Some antioxidant properties; aid in activity of protective enzymes.	Basil, citrus fruits, broccoli, orange and yellow vegetables
Omega-3 fatty acids	Inhibit estrogen; reduce inflammation.	Canola oil, flaxseed, walnuts, fatty fish
Phenolic acids	Inhibit nitrosamines; enhance enzyme activity.	Berries, broccoli, cabbage, carrots, citrus fruits, eggplant, parsley, peppers, teas, tomatoes, whole grains
Protease inhibitors	Suppress production of enzymes in cancer cells.	Soybeans
Quercetin	Inhibits cellular mutation, carcinogens, clot formation, and inflammation.	Grape skins, red and white wine, tea
Sulforaphane	Induces protective enzymes.	Broccoli
Terpenes	Stimulate anticancer enzymes.	Citrus fruits

APPETITE LOSS

EAT PLENTY OF
- *Fresh fruits and vegetables for vitamin C.*
- *Lean meats, seafood, poultry, nuts, seeds, and whole grains for zinc and B vitamins.*

CUT DOWN ON
- *Smoking and excessive alcohol, which dull the appetite.*
- *Liquids before meals.*
- *Bran and other high-fiber foods.*

The pleasant anticipation of eating that we call appetite is controlled by two centers in the brain: one is the hypothalamus, which stimulates the release of hunger-producing hormones until hunger is satisfied; the other is the cerebral cortex, the center of intellectual and sensory function. Thus, a healthy appetite reflects both an unconscious response and learned behavior.

Many disorders and circumstances cause loss of appetite; most are temporary conditions, such as a cold, an upset stomach, dental problems, or stress. A persistent loss of appetite, however, can reflect a more serious illness; for example, clinical depression, anemia, kidney disease, AIDS, or cancer.

In unusual cases, appetite loss stems from nutritional deficiencies, usually of vitamin C, thiamine, niacin, biotin, and zinc. Excessive drinking of alcohol not only reduces appetite but may also cause nutritional deficiencies. Smoking is another activity that blunts appetite.

Eating large amounts of bran, whole-grain products, and other high-fiber foods interferes with the absorption of zinc and other minerals; such foods also diminish appetite because they are filling. Drinking large quantities of liquid before a meal reduces appetite too.

Loss of appetite related to illness usually corrects itself with recovery. There are several strategies, however, that may help trigger an appetite when it is lost inexplicably. Avoid snacks between meals. Before a meal, have a lemon drop; sucking something sour increases saliva flow, which in turn stimulates appetite. Surround yourself with appetizing odors, such as the smell of bacon, spices like cinnamon, or a favorite food.

APPLES

BENEFITS
- *Low in calories and high in soluble fibers that help lower cholesterol.*
- *A good source of flavonoids.*

DRAWBACKS
- *Relatively low in nutrients.*
- *May contain pesticide residues.*

A fresh apple is an ideal snack. It's easy to carry, flavorful, filling, and low in calories; a 5-ounce piece of fruit has only 90 calories. Apples can be eaten fresh or cooked in myriad ways—baked into pies, crisps, and tarts; added to poultry stuffing; and made into jelly, apple butter, and sauce. Apple cider vinegar is an ingredient in many salad dressings. Pasteurized apple juice and fresh-pressed cider are popular drinks, while fermented apple cider, wine, and brandy are gaining in popularity.

Apple trees thrive in most temperate climates, but they are especially vulnerable to worms, scale, and other insects; they are usually sprayed with pesticides several times during the growing season. Apples should always be washed carefully before eating; some experts even suggest peeling them, especially if they have been waxed.

NUTRITIONAL VALUE
Despite the old saw "An apple a day keeps the doctor away," the average apple provides only 8mg of vitamin C, or 20 percent of the Recommended Nutrient Intake (RNI). The skin does

contain small amounts of beta carotene; the flesh adds some potassium and iron.

On a more positive note, apples are a good source of fiber, especially pectin (a soluble fiber that is used to thicken jellies), which helps lower blood cholesterol levels. Another type of soluble fiber in apples absorbs large amounts of water from the intestinal tract, which helps prevent constipation. Because applesauce is pleasant tasting and easily digested, doctors recommend it as an early baby food.

Fructose, the major sugar that occurs naturally in apples, is absorbed into the bloodstream more slowly than sucrose (table sugar); thus, diabetics can enjoy an apple without worrying about an abrupt increase in blood glucose levels.

Apples have long been called nature's toothbrush; while they don't actually cleanse the teeth, they still enhance dental hygiene. Biting and chewing an apple stimulates the gums, and the sweetness of the apple prompts an increased flow of saliva, which reduces tooth decay by lowering the levels of bacteria in the mouth.

DRIED APPLES

Usually served as a snack or used to make pies, dried apples are a more concentrated source of energy than the fresh form. It takes about 5 pounds of apples to make 1 pound of dried apple slices, which provide about 70 calories per ounce. Except for fiber and a small amount of iron, most nutrients are lost in the drying process. On the positive

APPLE HARVEST. *More than 2,500 varieties of apples grow in North America; others are imported. Popular ones include (clockwise from far left) Red Delicious, Crispin, Royal Gala, Granny Smith, Empire, Golden Delicious, Royal Gala, and Cox.*

side, dried apples are less likely to promote cavities than other dried fruits.

Sulfur dioxide is often added to dried apples to preserve their moistness and color; it can provoke an allergic reaction in a susceptible person.

Prunus Armeniaca

Apricots with an intense golden orange color will be the richest in beta carotene.

Apricot kernels contain cyanide and should not be eaten.

A handful of dried apricots makes a convenient and healthy snack that will provide plenty of energy.

FRAGRANT FRUIT. *One of the first fruits of summer, apricots are best eaten warm, right off the tree.*

APRICOTS

BENEFITS
- *A rich source of beta carotene, iron, and potassium.*
- *High in fiber, low in calories.*
- *Dried apricots and apricot leather are nutritious, fat-free snack foods.*

DRAWBACKS
- *Sulfite preservatives in some dried apricots can trigger an allergic reaction or asthma attack in people susceptible to these disorders.*
- *Dried apricots leave a sticky residue on teeth that can lead to cavities.*
- *A natural salicylate in apricots may trigger an allergic reaction in aspirin-sensitive people.*

Apricots are ideal for both snacks and desserts. They are tasty, easy to digest, high in fiber, low in calories (about 50 calories in 3 fresh apricots and 85 in 10 dried halves), virtually fat-free, and highly nutritious. Three fresh apricots or 10 dried halves also provide more than 25 percent of your Recommended Nutrient Intake (RNI) of vitamin A in its plant (beta carotene) form. When consumed from foods, beta carotene is an ANTIOXIDANT, a substance that protects against cell damage that occurs when the body uses oxygen. This damage is thought to be instrumental in aging and the development of heart disease, cancer, and other diseases.

Fresh apricots are rich in vitamin C, another antioxidant that also helps your body absorb iron. (Much of this vitamin C is lost, however, when apricots are canned or dried.) Regardless of form, apricots are high in iron as well as potassium, a mineral essential for proper nerve and muscle function that also helps maintain normal blood pressure and balance of body fluids.

Apricots contain a natural salicylate, a compound similar to the active ingredient in aspirin. People sensitive to aspirin may experience allergic responses after eating apricots.

DRIED APRICOTS

Ounce for ounce, dried apricots are more nutritious than the fresh or canned fruit. The reason: dried apricots are only 32 percent water, compared to 85 percent water in the fresh fruit. They are a more concentrated source of calories—50 calories in 4 ounces of fresh apricots versus 260 in 4 ounces (about 30 halves) of the dried. When eaten in moderation, dried apricots are a compact and convenient source of nutrition, ideal for snacks.

Apricots are often treated with sulfur dioxide before they are dried to preserve their color and certain nutrients. This sulfite treatment may trigger an asthma attack or allergic reaction in susceptible people. Unless dried apricots are labeled as sulfite-free, anyone with asthma should avoid them.

THE LAETRILE ISSUE

Laetrile, or amygdalin, is a highly controversial substance derived from apricot pits. Legally, it cannot be sold as a medical treatment, but it is available as a nutritional supplement, often called vitamin B_{17}, in health food stores. It is promoted in separate literature or by word of mouth as an alternative treatment for cancer, heart disease, allergies, liver disorders, and other diseases. However, numerous scientific studies have failed to find any benefit from laetrile. Indeed, laetrile from apricot pits and other sources can liberate cyanide. Consuming large amounts of laetrile carries a risk of cyanide poisoning; therefore, doctors warn that apricot pits in any form should not be ingested.

ARTHRITIS

EAT PLENTY OF
- *Salmon, sardines, and other fatty fish to counter inflammation.*
- *Fruits high in citrus bioflavonoids to reduce inflammation.*
- *High-fiber, low-calorie foods to help control weight.*

CUT DOWN ON
- *Vegetable oils and fatty beef and pork, which can add to inflammation.*

AVOID
- *Any foods that provoke symptoms.*

About one in seven Canadians suffers from some type of arthritis, any of more than 100 disorders characterized by joint inflammation, stiffness, swelling, and pain. The most common types are osteoarthritis, a painful condition in which joint cartilage gradually breaks down, and rheumatoid arthritis, a systemic disease that can cause severe pain and crippling. Both disorders have similar symptoms and respond to the same treatments.

Doctors do not understand why some individuals develop arthritis and others don't, but a combination of factors plays a role. People with osteoarthritis may have inherently defective cartilage that makes it vulnerable to normal wear and tear. Rheumatoid arthritis develops when an overactive immune system attacks connective tissue in the joints and perhaps other organs, causing inflammation and pain.

Until recently, doctors generally dismissed dietary treatments for arthritis as quackery; new research shows, however, that for many patients, diet can make a big difference.

Although evidence is sketchy, some studies indicate that beef, other types of red meat, and fatty foods and vegetable oils high in omega-6 polyunsaturated fatty acids can worsen arthritis inflammation in some patients. In a recent study, patients with severe rheumatoid arthritis were enrolled in a highly structured program that called for a low-fat, mostly vegetarian diet, regular exercise, and daily meditation. These patients experienced fewer symptoms and needed less medication than a matched group of patients who ate a regular diet. The researchers concluded that the diet accounted for the majority of benefits, which disappeared after the patients returned to their old eating habits.

BENEFICIAL OILS

At least two kinds of oils help fight inflammation: omega-3 fatty acids, found in salmon, sardines, and other coldwater fish; and gamma linolenic acid (GLA), derived from evening primrose, borage, and black currant and hemp seeds. Medical researchers have reported marked reduction in joint swelling, pain, and redness when rheumatoid arthritis patients take these oils. They also help in other types of inflammatory arthritis, including lupus.

Doctors advise getting omega-3 fatty acids from two or three servings of fatty fish a week instead of from fish-oil supplements. Excessive omega-3 increases the risk of bleeding problems, which can be hazardous for people taking arthritis drugs that interfere with normal clotting. GLA can be taken in capsules; the recommended daily dosage is about 500mg. Improvement usually occurs after 6 to 8 weeks.

FOOD ALLERGIES

Some patients with inflammatory arthritis have food allergies that can provoke a flare-up. Common offenders include shellfish, soy, wheat, corn, alcohol, coffee, and possibly certain food additives. Keep a diary to identify foods that provoke an attack. To test a particular food, don't eat it for two weeks, then try it again. If a flare-up occurs, eliminate the offending food from your diet.

THE WEIGHT FACTOR

Obesity greatly increases the risk and severity of osteoarthritis, and even a few pounds of excess weight strain the knees and hips, the most vulnerable weight-bearing joints. Losing weight and increasing exercise often improve symptoms of osteoarthritis.

Patients with rheumatoid arthritis often have the opposite weight problem; they may be too thin due to a lack of appetite, chronic pain, depression, or anemia. In such cases, a doctor may recommend calorie- and nutrient-enriched liquid supplements to counter any dietary deficiencies.

HELPFUL FOODS

Salmon and other oily fish to supply omega-3 oils. Eat three or more times a week.

Fresh green and yellow vegetables to provide beta carotene, vitamin C, and other antioxidants to reduce cell damage. Have at least two servings daily.

Grapefruit and other fresh fruits for citrus flavonoids, substances that are thought to increase the antioxidant effects of vitamin C; may have an anti-inflammatory effect. Eat daily.

Lentils and other legumes for zinc, a mineral essential for proper immune system function. Other good sources include oysters, wheat germ and whole-wheat products, and milk. Eat at least one high-zinc food each day.

Ginger to benefit from its anti-inflammatory effects. Eat one or two pieces of candied ginger or use 5g in cooking every two or three days.

Case Study

When Monica first developed rheumatoid arthritis in her fingers, she feared an end to her career as a legal secretary. Arthritis drugs helped, but did not stop the relentless spread to other joints.

Monica then heard about a promising study in which arthritis patients improved on a vegetarian diet, exercise, and meditation program developed by Dr. Dean Ornish, a California cardiologist who used it to treat heart patients.

Monica bought one of Dr. Ornish's books and put herself on the regimen. Within weeks, her symptoms subsided and the arthritis went into remission.

Monica understands that her arthritis has not been cured, but she's gratified that her altered lifestyle has eased her symptoms.

EXPERIMENTAL TREATMENTS

The 1994 reports of the "chicken-bone cure" for rheumatoid arthritis were premature, but they do appear promising. The goal of this treatment is to calm the overactive immune system by exposing it to large amounts of a substance similar to what it is attacking; in this instance, collagen made from chicken bones. In the initial study, all 28 patients with severe rheumatoid arthritis saw an improvement after a few weeks of consuming chicken-bone collagen broth.

Another promising approach entails rubbing painful joints with a cream containing capsaicin, a derivative of chilies. Capsaicin produces a stinging or burning feeling that distracts the person from the joint pain. But the effects of capsaicin are more than skin deep; it appears to also reduce inflammation.

Some European studies show a marked improvement in osteoarthritis when patients take glucosamine sulfate (GAS), a natural body compound vital in building and maintaining cartilage. Research to date shows no adverse effects when GAS is taken in dosages of 500mg three times a day. Scientists in Canada and the U.S. have set up clinical trials to verify the European results.

A CAUTIONARY NOTE

Because arthritis has no cure, many sufferers turn to alternative therapies. Some may help, others are worthless, often costly, and sometimes dangerous. Bee venom injections do nothing for arthritis. Chelation, normally used to remove toxic metals from the body, has been promoted in a series of 20 to 30 intravenous treatments as a remedy for rheumatoid arthritis, but there is no scientific evidence that it is effective. Herbal treatments, such as Chinese black balls sold under such brand names as Miracle Herb and Tung Shueh, have been found to contain the anti-anxiety drug diazepam (Valium) and mefenamic acid, a potent anti-inflammatory drug.

ARTICHOKES

BENEFITS
- *A good source of folate, vitamin C, and potassium.*
- *Low in calories, high in fiber.*

DRAWBACKS
- *May provoke allergic reaction in people sensitive to ragweed.*

Served either hot or cold, the globe artichoke is both a delicacy and a low-calorie, nutritious vegetable. Actually, a globe artichoke is the flower bud of a large, thistlelike plant, with only a few edible portions—the heart and the tender, fleshy part at the base of the tough outer leaves.

To prepare a fresh artichoke, the thorny top and leaf tips are trimmed away, and the vegetable is then boiled, steamed, or baked. It can be served in many ways, but one of the most popular is to dip the edible portion of the leaves in a sauce. It's this sauce that determines whether an artichoke is a healthful treat or a high-calorie indulgence. High-fat sauces like Hollandaise and melted butter are traditional favorites; a more healthful choice is lemon juice with a dash of olive oil.

A large artichoke provides 12 percent of the daily requirement of folate, 20 percent of vitamin C, 300mg of potassium, and about 2g of fiber. Artichokes contain cynarin, a chemical said to improve liver function and possibly lower blood cholesterol, but these claims are unproved. Also lacking proof are claims that artichokes lower blood sugar and stimulate bile flow.

Artichokes are members of the sunflower, or composite, plant family. People allergic to ragweed pollen may react to artichokes because of cross-reacting antigens that respond to both allergens.

EDIBLE THISTLE. *Globe artichokes (right) are no relation of the Jerusalem artichoke.*

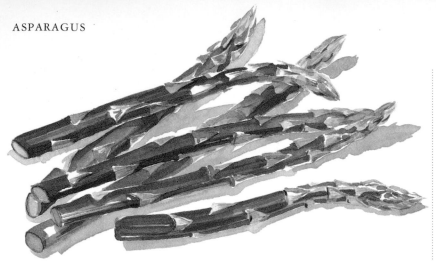

ASPARAGUS

BENEFITS
- *A good low-calorie source of folate and vitamins A and C.*
- *Stalks are high in fiber.*

DRAWBACKS
- *Contains purines, which may precipitate an attack of gout.*

Prized as a springtime delicacy for centuries, this edible member of the lily family is now so widely cultivated that it is available in every season. Lightly boiled or steamed, asparagus makes a tasty and nutritious appetizer, salad ingredient, or side dish.

The ancient Greeks and Romans thought that asparagus possessed medicinal qualities, curing everything from rheumatism to toothaches. None of these properties have been proven true, but asparagus does provide many essential nutrients: Six spears, or a half-cup serving, contain 90mcg (micrograms) of folate, almost one-half of the adult Recommended Nutrient Intake (RNI); as well as 20mg of vitamin C, or half of the RNI; and 750 IU of vitamin A (in the form of beta carotene), or about one-fifth of the RNI. Asparagus is low in calories (25 in six spears), high in fiber, and a useful source of protein.

Asparagus should be eaten as soon as possible after picking; it spoils quickly, and if unrefrigerated, it loses half its vitamin C and much of its flavor in just 2 or 3 days. If frozen quickly, asparagus retains most of its nutrients; canning destroys some flavor and nutrients while adding large amounts of salt.

GOUT sufferers may be advised to forgo asparagus because it contains purines, substances that can precipitate a painful attack of the disease. Some people notice that asparagus gives their urine a pungent odor; this harmless reaction occurs when the body metabolizes the sulfur compounds in the food. Studies show, however, that only about 40 percent of people have this problem.

ASTHMA

CONSUME PLENTY OF
- *Chicken soup, broth, and other fluids to help thin bronchial mucus.*
- *Foods high in omega-3 fatty acids to counter inflammation.*

AVOID
- *Any foods, including dairy products, or additives that seem to bring on attacks.*
- *Mushrooms, cheese, soy sauce, and yeasty breads if molds trigger attacks.*
- *Salicylates, an ingredient in aspirin, tea, vinegar, salad dressings, many fruits, and a few vegetables.*
- *Any food preserved with sulfites.*
- *Foods containing tartrazine, or yellow food dye 5.*

Asthma is a chronic lung condition that is a leading cause of childhood deaths, especially among city dwellers. The rising toll of asthma has puzzled doctors, but many attribute it to a combination of factors, such as the cost of asthma medications, which may be beyond the means of low-income families, improper use of asthma medications, and exposure to environmental pollutants.

Wheezing, chest tightness, labored breathing, and other asthma symptoms occur when the tiny muscles that control the airways to the lungs constrict, causing a bronchospasm. Normally, the airways narrow somewhat when exposed to smoke, pollutants, very cold air, or substances that are harmful if inhaled. In asthmatic people, however, the response is exaggerated and often triggered by otherwise harmless substances or activities, such as pollen and other allergens and exercise.

The reason some people have hyperreactive airways is unknown; heredity, however, is suspected of playing a role, because the disease runs in families. Many asthmatics also have hay fever and other allergies. Although stress and emotional upsets can trigger or worsen an attack, experts emphasize that asthma is a lung disease, not a psychological disorder; as such, it should be treated as a serious and sometimes debilitating physical condition.

Some asthma attacks are quickly reversed by taking a bronchodilator medication that eases symptoms by opening the constricted airways. Other episodes are more prolonged, and, as the airways become more inflamed and clogged with mucus, breathing becomes increasingly difficult. In such cases, an injection of epinephrine (Adrenalin) and a corticosteroid drug may be needed to stop the attack.

Although asthma is a chronic disease, the changes that occur during an attack are temporary, and the lungs generally function normally at other

Case Study

*W*hen Daniel suffered his first asthma attack, his parents misinterpreted his symptoms for a cold. But when they consulted a doctor, they learned that Daniel had asthma.

The doctor prescribed an inhalant, but he also stressed eliminating possible asthma triggers. As a result, the family cat was sent to live with Daniel's grandparents, and the entire house was placed off-limits to smokers. Despite these precautions, however, Daniel's attacks continued.

After careful questioning, the doctor began to suspect that an allergy to molds might be the trigger, and subsequent skin tests confirmed this. Daniel's parents were given a list of foods he should avoid, and an environmental hygienist checked the family home for hidden sources of molds.

times. When asthma starts during childhood, the frequency and severity of attacks tend to lessen as the youngster grows and may disappear by adulthood. Some adults, however, suffer a recurrence, often as an aftermath of a viral infection. In such cases, the asthma may be even more severe than it was in childhood.

ELIMINATING TRIGGERS

Doctors agree that the best treatment for asthma entails identifying and then avoiding its triggers. In some instances these are obvious—for example, exposure to tobacco smoke and other noxious fumes, cold air, exercise, or an allergy to animal dander. Seasonal asthma is usually due to various pollens, molds, and other environmental factors. Suspected allergens can usually be identified by blood and skin tests.

In many asthma sufferers, food AL-LERGIES can trigger attacks; in these cases, identifying the culprits may require considerable detective work, especially in children. Because food allergies vary from one person to another, there's no handy list of offenders. But sometimes a child unconsciously links an offending food with his asthma by fussing or refusing to eat it. Complaints such as "it makes my mouth feel funny" may point to a food allergy. More often, however, foods that trigger asthma are identified by keeping a careful record of the time and ingestion of all foods and drinks, as well as any asthma symptoms. After a few weeks, a pattern of offending foods may emerge. A doctor can then do confirming skin or other allergy tests.

For some people, environmental allergens that are inadvertently ingested are the problem, rather than the foods themselves. People allergic to ragweed, for example, may also react to pyrethrum, a natural pesticide made from chrysanthemums, or to other allergens related to plants.

Similarly, people allergic to mildew and other environmental molds may react to molds in foods; common offenders include cheese, mushrooms, hot dogs and other processed meats, and anything that is fermented, including soy sauce, beer, wine, and vinegar.

Salicylates—compounds in the same family as the active ingredient in aspirin and found naturally in many fruits—may trigger asthma. Yellow food dye 5 (tartrazine) is chemically similar to salicylate, although it is less potent.

More prevalent—and potentially deadly—asthma triggers are sulfites, preservatives that are added to many foods to prevent spoilage and preserve color and texture. They are especially common in dried fruits, dehydrated or instant soup mixes, instant potatoes, dough conditioners, wine, beer, and white grape juice. Anyone sensitive to sulfites should carefully check food labels for any ingredient ending in sulfite—for example, potassium bisulfite—as well as sulfur dioxide. In addition to precipitating an asthma attack, sulfites sometimes lead to anaphylaxis in people hypersensitive to them.

HELPFUL FOODS

There are no specific foods that prevent asthma, but some may lessen its complications. Omega-3 fatty acids, found in canola oil and salmon, mackerel, sardines, and other cold-water fish, have an anti-inflammatory effect and may counter bronchial inflammation. To fight bronchitis and other secondary lung infections, some nutritionists recommend eating extra servings of fresh vegetables and fruits for vitamin C, and lean meat, oysters, whole grains, and yogurt for zinc—nutrients that promote a healthy immune system.

Coffee and tea are sources of theophylline, a bronchial muscle relaxant used to treat asthma in people who are not sensitive to salicylates. A mild asthma attack can sometimes be aborted by drinking one or two cups of tea. Anyone taking a theophylline drug should avoid large amounts of tea to prevent an overdose.

POTENTIAL PROBLEMS

Like everyone else, asthma patients need to consume a healthful, balanced diet, but this is sometimes difficult if allergies require eliminating entire food groups (for example, milk and other dairy products). A dietitian can recommend substitutes or supplements to ensure maintaining good nutrition.

Asthma drugs can create nutritional problems. Long-term steroid use, for example, causes bone loss; vitamin D and calcium supplements may be needed to strengthen bones. Potassium deficiency is another potential problem; it can be prevented by eating ample citrus fruits, bananas, whole grains, and green leafy vegetables. Epinephrine and other bronchodilator drugs can cause feelings of nervousness, which are exacerbated by caffeine. It may be advisable to switch to decaffeinated coffee.

ATHEROSCLEROSIS

EAT PLENTY OF
- *Fresh fruits and vegetables for vitamin C and beta carotene.*
- *Wheat germ, lean poultry and seafood, and greens for vitamin E.*
- *Salmon, sardines, and other cold-water fish for omega-3 fatty acids.*
- *Apples, oatmeal, and whole-grain products for pectin and other types of dietary fiber.*

CUT DOWN ON
- *Fats, especially saturated ones.*
- *High-cholesterol foods.*

AVOID
- *Smoking, obesity, high alcohol intake, and physical inactivity.*

As we become older, our arteries lose some of their elasticity and stiffen. This can lead to a progressive condition referred to as arteriosclerosis, the medical term for hardening (sclerosis) of the arteries. These stiffened blood vessels usually become clogged with fatty plaque, the hallmark of atherosclerosis (*athero* is the Greek term for porridge, which describes the thick, cheesy appearance of the deposits).

Some degree of arteriosclerosis is a natural part of aging; indeed, it usually progresses slowly for many years without producing noticeable symptoms. But serious problems develop when these stiffened blood vessels become severely narrowed with plaque. Complications include CIRCULATORY DISORDERS, especially reduced blood flow to the lower legs and other extremities; angina, the chest pains caused by inadequate oxygen to the heart muscle; and HEART DISEASE and STROKE, which can result in disability and death.

Atherosclerosis is rare in underdeveloped parts of the world, but it is exceedingly common in industrialized Western societies. By the time they have reached their late forties, most men in these countries have some degree of atherosclerosis. In women the process is somewhat delayed, presumably due to the protective effects of estrogen during the reproductive years. After menopause, however, women quickly catch up with their male counterparts, and once in their sixties they are just as likely to develop severely clogged arteries as men are.

UNDERLYING CAUSES

Precisely what initiates atherosclerosis is unknown. Some experts theorize that it's an autoimmune disorder in which components of the immune system attack the artery walls and make them vulnerable to the buildup of fatty deposits. Others believe that a virus or some other environmental agent caus-

es the initial damage. Most agree, however, that a genetic susceptibility and a combination of lifestyle factors accelerate the process; these include a diet high in fats and cholesterol, cigarette use, excessive stress, and lack of exercise. Poorly controlled diabetes and high blood pressure also contribute to atherosclerosis and its complications.

Arteries can be narrowed by 85 percent (occasionally even more) without producing symptoms. Nevertheless, there is still a high risk of a heart attack or stroke because clots tend to form at the site of fatty deposits. Most heart attacks are caused by a clot blocking a coronary artery (a coronary thrombosis); similarly, a cerebral thrombosis, or a clot that blocks blood flow to the brain, is the most common type of stroke. Other manifestations include leg pains caused by reduced blood flow and decreased circulation to the hands.

DIETARY APPROACHES

Researchers agree that diet plays a critical role in both the development and treatment of atherosclerosis. CHOLESTEROL is the major component of atherosclerotic plaque, and numerous studies correlate high levels of blood cholesterol with atherosclerosis. Research indicates that atherosclerosis can be slowed and perhaps even reversed by lowering the amount of cholesterol that circulates in the blood—particularly the levels of low-density lipoproteins (LDLs), the type of cholesterol that collects in plaque.

Elevated triglycerides, another type of lipid that circulates in the blood, also may contribute to atherosclerosis. People with diabetes tend to have high triglyceride and cholesterol levels, which may explain why diabetics are so vulnerable to heart disease.

Dietary treatment for atherosclerosis entails limiting total fat intake to 20 to 30 percent of calories, with saturated fats (found mostly in animal products and palm, coconut, and palm kernel oils) comprising no more than 10 percent of calories. Some experts advocate even more stringent fat reduction; these include Dr. Dean Ornish, the California cardiologist who has developed a comprehensive lifestyle approach to treating heart disease, which combines a healthy low-fat diet with exercise and methods for dealing with stress. His atherosclerosis-reversal regimen limits fat calories to 10 percent of the diet and virtually eliminates saturated fats.

Although consumption of eggs, liver, and other high-cholesterol foods is not as instrumental as a high-fat diet in the development of atherosclerosis, a high intake of dietary cholesterol can raise the levels of blood lipids. Thus, experts generally recommend limiting dietary cholesterol to 300mg a day.

The omega-3 fatty acids in salmon, sardines, and other cold-water fish lower blood levels of triglycerides; they also reduce the tendency to form blood clots. Oat bran, pectin, guar gum, and psyllium all contain soluble FIBER that lowers cholesterol, probably by interfering with the intestinal absorption of bile acids, which forces the liver to use circulating cholesterol to make more bile. Recent studies indicate that AN-TIOXIDANTS, especially beta carotene and vitamins C and E, may protect against atherosclerosis by preventing LDL cholesterol from collecting in atherosclerotic plaque. The regular use of certain garlic preparations has also been shown to reduce blood cholesterol by 10 to 15 percent.

Diet is not the only factor that contributes to atherosclerosis. Maintaining an ideal weight, abstaining from smoking, increasing exercise, developing effective methods of coping with STRESS, and keeping BLOOD PRESSURE and blood sugar levels within normal limits are also important. Estrogen replacement appears to protect older women against atherosclerosis.

AVOCADOS

BENEFITS
- *A rich source of folate, vitamin A, and potassium.*
- *Useful amounts of protein, iron, magnesium, and vitamins C, E, and B$_6$.*

DRAWBACKS
- *Very high in calories, with 85 percent coming from fat.*

Although it is often mistaken for a vegetable, the avocado is a fruit—the reproductive part of the plant. The rich, buttery flavor and smooth texture of an avocado make it a complementary addition to vegetable, meat, and pasta salads. When mashed and seasoned, it can also be served as a dip (as in guacamole), or a sandwich spread. But despite its versatility and nutritional value, the avocado should be used sparingly. It contains approximately 200 calories in a 4-ounce serving, and it has more fat and calories than any other fruit. Because most of the fat in avocados is monounsaturated, it does not tend to elevate blood cholesterol levels, unlike the saturated oil that comes from palms and other tropical plants.

When served as part of an otherwise low-fat meal or snack, an avocado contributes a number of important nutrients. Four ounces, about one-half of a medium-size fruit, provides 500mg of potassium and more than one-third of the Recommended Nutrient Intake (RNI) of folate; it also supplies 10 percent or more of the RNIs for iron, magnesium, and vitamins A, C, E, and B$_6$.

Avocados should be

served raw; they have a bitter taste when cooked. But they can be added to hot dishes that have already been cooked—for example, tossed with a spicy pasta sauce or sliced atop a broiled chicken breast.

BAD BREATH

CONSUME PLENTY OF
- *Water, fruit juice, and sour foods to stimulate saliva flow.*

CUT DOWN ON
- *Sticky sweet foods to reduce plaque.*

AVOID
- *Garlic, onions, and other foods that have strong odors.*
- *Alcohol and tobacco products, which give the breath an unpleasant odor.*
- *Drugs that cause dry mouth.*

Halitosis, the transient bad breath that everyone develops occasionally, is usually a trivial problem caused by certain foods or drinks, smoking, or poor dental hygiene. Often, a chemical in food is responsible. The bad breath caused by eating onions and garlic, for example, is due to a number of smelly sulfur compounds they contain. Residues of wine, beer, and other alcoholic drinks produce a breath odor; and tobacco in any form makes the breath smell stale.

Saliva controls the mouth's bacteria population. A drop in saliva production, such as during sleep or the natural decline with age, allows bacteria, especially at the back of the tongue, to multiply and form plaque. This scenario accounts for morning breath and the bad breath experienced by many older people. More persistent DRY MOUTH may require treatment with artificial saliva, sold at drugstores.

Most bad breath can be remedied by good dental hygiene, eliminating the offending foods from the diet, and abstaining from alcohol and tobacco. If bad breath persists despite these measures, see your dentist first and, if no cause is found, your physician next.

Persistent bad breath may be a sign of an underlying illness. Some diseases, such as kidney failure, liver disease, and diabetes, cause certain odors. Other problems that can cause bad breath include tonsillitis, sinus and nasal problems, bronchitis and other respiratory infections, and some cancers. Disorders that reduce the flow of saliva, such as lupus, also cause bad breath.

QUICK FIXES

Mild bad breath can be camouflaged with a commercial mouth rinse or with foods or herbs that mask the odor. For example, chewing a few sprigs of parsley or peppermint, or anise, dill, or fennel seeds quickly freshens breath. Some people report good results from commercially available pills made from parsley seeds (Breath-asure).

Antiseptic mouth rinses control bad breath by reducing oral bacteria; products with chlorine dioxide are effective. Nonantiseptic rinses simply mask the odor. To make your own rinse, steep three whole (or ¼ teaspoon ground) cloves in hot water for 20 minutes. A commercial toothpaste with fluoride, baking soda, and hydrogen peroxide cleans the teeth and freshens the breath. To make your own, add a few drops of hydrogen peroxide to baking soda.

BANANAS

BENEFITS
- *A good source of potassium, folate, and vitamins C and B6.*

Healthful, filling, and tasty, bananas are one of nature's ideal snacks. The fruit, which is grown in most of the world's tropical areas, is harvested while still green. When stored at room temperature, most bananas ripen in a few days; the process can be hastened, however, by placing them in a plastic or paper bag along with an apple.

Because bananas are bland, easy to digest, and hypoallergenic, they are an ideal early food for babies. Bananas, along with rice, applesauce, and toast, are one of the foods in the BRAT diet recommended after a bout of DIARRHEA. Some ulcer patients report that bananas alleviate some of their pain, but this is unproven.

NUTRITIONAL VALUE

Bananas are exceeded only by avocados (which are high in fat) as a fruit source for potassium, a mineral instrumental in proper muscle function. Patients taking certain diuretic drugs for high blood pressure are usually advised to eat two or three bananas a day to help replace the potassium lost in the urine.

A relatively good source of vitamin B6, a medium (4-ounce) banana supplies one-third the Recommended Nutrient Intake (RNI), along with 10 percent or more of the RNIs for vitamin C and folate. It adds 2g of soluble dietary fiber, which helps to lower blood cholesterol levels. Bananas contain about 100 calories each, mostly in the form of fruit sugar and starch. Because the body quickly converts these to energy, they are a favorite of athletes.

PLANTAINS

These resemble large green bananas, but they never become as sweet. Plantains are baked or fried and served as a starchy side dish; they can also be a delicious addition to soups, stews, and meat dishes. Nutritionally, plantains are comparable to bananas, except that their content of vitamin A is much higher, providing approximately 20 percent of the RNI.

BASIC FOOD GROUPS

*The athlete who burns thousands of calories a day and the some-
what sedentary retiree are poles apart in their energy needs.
Still, both require the same balance of nutrients to stay healthy.*

The essence of a healthy diet can be summed up with three words: variety, moderation, and balance. To make it easy to follow these simple principles, Health Canada has devised the Food Guide Rainbow (see below), which divides foods into four basic groups and recommends a number of daily servings for each. These servings are of moderate size, and if a person selects a variety of foods from each group, there should be no problem in achieving a balanced diet. Still, even those who try to follow the Food Guide guidelines frequently find that they have ques-

5 GUIDELINES FOR HEALTHY EATING

In addition to the Food Guide Rainbow, Health Canada has established the following guidelines for healthy Canadians:

1. Enjoy a variety of foods.

2. Emphasize cereals, breads, other grain products, vegetables, and fruits.

3. Choose lower-fat dairy products, leaner meats, and foods prepared with little or no fat.

4. Achieve and maintain a healthy body weight by enjoying regular physical activity and healthy eating.

5. Limit salt, alcohol, and caffeine.

tions: "Where do fast foods like pizza fit in?," "Won't 12 servings of starchy grains a day cause me to gain weight?," and "Do these guidelines lower my cholesterol?"

THE NEED FOR VARIETY

To maintain health, the body needs a proper balance of carbohydrates, fats, and proteins for energy, growth, and repair or replacement of damaged cells. Also essential to maintain health are at least 13 vitamins and 16 minerals. Nutrition researchers believe that there are still other essential nutrients that have not yet been identified. Although it is not a nutrient, water—the most abundant sub-

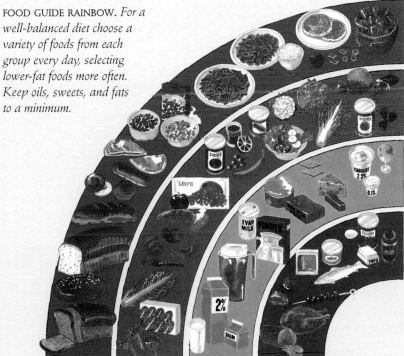

FOOD GUIDE RAINBOW. *For a well-balanced diet choose a variety of foods from each group every day, selecting lower-fat foods more often. Keep oils, sweets, and fats to a minimum.*

**Grain Products.
Have 5 to 12
servings per
day.** Choose
whole grain and
enriched products
more often.

**Vegetables and
Fruit. Have 5 to
10 servings per
day.** Choose
dark green and
orange vegetables
and orange fruit
more often.

**Milk Products.
Have 2 to 4
servings per
day.** Choose
lower-fat milk
products more
often.

**Meat & Alternatives.
Have 2 to 3 servings
per day.** Choose leaner
meats, poultry and fish, as
well as dried peas, beans
and lentils more often.

THE FOOD GROUPS: TAKING THE PATH TO HEALTHIER EATING

A balanced diet emphasizes a wide variety of grains and other complex carbohydrates, vegetables, fruits, and smaller amounts of meat and fish, dairy products, and fats. The chart below lists *the recommended daily amounts, in descending order, for the four Food Guide Rainbow groups (see Food Guide Rainbow, p.39), and suggests ways to improve your diet.*

FOOD GROUPS AND THEIR NUTRIENTS	TRY TO	AVOID
GRAIN PRODUCTS  **5 to 12 servings daily.** These foods provide complex carbohydrates (starches) and are a major source of B vitamins, magnesium, and many other minerals; enriched breads and cereals also provide iron; some products have been fortified with calcium.	Whenever possible, use whole-grain products. Combine grains with beans and other legumes to make a low-fat complete protein.	Frying any of the foods in this group. In addition, use butter, margarine, and other types of creamy spreads and sauces only in moderation.
VEGETABLES  **3 to 5 servings daily.** An assortment of these foods provides fiber and numerous vitamins and minerals, including vitamins A and C, folate, potassium, and magnesium, and they supply important plant chemicals that prevent tumor growth.	Include servings of broccoli, Brussels sprouts, cabbage, and other cruciferous vegetables 3 or 4 times a week. These foods, along with yellow or orange vegetables, contain protective bioflavonoids.	Frying vegetables in oil and with batter; serving with butter or cream sauces; overcooking, which destroys some nutrients.
FRUITS  **2 to 5 servings daily.** Like vegetables, fruits offer a broad range of nutrients, including beta carotene, vitamin C, potassium, fiber, and various bioflavonoids and other beneficial plant chemicals.	Eat a broad spectrum of fruits, including at least one citrus fruit per day. Incorporate them into your meals and eat them as snacks instead of products that are high in fat and sugar.	Consuming all fruit servings at once. Too much acidic food may lead to intestinal upsets.
MILK PRODUCTS  **2 to 4 servings daily.** Dairy products—such as milk, cheeses, yogurt, and other milk products—are the main source of calcium. They also provide protein and riboflavin and other B vitamins.	Opt for low-fat versions of dairy products, such as milk (skim or 1% fat), yogurt, and cheese. Look for brands that have been fortified with vitamins A and D.	Products or recipes that contain heavy cream, butter, whole milk, or full-fat cheese.
MEAT AND ALTERNATIVES  **2 to 3 servings daily.** This group provides the bulk of dietary protein, as well as the B vitamins, iron, phosphorus, magnesium, zinc, and other minerals.	Opt for poultry or fish. Limit red meats and fatty or processed meats, such as sausage and bologna; instead, choose lean meats and trim all fat before cooking.	Frying or sautéeing in fat; instead, cook by grilling, baking, roasting, or stir-frying.
OTHER FOODS  **Use sparingly.** This group includes margarine, butter, oils, sugar, chocolate, and other sweet or fatty foods. Only a very small amount of fat is necessary for the body to function properly.	Emphasize monounsaturated fats, such as canola and olive oils. Flavor with spices instead of frying in oils or using fatty spreads. Skim fat from meat juices, stews, and soups.	Fatty snack foods, such as potato chips, chocolate, pastries, and ice cream.

stance in the human body—is also essential to sustain life.

Keeping track of the daily intake of the more than 30 known essential nutrients is a daunting, if not impossible, task; fortunately, there's no need to do so. By consuming sensible portions from each of the food groups, most people will get all the nutrients that they need.

THE BASIC FOOD GROUPS

In Canada, public nutrition education is looked after by Health and Welfare Canada. Canada's Food Guide divides common foods into four categories: grain products, milk products, fruits and vegetables, and meat and alternatives.

The Food Guide describes the number and size of servings that should be consumed from each food group, making allowances for pregnant and breast-feeding women, males and females, age, body size, and activity level. Following the general concepts will result in a "nutritious diet." This means that energy needs will be fulfilled, micronutrient requirements (vitamins and minerals) will be met, and the macronutrients (proteins, fats, and carbohydrates) will be consumed in an appropriate ratio.

The optimal balance is arrived at by featuring an abundance of servings from the grain and fruit and vegetable groups, while limiting intake of fattier foods found in the milk and meat categories. If the guidelines are followed, no more than 30 percent of the total number of calories will come from fats.

The total number of servings a day adds up to a minimum of 14 and a maximum of 29, which sounds like a lot, but portions are quite small (see What Makes a Serving?, above) and the number of servings should be adjusted according to individual energy needs. A truly balanced diet is one that provides all the essential nutrients

WHAT MAKES A SERVING?

FOOD GROUP	SAMPLE SERVING
Grain products	I slice bread; ½ bagel, pita or bun; ½ cup pasta or rice; I bowl of hot cereal; I bowl of cold cereal
Vegetables	½ cup fresh, frozen, or canned vegetables; I medium-size vegetable; I cup salad; ½ cup juice
Fruits	½ cup fresh, frozen, or canned fruit; I medium-size fruit; ½ cup juice
Milk products	I cup milk; ¾ cup yogurt; 1½ oz of cheese
Meat and alternatives	2 to 3 oz lean meat, poultry, or fish; ⅓ to ⅔ can of fish; I to 2 eggs; ⅓ cup of tofu; 2 tbsp of peanut butter

while maintaining the ideal body weight. Thus, a person trying to shed a few pounds may have the maximum number of low-calorie fruits and vegetables and the minimum number of servings from the meat, dairy, and starch groups, which tend to be higher in calories.

RECOMMENDED NUTRIENT INTAKES (RNIs)

To meet the nutritional needs of most people, the Nutrition Research Division of Health and Welfare Canada established the Recommended Nutrient Intakes, or RNIs, for 9 vitamins, 6 minerals, protein, and energy.

The Nutrition Research Division also lists the estimated safe and adequate intakes of two other vitamins and five minerals. To determine a specific RNI, nutrition scientists establish a minimum value, below which deficiency develops, and a maximum amount, above which harm might occur. The RNI is set between these two values, with a margin of safety to ensure a reserve to carry a person through weeks or even months of inadequate intake.

Many people mistakenly assume that they must consume the full RNI of each nutrient daily. This is not true, because each RNI is actually more than a person needs. For example,

the RNI for vitamin C (40mg) is really four times what the average person needs to prevent scurvy. It should be noted that in Canada, deficiency diseases are rare, occurring mostly among people with other disorders—for example, thiamine deficiency is common among long-term alcoholics and the elderly.

THE MEDITERRANEAN DIET

Observing that the people of Greece, Italy, and other Mediterranean countries have much lower cholesterol levels and far fewer heart attacks than North Americans, researchers have tried to determine why. Many have concluded that the answer lies in their diet.

In contrast to the typical North American diet, wine is a regular feature of the Mediterranean diet. The bulk of the diet consists of pasta, bread, grains and other starches, fresh fruits and vegetables, nuts and beans.

Consumed regularly, about every other day, are cheese and yogurt, olives and olive oil. Sweets, eggs, poultry and fish are served frequently, a few times a week. Least often consumed is red meat, which is typically served in small portions, only a few times each month.

Although the Mediterranean diet does not specify serving sizes, as a general rule of thumb Western nutritionists recommend eating more pasta, grains, breads, fruits and vegetables, legumes, yogurt, cheese, and olives or olive oil, and less poultry and fish, sweets, eggs, and especially red meat.

More than 30 percent of total calories in the typical Mediterranean diet come from fats, mostly monounsaturated olive oil. Nutritionists note that the diet provides more fat and calories than what is generally recommended for most North Americans, but because so many Mediterranean people have physically demanding occupations, they are less likely to gain weight.

THE QUESTION OF SUPPLEMENTS

Millions of people take high-dose vitamin pills daily, especially beta carotene and vitamins C and E, the ANTIOXIDANT nutrients that have received so much media attention in recent years. But supplements are no substitute for good eating habits, and the vast majority of people can fulfill their nutritional needs by following the Food Guide Rainbow (see p.39).

Megadose supplements can actually be harmful. When taken in very large amounts, vitamins and minerals, like all drugs, carry a risk of adverse side effects and interactions. Many minerals, and vitamins A and D, are stored in the body and can build to toxic levels when taken in excess. The presence of large quantities of a particular vitamin or mineral in the intestinal tract invariably interferes with the body's absorption of other nutrients and can actually lead to deficiency diseases.

If supplements are needed, they should only be prescribed by a doctor. For example, a woman planning to conceive or who is already pregnant needs extra folate to protect her baby from neurological problems. Pregnancy also increases the demand for iron beyond what can be obtained from an ordinary diet. An older woman may need additional calcium and vitamin D to help prevent OSTEOPOROSIS.

HOW MUCH WATER DO WE NEED?

A healthy adult needs 2½ to 3 quarts of fluids a day. Some of this fluid comes from food, but six to eight glasses should come from water or other nonalcoholic drinks (avoid drinks high in sugar and caffeine). Prolonged exercise, hot weather, diarrhea, and a fever are among many conditions that demand extra fluid intake. In these cases drink extra fluids before signs of thirst occur (thirst is unreliable, especially in the elderly).

BALANCED MEALS. *Essential nutrients can be found in a variety of appetizing and appealing meals. For example (from left to right): chicken and vegetables with rice; pasta with vegetables; and salmon with potatoes, zucchini, and tomatoes.*

BEANS

BENEFITS
- *High in folate and vitamins A and C.*
- *Mature (shelled) beans are high in protein and iron.*

DRAWBACKS
- *Shelled beans can cause flatulence.*
- *Fava beans are toxic to some people.*

Green beans (which can also be yellow or purple) are harvested at an immature stage. Both the tender pods and small, soft seeds are eaten. In shelled varieties only the seeds are eaten. Some, such as lima beans, are harvested while they are still tender; others are left to mature (see LEGUMES). Most pod beans—snap beans, Italian green beans, long Chinese beans, purple and yellow wax beans, and green beans—can be eaten raw. More commonly, they are steamed or boiled. Shelled beans should always be cooked; they can be served hot or cold.

NUTRITIONAL VALUE

Limas and favas are good sources of protein, providing about 7g per half-cup serving. The same-size serving of baby or green lima beans contains 2mg of iron, more than twice as much as in favas and four times the amount in ½ cup of green snap beans. All these varieties are good sources of folate and vitamins A and C. Shelled beans have more thiamine, vitamin B_6, potassium, and magnesium; the soluble fiber in shelled beans may lower cholesterol, but the presence of carbohydrates such as raffinose may also cause FLATULENCE.

Warning: Some Mediterranean people lack an enzyme needed to protect red blood cells from damage by vicine, a toxic substance in fava beans that causes a type of anemia. People taking monoamine oxidase (MAO) inhibitors to treat depression should also avoid fava beans; the combination can raise blood pressure.

SPROUTING BEANS. *Among the most popular sprouts that can be grown at home are (from top to bottom) mung beans, chickpeas, green lentils, alfalfa, and soybeans.*

BEAN SPROUTS

BENEFITS
- *Some are high in folate; others are fair to good sources of protein, vitamin C, B vitamins, and iron.*

DRAWBACK
- *Alfalfa sprouts may provoke a flare-up of symptoms in lupus patients.*

Various types of sprouts are available in health-food stores, supermarkets, and salad bars. However, few live up to their reputation as the prototype of health foods. Some sprouts are much more nutritious than others. A cup of raw mung bean sprouts, for example, provides one-third of the Recommended Nutrient Intake (RNI) of folate and 30 percent of the RNI for vitamin C. In contrast, it takes approximately five cups of alfalfa sprouts to yield comparable amounts.

Warning: Most sprouts can be eaten raw. An important exception is the sprouted soybean, which contains a potentially harmful toxin that is destroyed by cooking. People with LUPUS should avoid alfalfa sprouts; alfalfa in any form can prompt a flare-up of symptoms.

BEEF AND VEAL

BENEFITS
- *Major sources of high-quality protein.*
- *Contain a wide range of nutrients, especially vitamin B_{12}, iron, and zinc.*

DRAWBACKS
- *Beef fat is highly saturated and can increase blood cholesterol levels and the risk of cardiovascular disease.*
- *A high-meat diet may raise the risk of colon cancer and other cancers.*
- *Rare beef is a source of* E. coli *and toxoplasmosis infections.*

Although its consumption has decreased dramatically in recent decades, beef is still a popular red meat. One of the most versatile meats, beef may be prepared by roasting, stewing, broiling, frying, and grilling. Beef, especially in the form of hamburgers, is the most common meat served in restaurants.

There is no question that beef is a highly nutritious food source; not only is it a leading source of high-quality protein, but a 4-ounce serving provides more than 100 percent of the Recommended Nutrient Intake (RNI) of vitamin B_{12}, an essential nutrient found only in animal products. Beef is also an excellent source of vitamin B_6, niacin, and riboflavin, as well as such essential minerals as iron and zinc.

A CASE OF LESS IS BEST
Beef's major nutritional drawback is the large amount of mostly saturated fat in many cuts, especially prime roasts and steaks. It is also a leading source of dietary cholesterol. Studies link a diet with large amounts of meat to an increased risk of heart attacks and certain cancers. Even well-trimmed lean beef has some hidden fat. Nonetheless, nutritionists stress that beef can be part of a healthful, low-fat diet if it is limited to small, fat-trimmed portions of round steak, brisket, and other lean cuts.

The way beef is cooked substantially affects its fat content. Trimming away all visible fat is an obvious beginning; roasting or broiling beef on a rack or spit allows the fat to drip free of the meat. Another approach is to cook stews and soups in advance, chill them so that the congealed fat can be removed easily, and then reheat before serving. Of course, controlling the size of the portion is important. A 16-ounce T-bone steak, rack of short ribs, or huge slab of prime rib roast each have 800 to 1,000 calories, with half or more of them coming from fat. In contrast, a modest 4-ounce serving of choice-cut eye of round provides about 200 calories, 70 of which come from fat.

The liver, kidneys, and other organ meats are the most concentrated source of iron and vitamins A and B_{12} in beef. At one time, women were urged to eat an occasional serving of liver to prevent iron-deficiency anemia. But enthusiasm for liver and other organ meats has been

---

ABOUT VEAL

Very young calves produce the delicate pink, low-fat meat of veal, which has always been considered a luxury meat in Canada. To ensure that the meat is fine grained and light textured, veal growers often resort to keeping calves confined in small, enclosed stalls or boxes, preventing them from eating grass. The calves are fed only milk, and after just a few weeks, the confined animals become painfully anemic. Media campaigns to raise public awareness of the cruel plight of veal calves has resulted in a sharp decline in veal consumption, which is now about 3 pounds per person a year compared to over 5 pounds a few decades ago.

---

dampened in recent years for several reasons: They are very high in fat and cholesterol, and they may further increase the risk of heart disease.

Another issue revolves around the fact that factory-reared animals are fed large amounts of antibiotics and hormones, which concentrate in the animals' liver. Some experts contend that these drug and hormone residues pose a health risk to humans who ingest them; others, however, insist that they are safe. Still, some countries cite these potential risks as a reason to bar the importation of Canadian and American beef.

A woman who consumes liver products frequently may store large amounts of vitamin A in her body. Although it is unlikely that this would endanger her health, it might cause serious birth defects if she becomes pregnant. This risk is compounded if the woman is also taking vitamin A supplements.

ANOTHER HEALTH ISSUE
Recent outbreaks of a deadly type of *E. coli* infection have been traced to contaminated beef. There are many strains of *E. coli* bacteria, including harmless ones that normally inhabit the human intestinal tract. But in 1982 researchers identified a different strain, later called 0157:H7, in the intestinal tract of cattle. This type of *E. coli* can easily invade meat during slaughtering. Grinding the contaminated beef further spreads the bacteria through the meat. The organism can survive in hamburgers and other contaminated beef that is served rare, so it's important to cook the meat thoroughly. When this strain of *E. coli* reaches the human intestinal tract, it can cause mild to severe diarrhea. More seriously, some people—especially children, the elderly, and individuals with weakened immune systems—develop hemolytic uremic syndrome, a life-threatening disorder characterized by the rapid destruction of red blood cells and kidney failure.

Recent studies indicate that approximately 55,000 North Americans are stricken with *E. coli* infections from beef each year. Although some infections have been traced to rare roast beef, and a few to unpasteurized milk, rare hamburgers are by far the most common source. Public health officials stress that virtually all beef-borne *E. coli* infections can be prevented by cooking beef, especially hamburger, until it is well-done, with no traces of pink, and by using only pasteurized milk.

SOCIAL ISSUES

The process of producing a pound of beef requires much more land and other resources than growing an equivalent amount of vegetable protein. Critics of our high beef consumption point to the increasing destruction of the Amazon rain forests, as well as our own ecological systems, to make room for more cattle ranching. The growing trend to raise meat animals in enclosed factories creates different environmental problems altogether—in particular, finding ways to dispose of animal waste without polluting our rivers and other natural resources.

BEER

BENEFITS
• *Is lower in alcohol concentrations than wine and hard liquor.*
• *Contains modest amounts of niacin, folate, vitamin B6, and some minerals.*

DRAWBACKS
• *Overconsumption can cause unwanted weight gain and obesity.*
• *Heavy drinking can lead to inebriation and alcoholism.*
• *Causes feelings of aggression in some people.*

Historians believe that humans began to brew beer some time around 5000 B.C. in what is now Iraq and Egypt. Barley, the grain that still dominates beer brewing, was abundant in that region. Nonetheless, almost every society worldwide has independently developed ways of making beer from local cereal grains: African tribes use sprouted corn, millet, and sorghum; Russians turn rye bread into a low-alcohol beer called kvass; the Chinese and Japanese use rice; and South and Central American Indians rely on corn to make their respective beers.

THE BREWING PROCESS

Although many societies around the world continue to use their traditional methods to make beer, modern brewing is a scientific process that begins with malting to convert grain starch into sugar that will ferment. To do this, the grain is sprouted in order to activate enzymes that will eventually turn the starch into sugar. The precise methods vary according to the type of beer being produced, but at some point the germination is stopped, the sprouts are removed, and the malted grain is then prepared for mashing. The malt is heated slowly to allow the enzymes to continue converting starch into a sugary broth called wort. The grain is allowed to settle, and the wort is heated and filtered through it into the brewing kettles. (The grains are then rinsed and salvaged for livestock feed.)

Hops, which are dried flowers from the hop vine, are added to the wort, and the mixture is boiled and then strained. (The used hops are added to livestock feed.) The wort is allowed to settle so that the protein, which clouds beer, can be removed; the clear liquid is then fermented with yeast and aged. Eventually, yeast residue is skimmed off and used as a nutritional supplement (brewer's yeast) or added to livestock feed. The process may be varied and other ingredients added to give beer a distinctive flavor, color, or aroma. Adding extra hops produces the British draft beer known as bitters; ale, a more concentrated beer, uses a type of yeast that rises to the top; stout is a bitter ale brewed from a dark malt.

The specific brewing method influences the nutritional quality of beer. The cloudy German *weisse bier,* for example, retains many of the B vitamins

found in brewer's yeast, but these are strained away to make clear beer. Native African beers remain unfiltered; as a result, they retain many of the nutrients found in the grains and roots and tubers that are their main ingredients. The type of yeast used by Canadian brewers contains selenium, an antioxidant mineral, and chromium, a mineral that aids carbohydrate metabolism.

Nevertheless, the nutritional value of beer is often overstated because most of the nutrients in grain are lost in the brewing process. About two-thirds of the 150 calories in 12 ounces of ordinary beer come from the alcohol itself, with one-third coming from sugars; in contrast, only a trace of protein remains after brewing and straining. A 12-ounce bottle of ordinary beer provides 10 percent or more of the RNIs of folate, niacin, vitamin B_6, phosphorus, and magnesium as well as significant amounts of chromium and selenium.

HOW MUCH IS ENOUGH?

Typically, the alcohol content of beer ranges from 3 to 8 percent, compared to an average of 12 percent in wine and about 40 to 50 percent in hard liquor. Some people who are very sensitive to alcohol will react almost immediately to even this modest amount, often with feelings of aggression. Many people, however, can consume a quart or more of beer without obvious mental or physical effects. Since drinking more than a quart of fluid produces an uncomfortable feeling of fullness, most beer drinkers usually stop before they become inebriated. Even so, drinking a quart of beer may yield up to 600 calories, which can result in weight gain, and the excessive urination resulting from the diuretic effect of the alcohol can wash away important vitamins and minerals before the body can absorb them. Contrary to popular belief, chronic overconsumption of beer can lead to problem drinking and alcoholism.

Beer is frequently served with nuts, potato chips, pretzels, and other salty foods. Because these increase feelings of thirst, they actually promote consumption of excessive amounts of beer. Foods that are high in protein, starches, vitamins, and minerals are better alternatives to balance the high-sugar content of beer; for example, eggs, meat, poultry, seafood, or such starchy foods as whole-grain bread or crackers, pasta, and legumes.

BEETS

BENEFITS
- *A good source of folate and vitamin C.*
- *The greens are a rich source of potassium, calcium, iron, beta carotene, and vitamin C.*
- *Low in calories.*

DRAWBACKS
- *Turn urine and stools red, a harmless condition that nonetheless alarms people who mistake it for blood.*

Beets are a highly versatile vegetable. They can be boiled and served as a side dish, pickled and eaten as a salad or condiment, or used as the main ingredient in borscht, a popular Eastern European cold summer soup. Beet greens, the most nutritious part of the vegetable, can be cooked and served like spinach or Swiss chard.

According to folklore, beets were believed to possess curative powers for headaches and other painful conditions. Even today, some naturalist practitioners recommend beets to prevent cancer and bolster immunity; they also suggest using the juice of raw beets to speed convalescence. Although beets are a reasonably nutritious food source, there is no scientific proof that they confer any special medicinal benefits.

A half-cup serving of beets provides 45mcg (micrograms) of folate, about

one-fourth the adult Recommended Nutrient Intake (RNI), and 5mg of vitamin C. The tops, if eaten while young and green, are more nutritious: 1 cup supplies 35mg of vitamin C, almost 90 percent of the RNI for adults; 720 RE of Vitamin A; and 160mg of calcium, 2.5mg of iron, and 1,300mg of potassium.

The most flavorful beets are small, with greens still attached. The best way to cook beet roots is to boil them unpeeled, which retains most of the nutrients as well as the deep red color. After the beets have cooled, the skins slip off easily; the root can be sliced, chopped, or puréed, depending upon the method of serving. Beets may also be canned and pickled with vinegar; some nutrients are lost in the processing, but the sweet beet flavor remains.

EFFECTS ON BODY WASTES

Many people become alarmed when they notice that their urine and stools have turned pink or even red after eating beets. This is a harmless condition that occurs in about 15 percent of people who lack the gut bacteria that normally degrade betalains, the bright red pigment in beets. The urine and stools usually return to their normal colors after a day or two.

BEGINNER FOODS—FEEDING A BABY

Proper early nutrition is extremely important. The eating patterns established in infancy not only determine how well a baby grows but also influence lifelong food habits and attitudes.

New parents probably worry more about feeding their baby than any other aspect of early child care. What if I can't breast-feed? How do I know if the baby is getting enough? Too much? Should I give the baby vitamins? When do I start solid food? Parents quickly learn that almost everyone is eager to answer such questions—grandparents, doctors, nurses, neighbors, babysitters, casual acquaintances—even strangers in the

FIRST MOUTHFULS. *Family mealtimes around the table give a newly weaned infant the opportunity to experience a variety of new tastes and food textures.*

supermarket. As might be expected, however, much of the advice is conflicting and adds to a parent's feelings of confusion and uncertainty. So let's begin with some general guidelines that should help ease some of the anxiety associated with feeding an infant:

First, get to know your baby. No two infants are alike. Some enter the world ravenously hungry and demand to be fed every hour or two. Others seem to prefer sleeping, and may even need to be awakened to eat.

Second, try to relax and enjoy your baby. It's natural for new parents to feel nervous and apprehensive,

not sure if they are doing everything the right way, but raising a baby should be a joyful experience.

Third, learn to trust your own judgment and common sense. If a baby is growing and developing at a normal pace, he's getting enough to eat. With a little practice, you'll learn how to adjust the diet to the baby's needs.

Finally, keep food in its proper perspective. It provides the essential energy and nourishment infants need to grow and develop. But food should not be a substitute for a reassuring hug or used as a bribe or reward for good behavior. If parents respond accordingly, even an

infant quickly learns how to use food as a manipulative tool, which can set the stage for later eating problems.

IN THE BEGINNING

Good infant nutrition actually begins before birth, because what the mother eats during PREGNANCY goes a long way toward determining her baby's nutritional needs. Skimping on food to avoid gaining excessive weight while pregnant can produce a low-birth-weight baby who not only has special nutritional needs but may also have serious medical problems. An anemic woman is likely to have a baby with low iron reserves. A woman who does not consume adequate folate may have a baby with serious neurological problems. Conversely, high doses of vitamin A just before and during early pregnancy can cause birth defects. Because of these potential problems, all pregnant women are strongly advised to have regular prenatal checkups and to eat a varied and balanced diet.

Physicians are in agreement that breast milk provides the best and most complete nutrition for full-term infants. (Premature and low-birth-weight babies may need special supplements.) Even if the mother plans to bottle-feed later, her baby benefits from just a few breast-feedings. Colostrum, the breast fluid that is secreted for the first few days after birth, is higher in protein and lower in sugar and fat than later breast milk. It has a laxative effect that activates the baby's bowels. Colostrum is also rich in antibodies, which increase the baby's resistance to infection.

Hormones released in response to the baby's suckling increase the flow of breast milk, and within a few days most women produce more than enough milk for their infants. This milk is easy to digest and provides just about all the nutrients that a baby normally needs for the first 4 to 6 months; however, many pediatricians recommend fluoride and vitamin D supplements beginning in the third or fourth month. In the past, iron supplements were given because breast milk contains very little of this mineral. Many doctors now feel that these are unnecessary; full-term babies born to women who are not anemic have enough iron reserves to last until they begin eating iron-fortified cereals and other foods (see Introducing New Foods in the First Year, p.51).

Many new nursing mothers often worry that their babies are not getting enough to eat. A baby who has regular stools and produces six or more wet diapers a day is most likely getting plenty of food. Although this varies considerably, breast-fed babies generally nurse every 2 to 4 hours for the first month or so. At one time, doctors felt that babies should be fed according to a regular schedule rather than on demand. This approach to nursing has fallen out of favor, and experts now agree that babies should be fed whenever they are hungry for the first 4 or 5 months. Some babies, however, may be overly sleepy or disinterested in food; a baby who is not feeding at least six to eight times a day may need to be awakened and stimulated to consume more.

Of course, growth is another important indicator of whether or not a baby is getting enough to eat. Remember, however, that babies and young children tend to grow in spurts, rather than showing a steady gain of a few ounces a week. During a growth spurt, an infant will want to nurse more often and longer than usual, which may completely empty the breasts. This will signal the mother's body to increase milk production. But the mother should not be concerned if, a week or two later, her baby is less interested in eating.

BOTTLE-FEEDING

Although more than half of all Canadian women now breast-feed for at least the first few weeks, this still leaves many who, for various reasons, elect to bottle-feed. They should be assured that commercial infant formulas provide all the essential nutrients and, when used according to the manufacturers' instructions, babies thrive on them. Babies under one year of age should not be given regular cow's milk because it is difficult for them to digest and it also may provoke an allergic reaction. The cow's milk in most infant formulas is modified to make it easier to digest. Despite this precaution, some babies are unable to tolerate it; these infants can usually digest a soy or rice formula.

THE ADVANTAGES OF BREAST-FEEDING

• In the early postpartum period, nursing stimulates uterine contractions that help prevent hemorrhaging and return the uterus to its normal size. Breast-feeding also helps a woman lose the extra weight gained during pregnancy.

• Breast milk is more convenient and economical than formula; it is sterile, portable, and always the right temperature.

• Nursing promotes a special kind of mother-infant bonding and closeness.

• Breast-fed babies have a reduced incidence of bacterial meningitis and respiratory and intestinal disorders. The benefits appear to extend beyond childhood; recent studies show that people who were breast-fed have a reduced incidence of allergies, obesity, diabetes, inflammatory bowel disease, asthma and other chronic lung disorders, heart disease, and some types of cancer.

• Women who breast-feed appear to have a reduced risk of premenopausal breast cancer and postmenopausal osteoporosis (loss of bone mass).

48

Generally, bottle-fed babies consume more at a feeding than breast-fed infants do; they may also gain weight more rapidly, although the breast-fed babies will eventually catch up with them. On average, most babies double their birth weight in 4 to 5 months, and triple it by the time of their first birthday.

Bottle-feeding requires more work than nursing; bottles, nipples, and other equipment must be sterilized. Some formulas are premixed and can be used straight from the can; others are concentrated or powdered, and must be mixed with sterile water. Formula mixed in advance should be refrigerated, but not for any longer than 24 hours; after that, the formula should be discarded. Any formula that is left in the baby's bottle after a feeding also should be thrown away; if not, there is a possibility of its being contaminated by microorganisms entering through the nipple opening.

INTRODUCING FOODS

There is no specific age at which solid foods should be started, but for most babies, 4 or 5 months is about right. Starting too early can be harmful because the digestive system may not be able to handle solid foods yet; also, the early introduction of solid foods seems to increase the risk of developing food allergies. An infant who is thriving solely on breast milk can generally wait until he is 5 or even 6 months old; after that, however, nursing alone will not provide adequate calories and the range of nutrients that a baby needs for normal growth.

There are several typical signs that indicate when a baby is ready to move on to solid foods: The baby chews at the nipple instead of simply suckling it; he swallows food instead of spitting it out because of improved coordination of the tongue and mouth muscles; and he drools more, which will facilitate swallowing.

Case Study

When Jason was born, his mother elected to breast-feed him, at least for the first few months. Jason seemed to be thriving, but every now and then he developed diarrhea and was unusually fussy. When the pediatrician examined Jason, she found him to be a healthy baby with no abnormalities that would explain the diarrhea and excessive fussiness.

The doctor's next step was to question Martha, Jason's mother, about her diet and habits, explaining that many substances in foods, drinks, and medications find their way into breast milk. Martha couldn't pinpoint anything that might be causing Jason's problems, so the doctor asked her to keep a food diary, and also to note any accompanying symptoms in Jason.

After a week, the problem became clear. Whenever Martha ate onions and garlic—common ingredients in many of her favorite dishes—Jason responded with diarrhea and fussiness.

Martha then tried a week of abstaining from onions and garlic, and Jason was his usual cheerful self with absolutely normal stools. This was enough to convince Martha to forgo onions and garlic until after Jason was weaned—a small price to pay for a happy, comfortable baby.

The first solid foods must be easy to digest and unlikely to provoke an allergic reaction—from both perspectives, infant rice cereal is a good choice. It can be mixed with formula, breast milk, or sterile water and fed with a spoon. For the first few feedings, put a very small amount of the cereal on the spoon, gently touch the baby's lips to encourage him to open his mouth, and try to place the cereal at the back of the tongue. Don't expect these feedings to go smoothly; even a baby who is ready for solid foods usually does a lot of spitting, sputtering, and protesting.

The baby should be hungry, but not ravenous. Some experts suggest starting the feeding with a few minutes of nursing or bottle-feeding, then offering a small amount of the moistened cereal—no more than a teaspoon or two—and finishing with the milk. After a few sessions, you can start with the cereal, then gradually increase the amount of solid foods at each feeding as you eventually reduce the amount of nursing or bottle-feeding.

Go slow in the beginning, introducing only one or two new items a week. If you use home-cooked foods, make sure that they're thoroughly puréed. In addition to iron-fortified rice cereal, try oatmeal and barley cereals; strained peas, carrots, sweet potatoes, and squash; applesauce, strained peaches and pears, and mashed bananas; and puréed chicken, turkey, lamb, and beef. Introduce vegetables before fruits, otherwise the baby may become hooked on the sweeter-tasting foods and reject the vegetables. If the baby refuses a particular food, don't force the issue; it's better to substitute something else and try again in a few weeks.

At about 5 months, fruit juice can be added to the diet, starting with apple juice. Hold off on orange juice and other citrus products for at least 6 months; these may provoke an allergic reaction. Other potentially allergenic foods should be delayed until the baby is 6 to 9 months old, or even later if there is a family history of allergies; such foods include corn, wheat products, berries, fish, and spinach. It's best to wait until after the first birthday to give the baby egg whites—one of the most allergenic foods—although the yolks can be tried somewhat earlier. Withdraw any food that provokes a rash, runny nose, unusual fussiness, diarrhea, or any other sign of a possible allergic reaction or food intolerance.

SELF-FEEDING

When they are about 7 or 8 months old, most babies have developed enough eye-hand coordination to pick up finger food and maneuver it into their mouths. The teeth are also beginning to erupt at this age; giving a baby an unsalted pretzel, teething biscuit, or cracker to chew on can ease gum soreness as well as provide practice in self-feeding. Other good starter finger foods include bite-size dry cereals, bananas, slices of apples and pears, peas, and cooked carrots, and small pieces of soft-cooked boiled or roasted chicken, ground beef, and turkey. The pieces should be large enough to hold but small enough so that they don't lodge in the throat and cause choking. For this reason, foods like grapes and peanuts should be avoided until the child is older.

As soon as the baby can sit in a high chair, he should be included in at least some family meals and start eating many of the same foods, even though they may need mashing or cutting into small pieces. Give the child a spoon, but don't be disappointed if he prefers using his hands. Try not to be too concerned about spills, which are inevitable; you can spread a plastic sheet on the floor to facilitate cleaning up (it should probably extend well beyond the high chair). At this stage it's more important for the baby to become integrated into family activities and master self-feeding than to learn neatness and proper table manners. These will come eventually, especially if the parents and older siblings set a good example.

WEANING

Giving up the breast or bottle is a major milestone in a baby's development, but not one that should be rushed. When a woman stops nursing is largely a matter of personal preference. Some mothers wean their babies from the breast to a bottle after only a few weeks or months; others continue nursing for 18 months or longer, even though the child is eating solid food and perhaps drinking milk from a cup. Similarly, some babies decide to give up their bottles themselves at 9 or 10 months; yet others will still want it—especially at nap or bedtime—until they are 2 years old or even older. In any event, a baby should not be given regular cow's milk in the first year of life. If a baby under a year old drinks milk from a cup, it should still be a formula.

DENTAL HYGIENE

Many parents mistakenly assume that baby, or primary, teeth aren't important because they are eventually replaced by permanent teeth. In fact, early dental decay not only threatens the underlying secondary teeth, it can cause severe toothaches. As soon as the first tooth erupts, parents should begin practicing preventive dental hygiene. Babies should not be permitted to fall asleep while nursing or sucking a bottle; this allows milk to pool in the mouth, and the sugar (lactose) in it can cause extensive tooth decay. Offering a little water at the end of a feeding rinses any remaining milk from the baby's mouth. The gums and emerging teeth can be wiped gently with a gauze-wrapped finger.

Sugar is the major cause of childhood tooth decay; avoid offering sugary soft drinks and sweet snacks. Fruit juice, boiled water, a chunk of cheese, or a piece of fruit are better alternatives that provide important nutrients without harming the teeth.

COMMERCIAL BABY FOODS

Most babies' introduction to solid food comes in the form of small jars of puréed vegetables, fruits, and meats. Older babies graduate to thicker and chunkier commercial foods prepared for toddlers. For a young baby, the commercial foods offer several advantages. They are safe, and most are now salt- and sugar-free. For the mother, they offer convenience. But they also have disadvantages. They are expensive, they offer the baby little incentive to develop chewing and self-feeding skills, and they have less nutritional value than freshly prepared foods. If you do elect to use commercial baby foods, follow these precautions:

• Never feed the baby straight from the jar and then save the remaining food; saliva on the spoon can transmit bacteria to the food and result in spoilage.

• Commercial baby food tastes bland; resist the temptation to season it with salt. Excessive salt can cause later health problems, especially if there is a family history of high blood pressure.

INTRODUCING NEW FOODS IN THE FIRST YEAR

During the first 3 months of life, breast milk or formula provides all the nutrients a newborn baby needs. The following chart summarizes the generally accepted guidelines for *introducing new foods to babies under a year old. It should be noted, however, that all babies are different; consequently, the timing varies considerably from one baby to another.*

1 to 3 MONTHS Total intake: About 2½ oz of formula or breast milk per pound of body weight.

First month: If giving breast milk, enough for weight gain and to yield regular soft stools and at least 6–8 wet diapers a day. If giving formula, 2–4 oz per feeding (every 2 to 4 hours).

Second and third months: 4–5 oz each feeding; six feedings a day.

MILK AND DAIRY	CEREALS AND OTHER STARCHY FOODS	VEGETABLES AND FRUITS	MEAT AND MEAT ALTERNATIVES	OCCASIONAL FOODS

4 to 6 MONTHS Total intake: About 30 oz per day of breast milk or formula, plus small amounts (1 or 2 teaspoons) of new foods (introduced one at a time) at two or three feedings a day.

By 4 months: 5–6 oz breast milk or formula each feeding five or six times a day.	**At 4 months:** Start with rice cereal, followed by oatmeal and barley. Begin with ½ teaspoonful or less; then gradually work up to 1 or 2 teaspoonfuls.	**At 4 to 5 months:** Start with small amounts of puréed vegetables (peas, carrots, squash, etc.); after a few weeks, add strained or puréed fruits (applesauce, bananas, peaches, pears, etc.).	**At 5 to 6 months:** Strained meats are usually one of the last foods to be added. The meat should be soft-cooked and puréed.	Babies tend to like bland foods, so salt is not needed. Salty or sugary drinks and snacks should be avoided; use boiled water instead. Small amounts of apple juice can be added at 5 to 6 months.

7 to 8 MONTHS Total intake: By the end of 6 months, about 30–40 oz of breast milk or formula; 2–4 oz. of cereal and/or puréed baby food should be given at each of the baby's three meals.

For breast milk, continue or wean to bottle. Give five or six feedings per day. For formula, 6–8 oz per feeding four or five times each day.	Other breads and cereals may be added, but avoid wheat products. Begin serving finger foods, such as dry toast squares or bite-size cereals. **Daily intake:** ¼ to ½ cup of starchy food over three meals.	Increase the variety of fruits and vegetables, but avoid corn, berries, citrus fruits, and spinach. **Daily intake:** Four ¼- to ½-cup servings of noncitrus juices, fruits, and vegetables.	Softened meat can be cut up into small pieces to be eaten as finger food. **Daily intake:** Two ½- to ¾-oz portions of meat, cheese, or other meat alternatives.	Citrus fruit juices tend to irritate the baby's skin and make stools acidic, so it is advisable to wait until at least 6 to 9 months.

9 to 12 MONTHS 750 to 900 total calories needed per day divided into three meals and two snacks.

Add yogurt and milk puddings. **Daily intake:** About 24 oz breast milk or formula per day (400–500 calories).	Wheat and mixed cereals may be added, as well as other starches, such as potatoes, rice, and well-cooked pasta. **Daily intake:** ½- to ¾-cup total a day.	A mixture of fruits (including juices) and vegetables distributed during meals and snacks. **Daily intake:** Six ¼-cup servings a day.	Egg yolks may be tried, but avoid whites until after the first birthday. Egg whites may cause an allergic reaction. **Daily intake:** Total of 2 oz of meat a day.	May use moderate amounts of butter (unsalted) and small amounts of jam on bread, toast, and crackers. Do not give peanut butter, which can cause choking.

51

BIOFLAVONOIDS

BENEFITS

- *Thought to function as antioxidants and also to enhance the antioxidant effects of vitamin C.*
- *Believed to be instrumental in proper capillary function.*
- *Some appear to be natural antibiotics and anticancer agents.*

DRAWBACKS

- *The benefits are largely unproved and may be overstated.*

Naturally occurring compounds in fruits and vegetables, the bioflavonoids are purported to have many health benefits. While animal experiments suggest that these compounds possess health attributes, there is insufficient human evidence to determine their role in nutrition. To date, more than 800 different bioflavonoids have been identified. Because many of these are the yellow pigments found in citrus fruits as well as other fruits and vegetables, they are often referred to as flavonoids, (*flavus* is the Latin term for yellow).

Bioflavonoids are also known as vitamin P, a name that nutrition scientists object to as it has not been proved that they are essential to human nutrition and health. But many researchers are studying bioflavonoids, and numerous theories have been advanced regarding their possible functions. Some experts believe that bioflavonoids:

Maintain capillaries. Capillaries are highly permeable mi-

BENEFICIAL PIGMENTS. *These and many other brightly colored fresh fruits and vegetables are rich in bioflavonoids.*

croscopic blood vessels that allow oxygen, hormones, nutrients, and antibodies to pass from the bloodstream to individual cells. If the capillary walls are too fragile, blood will seep out of the vessels and into the cells. This can result in easy bruising, brain and retinal hemorrhages, bleeding gums, and other abnormalities. Bioflavonoids are thought to prevent this by maintaining the proper degree of permeability.

Inhibit clot formation. Recent research indicates that some bioflavonoids are natural clot inhibitors and may be useful in treating phlebitis and other clotting disorders.

Protect against heart disease. Resveratrol and quercetin, bioflavonoids in grape skins, are thought to be the ingredients that account for the reduced risk of heart attacks among moderate wine drinkers.

Act as an antioxidant. Many bioflavonoids prevent cellular damage caused by free radicals, unstable molecules that are formed when the body uses oxygen. Some bioflavonoids are used as food preservatives to prevent oxidation of fats. Others are thought to enhance the antioxidant action of some nutrients.

Enhance the action of vitamin C. Bioflavonoids and vitamin C are present in the same foods, and the body metabolizes both in much the same way. This similarity has led some researchers to theorize that at least some of the functions attributed to vitamin C are actually due to bioflavonoids instead; others feel that the two work together in a synergistic manner in which one cannot be separated from the other.

Help prevent cancer. Laboratory studies indicate that some bioflavonoids stop or slow the growth of malignant cells; they may also help protect against cancer-causing substances.

Act as natural antibiotics. Some bioflavonoids destroy certain bacteria, retarding food spoilage and protecting humans from food-borne infections.

POTENTIAL MEDICAL USES

At least two bioflavonoids are under study for medicinal uses: hesperidin, a bioflavonoid in the blossoms and peels of oranges, lemons, and other citrus fruits, is being considered for treating easy bruising and other bleeding abnormalities; and rutin, found in buckwheat leaves and some other plants, is being studied for treating glaucoma and the retinal bleeding in diabetics as well as for reducing tissue dam-

age from frostbite, radiation exposure, and hemophilia. These and other bioflavonoids are available as nutritional supplements. Although their manufacturers are barred from promoting specific medical benefits, some alternative practitioners recommend these substances to treat various disorders.

DIETARY REQUIREMENTS

The Recommended Nutrient Intake (RNI) for bioflavonoids has not been established, but studies show that if a diet contains enough fruits and vegetables to supply 60mg of vitamin C, it will also provide adequate bioflavonoids. Foods that are high in bioflavonoids include apricots, blackberries, black currants, broccoli, cantaloupes, cherries, grapefruits, grapes, green peppers, oranges and lemons, papayas, plums, tangerine juice, and tomatoes, as well as coffee, cocoa, tea, and red wine.

BLACKBERRIES

BENEFITS
- *Low in calories and high in fiber.*
- *A good source of vitamin C and bioflavonoids; also contain folate, vitamin E, iron, and calcium.*
- *Contain anticancer chemicals.*

DRAWBACKS
- *Contain salicylates, which can cause a reaction in aspirin-sensitive people.*

When fully ripe, blackberries are sweet and juicy; less ripe berries are tart and taste best if cooked in pies or made into jam or jelly. Wild blackberries grow on bramble bushes; picking them carries a risk of thorn scratches and bee stings. There are cultivated varieties: boysenberries, which are dark maroon, and slightly tart, and loganberries, which are dark red, and very tart.

Their many seeds make blackberries high in fiber. A half-cup serving of raw berries has 40 calories and supplies 15mg of vitamin C, or 40 percent of the Recommended Nutrient Intake (RNI), as well as 10mcg (micrograms) of folate, 2.5mg of vitamin E, and small amounts of iron and calcium.

Blackberries contain ellagic acid, a substance that is believed to help prevent cancer. Cooking does not appear to destroy ellagic acid, so even jams may confer this health benefit.

People allergic to aspirin may find that they experience a similar reaction from eating blackberries. The reason for this is that blackberries are a natural source of salicylates, substances related to the active compound in aspirin.

BLEEDING PROBLEMS

EAT PLENTY OF
- *Spinach, potatoes, cabbage, oats and other whole grains, and organ meats for vitamin K.*
- *Lean meat, poultry, seafood, and other foods high in iron and vitamin B_{12}.*
- *Citrus and other fresh fruits and vegetables for vitamin C.*

CUT DOWN ON
- *Fatty fish and other sources of omega-3 fatty acids.*

AVOID
- *Alcohol, aspirin, and other drugs that suppress blood platelets and clotting.*

Some bleeding disorders, such as hemophilia, are hereditary; others develop as a result of nutritional deficiencies, the use of aspirin and other medications that suppress clotting, and as the consequence of certain diseases, including some cancers. Most of these bleeding disorders stem from some type of thrombocytopenia, the medical term for a reduced number of platelets, the blood cells instrumental in clotting. Symptoms vary, but they typically include easy bruising, frequent nosebleeds, and excessive bleeding from even minor cuts. Bleeding gums unrelated to dental problems are common. Affected women may experience very heavy menstrual periods. In some cases, there are no obvious symptoms, but blood tests reveal a low platelet count and reduced clotting time.

Treatment varies according to the underlying cause. Overuse of aspirin or other drugs that suppress normal platelet function or production is the most common cause of platelet abnormalities; stopping the offending medication usually solves the problem. In other cases, transfusions of platelets and other blood cells may be necessary.

NUTRITIONAL INFLUENCES

Bleeding disorders due to nutritional deficiencies are uncommon in Canada, but they do occur in some situations. For example, vitamin K—necessary for the blood to clot normally—is made by bacteria in the human intestinal tract; it is also found in spinach and other green leafy vegetables, potatoes, cabbage, whole grains, and organ meats. Sometimes prolonged antibiotic therapy destroys the intestinal bacteria that make vitamin K, resulting in bleeding problems. Increasing foods high in vitamin K may help, but more often supplements or injections of the vitamin are given.

Foods high in vitamin K should be limited by people taking anticoagulant medication such as coumadin, because the vitamin can counteract the desired effect of the drug. Omega-3 fatty acids, found in salmon and other oily fish, can suppress platelet function. People taking high doses of fish oil supplements have an increased risk of developing bleeding problems; the risk is compounded if they are also taking aspirin.

Vitamin C strengthens blood vessel walls; vitamin C deficiency can result in bleeding gums and easy bruising. Vitamin C deficiency is rare in Canada but may occur in alcoholics or people whose diet is devoid of fruits and vegetables.

Chronic blood loss can lead to ANEMIA, a blood disorder that is characterized by inadequate levels of red blood cells. In such cases, dietary sources should supply extra iron, folate, and vitamins B_{12} and C. Supplements may be needed as well, but these should be taken only under medical supervision.

BLOOD PRESSURE

EAT PLENTY OF

- *Fresh vegetables, fresh and dried fruits, whole-grain cereals, and legumes for potassium.*

CUT DOWN ON

- *Canned and other processed foods with added salt.*
- *Fatty foods.*

AVOID

- *Pickled and salty foods.*
- *Excessive alcohol.*

As blood circulates through the body, it exerts varying degrees of force on artery walls; doctors refer to this as blood pressure. About one in six Canadians has blood pressure that is too high, or hypertension. In its early stages, high blood pressure is symptomless, so many people don't realize they have a potentially life-threatening disease. However, if the condition goes unchecked, high blood pressure damages the heart and blood vessels and can lead to a stroke, heart attack, kidney failure, and other serious consequences.

In about 5 percent of cases, there's an underlying cause for the high blood pressure; for example, a narrowed artery

Case Study

Samuel, a 56-year-old high school teacher, was dismayed when a routine insurance examination revealed that he had mild high blood pressure, with blood pressure readings between 145–150/92–99 (see Understanding Blood Pressure Measurements, facing page). Before prescribing a drug, however, his physician wanted Samuel to change his diet and sedentary lifestyle and lose 10 pounds.

An exercise stress test showed that Samuel was able to safely embark on an exercise program. He was advised to start with a 20-minute walk every other day and to gradually work up to 3 miles in 45 minutes at least three times a week. He was also asked to consult a dietitian, who outlined a low-salt, high-fiber diet. After 3 months, Samuel's blood pressure was down to 138/85.

in the kidney, pregnancy, an adrenal gland disorder, or a drug side effect. Most often, however, there is no identifiable cause; this is referred to as primary, or essential, hypertension.

Blood pressure rises when the arterioles, the body's smallest arteries, narrow or constrict, requiring the heart to beat more forcefully in order to pump blood through them. Increased blood volume, often due to the body's tendency to retain excessive salt and fluids, raises blood pressure; so do high levels of adrenaline and other hormones that constrict blood vessels.

With age, blood pressure rises somewhat, but no one fully understands precisely what leads to hypertension, although a combination of factors seems to be involved. Because it tends to run in families, an inherited susceptibility is suspected. DIABETES, OBESITY, and certain other disorders increase risk. STRESS prompts a surge in adrenal hormones, leading to a temporary rise in blood pressure; some researchers believe that constant stress may play a role in developing hypertension. Other contributors include smoking, excessive ALCOHOL, and a sedentary lifestyle.

There is little doubt that keeping blood pressure at normal levels makes a difference in the quality and length of life. Cardiovascular disease death rates have been steadily declining in Canada since the mid-1960s, thanks largely to lifestyle changes and improvements in hypertension treatment. The 1992 death rates are almost half those of 1969 (this applies to all major categories of cardiovascular disease, as well as rates among both women and men).

DIET AND HYPERTENSION

Experts now agree that diet plays a role in both the prevention and treatment of high blood pressure. A high-salt diet contributes to the condition in people who have a genetic tendency to retain sodium; in these individuals, restriction of SALT beginning at an early age reduces the risk of developing hypertension. The experts disagree as to how much salt is too much; cutting back to a teaspoonful (about half the usual intake) seems to be a prudent approach. Most salt is consumed in processed foods; check labels carefully—look for the term "sodium" to find hidden salt. In addition to avoiding salty and pickled foods, substitute herbs and spices for salt in cooking and removing the salt shaker from the table.

Being even a few pounds overweight contributes to hypertension; losing excess weight is often all that is needed to return blood pressure to normal levels. Avoid crash diets, which don't work and can actually precipitate a heart attack. Instead, a nutritionist can help structure a sensible eating plan that results in a gradual weight loss.

A high-fat diet not only leads to weight gain but may also contribute to high blood pressure. Limit fat intake to 30 percent or less of total calories, with 10 percent or less coming from saturated animal fats. This means cutting back on butter and margarine; switching to skim milk, low-fat yogurt,

CHECK IT OUT

All adults over age 40 should have their blood pressure checked annually. But just one blood pressure measurement is insufficient to diagnose hypertension unless the reading is in the severe range. Some people also have "white coat" hypertension, in which their blood pressure rises when they are in a doctor's office but is normal at other times. In order to properly diagnose hypertension, several measurements are needed—taken at different times and perhaps in different places.

UNDERSTANDING BLOOD PRESSURE MEASUREMENTS

Blood does not flow through the body in a steady stream; instead, it courses in spurts. Thus, blood pressure is expressed in two numbers, such as 120/80. The higher number indicates the systolic pressure, the peak force when the heart contracts and pumps a few ounces of blood into the circulation. The lower number, the diastolic reading, measures pressure exerted when the heart is resting momentarily between beats.

A doctor usually uses a stethoscope and a sphygmomanometer to measure blood pressure. The cuff is tightened to stop blood flow, and as pressure is released, he listens for the sounds that indicate systolic and diastolic pressures. Equipment for home use has an internal listening device, and the pressure level is displayed digitally. Treatment is advised if several readings are 140/90 or above. Normal adult blood pressure is defined as below 140/85; hypertension is classified as follows:

• High normal or borderline: 140/85–89
• Mild: 140–159/90–104
• Moderate to severe: 160/105 and above.

Note: Some individuals have a normal systolic reading, but the diastolic pressure is elevated; they are classified as hypertensive. Other persons have isolated systolic hypertension.

Systolic reading | Diastolic reading

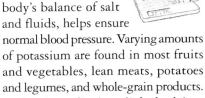

and other milk products; choosing lean cuts of meat; and shifting to low-fat cooking methods, such as baking and broiling instead of frying and sautéing.

Even moderate alcohol consumption—one drink a day for women, two for men—contributes to high blood pressure and increases the risk of a stroke. Although a glass of wine or other alcoholic drink daily seems to reduce the chance of a heart attack, consuming more than this seems to negate any benefit and may increase the risk.

Some foods or nutrients may protect against high blood pressure. Potassium, an electrolyte that helps maintain the body's balance of salt and fluids, helps ensure normal blood pressure. Varying amounts of potassium are found in most fruits and vegetables, lean meats, potatoes and legumes, and whole-grain products.

Certain studies have linked calcium deficiency and hypertension; the diet should provide at least two to three servings of low-fat milk products a day.

Other research appears to validate the claims that garlic may lower blood pressure. The amount of garlic necessary to lower blood pressure, however, can cause other problems, especially unpleasant breath and body odor.

Although garlic is available in odorless pills, it is not known if these pills produce the same benefits as eating garlic fresh or lightly cooked.

OTHER LIFESTYLE CHANGES

While a proper diet is instrumental in maintaining normal blood pressure, it should be combined with other lifestyle changes. One of the most important is regular aerobic exercise, which lowers blood pressure by conditioning the heart to work more efficiently. Consult a doctor before beginning any exercise program, however; you may need an exercise stress test to determine your safe level of activity. For most people a graduated walking program works well; start with a modest 15- to 20-minute walk three or four times a week and gradually build to a brisk 30- to 45-minute walk at least every other day.

If you smoke, make every effort to give up the habit. Nicotine raises blood pressure and has numerous other detrimental effects. Quitting can drop blood pressure by 10 points or more.

Use all medications with caution. Over-the-counter cold, allergy, and diet pills can raise blood pressure. In some women, birth control pills cause high blood pressure; less often, postmenopausal estrogen replacement has a similar effect. Switching to a lower dosage may solve the problem; if not, the drug may need to be stopped.

Experts continue to debate the role of stress in hypertension. There is no doubt that stress temporarily raises blood pressure, and some experts think that it may have a long-term effect. In any event, meditation, yoga, biofeedback training, self-hypnosis, and other relaxation techniques may help lower blood pressure. Along this same line, several studies have found that people with pets have lower blood pressure than non-pet owners, perhaps because stroking an animal is relaxing.

DRUG THERAPY

Doctors recommend 6 months of lifestyle changes to see if mild to moderate hypertension returns to normal levels. If not, drug therapy is often instituted. There are dozens of antihypertensive drugs, and doctors can usually find one or a combination that lowers blood pressure with minimal adverse side effects. The most widely used drugs are diuretics, or water pills, which reduce salt and fluid volume by increasing the flow of urine. Some classes of drugs reduce the heart's workload by helping to widen, or dilate, the arterioles to increase blood flow; others regulate nerve impulses to slow the pulse.

It is also important to treat disorders that contribute to high blood pressure; these include diabetes and elevated blood cholesterol, both of which compound the risk of developing heart attack and stroke. The dietary and other lifestyle changes that lower high blood pressure also help control diabetes and blood cholesterol levels.

BLUEBERRIES

BENEFITS
- *A good source of dietary fiber.*
- *Provide some vitamin C and iron.*
- *May protect against some intestinal upsets.*
- *May help prevent some urinary tract infections.*

DRAWBACKS
- *Can make stools dark and tarry, which may be mistaken for intestinal bleeding.*
- *May be allergens in susceptible persons.*

Unlike many berries that must be sweetened with sugar to make them palatable, blueberries are naturally sweet and can be eaten raw. Because cooking destroys vitamin C, eating blueberries raw preserves this ANTI-OXIDANT nutrient.

Dried blueberries have long been a popular folk remedy for diarrhea and other intestinal problems. Recent studies have found that blueberries contain anthocyanin, a substance that has mild antibiotic properties, especially against some strains of *E. coli,* intestinal bacteria that are a common cause of traveler's diarrhea and other infections.

Natural healers also advocate eating one cup of raw berries or drinking one to two cups of unsweetened blueberry juice a day to treat and prevent URINARY TRACT INFECTIONS. Again, recent research appears to support this advice. Blueberries are in the same plant family as CRANBERRIES, and both contain a substance that prevents bacteria from adhering to the bladder walls, where they can multiply. These berries also make urine more acidic, which helps destroy bacteria that invade the bladder and urethra. Eating large amounts of blueberries, however, can make the stool appear dark and tarry; this is a harmless situation but can be alarming, because it resembles intestinal bleeding.

Like many fruits, blueberries are potential allergens in susceptible people. Common symptoms are itchy hives and swollen lips and eyelids.

NUTRITIONAL VALUE

Although they are sweet and tasty, blueberries are not especially high in nutrients; one-half cup of the raw fruit provides 10mg of vitamin C, 0.7mg of iron, and small amounts of potassium, folate, and beta carotene, the plant form of vitamin A. However, a half-cup serving of blueberries provides 1mg of fiber and has only 40 calories, so they're an ideal low-calorie snack or dessert.

TASTY AND VERSATILE. *Blueberries can be added to muffins, fruit salads, and jams.*

BODY ODOR

CONSUME PLENTY OF
- *Lean beef, oysters, yogurt, and whole-grain cereals for zinc plus green leafy vegetables, nuts, and scallops for magnesium.*
- *Water and other nonalcoholic beverages, especially during periods of heavy sweating.*

CUT DOWN ON
- *Eggs, fish, liver, and legumes.*

AVOID
- *Onions and garlic.*
- *Alcoholic beverages.*

Sweating is one of the natural ways the human body maintains its normal temperature. The body has two types of sweat glands: apocrine, which are located in the armpits, face, scalp, and parts of the trunk; and eccrine, which are distributed throughout the body and give off a quart or more of perspiration a day. Apocrine sweat is scant, milky, and made up of water, carbohydrates, proteins, and lipids; these substances have a distinctive odor when they are broken down by the bacteria that live on the skin. In contrast, eccrine sweat is mostly water, with varying amounts of salt, potassium, urea, and other substances. It has little or no odor itself, but eccrine sweat can transmit the smells of alcohol and certain foods, especially garlic and onions, resulting in an unpleasant body odor.

A number of factors can influence sweat production, especially physical activity, hot weather, anxiety, and emotional stress. Many women experience drenching sweats during menopause, particularly at night. Fever can cause heavy sweating, as can AIDS, Hodgkin's disease, and certain other diseases. In order to replace the fluids lost through excessive sweating, it's good practice to drink plenty of water, fruit juices, and other nonalcoholic, caffeine-free beverages; otherwise, there's a risk of becoming dehydrated.

THE EFFECTS OF DIET

Chili peppers and other very spicy foods can provoke increased sweating; coffee, alcohol, and other stimulants may have a similar effect. Unlike the distinctive odors of garlic and onions, these foods do not ordinarily alter the odor of sweat. Because the body gets rid of some alcohol through the skin, however, overindulgence can result in a somewhat sour body odor.

Some people develop a defect in their ability to properly metabolize a substance called trimethylamine, a compound produced in the body from foods high in choline, such as eggs, fish, liver, and legumes. The skin will have a telltale fishy odor after such foods are eaten; eliminating them from the diet will solve the problem.

Some studies indicate that increasing the intake of zinc and magnesium may eliminate unpleasant odors from perspiration. Foods high in these important minerals include lean beef, oysters, yogurt, and whole-grain cereals. In addition, green leafy vegetables, nuts, and scallops are also excellent sources of magnesium.

LOCALIZED ODOR PROBLEMS

Areas that are normally encased in clothing—the feet, armpits, and genital and anal areas—are most affected by odor problems because bacteria and yeast organisms proliferate in moist, dark places. Daily washing with soap and water is usually all that is needed. In stubborn cases, however, washing with an antibacterial soap or one containing chlorhexidine may help.

Underarm odor can be controlled by daily bathing followed by application of an antiperspirant or deodorant. Shaving the underarms may also help by removing a haven in which bacteria can thrive. For severe cases of perspiration, a topical antibacterial cream may be prescribed by a doctor.

If foot odor is a problem, wash the feet daily with an antibacterial soap, dry them thoroughly, and apply a medicated foot powder. Wear white socks made of cotton or a fabric that wicks perspiration away from the skin, such as polypropylene. Shoes should be made of leather, canvas, or another material that allows air to circulate. In warmer months, sandals may be the preferred choice. Avoid wearing the same pair of shoes two days in a row; a dusting with an odor-absorbent powder, such as plain baking soda or boric acid, can also help.

Menstrual blood is odorless, but it develops an unpleasant smell after exposure to air. This can be avoided by using a tampon or by changing napkins frequently. The genital area is also vulnerable to yeast infections, which sometimes create a fishy or other unpleasant odor. Treatment entails using antiyeast creams, ointments, or oral medications.

BRAN

BENEFITS
- *Helps prevent constipation.*
- *Oat and rice brans help lower blood cholesterol levels.*
- *Promotes a feeling of fullness, which can lead to weight loss.*
- *May reduce the risk of some cancers, especially those associated with obesity.*

DRAWBACKS
- *Excessive bran reduces the absorption of calcium, iron, and zinc.*
- *Can cause intestinal irritation, bloating, and gas.*

Bran, one of the richest sources of dietary FIBER, is the indigestible outer husk of wheat, rice, oats, and other cereal grains. At one time most bran was discarded when grains were milled.

Then in the 1960s Dr. Dennis P. Burkitt, a British medical officer in Africa, published several scientific reports in which he theorized that bran and other types of fiber could prevent heart attacks, diverticulitis and other intestinal disorders, and cancers of the breast, colon, prostate, and uterus. He developed this theory after observing that these diseases are rare among rural Africans, who consume large amounts of whole grains. Prompted by a number of best-selling books and numerous media reports, bran became the fad food of the 1970s, and raw miller's bran was added to everything from bread, cereals, and muffins to such unlikely dishes as meat loaf and baked apples.

Since then, much of the enthusiasm for using raw bran has dissipated as researchers have learned more about its health benefits and possible hazards. We also know now that various types of bran have different properties and functions. Wheat bran, for example, is mostly insoluble; although it absorbs large amounts of water, it makes its way through the intestinal tract intact. When used in moderation, insoluble fiber helps prevent constipation by producing a soft, bulky stool that moves quickly and easily through the colon. Excessive amounts, however, can cause bloating and intestinal gas.

Dr. Burkitt had theorized that bran prevented colon cancer by reducing the amount of time required for the stool to travel through the bowel. But studies to document this protective effect have produced mixed results. An Australian study found that women taking large amounts of wheat bran actually had a slightly increased incidence of colon cancer. In contrast, a 4-year study involving 58 high-risk adults with pre-cancerous colon polyps found that those taking wheat bran achieved a reduction in the size and number of these growths.

On a more positive note, it appears that including wheat bran in a high-fiber diet can help prevent diverticulitis, an intestinal disorder in which small pockets bulging from the colon wall become impacted and inflamed. And because it helps prevent constipation, bran may also be beneficial for persons suffering from hemorrhoids.

Oat bran is high in soluble fiber, which is sticky and combines with water to form a thick gel. A number of researchers have reported that this type of fiber reduces blood cholesterol levels. It also appears to improve glucose metabolism in people with diabetes. This benefit, in turn, reduces their need for insulin and other antidiabetes medications.

More recently, there have been reports that rice bran also reduces cholesterol levels. Researchers are not sure, however, whether this benefit comes from the insoluble fiber found in the bran or from the highly unsaturated oil in the rice germ—which is not separated from the grain husks during the milling process.

All types of bran, as well as other high-fiber foods, play an important role in weight control by promoting a feeling of fullness without overeating. This may provide an explanation for the lowered incidence of some obesity-related cancers and heart attacks among populations whose diets are high in fiber.

POSSIBLE HAZARDS

When the benefits of bran were first announced, many people started adding three, four, or even more tablespoons of raw miller's bran to their daily diet. It soon became apparent that this practice could aggravate inflammatory bowel disease, a condition in which the colon is inflamed and pocked with small ulcers. In addition, the phytic acid in raw bran inhibits the body's absorption of calcium, iron, zinc, magnesium, and other important minerals. During bread baking, enzymes in yeast destroy much of the phytic acid. The heat present during processing also destroys most phytic acid in high-bran cereals. Thus, these processed products are safer than raw miller's bran.

There have been several reports of severe bowel obstruction in people who consumed large amounts of bran. Many nutritionists now advise a prudent approach: Eat whole-grain wheat bread, cereals, and other products that contain bran. Have oatmeal, muesli, and other cereals made with whole oats; similarly, substitute brown rice for the polished white variety. These foods are far more palatable than raw bran, which tastes like sawdust, and they are more nutritionally beneficial.

BREAD

BENEFITS
- *A good source of protein and complex carbohydrates.*
- *High in niacin, riboflavin, and other B complex vitamins.*
- *Some kinds provide good amounts of iron and calcium.*
- *Whole-grain breads are high in fiber.*

DRAWBACKS
- *Lacks many vitamins and minerals essential to maintain health.*
- *Often eaten with butter and other high-calorie spreads.*
- *People with celiac disease cannot tolerate the gluten found in many breads.*
- *May trigger an adverse reaction in people allergic to molds.*
- *Often high in salt.*

The popularity of bread is not new. Since prehistoric times, bread has been a staple food in virtually every society. As early hunter-gatherers settled into agricultural societies, they learned how to transform various grains into bread. This simple food required only stones to grind grain into flour or meal, water or another liquid to mix it into dough, and a means of baking or cooking it.

Over the centuries, each society developed its own unique types of bread. The huge variety of baked goods available to us at our supermarkets and bakeries today—different-shaped loaves of white, wheat, rye, pumpernickel, sourdough, and multigrain breads, bagels and muffins, croissants and matzos, tortillas, pita, and chapatis, among many others—represent a dietary melding of dozens of diverse cultures.

GIVING DOUGH A LIFT

The simplest and oldest breads are flat, or unleavened; they are made by mixing flour or meal with water and then baking, frying, or steaming it. Examples include matzo, tortillas, chapatis, and some types of crackers. The addition of yeast, baking soda, or other leavening agent to the flour-and-water mixture allows the dough to expand, or rise, and gives the bread a lighter, finer texture than unleavened types. Most of the breads baked in Canada are leavened.

The type of flour used and the manner in which it and the other ingredients interact give the various kinds of breads their unique textures and flavors. In many industrialized countries the most popular breads are made from wheat flour, which produces a product with a light texture. When wheat flour is kneaded with liquid, the gluten proteins absorb water to form an elastic dough that traps gas from the fermenting yeast; bubbles of carbon dioxide are formed, resulting in the light texture. Rye and some other flours contain vary-

ing amounts of gluten, but none come close to that of wheat—which is why breads made from other grains tend to be heavy and coarse. To make a lighter-textured bread from rye, barley, or other grains, some wheat flour is usually added to the dough.

Flavor and texture are also influenced by the type of liquid mixed into the dough—plain water, milk, beer, fruit juice, and water drained from boiled rice or potatoes are common choices. Sugar or honey may be added to "feed" the yeast and make the bread rise at a faster rate; it also results in a moister product. A small amount of salt is needed to strengthen the gluten and to temper the rate at which the yeast multiplies. Butter or some other fat is often added to flavor commercial breads; it also makes pastrylike breads, such as croissants, rich and flaky.

Bread sold in Canada is often mass-produced; such products contain various preservatives, emulsifiers, and bleaches or coloring agents to extend their shelf life and improve their appearance. These additives do not alter nutritional value, but most commercial bread may be too high in salt for people on low-sodium diets. Also, people who have celiac disease cannot tolerate the gluten in most bread. Similarly, people with food allergies may react to

specific ingredients; for example, people allergic to molds may react to sourdough or very yeasty breads. Some health food stores and specialty shops offer breads that are gluten-free; people with food allergies should always check labels for any offending ingredients.

NUTRITIONAL VALUE

Traditionally, bread has been called the staff of life, implying that it alone is all that is required for total nutrition. This is inaccurate, however. Bread does provide starch, protein, and some vitamins

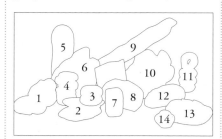

CHOOSING YOUR LOAF. *Breads from around the world include: croissant (1), pita (2), English muffin (3), crumpet (4), Italian (5), naan (6), raisin (7), whole wheat (8), baguette (9), crusty whole wheat (10), bagel (11), poppy-seed (12), pain de campagne (13), and brioche (14).*

and minerals, but it is far from being nutritionally complete because it lacks such essentials as vitamins A, B_{12}, C, and D. Many of the nutrients in the grain are destroyed by milling and processing, but some (typically calcium, iron, thiamine, riboflavin, and niacin) are added to restore the nutrients to their original levels or, in some cases, even increase them; consequently, enriched white flour often has more of the B complex vitamins than whole wheat. In general, however, whole-grain flours are more nutritious than their highly processed counterparts; they also provide more dietary fiber.

The addition of other ingredients also increases the nutritional value of bread. Depending upon the type, these may include eggs, molasses, raisins and other dried fruits, whole or sprouted grains, seeds, and cheese.

Some breads, such as the Cornell Triple Rich Formula developed by nutritionists at Cornell University in the U.S., are specifically formulated to increase their nutritional value. The Cornell formula 'adds soy flour, wheat germ, and dried nonfat milk to standard recipes for white and whole-wheat breads, increasing protein, calcium, and magnesium content without adding calories or markedly altering flavor. Multigrain breads that contain sprouts and seeds are also more nutritious than standard commercial products.

Contrary to popular belief, bread is not especially fattening; a typical slice of white or whole-wheat bread contains just 65 to 80 calories. But slathering bread with butter, margarine, or other fatty spreads does make it fattening; a

low-sugar jam or an all-fruit preserve is a more healthful spread.

THE WORLD'S BREADBASKET

The growing popularity of international breads is reflected in the many types sold in supermarkets, delis, and bakeries. Some common breads include:

Bagel. This doughnut-shaped roll, identified with Eastern European and Jewish communities, is boiled and then baked. Traditionally, bagels are made from a high-gluten white flour, but whole-wheat, rye, pumpernickel, sourdough, and other versions are also commonly available. They may be topped with caraway, sesame, or poppy seeds, chopped onions, or coarse salt.

Brioche. A light yeast roll that originated in France, brioche falls somewhere between bread and cake in terms of texture and taste. It is usually made with refined white flour and enriched with butter and eggs.

Chapati. A flat Indian bread that is made with whole-wheat or white flour and may be leavened or unleavened. Some are brushed with butter or oil, adding extra calories.

Ciabatta. Olive oil is added to this Italian raised bread, making it moist and chewy; oregano, basil, and various other herbs may also be added.

Cornbread. This bread is made from wheat flour, ground yellow cornmeal, eggs, milk, and sometimes sugar.

English muffin. High-protein white flour is used to make this round, honeycombed roll; it is cooked in a skillet or on a griddle.

Focaccia. An Italian yeast bread that is made from a dough similar to that of pizza, it is usually baked in a large disc and flavored with olive oil, onions, garlic, and other herbs. The added oil in this recipe contributes extra calories.

Matzo. Made from wheat flour, water, and salt, this crackerlike unleavened Jewish bread is traditionally served at Passover meals.

Multigrain. Often promoted as a health food, this bread is usually made with a combination of flours and added ingredients, such as sprouts, various seeds, and raisins. Some multigrain breads are more nutritious than other types, but a check of their labels will often show that many are comparable

DID YOU KNOW?

• Dry toast has just as many calories as a regular slice of bread; all that has been removed is some of the water.

• The Egyptians are credited with inventing raised, or leavened, bread—a type of sourdough exposed to natural yeasts in the air—in about 1500 B.C. During the California gold rush, bakers rediscovered the technique, which is still in use today.

• Although bakers had been using yeast for centuries, it was not until the 1850s that Louis Pasteur discovered that yeast is actually a living organism.

to ordinary breads.

Naan. Baked on the hot side of a tandoori oven, this flat yeast bread originated in India.

Pita. This flat, leavened Middle Eastern bread puffs up during baking and then flattens out to leave a hollow middle, or pocket.

Pumpernickel. This heavy rye German bread derives its dark color from molasses or caramel. One dense type is steamed and baked for hours, then sliced very thin.

Quick bread. Made from a variety of flours, it is leavened with baking powder or baking soda and rises as it bakes. Biscuits, muffins, scones, coffee cakes, and loaf breads are all quick breads.

Rye. All-rye bread is heavy and dense; most of the softer, deli-type rye breads are made mostly of wheat flour.

Sourdough. This bread is leavened with a "starter" and is usually made with white flour. True sourdough bread has a heavier, denser texture than yeast-leavened breads.

Tortillas. This unleavened Mexican bread is made of corn or wheat flour, salt, and water. Finely ground limestone is traditionally added.

THE LANGUAGE OF BREAD

Descriptions and definitions of breads vary widely, because there are no standard definitions. The following are some general guidelines for interpreting the labels:

• **White bread** is made from refined wheat flour,

to which nutrients, such as iron, calcium, and several B vitamins, have been restored.

• **Wheat bread** is also likely to be produced mostly from refined white flour, although it may contain varying amounts of whole-wheat flour, bran, and other ingredients.

• **Whole-wheat bread** will contain mostly whole-grain wheat flour, but unless it specifically states on the label "100 percent whole wheat," it too may contain some refined white flour.

• **High-fiber bread** is usually made from white wheat flour with varying amounts of added bran.

THE NUTRIENTS IN VARIOUS TYPES OF BREAD

The nutritional content of bread varies considerably according to the type of flour used and added ingredients. Listed in the chart | *below are some of the more common breads sold in Canada and their representative nutritional values.*

TYPE OF BREAD	CALORIES	FIBER (G)	CARBOHY-DRATE (G)	PROTEIN (G)	FAT (G)	VITAMINS AND MINERALS
WHITE						
1 slice. Made with enriched white flour; also contains wheat flour and sometimes eggs.	65	0.5	11.7	2.0	0.9	Fortified with iron, niacin, thiamine, and calcium.
RYE						
1 slice. Made with enriched white and rye flours.	65	0.9	12	2.1	0.9	Iron and thiamine.
PUMPERNICKEL						
1 slice. Good source of fiber. Made from rye and wheat flours and molasses.	80	4.3	15.4	2.9	0.8	Iron and thiamine.
WHOLE WHEAT						
1 slice. Made with white and wheat flours and shortening.	60	1.6	11.4	2.4	1.1	Iron and thiamine.
MULTIGRAIN						
1 slice. Made with several whole-grain flours, seeds, and sprouts.	65	1.0	11.7	2.5	0.9	Varying amounts of folate, thiamine, niacin, riboflavin, calcium, and iron.
OTHER						
Bagel, 1 medium. Made with enriched flour.	165	0.6	30.9	6	1.4	Varying amounts of iron, niacin, riboflavin, and thiamine.
English muffin, 1 plain muffin. Made with enriched flour.	135	0.3	26.2	4.5	1.1	Iron and thiamine; smaller amounts of calcium, niacin, riboflavin, potassium, and folate.
French, 1 slice. Made with enriched flour.	95	1	18	3	1	Varying amounts of iron, niacin, riboflavin, and thiamine.
Italian, 1 slice. Made with enriched flour.	80	1	15	3	1	Varying amounts of iron, niacin, riboflavin, and thiamine.
Pita, 1 pocket. Made with enriched flour. Whole-wheat pita is also available.	105	0.3	20.6	4.0	0.6	Thiamine, iron, and niacin.

BROCCOLI

BENEFITS

- *An excellent source of vitamin C.*
- *A good source of vitamin A and folate.*
- *Significant amounts of protein, calcium, iron, and other minerals.*
- *Rich in bioflavonoids and other plant chemicals that protect against cancer.*
- *Low in calories and high in fiber.*

DRAWBACKS

- *Overcooking releases unpleasant-smelling sulfur compounds.*

One of our most nutritious vegetables, broccoli also appears to protect against many common cancers. Over the last 20 years, numerous studies have found that people who eat an abundance of broccoli have a significantly reduced incidence of cancers of the colon, breast, cervix, lungs, prostate, esophagus, larynx, and bladder.

While other cruciferous vegetables (members of the cabbage family, whose flowers resemble crosses) are protective, broccoli seems to have more cancer-fighting compounds. Some of these block the action of hormones that stimulate tumors; others work by inhibiting tumor growth or by boosting the action of protective enzymes. The most interesting compound is sulforaphane, which shows decided anticancer activity in both cultured rat and human cells. Broccoli is also high in BIOFLAVONOIDS and other ANTIOXIDANTS, substances that protect cells against mutation and damage from unstable molecules.

Broccoli has an abundance of essential vitamins and minerals. A 1-cup serving of cooked broccoli contains only 40 calories, yet it provides almost twice

BROCCOLI HARVEST. *The tender flower heads, or florets, of broccoli are richer in beta carotene than the stalks, and the deeper the color, the higher their nutritional value.*

the Recommended Nutrient Intake (RNI) of vitamin C and one-third or more of the RNIs for vitamin A and folate. A cup of broccoli also provides 130mg of calcium, 1.2mg of iron, and 5g of protein. Because 1 cup of cooked broccoli provides 2.5g of fiber and contains natural laxatives, it is often suggested to prevent constipation.

Fresh broccoli is available year-round in most supermarkets; frozen broccoli is just as nutritious as fresh. Florets that are turning yellow, however, are past their prime and less nutritious.

Broccoli can be eaten raw, but most people prefer it cooked. Steaming or stir-frying it until crispy tender retains the most nutrients; boiling it in a large amount of water destroys many of the cancer-fighting compounds, vitamin C and other nutrients. Prolonged boiling also gives broccoli a cabbagelike odor.

BRUSSELS SPROUTS

BENEFITS

- *An excellent source of vitamin C.*
- *A good source of protein, folate, vitamin A, iron, and potassium.*
- *Contain bioflavonoids and other substances that protect against cancer.*

DRAWBACKS

- *Can cause bloating and flatulence.*

Brussels sprouts resemble small cabbages and share many of the same health benefits. Like BROCCOLI, CABBAGE, and other cruciferous vegetables, they contain chemicals that appear to protect against cancer. They are also very high in vitamin C; a cup of cooked Brussels sprouts provides 130mg, more than three times the adult Recommended Nutrient Intake (RNI); it also provides 20 percent or more of the RNIs of folate and vitamin A and more than 10

percent of the daily needs of iron and vitamin E. A 1-cup serving has about 40 calories, a third of which come from protein. Serving Brussels sprouts with a small amount of cheese, rice, or another grain adds complementary amino acids to make a complete PROTEIN.

THE CANCER FACTOR

Brussels sprouts have high amounts of BIOFLAVONOIDS and indoles, plant chemicals that protect against cancer in several ways. Bioflavonoids have an ANTIOXIDANT effect that helps prevent cellular damage and mutation caused by the unstable molecules released when the body uses oxygen. Bioflavonoids, along with indoles and perhaps other plant chemicals, inhibit hormones that promote tumor growth. Indoles are particularly active against estrogen, the hormone that stimulates the growth of some breast cancers.

Other studies indicate that bioflavonoids and indoles may protect against cancers of the prostate and uterus. Even if cancer does develop, these plant chemicals may slow tumor growth and spread of the disease.

SPROUTS AT THEIR BEST

When buying fresh Brussels sprouts, select small, bright green ones with tightly packed leaves. Those past their prime will have patches of yellow, an unpleasant sulfurous smell, and a bitter taste. Frozen Brussels sprouts retain most of their nutrients and flavor.

Sprouts can be boiled or steamed; to ensure that they are evenly cooked, cut a small cross into their base. When boiling, use a cup of water for each cup of sprouts. Bring it to a rapid boil, add the sprouts, and cook uncovered until they are crispy tender. Overcooking destroys vitamin C and gives sprouts a bitter taste. When steaming sprouts, uncover the steamer for a few seconds every 2 or 3 minutes to prevent a buildup of the sulfurous gases.

BUCKWHEAT

BENEFITS
- *A good source of iron and magnesium.*
- *High in starches, protein, and fiber.*

DRAWBACKS
- *Whole kernels are prepared with mixed egg or egg white, which may cause an allergic reaction in susceptible people.*

Although it's not a grain and is unrelated to wheat, buckwheat is generally used as if it were. Canadians are probably most familiar with buckwheat in pancakes, which are made from the flour of the plant's seeds. The hulled roasted seeds, commonly called groats or kasha, can be boiled to make cereal, pudding, or a side dish similar to bulgur wheat. Kasha porridge is a popular staple in Russia and the Middle East. The Russians also use buckwheat flour to make blini, a type of thin pancake, and the Japanese use it to make a type of noodles from the flour.

When cooked, the buckwheat groats have a nutty flavor that goes well with lamb and strong-tasting vegetables like cabbage or Brussels sprouts. Typically, the dry groats are mixed with a beaten egg, sautéed briefly, and then boiled in water. The protein in the egg white keeps the kernels from sticking together as the seeds expand and break their hulls. The amino acids from the egg also combine with the amino acids in buckwheat to provide a complete protein dish. To avoid the fat and cholesterol in eggs, discard the yolk. People with an allergy to eggs, however, should avoid this preparation method.

A half-cup serving of buckwheat groats contains about 90 calories, 3g of protein, and 51mg of magnesium, a mineral needed for proper energy metabolism. It also contributes 0.8mg of iron and some folate.

Sprouted buckwheat seeds are a nutritious and tasty addition to salads, stir-fried foods, and other dishes. Fresh unhulled seeds suitable for sprouting are available from health food stores.

BULIMIA

CONSUME PLENTY OF
- *Fresh vegetables, fruits, low-calorie beverages, and high-fiber foods to promote a feeling of fullness.*
- *Bananas, dried fruits, and a variety of fresh vegetables, fruits, and grains for potassium.*

CUT DOWN ON
- *Fats and other high-calorie foods.*

AVOID
- *Sweets and other foods associated with binges.*

Medically, bulimia is defined as recurrent episodes of binge eating—the rapid intake of unusually large amounts of food—an average of twice a week for at least 3 months. Although bulimia literally means "the hunger of an ox," the majority of bulimics do not have excessive appetites. Instead, their tendency to overeat compulsively seems to arise from psychological problems, possibly complicated by abnormal brain chemistry or a hormonal imbalance.

Far more women than men are affected by bulimia. Despite their overeating, most bulimics are of normal weight, although many have a frequent gain or loss of 10 or more pounds. Their ability to maintain normal weight is attributed to the other aspect of bulimia; namely, their ability to compensate for overeating by strict dieting and excessive exercise or by purging through self-induced vomiting or abuse of laxatives or enemas.

Some bulimics purge after eating any amount of food, especially those who also have the less-common eating disorder ANOREXIA, which is marked by self-starvation. About half of anorexics suffer from bulimia, and both disorders are characterized by a perfectionist focus on dieting and weight and a fear of being unable to control eating behavior. These disorders typically begin with a strict weight-loss diet. Driven by extreme hunger, the dieter may succumb to gorging, usually on sweet food that is high in calories, such as cake and ice cream. Then, feeling guilty and ashamed, the dieter may purge to compensate for the indiscretion. Before long, the dieter may be caught in a cycle of binging and purging, with binges often triggered by feelings of anxiety, stress, loneliness, or boredom. A binge may be brief, or it may last for several hours, with anywhere from 1,000 to 50,000 calories consumed.

Repeated purging can have serious consequences, including nutritional deficiencies and an imbalance of sodium and potassium, leading to fatigue, fainting, and palpitations. Acids in vomit can damage tooth enamel and the lining of the esophagus. Laxative abuse can irritate the large intestine and produce rectal bleeding. Overuse of laxatives disrupts normal bowel function, leading to chronic constipation when they are discontinued. Perhaps one of the most severe consequences, however, is depression and the high suicide rate that is common among bulimics.

TREATMENT
Like all eating disorders, bulimia can be difficult to treat and usually requires a team approach involving nutrition education, medications, and psychotherapy. If the patient appears to be suicidal or the intractable binge-purge behavior does not respond to outpatient therapy, hospitalization may be necessary. Don't expect instant success, however; treatment often takes 3 years or more, and even then, relapses are common.

Nutritional deficiencies must be treated early, especially if the body's potassium reserves have been depleted by vomiting or laxative abuse. Eating high-potassium foods, such as dried fruits, bananas, and fresh fruits and vegetables, usually restores the mineral; if not, a supplement may be needed.

Bulimics tend to favor diets high in fatty foods and sweets and low in protein, starches, fruits, and vegetables. Nutrition education typically begins with asking the bulimic to keep a diary to help pinpoint circumstances that contribute to binging. A nutrition counselor may also give the patient a strict eating plan that minimizes the number of decisions she must make about what and when to eat. This diet should emphasize foods high in protein and starches while excluding favorite binge foods until the bulimia is under control; then they can be reintroduced in small quantities. At this stage of treatment, the bulimic learns how to give herself permission to eat desirable foods in reasonable quantities, in order to reduce the feelings of deprivation and intense hunger that often lead to loss of control in eating.

Bulimics who abuse laxatives may need a special high-fiber diet to overcome constipation. Whole-grain cereals and breads, pasta, fresh fruits and vegetables, and adequate fluids should help restore normal bowel function.

Because chronic clinical depression often accompanies bulimia, treatment usually includes giving selective antidepressant drugs that restore normal levels of serotonin, a brain chemical instrumental in mood control and appetite. The most commonly prescribed drugs for bulimia are fluoxetine (Prozac), which also suppresses appetite, and sertraline (Zoloft). As patients recover from their depression, they are better able to control their compulsive eating.

Psychotherapy may be offered in several forms, including family and group therapy, as well as cognitive behavioral therapy to help the patient shift the central focus of her life away from food. Bulimics also learn to recognize the warning signs of a binge and how to deal with stress or situations that make them vulnerable to binges.

Participation in self-help groups can also be useful. In addition, alternative therapies, such as meditation, guided imagery, and progressive relaxation routines, can help patients become less obsessive about weight and their eating habits.

Case Study

After Alison gained 10 pounds, she went on a crash diet to lose the excess weight. But during her college finals, hunger drove her to gorge on two quarts of ice cream; filled with remorse, she forced herself to vomit. This incident was the first in what soon became a pattern of binging and purging.

Alison concealed her bulimia from friends, but a dental checkup revealed extensive enamel loss and eight new cavities. Upon questioning by her dentist, Alison tearfully admitted she was bulimic. At her dentist's urging, she sought help at an eating disorders clinic. It took Alison 2 years to overcome her bulimia, but by the time she graduated, she was again eating normally.

BURNS

CONSUME PLENTY OF
- *Foods high in protein and zinc, such as lean meat, poultry, fish and shellfish, eggs, and legumes, to promote healing and tissue repair.*
- *Water, broth, fruit juices, and other non-alcoholic beverages to replace fluids.*
- *Fresh fruits and vegetables rich in vitamin C to foster healing.*

AVOID
- *Tea and coffee.*
- *Alcohol in all forms.*

In order to promote healing and tissue repair, it is essential for victims of extensive burns to have a well-balanced diet that provides extra amounts of most nutrients. These victims also require extra fluids, sodium, and potassium to replace those substances that seep out through damaged skin; otherwise there is a danger of dehydration and an imbalanced body chemistry. Second- and third-degree burns that cause blistering and tissue damage are very serious; they have a high risk of becoming infected by germs that enter the body through the damaged skin.

Patients hospitalized with extensive burns are usually given intravenous fluids and antibiotics. If they are unable to eat, they will also be fed intravenously. A diet that provides extra calories, protein, and zinc is needed for tissue repair. Zinc, found in lean meat, shellfish, yogurt, and some fruits and vegetables, is essential for wound healing; it also bolsters the body's immune defenses to fight infection. To build and maintain healthy skin and ward off infection, the diet should also include vitamin C.

Tea, coffee, and other caffeinated beverages should be avoided; they have a diuretic effect that accelerates fluid loss. Alcohol should also be avoided because it, too, dehydrates the body; it also lowers immunity.

BUTTER AND MARGARINE

BENEFITS
- *Add flavor to many foods.*
- *Improve flavor, moistness, and texture of baked goods.*
- *Good sources of vitamins A and D.*
- *Margarine made with polyunsaturated oils has essential fatty acids.*

DRAWBACKS
- *High in calories, all of which come from fats, which increases the risk of obesity, cancers, and other diseases.*
- *Butter is high in cholesterol and saturated fats, which increase the risk of heart disease.*
- *Stick margarine contains trans fatty acids, which also appear to raise blood cholesterol levels.*
- *Either may be high in salt.*

Canadian eating habits have changed over the last few decades, and nowhere is this more obvious than in the supermarket dairy case. Where butter once reigned, we now have a puzzling array of margarines and other substitutes to choose from.

More Canadians than ever use margarine instead of butter because they believe it is the more healthful of the two spreads. Although most people agree that butter is more flavorful than margarine, they also know that it is relatively high in dietary cholesterol and that all of its calories come from fat (the dietary scourge of the 1990s). What's more, the fat in butter is mostly saturated. Saturated fats are presumed to raise blood cholesterol levels more than other types of fat. Also, numerous studies associate a high-fat diet with an increased risk of cancer. So all in all, it makes sense to switch to margarine.

But does margarine really live up to its reputation as being more healthful than butter? Doubts were raised in 1993, when Harvard researchers concluded that some types may actually increase the risk of heart disease more than butter. Understandably, this added fuel—and confusion—to the butter vs. margarine debate.

TRANS FATTY ACIDS
The cholesterol-raising culprits in some margarines are trans fatty acids. Low levels of these fats exist in most animal products, including butter. However, margarine is hydrogenated, a process in which hydrogen atoms are added to liquid fats to harden them; hydrogenation creates high levels of trans fatty acids. There is good evidence that trans fatty acids raise the levels of low-density lipoprotein (LDL) cholesterol, which may clog the coronary arteries.

The initial reports of the Harvard study proclaimed that butter was more "heart-healthy" than margarine, a position quickly disputed by researchers studying fat metabolism. These scientists conceded that hydrogenation raised levels of trans fatty acids in some margarines, but they cautioned that the saturated fats in butter were even more potent cholesterol-raising substances. Once again, the public was left confused by seemingly conflicting data.

In reality, however, the data are not as confusing as they seem. While trans fatty acids do appear to raise LDL cholesterol, they make up a small percent

COMPARISONS OF VARIOUS SPREADS

CALORIES (BY VOLUME AND BY WEIGHT)	FATS (G/TBSP)	CHOLES-TEROL (MG/TBSP)	NUTRIENTS
BUTTER, STICK			
108 per tbsp 203 per oz	Total fat 11 Saturated 7.1 Monounsaturated 3.3 Polyunsaturated 0.4	33	Vitamin A 459 IU Vitamin E 0.20mg
BUTTER, WHIPPED			
81 per tbsp 203 per oz	Total fat 9.2 Saturated 5.7 Monounsaturated 3 Polyunsaturated 0.3	24	Vitamin A 319 IU
MARGARINE, STICK			
100 per tbsp 203 per oz	Total fat 11 Saturated 2.2 Monounsaturated 5 Polyunsaturated 3.6	0	Vitamin A 460 IU Vitamin D 60 IU
MARGARINE, SOFT			
100 per tbsp 203 per oz	Total fat 11 Saturated 1.9 Monounsaturated 4 Polyunsaturated 4.8	0	Vitamin A 460 IU Vitamin D 60 IU Vitamin E 8mg
MARGARINE, IMITATION OR LOW-CALORIE (OFTEN LABELED "LITE") SOFT			
50 per tbsp 102 per oz	Total fat 5 Saturated 1.1 Monounsaturated 2.2 Polyunsaturated 1.9	0	Vitamin A 460 IU Vitamin D 60 IU Vitamin E 0.4mg

of the total fat intake in a typical diet, accounting for only 2 to 8 percent of total calories, compared to the 12 to 14 percent that come from saturated fats. Also, liquid and soft margarines are less hydrogenated than the stick types; therefore, they have lower levels of trans fatty acids. In short, because most of the calories in margarine are from unsaturated fats, it is still healthier than butter, but softer nonhydrogenated margarines are the best choice as they contain no trans fatty acids. A number of manufacturers now produce margarines that are nonhydrogenated. The general recommendation is to use a soft or liquid, preferably nonhydrogenated, margarine sparingly as a spread.

Check labels and select a product with at least twice as much polyunsaturated as saturated fat; margarines made from canola, safflower, sunflower, and corn oils are the best choices. For baking, use a stick margarine that lists polyunsaturated or monounsaturated oils as the first ingredients. Avoid products with hydrogenated or partially hydrogenated oils; they have more trans fatty acids than the other types do.

A MATTER OF CALORIES

Butter and margarine are a major source of fat calories in the Canadian diet. Many people think that butter has more calories than margarine, but ounce for ounce, butter and margarine have about the same calories (see Comparisons of Various Spreads, p.68); both are also 16 to 20 percent water. The calorie content of both butter and margarine can be reduced by adding extra water, air, or both, so anyone striving to cut fat intake should read product labels and select low-calorie items.

A QUESTION OF FLAVOR

It's no secret that butter tastes better than margarine, but it's also increasingly difficult to tell the difference. Whipped or light butter often loses

some of its natural flavor; conversely, mixing a little butter with margarine gives it a more buttery taste. Butter-substitute powders or sprinkles are virtually fat-free, deriving their flavor from the essence of butter. These products won't spread, but they melt when sprinkled on vegetables or other hot dishes.

Salt is used to flavor both butter and margarine; anyone on a low-sodium diet should look for unsalted varieties.

MODERATION IS THE KEY

Used sparingly, both butter and margarine can be incorporated into a healthful diet. A little butter goes a

THE APPEAL OF BUTTER. *Although it improves the texture and flavor of many foods and tastes better than margarine, butter is high in saturated fats.*

long way; a teaspoon imparts as much flavor as a tablespoon, with one-third the fat. Further reduce butter or margarine by combining it with herbs, spices, or low-fat ingredients; for example, top baked potatoes with chives and blended nonfat cottage cheese. When making cakes and other baked goods, cut the amount of butter or margarine by one-third to one-half; top whole-grain breads with fruit preserves.

CABBAGE

BENEFITS

- *An excellent source of vitamin C.*
- *Low in calories and high in fiber.*
- *May help prevent colon cancer and malignancies stimulated by estrogen.*
- *Juice helps heal peptic ulcers.*

DRAWBACKS

- *Can cause bloating and flatulence.*
- *Gives off strong, somewhat unpleasant sulfurous odor when cooked.*
- *Coleslaw is high in calories; sauerkraut is loaded with salt.*

Although not quite as nutritious as broccoli, Brussels sprouts, and cauliflower, cabbage outranks these plant relatives in consumption. In fact, in some parts of the world, cabbage consumption is on a par with that of potatoes. High in fiber and low in calories (a cup of cooked cabbage contains less than 30), cabbage is a rich source of vitamin C (with 50mg per cup); it also contributes significant amounts of potassium, folate, and beta carotene, a precursor of vitamin A.

It has long been known that people who eat large amounts of cabbage enjoy a low rate of colon cancer. This protective effect is assumed to come from BIO-FLAVONOIDS, indoles, monoterpenes, and other plant chemicals that inhibit tumor growth and protect cells against damage from unstable molecules released when the body uses oxygen. Some of these chemicals also speed up the body's metabolism of estrogen, which may explain why women whose diets provide ample amounts of cabbage and related vegetables have a reduced incidence of breast cancer. This chemical action may also protect against cancers of the uterus and ovaries.

Drinking large amounts of raw cabbage juice promotes healing of peptic ulcers. Researchers have demonstrated that this benefit comes from methionine, an amino acid found in small quantities in cabbage. It takes about a quart of cabbage juice a day for a week or more to notice any improvement. Unfortunately, drinking this much raw cabbage juice can cause bloating and intestinal gas, but this problem can be alleviated by using concentrated cabbage juice. Concentrating the juice can be tricky because methionine is destroyed by heating; however, other methods of extracting the substance from raw cabbage have been developed.

PREPARATION METHODS

Cabbage is served raw as coleslaw or in a mixed salad, steamed or boiled, and pickled into sauerkraut. Because it is made with large amounts of mayonnaise, commercial coleslaw is often very high in calories (about 200 per cup); the calories can be reduced dramatically by replacing the mayonnaise with a combination of nonfat yogurt, vinegar, oil, and sugar. Sauerkraut is soaked in salt brine and then fermented; to lower the sodium content, rinse it before heating. Sulfites are often used to preserve cabbage color; asthma sufferers or anyone allergic to sulfites should check the labels on cans or packages before eating sauerkraut.

Cabbage can be cooked in many ways: steamed, boiled, braised, stir-fried, or stuffed and baked. Steaming and stir-frying will preserve the most

TYPES OF CABBAGE

There are hundreds of different kinds of cabbage; the following are the most popular varieties in Canada and the United States:

- **Green** forms dense heads with green outer leaves.

- **Red** is similar to the green varieties, but the leaves are red or purple; it is much higher in vitamin C than other types.

- **Savoy** has ruffled yellow-green outer leaves and is less compact than other types. It is higher in beta carotene than the other varieties.

- **Bok choy,** or Chinese cabbage, forms a celerylike stalk of white leaves rather than a head; it is higher in calcium than others.

nutrients; these fast-cooking methods also reduce the sulfurous odor released when cabbage is heated. Don't cook cabbage in an aluminum pot, which causes a chemical reaction that discolors the vegetable and alters its flavor.

CAFFEINE

BENEFITS

- *Temporarily enhances mental alertness and concentration.*
- *Can improve athletic performance by temporarily increasing muscle strength and endurance.*
- *May abort an asthma attack by relaxing constricted bronchial muscles.*

DRAWBACKS

- *Is mildly addictive and can result in withdrawal symptoms.*
- *Can cause insomnia.*
- *Excessive amounts can produce tremors, palpitations, and feelings of anxiety.*
- *Diuretic effect increases urination.*
- *Lowers the body's absorption of calcium by increasing the amount lost in urine and stools.*

By far our most popular (and least harmful) addictive drug, caffeine is the stimulant in coffee, tea, chocolate, and colas and other soft drinks; it is also added to some painkillers, cold medications, and drugs used to promote mental alertness. Within a few minutes after caffeine is ingested, it is absorbed from the small intestine into the bloodstream and carried to all the organs in the body. It speeds up the heart rate, stimulates the brain, increases the flow of urine and the production of digestive acids, and relaxes smooth muscles, such as those that control the blood vessels and the airways.

Although caffeine in moderation is generally harmless, sudden withdrawal can cause headaches, irritability, and other symptoms that vary in severity

SOURCES OF CAFFEINE

Coffee is our most prevalent caffeinated drink; however, many other products also contain caffeine. The following chart shows how much caffeine can be found in some of the most common sources.

AVERAGE CAFFEINE CONTENT

COFFEE (5 oz)	MILLIGRAMS
Decaffeinated	1–5
Ground:	
Drip method	100–180
Percolated	75–170
Instant	65–120

TEA (5 oz)	
Brewed, 1 min.	9–33
Brewed, 3 min.	20–46
Brewed, 5 min.	20–50
Decaffeinated	1–5
Iced tea (from mix)	22–36
Instant	12–28

SOFT DRINKS (12 oz)	
Coca-Cola (Cherry, Classic, or diet)	46
Dr. Pepper (regular and diet)	39.6
Diet Pepsi	36
Mountain Dew	54
Pepsi-Cola	38.4
RC Cola (regular and diet)	48
Sunkist Orange	40

CHOCOLATE	
Baking chocolate (2 oz)	70
Cold chocolate milk (8 oz)	2–7
Hot cocoa (6 oz)	5
Milk chocolate candy (2 oz)	12
Sweet or dark chocolate (2 oz)	40

PAINKILLERS	
Anacin, 400mg aspirin	32
Bayer Select, 500mg acetaminophen	65
Excedrin, 500mg aspirin/acetaminophen	65

from one person to another. For example, in some caffeine-sensitive people, caffeine can trigger migraine headaches, while in others it can abort a migraine by relaxing the constricted blood vessels that are causing the throbbing head pain. People with some types of heart-valve disease are often advised to forgo caffeine because it can provoke palpitations or other cardiac arrhythmias.

The stimulant in caffeine enhances mental performance by increasing alertness and the ability to concentrate. For many people a cup of coffee helps them "get going" in the morning, and coffee or tea breaks during the day give them a boost when energy lags.

Athletes have long observed that one or two caffeine drinks an hour before competition can improve performance, especially in endurance sports like running a marathon. Studies confirm that 250mg of caffeine—the amount in two cups of strong coffee—increases muscle strength and endurance, presumably because caffeine increases the body's ability to burn fat for fuel. This benefit, however, is somewhat diminished by carbohydrate loading, a common precompetition tactic also aimed at improving endurance. Excessive pregame caffeine can also accelerate fluid loss through increased urination.

DETRIMENTAL EFFECTS

Ingestion of caffeine late in the day can result in a sleepless night, and excessive intake can lead to caffeinism, a syndrome marked by insomnia, feelings of anxiety and irritability, a rapid heartbeat, tremors, and excessive urination. These symptoms abate with the gradual withdrawal of caffeine. Otherwise, caffeine is relatively nontoxic; a fatal adult dose of the stimulant would require rapidly consuming the amount found in 80 to 100 cups of coffee.

Because caffeine, especially that in coffee, increases the production of stomach acid, ulcer patients are often advised to limit coffee (including de-caffeinated) consumption to one cup after a meal. Many ulcer patients can tolerate tea, however.

Caffeine can prompt a modest temporary rise in blood pressure; it also speeds up the heart rate. There's no need for most heart patients to eliminate coffee or tea from their diets, but they should use it in moderation—cardiologists generally advise no more than three or four cups a day.

Some studies have linked drinking more than six cups of coffee a day during pregnancy with a slightly increased risk of a miscarriage or having a low-birth-weight baby. The general recommendation is that pregnant women limit their daily caffeine consumption to 200mg—the amount found in two cups of coffee. This consumption should be spread over the entire day. For example, a woman might have a cup of coffee for breakfast, half a cup

after lunch, and another half cup with dinner. Because caffeine enters breast milk, nursing mothers should either eliminate caffeinated beverages or time their consumption so that at least 3 hours elapse before breast-feeding.

Caffeine reduces calcium absorption, which can increase the risk of OSTEO-POROSIS, especially in older women. Heavy coffee drinkers should either consume more milk, low-fat yogurt, and other high-calcium foods or consider taking calcium supplements.

Contrary to popular belief, caffeine does not stunt growth during childhood. But it can cause irritability and sleeplessness. Pediatricians generally advise that children consume no more than one cola or other caffeinated drink a day; however, even this may be excessive if a young child is sensitive to caffeine.

CAKES, COOKIES, AND PASTRIES

BENEFITS
- *In small amounts, a good source of quick energy.*
- *Delicious occasional snacks or desserts.*

DRAWBACKS
- *Most are high in fat and calories.*
- *Their high sugar content promotes tooth decay.*
- *Generally contain low amounts of most vitamins and minerals.*

Although high on most people's list of favorite foods, cakes, cookies, pies, and other pastries are low on the scale of nutritious choices. Most are high in fats, sugar and other sweeteners, and calories but relatively low in vitamins, minerals, protein, and starches. Certainly anyone who wants to avoid gaining

weight should minimize consumption of these foods. But this does not mean that they must be totally eliminated from a healthful diet; a small portion served as a special dessert or an occasional treat is not harmful, and it can be a tasty conclusion to an otherwise nutritious meal. Unfortunately, many individuals find it difficult to resist overindulging in such foods, often at the expense of more nutritious albeit less flavorful items.

Refined flour, sugar, fat, eggs, and milk or cream are the basic ingredients in most cakes, cookies, and pastries. Solid and highly saturated fats, such as vegetable shortening, lard, butter, and palm and coconut oils, are generally more suitable for baking than liquid vegetable oils and reduced-fat margarines. Thus, the fats found in most baked goods are the types that are most likely to raise the blood levels of the detrimental low-density lipoprotein (LDL) cholesterol.

HEALTHY ALTERNATIVES

In recent years commercial and home bakers alike have developed low-sugar, low-fat versions of many cakes, cookies, and pies. Some of these lack the flavor and texture of their traditional counterparts, but others are quite acceptable alternatives. Don't be afraid to experiment with your favorite recipes; in general, fat can be cut by one-third or more and sugar by up to one-half without substantially jeopardizing texture and flavor. Here are a few tips for cutting fat and sugar.

• Try using applesauce, strained prunes, mashed bananas, and other puréed fruits as substitutes for at least some of the fat in cookie and cake recipes. The fruit adds the moisture and texture generally contributed by fat; it also imparts sweetness and extra flavor.

• Reduce or even eliminate sugar in fruit pies; use extra cinnamon and other spices to perk up flavor.

• Cut the fat content in pies by using one crust; reduce it even further with a low-fat graham cracker crust or make a deep-dish crustless pie or cobbler. A low-fat graham cracker crust is a nutritious and flavorful alternative to the traditional butter crust used to make a fruit tart.

• Discard half the egg yolks and increase the number of whites when baking a cake or cookies; this increases the protein content and at the same time cuts down on fat and cholesterol.

• Substitute condensed skim milk for cream in frostings and pie fillings. Similarly, try strained yogurt cheese instead of high-fat cream cheese for toppings and fillings. Fruit and fruit sauces are still other options for low-calorie toppings.

• Increase the nutritional content and cut the fat calories in cookies by sticking with old favorites like oatmeal cookies or fruit bars. These can be made even more healthful by substituting applesauce or strained prunes for part of the fat, using whole-wheat flour, and loading them with raisins and other dried fruits instead of nuts.

• For a birthday or other festive occasion, serve a chocolate angel food cake with fresh berries and strawberry or raspberry sauce; it has virtually no fat and a fraction of the calories contained in a comparable piece of devil's food cake with chocolate cream frosting.

• Make a light and lemony cheesecake by using a combination of nonfat cottage and ricotta cheeses and condensed skim milk, lemon zest, and egg whites. Top with strained yogurt instead of sour cream.

The high sugar content promotes tooth decay and may pose a problem for some people with DIABETES. (Recent studies show, however, that most diabetics can tolerate some sweet foods, especially if they contain fat, which slows sugar metabolism.) Sweets also lessen one's appetite for foods that are more nutritious.

Carrot cakes, zucchini and banana breads, and other such commercial baked goods are often promoted as healthy alternatives. In fact, most of these contain only negligible amounts of the fruit or vegetable, are still high in fat and sugar, and are often topped with butter frosting. However, these can be made healthier by using low-fat substitutes for some ingredients (see Healthy Alternatives, above).

FATTENING BUT DELICIOUS. *Tasty homemade cakes and pastries are favorites at country fairs but should be reserved for occasional treats instead of eaten daily.*

CANCER

EAT PLENTY OF
- *Citrus and other fruits and dark green or yellow vegetables for vitamin C, beta carotene, bioflavonoids, and other plant chemicals that protect against cancer.*
- *Whole-grain breads and cereals and other high-fiber foods to promote smooth colon function.*

CUT DOWN ON
- *Fatty foods, especially those high in saturated animal fats.*
- *Alcoholic beverages.*
- *Salt-cured, smoked, fermented, and charcoal-broiled foods.*

AVOID
- *Foods that may contain pesticide residues and environmental pollutants.*

Recent research has dramatically changed our thinking about the role of diet in both the prevention and treatment of cancer. It's increasingly clear that certain dietary elements may help promote the development and spread of malignancies, while others slow or block tumor growth. The Canadian Cancer Society estimates that one out of three cancers may be related to diet, especially one high in fat and processed foods; they also believe that most of these cancers could be prevented by dietary changes.

PROTECTIVE FOODS

Compelling data associate a diet that provides ample fruits and vegetables with a reduced risk of many of our most deadly cancers. These foods are rich in BIOFLAVONOIDS and other plant chemicals; dietary FIBER; and ANTIOXIDANTS, vitamins A, C, and E, and selenium. All of these substances may slow, stop, or reverse the processes that can lead to cancer. They do so through several protective mechanisms: by neutralizing or detoxifying cancer-causing agents (car-

cinogens); by preventing precancerous changes in cellular genetic material due to carcinogens, radiation, and other environmental factors; by inducing the formation of protective enzymes; and by reducing the hormonal action that can stimulate tumor growth.

Equally important is a reduced intake of FATS. Numerous studies link a high-fat diet and obesity with an increased risk of cancers of the colon, uterus, prostate, and skin (including melanoma, the most deadly form of skin cancer). The link between fat consumption and breast cancer is more controversial. Experts stress that no more than 30 percent of total calories should come from fats, and many feel that even this is too high, advocating a 20 percent limit on fat calories. Often, it takes only a few simple dietary changes to lower fat intake; for example, choosing lean cuts of meat, trimming away all visible fat, substituting pasta and other vegetarian dishes for meat several times a week, adopting low-fat cooking methods, such as baking and steaming, and limiting the use of butter, margarine, mayonnaise, shortening, and oils.

Increased intake of fiber may protect against cancer in several ways. It speeds the transit of waste through the colon, which some researchers think cuts the risk of bowel cancer. A high-fiber, low-calorie diet also protects against obesity and the increased risk of cancers linked to excessive body fat.

HARMFUL HABITS

Doctors warn against heavy use of alcohol, which is associated with an increased risk of cancers of the mouth, larynx, esophagus, and liver. Excessive alcohol consumption hinders the body's ability to use beta carotene, which appears to protect against these cancers. Alcohol can also deplete reserves of folate, thiamine, and other B vitamins, as well as selenium. Folate is known to re-

EAT YOUR VEGETABLES (AND FRUITS TOO)!

The pigments and other chemicals that give plant foods their bright colors also seem to contribute to their cancer-fighting properties. Nutritionists now agree with the age-old urging of mothers and advise people to eat at least three different-colored vegetables and two different fruits daily. Choose from among the dark green leafy vegetables and the dark yellow, orange, and red fruits and vegetables. Include one serving of citrus a day, and strive to have a cruciferous vegetable. The members of the cruciferous (or cabbage) family include bok choy, broccoli, Brussels sprouts, cabbage, cauliflower, collards, kale, kohlrabi, mustard greens, rutabagas, and turnips.

duce proliferation of cancer cells; low levels of folate are also associated with an increased risk of cervical cancer. Researchers have found that giving folate supplements slows the proliferation of other precancerous cells.

Smoking, more than any other lifestyle factor, increases the risk of cancer; stopping the habit is the most important step that a smoker can take to avoid cancer. In addition to lung cancer, smoking is strongly associated with cancers of the esophagus, mouth, larynx, pancreas, and bladder; recent studies also link it to an increased risk of breast cancer. For people who find it impossible to stop smoking, there are a few dietary measures that can somewhat lower their cancer risk. One is to consume BROCCOLI or related cruciferous vegetables several times a week. These members of the cabbage family are known to be appreciably high in certain cancer-fighting compounds, including bioflavonoids, indoles, monoterpenes, phenolic acids, and plant sterols, precursors to vitamin D. In addition, sulforaphane, a chemical particularly abundant in broccoli, is one of the most potent anticancer compounds identified to date; various studies show that eating broccoli several times a week lowers the incidence of lung cancer among smokers compared to those whose diet does not include the vegetable.

Low levels of vitamin C are linked to an increased risk of many of the cancers related to smoking. Because smoking works to deplete the body's reserves of vitamin C, it's a good idea for smokers to increase their intake of citrus fruits and other good sources of this nutrient. Similarly, smoking can deplete the body's stores of folate and other B complex vitamins; increased consumption of lean meat, grains, fortified cereals, legumes, and green leafy vegetables may help counter this adverse effect.

People who eat large amounts of smoked, pickled, cured, fried, charcoal-broiled, and processed meats have a

high incidence of stomach and esophageal tumors. Smoked foods contain polyaromatic hydrocarbons which are known carcinogens. The salt in pickled foods can injure the stomach wall and facilitate tumor formation. Nitrites and nitrates in processed meats can form nitrosamines, established carcinogens. However, consuming these foods along with good sources of vitamins C and E reduces the formation of nitrosamines.

WHEN CANCER STRIKES

A qualified nutritionist should be part of any cancer treatment team, because both the disease and its treatment demand good nutrition as an aid to recovery. Surgery, which still remains the major treatment for cancer, also requires a highly nutritious diet for healing and recuperation. The cancer itself can cause nutritional problems that will require treatment along with the underlying disease; for example, colon cancer will often cause iron-deficiency ANEMIA because of chronic intestinal bleeding.

Weight loss is common among almost

all cancer patients. Most experience anorexia, or loss of appetite, as a result of the cancer itself; depression brought on by a diagnosis of a potentially fatal disease, as well as pain, understandably lessens any desire to eat. Cancer treatments, especially radiation and chemotherapy, curb appetite and produce nausea and other side effects. Surgery, too, can affect appetite and make eating undesirable, especially if it involves the digestive system. A dietitian or qualified nutritionist can devise a diet or recommend supplements to provide the calories, protein, and other nutrients needed to maintain weight and promote healing.

Dietary guidelines for cancer patients must take into account the stage and type of malignancy. In most cases of early or localized cancer, patients are generally advised to follow a diet that is low in fat; high in pasta, whole-grain products, and other starches; and high in fruits and vegetables. Fats, especially from animal sources, are discouraged because they are believed to support tumor growth. In contrast, fruits and vegetables contain an assortment of natural plant chemicals that are thought to retard cancer growth and spread.

Protein and zinc are essential for wound healing; therefore, surgery patients should eat two or more daily servings of lean meat, low-fat milk, eggs, fish, and shellfish. Many cancer patients find it difficult to tolerate red meat, however, because it takes on an unpleasant metallic taste; in such instances, substituting egg whites, poultry, and a combination of

CANCER-FIGHTING FOODS. *A variety of fresh fruits and vegetables, high-fiber legumes, and whole-grain breads are not only high in vitamins and minerals, but may also give protection against cancer.*

COPING WITH EATING PROBLEMS

In many instances, loss of appetite, nausea, and other eating problems of cancer patients can be dealt with by changing daily habits and routines. The following tips have worked for many people.

• Plan your major meal for the time of day when you are least likely to experience nausea and vomiting. For many cancer patients, this is in the early morning. Otherwise, eat small, frequent meals and snacks throughout the day.

• Let someone else prepare the food; cooking odors often provoke nausea. Food that is served cold or at room temperature gives off less odor than hot food.

• If mouth sores are a problem, eat bland, puréed foods—for example, custards, rice and other puddings made with milk and eggs, porridge, and blended soups. Avoid salty, spicy, or acidic foods. Sucking on zinc lozenges may speed the healing of mouth sores.

• Try to eat with others in a pleasant social atmosphere. Ask family members to bring home-cooked food to the hospital (but have them check with the dietitian first).

• Get dressed to eat, if possible, and strive to make meals visually attractive. A few slices of a colorful fruit give visual appeal to a bowl of oatmeal; a colorful napkin and bud vase perk up a tray of food.

• To overcome nausea, try chewing on ice chips or sucking on a ginger candy or sour lemon drop before eating. Sipping flat ginger ale or cola may also help.

• Rest for half an hour after eating, preferably in a sitting or upright position; reclining may trigger reflux, nausea, and vomiting.

• Pay extra attention to dental hygiene. If mouth sores hinder tooth brushing, make a baking soda paste and use your finger and a soft cloth to gently cleanse the teeth. Then rinse the mouth with a weak solution of hydrogen peroxide and baking soda. Diluted commercial mouth washes freshen the breath, but avoid full-strength products that can further irritate sores.

• If a dry mouth makes swallowing difficult, liquefy foods in a blender or moisten them with low-fat milk, sauces, or gravies.

• If diarrhea is a problem (as is often the case during chemotherapy), avoid fatty foods, raw fruits, whole-grain products, and other foods that can make it worse. Instead, eat bland, binding foods, such as rice, bananas, cooked apples, and dry toast.

legumes and grains will provide the needed protein and zinc. In some cases, supplements may be prescribed.

WISDOM OF THE BODY

Flying in the face of conventional wisdom, however, are recent recommendations from a growing number of cancer specialists who discourage urging some cancer patients to eat when they don't feel like it. In the past, forced feeding in the form of enriched dietary supplements, intravenous nutrition, or a gastric feeding tube was recommended to maintain nutrition, but these approaches usually did not result in weight gain or prolonged survival. Instead, many who were force-fed actually died sooner; experts now believe this may be because the feeding actually spurs tumor growth. Consequently, many medical scientists now believe that the anorexia and cachexia (a severe form of malnutrition and body wasting) that occurs in advanced cancer may be an example of the "wisdom of the body" as it attempts to starve the tumor. Although it may be difficult for family members and friends to watch loved ones stop eating and progressively lose weight, informed physicians now urge that, in some situations, cachectic patients be allowed to limit food intake while doctors undertake aggressive therapy to destroy the tumor. Once this is accomplished, appetite returns, and the lost weight is regained as recovery takes place.

THE LURE OF SUPPLEMENTS

Millions of North Americans take vitamin and mineral supplements, often in high doses and without consulting a doctor. Recent reports detailing the anticancer effects of antioxidants have resulted in greatly increased sales of high-dose supplements of beta carotene and vitamins A, C, and E. In theory, it is reasonable to assume that if a small amount of a nutrient protects against cancer, then a high dose should be even more protective. Unfortunately, this does not seem to be true. When consumed in the amounts that are generally found in foods, these nutrients do have an antioxidant effect, which prevents the potentially cancer-causing damage that occurs when the body uses oxygen. But when taken in the form of high-dose supplements, these substances may have an opposite effect; recent research indicates they may become pro-oxidants and may actually increase damage caused by free radicals, the unstable molecules released when the body uses oxygen. In addition, high doses of vitamin A can lead to toxicity.

The situation may be quite different, however, for patients who are undergoing cancer treatment. Some may need high-dose supplements, while others may be advised to avoid certain nutrients. This is why it's important to consult a registered dietitian or nutritionist regarding any dietary change and supplementation. There is no scientific evidence to suggest that alternative therapies, which include Japanese maitake, Chinese herbs, blue-green algae, and shark cartilage extracts, have any value in cancer treatment.

CARBOHYDRATES: THE BACKBONE OF A HEALTHY DIET

*Starches and sugars are our major source of energy.
In their natural state, they are also low in
calories and high in fiber, vitamins, and minerals.*

Almost all of the starches and sugars that humans burn for energy come from plants; the only major exception is lactose, the sugar in milk. In effect, each plant is a complex food factory that takes water from the soil, carbon dioxide from the air, and energy from the sun to make glucose, a simple sugar that is later converted into starch. As the plant develops and grows, it also makes various vitamins, minerals, and chemicals, as well as some fat and protein. Consequently, we can get our carbohydrates and most of the other nutrients needed to sustain life from thousands of different grains, seeds, fruits, and vegetables.

In general, carbohydrates are classified according to their chemical structure and digestibility; they are divided into two groups:

Simple carbohydrates, or sugars, form crystals that dissolve in water and are easily digested. Naturally occurring sugars occur in a variety of fruits, some vegetables, honey, and maple sap. Processed sugars include table sugar, brown sugar, and molasses.

Complex carbohydrates have a range of textures, flavors, colors, and molecular structures. Composed of complex chains of sugars, these carbohydrates are further classified as starches and fiber. Our digestive system can break down and metabolize most starches, which are found in an array of grains, vegetables, and some fruits. The digestive system lacks the enzymes or or-

---

BENEFITS
- *They are converted to glucose, which the body uses for energy.*
- *Starchy foods are low in cost, yet high in nutritional value.*

DRAWBACKS
- *Simple carbohydrates (various sugars) are low in nutritional value; in addition, they usually promote dental decay.*

---

ganisms that are needed to break down most fiber, including cellulose and other woody parts of the plant skeleton, and pectin and other gums that hold plant cells together. But dietary fiber is still important because it promotes smooth colon function and may help prevent some types of cancer, heart attacks, and other diseases.

HOW CARBOHYDRATES WORK

Our body metabolizes both simple and complex carbohydrates into glucose, or blood sugar, the body's primary source of fuel. Carbohydrates are high-quality fuels because—compared to proteins or fats—relatively little work is required of the body to break them down in order to release their energy.

Glucose, the only form of carbohydrates that the body can use immediately, is essential for the functioning of the brain, nervous system, muscles, and various organs. At any given time the blood can carry about an hour's

supply of glucose. Any glucose that is not needed for immediate energy is converted into glycogen and stored in the liver and muscles; when it is required, the liver turns the glycogen back into glucose. The body can store only enough glycogen to last for several hours of moderate activity.

The glycemic index is a measure of how quickly the energy from a carbohydrate food is made available for use as glucose, as reflected by the raising of the blood sugar level. Sugars are rapidly converted into glucose to provide energy. In contrast, starches vary widely in the glycemic response they generate, with the size of a food particle and the duration of cooking, if any, having a significant effect. The bigger the particle size, the more difficult it is to digest and the more slowly glucose is released into the bloodstream, yielding a lower "glycemic index." For example, stone-ground whole-grain bread has a larger particle size, and a lower glycemic index, than finely milled bread, whether white or whole-grain.

When glucose reserves run low, the body turns first to protein and then to fat to convert them into glucose. Burning protein, however, robs the body of lean muscle tissue. In addition, if the body has to burn fat in the absence of carbohydrates, toxic byproducts called ketones are released; these can lead to a potentially dangerous biochemical imbalance.

THE IMPORTANCE OF STARCHES

Complex carbohydrates form the basis of the human diet worldwide. In Canada and many other industrialized countries, however, the bulk of calories comes from meat and other high-protein foods, fats, and simple carbohydrates (often in the form of processed sugars). Until recently, starchy foods have been shunned as being fattening, dull, and nutritionally unimportant. We now know that this is a serious misconception, which may account, at least in part, for our modern epidemics of OBESITY, DIABETES, HEART DISEASE, and some types of CANCER.

Despite carbohydrates' undeserved reputation as being fattening, both carbohydrates and proteins provide 4 calories per gram, compared to 9 calories per gram of fat. Sugar and starches are fattening only when they are consumed with fatty additions or are eaten in quantities much larger than the body can readily use, in which case they are converted and stored as body fat. Overeating is unlikely to be a problem if meals are built around starchy and fibrous foods, which tend to be filling. In contrast, meat and other high-protein foods come pack-aged with fat and are more likely to cause weight gain.

Most grains, vegetables, and fruits also provide essential vitamins and minerals, making them even more important nutritionally. In contrast, pure sugars can be used for energy but offer no nutrients.

HOW MUCH DO YOU NEED?

The prevailing scientific wisdom is that approximately 55 to 60 percent of calories should come from carbohydrates drawn from a wide spectrum of grains and other starches, vegetables, and fruits. Only about 10 percent of these calories should be from processed sugars. Unfortunately, the typical North American diet now gets 20 percent of its calories from sugar, 20 percent from protein, 35 percent from fat, and only 25 percent from starches.

There are encouraging signs of improvement, however. Recent surveys show that an increasing number of people are eating more bread, cereals, pasta, grains, and legumes and are cutting back on meat. Although so-called refined carbohydrates, such as white flour and white rice, are just as good energy sources as whole-wheat flour and brown rice, processing removes many essential nutrients, including the B vitamins, iron and other minerals, and dietary fiber. The best approach is to build a diet around whole or lightly processed grains and raw or slightly cooked vegetables and fruits.

CARBOHYDRATE LOADING

Nutrition can have a significant impact on athletic performance and vice versa. Regular exercise increases the body's ability to utilize glucose efficiently and to store glycogen in muscle tissue. Thus, the fitter you are, the greater your ability to store the extra glycogen that is particularly needed for endurance events, such as running a marathon or cross-country skiing.

Therefore, although a well-balanced diet is important for anyone interested in complete nutrition, a diet high in carbohydrates is particularly beneficial for athletes. In general, nutritionists recommend that athletes who train exhaustively on a daily basis should aim for a diet with 65 to 70 percent of calories coming from carbohydrates. Further, 80 to 85 percent of these carbohydrates should come from starches, such as pasta, bread, cereals, grains, potatoes, and beans, with the balance coming from fruit and other sugary foods.

Athletes seeking to develop plentiful stores of glycogen have turned to "carbohydrate loading" before major athletic events. This involves consuming a diet that is very high in carbohydrates for 3 days, then really loading up the night before the event on a large meal of pasta, bread, and other starchy foods. This dietary strategy is useful in endurance sports or those that require an end burst of energy, such as competitive rowing.

SPECIAL CONCERNS

Carbohydrates can be incorporated into almost any diet, but people with certain diseases may need to

DID YOU KNOW?

• Carbohydrates make up about 75 percent of total calorie intake worldwide. In the developed world, however, they comprise only 45 percent of the diet, with almost half coming from sugars.

• Legumes, such as dried beans and peas, provide the best food value per dollar spent.

• Just because you don't see "sugar" listed as an ingredient on a food label doesn't mean it's not there. Look for words ending in "ose" (sucrose, lactose, maltose, fructose, glucose, and dextrose) and anything described as "syrup" (such as corn or malt syrup), as well as honey and molasses.

• Maltose is found in sprouting grains, malted wheat and barley, and malt extract.

• Glycogen is the form in which carbohydrates are stored in humans and animals, but it can be quickly converted back to glucose. Because it has a structure similar to starch, it is sometimes referred to as animal starch.

• After harvesting, the sugar in corn and other starchy vegetables is gradually converted to starch, which explains why these foods lose their sweetness. In contrast, the starch in bananas and other starchy fruits turns to sugar, increasing their sweetness.

CARBOHYDRATES IN THE DAILY DIET

Carbohydrates should provide about 55 to 60 percent of your total energy intake, with a balance of starchy foods, vegetables, and fruits. The Food Guide Rainbow (see p.39) recommends that a person with an energy need of 1,800 or more calories per day should eat 5 to 12 servings of starchy foods, 5 to 10 servings of fruits and vegetables. Below are three

suggested combinations of carbohydrate foods that would fulfill the recommended number of servings for the average person. These are spread over the traditional three meals a day, but if desired, some can be switched to between-meal snacks. Follow Canada's Food Guide for recommendations to create your own combinations.

1 bowl cold whole-grain cereal
1 slice toast
½ grapefruit

2 slices whole-grain bread
1 large bowl of salad with lettuce,
  green pepper, cucumber, and tomato
1 apple

1 baked potato
½ cup broccoli
½ cup carrots
1 peach
2 oatmeal cookies

½ cup orange juice
1 bowl cooked whole-grain cereal
¼ cup raisins
1 muffin

Large three-bean salad (chickpeas, red
  kidney beans, and string beans)
½ cup rice
1 banana

Bowl of pasta with tomatoes, eggplant,
  peas, and tomato sauce
1 cup spinach salad
½ cup berries

1 medium-size orange, sliced
2 slices French toast
½ cup applesauce

2 corn tortillas filled with beans,
  lettuce, tomato, and salsa
½ cup fruit salad
3-4 tea biscuits

1 sweet potato
½ cup lima beans
½ cup squash
½ cup pineapple
1 roll

make some adjustments. People with DIABETES, for example, should include a balance of protein, fat, and high-fiber starchy foods, such as whole-grain bread, beans, peas, and lentils, at each meal. This balance provides for a steady supply of glucose, rather than the typical sharp rise that occurs after an all-carbohydrate meal. Contrary to popular belief, sugar does not cause diabetes, nor do diabetics have to completely avoid sugar. They do, however, have to monitor the blood level of glucose, but whether the glucose originates from table sugar or from starch is not relevant.

Sugar does contribute to DENTAL DISORDERS.

Those with HEART DISEASE need to emphasize high-fiber complex carbohydrates in their diet. Soluble FIBER, such as that found in oat bran and fruit pectin, helps lower high cholesterol levels and plays an important role in preventing ATHEROSCLEROSIS, the buildup of fatty deposits in coronary arteries and other blood vessels.

CANCER patients are often advised to increase their intake of carbohydrates and decrease fat intake, especially if they have cancers of the breast,

colon, uterus, prostate, or skin. Increasing evidence suggests that fat in general, and animal fat in particular, may influence body chemistry in such a manner as to support tumor growth.

People with CELIAC DISEASE should avoid all foods containing gluten, a protein found in wheat, rye, and to a lesser extent, other cereal grains. Because carbohydrates are easy to digest, they often make up the bulk of the diet for people with various DIGESTIVE DISORDERS. Depending on the nature of the disorder, high- or low-fiber foods may predominate.

CARROTS

BENEFITS
- *An excellent source of beta carotene, the precursor of vitamin A.*
- *A good source of dietary fiber and potassium.*
- *Help prevent night blindness.*
- *May help lower blood cholesterol levels and protect against cancer.*

DRAWBACKS
- *Excessive intake can give skin a yellowish tinge.*

Native to Afghanistan, carrots are our most abundant source of beta carotene, an ANTIOXIDANT nutrient that the body converts to vitamin A. One large carrot provides 17mg of beta carotene and more than six times the Recommended Nutrient Intake (RNI) of vitamin A—a nutrient essential for healthy hair, skin, eyes, bones, and mucous membranes. Vitamin A also helps prevent infections in the body. Antioxidants, such as beta carotene and vitamin A, are essential to the diet because they protect against CANCER.

A recent U.S. government study found that research volunteers who ate 7 ounces (about one cup) of carrots a day had an average 11 percent reduction in their blood cholesterol levels after only 3 weeks. Lowered cholesterol levels, in turn, decrease the risk of HEART DISEASE. Additional research is necessary to verify this and to identify the cholesterol-lowering substance in carrots. Meanwhile, eating a prudent amount of carrots does no harm and may confer major health benefits against cancer and heart disease.

SEEING IN THE DARK

Carrots will not prevent or correct our most common vision problems, such as myopia and farsightedness. But a deficiency of vitamin A does cause night blindness, an inability of the eyes to adjust to dim lighting or darkness. Vitamin A combines with the protein opsin in the retina's rod cells to form the substance rhodopsin that the eye needs for night vision. Eating one carrot every few days provides enough vitamin A to prevent or overcome night blindness.

COOKED OR RAW?

Naturally sweet, carrots make an ideal high-fiber, low-calorie snack food. Interestingly, cooking actually increases carrots' nutritional value, because it breaks down the tough cellular walls that encase the beta carotene. To convert beta carotene to vitamin A, the body needs at least a small amount of fat, because vitamin A is soluble in fat, not water. Adding a pat of butter or margarine to cooked carrots ensures that the body will fully utilize this nutrient. People allergic to raw carrots can usually eat cooked carrots with no difficulty. Cooked and puréed carrots are an ideal BEGINNER FOOD, as they are naturally sweet and high in nutrients.

Carrots also contain carotenoids other than beta carotene, as well as BIOFLAVONOIDS. The beneficial effects of carrots may not be reproduced by taking isolated supplements. Excessive intake of carrots may produce high levels of these pigments, giving the skin a yellow tinge. This harmless condition, called carotenemia, disappears in a few weeks of reducing carrot intake. If the yellow skin persists, or if the white portions of the eyes are also discolored, the problem may be jaundice, a symptom of a LIVER DISORDER.

CAULIFLOWER

BENEFITS
- *An excellent source of vitamin C.*
- *A good source of folate and potassium.*
- *Low in calories and high in fiber.*

DRAWBACKS
- *More expensive than vegetables with comparable nutrients.*
- *May cause bloating and flatulence.*

Cauliflower is a rich source of nutrients, especially vitamin C and folate. A cup of cauliflower florets has more than the Recommended Nutrient Intake (RNI) of vitamin C, one-third of the RNI for folate, and reasonable amounts of potassium and vitamin B_6; it also has BIOFLAVONOIDS, indoles, and other chemicals that protect against cancer.

Filling, high in fiber, and low in calories (25 in a cup of florets), cauliflower is an ideal snack food for weight watchers. Raw cauliflower has more folate than when cooked (80 percent of this B vitamin is lost in cooking).

To retain flavor and reduce nutrient loss, cook cauliflower rapidly by boiling or steaming. Too much cooking turns cauliflower mushy and releases sulfurous compounds, resulting in an unpleasant odor and bitter taste. Boiling the vegetable in an open pot helps disperse these compounds. To avoid discoloring the cauliflower, don't cook it in aluminum or iron pots.

When buying cauliflower, look for a head with firm, compact florets. If it is fresh, the leaves will be crisp and green, and the head, or curd, snowy white. Broccoflower is a hybrid of cauliflower and broccoli; it resembles cauliflower but is green and has a milder flavor. Another variety, purple cauliflower, has more vitamin A than the white kind.

KING OF THE CABBAGES. *Cauliflower, a cruciferous cancer-fighting vegetable, was grown in ancient times in the Middle East.*

CELERIAC

BENEFITS
- *A good source of fiber, including the soluble type that lowers elevated blood cholesterol levels.*
- *A good source of potassium; also provides some vitamin C.*
- *Low in calories.*

DRAWBACKS
- *Not readily available in many supermarkets and produce stores.*

A winter root vegetable, celeriac is a member of the parsley family and is closely related to celery; in fact, its other names include celery root, knob celery, and German celery. Fresh celeriac resembles a large, round, knobby turnip, but when the tough outer skin is peeled away, the flesh is white, with a flavor and odor similar to celery.

Celeriac is something of a novelty vegetable in Canada, but its mild, celerylike flavor lends itself to a variety of dishes. For example, it is often grated raw into salads, boiled and puréed to add body and flavor to soups and stews, chopped into poultry stuffing, or sliced, dipped in an egg batter, and sautéed to serve as a meat substitute. The French cut celeriac into thin strips, blanch them, and toss them with a mustard mayonnaise to make an alternative to celery salad.

A half-cup serving of cooked celeriac contains less than 20 calories, yet it provides about 500mg of potassium; it also contains 1mg of iron and 5mg of vitamin C. Celeriac is respectably high in fiber, including the soluble fiber that lowers elevated levels of blood cholesterol, therefore reducing the risk of a heart attack.

CELERY

BENEFITS
- *Low in calories and high in fiber.*
- *A good source of potassium.*
- *May reduce inflammation and protect against cancer.*

DRAWBACKS
- *High in plant nitrates.*

Dieters tend to eat lots of celery because it is so low in calories, however, it is a misconception that chewing the stalks consumes more calories than the vegetable provides. Two stalks of celery contain less than 10 calories, yet their high fiber content makes them very filling. Celery is a good source of potassium; it also contributes small amounts of vitamin C, some folate and vitamin A. Although it is not very high in nutrients, it adds a unique flavor to a variety of foods—from soups to salads and poultry stuffing. Celery is about 95 percent water; this liquid is often extracted and combined with other vegetable juices to make a nutritious drink.

Celery leaves are the most nutritious part of the plant, containing more calcium, iron, potassium, and vitamins A and C than the stalks. The leaves should be salvaged for soups, salads, and other dishes enhanced by the flavor of celery.

MEDICINAL PROPERTIES

Traditionally, herbalists have advocated fresh celery and celery seed tea to treat gout and other forms of inflammatory arthritis, as well as high blood pressure and edema. Polyacetylene, compounds found in celery, are said to reduce production of certain prostaglandins, body chemicals that are instrumental in producing inflammation. There is no proof, however, that celery actually eases arthritis pain. Nor is there any proof that celery lowers blood pressure and increases urination.

Celery may help reduce the risk of certain cancers. The polyacetylenes in celery destroy benzopyrene, a powerful substance that causes cancer. This benefit may be partially offset by celery's high levels of plant nitrates, substances that the body converts into nitrosamines, which are linked with an increased risk of cancer. However, many researchers believe that this is a minor risk because most plants high in nitrates and other potentially cancer-causing substances also contain chemicals that neutralize any harmful effects. Cooking celery by boiling, braising, or steaming lowers nitrate levels.

CELIAC DISEASE

CONSUME PLENTY OF
- *Low-fat milk, eggs, fish, meat, and poultry for protein.*
- *Vegetables and fruits for vitamins and minerals.*
- *Legumes, potatoes, and rice for starches, minerals, and protein.*
- *Bread, cereal, and baked goods made from corn, potato, rice, soybean, tapioca, and buckwheat meals or flour.*

AVOID
- *Bread, pasta, cereals, cakes, and other wheat, rye, or barley products.*
- *Foods using wheat products as a thickening agent or coating, such as breaded foods, meat loaf, frankfurters, sausages, sauces, and soups.*
- *Beverages containing gluten, such as beer, malted drinks, and chocolate milk.*
- *Almost all commercial salad dressings except pure mayonnaise.*

Celiac disease, also known as celiac sprue or nontropical sprue, is a hereditary disorder that affects about 1 out of every 2,000 Canadians. Typically, the disorder becomes apparent when a baby or young child starts eating foods containing wheat, rye, barley, and in some cases, other cereal grains. A gluten protein called gliadin, which is found in these grains, combines with antibodies in the digestive tract to damage the walls of the small intestine and interfere with the absorption of many nutrients, especially fats and certain starches and sugars.

Children with celiac disease are usually plagued with such symptoms as stomach upsets, diarrhea, abdominal cramps, bloating, mouth sores, and an increased susceptibility to infection. Their stools are pale and foul-smelling, and they float to the top of the toilet bowl, indicating a high fat content. The child's growth may be stunted; some children develop anemia and skin problems, especially dermatitis. Diagnosis, based on the symptoms, is confirmed by an inspection of the small intestine with a special viewing instrument and an intestinal biopsy indicating abnormalities characteristic of celiac disease.

Individuals who develop celiac disease later in life may have had a mild or symptomless form of the disease in childhood. In unusual cases, adults with no prior history of gluten sensitivity develop the condition after surgery on the digestive tract. Women with celiac disease often fail to menstruate (amenorrhea) and may also have problems getting pregnant.

Once the disease has been identified, patients are advised to permanently eliminate any foods that contain gluten from their diet. A registered dietitian can assist in planning nutritionally balanced meals that are gluten-free. Most doctors also prescribe a vitamin and mineral supplement to counter any nutritional deficiencies, especially for the first several months. If anemia is a problem, iron and/or folate supplements will also be recommended.

AVOIDING GLUTEN

Hundreds of everyday foods contain gluten: breads, cakes, rolls, muffins, baking mixes, pasta, sausages bound with bread crumbs, foods coated with batter, sauces and gravies, soups thickened with wheat flour, and most breakfast cereals, as well as some candies, ice creams, and puddings. Many baby foods are thickened with gluten, although most commercial first-stage foods are gluten-free.

Always read labels on packaged foods. Avoid ingredients such as flour-based binders and fillers and modified starch. Be suspicious of any label that specifies "other flours" because they are likely to include at least some wheat derivatives. Beer is made from barley and should be avoided, along with malted drinks.

Outside the home, order only plain foods, such as broiled fish or meat, steamed vegetables, and a baked potato—all without any sauces or dressings. Even communion wafers contain some gluten. However, gluten-free wafers are now available; check with your pastor.

Contrary to popular belief, people with celiac disease can eat pasta, bread, cake, and other baked products, but they must look for gluten-free items, such as Jerusalem artichoke pasta and baked goods made with corn, rice, potato, or soy flours. Gluten-free flour is now available. In general, it is better to prepare most foods at home to assure a healthy diet without risking exposure to gluten.

It was once believed that oats also contained the offending gliadin protein, but recent analyses have shown that they do not. Thus, doctors are now allowing patients to experiment with oatmeal and other oat products; if they provoke symptoms, however, they should still be avoided.

Case Study

Susan had been a healthy infant. She was breast-fed by her mother for 5 months, after which rice cereal and puréed vegetables and fruits had been added to her diet. When she started teething, her mother gave her pretzels and teething crackers to chew. Instead of relieving her discomfort, Susan became more irritable; her mother attributed this to teething.

Over the next few months, Susan had repeated bouts of diarrhea and developed a bloated abdomen. At her checkup the pediatrician was surprised at her loss of some weight. After blood tests and a laboratory examination of Susan's stools, a biopsy confirmed celiac disease.

Susan's mother was referred to a clinical dietitian, who outlined a gluten-free diet. As Susan grew, she had follow-up visits with the dietitian. At an early age Susan learned that she must follow a special diet for life—even in preschool and at the homes of her playmates. However, Susan can also look forward to normal growth and health.

CEREALS

BENEFITS

- *High in complex carbohydrates.*
- *Many are high in fiber.*
- *Some are reasonable sources of protein; adding milk makes a bowl of cereal a high-protein dish.*
- *Enriched cereals are high in iron, niacin, thiamine, and riboflavin, along with other B vitamins.*
- *Iron-fortified infant cereals are ideal introductory solid foods.*

DRAWBACKS

- *Many commercial varieties are high in salt, sugar, and fat.*
- *Bran cereals can reduce the absorption of iron, zinc, and other minerals.*
- *High-bran products may cause bloating and flatulence.*

Served hot or cold, cereals are a healthful, low-calorie breakfast main dish. Many also make popular snacks and are used as ingredients in meat loaf, muffins, and cookies. Since ancient times oatmeal and other cooked cereal porridges have been valued as much for their economy and ease of preparation as for their nutrition.

The first ready-to-eat cold cereals in North America were developed as health foods by the Western Health Reform Institute in Battle Creek, Michigan, which was founded by the Seventh-Day Adventists in 1866; the Adventists were seeking a vegetarian alternative to the traditional cooked breakfast of ham or bacon and eggs. It took another 30 years, however, for cold cereals to gain much of a following. In 1899 Dr. John Harvey Kellogg, the manager of the Battle Creek Sanitarium (a health clinic that specialized in the treatment of digestive diseases), and his brother invented a wheat-flake cereal to improve bowel function. A few years later they developed another cereal made of cornflakes. Adding

to these developments, one of Dr. Kellogg's patients, C.W. Post, came up with a wheat and barley mixture that he called Grape Nuts. Food companies founded by the Kellogg brothers and Post remain North America's leading producers of cold cereals, with dozens of different brands.

Although prepared cereals are gaining popularity in Europe and other parts of the world, they are generally considered a North American product with one notable exception—the granola-type mixture of oats, wheat flakes, nuts, and dried fruits invented by Dr. Max Bircher-Benner, a Swiss pioneer of the natural health-food movement in Europe. Variations of his muesli, which is served either hot or cold, are now popular in Canada as well as in most European countries.

SOMETHING FOR EVERY TASTE. *Cold cereal with fruit and low-fat milk provides a flavorful low-calorie breakfast; for a heartier start, try oatmeal or other cooked cereal. Fruit adds flavor and extra vitamins and minerals.*

Wheat, corn, rice, oats, and barley are the most familiar grains used to make cereals. Most flaked cereals are varying combinations of flour, water,

sugar, and salt that are mixed into a dough, rolled thin, and then toasted. Some cereal preparations are spun into different shapes, such as tiny doughnuts or cartoon characters; in others, the grains are shredded or exploded.

NUTRITIONAL VALUE

Cereals are one of the most popular members of the complex CARBOHY-DRATE, or starch, food group. More than 90 percent of all commercial cereals are fortified with various vitamins and minerals, especially iron, niacin, riboflavin, thiamine, and perhaps calcium. Iron-fortified rice or barley cereal is often a baby's first solid food. An in-

CALORIES AND OTHER NUTRIENTS IN CEREALS					
CEREAL TYPE (SERVING SIZE)	CALORIES	STARCHES (G)	SUGARS (G)	PROTEIN (G)	FIBER (G)
Barley nuggets (½ cup)	140	23	3	6	6
Bran (1 cup)	120	21	5	6	9
Bran flakes (⅔ cup)	90	23	5	3	5
Corn flakes (1 cup)	100	24	2	2	1
Oat bran (½ cup)	110	21	7	2	4
Oatmeal (1 cup)	110	23	1	5	2
Rice, crisped (1 cup)	100	22	23	2	1
Rice, puffed (1 cup)	60	12	1	2	1
Wheat flakes (⅔ cup)	100	24	2	3	3
Wheat, shredded (2 biscuits)	85	18	1	2	1

creasing number of super-fortified products provide 100 percent of the Recommended Nutrient Intakes (RNIs) of a dozen or so vitamins and minerals, many of which are not found in the original grains; in effect, a bowl of one of these cereals equals a vitamin pill plus a little processed grain. In addition, these cereals are usually sweetened with sugar, corn or maple syrup, honey, or fruit juice. The granola-type cereals are often high in fat from added oils; many commercial cereals are also high in salt.

Some cereals, especially those promoted for their health values, have added dried fruits and nuts. In reality, however, the fruits and nuts comprise only a small percentage of the total ingredients, usually not enough to justify the higher cost of these commercial products. An economical and healthful approach is to buy plain cereal and add your own fresh fruits, raisins, seeds, nuts, or other ingredients. To make a low-fat granola, mix uncooked rolled oats with an assortment of dried fruits and seeds, sweeten with a small amount of brown sugar, and toast for a few minutes in a warm oven.

Unfortified cereals, such as oatmeal, provide most of the B vitamins, minerals, starches, and fiber found in the original grains. Oat cereals are high in soluble bran, a type of FIBER that helps lower blood cholesterol levels, thereby reducing the risk of HEART DISEASE. Some cereals, especially those made from whole grains or with added bran, are high in dietary fiber. Bran helps prevent constipation and may also reduce the risk of some cancers, including colon cancer. On the other hand, consuming excessive bran reduces the body's absorption of iron, zinc, and other essential minerals; it can also cause bloating, abdominal discomfort, and intestinal gas and flatulence.

Most cereals are relatively low in calories, but this varies considerably, depending on the ingredients and how they are served. Serving whole milk can more than double the calorie content of many cereals. Using skim or 1 percent fat milk saves calories and, for older children and adults, it is more healthful than whole milk. When comparing the calorie content of cereals, pay attention to serving size; some are low in calories only when consumed in very small amounts (see Calories and Other Nutrients in Cereals, above).

CHEESE

BENEFITS
- *High in protein and calcium.*
- *A good source of vitamin B$_{12}$.*
- *Cheddar and other aged cheeses may fight tooth decay.*

DRAWBACKS
- *Most are particularly high in saturated fat and sodium.*
- *Some may trigger migraines or allergic reactions in susceptible people.*

One of our most versatile and popular foods, cheese is used for everything from snacks and appetizers to main courses and desserts. It's an ancient food that can be made from the milk of almost any animal—cows, sheep, goats, yaks, camels, even buffaloes.

Cheese is made by culturing milk with bacteria, then adding rennin or another enzyme to curdle it. When the liquid whey is drained away, the remaining curds can be used as cottage or farmer's cheese. Or the curds may be mixed with other ingredients, injected with special molds or bacteria, soaked in wine or beer, pressed or molded, or smoked or aged to make any of hundreds of different cheeses.

On average, it takes about 4 quarts to make a pound of Cheddar, Muenster, Swiss, or other firm cheese. A typical 1-ounce serving of cheese contains 100 calories, 180 milligrams of calcium, and 8 grams of fat. Cottage cheese has the fewest calories—about 90 in a half-cup serving, but it has only half the calcium of milk. Cream cheese, Brie, and other soft cheeses are comparable to hard cheeses in calories and fat, and they also have much less calcium.

EAT IN MODERATION

Despite the high nutritional content of cheese, most people—especially those with a weight or cholesterol problem—should use it as an occasional treat or

garnish rather than as a staple food. Exceptions include children and pregnant women who need the extra calories and calcium, adolescents going through a growth spurt, and thin older women threatened by OSTEOPOROSIS, a weakening of bones especially common in older women. Many people who cannot digest milk because of lactose intolerance can eat cheese, especially the hard ones; the bacteria and enzymes used to make cheese also break down a reasonable amount of the lactose (milk sugar).

Ending a meal or snack with a small piece of Cheddar or other aged cheese may help prevent cavities by neutralizing the mouth acids that promote dental decay. Given the high fat content of cheese, however, rinsing or brushing are better ways to fight cavities.

HEALTH HAZARDS

Doctors often advise patients with heart disease, elevated blood cholesterol, or HIGH BLOOD PRESSURE to eliminate cheese from their diets. Because most cheese is high in cholesterol and its fat is highly saturated, it increases the risk of ATHEROSCLEROSIS, the clogging of arteries with fatty

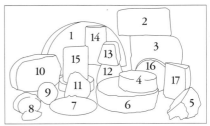

CHEESES FROM AROUND THE WORLD.
*Cheddar (1), Emmental (2), Jarlsberg (3),
Camembert (4, 6), Ricotta (5), Cottage
cheese (7), Mozzarella (8), Crottin de
Chavignol (9), Ticklemore (10), Coeur de
chèvre (11), Natural pyramide (12), Ash
pyramide (13), Chèvre (14), Feta (15),
Little Rydings (16), Peccorino (17).*

deposits. Most cheese is also very high in salt, a hazard for people with high blood pressure.

Aged cheese can trigger a MIGRAINE headache in some susceptible people. The likely culprit is tyramine, a naturally occurring chemical in Cheddar, blue cheese, Camembert, and certain other ripe cheeses. Tyramine also interacts with monoamine oxidase (MAO) inhibitors, drugs sometimes used to treat depression, and can cause a life-threatening rise in blood pressure. People taking MAO inhibitors should get a list of foods to avoid from their doctor.

People who are allergic to penicillin may react to blue cheese and other soft cheeses that are made with penicillin molds. Also those individuals allergic to cow's milk may react to cheese, especially cottage and other fresh cheeses. Cheeses made from goat's or sheep's milk are less likely to be allergenic.

Pasteurized milk must be used to make commercial cheese in Canada. Occasionally, however, health food stores and specialty shops sell imported or homemade unpasteurized cheese. Such cheeses can harbor dangerous salmonella and other bacteria; a recent case in point involved several food poisoning deaths in the United States that were later traced to imported cheese made from raw milk.

LOW-FAT CHEESES

Fat gives cheese its rich texture and delicious taste, but it also adds calories and cholesterol. About 70 to 80 percent of the calories in cheese comes from fat. Even reduced-fat or part-skim milk cheeses are high in fat; more than 50 percent of the calories in part-skim milk mozzarella come from fat. Truly low-fat cheeses, less than 3 grams of fat per ounce, are rare, often lack flavor, and tend to be high in salt to improve flavor; sodium phosphate may be used as an emulsifier for a smoother texture. Cholesterol-free imitation cheeses are often made of soy, or tofu; they still can be high in fat and sodium.

Fresh cheeses made from skim milk—for example, nonfat ricotta and cottage cheese—are low in fat and calories. Whipped or blended versions of these cheeses can be substituted for regular cream cheese, which is 90 percent fat. Strained nonfat yogurt is another possible alternative. To make it, line a strainer with cheesecloth, fill it with yogurt, and allow the whey to drain for several hours.

CHERRIES

A member of the plant family that includes plums, apricots, peaches, and nectarines, cherries are generally lower in vitamins and minerals than their larger cousins. Still, the flavor and low calorie content of the various sweet varieties make cherries an ideal snack or dessert during the relatively short time they are in season. Sour cherries, which are more nutritious than the sweet types, are used mostly for making jams and other preserves or are baked into pies and other pastries.

A cup of pitted sweet cherries contains about 140 calories and has 20mg of vitamin C, or 50 percent of the Recommended Nutrient Intake (RNI); it also contributes 500mg of potassium. Canning reduces these nutrients; a cup of canned sweet cherries in light syrup has 6mg of vitamin C and 150mg of potassium. Cherries are a good source of pectin, a soluble fiber that helps control blood cholesterol levels.

Sour cherries, which must be cooked and sweetened to make them palatable, are comparable to the sweet varieties in vitamin C and potassium, but they are much higher in beta carotene; one cup in light syrup has enough beta carotene to supply about 20 percent of the RNI for vitamin A.

Folk healers used to advocate sour cherries to treat gout, as do some alternative practitioners today; these practitioners sometimes suggest the juice of wild chokecherries to prevent or alleviate an attack of gout. There is no scientific basis for such claims, however.

People who are allergic to apricots

DID YOU KNOW?

- Maraschino cherries are made by bleaching the fruit (usually the yellow Queen Anne variety) in a sulfur dioxide brine, then toughening it with lime or calcium salt. The cherries are then dyed bright red, sweetened, flavored, packed in jars, and canned.
- Dried cherries can be used to replace some of the fat in hamburgers. Because cherries have antioxidant properties, cherry burgers last longer in the refrigerator before spoiling.

and the other members of the plum family may also suffer a reaction to cherries; the most likely symptoms are hives and a tingling or itching sensation in or around the mouth.

VARIETIES OF CHERRIES

There are more than 1,000 varieties of cherries worldwide. The most popular sweet cherries in Canada and the United States are Bing and other dark colored varieties, ranging from deep maroon to almost black, and Lamberts, which are a bright crimson. Queen Annes are yellow with tinges of red, large, and very sweet. Sour varieties, or pie cherries, are smaller than the sweet types.

When buying fresh cherries, look for plump, firm fruit with green stems. Both sweet and sour cherries spoil quickly and have a relatively short season. Imported cherries, available off-season in some areas, are not as flavorful as the local fruit that is picked and marketed at the height of its ripeness.

CHERRY RIPE. *The yellowish Queen Anne cherries (right) are very sweet and ideal for a snack, while the scarlet Morello cherries (left) are sour and make delicious pies. Bing cherries (foreground) are best eaten raw, and the versatile Dukes (center, back) can be cooked or eaten raw.*

CHESTNUTS

BENEFITS
- *Rich in folate and vitamins C and B6.*
- *Good source of iron, phosphorus, riboflavin, and thiamine.*
- *Much lower in fat and calories than almost all other nuts.*

DRAWBACKS
- *Tend to be expensive and are sometimes difficult to find.*

Unlike most other nuts, chestnuts are made up almost completely of carbohydrates, and they are low in fat and calories. They are also high in a number of important nutrients: A ¾-cup serving provides more than 40 percent of the adult Recommended Nutrient Intake (RNI) of vitamin C, 35 percent of the RNI of folate, and also provides some vitamin B_6 RNI. The same size serving, which contains 240 calories, 3g of protein, and 2g of fat, also contributes more than 10 percent of the RNIs for iron, phosphorus, riboflavin, and thiamine.

HIGH IN NATURAL SUGAR

After chestnuts are picked, their starch begins to turn to sugar, giving the nuts their mild, sweet flavor. Chestnuts are almost always cooked, either by roasting or boiling, before they are eaten. When heated, the nuts swell and crack their thin, soft shells, which makes them very easy to peel.

Chestnuts are often used in baked desserts. Roasted nuts can be dried and ground into a flour that makes a rich, flavorful crust for tarts or pies. Boiled chestnuts, which have a consistency similar to that of potatoes, can be

mashed or puréed to add to cake batter or used as a pastry filling. They are also served as part of a traditional Thanksgiving dinner, either as a side dish or added to turkey stuffing. Marrons glacés, a delicacy available in gourmet shops, are peeled whole chestnuts preserved in a sweet syrup.

The chestnut develops inside a prickly burr that is gathered after it falls from the tree in early autumn. It should not be confused with the horse chestnut, which is inedible. At one time, the American chestnut tree grew abundantly in the more temperate regions of North America, but a blight in the early 1900s destroyed almost all of these trees. Since then, a hybrid of the American tree and the Oriental chestnut tree has been introduced; however, most of the chestnuts now sold in supermarkets in Canada are actually imported from Italy and Spain; other major producers are China and South Korea.

WATER CHESTNUTS

These crunchy vegetables, which are served in many Asian dishes, salads, and soups, are unrelated to chestnuts; in fact, they are not nuts nor do they grow on trees. Instead, they are tubers that grow wild in marshes or the shallow water along lake banks in China, Japan, and the East Indies. The Chinese also cultivate water chestnuts as a second crop in their rice paddies.

Most water chestnuts sold in North America are imported from China. They contain moderate amounts of protein and vitamin C, but they are not as nutritious as potatoes and other tuberous vegetables.

CHILDHOOD AND ADOLESCENT NUTRITION

*During the first few years of life, it's vital to meet a child's
nutritional needs in order to ensure proper growth
and also to establish a lifelong habit of healthy eating.*

Eating a meal should be both a healthy and an enjoyable occasion—a fact that many parents may overlook when planning a meal for their growing children. Instead of a fast meal (especially one short in nutritional value) that family members eat at different hours, mealtimes should promote family togetherness.

Relaxed dining experiences with good food and conversation (that doesn't involve criticizing table manners or pleading with children to eat) help to foster family relationships as well as good digestion. You should try to schedule meals so that they don't conflict with other activities; children will be less likely to gobble their food and rush to leave the table. You can also involve children in family meals by having them help out with simple mealtime tasks, such as peeling potatoes, preparing salads, or setting the table. If mealtime is a pleasant event, children may practice healthful eating habits later on in life.

THE GROWING YEARS

Between the ages of 2 and 20, the human body changes continuously and dramatically. In general, muscles grow stronger, bones grow longer, height may more than double, and weight can increase as much as five-fold. The most striking changes take place during puberty, which usually occurs between the ages of 10 and 15 in girls and slightly later—between the ages of 12 and 19—in boys. Sexual development and maturity take place at this time, which, along with the adolescent growth spurt, result in a startling physical transformation.

Children need energy throughout the growing years: typically 1,300 calories a day for a 2-year-old, 1,700 for a 5-year-old, 2,200 for a 16-year-old girl, and 2,800 for a 16-year-old boy. For a guide to their nutritional needs, see Food for Growing Up, p.92.

The amount of food that a child needs

DO'S AND DON'TS: ENCOURAGING GOOD EATING HABITS

- Do set a good example for your child to copy. Share mealtimes and eat the same healthy foods.

- Do discourage snacking on sweets and fatty foods. Keep plenty of healthy foods, such as fruits, raw vegetables, low-fat crackers, and yogurt, around for children to eat between meals.

- Do allow children to follow their natural appetites when deciding how much to eat.

- Do encourage children to enjoy fruits and vegetables by giving them a variety from an early age.

- Don't give skim or 1-percent-fat milk to children under the age of 5 unless your doctor prescribes it; at this stage children need the extra calories in whole milk.

- Do ask children to help prepare meals. If parents rely mostly on convenience foods, children may not learn to enjoy cooking.

- Don't add unnecessary sugar to drinks and foods.

- Don't accustom children to extra salt by adding it to food or placing the shaker on the table.

- Don't give whole nuts to children under the age of 5, who may choke on them. Peanut butter and chopped nuts are fine as long as the child is not allergic to them.

- Don't force children to eat more than they want.

- Don't use food as a bribe.

- Don't make children feel guilty about eating any type of food.

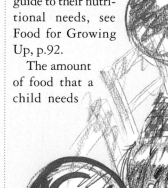

varies according to height, build, gender, and activity level. Left to themselves, most children will usually eat the amount of food that's right for them; however, it is up to the parents to make sure that their children have the right foods available to choose from. Don't fall into the age-old trap of forcing them to eat more food than they want or need. Yesterday's notion of "cleaning your plate" and "starving children in Africa" can lead to overeating and weight problems or to a life-long dislike of particular foods. Parents may find it better to serve smaller portions in the first place or to allow children to serve themselves.

CHANGES IN APPETITE

In most children, appetite slackens as the growth rate slows after the first year; it will then vary throughout childhood, depending on whether the child is going through a period of slow or rapid growth. It is perfectly normal for a young child to eat ravenously one day and then show little interest in food the following day.

Eating patterns change with the onset of the adolescent growth spurt; teenagers usually develop voracious appetites to match their need for additional energy. At the same time, many develop erratic eating habits—for example, skipping breakfast, lunching at school or at a fast-food restaurant, then snacking almost nonstop until bedtime. Although snacking is not the ideal way to eat, a "food on the run" lifestyle won't necessarily cause nutritional problems as long as the basic daily requirements for protein, carbohydrates, fats, and various vitamins and minerals are met. You can generally keep your teenager out of nutritional danger by providing snacks that are high in vitamins, minerals, and protein but low in sugar, fat, and salt. This basically means buying healthful snack foods, such as fresh and dried fruits, juices, raw vegetables, nuts, cheese, whole-grain crackers, unadulterated popcorn, and yogurt—not candy, cake, cookies, potato chips, corn chips, and soda pop.

THE QUESTION OF SWEETS

Sugary foods can provide a quick burst of energy, but they can also spoil the appetite for healthier foods and cause tooth decay without contributing any valuable nutrients. However, banning candies altogether can be troublesome; children may feel left out when their friends have them and so develop a pattern of eating candy in secret. There is no harm in letting children have candy occasionally, as long as you don't offer sweets as bribes or rewards for good behavior. For a sweet treat, cookies or ice cream is better than candy because there are some nutrients in the milk and grains used to make these snacks. If your family has dessert as a regular part of the menu,

PARTY TIME. *Sharing treats at a birthday party or other festive occasion with family and friends helps children to develop good table manners as well as a regard for others.*

FOOD FOR GROWING UP

As children grow, their nutritional needs change; some needs vary between the sexes. The chart below gives an overview of the Recommended Nutrient Intakes (RNIs) of certain nutrients for children from ages 1 to 18. This information was compiled by the Nutrition Research Division of Health Canada. Height and weight estimates for each age group and sex are also included.

AGE	1–3	4–6	7–10	11–14	15–18
HEIGHT (IN)	35	44	52	62	BOYS: 69 GIRLS: 64
WEIGHT (LB)	29	44	62	BOYS: 99 GIRLS: 101	BOYS: 145 GIRLS: 120
CALORIES Boys Girls	1,300 1,300	1,800 1,800	2,000 2,000	2,500 2,200	3,000 2,200
PROTEIN (G) Boys Girls	16 16	19 19	26 26	49 46	58 47
VITAMIN A (RE) Boys Girls	400 400	500 500	700 700	1,000 800	1,000 800
VITAMIN D (MCG)	10	5	2.5	2.5	2.5
VITAMIN E (MG) Boys Girls	4 4	5 5	7 7	10 8	10 8
VITAMIN C (MG)	20	25	25	30	40
NIACIN (MG) Boys Girls	9 9	13 13	13 13	20 16	23 15
THIAMINE (MG) Boys Girls	0.7 0.7	0.9 0.9	1.0 1.0	1.1 0.9	1.3 0.8
RIBOFLAVIN (MG) Boys Girls	0.8 0.8	1.1 1.1	1.2 1.3	1.5 1.3	1.8 1.3
FOLATE (MCG)	50	70	90	130	200
VITAMIN B$_6$ (MG)	1.0	1.1	1.4	1.7	2.0
VITAMIN B$_{12}$ (MCG)	0.5	0.8	1.0	1.0	1.0
CALCIUM (MG)	500	600	700	1,100	800
IRON (MG) Boys Girls	6 6	8 8	8 8	10 13	10 13
ZINC (MG)	4	5	7	9	12

emphasize fruits, yogurt, or custards instead of pastries and other sweets.

FOODS FOR TODDLERS

After the first year children can eat most of the dishes prepared for the rest of the family. However, because toddlers often have high energy requirements and a small stomach, they may need five or six small meals or snacks a day. Schedule a toddler's snacks so they don't interfere with food intake during meals. An interval of about an hour and a half is usually enough to satisfy hunger without spoiling meals.

Toddlers often go on food jags—for example, eliminating everything that's white or green. Such food rituals are often short-lived, although they can be annoying or worrisome if they get out of hand. Try to respect the child's preferences without giving in to every whim; offer a reasonable alternative. If, for instance, lunch is rejected with a demand for a peanut butter sandwich, resist the temptation to make a substitution but offer to fix the sandwich for a later snack.

BALANCE AND VARIETY

Children need a wide variety of foods. CARBOHYDRATES—breads, cereals, fruits, and vegetables—should make up the major part of the diet. PROTEIN foods can include meat, fish, milk, grains, soy products (such as bean curd), and combinations of grains and legumes. Milk is an important source of calories, minerals, and vitamins. Children 4 to 9 years old should have 2 to 3 milk product servings every day (some of the milk may be in the form of cheese or yogurt). Grilled and baked foods are preferable to fried and fatty ones for children of all ages.

FATS are probably the most misunderstood food group. Although everyone should avoid excess fat, we all need a certain amount for important body functions. Several vitamins (A, D, E, and K) can be absorbed only in

SNACKS AND FAST FOODS

Stock up on healthful snacks that children and teenagers can nibble on throughout the day.

• Breads and crackers with such spreads as peanut butter, low-fat cheese, canned tuna or sardines, and lean cold cuts.

• Rice cakes and whole-grain crackers or breadsticks.

• Fresh and dried fruits.

• Yogurt.

• Sticks of carrot, celery, or other raw vegetables and cherry tomatoes with nutritious dips.

• Plain popcorn.

• Breakfast cereals.

• Water, milk, or fruit juice.

the presence of fat, and fats are necessary for the production of other body chemicals, including the hormones that transform boys and girls into men and women. Excessive fat intake may well lead to obesity and many adult diseases; even so, about 30 percent or less of total calories should come from fat.

Many parents have a battle when it comes to getting children to eat vegetables, but you can win children over by appealing to their taste for bright colors and interesting textures. Who wouldn't choose crisp, raw carrot sticks over soggy, limp cabbage? Innovative cooks can substitute minced vegetables (zucchini, eggplant, mushrooms) for ground meat in spaghetti sauce, or chop chickpeas with grains and other vegetables to make "vegeburgers."

FOODS FOR TEENAGERS

Adolescents need more of everything to keep up with the massive teenage growth spurt: calories and protein for growth and to build muscles; and protein, calcium, phosphorus, and vitamin D for bone formation. For many teenagers the demands of school and social life mean that they eat many meals away from home; suddenly they have the responsibility of choosing perhaps the major part of their diet. Some use food to establish an identity, such as by becoming a VEGETARIAN or going on a diet. Iron-deficiency ANEMIA is fairly common in adolescent girls; the cause is not always clear and may be a problem of absorption rather than the amount of iron in the diet. ANOREXIA and certain other eating disorders are a risk for a small group of adolescents, especially girls.

OBESITY (defined as being 20 percent or more above desirable weight) is a problem for both boys and girls, but weight control can be complicated for adolescents. They still need calories for growth, together with the necessary balance of proteins, carbohydrates, and fats. The best approach to controlling weight in obese youngsters is serving smaller portions and encouraging regular, vigorous exercise, which reduces body fat while building lean tissue.

Calcium is important for forming strong, healthy bones during adolescence and preventing OSTEOPOROSIS later in life. Youths 10 to 16 years old need 3 to 4 milk product servings a day—the equivalent of 2 cups of milk and 1½ ounces (2 slices) of cheese or ¾ cup of yogurt—every day. A rich supply of calcium is found in canned sardines and salmon (where the fish is eaten bones and all), fortified breakfast cereals, and dark green leafy vegetables, such as kale.

Teenagers often prefer snacks loaded with fat, sugar, and salt: potato chips, French fries, hamburgers, hot dogs, pizza, chocolate, and candy bars. These foods are high in sodium and yield a poor balance between calories and nutrition; a steady diet of them is low in vitamins A and C, calcium, and dietary fiber. Encourage teenagers who frequent fast-food restaurants to choose some fresh vegetables and fruits from the salad bar.

Offer your teenager a variety of appealing, healthful snack foods to choose from at home. Teenagers who skip breakfast may start the school day feeling lethargic; slip a breakfast of fruit, cheese, and dried cereal or trail mix into their backpacks to eat on the way to school.

HEALTHY GRAZING. *An assortment of fresh and dried fruits, trail mix, whole-grain crackers and cheese, and juice can easily be tucked into an adolescent's backpack and provide a healthy alternative to candy and other sweets.*

CHILIES

BENEFITS

- *An excellent source of vitamins A and C.*
- *May help relieve nasal congestion.*
- *May help prevent blood clots that can lead to a heart attack or stroke.*

DRAWBACKS

- *Require careful handling during preparation to prevent irritation of the skin and eyes.*
- *May irritate hemorrhoids in susceptible people.*

A popular ingredient in Southwestern cooking, chilies, or hot peppers, add spice and interest to many foods; some of the milder varieties are consumed as low-calorie snacks.

The heat in chilies comes from capsaicinoids, substances that have no odor or flavor themselves but impart their bite by acting directly on the mouth's

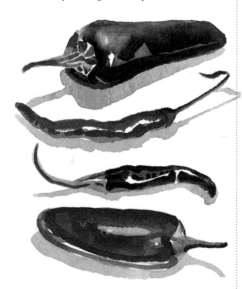

pain receptors. This results in the teary eyes, runny nose ("salsa sniffles"), and sweating experienced by most people who indulge in the hotter varieties. For those with a cold or allergies, eating chilies can provide temporary relief from nasal and sinus congestion. Cap-

A CONSUMERS' GUIDE TO CHILIES

Not all chilies are equally hot; the following is a ranking from the mildest to the hottest.

MILD TO MODERATELY HOT:

- **Anaheim.** These long, slender red or green chilies are among the most popular in the North America.
- **Ancho.** Also called dried poblano, these dark red, heart-shaped peppers are usually dried.
- **Cherry.** These small, round red chilies are often pickled.
- **Poblano.** Green chilies with a small, tapered shape; they are usually roasted, and may be stuffed or added to a variety of dishes.

HOT:

- **Cascabel.** These round red or green chilies are usually dried.

VERY HOT:

- **Cayenne.** These long red chilies are dried and often ground into a hot pepper spice.
- **Habanero.** Shaped like red, yellow, or orange lanterns, these are considered the hottest of cultivated chilies.
- **Jalapeño.** These tapered green or red chilies are sold fresh, canned, or pickled.
- **Serrano.** These small, bullet-shaped green or red chilies are often used in hot salsas.

saicin and other capsaicinoids are concentrated mainly in the white ribs and seeds, which can be removed to produce a milder flavor.

Handle chilies with care. Wear thin gloves and wash all utensils well with soap and water after use. Even a tiny amount of capsaicinoids causes severe irritation if it is transferred to the eyes.

Chilies are more nutritious than sweet peppers, and the red varieties generally have a higher nutritional content than the green ones. They are very good sources of ANTIOXIDANTS, especially vitamins A and C. Just one ounce of chilies contains 70mg of vitamin C, more than 100 percent of the Recommended Nutrient Intake (RNI), as well as about 70 percent of the RNI for vitamin A. Chilies also contain BIOFLAVONOIDS, plant pigments that some researchers believe may help prevent cancer. In addition, recent research indicates that capsaicin may act as an anticoagulant, perhaps helping to prevent blood clots that can lead to a heart attack or stroke. Incorporated into creams, capsaicinoids alleviate the burning pain of shingles. They may also reduce the mouth pain associated with chemotherapy. Commercially

available poultices for relief of lower back also contain capsaicin.

Contrary to popular belief, there is no evidence that chilies can cause ulcers or produce other digestive disturbances. They can, however, cause rectal irritation in some people with hemorrhoids.

CHOCOLATE AND CANDY

BENEFITS

- *Flavorful source of quick energy.*
- *Eating chocolate elevates some people's moods.*

DRAWBACKS

- *Chocolate is high in calories and fat.*
- *Sugary candies can cause tooth decay.*
- *Spoil the appetite for more healthful food choices.*
- *Chocolate may trigger migraine headaches.*
- *Licorice may raise blood pressure in susceptible people.*

Chocolates and candies are nutritionally limited food sources, even though they have been enjoyed by people worldwide for centuries. But despite their nutritional drawbacks, there is no harm in occasionally adding them to an otherwise healthy and balanced diet.

CHOCOLATE

The returning crew of Columbus's fourth voyage in 1502 brought the first cocoa beans from the New World to Europe. The Spanish eventually combined them with vanilla and other flavorings, sugar, and milk to arrive at a concoction that, as one writer noted at the time, people "would die for."

For the first couple of centuries after its introduction in Europe, chocolate was served only as a beverage. A solid form—probably more like marzipan than the chocolate we know—was touted as an instant breakfast in 18th-century France. The stimulant effects of chocolate were thought to make it a particularly useful food for soldiers standing watch during the night.

The chocolate bar, first marketed in about 1910, captured the public imagination when it was issued to the U.S. armed forces as a "fighting food" during World War II.

THE SOURCE OF CHOCOLATE

Chocolate is harvested from the pods and beans of the cocoa tree, an evergreen that originated in the river valleys of South America. Native Central and South Americans valued cocoa so highly that they used cocoa beans as currency. Today about three-fourths of the world's chocolate is grown in West Africa and most of the rest in Brazil.

After cocoa beans are harvested, an initial phase of fermentation and drying is followed by low-temperature roasting to bring out the flavor. Various increasingly complicated manufacturing processes follow, depending on whether the final product is to be solid chocolate or cocoa powder.

In 1828 the Van Houten family of chocolate purveyors in Amsterdam, seeking to make a less-oily drinking chocolate, invented a screw press to remove most of the cocoa butter from the beans. Not only did it make a better drink, but they also found that by mixing the extracted cocoa butter back into ground cocoa beans, they could make a smoother, more unctuous solid paste that would absorb sugar; this eventually led to "eating chocolate."

COMPONENTS

An ounce of solid chocolate contains about 150 calories and 2 or 3 grams of protein. The original bean has significant amounts of vitamin E and the B vitamins. These nutrients, however, are so diluted as to be negligible in modern processed chocolate. Sweet or semisweet chocolate contains between 40 and 53 percent fat, or cocoa butter. Both chocolate and cocoa powder supply chromium, iron, magnesium, phosphorus, and potassium, but fat and calories make chocolate an inappropriate source of these minerals except when used in emergency rations.

A chemical composition that prevents it from quickly turning rancid made cocoa butter valuable as a long-lasting food and cosmetic oil.

Chocolate is a solid at room temperature, but since its melting point is just below the human body temperature, it begins to melt and release its flavor components as soon as it is placed in the mouth.

White chocolate, a mixture of cocoa butter, milk solids, and sugar, contains no cocoa solids. Unlike milk chocolate, white chocolate does not keep well, because it lacks the compounds that prevent milk solids from becoming rancid over time.

THE FEEL-GOOD FACTOR

Chocolate contains two related alkaloid stimulants, theobromine and caffeine, in a ratio of about 10 to 1. Theobromine, unlike caffeine, does not stimulate the central nervous system; its effects are mainly diuretic. Commercial chocolate products contain no more than about 0.1 percent caffeine and are much less stimulating, volume for volume, than a cup of decaffeinated coffee. Unsweetened baking chocolate for home use is a more concentrated source of caffeine. Chocolate is also rich in phenylethylamine (PEA), a naturally occurring compound that has effects similar to amphetamine. This compound can also trigger MIGRAINE headaches in susceptible people.

Some people (more often women) have a tendency to binge on chocolate after emotional upsets. No scientific basis for this behavior has been proved. However, psychiatrists have theorized that "chocoholics" may be people who have a faulty mechanism for regulating their body levels of phenylethylamine; others attribute chocolate cravings to hormonal changes, such as those that occur during puberty or a woman's premenstrual phase.

After centuries of investigation, chocolate's once-vaunted aphrodisiac qualities can be discounted. But in its

MELTS IN THE MOUTH. *The finest chocolate gets its unique and appealing texture from pure cocoa butter. Its distinct flavor comes from a high proportion of cocoa solids.*

myriad modern forms, chocolate is an endless temptation and, for those who can withstand the caloric assault, a culinary source of pleasure.

CANDY

Our preference for sweet tastes is evident in the womb and is considered to be part of human evolution. For instance, edible berries and fruits tend to be sweet as opposed to the bitter taste of many poisonous plants.

Commercial candy production is believed to have begun when marzipan (a paste made of almonds and sugar) was brought to Italy and Spain through trade with the Arabs and Moors during the Middle Ages. In fact, the word *candy* is derived from the Arabic pronunciation of *khandakah,* the Sanskrit word for sugar.

European candies were first compounded by druggists who preserved herbs in sugar. Candies were rare treats, however, until the widespread cultivation of sugar cane and the development of large-scale refining processes in the 17th and 18th centuries. Modern candies are mostly variations on three basic forms: taffy, from the Creole French word for a mixture of sugar and molasses; nougat, from the Latin word for nutcake; and fondant, from the French for melting (which can be recognized in the texture of fudges and soft-centered chocolates and bars).

NUTRITIONAL DRAWBACKS

All candies are packed with simple sugars—sucrose, corn syrup, fructose—which supply about 375 calories in a 3½-ounce serving and provide quick energy because they are rapidly converted to glucose, or blood sugar. The calorie content of candies varies greatly, however, depending on their other ingredients, such as nuts, fruits, and fat. Although you should count candy calories in your overall daily consumption, don't expect to obtain any useful nutrition from candy.

Practically all hard candies are made with artificial flavors and colorings. In addition, the least expensive candies sold as chocolate often prove to be made of artificial chocolate and vanilla flavoring, with added vegetable fat. It pays to read labels, even with candies, to make sure you know what you're eating.

ADDITIVES AND SENSITIVITIES

There is no scientific evidence that the rigorously tested food dyes allowed in candy by Health Canada cause allergies or adverse reactions in adults or children. These additives are included in minute amounts, and the quantity in an individual serving is not significant. Some people may be hypersensitive to the ingredients in a particular candy, but since candy is not an essential part of the diet, it's easy enough to avoid the offending sweet. Many studies now show that sugar does not cause hyperactivity, but some food dyes in candies

may exacerbate existing hyperactivity.

Natural licorice is known to raise blood pressure in certain people. The effect takes place mainly through the mechanism of salt retention. If you know you're hypertensive, you may be better off avoiding licorice.

SWEETS AND TOOTH DECAY

Sweets and sugary foods form an acid bath that is corrosive to tooth enamel and create an environment where destructive, caries-causing bacteria flourish. The effect is less harmful if you brush your teeth regularly to remove dental plaque. Candies that linger in the mouth are more damaging than those that are quickly swallowed. Chocolate is less likely to cause tooth decay than hard candies. Nevertheless, the sugar in chocolate can do damage.

Sugarless chewing gum is preferable to the sugary kind for adults. (The wisdom of exposing children to artificial sweeteners is questionable.) Gums sweetened with xylitol, a sugar alcohol, have been promoted as "tooth friendly" because xylitol favorably changes the composition and stickiness of dental plaque. When you can't brush after a meal, chewing sugarless gum may help to stimulate the saliva flow and flush food particles out of the mouth. But although gum may be free of caries-inducing sugar, such sweeteners as xylitol and other sugar alcohols typically contain just as many calories as sugar.

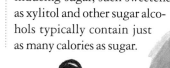

JELLY BEANS, SUCKERS, AND OTHER CANDY. *Bright colors and a variety of shapes add to their appeal.*

CHOLESTEROL: SORTING THE FACTS FROM THE MYTHS

*By now, most people know that high levels of blood
cholesterol increase the risk of a heart attack. Still, confusion
abounds over the role of diet in affecting cholesterol.*

Although often portrayed as a dietary pariah, cholesterol is essential to life. The body needs it to make sex hormones, bile, vitamin D, cell membranes, and nerve sheaths. These and other functions fall to serum cholesterol, a waxy, fatlike compound that circulates in the bloodstream. The liver manufactures about a gram each day, which is all the body requires.

Dietary cholesterol is found only in animal products. The body does not need this cholesterol, but anyone other than a strict VEGETARIAN who excludes all animal products will consume varying amounts of it. Many factors—exercise, genetics, gender, and other components of the diet—influence how the human body processes dietary cholesterol; some people can consume large amounts but have normal blood levels, while others eat very little but have high blood cholesterol.

GOOD VS. BAD CHOLESTEROL

To travel through the bloodstream, cholesterol molecules attach themselves to lipid-carrying proteins, or lipoproteins. Two types of lipoproteins are the major transporters of cholesterol: low-density lipoproteins (LDLs) carry two-thirds of it; most of the remainder is attached to high-density lipoproteins (HDLs). LDLs tend to deposit cholesterol in the artery walls, leading to ATHEROSCLEROSIS and an increased risk of HEART DISEASE. In contrast, HDLs collect cholesterol

from the artery walls and other tissues and take it to the liver to be metabolized and eliminated from the body. This is why LDLs are often called the "bad" cholesterol and HDLs the "good." A third type, very-low-density lipoproteins, VLDLs, carry a small amount of cholesterol and triglycerides.

A blood cholesterol test measures the amount of cholesterol in the blood. This can be expressed in terms of milligrams (mg) of cholesterol per deciliter or millimoles (mmol) of cholesterol per liter. The multiplication factor 0.026 converts the milligram system to the millimole system. A value below 200mg/dl (5.2 mmol/l) is considered desirable. If the total is more than 200mg, LDL and HDL levels should be measured individually. LDL levels should be below 130mg/dl; 130 to 159 is classified as borderline high, over 160 is considered high risk for coronary artery disease and a heart attack. HDL levels should be at least 45mg/dl, and the higher the better. In assessing cardiovascular risk, doctors calculate the LDL/HDL ratio by dividing the total cholesterol by the HDL figure. A desirable ratio is less than 4.5. For example, if your total cholesterol is 220 and your HDL level is 55, then your ratio is 4.0, putting you in a low-risk category.

HOW DIET CAN HELP

Experts agree that dietary modification is appropriate if the total choles-

terol count is greater than 200mg/dl (5.2 mmol/l) or if the LDL level exceeds 130mg/dl (3.4 mmol/l). Reducing intake of saturated FATS has the greatest effect on lowering blood cholesterol levels. A diet that limits fat intake to 20 percent or less of total calories and restricts saturated fats to 7 percent or less can lower total blood cholesterol an average of 14 percent. Most people can significantly lower intake of saturated fats by cutting down on or eliminating fatty meats, whole milk and other dairy products, and baked goods made with tropical (coconut, palm, and palm kernel) oils.

Stricter diets yield even better results. For example, the vegetarian low-fat (less than 10 percent of calories) program developed by Dr. Dean Ornish can lower LDL cholesterol by up to 70mg/dl. The Ornish program also calls for daily exercise and meditation.

It isn't just what you don't eat that matters; consuming foods that have a cholesterol-lowering effect also helps. Oat bran and dried beans and peas are high in a soluble fiber, which lowers cholesterol. The pectin in apples and other fruits also lowers cholesterol, as does, apparently, the soy protein found in tofu, tempeh, and soy milk.

Two or three servings a week of salmon, sardines, shrimp, lobster, and other cold-water fish or seafood are linked with a reduced risk of heart attacks and strokes. Initially, it was thought that the omega-3 fatty acids in seafood reduced cardiovascular risk by lowering blood cholesterol levels; however, recent studies suggest that their benefit comes from interfering with blood clotting and from possible changes in the way the liver metabolizes other lipids.

At one time, increasing the intake of polyunsaturated fats—corn, cottonseed, safflower, soy, and sunflower oils—was advocated to lower cholesterol, but more recent studies have found that these oils reduce the levels of the protective HDLs while having little effect on the harmful LDLs. In contrast, monounsaturated fats found in canola and olive oils have the opposite effect, cutting LDLs without altering HDL levels.

The role of dietary cholesterol is still unclear; recent studies indicate it is not as potent in raising blood cholesterol as saturated fats are (see Eating to Keep Cholesterol in Check, right). Still, some experts recommend limiting dietary cholesterol intake to 300mg a day—the amount in one and one-half egg yolks, 4 ounces of beef liver, or a combination of 2 cups of whole milk (60mg), a 6-ounce steak (180mg), and 1 cup of ice cream (60mg).

OTHER APPROACHES

Increased exercise, weight loss, and stress reduction can all lower cholesterol or improve the LDL/HDL ratio. Women are protected from developing coronary artery disease during their reproductive years by estrogen, and new research indicates that postmenopausal hormone replacement extends this protection into old age.

Moderate ALCOHOL intake lowers the risk of heart attack. This may be due to alcohol's ability to raise HDL, its tendency to reduce the stickiness of platelets, or the presence of antioxidants, such as resveratrol, in red wine.

If dietary and other lifestyle changes fail to reduce blood cholesterol, drugs may be prescribed.

EATING TO KEEP CHOLESTEROL IN CHECK

There's no doubt that what you eat influences the levels of cholesterol and other lipids in your blood. Numerous studies document that diets high in animal products and other saturated fats tend to elevate cholesterol levels, in contrast to the low levels found in people whose diets consist largely of starches, fruits, and vegetables. Individuals with a family history of heart disease should be diligent in structuring a diet that limits the cholesterol-raising foods and emphasizes the cholesterol-lowering foods indicated below.

FOODS THAT MAY RAISE CHOLESTEROL

Hard margarine and vegetable shortening, which are high in saturated fats and trans fatty acids.

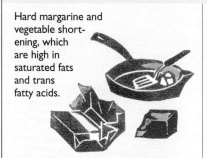

Fatty meat and meat products, such as marbled beef, pork and lamb chops, hamburgers, bacon, frankfurters, salamis, and other cold cuts.

Cookies, cakes, pastries, and chocolates, especially those made with saturated tropical oils.

Dairy products, such as cheese, cream, and butter, which are high in saturated fats.

FOODS THAT MAY LOWER CHOLESTEROL

Whole-wheat, pumpernickel, rye, and multigrain bread and rolls.

Fruits, such as oranges, apples, pears, bananas, and such dried fruits as apricots, figs, and prunes.

Oatmeal and breakfast cereals that contain oat or rice bran, as well as tofu and other soy products.

Vegetables, such as sweet corn, onions, garlic, lima beans, kidney beans, and other legumes.

CHRONIC FATIGUE SYNDROME

EAT PLENTY OF
- *Pasta, rice, and whole-grain cereals and breads for complex carbohydrates.*
- *Lean meat, fish, poultry, and other high-protein foods.*
- *Fruits and vegetables for vitamin C.*
- *Salty foods (if low blood pressure is part of the diagnosis).*

CUT DOWN ON
- *Caffeine, especially near bedtime.*

AVOID
- *Alcohol.*

Currently one of the most controversial disorders, chronic fatigue syndrome (CFS) has many flulike symptoms, no apparent cause, and no proven cure. It is marked by persistent, debilitating fatigue as well as other baffling symptoms that include headaches, muscle aches and weakness, tender lymph nodes, sore throat, joint pain, sleep that doesn't lead to feeling refreshed, difficulty concentrating, post-exercise exhaustion that lasts for 24 hours, and short-term memory problems. There may also be a chronic or recurring low-grade fever.

There is no laboratory test for CFS, so a doctor must systematically rule out all other medical causes that produce similar symptoms. According to diagnostic criteria set up by the Centers for Disease Control and Prevention (CDC) in the U.S., the chronic fatigue and at least eight other nonspecific symptoms must persist for at least 6 months.

Although some claim that CFS is a new disorder (for example, the "yuppie flu" of the 1980s), doctors since the 1800s have reported similar disorders but given them different names, including hypoglycemia (low blood sugar), chronic Epstein-Barr virus, myalgic encephalomyelitis, and post-viral fatigue syndrome. Many theories regarding possible causes have been advanced, but none have been proved. In many cases, CFS develops in the aftermath of a viral illness, such as mononucleosis or the flu, but no single viral cause has been identified. Other possible contributing factors include prolonged stress, hormonal imbalance, low blood pressure (hypotension), allergies, immune system disorders, and psychological problems. Some experts suggest CFS is a group of ailments that share similar symptoms. In any event, the Myalgic Encephalomyelitis Association of Canada estimates that some 20,000 to 35,000 Canadians suffer from the disease. At least two-thirds of the sufferers are white middle-class women. Most CFS patients eventually recover, but it may take a year or more to do so.

MEDICAL TREATMENT

Various medications are prescribed to treat CFS symptoms, but none appear to cure the disorder. Aspirin and other painkillers may alleviate headaches, joint pain, and muscle soreness, and antidepressant drugs help some patients. Some doctors advocate antiviral drugs, such as acyclovir, or injections of gamma globulin, a substance containing antibodies from the blood serum of a number of people, but studies have failed to document their value.

NUTRITIONAL APPROACHES

Doctors stress the importance of a well-balanced diet that has ample starches, fruits, and vegetables to get the carbohydrates the body needs for energy, and lean meat and other high-protein foods to help build and maintain muscle tissue. Fresh fruits and vegetables also supply the vitamins needed to resist infection. Alcohol, which lowers immunity, should be avoided, and caffeinated drinks should be used in moderation to minimize sleep problems.

One study indicates that low blood pressure may contribute to the fatigue experienced by CFS patients. Usually, blood pressure rises slightly during periods of stress or physical activity. But in some people, blood pressure remains constant or goes down, resulting in fatigue. These individuals may be salt-resistant and need a higher salt intake to raise blood pressure. Researchers have noted that many CFS patients have low-salt diets, which may explain their hypotension and fatigue. Symptoms became less severe when the patients increased their intake of salty foods, such as pickles, olives, and processed foods, or took table salt tablets.

Some alternative practitioners advocate injections of vitamin B_{12}, along with supplements of vitamins A and C, iron, and zinc, to treat CFS. But a balanced diet is preferable to taking supplements, which should be used only under medical supervision.

An approach that appears hopeful is for patients to take a combination of evening primrose oil and fish oil; in one study, 85 percent reported some improvement after 15 weeks. Otherwise, caution is needed when taking herbal remedies, because many contain potentially harmful stimulants.

DO'S AND DON'TS

- Do obtain an accurate diagnosis, preferably from a physician who has experience in treating CFS.
- Do keep a detailed diary of your progress, noting symptoms and how foods and activities affect your physical well-being.
- Do establish a sensible and balanced program of treatment that covers both diet and exercise.
- Don't nap during the daytime; instead, adopt a lifestyle that allows you to get between 7 to 9 hours of sleep each night.
- Do look for a support group.

CIRCULATORY DISORDERS

EAT PLENTY OF

- *Oily fish, such as salmon and sardines, for omega-3 fatty acids.*
- *Citrus and other fresh fruits and vegetables for vitamin C.*
- *Seeds, nuts, seafood, wheat germ, and fortified cereals for vitamin E.*

CUT DOWN ON

- *Meat and saturated fats.*

AVOID

- *Smoking and excessive alcohol use.*

The most common circulatory, or vascular, disorders are high BLOOD PRESSURE and ATHEROSCLEROSIS; others include various clotting abnormalities and diseases marked by reduced blood flow. Some of the more common are aneurysms, intermittent claudication, phlebitis, and Raynaud's disease.

ANEURYSMS

These balloonlike bulges form in weakened segments of the arteries, especially the aorta, the body's largest artery, which arises from the heart. Many aneurysms are due to a congenital weakness, while others are caused by atherosclerosis and high blood pressure.

There is no specific dietary treatment for an aneurysm, but following a low-fat, low-salt diet can help prevent those caused by atherosclerosis and high blood pressure. Consuming ample fresh fruits and vegetables will provide the vitamin C needed to build and maintain strong blood vessels.

INTERMITTENT CLAUDICATION (LEG PAIN)

Severe leg pain and cramps induced by walking are symptoms of intermittent claudication. A lack of oxygen due to inadequate blood flow causes the pain.

Atherosclerosis is responsible for most intermittent claudication; it is also common in DIABETES patients. Adopting a very-low-fat diet and an exercise program (for example, the regimen developed by cardiologist Dean Ornish) has helped many patients. Including onions and garlic in the diet is said to improve blood flow. Patients with severe blockages, however, may require surgery to remove them.

PHLEBITIS

Any inflammation of a vein is referred to as phlebitis; the large, superficial veins in the lower legs are the most commonly afflicted. Although painful, this type of superficial phlebitis is not as dangerous as when veins located deeper in the legs become inflamed, setting the stage for thrombophlebitis. In this condition, clots form at the site of inflammation; pieces may break away and travel to the heart and lungs.

Phlebitis can be treated with aspirin and other anti-inflammatory drugs and by applying warm compresses. Clot-dissolving drugs may be administered for thrombophlebitis; other measures may be required to prevent clots from reaching vital organs.

A diet that includes several servings a week of fatty fish or other sources of omega-3 fatty acids, as well as foods high in vitamin E, helps reduce inflammation and clot formation. Gamma linolenic acid, a substance in evening primrose and borage oils, has a similar effect; but check with a doctor before taking these, as they may interact with prescribed drugs.

RAYNAUD'S DISEASE

This condition is characterized by periods of numbness, tingling, and pain in the fingers and toes due to constriction or spasms in the small arteries that carry blood to the extremities.

Typically, Raynaud's disease is set off by exposure to the cold; in some individuals, however, periods of stress may trigger an attack. For unknown reasons, two-thirds of all Raynaud's sufferers are women. Smoking is blamed in many cases, but the disorder also occurs among nonsmokers. Some victims may also have lupus, rheumatoid arthritis, and other inflammatory autoimmune disorders.

Avoiding exposure of the hands and feet to cold temperatures can usually prevent or minimize attacks. Of course, not smoking and avoiding secondhand smoke is critical. Consuming foods that are high in omega-3 fatty acids and vitamin E may help.

CIRRHOSIS

EAT PLENTY OF

- *A combination of grains and legumes instead of meat for protein.*
- *Carbohydrates for energy.*
- *Cereals, breads, potatoes, and legumes for B-complex vitamins.*
- *Fruits and vegetables for vitamin C.*

CUT DOWN ON

- *Animal protein, salt, and fats.*

AVOID

- *Alcohol and salty processed foods.*

In cirrhosis, a chronic progressive disease, normal liver cells are replaced by scar tissue. Prolonged, heavy alcohol use is the most common cause, but cirrhosis may also result from hepatitis, inflammation or blockage of the bile ducts, inherited conditions, or a reaction to a drug or environmental toxin.

In its early stages, cirrhosis does not usually produce symptoms, but as the liver is increasingly infiltrated with fibrous tissue, a person may experience fatigue and nausea, and have a poor appetite. Later, JAUNDICE may develop and fine, spidery blood vessels appear on the skin. The liver damage is irreversible, but the progress of cirrhosis can be arrested and the complications treated with diet and other measures.

DIET AND LIVER REPAIR

Whether or not alcohol intake is the cause of cirrhosis, it is essential to stop drinking entirely to prevent further liver damage. Although the scar tissue cannot be replaced, the liver does have a remarkable ability to repair itself. To achieve this and regain lost weight, a daily intake of 2,000 to 3,000 calories is necessary. Most people with cirrhosis, however, have little appetite; thus, frequent small meals may be more tempting than three large ones.

PROTEIN intake must be carefully controlled. Too little protein and the liver cannot generate new, healthy cells; too much will overload the liver, resulting in a buildup of ammonia in the bloodstream, causing brain complications leading to coma and death. An individual with cirrhosis should eat about 40g of protein per day (compared with the 50g recommended for a healthy adult). Low-grade or incomplete proteins (such as those in dried peas, legumes, and cereals) are preferable to high-grade animal proteins, which are usually combined with fat that is difficult for a cirrhotic liver to process. A good supply of CARBOHYDRATES is needed to meet the body's energy needs. Moderate amounts of polyunsaturated fats (oily fish, corn oil, safflower oil) also provide needed calories without overburdening the liver.

Nutritional deficiencies are common among cirrhosis patients. Enriched cereals, breads and pasta, and fruits and vegetables will help replace depleted vitamins and minerals. Often, a doctor will also prescribe supplements.

FLUIDS AND SALT

The orderly flow of body fluids is an early casualty of cirrhotic damage. In a healthy individual, the blood supply circulates through vessels in the liver at the rate of $1\frac{1}{2}$ quarts every minute. In cirrhosis, rigid scar tissue forms on the liver, hindering the blood from passing freely. As the blood backs up, the pressure in the supplying vessels increases, which forces plasma out of the blood vessels and into the surrounding tissue of the abdominal cavity. People with cirrhosis often have distinctive abdominal swelling, known as ascites. The volume of blood in the vessels throughout the body is therefore decreased, and when the kidneys register the fall in blood flow, they send out a signal for help in the form of the hormone aldosterone. Far from helping, this causes the body to retain sodium (instead of excreting it in the urine in the normal manner), which in turn produces a further damming of fluid and worsens the ascites. The whole body becomes puffy and swollen, and the vicious cycle continues with other complications that arise as the blood seeks a way to bypass the obstruction in the liver. This entails increasing blood flow in vessels in neighboring organs, such as the veins of the esophagus. Some cirrhotic patients suffer from varices (varicose veins) in the esophagus, which can rupture and cause severe bleeding.

People with cirrhosis should eat little salt, especially if ascites is present, and drink about four to six glasses of fluids a day. Use herbs and spices on food instead of salt. If varices are present in the esophagus, the food should be soft and thoroughly chewed.

COCONUTS

BENEFITS
- *A useful source of iron and fiber.*
- *High in easy-to-digest fatty acids.*

DRAWBACKS
- *High in saturated fats and calories.*

The coconut, the seed of a palm tree that grows mostly in tropical coastal areas, yields numerous food and nonfood products. The oil is used in vegetable shortening, nondairy creamers, some margarines, and many commercial baked goods; it is also an ingredient in shampoos, moisturizing skin lotions, soaps, and various cosmetics. The creamy coconut meat that lines the interior of the nut's hard outer shell is eaten raw or used to flavor ice cream, confectionery products, and baked goods. Coconut milk, the sweet white fluid from the heart of the nut, is served as a beverage or used as a marinade. An 8-ounce serving of fresh milk has only 60 calories, mostly from sugars.

Dried coconut meat, or copra, is rich in oil. In fact, more than 90 percent of the fatty acids in coconuts are classified as saturated; remarkably, coconut oil is more highly saturated than the fat in butter or red meat. This high level of saturation results in an oil that resists turning rancid, making coconut oil ideal for commercial baking. However, it is also a major drawback; saturated fats tend to raise blood cholesterol levels. In light of this, people who have elevated cholesterol levels or any other cardiovascular risk factors are typically advised to avoid products made with coconut oil.

On the plus side, the fatty acids are easy to digest, and a half cup of coconut meat has about 1mg of iron and a fair amount of fiber.

BUYING TIP. *When shopping for a coconut, choose one with a firm shell; check it carefully to make sure there are no dark or soft spots on it.*

COFFEE

BENEFITS
- *Stimulates the central nervous system.*
- *Can help you stay awake and alert.*

DRAWBACKS
- *Reduces women's fertility.*
- *May contribute to difficulty falling asleep and disturbed or reduced sleep.*
- *Drinking large amounts can cause irritability and jittery nerves.*
- *Increases excretion of calcium.*

Our major source of CAFFEINE, coffee is the substance millions of Canadians use to stay alert. In addition to caffeine, coffee contains nearly 400 other chemicals, including trace amounts of several vitamins and minerals, tannins, and caramelized sugar. Coffee is not entirely calorie-free; while a 6-ounce cup of sugar-free black coffee has only 4 calories, some coffee drinks have more fat and calories than a rich dessert. A cup of whole-milk mocha topped with whipped cream is on a par with a hot fudge sundae.

A dedicated coffee drinker might consider reducing caffeine from other sources—for example, giving up caffeinated soft drinks from the diet.

POSSIBLE HAZARDS

Coffee, like any food, is best consumed in moderation. The following are possible hazards linked to coffee.

Infertility. A recent study found that women who drank more than 3 cups of coffee (300mg caffeine) a day reduced their chances of conception by approximately 25 percent.

Heart problems. Caffeine prompts a temporary rise in blood pressure; it can also provoke cardiac arrhythmias in susceptible persons.

Bone loss. Coffee increases calcium excretion in the urine. To compensate for this loss, heavy coffee drinkers should consume extra calcium-rich foods.

CHERRIES AND BEANS.
The fruits of coffee bushes are called cherries, because they turn red as they ripen and they grow in clusters. Each cherry contains two beans.

Caffeine withdrawal. Heavy coffee consumers who stop drinking coffee abruptly may suffer headaches, irritability, and other withdrawal symptoms for a few days. Cut back gradually.
Cholesterol problems. Cafestol and kahweol, compounds in coffee, can boost cholesterol synthesis by the liver. These are found in highest concentrations in Scandinavian and Turkish coffees, as well as French-press brews.

DECAFFEINATED COFFEE

Many people drink decaffeinated coffee to escape the insomnia and jittery nerves caused by caffeine. But even decaffeinated coffee has up to 5mg of caffeine in a 5-ounce cup. People with sleep problems are better off avoiding coffee.

COLDS AND FLU

CONSUME PLENTY OF
- *Fruits and vegetables for vitamin C.*
- *Wheat germ, dried peas and beans, seafood, and meat for zinc.*
- *Garlic and hot peppers (chilies), which may act as natural decongestants.*
- *Fluids to loosen phlegm.*

AVOID
- *Alcohol in any form.*

The runny nose, cough, loss of taste and smell, sore throat, and blocked ears of a cold are hard to escape; most people suffer two or three bouts a year. That's why it's called "the common cold."

In the winter months, flu (short for influenza) inflicts a similar misery on people; what makes flu worse is the presence of fever as well as muscle and joint aches. The complications of flu—especially pneumonia—can be serious. More than 200 Canadians die from flu or its complications each year.

Colds and flu are highly contagious respiratory infections that are caused by viruses. More than 200 cold viruses (rhinoviruses) have been identified; unfortunately, developing immunity to one does not protect you from the others. There are fewer flu viruses, but they undergo frequent mutations—that is, they change their protein structure just a little—each year as they sweep around the globe. Thus, each flu season is different. This is why new flu vaccines are produced yearly that protect against the prevailing strains of the virus. Doctors recommend annual flu shots for everyone over the age of 65, people of any age who have a circulatory, respiratory, kidney, metabolic, or immune disorder, and residents in communal-living facilities.

CATCHING THE "BUG"

Colds and flu are spread when virus-laden fluid droplets are released into the air by coughing and sneezing or transferred to surfaces by touch. British researchers have shown that the cold virus is activated at temperatures slightly below 98.6°F (37°C), the normal temperature for humans. So it seems that the old wives' tales about catching cold have a grain of truth: If you sit in a draft, your temperature may drop just enough to activate the cold viruses that have been biding their time in your nasal passages.

When you breathe overly dry air (especially in planes and artificially ventilated office buildings), your nasal passages may form tiny cracks that provide an entryway for viruses. The best defense is plenty of fluids to rehydrate the tender membranes; in an office, try using a humidifier or opening the window a crack to improve air quality.

You're more vulnerable to colds and flu when your immune system is depressed by another illness, stress, or fatigue. Preventive steps include avoiding alcohol, getting plenty of rest, and reducing stress levels.

THE ROLE OF DIET

While there's no cure for colds or flu, eating properly may help to prevent them, shorten their duration, or make symptoms less severe. For example, in one study, persons who sucked on zinc-enriched lozenges during their colds were free of symptoms a full 4 days earlier than a comparable group who weren't given the lozenges. Rich food sources of zinc include wheat germ, dried peas and beans, oysters and other seafood, meat and poultry, dairy products, and tofu.

More than two decades of extensive research have failed to substantiate claims that megadoses of vitamin C can prevent and cure colds. It's known, however, that vitamin C has a slight antihistaminic effect, so drinking more citrus juice or taking a supplement of 500 to 2,000mg a day may help reduce nasal symptoms. Perhaps more promising are Israeli findings that elderberry extract and lozenges attack cold and flu viruses. Elderberry products are available under the name of Sambucol in health-food stores.

During a cold or the flu, drink a minimum of 8 to 10 glasses of fluids a day in order to replenish lost fluids, keep mucous membranes moist, and loosen phlegm. Abstain from alcohol, which dilates

THROAT SOOTHER.
Add honey and lemon to hot water or weak tea to loosen mucus and ease pain.

WHEN TO SEE A DOCTOR

Most colds and bouts of flu go away by themselves, but a doctor should be seen if you have:

• A cough that produces green, yellow, or bloody phlegm.

• A severe headache or pain in the face, jaw, or ear.

• Trouble swallowing or breathing.

• A fever over 100°F (38°C) that lasts more than 48 hours.

small blood vessels and makes the nose and sinuses feel stuffed up. Alcohol may also produce adverse effects when taken with many drugs, especially cold and cough remedies, and reduces the body's immune response, its ability to fight infection.

The debate about whether to starve a cold and feed a fever (or vice versa) is obsolete; doctors recommend eating when you feel hungry. The following foods may be helpful and comforting. **Chicken soup.** Grandma was right! Not only is it soothing and easy to digest, but chicken soup also contains cystine, a compound that helps to thin out the mucus, relieving congestion. **Spicy foods.** Hot peppers, or chilies, contain capsaicin, a substance that can help reduce nasal and sinus congestion. Garlic, turmeric, and other hot spices have a similar effect.

COLITIS

EAT PLENTY OF
- *Poached fruits and steamed vegetables to help prevent constipation.*
- *Eggs, fish, poultry, and lean meat for high-grade protein and iron.*

CUT DOWN ON
- *Fats, oils, and caffeine.*

AVOID
- *Raw fruits and vegetables, whole grains, bran, seeds, and nuts.*
- *Foods that provoke symptoms.*
- *Alcohol in all forms.*

Colitis, also called ulcerative colitis or inflammatory bowel disease, is a chronic inflammatory disease that causes bleeding ulcers in the colon and rectum. Symptomatic flare-ups alternate with periods of symptom-free remission. In mild cases of colitis, patients may have normal bowel movements with a mucous discharge; more commonly, the disease also causes abdominal cramps and bloody diarrhea. When the disease is severe, violent and persistent bloody diarrhea is accompanied by fever, malaise, loss of appetite and weight, and ANEMIA.

Although colitis may strike at any age, it most often develops between the ages of 15 and 30. The cause remains unknown, although infection, the immune system, heredity, and diet have all been implicated.

FOOD AND COLITIS

Modification of the diet is a mainstay of colitis treatment. Because individuals vary greatly in their response to foods, each person must develop an eating plan based on personal experience. Fundamental to the diet plan is a food diary that lets the patient key symptoms to specific foods. It is also important to consult a qualified dietitian to ensure that the meal plan provides good nutrition. Vitamin and mineral supplements are often needed to compensate for a restricted diet and possible absorption problems.

Foods that irritate the bowel often include those high in insoluble fiber, which is found in bran, whole grains, nuts, seeds, dried fruits, and the skins of potatoes, fresh fruits, and vegetables. Less irritating are pectin and other types of soluble fiber, which can be obtained from poached peeled fruits and cooked leafy green vegetables.

Fatty foods are hard to digest, so keep FATS and oils to a minimum and avoid fried and sautéed foods, as well as such obviously fatty items as bacon, potato chips, and most cheeses.

Depending on how your intestines tend to react, you may also be better off avoiding caffeinated drinks, as well as decaffeinated coffee and colas, alcohol, highly spiced foods and seasonings (such as horseradish and mustard), and beans, cabbage, and other vegetables that may produce gas.

Many people with ulcerative colitis have an INTOLERANCE to dairy products during symptom flare-ups; some, however, can use lactose-free products.

The diet should provide enough calories, protein, and other nutrients to make up for the strict limitations. Eggs, fish, poultry, and lean meat supply high-grade protein. Red meat, especially liver, is an important source of iron for people who are constantly losing blood from the bowel. Eat as much as you want of puréed, canned, or soft-cooked vegetables and fruits that are strained to remove seeds and skins.

During a severe flare-up, a very-low-residue bland diet (a diet low in fiber designed to avoid producing stools) might include clear broth, weak tea, toasted white bread, soft-cooked eggs, gelatins, and cooked cream of rice or cream of wheat. As healing progresses,

Case Study

*A*t the age of 30, Jim began to notice a change in his bowel habits. He often experienced cramps and had unexpected urgency to move his bowels. With time, these episodes become more frequent and were climaxed by watery diarrhea. When Jim noticed blood in the toilet bowl, he became frightened and called his doctor.

After a series of tests, including X-rays and a colonoscopy to examine the lining of the bowel, the diagnosis was ulcerative colitis. Jim's doctor prescribed medication to help ease the diarrhea. He also referred Jim to a registered dietitian, who showed him how to use a low-residue diet to manage the disease. Although Jim occasionally misses some of the crunchy, spicy, and fried foods that he used to enjoy, he has adapted well to the limitations of his new diet and has had only a few bouts of diarrhea since he changed his lifestyle.

soft-cooked fish, poultry, and lean meats can be added, along with baked or boiled skinless potatoes and, eventually, poached fruits and steamed vegetables. In very severe cases, liquid diets given orally or intravenously, or by a nasogastric tube, may be necessary to prevent malnutrition.

DRUG THERAPY

In mild to moderate colitis, when ulceration is limited to the lower part of the bowel, the use of steroid enemas can bring about remission within a few weeks. For more extensive disease, the anti-inflammatory drug sulfasalazine (which combines an aspirinlike drug with a sulfa compound) may produce remission. Anyone taking this drug should eat folate-rich foods, such as liver, leafy greens, and poached fruits.

Corticosteroid drugs, such as prednisone, are prescribed to bring severe colitis symptoms under control, at which time sulfasalazine is used to maintain remission. Because steroids promote fluid retention, patients taking these medicines should reduce their salt intake; they may also need extra calcium to prevent OSTEOPOROSIS.

CONSTIPATION

CONSUME PLENTY OF
- *Fresh fruits and vegetables, grains, and other high-fiber foods.*
- *Fluids (at least 8 glasses a day).*

CUT DOWN ON
- *Sugar and refined starchy foods.*

AVOID
- *Alcohol in all forms.*
- *Any foods that provoke constipation.*

Many people wrongly assume that they are constipated because they don't have a daily bowel movement. In fact, it's perfectly normal for bowels to move as often as three times a day or as infrequently as once in 3 or 4 days. The important factors are regularity and easy passage of a reasonably soft but well-formed stool.

There are two types of constipation: atonic occurs when the colon muscles are weak and lack tone; spastic (sometimes called IRRITABLE BOWEL SYNDROME) is characterized by irregular bowel movements. Atonic constipation, the more common of the two, develops when the diet lacks adequate fluids and fiber; a sedentary lifestyle is another common cause. Spastic constipation can be caused by stress, nervous disorders, excessive smoking, irritating foods, and obstructions of the colon.

Adults should drink 8 glasses of nonalcoholic fluids every day. When a low-fiber diet coincides with a low fluid intake, the stool becomes dry and hard, and increasingly difficult to move through the intestinal tract.

Regular physical activity helps to stimulate bowel movements, whereas prolonged inactivity can cause constipation. Several medications, especially codeine and other narcotic painkillers, reduce peristalsis, the rhythmic muscle movements that push digested food through the bowel. Drinking alcohol has a similar effect in some people. Poor toilet habits, such as putting off going to the toilet despite an urge to defecate, can also cause constipation. Excessive laxative use reduces normal colon function. If a laxative is needed, one made of psyllium or another high-fiber stool softener is probably the best choice.

RECIPE FOR RELIEF

Increasing intake of dietary fiber, especially the insoluble type that absorbs water but otherwise passes through the bowel intact, is instrumental in preventing constipation. Whenever possible, try to use the whole vegetable; fiber tends to be concentrated in the peelings, stems, and outer leaves— parts

---

THE PROBLEM OF HEMORRHOIDS

Chronic constipation, obesity, pregnancy, and an inherited predisposition are common causes of hemorrhoids—varicose veins in the anal area. Most hemorrhoids are symptom-free, but some cause itching, pain, and bleeding, especially during bouts of constipation. Straining to pass a hard stool can rupture one of the distended veins and result in considerable bleeding; more often, the stool contains small amounts of bright red blood. The blood loss itself is usually inconsequential, but any rectal bleeding should prompt medical investigation to rule out colon cancer or polyps.

Avoiding constipation and maintaining a normal weight will often eliminate hemorrhoid symptoms. Some sufferers find that curries, chilies, and other hot, spicy foods increase discomfort during bowel movements; citrus fruits and other acidic foods may also be irritating.

In severe cases, chronic blood loss from hemorrhoids can cause ANEMIA; a doctor may prescribe iron supplements and removal of the hemorrhoids. Eating iron-rich foods can help restore the body's iron reserves.

---

that many cooks discard. But any increase in high-fiber food consumption should be gradual and accompanied by more fluids to help prevent bloating and FLATULENCE.

Avoid the temptation to add miller's BRAN to foods—this can cause uncomfortable gas and bloating; it also reduces the absorption of iron, calcium, and other minerals. Instead, try an ounce or two of prunes or dried figs.

Convenience and Fast Foods: Eating on the Run

Instead of "cooking from scratch," many Canadians are relying on processed and prepared foods. Some see this as unhealthy, but others say convenience doesn't rule out good nutrition.

Technological advances have dramatically enhanced the quality and increased the range of processed foods. Vacuum-packed or frozen precooked meals ready for the microwave oven, instant mashed potatoes and hot cereals, jars of prepared baby foods, and envelopes of soup, dessert, and sauce mixes are just a few of the time-saving foods that many people rely on. In addition, delicatessens and fast-food and take-out restaurants are everywhere, even in hospitals and schools. According to food industry statistics, fast-food restaurants serve about 60 million North Americans each day.

Some critics blame this growing reliance on convenience and fast foods, which are typically high in fat and calories, for the fact that more than 40 percent of adult Canadians are overweight. Of these, some 28 percent are obese. But defenders point out that most fast-food establishments offer a choice of low-calorie, healthful foods as well as the traditional hamburgers, French fries, and milk shakes. The fact is, convenience and fast foods are here to stay; however, anyone who follows the basic rules of variety, moderation, and balance can work them into a healthful, nutritious diet.

CONVENIENCE FOODS

Almost everyone consumes at least some convenience foods, defined as items that require little or no preparation; examples range from ready-to-eat breakfast cereals, instant soup mixes, and canned or frozen goods to prepackaged heat-and-serve meals. Nutritionally, some of these products do not measure up to home-cooked meals prepared with fresh ingredients, but this varies greatly among foods. Instant soups, for example, typically contain a few dehydrated vegetables and a lot of artificial flavorings, emulsifiers, fillers, and preservatives. Home-made and even canned soups are more nutritious and contain fewer additives. Most convenience foods also tend to contain more sugar, salt, and fat than comparable dishes prepared at home.

Processing strips vitamins and minerals from some foods, but there are exceptions in which convenience foods are actually more nutritious than their fresh counterparts. Vegetables and many fruits harvested and quick-frozen at their peak often have more vitamins than those picked before maturity, shipped for long distances, and then allowed to sit on store shelves. Most CEREALS and BREADS are made with enriched flours, so they may provide nutrients that are not found in the original grains.

Many food processors have been prompted by consumer demands to enhance the nutritional quality of their products by adding healthful ingredients (for example, dietary fiber to cereals or calcium to orange juice) or by reducing fat, sugar, and salt. Although some claims of low-fat, no cholesterol, and "lite" are exaggerated, an informed shopper who knows how to decipher food LABELING can make healthful choices.

THE PRICE OF CONVENIENCE

Most convenience foods carry a higher price tag than the total cost of their ingredients. For many people, however, the extra cost is worth the savings in time and effort. Still, they may

---

DO-IT-YOURSELF CONVENIENCE FOODS

A growing number of cooks are discovering that they can make their own convenience foods—all it takes is a freezer and planning. Instead of discarding leftovers, for example, make up a frozen prepackaged meal that can be popped in the microwave at a later date. Chances are it will taste better (and cost less) than commercial TV dinners. This approach also allows you to control the amount of fat, salt, and other ingredients.

If you're making a soup or stew, double the recipe and then freeze the extra portion. Similarly, buy extra fresh vegetables that are in season and freeze them for later use. Be sure to date the packages, and use the oldest first.

HOW TO BALANCE CONVENIENCE AND FAST FOODS WITH OTHER MEALS

Fast foods are readily available and can save time, but from a nutritional standpoint, they are usually high in calories, fat, salt, or sugar, or all four; many also lack important vita- *mins and minerals. The table below suggests ways to compensate for any nutritional excesses or deficiencies in the fast food in another meal.*

ADVANTAGES	DISADVANTAGES	HEALTHY BALANCE
CHEESEBURGER (4 OZ MEAT) AND FRENCH FRIES (3 OZ)		
High in protein and starchy complex carbohydrates. Also contains vitamin B₁₂, riboflavin, iron, potassium, and calcium. 	High in calories (about 800), fat, and sodium. Fat content will increase if mayonnaise dressing is included. Low in fiber, vitamins A, C, and D, beta carotene, and folate.	Salad made with a variety of fresh vegetables and dressed with olive oil and lemon juice. This meal is low in calories and fat while providing high amounts of vitamins A, C, and E, folate, and beta carotene.
FRIED CHICKEN		
High in protein. Some carbohydrates in batter. 	Calories will vary depending on whether it is skinless and dark or white meat (the skin and dark meat are higher in fat). Regardless, fried chicken is high in fat, calories, and often sodium.	Black beans and rice with spices and vegetables, such as onions, red and green peppers, and tomatoes. Provides protein, fiber, and vitamins A, C, and the B complex.
BURRITO		
Depends upon the filling. A good source of carbohydrates and protein. If cheese, tomatoes, onions, peppers, and other fresh vegetables are added, vitamins A and C and calcium will be provided. 	Tends to be high in calories and fat. While meat fillings will increase protein levels, they tend to be quite fatty. Toppings such as guacamole and sour cream add to the fat content.	Pasta with steamed vegetables, including spinach or broccoli. Pasta will supply carbohydrates and fiber. Vegetables will supply vitamins A, C, and the B complex.
FISH SANDWICH		
High in protein; also provides starchy carbohydrates from bread or roll. 	Since these are often dipped in batter and fried, they are high in fat and calories. Tartar sauce increases the fat content.	Pasta salad with feta cheese and broccoli, spinach, or other fresh or steamed vegetables will provide calcium, fiber, and vitamins A and C.
PIZZA		
Depends on the topping. A good source of starchy carbohydrates. A plain slice has protein, calcium, vitamin A, niacin, and riboflavin. Adding fresh vegetable toppings, such as red peppers, will add vitamins A and C. 	Usually high in fat. May be high in sodium as well. Meat toppings, such as pepperoni, sausage, bacon, ham, or meatballs, will increase the levels of protein but will also add fat and salt.	Grilled or baked fish with brown rice and steamed vegetables and fresh fruit for dessert. This balanced meal will provide vitamins A and C, folate and other B vitamins, potassium, iron, and fiber.
DELICATESSEN SANDWICH		
This depends on the type of bread, filling, and size. Turkey breast or other low-fat meat with mustard, lettuce, and tomato on whole-grain bread offers a fairly balanced meal. 	Fatty meats, such as salami or cold cuts, will be high in calories, salt, and fat. Lean meat mixed with mayonnaise (such as chicken salad) is also high in fat. Avoid fatty dressings.	Homemade vegetable and rice soup (or perhaps a lentil soup or minestrone) will provide protein, fiber, potassium, and vitamins A and C.

worry about the nutritional value of frozen dinners, breakfast bars, and other convenience foods. To answer such concerns, many food manufacturers now produce special products; indeed, various commercial diet and fitness programs offer complete lines of convenience foods. Some of these are low in calories and sodium, while others are designed to meet the special needs of people with nutrition-related problems like diabetes and food allergies. It's important to check labels and ingredient lists, however; a "lite" meal may still have unacceptable amounts of fat, salt, and sugar, and a low-fat product may be high in sugar. Also, special health or dietary items tend to be more expensive than the regular lines, even though their components may be similar.

Combining convenience foods with fresh ingredients can save both time and money while increasing interest and nutritional value. For example, you can build a tasty and nutritious meal around a frozen entrée by adding a green salad and seasonal vegetables that take only minutes to prepare.

FOODS FOR CHILDREN

Most parents rely upon at least some convenience items when introducing BEGINNER FOODS into a baby's diet. Instant cereals and jars of puréed fruits, vegetables, and meats are certainly easier and perhaps safer than homemade baby foods. More questionable are the convenience foods that many older children seem to prefer. Favorites like hot dogs and cold cuts are usually loaded with fat, salt, and preservatives; instant puddings may provide milk, but they are also high in sugar, fats, emulsifiers, and artificial flavorings and colorings. Cereals that have a lot of sugar further encourage a child's taste for sweets.

When feeding children, emphasize foods made with minimal processing; for example, chicken is a better pick

---

"JUNK" FOOD?

Sweets, hamburgers, hot dogs, French fries, potato chips, and soda pop are often called "junk" foods. However, nutritionists believe that any food, in moderation, can be part of a healthful diet, while too much of a nutritious item can be a hazard.

Even "junk" foods have some nutritional merit. A hamburger, for example, has protein, iron, and B vitamins. Add lettuce and tomato for vitamin C. Having a salad instead of French fries cuts calories and supplies even more nutrients. Juice or low-fat milk are substitutes for soda pop.

---

than hot dogs, yogurt is more healthful than puddings, uncoated oat cereals or low-fat granola is a wiser choice than sweetened children's cereals.

FAST FOODS

Fast foods are usually defined as ready-to-eat dishes sold by commercial establishments that may or may not have on-site dining accommodations. The first fast-food establishments in North America were employee cafeterias. At the same time, street food carts, food stands, and delicatessens started springing up in urban areas. In 1919, the first franchised fast-food chain (A&W) was established in the U.S.; however, it was not until McDonald's came on the scene that the industry in North America began to take off. Since then, McDonald's, the number-one chain, markets its food in almost every country in the world and has been joined by scores of other franchised fast-food operations.

Most Canadians eat fast foods, at least occasionally; a government survey found that we spend an average of just under $1,500 a year per household eating out. The most popular fast

---

foods are mass produced inexpensively; these include hamburgers, French fries, deep-fried chicken and fish sticks, pizza, hot dogs, tacos, soft drinks, and ice cream bars. Chinese, Mexican, and other ethnic foods, too, are gaining popularity in the fast-food market. While many of these foods provide enough protein, adequate iron, and most B vitamins, they are very high in fat and salt. A diet built around such foods fosters obesity and may also lack adequate fiber, calcium, and vitamins A and C.

Recognizing these shortcomings, many fast-food establishments have added SALAD BARS or prepackaged salads to their menus. However, most fast-food outlets do not provide nutrition labels and lists of ingredients. Some will identify low-calorie and salt-reduced items or provide nutritional information upon request; yet most decline to give detailed lists of ingredients and nutritional analyses. Despite such shortcomings, however, a nutrition-conscious diner can get a balanced meal at a fast-food restaurant by choosing wisely. (See How to Balance Convenience and Fast Foods With Other Meals, p.107.)

THE SAFETY FACTOR

Every now and then, an outbreak of food poisoning is traced to a fast-food establishment. Any meal that is mass produced and then allowed to stand for any length of time is vulnerable to contamination. Especially deadly, particularly to young children, is a type of *E. coli* infection contracted by eating undercooked contaminated BEEF.

People who take out fast food and wait several hours before eating it are courting danger. Any food that is not consumed right away should be refrigerated, and then thoroughly reheated before it is eaten. If you're eating in a restaurant, decline any precooked item that has grown cold or looks like it has been sitting around.

CORN

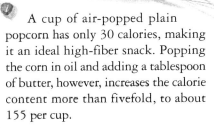

BENEFITS
- *A good source of folate and thiamine.*
- *A fair amount of vitamins A and C, potassium, and iron.*
- *Air-popped unbuttered popcorn is low in calories and very high in fiber.*

DRAWBACKS
- *The niacin in corn is not released in the human digestive tract.*
- *Corn lacks lysine and tryptophan, two essential amino acids needed to make a complete protein.*

Indigenous to the Western Hemisphere, corn is our most abundant grain crop; worldwide, it is exceeded only by wheat as a cereal grain. Most of the corn grown in Canada and the United States is field, or dent, corn, which is allowed to mature on its stalk, dried, and used as animal feed or processed into flour to make cereals. Flint corn, another field variety, keeps better than dent corn and is used to make cornmeal. Flour corn has soft, starchy kernels that are easily ground into flour, making it a favorite with Native peoples to make tortillas and other corn dishes.

Sweet corn, which is harvested while still immature, is the type consumed as a vegetable. It can be cooked in several different ways: on the cob or with the soft kernels removed and served fresh or frozen or canned for future use.

Corn is high in starch and protein, but it lacks two essential amino acids—lysine and tryptophan; as a result, it is not a suitable protein substitute. In undeveloped countries, children are sometimes fed a diet made up mostly of corn, which can lead to two deficiency diseases: kwashiorkor, caused by inadequate protein, and pellagra, resulting from a deficiency of niacin. When corn is consumed along with beans and other legumes, however, it provides a complete protein.

Most of the niacin in corn is in the form of niacytin, which is not broken down in the human digestive tract. Early nutrition researchers were puzzled by the fact that Mexicans and South Americans did not develop pellagra, even though their diets were made up mostly of corn. It was later discovered that combining the corn with an alkaline substance releases the niacin in niacytin; thus, the practice of mixing cornmeal with lime water to make tortillas prevented pellagra. Similarly, Indians in Colombia and other parts of South America ground their corn with alkaline potash to loosen the bran, another practice that released niacin and prevented pellagra.

While corn may not be a complete food, it is by far our most important farm crop; not only is it fed to pigs, cattle, and other meat animals, but it is also used in more than 800 different processed foods (see Common Corn Products, right). This is why people who are allergic to corn have difficulty finding corn-free processed foods.

POPCORN

A popular snack food, popcorn is a special variety that grows on a cob smaller than those of sweet or field corn. As the kernels are heated rapidly, the moisture inside them is converted to steam. When the steam pressure builds to a certain point, it bursts the outer shell and the interior turns into a fluffy mass of starch and fiber many times larger than the original kernel.

A cup of air-popped plain popcorn has only 30 calories, making it an ideal high-fiber snack. Popping the corn in oil and adding a tablespoon of butter, however, increases the calorie content more than fivefold, to about 155 per cup.

COMMON CORN PRODUCTS

PRODUCT	EXAMPLES
Breakfast cereals	Cornflakes and other ready-to-eat cereals.
Cornmeal	Corn bread, corn chips, muffins, polenta, tortillas, and other dishes made from ground corn.
Flour	Fillers and thickeners; combined with wheat flour to make breads and other baked goods.
Grits and hominy	Cooked cereal; starchy vegetable dish.
Oil	Cooking oil, margarine, salad dressings, and shortenings.
Starch	Thickener in baked goods, candy, chewing gum, gravies and other sauces, and puddings.
Sugar and syrup	Sweetener in baked goods, jams and jellies, soft drinks, beer, ale, and many other products.

CRANBERRIES

BENEFITS

- *A fair source of vitamin C and fiber.*
- *Juice helps prevent or alleviate cystitis and urinary tract infections.*
- *Contain bioflavonoids, thought to protect eyesight and help prevent cancer.*

DRAWBACKS

- *Must be prepared with large amounts of sugar to make them palatable.*

Once served mostly as a condiment at Thanksgiving and Christmas, cranberries are now consumed throughout the year as juice, a dried snack fruit, and an ingredient in muffins and other baked goods. Cranberries belong to the same family as blueberries and huckleberries, but unlike these fruits, they are too tart to eat raw. Even when sweetened, cranberries retain a fresh tartness that complements poultry and pork.

Cranberries are a native North American plant. Although they still grow wild in boggy areas, most are cultivated in British Columbia, which ranks as the third largest cranberry-producing area in the world, behind Massachusetts and Wisconsin. When buying fresh cranberries, look for firm, bright red fruit. Berries that are at their peak will bounce when dropped; those that don't are likely to be soft and past their prime.

ROLE IN CYSTITIS

Cranberry juice has long been used as a home remedy for cystitis and also to prevent kidney and bladder stones. Until recently, this benefit was attributed to quinic acid, a substance that increases urine acidity and prevents the formation of calcium stones. It was also thought that this acidity helped prevent cystitis. New studies show, however, that cranberries also contain a natural antibiotic substance that makes the bladder walls inhospitable to the

Vaccinium macrocarpon

The American, or large, cranberry fruits from September onwards.

Delicate mauve flowers make their appearance in summer.

BEYOND THANKSGIVING. *Cranberries are now consumed year-round in many forms.*

organisms responsible for urinary tract infections. This prevents the bacteria from forming colonies; instead, they are washed out of the body in the urine. (Interestingly, BLUEBERRY juice has a similar protective effect.)

Many urologists and gynecologists now advise patients who suffer recurrent or chronic bladder infections to drink a couple of glasses of cranberry juice daily as a preventive measure. See a doctor, however, if symptoms develop or persist; prescription antibiotics are usually necessary to cure an established urinary infection.

Commercial cranberry juice is often too diluted to be effective in preventing or treating urinary infections; it also contains large amounts of sugar or other sweeteners. Use a juicer to make your own cranberry juice. To reduce the amount of sugar needed, dilute a cup of concentrated juice with 2 to 3 cups of apple juice and then sweeten to taste.

OTHER BENEFITS

Cranberries provide fiber, along with some vitamin C; they also contain BIO-FLAVONOIDS, plant pigments that help counter the damage of unstable molecules that are formed when oxygen is used by the body. European researchers have found that one of these bioflavonoids, anthocyanin, promotes formation of visual purple, a pigment in the eyes instrumental in color and night vision. Other studies suggest anthocyanin has an anticancer effect.

CRAVINGS

EAT PLENTY OF
- *Low-fat starchy foods to satisfy a carbohydrate craving.*
- *High-fiber foods to avoid feeling hungry.*

EAT IN MODERATION
- *Foods you might crave, especially sweets, chocolates, and salty items.*

AVOID
- *Becoming overly hungry, which can lead to overindulgence.*

All of us occasionally have an irresistible urge for a certain food or beverage. But merely having a sudden need for a particular food does not constitute a true craving, nor does indulging in an occasional chocolate, ice cream, or other favorite food. A craving goes much deeper—it's an insistent desire that you can't ignore, even though satisfying it may entail considerable inconvenience or even danger.

Occasional cravings may be in response to stress, hormonal changes, or excessive hunger. More obsessive cravings, however, can stem from a specific illness, addiction, or deep-seated psychological problem.

Recent research suggests that hormonal changes are responsible for many food cravings, especially those that develop during periods of stress, pregnancy, or different phases of a woman's menstrual cycle. Following this theory, fluctuating hormonal levels may influence the brain's production of serotonin and other chemicals—changes that can trigger an intense desire for specific foods. Under these circumstances, a person usually craves chocolate and other sweets; researchers think this is because sugars are a quick source of glucose, which the brain needs for energy. Eating a diet high in starchy foods along with moderate amounts of protein may prevent the intense craving for sweets because these complex carbohydrates and protein are metabolized more slowly than sugars, thus providing a steady supply of glucose.

PREGNANCY CRAVINGS

Pregnant women often develop strange food cravings, especially for pickles and other salty foods. In this instance, the craving reflects a physical need. During PREGNANCY, a woman's volume of blood doubles, and as a result she needs extra sodium to maintain a proper fluid balance. Normally, adding salt to food to taste supplies the necessary sodium. As for other cravings, there's usually no harm in satisfying them in moderation, provided overall nutritional needs are met. But if the cravings are for bizarre indigestible items like laundry starch, soil, clay, and ice, it constitutes pica (see Pica—A Bizarre Phenomenon, below) and may reflect a serious medical or psychological problem.

A craving for ice (during pregnancy and at other times as well) is a common sign of iron deficiency; conversely, the deficiency can be caused by eating starch, clay, and other substances that bind to iron and prevent its absorption. In either instance, taking iron supplements to counter the deficiency usually puts an end to the craving.

Cravings are also influenced by cultural traditions, some of which are still practiced in places like the rural American South or among recent immigrants. For example, some folk healers urge pregnant women to eat clay for an easier delivery; others maintain that consumption of soil provides needed iron. Such practices, however, are dangerous for both the mother and her fetus.

TO GIVE IN OR TO DENY?

Some experts believe that food cravings reflect the "wisdom of the body"; we feel an urge to eat particular foods to fulfill a nutritional need. In general, however, we tend to crave foods that are not particularly nutritious, and in such instances, psychological factors are probably more influential than physical needs. For some individuals, food may fill an emotional void, leading a person to turn to certain foods during

---

PICA—A BIZARRE PHENOMENON

For unexplained reasons, some children develop intense cravings for nonfood items, such as paint chips, soil, clay, or laundry starch. This phenomenon is known as pica, which comes from the Latin term for magpie—a bird that will eat almost anything.

Childhood pica should be distinguished from a child's natural curiosity about objects in his environment. A young child's normal tendency is to learn about new things by putting them in his mouth, but he's not obsessive about it. In contrast, a child with pica craves certain nondietary substances, often paint chips, soil, or clay, and will go to great lengths to get them. This can have serious consequences, including lead poisoning, intestinal obstruction, worm infestations, and even death if poisonous substances are consumed. Young children with pica are sometimes mentally retarded or emotionally disturbed; others are normal, but they may lack appropriate intellectual stimulation or love and nurturing.

Adult pica sometimes develops during pregnancy; it may also reflect an emotional problem or nutritional deficiency. In any event, pica at any age requires treatment to overcome it.

periods of stress or sadness. The power of suggestion is another possible trigger, which is why just a brief whiff of a favorite food can result in an intense desire for it, even though you may not be particularly hungry at the time.

People often make the mistake of trying to deny a craving. Some individuals may succeed, but more often than not, denial fosters an even stronger desire for the food. Unless the object of the craving poses a serious health risk (for instance, a person with high blood pressure craving salty foods), experts say it is better to satisfy the longing, but to do so in moderation. A healthier approach is to anticipate the craving and to satisfy it in advance. For example, if a woman invariably develops a strong craving for sweets during her premenstrual phase, she can lessen it somewhat by increasing her intake of starchy foods, which raise blood glucose levels. Eating more fruits, which are high in natural sugars, may also satisfy the desire for sweets.

Some medications, particularly steroids and other hormonal preparations, can promote food cravings. These drug-related cravings, however, are usually nonspecific; the person may simply feel ravenously hungry and crave eating in general instead of a particular food, such as chocolate or pickles.

Avoiding becoming overly hungry can also forestall cravings for sweets or fatty foods. Hunger is the body's way of letting you know it's running short of fuel; it's a powerful instinct that is almost impossible to deny for any length of time. This is one reason why dieters often find it so hard to adhere to an overly restrictive regimen; their resolve may be strong, but it's almost impossible to deny the body's instinct for self-preservation against starvation. Eating small, frequent meals on a regular schedule is the best way to avert hunger and the subsequent strong cravings that can lead to overeating.

CROHN'S DISEASE

TAKE PLENTY OF
- Lean meat, fish, and poultry for the protein necessary for healing.
- Under a doctor's supervision, vitamin, mineral, and other nutritional supplements.

CUT DOWN ON
- High-fiber foods, especially if the bowel is partially obstructed.

AVOID
- Alcohol in any form.
- Any food that worsens symptoms.

Also known as ileitis, Crohn's disease is a type of inflammatory bowel disease that can affect any part of the intestinal tract, from the mouth to the anus. However, it most commonly attacks the colon and the lower part of the small intestine, or the ileum.

Crohn's disease is a chronic condition that may recur after lengthy periods of remission. Common symptoms are abdominal pain, often in the lower right area, and diarrhea. Typically, diseased portions of the intestine are interspersed with normal segments; fistulas (abnormal passageways between portions of intestines) are common. The diseased portions may become obstructed, an emergency situation. There may also be weight loss, fever, and intestinal bleeding persistent enough to cause anemia. Children with Crohn's disease may suffer stunted growth and delayed sexual development.

There are many theories about the causes of Crohn's disease, but none have been proved. Some scientists believe that the immune system is affected by a virus or a bacterium that triggers an inflammatory reaction in the intestinal wall. Crohn's disease appears to run in families; about 20 percent of those who have the disease have a blood relative with some form of inflammatory bowel dis-

Case Study

Peter is a 34-year-old aircraft engineer for whom alternating shift work is a way of life. When he began experiencing repeated episodes of abdominal cramps and diarrhea, he blamed them on a new shift. However, the digestive problems continued for several months, and when he started losing weight too, Peter decided to consult a doctor.

After a series of tests, Peter's doctor diagnosed Crohn's disease. He prescribed a multivitamin supplement and low-dose steroid drugs. Fried foods worsened Peter's symptoms, so the doctor recommended avoiding them. He also stressed the importance of regular balanced meals, rather than reliance on fast foods and vending machine snacks. Within 6 weeks on the new regimen, Peter's symptoms were much improved. He was able to tolerate his food better and began to regain his lost weight.

ease. Symptoms can flare up in periods of unusual or prolonged stress, but stress doesn't appear to cause the disease.

MEDICAL TREATMENT

Crohn's disease has no cure, but a combination of antibiotics and steroids usually alleviates symptoms. Surgery is often needed to correct complications, such as an intestinal blockage, perforation, and abscesses. Sometimes it is necessary to remove the diseased section of bowel; unfortunately, this does not prevent recurrences in other portions of the intestinal tract.

NUTRITIONAL APPROACHES

Nutritional deficiencies are common in individuals with Crohn's disease for several reasons. During a flare-up, symptoms squelch appetite, and a person is unlikely to consume enough food to maintain weight and good nutrition. Nutrition can be a problem even during periods of remission; if the small intestine is damaged by inflammation, vitamins and nutrients are not absorbed properly. Surgical removal of portions of the intestine further impairs the body's ability to absorb nutrients.

Although some doctors advise patients to avoid all fried foods, dairy products, spices, and high-fiber foods, there is no specific diet for Crohn's disease. The overall objective is to consume adequate calories, vitamins, and minerals without exacerbating symptoms. Try eliminating any food that seems to create problems for several weeks, and keep a diary of symptoms to determine whether giving it up is helpful. Eliminate only one type of food at a time, such as milk and other dairy products.

High-fiber foods are generally discouraged because they may be irritating to the intestines, and they can also exacerbate diarrhea. Alcohol should be avoided as it can worsen intestinal bleeding; it lowers the body's immunity; and it can contribute to malnutrition.

Consuming six or more small meals a day is less likely to provoke symptoms than having three large ones. Eat slowly and chew each mouthful thoroughly in order to improve digestion.

Even patients who can consume a normal diet may develop nutritional deficiencies because of poor absorption of nutrients; thus, many patients need to take a daily multivitamin and mineral supplement. High-dose vitamins should only be taken under a doctor's supervision. Those who develop vitamin B_{12} deficiency, for example, often need to take it by injection if they lack the intestinal substances to metabolize it.

SPECIAL SUPPLEMENTS

Patients with severe symptoms or who have had extensive surgery may need a special high-calorie liquid formula, either as a nutritional supplement or as a replacement for normal meals. Again, such supplements should be prescribed by a doctor or clinical dietitian. In unusual cases, an elemental diet—a low-fat, easy-to-digest formula—may be prescribed. Unfortunately, an elemental formula often has an unpleasant taste, but if the patient is unable to drink it, it can be given through a feeding tube (known as enteral nutrition).

The most severe cases of Crohn's disease may require total parenteral nutrition (TPN), in which all nutrients are given intravenously. TPN is most beneficial for patients who need to rest their intestinal tract so it can heal or who are unable to absorb enough nourishment from their regular diets. This approach is also beneficial in treating a child whose growth is being stunted by inadequate nutrition. Because it can be administered at home, TPN allows for a more normal lifestyle. A recent study has shown that enterically coated fish oil supplements significantly reduced the rate of flare-ups in Crohn's disease patients over a one-year period.

CUCUMBERS

BENEFITS
- *Low in calories.*
- *A good source of fiber.*
- *A fair source of vitamin C and folate.*

DRAWBACKS
- *Some are coated with wax to extend shelf life.*

Cucumbers belong to the same plant family as melons, pumpkins, and winter squash, but they are not as nutritious. An 8-inch slicing cucumber provides only about 15 percent of the Recommended Nutrient Intake (RNI) of vitamin C and smaller amounts of folate and potassium. The skin contains some beta carotene, but cucumbers are often peeled, especially if they've been sprayed with wax to retard spoilage.

Because cucumbers are approximately 95 percent water, they are very low in calories; a cup of slices contains less than 15 calories. Folk healers often recommend cucumbers as a natural diuretic, but any increased urination is probably due to their water content rather than an inherent substance.

In Canada cucumbers are used mostly as a salad ingredient or as PICKLES. Commercially, they are used mainly to make pickles and relishes; cucumber juice contains some alpha hydroxy acids, which improve the effectiveness of facial masks, and other cosmetic products.

In many countries cucumbers are an important staple; worldwide, they rank ninth among vegetable crops with multiple uses. In India and Central Europe, for example, they are diced and mixed with herbs and yogurt to serve as a salad. They are also stuffed and baked or served as a cooked side dish.

CURRANTS

BENEFITS
- *An excellent low-calorie source of vitamin C and potassium.*
- *High in bioflavonoids.*

DRAWBACKS
- *Fresh currants are highly perishable and are available for only a few weeks in the summer.*

The several varieties of fresh currants are actually berries that are related to GOOSEBERRIES. The fruit marketed as dried currants is a variety of GRAPE, and thus a type of raisin.

Red and white currants are the most common types available in North America, usually for only a short time during the summer. Black currants (cultivated mostly in Europe) lead both the red and white types in nutritional value. A cup of black currants provides a whopping 260mg of vitamin C, more than eight times the Recommended Nutrient Intake (RNI), as well as 490mg of potassium. This compares with 55mg of vitamin C and 340mg of potassium in a cup of red or white currants (also good amounts of these essential nutrients). All types are low in calories, about 70 in a cup of fresh berries. Currants are also a good source of fiber, providing about 2g per cup.

Because they are quite tart, fresh currants usually are not eaten raw; instead, they are used in baking or to make jams, jellies, and sauces. Diluted and sweetened black currant juice is a refreshing beverage that is very high in vitamin C. The juice can be fermented and made into liqueurs and cordials.

MEDICINAL USES

All varieties of currants are rich in BIO-FLAVONOIDS, pigments that are thought to boost the ANTIOXIDANT effects of vitamin C; they also help inhibit cancer growth and may possibly prevent other diseases. Europeans have long valued black currants for their antibacterial and anti-inflammatory properties, which are thought to come from anthocyanin, a bioflavonoid in the berry skins. In Scandinavia a powder made from dried black currant skins is used to treat diarrhea, especially that caused by *Escherichia coli,* a common cause of bacterial diarrhea. Europeans also use black currant syrup to ease the inflammation of a sore throat.

CYSTIC FIBROSIS

CONSUME PLENTY OF
- *Fish, poultry, eggs, meat, and other high-protein foods for growth.*
- *Starchy foods and a moderate amount of sweets for energy.*
- *Fat (as much as can be tolerated) for extra calories.*
- *Salt to replace that lost in sweat.*
- *Fluids to prevent constipation.*

AVOID
- *Low-calorie products.*

A genetic disease that afflicts about one in every 2,500 children born in Canada, cystic fibrosis affects the glands that produce mucus, sweat, enzymes, and other secretions. The most serious consequences of the disease occur in the lungs, pancreas, and intestines, all of which become clogged with thick mucus. As the lungs become congested, they are especially vulnerable to pneumonia and other infections. When the ducts that normally carry pancreatic enzymes to the small intestine become clogged, difficulty in breaking down fats and protein is the result, along with other digestive problems. Abnormal amounts of salt are lost in sweat and saliva, which can lead to serious imbalances in body chemistry.

At the moment there is no cure for cystic fibrosis, although scientists are testing gene therapy as a means of correcting the underlying genetic defect. In the meantime, a combination of an enriched diet, vitamin supplements, replacement enzymes, antibiotics and other medications, and regular postural drainage to clear mucus from the lungs has greatly improved the outlook for people with cystic fibrosis.

NUTRITIONAL NEEDS

Since diet is critical in the overall treatment of cystic fibrosis, the treatment team usually includes a clinical dietitian. In order to grow properly, children with cystic fibrosis typically need to consume many more calories than are normally recommended. (The level of consumption necessary varies considerably from one child to another, however; some can get by on a regular diet, but most need to increase their calorie intake two- or three-fold.)

In the past it was almost impossible to meet these markedly increased calorie demands because of the body's inability to digest and absorb fats and protein. The development of improved enzyme preparations to supplement or replace those normally produced by the pancreas has helped solve this problem. These supplemental enzymes, in the form of tablets, capsules, or powder, must be taken with every meal and snack to aid digestion.

There is no special diet for cystic fibrosis; rather, the child is encouraged to take larger portions during meals and have more frequent snacks. Babies with the disease may be given a special formula that contains predigested fats. For older children, high-protein foods, such as meat, poultry, fish, eggs, and milk, are emphasized, along with as much fat as the child can tolerate to help meet the need for extra calories. Vitamin and mineral supplements are often necessary, but these should be taken only under the supervision of a doctor or clinical dietitian experienced in treating cystic fibrosis.

Salt is also an essential part of the diet, because cystic fibrosis affects the sweat and salivary glands, causing them to excrete abnormal amounts of sodium and chloride in perspiration and saliva. This situation can be especially critical during hot weather or exercise, when it may be necessary to consume extra salt. Otherwise, adding moderate amounts of salt to flavor foods should be sufficient to maintain adequate levels of sodium.

If digestive problems develop despite taking enzymes, supplements of predigested fats may be prescribed, and in some cases, calorie-enriched supplements may be necessary. Usually these can be taken by mouth, but in severe cases they are administered at night through a feeding tube. Intravenous feeding (parenteral nutrition or hyperalimentation) is rarely necessary, but if required, it can be given at home.

Some people with cystic fibrosis may also develop DIABETES if the pancreas becomes so clogged that it can no longer make adequate insulin, the hormone needed to metabolize carbohydrates. In such cases, insulin injections are added to the regimen. Constipation and even intestinal obstruction are common in cystic fibrosis. It's important to consume adequate water and other fluids, but large amounts of high-fiber foods generally are not recommended because they are filling and do not provide adequate calories. Instead, a doctor may prescribe a special laxative to prevent constipation.

DIETARY DIFFERENCES

Parents often find it difficult to reconcile the dietary recommendations for a child with cystic fibrosis with what is urged for healthy people. It's important to understand that the nutritional needs of a person with cystic fibrosis are very different from those of a healthy person. A high-calorie diet with as much protein and fat as can be tolerated is necessary to compensate for the large quantity of nutrients lost because of digestive problems

caused by the disease. Prescription enzymes that improve absorption of fats and protein have made a big difference in living with cystic fibrosis. Fats provide more calories per unit than other nutrients, so they are a critical source of energy. The body also needs fat in order to absorb vitamins A, D, E, and K.

In the absence of diabetes, it's not necessary to restrict sweets and other sugary foods. These simple carbohydrates are more easily absorbed than starches, so they are an important source of energy. However, sweet snacks should be accompanied by a source of protein to provide balance and the amino acids that are needed for growth, immune function, and repair and maintenance of body tissue.

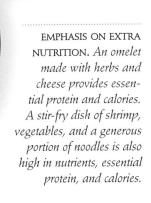

EMPHASIS ON EXTRA NUTRITION. *An omelet made with herbs and cheese provides essential protein and calories. A stir-fry dish of shrimp, vegetables, and a generous portion of noodles is also high in nutrients, essential protein, and calories.*

DATES

BENEFITS
- *An excellent source of potassium.*
- *A good source of iron and calcium.*
- *High in fiber.*

DRAWBACKS
- *High sugar content and stickiness promote tooth decay.*

Prized for their sweet fruits, date palms are among the oldest cultivated trees; they have been grown in North Africa for at least 8,000 years. These desert trees are extraordinarily fruitful, producing up to 200 dates in a cluster.

Fresh dates are classified according to their moisture content, falling into three categories: soft, semisoft, and dry. Most varieties in North America are semisoft, which are marketed fresh as well as dried after part of their moisture has evaporated.

With 60 to 70 percent of their weight coming from sugar, dates are one of the sweetest of all fruits. One-half cup (about 12 medium dates) contains about 275 calories—many more than most fruits. They are very high in potassium; 12 dates provide 650mg, several times more than a comparable amount of other high-potassium foods, such as bananas and oranges. Twelve dates also provide 6 percent or more of the adult Recommended Nutrient Intakes (RNIs) of iron, niacin, and vitamin B_6, as well as 2g of fiber. However, dates have almost no vitamin C.

Dates contain tyramine, an organic compound found in aged cheese, certain processed meats, red wine, and other products. Anyone taking monoamine oxidase (MAO) inhibitors to treat depression should avoid dates, because tyramine can interact with these drugs to produce a life-threatening rise in blood pressure. In some people, tyramine can also trigger migraine headaches.

It's important to brush your teeth after eating dates. Both the dried and fresh fruits are very sticky, and because of their high sugar content, they can lead to dental decay if bits are allowed to adhere to the teeth.

DEHYDRATION

CONSUME PLENTY OF
- *Water, juice, milk, and other fluids, especially in warm weather or during intense exercise workouts.*
- *Fruits and vegetables high in water.*

CUT DOWN ON
- *Caffeine, which has a diuretic effect.*

AVOID
- *Alcohol and diuretic drugs.*

WATER is by far the single most important component of the human body—on average about 60 percent by weight. Outside human cells, water transports nutrients and wastes; it also acts as a lubricant and shock absorber. Inside the cells, water is the solvent in which all chemical reactions take place. During respiration and perspiration, water removes excess heat from the body.

While humans can survive for several weeks without food, lack of

WATER TO GO. *Water has become a popular portable beverage, especially during hot weather.*

water, or dehydration, can be fatal in just a few days. If you lose more than about $1\frac{1}{2}$ cups of water through perspiration or excretion, thirst prods you to find water. Similarly, eating salty foods also triggers thirst, because the body needs to maintain a delicate balance between fluids and sodium and other salts. Even so, feelings of thirst that prompt a person to drink lag behind the body's actual need for water; by the time you feel thirsty, you may already be dehydrated. This fact can be critically important during periods of rapid water loss, such as prolonged exercise, diarrhea, or severe bleeding. In such cases, kidney damage may develop before thirst sets in.

Everyone should drink at least six to eight glasses of nonalcoholic fluids a day. Consuming fresh fruits and vegetables also increases fluid intake. Athletes and outdoor workers should drink extra fluids before, during, and after prolonged physical activity.

Those at risk for dehydration (or their caregivers) need to pay special attention to fluid intake. Babies, for example, can quickly become dehydrated, because they perspire over a large surface area in relation to their fluid volume. Furthermore, they are unable to tell you when they are thirsty. Elderly

people risk dehydration because body tissues lose water with aging; they also become less sensitive to thirst. Consequently, severe bleeding or illnesses that cause fever, vomiting, and diarrhea are especially hazardous to both the very young and the elderly.

People on high-protein weight-loss diets or body-building regimes also risk dehydration, because the body uses more water to get rid of protein waste products. Dieters who use diuretics to shed excess pounds through fluid loss are fooling themselves. The weight will be gained back as soon as the body restores its fluid balance.

DENTAL DISORDERS

EAT PLENTY OF
- *Calcium-rich foods, such as low-fat milk, yogurt, and cheese.*
- *Fresh fruits and vegetables for vitamins A and C, and for chewing in order to promote healthy gums.*

CUT DOWN ON
- *Dried fruits and other sticky foods that lodge between the teeth.*

AVOID
- *Sweet drinks and snacks.*
- *Steady sipping of acidic drinks for prolonged periods.*

In addition to brushing and flossing, a prudent diet (with natural or added fluoride) protects teeth from decay and keeps the gums healthy. Tooth decay (cavities and dental caries) and gum disease are caused by colonies of bacteria that constantly coat the teeth with a sticky film called plaque. If plaque is not brushed away, these bacteria break down the sugars and starches in foods to produce acids that wear away the tooth enamel. The plaque also hardens into tartar, which can lead to gum inflammation, or gingivitis.

A well-balanced diet provides the minerals, vitamins, and other nutrients essential for healthy teeth and gums. Fluoride, occurring naturally in foods and water, or added to the water supply, can reduce the rate of cavities by as much as 60 percent.

DENTAL HEALTH GUIDELINES
Make sure that children's teeth get off to a good start by eating sensibly during pregnancy. Particularly important are calcium, which helps to form strong teeth and bones, and vitamin D, which the body needs to absorb calcium. Low-fat dairy products, canned fish (such as sardines or salmon consumed with the bones), and dark green leafy vegetables are all excellent sources of calcium. Vitamin D is obtained from egg yolks, fortified dairy products, and moderate exposure to the sun.

To a large extent, dental caries can be prevented by giving children fluoride in the first few years of life. Pediatricians usually recommend fluoride supplements for babies. Adults also benefit from fluoride; the amount provided in the water or in fluoridated toothpaste is usually adequate.

In addition to calcium and fluoride, minerals needed for the formation of tooth enamel include phosphorus (richly supplied in meat, fish, and eggs) and magnesium (found in whole grains, spinach, and bananas). Vitamin A also helps build strong bones and teeth. Good sources of beta carotene, which the body turns into vitamin A, include orange-colored fruits and vegetables and dark green leafy vegetables.

Children are particularly vulnerable to tooth decay; parents should provide a good diet throughout childhood, brush children's teeth until they're mature enough to do a thorough job by themselves (usually by 6 or 7 years old), and supervise twice-daily brushing and flossing thereafter. Parents should never put babies or toddlers to bed accompanied by a bottle of milk (which contains the natural sugar lactose), juice, or other sweet drink, nor should they dip pacifiers in honey or syrup.

THE SUGAR FACTOR
Sucrose, most familiar to us as granulated sugar, is the leading cause of tooth decay, but it is far from the only culprit. Although sugary foods, including cookies, candies, and sodas, are major offenders, starchy foods (such as breads and cereals) also play an important part in tooth decay. When starches mix with amylase, an enzyme in saliva, the result is an acid bath that erodes the enamel and makes teeth more susceptible to decay. If starchy foods linger in the mouth, the acid bath is prolonged, and the potential for damage is all the greater.

Dried fruits can have an adverse effect on teeth, because they are high in sugar and cling to the teeth. Even unsweetened fruit juices can contribute to tooth decay—they are acidic and contain relatively high levels of simple sugars. Drinks containing artificial sweeteners can also do harm because they increase the acidity of the mouth.

Fresh fruit, although both sweet and acidic, is much less likely to cause a problem, because chewing stimulates the saliva flow. Saliva decreases mouth acidity and washes away food particles. Thus, a chronically DRY MOUTH also contributes to dental decay, because saliva flow is reduced during sleep, and therefore, going to bed without brushing the teeth is especially harmful. Certain drugs, including those used for high BLOOD PRESSURE and some tranquilizers, also cut down saliva flow.

HELPFUL FOODS
You can protect your teeth by concluding meals with foods that do not promote cavities and may even prevent

them. For instance, Cheddar and some other aged CHEESES help prevent dental decay if consumed at the end of a meal. The tannins and cocoa in CHOCOLATE help to reduce the impact of its sugar. Chewing sugarless gum stimulates the flow of saliva, which decreases acid and flushes out food particles.

GUM DISEASE

More teeth are lost through gum disease than through tooth decay. Gum disease is likely to strike anyone who neglects oral hygiene or eats a poor diet. Particularly at risk are individuals with ALCOHOLISM, MALNUTRITION, or AIDS, or who are being treated with steroid drugs or certain cancer chemotherapies. Regular brushing and flossing help to prevent puffy, sore, and inflamed gums.

Gingivitis, a very common condition that causes the gums to redden, swell, and bleed, is typically caused by the gradual buildup of plaque. Treatment requires good dental hygiene and removal of plaque by a dentist or dental hygienist. Left untreated, gingivitis can lead to periodontitis—an advanced infection of the gums that causes teeth to loosen and fall out.

Bleeding gums may also be a sign that your intake of vitamin C is deficient. Be sure that your diet includes plenty of fresh fruits and vegetables every day; munching on hard, fibrous foods, such as a celery stick or carrot, stimulates the gums.

DEPRESSION

EAT PLENTY OF
- *High-grade proteins, such as meat, dairy products, eggs, and fresh fish for tryptophan and choline to promote good nervous system function.*

CUT DOWN ON
- *Alcohol, which can be a depressant.*
- *Caffeine, which can interfere with sleep and mood.*

AVOID
- *Foods and drinks that contain tyramine (if you are taking MAO inhibitors).*

Throughout a long and productive life, Winston Churchill lived in dread of visitations by the "black dog," as he called his periodic bouts of paralyzing depression. Other writers, seeking to describe the anguish of clinical depression, have told of trying to find the way through a thick yellow fog or being kept from the sunlight by a trailing black cloud. Clinical depression is quite different from the normal "down" reaction to disappointment. Depression is a serious disorder, probably caused by a disturbance in brain chemistry. It can strike out of the blue and—for a few of the more fortunate sufferers—can disappear just as mysteriously. Many sufferers can benefit from medications to lift their mood.

One of the classic signs of depression is a dramatic change in eating patterns. Some people lose all desire to eat, while others develop voracious appetites, especially for carbohydrates. People with

---

Case Study

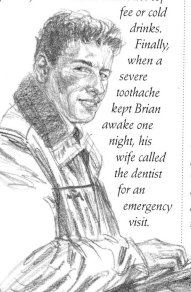

Brian, a 25-year-old mailman, knew he should see a dentist when he began to experience persistent throbbing pain in one of his molars. The pain was especially bad when he drank hot coffee or cold drinks. Finally, when a severe toothache kept Brian awake one night, his wife called the dentist for an emergency visit.

Neglect of a cavity had allowed an abscess to form at the base of Brian's molar. The dentist gave him a pain reliever and began treatment with antibiotics. Because of some unhappy childhood experiences with dental treatment, Brian had put off going to the dentist for several years. He was surprised to find, thanks to the dentist's up-to-date equipment and gentle approach, that treatment for his abscess was practically painless.

With the abscess successfully treated, Brian and the dentist agreed on a comprehensive plan to take immediate care of several long-standing problems. In addition, Brian vowed to maintain his dental health with regular appointments. The dentist advised Brian to snack on fresh fruits or vegetables, instead of the candy bars he sometimes used for pick-me-ups, and to chew only sugarless gum. He also reminded him to keep a toothbrush at work for daytime hygiene and to make sure that his meals included a balance of lean meat or fish and vegetables with fruits and cheese for dessert. He cautioned Brian to avoid soft foods that didn't require chewing.

depression typically have little energy. Other common signs of depression include an unshakable feeling of sadness, inability to experience pleasure, early morning awakening or multiple awakenings throughout the night, insomnia, excessive sleepiness, other sleep disorders, inability to concentrate, and indecisiveness. Feelings of worthlessness or excessive guilt may be accompanied by recurrent thoughts of death. An individual who has some or all of these symptoms nearly every day for more than two weeks may be suffering from major depression.

Elderly sufferers do not always have the classic signs of depression; instead, they may show signs of dementia, complain of aches and pains, and appear agitated, anxious, or irritable. If you notice the symptoms of depression in someone close to you, try to persuade the person to see a doctor.

Depression is more common in people with Parkinson's disease, stroke, arthritis, thyroid disorders, and cancer. In these cases, it can be difficult to sort out whether the individual is feeling depressed because he has a serious illness or whether the underlying disease has triggered a chemical change in the brain. Depression also can be a side effect of many medications taken for other existing conditions; these include beta blockers for hypertension, digoxin and other drugs for heart disease, indomethacin and other painkillers, corticosteroids (including prednisone), anti-parkinsonism drugs, antihistamines, and oral contraceptives and other hormonal agents.

DIETARY FACTORS

Individuals with depression often fail to take care of themselves, neglecting their appearance and eating irregularly. Nutritious food is needed by the human body to cope with any disease, but unfortunately, depressed people are especially likely to be careless about their nutrition. The resulting poor nourishment may impede recovery.

As yet, however, there is really no scientific evidence to back claims that poor diet actually causes emotional problems, including depression. Even acting on possibly valid claims may be dangerous to health. For example, there is some evidence that the amino acid tryptophan, a substance needed to make the neurotransmitter serotonin, can help induce sleep and play a role in treating certain types of depression. As a result, tryptophan supplements were touted in the late 1980s as a panacea for depression and insomnia. Tragically, this led to several thousand cases—nearly two dozen of them fatal—of a rare muscle disorder. The problem was caused by a manufacturing error that led to the introduction of a contaminant into the supplements. Consequently, both the Canadian and U.S. governments have banned the sale of tryptophan supplements. Nevertheless, adequate tryptophan is available in a healthful balanced diet; it is especially abundant in turkey, but it is also found in meat and other animal products.

Choline, a nutrient that is grouped with the B vitamins, has been studied in the management of depression and other psychiatric problems. It may be just as well that the results of the studies were doubtful, because choline supplements usually cause an unpleasant fishy odor in individuals who take them. Choline is abundant in many foods, including the lecithin in eggs, liver, and soybeans. Unlike the supplements, dietary forms of choline do not cause a fishy odor.

When some sugar-sensitive people eat large quantities of sweets, they may experience an energetic "high" followed by a "low" with weakness and "jitters" when the sugar is metabolized. If you believe that you may be oversensitive to certain foods, keeping a food diary over a period of weeks could help you to link food intake and sensitivity with mood swings. Eliminating the culprits may help to stabilize your moods.

DRUG-FOOD INTERACTIONS

Antidepressant drugs in the class called monoamine oxidase (MAO) inhibitors can have serious side effects when taken with certain foods. These drugs include phenelzine (Nardil) and tranylcypromine (Parnate). If you're taking one of these drugs, your blood pressure could rise dangerously if you eat foods rich in tyramines.

Tyramine-rich foods that should be avoided completely include beer and ale; avocados, bananas, and figs; bean curd and soy sauce; fish roe (including caviar) and dried fish; Cheddar and other ripened cheeses (soft varieties, such as cottage cheese, are fine); such organ meats as liver; liquid and powdered protein dietary supplements; preserved meats (bologna, pepperoni, and salami); and certain wines (including Chianti and champagne).

Coffee, tea, colas, chocolate, weight-loss dietary supplements containing cocoa, yeast, yeast extracts, fava beans, and ginseng contain small amounts of tyramine but are generally safe if taken only occasionally and in small amounts.

DRUGS AND WEIGHT

Another class of antidepressant drugs, called selective serotonin reuptake inhibitors, can reduce appetite, leading to a slight but ongoing weight loss. These drugs include fluoxetine (Prozac), sertraline (Zoloft), and paroxetine (Paxil). You may need to make a special effort to maintain weight during treatment with any of these medications.

Tricyclic antidepressants, which can cause weight gain, include imipramine (Tofranil), amitriptyline (Elavil), and nortriptyline (Pamelor). If you are overweight to begin with or gain weight while taking any of these drugs, ask your doctor to suggest an alternative.

DIABETES

CONSUME

For insulin-dependent diabetes

- *Regular meals and snacks to avoid fluctuations in blood sugar levels.*
- *A balance of starches, protein, and fats at each meal.*
- *Oats, fruits, and other foods that are high in soluble fiber.*

For non-insulin-dependent diabetes

- *Low-fat, high-fiber foods to achieve and maintain a normal weight.*

CUT DOWN ON

- *Bran cereals, which can reduce the absorption of iron, zinc, and other minerals.*
- *Miller's bran and supplements, which may cause bloating and flatulence.*
- *Excessive sweets and sugar, which produce a rapid rise in blood sugar.*
- *Saturated fats and foods that are high in cholesterol.*
- *Salty foods to prevent a rise in blood pressure.*

AVOID

- *Smoking and alcohol.*
- *Any abrupt changes in diet and exercise.*

About 1.5 million Canadians have diabetes mellitus, a serious, chronic disease that impairs the body's ability to derive energy from blood sugar, or glucose. Persons with diabetes either cannot produce or cannot respond to insulin, a hormone instrumental in glucose metabolism. Because all human body tissues must have a steady supply of glucose, diabetes can affect every organ. In particular, it can lead to heart disease, kidney failure, blindness, and nerve problems. In Canada, diabetes is the cause of 50 percent of all nontraumatic amputations and one of the leading causes of death, both of which can often be prevented by early, effective treatment.

There are two kinds of diabetes. About 10 percent of Canadians with diabetes have type I, or insulin-dependent diabetes mellitus (IDDM), which is also called juvenile-onset diabetes because it often develops in children and young adults. In this autoimmune disease, the body's mechanisms for protecting itself from foreign organisms are turned against its own healthy tissue. Because this type of diabetes often develops in the aftermath of an infection, such as chicken pox, some researchers theorize that after destroying the invaders, the immune system keeps on attacking but turns on body tissue. The result is destruction of the cells that produce insulin in the pancreas.

About 90 percent of Canadians with diabetes have type II, or non-insulin-dependent diabetes mellitus (NIDDM). Also termed adult-onset diabetes, this form occurs in overweight middle-aged and older adults. Although these people often have adequate or even high levels of insulin, they cannot use it properly.

When the first symptoms of type I diabetes strike (see Case Study, right), an urgent call to the doctor is the norm. In contrast, the early symptoms of type II diabetes are hardly noticeable. Some people are aware only of gradually increasing fatigue. Others may note drowsiness, increased thirst, blurred vision, slow healing of cuts, itchy skin, or frequent skin infections. Type II diabetes may go undiagnosed until there is a serious complication, such as a heart attack or stroke. The Canadian Diabetes Association (CDA) estimates that 750,000 Canadians have type II diabetes and don't know it. Although they may not experience any obvious symptoms, the disease may be damaging the heart, blood vessels, nerves, kidneys, eyes, and other organs. While much of this damage is permanent, it can be prevented with early treatment. Therefore,

Case Study

*A*my, a normally energetic teenager, began to suffer from fatigue, irritability, unusual thirst, increased urination, and hunger, despite losing weight. When she started vomiting, her parents made an immediate doctor's appointment. Blood tests revealed that she had type I diabetes.

To stabilize her condition, Amy was hospitalized and given fluids, glucose, and insulin. She and her parents were counseled by a diabetes educator and a registered dietitian. Amy learned how to give herself insulin injections and check her blood sugar levels with a glucose monitor several times a day in order to adjust her medication to keep her blood glucose levels stable. Her family paid special attention to the instructions on planning meals and snacks to ensure good nutrition with adequate calories for growth and energy.

However, there were some setbacks. Amy caught a cold, her blood sugar went out of control, and she ended up back in the hospital. She learned that any infection or stress affects the body's glucose needs, and the diabetes educator showed Amy and her mother how to adjust her insulin dosage. Amy also learned that her insulin needs rose during menstruation. With practice and sessions with her diabetes educator, Amy has resumed her activities and is successfully controlling her condition.

adults over the age of 50 should have their blood sugar levels tested every 2 years, or more often if they are overweight or if their doctors recommend it.

Diabetics must carefully balance food intake and exercise. Most people with type II diabetes can manage with diet and exercise alone; however, some may need oral medications to improve the effect of their own insulin, and a few may need insulin injections. Type I diabetics require daily insulin injections for survival. (Insulin must be injected because it's made up of proteins that are broken down in the intestinal tract.)

People with diabetes should carry an ID card describing their illness, their usual treatment, including medications and doses, and measures to be taken in an emergency.

THE WEIGHT CONNECTION

The prevalence of type II diabetes is increasing as more Canadian baby boomers move into the high-risk age groups and become increasingly overweight. Not every overweight person will get diabetes, but 85 percent of type II diabetics weigh more than they should. Extra fat, especially abdominal fat in the "apple-shape" body, causes insulin resistance. Newly diagnosed, overweight type II diabetics may banish the disease by dieting to reach and maintain their ideal weight. Even if they don't reach their ideal weight, any loss makes the disease easier to control with diet and exercise alone.

DIET AND DIABETES

A fundamental element in managing diabetes is diet. A good one can stop symptoms, stabilize blood sugar levels,

and lower the risk of complications. The CDA urges every patient to consult a registered dietitian to work out a diet tailored to individual tastes and needs. The CDA now emphasizes meal plans that take into consideration the overall diabetes management as well as age and related health concerns, such as elevated blood cholesterol levels and hypertension. In order to maintain normal blood glucose levels, meals and snacks must be balanced to provide a mixture of CARBOHYDRATES, FATS, and PROTEINS. Children must have adequate calories for growth; a teenager's meal plan should allow flexibility to match an often erratic schedule. Adults may need to reduce fat, cholesterol, and protein intake to protect against heart and kidney disease. An overweight person with type II diabetes needs to focus on

weight loss by cutting 200 to 300 calories from his daily diet and increasing exercise to burn up more.

For most diabetics, complex carbohydrates (vegetables, breads, cereals, and pasta) should make up the bulk of the diet. Because their FIBER content slows the release of glucose, high-fiber starches—such as whole-grain bread, beans, peas, and lentils—help suppress a sharp increase in blood sugar after high-carbohydrate meals. High-grade protein (lean meats, meat substitutes, and low-fat dairy items) should supply 10 to 20 percent of daily calories. FRUITS are a nutritious source of simple sugar. If using canned fruits, buy

121

them packed in natural juices instead of syrup. Ounce for ounce, dried fruits have more concentrated sugar than fresh. Be careful to limit salt and salty foods if you have high BLOOD PRESSURE, a complication of diabetes.

In contrast to earlier CDA recommendations, the new dietary guidelines allow leeway in eating simple carbohydrates. It is no longer an iron-clad rule that syrups, sugars, and sweeteners must be avoided in favor of vegetables, breads, cereals, pasta, and other complex carbohydrates. The emphasis is now on monitoring total carbohydrate consumption rather than the source of

---

PREGNANCY-RELATED DIABETES

Gestational diabetes mellitus can complicate pregnancy for both mother and baby. The effects of hormonal changes and weight gain during pregnancy increase demands on the pancreas and lead to insulin resistance. Gestational diabetes can strike any expectant mother but is most likely in those who are over 30 years of age and overweight, as well as those who have had a previous baby weighing more than 9 pounds or a family history of gestational or type II diabetes.

All women should have a blood test for diabetes between the 24th and 28th weeks of pregnancy. If gestational diabetes is diagnosed, the mother will need to modify her diet and monitor weight gain carefully; she may require daily insulin injections for the rest of the pregnancy. Although this type of diabetes usually disappears almost immediately after childbirth, women who have had it are at high risk for type II diabetes in later years.

---

the carbohydrate: A cookie will have no more effect on blood glucose than mashed potatoes, provided the total amount of carbohydrate is the same. Still, all carbohydrates are not equal when it comes to nutrition. Starches provide vitamins, minerals, and fiber, whereas sugar and sweeteners provide mostly calories; therefore, starches should make up the bulk of the diabetic diet, and sugar only a small amount.

FOOD CHOICES

The CDA has produced the Good Health Eating Guide that classifies foods into seven distinct categories: starchy foods, fruits and vegetables, milk, sugars, protein foods, fats and oils, and extras. Each food choice within a category has about the same nutrient composition, therefore food choices are readily exchanged.

The CDA has also assigned easily recognized symbols to each food category. A starch choice is indicated by a square, a fat choice by a triangle, and a sugar choice by a star. Food producers can now cater to the diabetic market by labeling foods with the appropriate symbols. A serving of chips, for example, may be marked with a square and two triangles, indicating that it represents one starch and two fat food choices. To properly plan meals, diabetics must develop a familiarity with food choices as described in the Good Health Eating Guide and follow a dietitian's advice about the number of choices from each category that is required for proper insulin balance.

WARNING ON FIBER

Some diabetics have gastrointestinal complications that delay the passage of food; this can interfere with blood glucose control by delaying the absorption of nutrients and oral diabetes medications. Patients with this problem should avoid whole grains and some of the other high-fiber foods. To prevent con-

---

stipation, poached fruits, steamed leafy vegetables, and other sources of soluble fiber can be substituted. A diabetes educator or nutritionist can provide extra help in low-fiber meal planning.

DIARRHEA

CONSUME PLENTY OF

- *Water, mineral water, herbal teas, ginger ale, apple juice, broth, or low-sugar sports beverages to replace lost fluids, salts, and minerals.*
- *Binding foods in the BRAT diet.*
- *Skinless baked potatoes, boiled or poached eggs, and other bland foods as the bowels return to normal.*

AVOID

- *Citrus juices.*
- *Most other foods, especially salads, fruits, and whole grains, until bowel function normalizes.*
- *Alcohol, which is dehydrating, and caffeine, which stimulates the bowel, for 48 hours after the symptoms disappear.*

Acute infectious diarrhea is one of the world's most common ailments. An estimated 5 billion cases occur every year, and in North America, diarrhea is runner-up only to the common cold as a cause for absences from work. Although diarrhea causes fatalities—due to dehydration—it is seldom a threat in affluent, well-nourished societies, except to such vulnerable groups as babies, the elderly, and invalids. In the developing countries, many deaths have been prevented with the use of a homemade rehydration fluid that has been promoted through the World Health Organization (WHO) efforts.

THE DEFINITION

Diarrhea—the frequent passage of loose, watery stools—is not a disease but a symptom of an underlying problem. It is most commonly brought on

WHEN TO CALL A DOCTOR

Mild diarrhea can usually be self-managed. But call your doctor promptly for any of the following:

• Diarrhea that lasts more than 2 days (1 day for a child under two, a frail elderly person, or someone with DIABETES) or if it worsens during that time.

• The appearance of blood, mucus, or worms in the feces.

• Severe abdominal pain.

• Diarrhea that is accompanied by vomiting or fever.

by FOOD POISONING, especially among TRAVELERS. Transient looseness can be caused by overconsumption of laxative foods (such as prunes), heavy use of sugarless chewing gum sweetened with sugar alcohol (such as sorbitol), and over-the-counter indigestion remedies containing magnesium. Emotional stress that causes IRRITABLE BOWEL SYNDROME may disrupt the normal bowel pattern with alternating diarrhea and constipation; similar symptoms occur in COLITIS and CROHN'S DISEASE, both inflammatory bowel disorders. In many instances, however, diarrhea develops without any identifiable cause. Unless the problem persists or recurs often, this is not a cause for concern.

DIETARY MANAGEMENT

Most cases of diarrhea are minor and short-lived and can be managed at home with simple dietary measures. Start by eliminating all solid foods and sipping warm or tepid drinks to prevent dehydration. Drinking half a cup of fluid every quarter hour or so is usually enough. Suitable drinks include water, mineral water, herbal teas, and ginger ale. Clear broths also help replace salts and other minerals lost with the diarrhea. You can make your own rehydration fluid by mixing $\frac{1}{4}$ teaspoon of baking soda, a pinch of salt, and $\frac{1}{4}$ teaspoon of corn syrup or honey in an 8-ounce glass of water or juice. If, instead, you choose a commercial sports drink for rehydration, check the label to make sure that the sugar content is low; anything over 10 percent can aggravate diarrhea.

When you feel like eating (but preferably not within the first 24 hours), start with bland, binding foods; most doctors recommend the BRAT diet (pictured below). Apples and other fruits high in pectin (a soluble fiber) help counteract diarrhea; that's why unsweetened applesauce is a traditional home remedy. Other suitable foods include salted crackers and chicken-rice soup to help replenish lost sodium and potassium. As the bowels return to normal, add such items as skinless baked potatoes and boiled or poached eggs.

Avoid milk products until symptoms disappear; some of the organisms that cause diarrhea can temporarily impair the ability to digest milk. Although cooked and pureed fruits and vegetables can usually be tolerated, don't eat raw fruits, high-fiber vegetables, and fats until bowel movements are back to normal. Because alcohol has a dehydrating effect and caffeine stimulates the bowel, both should be avoided for 48 hours after diarrhea stops.

RECURRENT DIARRHEA

Some people have recurrent or chronic diarrhea due to malabsorption of a particular nutrient. For example, in lactose INTOLERANCE, the sugar in milk passes intact into the colon, where it is fermented by bacteria, producing hydrogen gas, along with water retention, bloating, and diarrhea. If you think milk products may be causing episodic diarrhea, keep a food diary so you can see if there is a direct relationship between suspected foods and symptoms. In all cases of recurrent or chronic diarrhea, you should see your doctor.

Diarrhea is sometimes a side effect of treatment with antibiotics, which can kill off the normal intestinal bacteria along with infecting pathogens. In the past, it was debatable if eating yogurt was beneficial; however, recent studies indicate that the cultures in yogurt can, indeed, help restore "friendly" intestinal bacteria. Also, let your doctor know if you have diarrhea; he may be able to switch you to another antibiotic. Bowel movements will usually return to normal within a few days.

OTC REMEDIES

Over-the-counter (OTC) antidiarrheal drugs may give some relief when diarrhea has no obvious cause or is due to a minor illness, such as a flu, but many physicians believe that you will heal faster by letting nature take its course. Never use a nonprescription antidiarrhea product for more than 2 days without consulting your doctor.

THE BRAT DIET. *The diet's name is an acronym for its components—bananas, rice, applesauce, and toast.*

DIETING AND WEIGHT CONTROL

*There's no easy way to lose weight—crash diets
only worsen the problem. A successful diet allows gradual
weight loss and fosters a commitment to sensible eating.*

Despite what amounts to a national obsession with dieting, thinness, and fitness, we may be losing the battle of the bulge. Statistics show that more than 40 percent of adult Canadians are overweight. Of these, some 28 percent are obese, defined as being 20 percent or more over desirable weight for the body's size.

The only way to achieve successful weight control is through a lifelong commitment to sensible eating and regular EXERCISE. Losing extra weight is not an easy or quick task. The best way to trim down involves consuming fewer calories and expending more of them by exercising; thus the body uses up more energy than it takes in and depletes its fat stores. FAD DIETS don't work. Drastic measures to reduce in a hurry may produce dramatic results in the first week or two, but this is mainly because the body is losing water. Water weight rapidly comes back as soon as normal eating is resumed.

When dieting, experts suggest a goal of losing about a pound a week. There are 3,500 calories in a pound of stored fat, so reducing your intake by 500 calories a day can achieve this goal, provided you keep to a low-fat, balanced diet and exercise daily.

COMMON FALLACIES

Many people try diet pills and capsules, but science has yet to devise a magic pill for weight loss that is also safe to take. Some pills may help con-

trol the appetite, but they can also have serious side effects. Be wary of so-called "fat blockers" that claim to absorb fat, as well as "starch blockers" that promise to block starch digestion. These claims have not been proven. Also be wary of herbal weight-loss products—many of these are loaded with stimulants such as ephedrine that can provoke cardiac arrhythmias and other serious side effects.

Crash diets that replace healthful meals with low-calorie drinks do not provide a balance of essential nutrients. Instead, these diets encourage the yo-yo phenomenon, in which a person loses weight quickly and then gains it all back as soon as he returns to his normal eating habits. As a yo-yo dieter returns to his former weight, he will also have an increased percentage of body fat, which makes it harder to lose weight in the future. A change in body metabolism may unfairly be blamed for the extra weight, but it is probably due to repeated cycles of the deprivation that occurs while dieting, followed by food binging.

Fasting, even when plenty of water is consumed, can be very dangerous; it may lead to lowered blood pressure and heart failure. Weight loss is rarely sustained once eating is resumed.

Phony devices and gadgets that are promoted for weight loss are a waste of money, and some of them can even be dangerous. Far-fetched examples include weight-loss earrings that sup-

posedly stimulate acupuncture points that control hunger, as well as appetite-suppressing eyeglasses said to project an image onto the retina that dampens the desire to eat.

HEALTHY WEIGHT LOSS

A healthy diet for permanent weight loss must provide all the nutrients the body needs. The diet should be based on nutritious but lower-calorie foods, including vegetables, fruits, low-fat or nonfat dairy products, breads and cereals, fish, poultry, and small amounts of lean meat. Grains and other filling high-fiber foods can help stave off hunger. Unhealthy high-calorie foods should be cut back or eliminated. These include candy, cakes, cookies, and other sweet desserts, as well as nondiet soda pop and other sweetened drinks. Snack foods that are high in fat and salt, such as potato chips, salted nuts, and the like, also should be eliminated; alcohol, fatty meats, cheese, whole milk, cream, sauces, and fatty spreads should be restricted.

FAT-FIGHTING TIPS

The most effective way to reduce calorie intake is to cut down on fats; they are our most concentrated source of calories, providing more than twice as many as calories as protein or carbohydrate. Start by replacing some of the meat in your diet with fish or poultry. Remove the skin from poultry before you cook it, and banish the frying pan.

Prepare fish and poultry by steaming, grilling, baking, or microwaving. Select lean cuts of meat and trim off all the visible fat; stay away from sausages, bacon, and cold cuts (even low-fat versions tend to be high in fat).

Olestra, a new fat substitute, has been approved in the U.S. but not in Canada for use in fatty snack foods, such as potato chips. This synthetic compound of sugar and vegetable oil could well become the NutraSweet of fatty snack foods. Its use in food remains controversial, however. Olestra may cause such symptoms as cramps and diarrhea. Studies also indicate that it impairs the absorption of carotenoids, as well as the fat-soluble vitamins A, D, E, and K. These nutrients are important to retain; they have been linked to a decreased risk of cancer and other diseases.

Food companies have become more skilled at reducing fat without eliminating taste in many nonfat and low-fat dairy products. Try some of the new nonfat cheeses and yogurts. For a sweet dessert, consider nonfat frozen yogurt instead of ice cream.

Don't deprive yourself so much that you can't stick to your diet. Allow for an occasional treat of "forbidden foods," but don't binge. If your favorite snack is chocolate chip cookies, have one or two after every successful week of weight loss. This reward may help you to continue taking off the pounds.

During the first week of dieting, you may lose up to 3 pounds, due to an initial loss of water. After that, aim for a steady loss of 1 or 2 pounds a week. This allows you to lose weight without becoming overly hungry. Exercise raises the body's basal metabolic rate, thereby increasing energy expenditure even when not exercising.

Burn up calories by increasing your EXERCISE program. If you exercise less than twice a week, you should work up gradually to a program of sustained exercise for 20 to 30 minutes a day, 3 to 5 days a week.

BALANCING YOUR WEIGHT-LOSS DIET

Make sure you eat nourishing foods while you diet. Follow the recommendations in the Food Guide Rainbow in BASIC FOOD GROUPS (see p.40) and select a wide variety of the foods shown below. This sensible approach will provide optimum levels of nutrients while still allowing you to shed pounds.

FOOD TYPES	TIPS

STARCHY FOODS

Make rice, bread, potatoes, cereals, pasta, and other starches the staple foods in your diet; everything else revolves around them. Contrary to popular belief, starchy foods are not fattening. Breads and cereals contain no more calories per gram than lean meat and far less than fats.

Choose specialty breads that taste good on their own without spreads. Serve pasta and rice with tomato-based vegetable sauces, avoiding any made with cheese, cream, butter, or lots of oil.

FRUITS, VEGETABLES, AND SALADS

Include a wide variety of fresh fruits, vegetables, and salad greens.

Go easy on dried fruit, which is high in sugar, and avocados, which are high in fat. Avoid fattening salad dressings, such as mayonnaise; make your own based on lemon or lime juice and low-fat yogurt. Do not eat fried potatoes, such as French fries, or potatoes baked with a cheese sauce or served with sour cream.

MILK, CHEESE, AND YOGURT

Eat moderate amounts of low-fat dairy products.

Choose skim or 1% fat milk, nonfat yogurt, and low-fat cheeses, such as part-skim farmer's cheese and nonfat cottage cheese and ricotta. Avoid milk shakes made with ice cream; try nonfat frozen yogurt instead.

PROTEIN

Choose lean meat with all visible fat trimmed off, poultry with the skin removed, fish, and lentils, split peas, dried beans, and other legumes.

Steam, grill, bake, or poach—but do not fry. Eat nuts, nut butters, and seeds in moderation. Avoid high-fat meat products, such as hot dogs, sausages, bacon, and hamburgers. White fish, such as cod, is less fattening than oily fish. Avoid fish canned in oil.

FATTY AND SUGARY FOODS

Use low-fat spreads. Use oil, even olive oil, sparingly. Cutting down on fats is the best approach when you are trying to diet. The occasional (once or twice a week) sugary treat will do no harm, as moderate amounts of sugar do not cause obesity.

Avoid potato chips, cookies, cakes, and pies, as they contain a lot of hidden fat.

DIGESTIVE AND MALABSORPTION DISORDERS

CONSUME PLENTY OF

- *Fresh fruits, vegetables, whole-grain products, and other high-fiber foods to speed the digestive process.*
- *Fluids (at least six to eight 8-ounce glasses of water, juices, or other nonalcoholic fluids daily).*

CUT DOWN ON

- *Coffee, tea, colas, and other sources of caffeine.*
- *Refined carbohydrates.*
- *Fried foods and other high-fat foods.*

AVOID

- *Alcohol in all forms.*
- *Miller's or raw bran, which irritates the colon and interferes with the absorption of iron and other minerals.*
- *Any foods or beverages that provoke a flare-up of symptoms.*

Digestion refers to the overall process by which food is broken down mechanically and chemically and is converted to forms that can be absorbed by the body through the bloodstream. Only water, salt, and simple sugars, such as glucose, can be absorbed unchanged. Starches, fats, and proteins must be broken down into smaller molecules before they can be used. Proteins called enzymes aid in the breakdown of food.

The digestive process actually begins in the mouth. As food is broken into small pieces by chewing, it is mixed with saliva, which moistens it and supplies enzymes that start breaking down carbohydrates. Once the food has been sufficiently chewed, it is carried through the esophagus, which has a ring of muscles at its base that relaxes to open the passage to the stomach. The ring normally closes to prevent food and

HEALING HERBS

Some herbs are known to help troubled digestion. Ginger, for example, is reputed to ease nausea. Many of the HERBS and SPICES that are traditionally used in cooking aid digestion, so use plenty of mint, dill, caraway, horseradish, bay, chervil, fennel, tarragon, marjoram, cumin, cinnamon, ginger, and cardamom. Chamomile tea or angostura bitters, a tincture of the bitter gentian root, also may help. A teaspoon of bitters can promote digestion and alleviate flatulence.

stomach acid from returning to the esophagus. In some cases the ring fails to close properly and food is regurgitated, a process that is referred to as reflux; this can occur in individuals with a HIATAL HERNIA. Reflux can cause IN-DIGESTION AND HEARTBURN, the most common digestive disorders.

When the food reaches the stomach, it is churned by the stomach's muscular walls and broken down into smaller pieces. In addition, the stomach walls secrete gastric acid and an enzyme called pepsin that breaks down protein. Special mucus-producing cells within the stomach ordinarily prevent it from digesting its own tissues with these strong digestive juices. However, if these mechanisms fail for any reason, an ULCER can arise.

By the time the food leaves the stomach, it has been converted into a semifluid called chyme. Digestion continues in the duodenum, the first few inches of the small intestine, where bile from the liver and enzymes from the pancreas break down fats and proteins. The intestines are muscular tubes that move food with rhythmic contractions known as peristalsis. The 20-foot-long small intestine is lined with millions of hairlike projections called villi. These have surface membranes that allow digested nutrients to pass through them and into attached tiny blood vessels. Protein in the form of amino acids and sugar in the form of glucose are absorbed directly into the bloodstream for transport to cells throughout the body. While smaller fat molecules also go directly into the blood, larger ones enter the lymph system.

Fiber and other undigested waste products move into the large intestine, or colon, where most of the water needed by the body is reabsorbed. It's important to drink at least six to eight glasses of water, juices, and other nonalcoholic fluids a day; otherwise, the fecal mass moving through the colon becomes dehydrated, resulting in CON-STIPATION. Fiber absorbs large amounts of water, and it, along with some of the starches from vegetables and fruits, becomes fermented in the large bowel and provides the bulk that helps stimulate the colon muscles.

Depending on the contents of a meal and a person's individual metabolic rate, it may take from 2 to 6 hours for a meal to be fully digested and its nutrients absorbed. Simple sugars are broken down rapidly and may enter the bloodstream just minutes after eating. Starches require about an hour or longer to be digested; proteins need 2 to 3 hours. Fat takes from 4 to 6 hours to be digested and absorbed. For this reason, protein and fat will satisfy hunger for much longer periods of time than sugars and carbohydrates do. It takes another 8 to 24 hours for the undigested waste to move through the colon.

The intestine has a remarkable ability to heal itself. It replaces its lining every 72 hours and reacts swiftly to expel harmful substances. However, a diet high in refined and nutritionally deficient foods, typically found in Western countries, can lead to digestive problems ranging from unpleasant but minor episodes of indigestion and FLATULENCE to more serious disorders such as DIVERTICULITIS.

DIGESTIVE DISORDERS

The digestive system has a relatively small repertoire of symptoms, principally nausea, vomiting, pain (such as heartburn), bloating, cramping, DIARRHEA, constipation, and flatulence. The onset of such symptoms may simply reflect a normal response to an unusual meal or may be associated with some lifestyle factor, such as eating an improper diet or dealing with the stresses of daily life. Excitement, disappointment, fear, anxiety, and other strong emotions can cause some upset in the digestive system; this should not cause alarm if it is transient.

Since the digestive system has a limited set of symptoms for expressing distress, however, the same symptoms may also reflect any one of a number of very serious disorders, including GASTRITIS, or inflammation of the stomach lining; problems in the intestines, such as ulcerative COLITIS or CROHN'S DISEASE (both are inflammatory disorders); diverticulitis, an inflammation and infection of small sacs protruding from the intestinal wall; IRRITABLE BOWEL SYNDROME, a functional disorder that affects movement within the intestines; or CANCER anywhere in the digestive tract. Similarly, nausea and vomiting may be triggered by an adverse reaction to a medication, emotional upset, mild viral infection, ear disorder, migraine headache, and motion sickness, as well as a host of other serious disorders, including a heart attack and intestinal obstruction.

Any persistent symptoms that do not respond within a reasonable period of time to dietary change or efforts at stress management should cause concern and prompt a visit to a doctor.

MALABSORPTION DISORDERS

A similar group of symptoms, especially diarrhea and bloating, also indicate a malabsorption problem, which occurs when the digestive tract is unable to properly utilize one or more components of the diet. Depending on the severity of the problem, the person may experience weight loss, muscle wasting, and evidence of vitamin and mineral deficiencies. While some malabsorption problems are congenital, others may occur because of illness or its treatment. Problems may arise from the digestive tract itself, or from disorders of the heart and blood vessels, the endocrine glands, or the lymph system.

Some malabsorption conditions involve a single nutrient, as in CELIAC DISEASE, when the body is unable to absorb gluten (a protein found in wheat, rye, and barley), and INTOLERANCE TO MILK, when the body is unable to digest lactose. Others involve an array of nutrients. For example, in CYSTIC FIBROSIS, enzymes needed to digest protein, carbohydrate, and fat are either missing completely or are present only in reduced amounts.

People with malabsorption problems may be in danger of malnutrition. They may avoid certain foods in order to prevent symptoms, therefore failing to get adequate nutrients. Or the side effects of the disorder may lead to malnutrition. For example, when fat is not properly absorbed, it is discharged from the body as waste and takes with it the fat-soluble vitamins A, D, E, and K.

A registered dietitian can help individuals with malabsorption problems plan meals. A doctor may prescribe vitamin and mineral supplements or other treatments to provide the missing digestive component or minimize the damage caused by its absence.

Case Study

Margot enjoyed the Rotary Club dinners she attended with her husband. She especially looked forward to sampling the trays of cheese and hors d'oeuvres, and having a cocktail or two while visiting with friends. Unfortunately, she often felt bloated after the rich meals, and would develop embarrassing flatulence and burning pains, which she attributed to her hiatal hernia. Eventually, her discomfort prompted her to see a doctor, who advised her to lose weight, eat smaller meals, and avoid fatty foods and alcohol.

She followed the doctor's suggestions, and the bouts of indigestion became less frequent. It wasn't long before Margot began to enjoy after-dinner socializing free of heartburn and gas.

DIVERTICULITIS

EAT PLENTY OF
- *Seedless fresh fruits and vegetables.*
- *Whole-grain cereals and bread.*

CUT DOWN ON
- *White bread, polished rice, cookies, cakes, and other foods high in sugar and refined starches.*

AVOID
- *Alcoholic beverages.*
- *Beverages and foods high in caffeine.*
- *Seeds and nuts.*
- *Celery, corn, and other foods with strings or hulls.*

Diverticula are small pouches that form in the wall of the large intestine, creating a condition called diverticulosis. The specific cause remains unknown, but the disease occurs most often in people who are over age 60 and overweight. Weakening of the intestinal wall as a person ages is believed to contribute to the formation of the pouches. As pressure builds up in the large intestine—for example, during a bout of constipation—the weakened areas balloon outward, forming pouches.

The pouches or sacs are not a problem in themselves, producing no symptoms until they become infected or inflamed. Infection or inflammation can occur when waste flowing through the intestines is diverted into one of the sacs and becomes impacted. The resulting condition is called diverticulitis, or inflammation of the diverticula. It can be painful and serious, and may lead to complications, such as abscesses, intestinal obstruction, or perforation of the intestinal wall. In addition to abdominal cramps and pain, other symptoms of diverticulitis include gas, flatulence, fever, and rectal bleeding. Constipation may sometimes alternate with diarrhea.

Diverticulitis occurs primarily in the industrialized Western world, where diets that are high in fat and low in fiber are common. Inadequate consumption of dietary fiber can cause stools to become hard and compact, resulting in constipation. This may provoke unnatural contractions of the large intestine, which in turn leads to the formation of diverticula.

THE ROLE OF DIETARY FIBER

A diet rich in vegetables and whole-grain cereals may help to prevent diverticulitis, which is known to be less common among vegetarians than those who include meat in their diet. Vegetarian diets are typically higher in fiber-rich foods, such as vegetables, fruits, cereals, and grains. However, excessive fiber, particularly too much BRAN, can create other digestive problems; for example, studies have suggested that it can irritate the colon. If you have diverticular disease, do not start taking fiber supplements without first discussing this with your doctor.

While emphasizing high-fiber foods, cut down on foods prepared with refined carbohydrates, and avoid alcohol and high-caffeine drinks, which can irritate the colon. Foods containing nuts, seeds, hulls, or strings (such as celery) should be avoided, since they are easily trapped in the sacs. For example, choose blueberries for dessert rather than strawberries. If you prepare tomato sauce for a pasta dish, be sure you remove the seeds by cutting the tomatoes in half and gently squeezing them. Drink plenty of water; along with a high-fiber diet, increased fluid intake (at least eight glasses every day) produces bulky, soft stools that move easily through the intestinal tract.

SOOTHING HERBS

Chamomile or peppermint tea, traditionally recommended by herbalists to treat digestive problems, may be useful in relieving some of the symptoms of diverticulitis. Both are known for their soothing effect on the stomach and are said to aid digestion. Peppermint in particular is claimed to help relieve indigestion and gas. Psyllium seeds, which are often included as an ingredient in stool softeners, may ease symptoms, but be sure to consult your doctor first.

FOODS TO AVOID. *Any foods that have hulls, seeds, strings, or other fibrous parts can become trapped in the diverticula, leading to inflammation and other intestinal symptoms.*

DRY MOUTH

CONSUME PLENTY OF
- *Fluids, such as water, juice, and tea.*
- *Foods with a high moisture content, such as fruits and sherbets.*
- *Soft foods, such as puddings.*

CUT DOWN ON
- *Plain dry meats, especially beef, pork, and lamb.*
- *Plain crackers and dry breads.*
- *Bananas and other foods that may stick to mouth structures.*

AVOID
- *Alcohol and caffeine.*
- *Spicy and acidic foods.*

Medically known as xerostomia, dry mouth is caused by a shortage or thickening of saliva. Depending upon the severity of the condition, symptoms typically range from increased thirst to heightened sensitivity of the tongue and mouth, and difficulty in chewing and swallowing food.

A chronic dry mouth increases the risk of DENTAL DISORDERS, such as cavities, gingivitis, and periodontal disease. It can also cause BAD BREATH. Dry mouth is a common complaint among older people, because saliva flow naturally declines with age. It may also arise from an illness or as a side effect of drugs or radiation treatments. In addition to cancer chemotherapy, drugs that cause dry mouth include antihistamines taken for allergies, diuretics that are taken for hypertension, tricyclic antidepressants, codeine and other opiates, and anticholinergic drugs (such as atropine) that are taken to reduce muscle spasms.

Of the diseases that cause dry mouth, Sjögren's syndrome is the most prevalent, affecting approximately 5 million North Americans. It is an autoimmune disorder in which a destructive inflammatory process attacks the tissues that typically secrete moisture. In addition to dry mouth, the individual may also experience dryness of the eyes, nose, and vaginal tract. Sjögren's syndrome often occurs in conjunction with other autoimmune problems, such as rheumatoid ARTHRITIS, LUPUS, and scleroderma.

COPING WITH A DRY MOUTH

Keep lips moist with a simple salve, such as petroleum jelly. In addition, different types of nonprescription artificial saliva formulas are available from pharmacies, including sprays, drops, and ointments. Check the list of ingredients, however, because some contain large amounts of sugar, which can add to dental problems.

Drinking ample fluids can ease the effects of dry mouth. Have a bottle of water or other sugar-free beverage handy for frequent small sips, and always drink plenty of fluids with meals. In addition, you may be able to promote salivation by consuming tart or sour liquids, such as lemonade. Sipping hot fluids (for example, tea with lemon), licking a fresh lemon, sucking sugar-free sour candies, or chewing sugarless gum may help promote salivation as well as thin the saliva already present.

What you eat—as well as how you eat it—can also help you cope with dry mouth. For example, dry foods are easier to swallow when served in a liquid, such as a broth or gravy. Bread or crackers can be dunked into broth, tea, or milk to moisten them. If you have difficulty swallowing, foods can be ground or pureed to a palatable consistency.

In general, meals should emphasize soft, moist foods, such as soft-cooked fish and chicken, vegetables cooked in broth or sauces, and canned or fresh fruits that have a high moisture content. Unfortunately, some people find that citrus fruits, which are loaded with juice, are irritating to the mouth. Similarly, very spicy or salty foods may provoke burning or irritation.

Case Study

*K*aren, a 55-year-old bank teller, developed a taste for gardening after she moved to a home with a lovely backyard. But as her first spring there progressed, she was increasingly troubled by allergies that produced a runny or stuffy nose, sneezing, and itching. She decided to self-treat with nonprescription antihistamine pills. Although these stopped the allergy symptoms, the pills made her sleepy and produced a dry mouth. Karen was constantly thirsty, and as a result of sipping water all the time, she was urinating more often and even awakening several times during the night to go to the bathroom.

Finally, Karen consulted her doctor, who told her to stop taking the antihistamines. Instead, he prescribed an inhalant to be used twice a day to prevent nasal allergy symptoms. This alleviated her dry mouth and allowed Karen to enjoy her gardening in comfort.

EAR DISORDERS

EAT PLENTY OF
- *Vegetables and fruits to help bolster immunity against infection.*

AVOID
- *Foods high in saturated fats to prevent hearing loss due to atherosclerosis.*
- *High-salt foods that can cause a buildup of inner ear fluid.*
- *Aspirin and other nonsteroidal anti-inflammatory painkillers if you have ringing in the ears or Ménière's disease.*

The ear does more than tune us into the sounds around us; the complex fluid systems of the inner ear also help us to maintain our balance. Although there's a good deal of overlap, the three main categories of ear disorders are infections, hearing loss, and inner ear problems that produce VERTIGO and dizziness.

EAR INFECTIONS

Young children are especially vulnerable to middle ear infections (otitis media) because fluid tends to collect in this part of the ear, providing an ideal breeding place for bacteria. Breast-fed babies have fewer problems with ear infections, partly because of the antibodies in their mothers' milk, but also because the head-up position at the breast allows milk to follow a natural course downward rather than back up into the ear.

In older children and adolescents, ear infections often take the form of swimmer's ear, in which excess moisture lets bacteria multiply in the softened skin of the ear canal. Children with seasonal allergies are prone to ear infections during the HAY FEVER season, when the ears become congested. In some cases, food allergies may also cause ear congestion, and consequently infections.

Bacterial ear infections can be treated with antibiotics. Severe, recurrent infections are sometimes treated with surgery to implant a tiny tube to drain the fluid. However, most children outgrow these infections as they mature. A balanced diet that includes ample fruits and vegetables helps build immunity.

HEARING LOSS

Hearing loss takes two main forms: conductive deafness, in which a barrier hinders the transmission of sounds to the inner ear, and nerve deafness, which occurs when the auditory nerve is damaged. In people with high blood cholesterol levels, nerve deafness may be the result of ATHEROSCLEROSIS in the tiny blood vessels of the inner ear. Doctors recommend a low-fat diet to prevent the buildup of plaque in the ear vessels.

OTHER EAR DISORDERS

Ringing in the ears—tinnitus—may be just a transient nuisance during a cold, or it can be a relentless torture. Aspirin and certain other drugs can cause tinnitus, especially when used in high doses or for long periods. If you develop tinnitus as a drug reaction, ask your doctor to suggest an alternative.

Ménière's disease is an ear disorder caused by excessive fluid in the inner ear. Its symptoms include dizziness, vertigo, and nausea. The disease is not curable, but diuretics to rid the body of excess fluid can help to prevent attacks. Antihistamines stop vertigo, and home remedies, such as GINGER, can relieve nausea. Too much salt in the diet can affect the body's fluid balance, so doctors recommend a low-salt diet to avoid buildup of inner ear fluid.

ECZEMA

EAT PLENTY OF
- *Legumes, brown rice, wheat germ, and other foods high in vitamin B6.*

AVOID
- *Foods that trigger or worsen eczema.*
- *External causes, such as wearing wool clothing next to the skin.*

Eczema is an itchy, scaly rash often caused by sensitivity to foods, chemicals, and other triggers. The rash of eczema (also called atopic dermatitis) is not always a true allergic reaction, but as in an allergy, the immune system reacts to a normally harmless substance. The symptoms of sensitivity vary from one person to another and can appear anywhere from a few minutes to several hours after exposure to the offending food or substance. Eczema runs in families, often along with a tendency to develop ASTHMA, HAY FEVER, or HIVES.

THE ROLE OF DIET

Certain foods trigger eczema in some people. Common culprits include eggs, dairy products, seafood, walnuts, and pecans. A food diary may help to pinpoint the offending items.

Cow's milk can cause eczema in babies and small children; they may be able to tolerate goat's milk or soy-based products. Many children outgrow their sensitivities by the age of 6, but others have lifelong recurrences.

MANAGING ECZEMA

There are researchers who believe a diet rich in vitamin B6 offers some protection against sensitivity rashes. Good sources include vegetable oil, eggs, oily fish, legumes, brown rice, wheat germ, and leafy green vegetables.

In an experimental study, patients found that their eczema symptoms improved when they took supplements of evening primrose oil, which is rich in gamma linolenic acid. These results have not been confirmed in large numbers of people, so these and other vitamin and mineral supplements are not medically approved eczema treatments.

ENVIRONMENTAL TRIGGERS

Chemicals in the environment probably trigger eczema more often than foods do. Common offenders include nickel, which is often used for making costume jewelry, and latex, which is used in household and industrial rubber gloves and many other products.

People in certain jobs are at high risk for developing eczema. Acrylic adhesives are a hazard for manicurists and their customers, for dental technicians,

and for people whose hobby is model building. Athletes and others who favor casual footwear sometimes suffer from skin rashes on the feet caused by the adhesives used in bonding sneakers. Buying another brand of sneaker may solve the problem.

Woolen clothing worn next to the skin can cause a rash. Those who are sensitive to wool should also try to avoid skin-care products based on lanolin, the natural oil that occurs in wool.

It makes sense to avoid known triggers. If your rash is worse in either hot or very cold weather, avoid extremes of temperature. Buy only soaps, detergents, and toilet papers that are free of dyes and perfumes.

EGGPLANTS

BENEFITS
- *Low in calories (unless cooked in fat).*
- *Meaty flavor and texture lends itself to vegetarian dishes.*

DRAWBACKS
- *Soak up fat during cooking.*
- *Provide minimal nutrients.*

Although eggplants provide very little nutrition, they are among our most versatile vegetables and a component of many popular ethnic dishes, including Indian curries, Greek moussakas, Middle Eastern baba ghanoush, and French ratatouille, among others. Eggplants are filling, yet very low in calories—a cup of the raw vegetable contains less than 40 calories. There is a drawback, however—eggplants' spongy texture allows them to soak up fat like a sponge. In one experiment a deep-fried eggplant soaked up four times as much fat as French fried potatoes did.

The tastiest eggplants are young and firm, with thin skins and a mild flavor. Larger ones are more likely to be seedy, tough, and bitter. The most familiar varieties have deep purple skins, but there are also light violet and white (the type that inspired its name) eggplants.

Eggplants are members of the nightshade family, which also includes tomatoes, potatoes, and peppers. Some develop a bitter flavor, which can be eliminated by salting the eggplant before cooking. Slice or cube the vegetable, sprinkle with salt, let stand for 30 minutes, then drain and blot dry. The salt draws out some of the moisture as it reduces bitterness. Eggplants can be stuffed and baked or broiled, roasted, or stewed. If sautéing, use a nonstick pan and minimal oil.

DIFFERENT SHAPES. *Most eggplants are purple and elongated, but the Italian rosa bianca has a round shape.*

EGGS

BENEFITS

- *An excellent source of protein, vitamin B₁₂, and many other nutrients.*

DRAWBACKS

- *Yolks are high in cholesterol.*
- *A common cause of food allergy.*
- *A risk of salmonella if not fully cooked.*

The egg is one of nature's best designs, providing everything that a developing chick requires. Its protective shell is not only strong enough to support the mother hen's weight as it allows heat to transfer from her body to the chick, but it also supplies 100 percent of the chick's dietary requirements of protein, vitamins, and minerals.

Regardless of concerns about their high cholesterol content and possible salmonella contamination, eggs remain a popular and inexpensive source of nourishment. Any fear of salmonella poisoning can be put aside by thoroughly cooking them; fortunately, an egg's overall nutrient content is not affected by the cooking process.

Like other animal proteins, those supplied by eggs contain all the essential amino acids. Eggs also provide a broad spectrum of vitamins and minerals. In particular, they are an excellent source of vitamin B_{12}, which is essential for proper nerve function. Because dietary needs for vitamin B_{12} are often fulfilled by meat, vegetarians especially rely on eggs as an important source of this vitamin.

Lecithin—a natural emulsifier found in eggs—is rich in choline, which is involved in moving cholesterol through the bloodstream as well as aiding fat metabolism. Choline is also an essential component of cell membranes and nerve tissue. Although the body can make enough choline for its normal

needs, some researchers have suggested that dietary sources may be helpful in reducing the accumulation of fat in the liver as well as repairing some types of neurological damage.

THE CHOLESTEROL ISSUE

To help keep blood cholesterol in check the general recommendation is that adults consume no more than four egg yolks a week, including those in baked goods. A large egg contains about 70 calories, 6g of protein, 5g of fat (of which less than 2g is saturated fat), and about 210mg of cholesterol.

Adults should limit their cholesterol

intake to 300mg a day; therefore, even individuals who limit their egg consumption to four yolks a week should still consume other animal products in moderation to keep their average weekly cholesterol intake below the limit.

Only the yolks of eggs contain cholesterol; therefore, egg whites need not be restricted. In fact, the whites can be used to replace whole eggs or just the yolks in many recipes without detriment to their taste or texture. For example, you can replace one whole egg with two whites, or you can substitute beaten whites instead of a whole egg to coat foods for frying.

CONFUSING EGG LABELS

Labels such as "farm-laid" or "country-fresh" can conjure up misleading images; the hens that laid the eggs may well have been confined to cages. Although the term "free range" may suggest chickens pecking freely in a farmyard, it can be legally applied to the eggs of caged hens as long as they have daytime access to open runs.

Whatever the labeling, always open the carton to inspect the eggs before you buy them. Reject any eggs that have cracked or blemished shells. It is a myth that brown eggs are more nutritious than white ones, even though many supermarkets charge a higher price for brown eggs. Both are equally nutritious; they just come from different breeds of chicken.

STORAGE

Keep eggs in the main part of the refrigerator, which is cooler than the shelves on the inside of the door. Store the pointed end of the egg down, so that the yolk remains centered in the

EGGS OF THE WORLD. *Chicken eggs are most often used in Canadian homes, but in other countries, quail, duck, and goose eggs are eaten as well.*

shell away from the air pocket at the larger end. Leave eggs in their original dated carton to keep track of when you bought them. Refrigerated eggs can be kept safely for up to 3 weeks.

EGGS AND ALLERGIES

Eggs are among the foods most likely to trigger allergic reactions. People who know that they are allergic to eggs should be on the lookout for obvious sources, such as mayonnaise and sauces; pancakes, waffles, and bakery items; and sherbets and ice cream. They should carefully read food labels for telltale terms, such as albumin, globulin, ovomucin, and vitellin, which are all ingredients derived from eggs. They should also avoid flu shots and other vaccines incubated in eggs.

THE SALMONELLA SCARE

Occasionally, an egg may be found to harbor salmonella bacteria, which can be passed on by the hen or enter through cracked shells. Although the risk of food poisoning is relatively low, it's best to avoid eating raw or partly cooked eggs in any form. People at special risk include the frail elderly, young children, the sick, pregnant women, and anyone with lowered immunity.

Caesar salads, fresh mayonnaise, egg-based sauces and dressings, and mousses can all contain raw or partly cooked eggs. To be certain that eggs have been cooked long enough, boil them for at least 7 minutes, poach them for 5 minutes, or fry them for 3 minutes on each side. Both the yolk and the white should be firm. Omelettes and scrambled eggs should be cooked until firm and not runny.

EPILEPSY

About 300,000 Canadians have some form of epilepsy, recurrent seizures triggered by abnormal electrical impulses in the brain. Some seizures are so mild and fleeting that they are barely noticeable; others last for several minutes, during which the person falls down and is seized by convulsive movements. The frequency of seizures also varies from person to person; some epileptics suffer many seizures each day, while others may go for months between episodes.

Neurologists generally discount any link between diet and epilepsy, with some exceptions. Epileptics who also have MIGRAINE headaches that are triggered by certain foods often cease to have seizures when the offending foods are eliminated from the diet. Some diabetics suffer seizures when their blood sugar levels drop suddenly. Large amounts of alcohol consumed in a short time can cause seizures. Although evidence is sketchy, there have been reports of aspartame triggering seizures in people who already have epilepsy.

THE HIGH-FAT DIET

A rigid diet that appears to halt seizures in children whose seizures cannot be controlled by drugs has been hailed as a new breakthrough. In reality, however, the diet dates to the early 1900s, when doctors devised a dietary treatment for epilepsy based on the ancient observation that seizures ceased during periods of prolonged fasting. Fasting is hardly a practical long-term treatment for chronic seizures, but researchers found that a high-fat diet mimicked fasting metabolism without starvation.

With the development of effective anticonvulsant drugs, the dietary treatment was dropped. But neurologists at Johns Hopkins hospital have refined a dietary treatment for severe epilepsy. After about 24 hours of fasting, the body depletes its reserves of glucose and starts to burn stored fat for energy. However, burning fat in the absence of glucose gives off waste products called ketone bodies, which build up in the blood and are excreted in the urine. Very high blood levels of ketones can upset body chemistry, and even lead to a coma and death. But at lower levels they can eliminate seizures. Carefully structuring the diet by allowing only a sprinkling of carbohydrates can result in a therapeutic level of ketones in the bloodstream.

This regimen, called the ketogenic diet, appears to work best in young children, especially those 20 percent whose seizures are not adequately controlled by drugs. The diet provides about 75 percent of the calories generally recommended for healthy children, and most of these come from fats. A small amount of protein is added to allow for at least some growth, but carbohydrates are kept to a minimum. Fluid intake is restricted. The diet must be carefully tailored and then followed exactly; a small deviation can bring on seizures. To begin, the child is hospitalized for 2 or 3 days of fasting, after which the ketogenic diet is gradually introduced. The diet can be difficult to follow, but after 2 to 3 years, most patients can resume a normal diet and still be seizure-free.

Case Study

*S*ix-year-old Megan suffered from what are known as absence, or petit mal, seizures. One minute she'd be fine, and the next she would stare into space, unaware of her surroundings. Although she was taking three different drugs, she still had several episodes an hour. Because she was unable to focus her attention, Megan was regressing in both school and social skills. The medications upset her stomach so much that she was losing weight and was not growing properly. She slept 12 to 14 hours a day, but she was always tired. Megan's neurologist felt he had exhausted his options and suggested surgery to destroy the malfunctioning part of her brain.

Megan was referred to the Johns Hopkins Pediatric Epilepsy Center in Baltimore. Instead of neurosurgery, doctors there suggested that she try their high-fat ketogenic diet. At first her parents were skeptical, but after Megan spent a week in the hospital to initiate the diet, her seizures stopped. She was gradually weaned off her seizure medications and was eager to help her mother prepare her "magic diet" foods. Her teachers and classmates immediately noticed that Megan seemed to be a new person—her concentration and memory improved, and she quickly began to make up for her lost learning time.

After more than 4 years of dealing with drugs that didn't work and their side effects, Megan's parents call the diet a fantastic alternative. Megan herself sums up her progress when she says "I can remember things now. I'm doing just great!"

Exercise and Diet to Boost Energy and Lift Mood

*Regular physical activity does wonders for your health,
your shape, and your mood. No matter what your age, health,
and level of fitness, there's a form of exercise to suit you.*

Exercise burns calories; it also keeps bones healthy, improves cardiovascular performance, enhances digestion, tones the muscles and the skin, and increases your chance of getting a restful night's sleep. In addition to its physical benefits, exercise activates the brain to release endorphins, morphinelike natural tranquilizers that soothe pain and create a sense of emotional well-being. Endorphins are responsible for the "runner's high" that many athletes experience. They help to explain why exercise has a positive impact on your state of mind and ability to manage stress.

The paradox of exercise is that by expending energy you can increase energy. By improving the heart's performance and ability to pump blood, aerobic exercise makes your body more energy-efficient, and you consume less oxygen when going about normal daily activities. In effect, it is like tuning up a car's engine and getting better gas mileage. If you are unused to regular exercise, however, you may feel a bit stiff or sore and fatigued at first. Start slowly, perhaps only 5 to 10 minutes three times a week, and gradually build up the intensity and duration of your workout. After a few weeks of following a regular exercise regimen, most people report a surge of energy.

In this sedentary society, you need to schedule regular exercise to keep your body trim and improve your health. If you eat more food than your

---

CONSUME PLENTY OF

- *Starchy foods, such as pasta, legumes, brown rice, potatoes, and whole-grain breads, for complex carbohydrates to provide a steady source of energy.*
- *Fruits for vitamins, minerals, and natural sugars for quick energy.*
- *Vegetables and legumes for vitamins and minerals.*
- *Lean meat, low-fat milk and dairy products, and other high-protein foods to maintain muscles.*

CUT DOWN ON

- *High-fat foods.*

---

body uses up in energy, the surplus calories are stored as fat. The only way to lose weight and keep it off is to combine a healthy low-fat diet with regular aerobic exercise, such as brisk walking, jogging, cycling, swimming, or aerobic dancing. By speeding up breathing and raising your heart rate, aerobic exercise helps to burn body fat. Undertaking an exercise program, however, doesn't give you a license to eat all the French fries, fudge, and brownies you can lay your hands on. On the contrary, a balanced diet is essential to provide the energy you need to sustain a regular exercise program.

When you exercise aerobically, your body first burns the glucose circulating; it then turns to the glycogen stored in the muscles and the liver, as

well as some fatty acids. Thus, a longer exercise session of at least 20 minutes burns more fat and helps to shed weight and keep it off. Endurance training increases the amount of fatty acids being burned. Therefore, the best way to promote fat burning is steady, sustained effort, in which you exercise for long periods—at least 25 to 30 minutes at a time—at 30 to 40 percent of your maximum capability.

DIET BASICS

The human body converts CARBOHYDRATES to glucose, its most important source of energy. The levels of glucose stored in the liver and muscles are directly related to a person's ability to sustain prolonged, vigorous exercise. Glucose stores can be increased in a relatively short time by modifying the diet. For example, some experts in SPORTS NUTRITION advise athletes to eat high-carbohydrate meals for several days before an endurance event. However, carbohydrate loading is unnecessary for most people; consuming 55 to 60 percent of calories in the form of carbohydrates (mostly starches) will provide the energy needed for moderate to vigorous exercise.

PROTEIN builds, maintains, and repairs the body's tissues. It can also be converted to energy but is a less efficient source than carbohydrates.

While FATS are the most concentrated source of calories, they are actually a less efficient source of energy

CREATING AN EXERCISE PROGRAM

• Don't try to cram exercise into a crowded schedule. Instead, substitute it for a less important activity, such as watching television. Alternatively, increase exercise by walking or bicycling at least part of the way to and from work, or try working out at lunchtime.

• Pick an exercise you'll enjoy. Try cross-training for variation and to ward off boredom. Take a brisk walk one day, go to the gym and lift free weights the next. Enroll in a yoga class for stretching and flexibility, play tennis or go swimming on weekends, and so forth.

• Whatever your exercise plan, begin slowly and build up gradually. Anyone who is over 40, seriously overweight, or has high blood pressure, heart disease, bone or joint disease, diabetes, or any other potentially serious condition should see a doctor before starting to exercise. Smokers of any age should also have a checkup. In such instances, an exercise stress test may be necessary to determine a safe level of exercise.

• Some people do better exercising alone. If that's true of you, go to a gym or health club and try the various machines to see which you prefer. Then consider buying a treadmill or some other exercise machine to use at home. If you're the type who needs the motivation of a group, take classes at a health club or join a dance group in your community.

than carbohydrates because they take longer to digest and metabolize. Doctors and nutritionists advise limiting fat intake to no more than 30 percent of daily calories, with most of these coming from vegetable oils.

Despite some extravagant claims, VITAMINS don't provide energy. They are needed, however, to power many of the metabolic processes by which the body transforms food into energy. A diet that includes an ample supply of vegetables, legumes, fruits, and whole-grain products will provide adequate vitamins and minerals. Some fruits also provide sugars that are quickly converted to energy.

FIT FOR LIFE. *Exercise not only maintains strength and muscle tone, it also helps prevent disease and slows aging. Almost anyone, regardless of age or level of fitness, can find an appropriate form of exercise.*

EYE DISORDERS

CONSUME PLENTY OF
- *Carrots, sweet potatoes, and dark green vegetables for beta carotene.*
- *Citrus fruits, melons, tomatoes, and dark green vegetables for vitamin C.*
- *Whole grains, seeds, nuts, green vegetables, avocados, potatoes, bananas, fish, poultry, and lean meat for B vitamins.*
- *Vegetable oils, wheat germ, liver, fish, fresh green leafy vegetables, legumes, and dried fruits for vitamin E.*
- *Whole-grain cereals, seafood, lean meat, poultry, and eggs for selenium and zinc.*

CUT DOWN ON
- *Saturated fats.*

The role of ANTIOXIDANT nutrients and BIOFLAVONOIDS in vision loss and other degenerative problems associated with aging is becoming increasingly clear. With advancing age, the production of free radicals, unstable molecules that form when the body uses oxygen, increases. These molecules cause eye damage like that which results from exposure to radiation, and contribute to such degenerative disorders as cataracts and macular degeneration.

AGE-RELATED DISORDERS

Cataracts develop when the lens—the transparent membrane that allows light to enter the eye—yellows, hindering the passage of light rays through it. Vision becomes hazy, cloudy, or blurry; if untreated, the lens may become completely opaque, resulting in blindness.

Although aging is the most common cause of cataracts, they can occur at any time of life, even in infancy. Smoking and diabetes can hasten their development. But a diet that provides ample antioxidants—in particular, vitamins C and E and the mineral selenium—appears to slow their progression.

Another eye disease that comes with aging, macular degeneration, is one of the most common causes of legal blindness among older North Americans. It entails a gradual, painless deterioration of the macula, tissue in the central portion of the retina. The first symptom is usually blurring of central vision; eventually, the person may have only limited side vision. The cause of macular degeneration is unknown, but recent research suggests that a diet high in antioxidant nutrients may help prevent or slow the disorder.

Some studies also suggest that riboflavin and vitamin B6 may help protect the eyes from age-related macular degeneration. Research also shows that a diet high in saturated fats increases the risk of age-related macular degeneration. Scientists theorize that saturated fats may clog the arteries in the retina in the same way that they contribute to atherosclerosis in larger blood vessels, such as the coronary arteries.

DIABETIC RETINOPATHY

Certain similarities between macular degeneration and diabetic retinopathy—the infiltration of the retina with tiny ruptured blood vessels—suggest that antioxidant nutrients may also be beneficial in this common complication of DIABETES. Diet is critical in maintaining tight control of blood glucose levels, which also reduces the risk of diabetic retinopathy. A diet high in starches, fruits, and vegetables, with moderate amounts of protein and minimal fat, not only keeps diabetes in check but may also help prevent eye damage and the other serious complications of the disease.

NIGHT BLINDNESS

The eyes need vitamin A and its precursor, beta carotene, as well as bioflavonoids, to make the pigments that absorb light within the eye. A deficiency in vitamin A or a failure to utilize it properly impairs the eye's ability to adapt to darkness and leads to night blindness. This does not entail a total loss of night vision, but rather difficulty seeing well in dim lighting.

Vitamin A deficiency is uncommon in Western industrialized countries, but it remains a major problem in many underdeveloped areas of the world. Organ meats, fortified margarine, butter, and other dairy products are good sources of vitamin A. Dark yellow or orange foods, such as carrots, sweet potatoes, and apricots, as well as dark green leafy vegetables, are the richest sources of beta carotene, which the body converts to vitamin A.

Failing night vision should not be self-treated with vitamin A or beta carotene supplements; the problem may stem from a DIGESTIVE or MALABSORPTION DISORDER that prevents the body from using the vitamin. Treatment of the underlying cause usually cures the night blindness. An exception is night blindness caused by retinitis pigmentosa, a genetic disease. However, recent research suggests that vitamin A may, in fact, slow the progressive vision loss of this incurable disease.

CONJUNCTIVITIS

Commonly called pink eye, conjunctivitis is an irritation or infection of the membrane that lines the front of the eyeball and eyelid. Typical symptoms include redness, itchiness, a burning sensation, a thin watery discharge, and a yellow crust that forms during sleep.

Viruses are responsible for most conjunctivitis, but in recurring cases an ALLERGIC REACTION may be the cause. Some people, for example, suffer conjunctivitis as part of HAY FEVER; others react to certain foods. If you suspect a food is causing the conjunctivitis, try eliminating that food from your diet for a few weeks. If the eye irritation disappears only to return when you reintroduce the food into your diet, you have probably identified the offending culprit, which you can then avoid.

FAD DIETS

*Each year, yet another miracle diet comes on the scene.
Despite all the hype and claims, none ever lives up to its
promises of painless weight loss and renewed health.*

Canadians spend more than $300 million each year on commercial weight-loss programs, and experts agree that this is not only a waste of money but also a threat to health. Most fad diets promise fast weight loss, but some address other concerns: Some play on common misconceptions (the body needs to be detoxified periodically) or groundless fears (our foods are filled with harmful additives or fail to provide essential nutrients). Other diets are outgrowths of religious or philosophical tenets—for example, macrobiotic or Ayurvedic regimens.

In general, purveyors of fad diets take advantage of a person's insecurity about what constitutes good nutrition. Some have medical degrees, but many are naturopaths (self-styled nutritionists) who appear sincere but whose real goal is to sell special dietary products. You should be wary of any regimen that rejects the principles outlined in BASIC FOOD GROUPS or makes unrealistic promises. Although a nutritious, balanced diet is necessary to maintain health, no diet or supplement will cure cancer or restore lost youth. Be cautious, too, of regimens driven by an obvious profit motive; for example, any that require membership fees, costly books or supplements, special food, or exercise equipment. These are often sold through television infomercials or by telephone solicitors.

Before undertaking any major dietary change, it's a good idea to check with a doctor, registered dietitian, or qualified nutritionist. These professionals can quickly ascertain whether a diet is nutritionally sound.

CRASH WEIGHT LOSS

At any given time, more than 3 million Canadians are on some kind of weight-loss diet, and a similar number either plan to diet or think they should. All too often these dieters turn to some sort of crash plan that promises fast results. In recent years there have been the Scarsdale, Fit for Life, Bloomingdale's, Hamptons, Aspen, Mediterranean, Atkins, Stillman, Air Force, grapefruit, rice, drinking man's, high-fat, pasta, high-fiber, high-protein, water, chocolate-lover's, cabbage soup, and macrobiotic diets—to name a few.

All these diets promise relatively painless weight loss; indeed, most people will lose weight if they follow any one for more than a few weeks. Although the focus varies from one diet to another, they all restrict the total intake of calories, including diets that proclaim you can eat all you want. In most of these diets, the food choices tend to be limited and so boring that there's little temptation to overeat. The fruits and rice diet, for example, allows for large amounts of most fresh fruits and moderate portions of rice. After a few days of this monotonous fare, most people are so sick of fruits and rice that they end up eating even less than the diet's allotted portions.

This restricted approach to DIETING AND WEIGHT CONTROL not only carries a risk of nutritional deficiencies but is doomed to failure, because it does not instill a permanent change in eating habits. As soon as former eating habits are resumed, the unwanted weight is rapidly regained.

Losing weight often becomes more difficult with each successive attempt; this is commonly referred to as the yo-yo effect. If a person seriously wants to lose weight and keep it off, the only truly successful way is to adopt sensible, permanent EXERCISE AND DIET habits that balance food intake with expended energy.

COMMON DIET MYTHS

Many alternative practitioners recommend periodic detoxification diets; they believe that these diets cleanse the digestive system and rid the body of waste products. A typical detoxification regimen calls for a few days of fasting, during which the person consumes only distilled water, fruit juice, raw fruit, and perhaps spirula (a type of algae), bran, various supplements, and herbs or herbal teas. In many regimens, enemas are advocated to further cleanse the colon, as well as saunas or sweat baths to rid the body of "toxins" through the skin. Some practitioners also recommend chelation, which entails administering a drug that binds with minerals to remove them from the body.

There is no scientific evidence that the body needs detoxification—it has its own highly efficient waste-removal systems. Indeed, detoxification regimens not only upset the body's natural waste removal, they can also be harmful. Enemas disrupt normal colon function and can upset the body's natural chemical balance. Fasting, especially during an illness, deprives the body of the energy and nutrients it needs to heal itself. Chelation therapy is justified in cases of lead, mercury, or other metal poisoning, but not in the treatment of arthritis, atherosclerosis, and other diseases.

DIET AND PHILOSOPHY

Most religion-based dietary regimens are generally healthy; in fact, studies show that people who follow the vegetarian regimens of Seventh-Day Adventists or Buddhists often live longer and enjoy a lower incidence of obesity, heart disease, cancer, and other serious diseases than do those who consume a typical Western diet.

This doesn't apply to some restrictive diets, such as the most extreme levels of the macrobiotic regimen. In the 1900s the macrobiotic diet was developed by the American-Japanese writer George Ohsawa, who credited the diet with curing his tuberculosis. His dietary system classified all foods according to the Chinese system of opposing forces, as yin or yang, instead of using protein, carbohydrate, and fat designations. The philosophy is to balance foods according to their yin and yang qualities. Foods should also be seasonal and locally grown. Geography and methods of preparation, too, are classified as yin and yang; for example, a person living in a warm (yang) area should emphasize yin foods, and vice versa. Yin foods should predominate during the warm summer months, yang foods during the winter months.

There are seven increasingly restricted levels of macrobiotics. Brown rice and herbal teas are basic items in all levels. Grains, vegetables, and fruits make up the bulk of the diet; fish and some meat are permitted on the lower levels, dairy products and all processed foods are avoided on every level.

The liberal, lower-level macrobiotic diets are low-fat, mostly vegetarian regimens that meet all or most of our nutritional needs. In contrast, the extreme upper-level macrobiotic diets are deficient in many nutrients, such as vitamin B_{12}, iron, and calcium.

Warning: Long-term use of the extreme upper-level diets can result in anemia and other deficiency diseases. Some alternative practitioners recommend a limited macrobiotic regimen for AIDS and cancer patients—a practice that may prove dangerous. People with these life-threatening diseases generally need more, not less, nutrition. A strict macrobiotic diet should also be avoided by a pregnant or breast-feeding woman, children, or anyone needing extra calories.

MACROBIOTIC STAPLES

There are seven levels of macrobiotic diet. The less extreme levels are mainly vegetarian (although they may allow fish and some meat), consisting of large amounts of unrefined cereals and small amounts of seasonal and locally produced fruits and vegetables. The most extreme level, now rarely followed, consists of brown rice only. Several deaths from malnutrition have been attributed to this regimen. A suitable macrobiotic diet can include the following foods:

Whole-grain cereals. Brown rice, oats, barley, wheat, buckwheat, corn, rye, millet, and products made from these, such as wholewheat flour, bread, and pasta; couscous; oatmeal.

Fruits. A mixture of fresh seasonal fruits, which should include some citrus fruits. To ensure freshness, buy frequently and, where possible, choose local produce.

Vegetables and seaweed. A wide variety of fresh vegetables is recommended. Seaweed is used to enhance the flavor and nutritional value of many dishes.

Seeds, nuts, flavorings, and fish. Sesame, sunflower, and pumpkin seeds, peanuts, almonds, hazelnuts, walnuts, and dried chestnuts. In moderation, sea salt, ginger, mustard, tahini, cider vinegar, garlic, lemon juice, and apple juice can all be used to enhance the flavor of a dish. For nonvegetarians, three small portions of fresh seafood can be included every week. The yang qualities of fish and shellfish should be balanced by helpings of green leafy vegetables, grains, or legumes at the same meal.

Legumes. Lentils, chickpeas, beans, peas, and soy products, such as tofu (bean curd).

Soups. Often made with beans, lentils, and special Asian seasonings, such as miso (made from fermented soya beans), shoyu (a dark soy sauce), and dried seaweed.

FATS: AN ABUNDANCE OF FACTS AND FALLACIES

*Each year brings a new tide of conflicting information
about fats. Some claims are false, others are based on incomplete
data, yet still others raise important health concerns.*

In all the debate about dietary fats, there are three facts beyond dispute: one, in small amounts, fats are essential to maintain health; two, the typical North American diet is much too high in fats of all kinds; and three, the fat debate is a gold mine for commercial exploitation of the popular pursuit of low-fat and fat-free alternatives to traditional foods.

Lipids is the term applied interchangeably to fats, oils, waxes, sterols, esters, and similar substances that usually cannot be dissolved in water but will dissolve in an organic solvent. Dietary fats and oils are members of the same chemical family, the triglycerides. They differ in their melting points: at room temperature, fats are solid, whereas oils are liquid. In other respects they can be considered as a single class of compounds, and for simplicity can be referred to as fats.

Natural fats, whether they are derived from animal or plant sources, are composed of three fatty acid molecules (a triglyceride) bound by one glycerol (a type of alcohol) molecule. The nature of a fat depends on which specific combination of fatty acids is drawn from a basic pool of about 25.

All fats contain the same number of calories by weight; that is, about 250 calories per ounce, or 9 calories per gram. Volume for volume, however, the calorie count can differ substantially. For example, a cup of oil weighs more—and therefore has more calories—than a cup of whipped margarine, into which air has been added to increase its volume. In addition, if the whipped margarine is one of the low-calorie versions, a considerable percentage of its weight will come from added water.

A diet rich in high-fat foods results in more weight gain than a diet made up mainly of carbohydrates with some protein. Not only are fats a more concentrated source of calories than the other food groups, but recent studies indicate that the body is also more efficient in storing fats than carbohydrates and protein.

HOW WE USE FATS

It is important to distinguish the fat consumed in foods—dietary fat—from body fats circulating in the blood or stored as adipose tissue, which is made up of cells specially adapted for that purpose. Even if the diet contains no fat whatsoever, the body will convert any excess protein and carbohydrate to fat and store them as such. When our weight remains steady, it's because we are making fat and using it up at equal rates. If our food intake exceeds our need for energy, then no matter what the composition of the diet, we synthesize more fat than we use and gain weight.

The average woman's body is about 20 to 25 percent fat by weight; the average man's is 15 percent. The greater proportion of fat in women is an evolutionary adaptation to meet the demand for extra calories needed to bear and nourish children.

Most body cells have a limited capacity for fat storage. The fat cells (adipocytes) are exceptions; they expand as more fat accumulates. An obese person's fat cells may be 50 to 100 times larger than those of a thin person. In addition, overweight infants

BENEFITS

- *Supply the fatty acids the body needs for many chemical activities, including growth, metabolism, and the manufacture of sex hormones and cell membranes.*
- *Transport the fat-soluble vitamins A, D, E, and K in the body.*
- *Add flavor, aroma, and smooth, pleasing texture to foods, making eating more enjoyable.*
- *Satisfy feelings of hunger.*
- *An important source of energy for basal metabolism.*

DRAWBACKS

- *A high-fat diet easily leads to weight gain.*
- *Saturated fat is linked to elevated blood cholesterol levels and an increased risk of heart disease, stroke, and circulatory disorders.*
- *A high fat intake may increase the risk of developing certain cancers, particularly of the colon, prostate, breast, and ovaries.*

THE FAMILY TREE OF FATS

Fats and oils contain many different fatty acids that affect the body in varying ways. Most simply, they are classified as saturated or unsaturated based on their molecular structure.

Unsaturates are further subdivided into monounsaturates and polyunsaturates. Trans fatty acids are created in food processing and also occur naturally in beef, lamb, and dairy products.

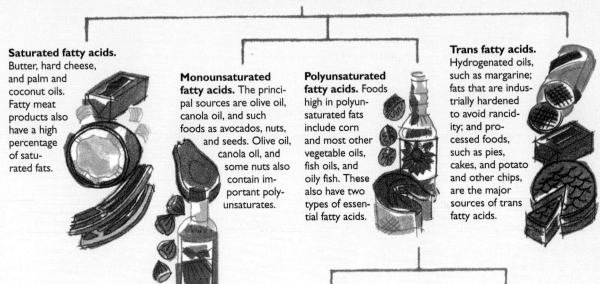

THE FATS IN EVERYDAY FOODS

Saturated fatty acids. Butter, hard cheese, and palm and coconut oils. Fatty meat products also have a high percentage of saturated fats.

Monounsaturated fatty acids. The principal sources are olive oil, canola oil, and such foods as avocados, nuts, and seeds. Olive oil, canola oil, and some nuts also contain important polyunsaturates.

Polyunsaturated fatty acids. Foods high in polyunsaturated fats include corn and most other vegetable oils, fish oils, and oily fish. These also have two types of essential fatty acids.

Trans fatty acids. Hydrogenated oils, such as margarine; fats that are industrially hardened to avoid rancidity; and processed foods, such as pies, cakes, and potato and other chips, are the major sources of trans fatty acids.

Omega-6 (linoleic acid and its derivatives). Good sources include corn, safflower, soybean, and sunflower oils.

Omega-3 (linolenic acid and its derivatives). Good sources include rapeseed and evening primrose oils, flaxseed, walnuts, and oily fish, such as sardines, mackerel, and salmon.

FAT CHEMISTRY. *Fatty acids are made up of carbon, hydrogen, and oxygen in varying proportions. A fat is saturated when its molecules hold the maximum amount of hydrogen. Monounsaturates have a little less, while polyunsaturates have the least. Trans fatty acids can be created by the hydrogenation process.*

---

and children accumulate more fat cells than their thin counterparts. Once in place, fat cells will never go away, although they will shrink if fat is drawn off to be used for energy production. One theory has it that shrunken fat cells emit a chemical plea for replenishment, which could explain why many people spend their lives on a roller coaster of weight loss and gain.

WHY WE NEED FATS

Fats add flavor and a smooth, pleasing texture to foods. Because they take longer to digest, fats continue to let us feel full even after the proteins and car-

bohydrates have been emptied from the stomach. Fats also stimulate the intestine to release cholecystokinin, a hormone that suppresses the appetite and signals us to stop eating.

Stored body fats provide a fuel reserve for future needs—one pound of body fat provides enough energy to last 1½ to 2 days. The chemical structure of fats allows them to store about twice as much energy in a given weight as carbohydrates do. This means that if a 120-pound woman's fat supply were converted into its energy equivalent in carbohydrates, her weight would balloon to 150 pounds.

The layer of fat just beneath the skin (about half of the total stored amount) provides insulation against changes in temperature. While very thin people may be oversensitive to cold, those carrying extra fat often suffer more in hot weather. This subcutaneous fat is also instrumental in the manufacture of vitamin D when the skin is exposed to the sun.

Deposits of fat that surround the vital organs hold them in place and help cushion them against injury. These protective deposits are among the last to be depleted if the body's energy stores run low.

REDUCING YOUR FAT INTAKE

• Limit meat to 3 or 4 ounces per serving. Buy lean cuts that contain no more than 9 percent fat (look for products that state fat content on the label). Trim all visible fat before cooking. Buy extra-lean ground beef, or better still, select a lean cut and ask the butcher to grind it for you.

• Remove the skin from poultry before eating it. (In some instances, this can be done before cooking.)

• Don't buy prebasted turkey; it's often injected with coconut oil, butter, or other fats.

• Broil, bake, or roast meat, fish, and poultry. Use a roasting rack to drain off the fat as the meat cooks.

• Cook stews and soups in advance; chill and skim off the congealed fat, and reheat before serving.

• Avoid fried foods. Use a nonstick pan and vegetable oil spray for sautéing.

• Buy low-fat (1 percent) or skim milk, low-fat cheese and cottage cheese, and fat-free yogurt.

• Toss salad with fat-free dressings or make your own with lemon juice or vinegar, mustard, herbs, and spices. If oil is called for, use olive oil.

• Buy a low-fat or even a fat-free substitute for mayonnaise.

• Cook rice in a fat-free broth; flavor it with chopped fresh herbs and scallions instead of butter.

• Mash potatoes with low-fat yogurt or buttermilk; add chives and parsley for extra zip.

• Serve higher-fat foods in smaller portions; compensate with larger servings of low-fat items, such as pasta, vegetables, and fruits.

• Eliminate the use of nondairy creamers and toppings; these products are usually high in saturated fats because they are made with palm oil or coconut oil.

• Serve fat-free frozen yogurt instead of ice cream or consider other fat-free dessert alternatives, such as fresh fruits, and gelatins, and angel food cake.

Fats also supply the fatty acids that are essential for numerous chemical processes, including growth and development in children, the production of sex hormones and prostaglandins (hormonelike chemicals that are responsible for regulating many body processes), the formation and function of cell membranes, and the transport of other molecules into and out of the cells. Interestingly enough, fat does not supply energy for the brain and nervous system, both of which rely on glucose for fuel. Like certain vitamins and amino acids, some fatty acids must be obtained from the diet, because the body cannot synthesize them. As a result, our need for essential fatty acids is met by linoleic acid (found in vegetable oils, especially corn, safflower, and soybean oils), which is then converted in the body into arachidonic acid, an essential fatty acid. Finally, fats are needed for the transport and absorption of the fat-soluble vitamins A, D, E, and K.

DIETARY INTAKE

In developing countries fats make up 10 percent of daily calories. In North America daily fat intake has increased from about 30 percent of the daily diet 100 years ago to 35 to 40 percent today. This is the equivalent of approximately a fifth of a pound of pure fat a day and is more than six to eight times what we actually need. The Heart and Stroke Foundation of Canada recommends that adults restrict their total fat intake to no more than 30 percent of each day's calories. Some authorities believe this should be lowered to 20 percent, but others feel this is an unrealistic goal for most people. For healthy children over the age of 2, The Canadian Paediatric Society recommends a diet that provides no more than 30 percent of energy as fat, and no more than 10 percent of energy as saturated fat, which is needed for growth and proper brain development.

A tablespoon of vegetable oil provides enough linoleic acid and fat to transport all the fat-soluble vitamins we need in a day; any more than this is unnecessary. Reducing dietary fat is difficult, however, as two-thirds of it is hidden in lean meat, cheese, fried foods, sauces, nuts, pastries, and so on. (See Reducing Your Fat Intake, left.)

SATURATION

The types of fats consumed may be more important than total fat intake. For years nutritionists have recommended unsaturated over saturated fats (see The Family Tree of Fats, p.141). In general, saturated fats (but not palm, palm kernel, and coconut oils) are solid at room temperature; most animal fats (beef, butter, and cheeses) are saturated. Monounsaturated fats are liquid at room temperature and solid or semisolid under refrigeration (margarine and olive and peanut oils). Polyunsaturated fats are liquid (corn and sunflower oils) unless hydrogen is added in the process called hydrogenation, as in the manufacture of margarine.

Highly saturated fats raise blood CHOLESTEROL levels because they interfere with the removal of cholesterol from the blood. Monounsaturated and polyunsaturated fats, by contrast, either lower blood cholesterol or have no effect on it. When polyunsaturated fats are hydrogenated to make them firm, they become like saturated fats in their effects on blood cholesterol.

Cutting down on saturated fats involves choosing vegetable fats over animal fats and favoring monounsaturates over polyunsaturates. Remember that a food labeled as 95 percent fat free may still derive most of its calories from fat. The fat free calculation is based on total weight which includes the weight of water in the food.

REGIONAL DIETS AND HOW THEY IMPACT ON HEALTH

In an attempt to pinpoint a cause of heart disease, diabetes, and certain cancers that are so prevalent in Western societies, researchers are increasingly looking at data from other cultures whose diets are quite different from our own.

The Japanese Diet

It is no coincidence that the Japanese, whose diet contains just over 30 percent fat (mostly polyunsaturated), compared with 35 to 40 per-

cent in North America—and even more in Britain, Germany, and many other European countries—should enjoy one of the lowest rates of heart disease in the world.

Japanese cuisine emphasizes fish in such forms as sushi, sashimi, and tempura; on average, the Japanese consume 100g (3.5 ounces) of fish a day. The staple food, however, is rice. A basic meal includes steamed rice, soup (such as miso, made with soybean paste), and small side dishes that may contain meat, vegetables (including seaweed), seafoods, fish, eggs, chicken, and noodles, in different sauces and combinations.

As in the West, the Japanese eat three meals a day. Traditionally, breakfast consists of rice and a miso soup made of such ingredients as seaweed, tofu, or leeks, and a side dish, such as grilled fish. A typical lunch might be chicken and vegetables cooked in a soup stock blended with eggs and served on rice. Dinner, the most important meal of the day, might include a small portion of grilled fish as well as a meat dish, such as stewed beef and bean sprouts, served with boiled greens, miso soup, and rice.

The Mediterranean Diet

Although people living in France, Greece, Spain, and Italy eat slightly more fat than North Americans, most of it is unsaturated. Amazingly, their risk of fatal heart disease is less than half that of North Americans.

The staple foods of the Mediterranean countries are rice, bread, potatoes, pasta, and cereals, such as couscous, accompanied by plenty of vegetables. Olive oil is widely used in cooking; other sources of fat include nuts, seeds, and oily fish, such as sardines. It should be noted that butter consumption in Spain, Portugal, Italy, and Greece (but not in France) is relatively low.

The Mediterranean breakfast is light, often made up of rolls, coffee, and fruit juice or fruit. Lunch may

include a protein dish of meat, fish, or poultry, bread or pasta, and sometimes a vegetable. Dinner is often an extended meal of several courses, accompanied by wine. At both lunch and dinner, salad is served, often as a separate course.

People living in southern Europe eat more legumes, nuts, and vegetables than North Americans; on average the Mediterranean diet includes five or more servings of fruits and vegetables a day.

The Western Diet

The typical diet in Canada and other industrialized countries is high in saturated fats from animal sources.

North Americans tend to eat two or more portions of meat, fish, or poultry a day and drink a pint or more of milk or its equivalent in cheese, yogurt, or other milk products. Other popular sources of fat include butter or margarine, mayonnaise, and snack foods, especially potato chips, French fries, ice cream, and baked goods. People are now eating more vegetables, fruits, and starchy foods, but still less than the recommended amounts.

A COUSIN OF CELERY. *Fennel may look like celery with a fat bulb, but it has its own distinctive flavor that is an asset to a variety of dishes.*

FENNEL

BENEFITS
- *An excellent source of vitamins A and C (especially the leaves).*
- *A good source of potassium, calcium, and iron.*
- *High in fiber and low in calories.*

DRAWBACKS
- *The oil in fennel seeds can irritate skin.*

Filling, yet low in calories, fennel is an ideal snack food for people trying to lose weight. Although it has a distinctly different flavor, its stalks can be mistaken for celery. Both vegetables are members of the parsley plant family, and like celery, fennel is very high in fiber and low in calories—a 1-cup serving has only 25 calories. Fennel is much more nutritious than celery, however; a 1-cup serving fulfills one-third of the Recommended Nutrient Intake (RNI) of vitamin A (because of its beta carotene content), and half of the RNI of vitamin C; the leaves contribute even more of these vitamins. One cup of chopped fennel also provides 15 percent or more of the RNIs of iron and calcium, as well as potassium and other minerals.

The sweet, licoricelike flavor of fennel is similar to that of anise; in fact, although it is unrelated to this herb, fennel is sometimes called anise. The licorice flavor goes especially well with fish; try baking or grilling it on a bed of fennel stalks. All parts of the plant are edible, and it can be prepared in many ways: raw in salads or braised, steamed, baked, or sautéed as a side dish. Stuffed and baked bulbs are a flavorful vegetarian entrée; the chopped leaves make a colorful and nutritious garnish for tomato soup and other vegetable dishes.

Aromatic fennel seeds are one of our oldest spices; they also are used to make a refreshing tea that is said to alleviate bloating, FLATULENCE, and other intestinal problems.

FEVER

TAKE PLENTY OF
- *Fluids.*
- *Frequent small, light, bland meals.*

Although normal body temperature is generally spoken of as 98.6°F (37°C), human temperature tends to vary over the course of the day, from about

97.6°F (36.4°C) in the morning to about 99.5°F (37.5°C) in the late afternoon—and what's normal for one person can vary above or below the average temperature by as much as one degree. Although minimal increases of a degree or so may simply be caused by hot weather or being bundled up in too much clothing, most people can feel a difference in their body temperature that they will call a fever once it reaches 100.5°F (38°C) or 101°F (38.5°C).

Fever is not a disease in itself, but rather a symptom of some underlying problem, most commonly an infection. Depending on the cause, a fever is often accompanied by other symptoms, such as sweating, shivering, thirst, flushed skin, nausea, vomiting, and DIARRHEA.

Experiencing a fever alone does not necessarily require treatment—it is one of the body's natural ways of fighting disease and, generally, should not be suppressed unless it is very high or accompanied by other symptoms. When fever-lowering medication is indicated, either acetaminophen or aspirin may be effective. But aspirin should never be given to anyone under the age of 18 without a doctor's approval; aspirin given during a viral infection increases the risk of developing Reye's syndrome, a potentially life-threatening disease affecting the brain and liver. Keep in mind that children's fevers can rise rapidly, so even a high temperature over 102°F (39°C) does not necessarily reflect the severity of an illness.

NUTRITIONAL NEEDS

There is no medical basis for the saying "feed a cold and starve a fever." If anything, you need more calories than normal if you have a raised temperature because your metabolic rate rises as the fever rises. Also, the body needs extra calories and nutrients to fight off the infection or other illness. A patient with a raised temperature should drink plenty of liquids, such as diluted fruit

juices, and if not suffering from diarrhea or vomiting, should also be encouraged to eat light, nourishing meals.

If diarrhea is a problem, solid foods should be avoided until the bowels stabilize. Then, small servings of bland foods, such as ripe bananas, applesauce, white toast dipped in chicken or beef broth, chicken-rice soup, rice cereals, boiled or poached eggs, and baked potatoes, can be eaten.

Sweating, the body's response to an elevated temperature, results in the loss of fluid, which is worsened if there is diarrhea or vomiting. So it is important to drink at least eight 8-ounce glasses of fluid daily to prevent dehydration. If a feverish person does not feel thirsty, it may be easier to sip a few teaspoons of fruit juice diluted with an equal volume of water every few minutes rather than to drink a whole glass at once. Or the patient, especially if a child, can be given a frozen fruit juice bar to suck on.

Warning: Feverish infants can get dehydrated very quickly, because they have a large body surface in proportion to their fluid volume. When babies have high temperatures, parents should give frequent bottles of plain water.

WHEN TO CALL A DOCTOR

Consult a doctor about a fever in the following circumstances:

• If an infant under the age of 3 months has a fever that is higher than 100°F (38°C).

• If a child or adult under 60 has a fever above 103°F (39.5°C).

• If an adult over 60 has a fever over 102°F (39°C).

• If a fever of 101°F (38.5°C) persists for more than 3 days.

• If a child or adult has a fever of 101°F (38.5°C) that is accompanied by severe headache, nausea and vomiting, a stiff neck, change in alertness, or hypersensitivity to light.

FIBER

BENEFITS
• *Helps prevent constipation.*
• *Relieves the symptoms of diverticulosis and hemorrhoids.*
• *May help reduce risk of colon cancer.*
• *Plays a role in lowering elevated blood cholesterol levels.*
• *Useful as a means of controlling weight.*

DRAWBACKS
• *Too much fiber can cause bloating and other digestive problems.*
• *Some high-fiber foods can cause gas.*
• *Excessive fiber may lead to iron, zinc, and other mineral deficiencies.*

Dietary fiber (also called roughage) is the indigestible component of plant foods. The effects of fiber appear to have been known since biblical times, but only in recent years have scientists begun to understand its importance in the daily diet as a means of preventing disease and maintaining health. Although fiber is not a magic bullet that can prevent or cure everything from cancer to indigestion, research does suggest that the typically low-fiber diets consumed in Western industrialized countries may contribute to such widespread illnesses as coronary artery disease, diabetes, and diseases of the large intestine, including cancer.

The typical Canadian diet is estimated to provide about 15g of fiber a day. The Canadian Cancer Society recommends a daily consumption of about 30g of dietary fiber from a wide variety of high-fiber foods. But they do not recommend taking a whopping dose of bran or a fiber supplement once a day.

DIETARY SOURCES

Most dietary fiber comes from fruits, vegetables, dried beans, peas and other legumes, cereals, grains, nuts, and seeds. The outer layer of a grain, which contains the most fiber, is removed in

INCREASING FIBER INTAKE

- Eat the skins of potatoes, apples and other fruits, and vegetables.
- Serve vegetables raw or steamed.
- Use whole-grain cereals and breads and brown rice; avoid products made from white or highly processed flour.
- If you can't tolerate a particular high-fiber food, substitute something else; for example, replace beans with another vegetable.

the refining process. This explains why whole-grain products, such as brown rice and whole-wheat bread, are such good sources of fiber.

Fiber falls into two broad categories: soluble and insoluble. The soluble fibers dissolve in water and become sticky. They include pectin, which is contained in fruits, nuts, legumes, and some vegetables; guar, carrageenan, and other gums found in seaweed and algae; and mucilages, which are present in plant seeds and some plant secretions. Insoluble fiber does not dissolve, passing through the digestive tract chewed but otherwise largely unchanged. Insoluble fibers include cellulose, which is found in bran, whole grains, and vegetables; hemicellulose, contained in fruits, nuts, whole grains, and vegetables; and lignin, a woody substance that is also found in bran, nuts, whole grains, and the skins of fruits.

ROLE IN GOOD HEALTH

As it passes through the digestive tract, fiber acts as a sponge, absorbing many times its own weight in liquid. The result is that stools are softer and bulkier and can pass through the intestines more rapidly and be expelled more easily, thus decreasing the likelihood of constipation. This quick passage also helps prevent related bowel disorders, such as diverticulosis and hemorrhoids, which can occur from the increased

pressure created by hard stools. It has also been theorized that fiber protects against cancer of the colon by causing stools to pass more quickly, thus reducing contact with cancer-causing agents being carried in them. In addition, some researchers speculate that the increased water content of high-fiber stools is also protective because it dilutes these carcinogens. This theory remains unproved, however, and there may be other substances in high-fiber foods that protect against cancer.

Some of the soluble fibers—pectin, oat bran, guar, and others—can lower blood cholesterol levels; in turn, this decreases the risk of coronary artery disease and heart attacks due to atherosclerosis, the buildup of fatty plaque in arteries. Simply adding soluble fiber to the diet is not enough, however; fat consumption must also be reduced.

Although insoluble fibers have little or no effect, some soluble fibers also help to control blood sugar levels in people with diabetes. Increasing fiber will not cure diabetes, but a diet that is high in complex carbohydrates and fiber can allow some diabetics to lower their medication doses.

Because it is filling and low in calories, eating fiber is helpful when you're trying to lose or control your weight. It provides a welcome feeling of fullness, although this tends to wear off rather quickly as it passes through the digestive system. The best way to use fiber for weight loss is to consume a balanced diet that also includes modest amounts

of protein and fat in each meal. Because the body metabolizes these more slowly than fiber, you will not become hungry again as quickly.

HOW MUCH IS TOO MUCH?

Increasing the amount of fiber in the diet should be done gradually, and its intake should be spread throughout the day. Suddenly increasing fiber intake from 10g to 30g a day, for example, can provoke such unpleasant symptoms as bloating and gassiness. Similarly, consuming a large amount of fiber at once can lead to abdominal cramps or even a bowel obstruction, particularly among older or sedentary persons who already have sluggish bowel function.

Fiber pills are not a good alternative to actually consuming fiber through your diet. Pills and other types of supplements lack the other nutrients and substances found in high-fiber foods, and it is possible that these, too, are instrumental in disease prevention, not just the fiber itself.

Too much bran and other insoluble fibers can prevent the digestive system from absorbing certain minerals properly, particularly calcium, iron, and zinc. This is rarely a problem and is unlikely to occur unless more than 35g of fiber a day are consumed.

Fiber may be directly anticarcinogenic. Wheat bran, for example, binds nitrite, making it unavailable to form cancer-causing nitrosamines, and fiber may prevent carcinogens from entering cells.

FIBER IN THE DAILY DIET

A well-balanced diet will provide all the fiber you need, without supplying too much. While it has little or no nutritional value, fiber forms an essential link in the body's digestive chain. Soluble and insoluble fiber are equally important. Some plant foods provide both types—apple peel, for instance, has insoluble cellulose, while the flesh is an excellent source of the soluble fiber pectin. Wheat bran, whole grains, and dried fruits are particularly good sources of both forms.

FIGS

Figs have provided sugar in the Mediterranean diet for at least 6,000 years. Introduced to North America in about 1600, figs were planted throughout California by Spanish missionaries in the 1700s but were not cultivated commercially until the 20th century.

Not fruit but flower receptacles, figs bud like other fruit blossoms on the bare branches. The true fruits are the seedlike achenes that develop, along with the inconspicuous flowers, inside the fleshy bulb.

Neither bees nor wind contribute to the pollination of figs. Instead, a unique species of wasp, only about $1/8$ inch long, pollinates the flowers as it enters and exits through the small pore on the rounded end of the fig. Commercial fig growers depend on this symbiotic relationship and foster it by tying wild figs containing wasp eggs to the branches of their cultivated trees. This method of ensuring fertilization has been used at least since it was recorded in ancient times by a pupil of Aristotle.

Traditionally, figs were ripened by rubbing their skins with oil, which stimulated production of the maturing agent, ethylene. North American fig growers no longer follow this practice, as it detracts from the taste of the fruit.

Because fresh figs typically bruise easily and spoil rapidly, most are dried

Ficus carica

Fig trees usually bear two crops of fruit each summer.

The fig tree, often mentioned in the Bible, was said to grow in the Garden of Eden. After their fall, Adam and Eve used its leaves to preserve their modesty.

BIBLICAL FRUIT. *Figs, both dried and fresh, have been a popular delicacy in the Mediterranean area at least since biblical times. Fresh figs are at their best just picked from the tree.*

or canned. Although high in calories—260 in five pieces—dried figs are a highly nutritious snack food, contributing about one-fifth of the Recommended Nutrient Intakes (RNIs) of calcium, iron, and magnesium, as well as 5g of fiber, more than 750mg of potassium, and reasonable amounts of vitamin B_6 and folate. Consuming figs with a citrus fruit or another source of vitamin C will increase the absorption of their iron.

Fresh California figs are available only for a short time after they are harvested in late summer or early fall. Although expensive, their delicate flavor and high nutrient content are worth a splurge. Examine the figs carefully before buying them, however; the fruit should be soft but not mushy, with no bruises or signs of mold.

Both fresh and dried figs are high in pectin, a soluble FIBER that helps lower blood cholesterol. Figs may also have a laxative effect, so they are especially beneficial to people who suffer from chronic constipation; in others, however, overindulging can provoke diarrhea.

Fig bars are more nutritious and lower in fat and sugar than most cookies; two bars contain less than 100 calories. Because their fruity centers tend to stick to teeth—like plain dried figs—it's important to brush after eating.

FISH

BENEFITS
- *An excellent source of complete protein, iron, and other minerals.*
- *Some are high in vitamin A.*
- *Contains omega-3 fatty acids.*

DRAWBACKS
- *Some may harbor PCBs, mercury, and other pollutants.*
- *Often expensive.*

Although a forkful of fish is a gold mine of concentrated nutrients, Canadians consume an average of only 16 pounds a year, compared to our annual per capita intake of about 50 pounds of beef and 55 pounds of chicken. While these statistics seem to indicate a clear culinary preference for beef and chicken, there are important health benefits to be gained from eating more fish and less meat.

The average Western diet provides about twice as much protein as necessary; in itself, this might not be a problem except that our typical protein choices of red meat and dairy products come packed with huge quantities of saturated FATS. In contrast, fish and SHELLFISH have more protein, fewer calories, and less fat per serving than most meats. The fats in fish are particularly high in polyunsaturates, which remain liquid even when chilled. (If fish had a lot of saturated fat, it would congeal into a solid mass and prevent them from moving in their cold-water habitat.) And although fish contains cholesterol, since it lacks saturated fat, it is no more likely to increase blood cholesterol than skinless poultry is.

HEALTH BENEFITS
Eating fish three times a week has been associated with a significant decrease in the rate of heart disease. This became apparent when scientists noted that coronary artery disease (a leading cause of death in Canada and most Western countries) was almost nonexistent among the Eskimos of Greenland, Japanese fishermen, and Native people of the Pacific Northwest. The one factor that these three groups had in common was a diet that relied heavily on fish for protein. When researchers examined the effects of different diets in other populations, they found that men who ate fish regularly two or three times a week were much less likely to suffer heart attacks than men who shunned fish.

It's not yet known whether the effect is due to one factor or many, but evidence so far points to the beneficial action of fish oils. Fish oils are rich in a type of unsaturated fat that is known as omega-3 fatty acids. These fatty acids alter the chemical composition of the blood by increasing levels of HDL (the cholesterol that helps to prevent heart attacks) and decreasing levels of LDL ("bad" cholesterol) and triglycerides. Fatty acids also make blood platelets less likely to stick together and form clots, and they increase the flexibility of red blood cells, enabling them to pass more readily through tiny vessels.

The human body uses omega-3 fatty acids to manufacture prostaglandins, chemicals that play a role in many processes, including inflammation and other functions of the immune system. Several studies have found that a diet that includes fish oil equivalent to the amount in an 8-ounce daily serving of fish could relieve the painful symptoms of rheumatoid arthritis. This positive change was not permanent; symptoms quickly returned to their original level when the participants in the studies stopped eating the experimental diet. Doctors treating the patients believe that the beneficial effect was due to fish oil components, especially one termed eicosapentaenoic acid (EPA). This fatty acid seems to promote the production of forms of prostaglandins and other substances that are less active in inflammation than those derived from saturated and polyunsaturated fats.

NUTRITIONAL VALUE
All fish are rich in nutrients, especially in the water-soluble B vitamins. Oily fish are particularly rich in vitamins A, D, and K. Fish also supply a wealth of minerals: iodine, magnesium, calcium, phosphorus, iron, potassium, copper, and fluoride. In addition, the bones in canned salmon and sardines are an excellent source of calcium.

Fish are high in protein because they carry a massive bulk of muscle on a much more spindly skeleton than land animals do. Contrary to popular belief, it's not necessarily true that the darker the flesh, the oilier the fish; the dark color is, in fact, due to the presence of myoglobin, a pigment that stores oxygen in the muscles. The flesh of salmon and trout gets its appealing pink color from astaxanthin, a carotenoid pigment derived from the crustaceans and insects the fish feed on. The diet of farmed fish is fortified with carotenoids to enhance the pink color of the flesh.

There is no difference in nutrient content between fish that are farmed and those caught in the wild. However, some farmed fish, such as salmon and trout, have a texture that is mealier than that of their wild counterparts.

HOW MUCH IS ENOUGH?
Although the Heart and Stroke Foundation of Canada makes no specific recommendations about fish consumption, the general scientific consensus is that at least three servings of fish a week are required to provide the benefits attributed to omega-3 fatty acids. Fish oil supplements have not under-

A HEALTHY CATCH. *Oily fish, such as tuna (tail up), salmon (top), and mackerel (lower pair), are high in health-giving omega-3 fatty acids.*

FISH FACTS AND FOOD VALUES

NUTRIENTS PER 3 OZ	DID YOU KNOW?

WHITE FISH, SUCH AS COD, HADDOCK, SOLE, AND FLOUNDER

Calories: 100–160
Protein: 17–23g
Fat: 0.8–1.3g
Iron: 0.3–1.1mg

These fish are rich in vitamin B$_{12}$, and they contain a low to fair level of omega-3 fatty acids.

OILY FISH, SUCH AS HERRING, MACKEREL, SALMON, AND TROUT

Calories: 180–215
Protein: 18–21g
Fat: 5.6 (salmon) to 14.3g (herring)
Iron: 0.8–1.0mg

Oily fish are an excellent source of omega-3 fatty acids and vitamin B$_{12}$. Some of these fish also contain small amounts of calcium.

CANNED FISH, SUCH AS ANCHOVIES, SARDINES, AND TUNA

Calories: 100–210, depending on whether the fish is canned in oil or water.
Protein: 17.7–23g
Fat: 2.1 (tuna in water) to 8.4g (sardines in oil)
Iron: 0.5 (tuna in water) to 3.6mg (anchovies)

Canned tuna contains only small amounts of omega-3 fatty acids. Anchovies are high in sodium and purines; they should be avoided by those with gout or high blood pressure. Similarly, sardines contain purines and should not be consumed by gout patients.

SMOKED FISH, SUCH AS SALMON, MACKEREL, AND KIPPERS (HERRING)

Calories: 100–180
Protein: 18.6g
Fat: 7.8–15.1g
Iron: 1.2mg

Smoked fish, while tasty, tend to be packed with sodium; thus, they should either be consumed occasionally in very small amounts or avoided entirely by people with high blood pressure.

FROZEN FISH STICKS

Calories: 150–215
Protein: 8.6–13.3g
Fat: 7.6–12.8g
Iron: 0.3mg

Fish sticks are an extremely popular frozen food product, especially with children, who might not otherwise be willing to try fish. However, as they are dipped in batter, often fried, and then served with tartar sauce, they tend to be high in fat. To lower the fat content, try baking them in an oven rather than frying in oil, and flavoring them with lemon instead of a high-fat sauce.

CAVIAR, BLACK AND RED, GRANULAR

Calories: 215–225
Protein: 21–23g
Fat: 12.8–15.6g

Beluga caviar is the highest quality caviar, and also the most expensive; the sturgeon that produce these eggs can weigh as much as 3,500 pounds and can be up to 100 years old. Caviar is highly perishable and should be bought fresh, stored in a refrigerator, and served in a tub of ice. It is very high in sodium and calories; a mere teaspoonful contains 40 calories. This delicacy should be avoided by those trying to watch their weight or anyone with high blood pressure.

---

gone the rigorous testing that drugs are subjected to and therefore are not recommended. Advertisements fail to mention that the supplements are usually high in calories and cholesterol; also, they are often high in vitamins A and D, which can be dangerous when taken in large doses. Use a fish oil supplement only if your doctor prescribes a specific brand and monitors your health.

POTENTIAL HAZARDS

The rising popularity of sushi bars and restaurants attests to a venturesome attitude toward eating. Although chefs trained in the art of preparing the Japanese rawfish specialty usually maintain rigorous standards of freshness and cleanliness, eating raw fish carries certain risks. Both freshwater and saltwater fish can be intermediate hosts for parasitic worms. Many of the fish used to make sushi are chilled to a temperature that kills parasites; nonetheless, sushi-eaters should be aware that there is a risk of infection.

Parasites are also sometimes present in raw fish preparations, such as Dutch "green" herring and Scandinavian gravlax (pickled salmon). However, the pickling process used in pickled herring and properly made gravlax eliminates worms and eggs.

Oily fish, such as fresh herring and mackerel, must be cooked or processed soon after they are netted. If kept too long before cooking, they can spoil and cause scombroid poisoning—accompanied by a rash and stomach upset—due to bacterial growth on the fish.

Shellfish from waters polluted by human waste bring a threat of viral hepatitis as well as bacterial infections that can cause severe gastrointestinal upset. Shellfish farms are required to meet strict health standards to ensure that their products are safe. The old rule of eating oysters only in the "R" months remains a sound one; oysters taken during warm non-R months—

May, June, July, and August—are more likely to be contaminated.

Coastal waters are, at times, tinged red by marine microorganisms in the phenomenon known as the "red tide." Ask where shellfish comes from; you should never eat any from red tide areas. Shellfish ingest the microorganism, which produces a toxin that is not destroyed by cooking. Eating contaminated shellfish brings on symptoms of poisoning within 30 minutes: facial numbness, breathing difficulty, muscle weakness, and sometimes partial paralysis. Ciguatera poisoning is similar, and is caused by a heat stable toxin produced by a species of plankton. The plankton are consumed by fish, which then pass the poison on to the humans who eat them. In some cases, the effects of this toxin have lasted more than 20 years.

Large, long-lived fish, such as tuna and swordfish, may accumulate heavy-metal contaminants—especially mercury—which are toxic to the human nervous system and can be dangerous for unborn babies. Because of this potential hazard, women should avoid fresh tuna and swordfish during pregnancy. Tuna that is processed for canning is routinely inspected, however; you can be confident that this and other canned fish products available on supermarket shelves are safe to eat.

Some species of fish caught in certain areas may show high levels of PCBs and other industrial pollutants; they are best avoided. Pregnant women are probably best advised not to eat striped bass, especially from the northeastern regions, which may accumulate oil residues.

A final word of caution: If you're serving fish to young children or elderly family members, flake the flesh to make sure there aren't any fine bones that could get stuck in the throat.

BUYING FISH

Unlike most other perishable food items, fish is not subject to mandatory

---

FUGU: DINING WITH DEATH

The Japanese specialty fugu—puffer fish, or blowfish—can turn a dinner into a fatal game of Russian roulette. The ovaries, roe, and liver of the puffer fish contain a deadly toxin. A slip of the knife during preparation can allow this poison to contaminate the flesh. The toxin is so powerful that consuming just a drop quickly brings on paralysis followed by death. Fugu is never served in Japanese homes, and restaurant chefs must endure a 7-year apprenticeship before they are entrusted with preparation of the dish. Despite these precautions, fugu is the major cause of fatal food poisoning in Japan, causing dozens of deaths every year, according to official statistics. Japanese food scientists claim to be developing a non-toxic variety of fugu; it remains to be seen, however, whether consumers will want the delicacy once the danger is removed.

---

evaluation and grading by federal government inspectors to ensure safety and acceptable quality. Instead, processors, packers, and brokers subscribe to a voluntary program of inspection by Fisheries Canada. Self-monitoring in the fishing industry has been very reliable. For added insurance, the following should be observed:

Buy canned tuna that is packed in water; oil-packed tuna is substantially higher in calories. Be sure to thoroughly drain the oil from other canned fish, such as sardines and anchovies.

When buying fresh fish, look for bright, glossy skin; clear, bulging eyes; tight scales; and firm flesh. There should be only a clean, briny aroma—

no whiff of iodine, ammonia, or strong "fishiness" should be present. Buy fish only at markets that keep them covered (both top and bottom) with ice.

COST AND PREPARATION

Many shoppers recoil from the price per pound of fish and don't stop to consider the actual cost-value ratio. Although fresh fish can be expensive to buy, it is economical to use. If you buy a whole fish, use the head, bones, and skin to make stock for a low-fat fish soup or stew. You can combine fish with carbohydrates to make a small amount go a long way: a single poached salmon steak flaked into spinach noodles can serve a small group; one or two fillets of cod mixed with leftover mashed potatoes, scallions, and herbs can make a family meal of fish cakes.

Fish requires little preparation, and it cooks quickly. Steaming, poaching, baking, and grilling are methods that will preserve the flavor of fish without adding calories. Avoid dishes that demand lavish amounts of buttery sauces; these sauces spoil the low-fat value of the fish and mask its unique character.

FORMS OF FISH

While beef has an elaborate spectrum of grades and cuts, fish at the market come in only a few forms:

Whole fish, which are also called "round" fish, are purchased in the form in which they were caught.

Whole drawn fish have been gutted via a small opening so they remain whole in appearance. The heads and tails are left intact, but the gills and scales are often removed.

Whole dressed fish are first split and gutted, then scaled. Also, the fins, heads, and tails may be removed.

Fillets are the deboned meaty pieces of fish stripped away from the backbone.

Steaks are cross-cut slices of a dressed large round fish containing a section of backbone at the center.

FLATULENCE

CONSUME PLENTY OF
- *Yogurt made with live cultures.*
- *Peppermint and fennel teas.*

CUT DOWN ON
- *Fatty foods.*
- *Dried beans and other legumes, onions, broccoli and other members of the cabbage family, and any other foods that exacerbate the problem.*
- *Fruits and fruit-based sweeteners, such as sorbitol and fructose.*

AVOID
- *Milk if you are lactose intolerant.*
- *Carbonated drinks, chewing gum, and drinking straws, which all encourage swallowing air.*
- *Bran and high-fiber laxatives.*
- *High doses of vitamin C.*

Excessive gas, or flatulence, causes uncomfortable abdominal bloating, which can be relieved only by bringing the gas up from the stomach (burping) or expelling it through the anus. Although it is embarrassing, this experience is the completely natural result of intestinal bacteria acting on undigested carbohydrates and proteins. The average person has more than 13 episodes a day, most of which pass unnoticed. It's only when certain malodorous gases are released that the problem becomes unpleasant.

Flatulence seems to worsen with age, and some individuals are simply more susceptible to gas than others. Eating smaller portions, chewing food thoroughly, and not gulping liquids should minimize episodes. Some experts also believe that reducing the amount of air in the digestive tract may help to prevent flatulence, so they advise against drinking carbonated beverages, chewing gum, or drinking through a straw, which promotes swallowing air.

Some foods are especially notorious gas producers; topping the list are those that produce methane gas when fermented by intestinal bacteria. Soybeans, kidney beans, lentils, and dried peas can result in unpleasant-smelling flatus. Except for lentils and split peas, which do not need to be presoaked, soaking dried beans for at least 4 hours (preferably 8 or more hours) before cooking them in plenty of fresh water helps to reduce the indigestible sugars, raffinose and stachyose, that cause gas.

Many people also experience flatulence after eating onions and Brussels sprouts, broccoli, cauliflower, and other members of the cabbage plant family; you may be able to reduce gas production by adding such spices as anise, ginger, rosemary, bay leaf, and fennel seeds during cooking. Some cooks add kombu seaweed, available in Asian markets and natural food stores, to cooking water for the same purpose.

Passing gas can be an uncomfortable side effect of a well-intentioned move toward a healthier, high-fiber diet. Nutritionists suggest increasing fiber intake gradually, and they recommend not using bran and high-fiber laxatives. In addition, sorbitol, fructose, and other sweeteners cause flatulence in some people, as can doses of vitamin C.

Beano, a relatively new product made from natural enzymes, is available in pharmacies as drops or tablets. It helps reduce flatus when a few drops are sprinkled on gas-producing food or a tablet is taken before a meal. A cup of peppermint or fennel tea after a meal sometimes helps improve digestion and reduce flatulence. Some people find that eating yogurt made with live cultures cuts down on flatulence. Yoga, particularly the knee-to-chest pose, is also said to alleviate the condition.

Sometimes flatulence is due to a medical disorder; if the problem is severe and persists, it could be a symptom of food ALLERGIES, CROHN'S DISEASE, INTOLERANCE TO MILK, or IRRITABLE BOWEL SYNDROME (IBS).

FLOURS

BENEFITS
- *A concentrated source of starch.*
- *Enriched flours are a good source of calcium, iron, and B vitamins.*

DRAWBACKS
- *Substantial vitamins, minerals, and fiber are lost during milling.*
- *Whole-grain flours may contain insect parts and eggs.*

People have been grinding various seeds, as well as dried fish and other foods, to make flour for thousands of years. Initially, the seeds were roasted and ground between two stones to make them easier to eat; eventually, water was added to the flour, and the paste baked into a type of crude BREAD. As agricultural societies developed, they devised increasingly sophisticated methods of grinding and sifting grains and seeds. Today huge, fully automated mills are responsible for producing tons of flour, which are then transformed into breads, PASTA, pastries and other baked goods, and thickening agents and other food ADDITIVES.

NUTRITIONAL VALUE

In general, flour is a more concentrated source of calories than the original GRAINS, seeds, or other raw materials because the moisture has been removed. For example, 1 pound of potato flour contains 1,600 calories, compared to 350 in a pound of raw potatoes; 1 cup of cornmeal has about 400 calories, compared to 100 in a cup of cooked corn. This increased density of calories is the reason food relief organizations often prefer to provide flour made from grains, legumes, tubers, or dried fish rather than the raw products.

On the other hand, many nutrients are lost in flour milling and processing. Wheat flour, our most common variety, is milled by using steel rollers to crack the grain, sifting out the bran and germ, and putting the remaining part of the seed (the endosperm) through a series of rollers and sifters to make a fine, powdery product. Removing the bran and germ from wheat reduces the fiber and the amounts of 22 vitamins and minerals found in the whole grain. Because of this depletion, wheat flour is usually enriched with iron, riboflavin, thiamine, and niacin (important nutrients that might not be provided otherwise). Manufacturers may also add calcium and vitamin D; the product label specifies whether or not the flour is enriched and what nutrients have been restored or added.

Whole-grain flour, which is made by restoring the germ and bran at the end of the process, provides more fiber, protein, vitamin E, and trace minerals than enriched white varieties do. Depending upon the type of flour, other ingredients are added; these include salt and baking soda or baking powder to make self-rising flour, extra gluten for special baked products, and benzoyl peroxide or other bleaching agents.

TYPES OF FLOURS

Almost any type of grain or seed can be ground into flour, although those with a high fat or moisture content must first be defatted and roasted or dehydrated.

Because most grains lack gluten, the protein that makes flour ideal for baking, they are usually mixed with varying amounts of wheat flour, which is high in gluten. Some of the more common flours include the following:

Amaranth is higher in protein, including the amino acid lysine, than most other flours.

Arrowroot, made from maranta roots, is one of the most digestible flours.

Barley, a soft, bland flour, is used for unleavened baked goods.

Buckwheat, made from the same seeds as kasha, is high in lysine.

Cornmeal is not as nutritious as many other types of flour, but it provides a complete protein when combined with beans and other legumes.

Cottonseed flour, made from hulled seeds after oil is extracted, contains very high levels of protein.

Fish flour is produced from whole dried defatted fish; it contains very high levels of calcium and protein.

Oat, which is high in soluble fiber, is used mostly in cereals and breads.

Potato, made from steamed and dried potatoes, is used in baking and is also a common thickening agent.

Rice is manufactured mostly from broken polished grain; typically, this flour is used to make noodles, cookies, and unleavened baked goods.

Rye is high in fiber if the bran and germ have been retained. It is usually combined with wheat flour to form a mixture used in bread-baking.

Soy, made from soybeans, is often combined with wheat flour to increase the protein content of baked goods.

Triticale, a hybrid of wheat and rye, is also very high in protein; it is often mixed with wheat flour to increase its nutritional content.

FLAVORFUL FLOURS. *By combining whole-grain and refined flours, bakers can produce a tastier, more nutritious product that still has a fine texture.*

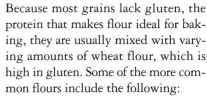

FLUORIDATION: A CONTROVERSY THAT WON'T GO AWAY

*There's no doubt that adding small amounts of fluoride
to drinking water strengthens teeth and bones.
But critics charge that the risks outweigh these benefits.*

One of the most enduring public health controversies of our time revolves around the fluoridation of public drinking water. Numerous studies show that when fluoride—a mineral that strengthens teeth and bones—is added to drinking water, the incidence of childhood dental decay drops by 50 percent. To capitalize on this protection against cavities, fluoride is also added to most toothpastes. Furthermore, pediatricians often recommend fluoride supplements for breast-fed babies to compensate for the inadequate levels in mother's milk.

The results have been dramatic. Children who lack adequate fluoride almost always have one or more dental cavities by the age of puberty, a fate escaped by more than 50 percent of youngsters who receive the mineral from drinking water or other sources.

Fluoride can be found naturally in soil, water, and many foods, but the amounts vary greatly from one source to another. The volcanic soil in parts of the U.S. West and Southwest are high in fluoride; consequently, water in these areas also contains sufficient amounts of the mineral. In other regions where there is less than 1 part of fluoride to 1 million parts (ppm) of water, health officials may advocate fluoridation to bring it up to that level.

Despite the proven benefits and low cost of water fluoridation, many pub-

---

BENEFITS
- *Strengthens teeth and reduces the risk of dental decay.*
- *Helps bones retain calcium.*

DRAWBACKS
- *Excessive amounts can cause tooth mottling and weakened bones.*

---

lic water systems in North America forgo it, usually due to strong public opposition. This stems from fears that fluoridation creates more serious health problems.

FLUORIDE TOXICITY

Even a small overdose of fluoride is toxic, and in time can cause fluorosis, a disorder in which the teeth become mottled and wear unevenly. Bones may also become discolored, thickened, soft, and may fracture easily. The effects are cumulative; it may take years of ingesting excessive fluoride to develop fluorosis. Toxicity can occur from various sources; for example, when children frequently eat fluoridated toothpaste, when drinking water contains large amounts of naturally occurring fluoride, or when the diet provides high fluoride foods.

One part of fluoride per million parts of water or food is safe; at this level, an adult might ingest up to 2mg per day, and a child, somewhat less. Fluorosis develops when a person consumes more than 20mg of fluoride

a day over an extended period of time. This might happen when the ratio of fluoride in water reaches 2.5 ppm, or when fluoride in food exceeds 30 to 40 ppm. Very few foods are in this range; the richest source is dried seaweed, which has more than 300 ppm. Dried tea leaves have about 30 ppm, but this amount is greatly diluted when brewed in tea. Still, a person who drinks a lot of tea made with water that is already high in fluoride has an increased risk of fluorosis.

Opponents of water fluoridation also charge that the mineral can cause cancer, but there is no scientific evidence to back this assertion. Long-term studies in some 30 countries have failed to show an increased cancer risk associated with fluoride.

OTHER SOURCES

Wheat germ and soybeans are high in fluoride. Most other foods naturally contain varying amounts, depending on where they are grown.

Grains and vegetables taken from fluoride-rich soil will have higher-than-average amounts of the mineral, but it is unlikely that anyone could eat amounts of these foods large enough to cause a problem.

Good animal sources of fluoride include such foods as cheese, eggs, chicken, lean beef and lamb, and pork. Fish and seafood are also good sources, especially canned sardines and salmon eaten with the bones.

FOOD POISONING

CONSUME PLENTY OF
- *Diluted sweetened drinks to replace lost body fluids and provide energy.*
- *Bananas, rice, cooked apples, and dry toast (the BRAT diet) for 24 to 48 hours after symptoms have subsided.*

AVOID
- *Overhandling any food.*
- *Having raw and cooked foods touch, such as on food preparation surfaces.*
- *Raw or undercooked eggs, such as in mayonnaise, sauces, mousses, cold desserts, or unbaked cake batters.*
- *Old leftovers or foods that are past their expiration date.*

Next to the common cold, food poisoning is our most prevalent infection, afflicting perhaps as many as 90 million North Americans. Health Canada monitors the incidence of food poisoning, but the number of reported cases—up to 1 million a year—shows trends and does not reflect the actual number of cases, which is several times this figure.

In all, more than 250 diseases can be spread through contaminated food. The term "food poisoning" is now generally applied to illness (most often gastroenteritis, but occasionally nervous system complications) resulting from bacterial or viral contamination of food. Bacteria can cause disease either through their rapid multiplication inside the body (bacterial infection) or through toxins that they may produce (bacterial intoxication). While heat destroys bacteria in food, some toxins, such as those produced by staphylococcal organisms, are heat stable. Infestation with parasites from raw or undercooked meat and FISH can also cause food poisoning. Thanks to strict regulations controlling food processing and the use of additives, illness due to deliberate adulteration of foods is a thing of the past.

There are many opportunities for contamination to occur along the trail of harvesting, processing, packing, transporting, and displaying food for sale. Most cases of food poisoning are caused by bacterial contamination, usually traceable to faulty handling and preparation in the home or in food service outlets. The microorganisms most often involved are *Clostridium botulinum*, *Clostridium perfringens*, *Escherichia coli*, *Listeria monocytogenes*, *Salmonella* strains, and *Staphylococcus aureus*.

TYPICAL SYMPTOMS

Food poisoning usually causes nausea and vomiting, diarrhea and cramps, headache, and sometimes fever and prostration. The infection can be serious in vulnerable people, especially in infants and young children, people with chronic illness (including AIDS and other immune system disorders), and the frail elderly. Call the doctor if someone you know in these groups has symptoms of food poisoning. Otherwise, most cases clear up without medical help, although DEHYDRATION may occur unless fluids lost as a result of vomiting and DIARRHEA are replaced.

Botulism is a rare but grave form of food poisoning caused by a nerve toxin from *C. botulinum*. Symptoms of nerve and muscle impairment are double vision and difficulty in speaking, chewing, swallowing, and breathing; any of these call for immediate medical attention.

The body rids itself of the organisms that cause food poisoning through vomiting and diarrhea. Unpleasant though they may be, it's best to let nature run its course. Don't tax your digestive system with food until it's able to handle it. Prevent fluid depletion by sipping a mixture of apple juice and water, weak tea, or a rehydration fluid.

When you're confident that your system has settled down, reintroduce

Case Study

*O*n her way back from playing tennis, Jean dropped in on her neighbor, who was baking a cake. Jean dipped her finger in the batter, licked it, and declared the mixture first-rate. Later that evening she was delighted when her neighbor and friends arrived with the frosted cake for a surprise birthday party.

The next morning Jean awoke with a splitting headache, nausea, and diarrhea, which continued throughout the day. As symptoms abated, she drank diluted apple juice and tried a dry salty cracker. The next morning she managed to finish some applesauce with rice cereal.

When Jean inquired, she learned that none of her friends had stomach problems. She concluded that it could have been her rash sampling of the uncooked, egg-rich cake batter that gave her a dose of salmonella. Within a few days Jean was back to her regular diet and her tennis game, and had resolved to sample no more raw batter.

155

WHAT'S YOUR POISON?

If you have symptoms of food poisoning, try to figure out when you ate a suspect meal, as this can help determine which bacteria are responsible. If a fever develops or the symptoms persist for more than a couple of days, consult your doctor.

MICROORGANISMS	SYMPTOMS
CAMPYLOBACTER JEJUNI	
Infection usually stems from contact with infected animals or contaminated food (in many cases, from raw or undercooked poultry).	Fever, nausea, abdominal pain, and diarrhea, which may be bloody. Symptoms typically come and go; there may also be an enlarged liver and spleen.
CLOSTRIDIUM BOTULINUM (BOTULISM)	
Home-canned foods, improperly packed and sterilized canned products, and contaminated vegetables, fruits, fish, and condiments. More rarely it is found in beef, pork, poultry, milk products, unpasteurized honey, and garlic bottled in oil.	Within 18 to 36 hours, double vision and difficulty with muscular coordination, including chewing, swallowing, breathing, and speech. Progressive muscle weakness and paralysis can lead to respiratory failure and death.
CLOSTRIDIUM PERFRINGENS	
Outbreaks have often been associated with contaminated meat.	Severe diarrhea, abdominal pain, bloating, and flatulence appear in 8 to 24 hours.
ESCHERICHIA COLI (E. COLI)	
Undercooked beef or unpasteurized milk. Most cases have been traced to contaminated ground beef, but a few cases have been linked to rare roast beef.	Bloody diarrhea and vomiting. In severe cases, seizures, paralysis, and even death. Symptoms appear within 24 to 48 hours. Patients may require hospitalization.
LISTERIA MONOCYTOGENES	
Organism found in the soil and intestinal tracts of humans, animals, birds, and insects. Infection usually follows eating contaminated dairy products and raw vegetables.	Adults may develop meningitis, with headache, stiff neck, nausea, and vomiting. Eye inflammation and swollen lymph nodes sometimes develop; in unusual cases, the heart is involved. Symptoms usually appear in 8 to 24 hours.
SALMONELLA	
Infected meat-producing animals, undercooked poultry, and raw milk, eggs, and egg products are common culprits.	Within 12 to 48 hours, nausea, abdominal pain, diarrhea, vomiting, and fever; symptoms typically last 1 to 4 days.
STAPHYLOCOCCUS AUREUS	
Commonly spread by food handlers with skin infections who transmit the organism to such foods as custards, cream-filled pastries, milk, processed meat, and fish; poison is caused by a toxin rather than the bacterium.	Within 2 to 8 hours, severe nausea and vomiting. There may also be diarrhea, abdominal cramps, headache, and fever. Shock, prostration, and electrolyte imbalance may occur in extreme cases.
TRICHINELLA	
Raw or undercooked pork that has been fed contaminated meat; bear meat.	Within 24 to 48 hours, fever and diarrhea, with pain and respiratory problems.

foods on the BRAT diet (see p.123): bananas, rice, applesauce, and dry toast for 24 to 48 hours. Then try other bland foods, such as soft-cooked chicken and mashed potatoes. Avoid fresh fruits, especially citrus fruits, for a few more days.

SIMPLE PRECAUTIONS

Foods of animal origin are the most susceptible to contamination. The muscles of healthy animals are free of bacteria, but they provide a rich culture medium for the growth of bacteria picked up in handling and processing. The skin prevents bacteria from penetrating the flesh of a living animal, but microorganisms can be transferred from the skin to the muscle when the carcass is cut up. Meats that are dressed with their skin, such as poultry, are the most prone to spoilage, because bacteria remain on the skin despite thorough washing after slaughter.

Be careful when handling meat, fish, shellfish, and especially poultry. Wash hands thoroughly with hot water and soap before starting any food preparation, and repeat as necessary throughout the process. Also, remove rings, and make sure fingernails are clean both before and after food preparation. Use hot, soapy water to thoroughly wash food preparation surfaces, such as chopping boards and countertops. Never allow cooked food to touch an unwashed surface where traces of raw food remain.

Always keep raw foods away from other foods, and separate starchy foods and dairy products to prevent cross-contamination. If you don't intend to eat food immediately after preparing it, refrigerate or freeze it. Never leave food for longer than 2 hours at temperatures between 45°F (7°C) and 140°F (60°C), which are ideal for bacterial growth. Always cook hamburger to an internal temperature of 155°F (68°C).

Discard food that smells bad or is discolored. Don't use food from damaged cans or containers. Never taste foods that look "off"; don't even sniff them. Most important, never buy or use a can if the ends are bulging. This can only be caused by the pressure of gases produced by bacterial metabolism.

GOOD VS. BAD GERMS

It may seem puzzling that the bacteria and yeasts used in fermentation produce healthful foods, while some of their relatives cause various, sometimes lethal, forms of sickness. The reason is that the beneficial bacteria (for example, *Penicillium roqueforti,* which makes the blue veins in some cheeses) inhibit the growth of unwanted organisms, crowding out potentially harmful members of the clostridium, bacillus, and streptococcus families. This inhibitory action is the principle behind antibiotic treatment. It doesn't seem possible that cheese can have a truly medicinal effect, because the numbers of microorganisms in a serving are comparatively small, whereas the antibiotics used to fight infection are highly purified and concentrated extracts. Nevertheless, cheese may slow the growth of bacteria that cause tooth decay.

FRACTURES

CONSUME PLENTY OF

- *Low-fat milk and dairy products, sardines (with bones), and other high-calcium foods.*
- *Fortified milk, eggs, liver, and oily fish for vitamin D.*

CUT DOWN ON

- *Whole grains and other high-fiber foods that reduce calcium absorption.*

AVOID

- *Tea, cocoa, spinach, chard, rhubarb, and bran, which contain substances that bind with calcium.*
- *Alcohol, which slows healing.*

Broken bones have a remarkable ability to regenerate themselves, and unlike other wounds, they heal without forming scar tissue. In fact, the healed bone is often larger and stronger than it was originally.

Broken bones can occur at any age, but older people, especially women with OSTEOPOROSIS, are especially vulnerable to fractures. Even minor accidents that ordinarily would not inflict serious damage can cause fractures in people whose bones are weak and brittle. In fact, many older people with advanced osteoporosis, as well as those with cancers that affect the bones, often suffer spontaneous fractures.

Contrary to popular belief, broken bones heal at any age, although the process usually takes longer in an older person, often a full year compared to 6 to 9 months in a child or young adult. To facilitate bone healing, however, the diet must provide an ample supply of calcium, the major mineral in bones; vitamin D, which the body needs to absorb calcium; protein, which is also necessary to build bone; and zinc, which promotes healing. Milk and dairy products are our best sources of calcium; choose low-fat versions to avoid unwanted weight gain. Other foods that are rich in calcium include

BONE BUILDERS. *Eat ample high-calcium foods, such as milk and yogurt, tofu, broccoli, and canned sardines (with bones), plus eggs or other foods high in vitamin D.*

canned sardines and salmon, provided that the bones are also consumed.

Good plant sources of calcium include broccoli, kale, lamb's quarters, mustard greens, Chinese cabbage, dates, and almonds. Care is needed, however, because some plants high in calcium also contain substances that hinder its absorption; for example, rhubarb, sesame seeds, spinach, beet greens, and chard are high in calcium, but they contain oxalates, which bind to calcium. Similarly, bran and brown rice contain phytic acid, which increases excretion of the mineral. Tea, cocoa, and many whole-grain products are also high in oxalates; limit their consumption when recuperating from a fracture. Excessive intake of high-fiber foods reduces calcium absorption as well.

The human body has the ability to produce vitamin D, provided that the skin is exposed to the sun. For a young person, 10 to 15 minutes of midday sun two or three times a week is usually adequate. The elderly, on the other hand, require about 30 minutes of sun exposure. In the event that exposure to sunlight is not possible, adequate levels of vitamin D must come from foods in the diet instead. Fortified milk, eggs, liver, and oily fish are particularly good dietary sources of vitamin D.

FRUITS

BENEFITS
- *Excellent sources of vitamin C, beta carotene, and potassium; lesser amounts of other vitamins and minerals.*
- *Contain bioflavonoids, which may protect against cancer and other diseases.*
- *High in fiber and low in calories.*
- *A source of natural sugars that provide quick energy.*

DRAWBACKS
- *May contribute to dental decay, especially when dried.*
- *Some provoke allergic reactions and asthma attacks in susceptible people.*
- *Vulnerable to spoilage.*

For much of human history, fruits have been a favorite food, and with good reason: they're tasty, easy to digest, a good source of quick energy, and packed with vitamins and minerals. They can be served alone or teamed with other foods in almost any course—from a refreshing summer soup to a hearty dessert—to add flavor and interest to meals.

Anthropologists theorize that apes and early humans alike favored the sweet-tasting fruits, because both species observed that such foods were less likely to be poisonous than those that were bitter. Early hunter-gatherers foraged for wild fruits and berries, but as agrarian societies developed, humans learned to cultivate dates, figs, apples, and other fruit-bearing bushes and trees. They also developed methods to dry many fruits so that they could be enjoyed during the off-season.

NUTRITIONAL VALUE
Today fruits are lauded for their nutritional value as well as for their pleasing flavor. Numerous studies demonstrate that people who eat ample amounts of fruits (the Food Guide Rainbow, p.39, recommends up to five servings a day) enjoy a reduced incidence of cancer,

heart attacks, and strokes. Researchers believe that the high amounts of AN-TIOXIDANTS, especially vitamins C and A (in the form of its precursor, beta carotene), in most fruits protect against these and possibly other diseases. Antioxidants work by preventing the cell damage caused by free radicals, unstable molecules that are released when the body uses oxygen. Fruits are also high in BIOFLAVONOIDS, phytochemicals with antioxidant properties that may prevent or retard tumor growth.

Citrus fruits are among the richest sources of vitamin C; thus, nutritionists recommend at least one daily serving of an orange, grapefruit, tangerine, or other citrus fruit. A serving is one medium-size fruit or an 8-ounce glass of pure juice. (Canned fruits lose much of their vitamin C but provide other important vitamins and minerals.)

If you believe you are ALLERGIC to citrus fruits, especially orange or grapefruit juices, try an experiment. After having someone else carefully peel one of these fruits, eat a small piece to see if it provokes symptoms. If not, chances are that you are allergic to an oil in the citrus skins, not to the fruits themselves. When the fruits are squeezed, some of this oil is released into the juice; people allergic to citrus juice often have no problems with the peeled fruits, provided they aren't exposed to the oil on their skin or in the fruits. For those who cannot tolerate (or don't like) citrus, other fruits that are high in vitamin C include cantaloupes and other melons, kiwifruits, strawberries, raspberries, mangoes, and papayas. Cranberry juice is another excellent source.

Fruits with orange or deep yellow flesh—including apricots, cantaloupes,

and mangoes—get their color from the yellow-orange pigment that harbors beta carotene, which the body converts to vitamin A. Other carotene pigments, such as lycopene in red fruits, or bioflavonoids such as quercetin in grapes, are thought to protect against heart disease. In fact, recent studies indicate that quercetin or resveratrol may be the ingredients in wine responsible for the noted reduction in heart disease and stroke among moderate wine drinkers.

A VERSATILE FOOD CHOICE. *Whether you prefer bananas, figs, grapes, oranges, pears, pineapples, plums, or raspberries, fruits offer many nutritional benefits and are a welcome addition to any meal.*

Many fruits are high in potassium, an electrolyte essential to maintaining a proper balance of body fluids. Adequate potassium also appears to reduce the risk of developing high blood pressure. People taking diuretic drugs, which increase the excretion of potassium in the urine, are advised to eat extra servings of bananas, melons, apricots, peaches, and dried fruits to maintain adequate levels of this mineral.

Most fruits are low in calories and high in fiber, a fact that enhances their appeal to individuals who are weight conscious. Apples, grapes, and many other fruits contain pectin, a soluble fiber that helps regulate blood cholesterol levels. Berries, citrus, and dried fruits are especially high in both soluble and insoluble fibers.

THE PESTICIDE ISSUE

Because fruit trees are particularly vulnerable to a variety of worms, flies, and other destructive insects, most growers use pesticide sprays to keep them in check. Many people worry that residues of these pesticides pose a substantial health risk. Experts stress that the pesticides used in Canada meet specific safety standards and that the health benefits of eating fruits outweigh any risk. Even so, fruits should be washed well before eating, and some should be peeled. These include apples that have been sprayed with a wax to extend their shelf life and to make them shiny and more attractive. The wax itself is harmless, but it forms a seal over the skin

WHAT MAKES A BERRY?

When botanists talk about berries, they are often referring to something very different from what we normally envision. All fruits represent the ripened ovary of a pollinated female flower. Botanically, berries are defined as fruits that develop from a single ovary; thus, technically speaking, such fruits as grapes, bananas, and persimmons are berries. In contrast, strawberries and raspberries are a type of aggregate fruit; they are formed from numerous ovaries contained in a single flower. Blueberries and cranberries are classified as false berries; they contain many seeds and are formed by the joining of an ovary and the base of the flower (receptacle).

that prevents any pesticide residue from being washed away.

Citrus fruits are often coated with fungicides and other pesticides to prevent mold growth and fruit fly infestation. Ordinarily, this practice would not pose a health problem because the peels are discarded. But if you are using the zest of fresh citrus peels or making marmalade or candied peel, be sure to remove any pesticides by washing the fruit thoroughly in soapy water and then rinsing it. This is also a good precaution to follow before squeezing the juice from citrus fruit.

Imported fruits may be more hazardous than those grown locally, because pesticides that may be banned in Canada may be used abroad. There are safety standards for imported foods, which are also subject to inspection, but not every batch of imported food can be tested for pesticide residues. Consequently, consumer groups warn against eating imported fresh produce. It's probably unnecessary to go this far; shunning imported fruits not only limits one's choice, it means forgoing many nutritious and wholesome foods. Nevertheless, it's a good idea to be extra diligent about washing imported fruits and other produce before eating it.

Anyone who is uncomfortable eating foods that have been treated with pesticides can buy ORGANIC produce that has been grown without these substances. At one time, organic foods were found mostly in health-food stores, but now many supermarkets also offer them. Be prepared to pay more for organic produce, however, and don't expect it to look as pretty as foods grown with pesticides. Inspect the foods carefully for moldy or blighted spots; these may harbor natural cancer-causing agents.

FRUIT PROCESSING

Historically, the most common methods of preserving fruits entailed drying or making them into wine. Today we have numerous methods of processing and preserving fruits, some of which alter their nutritional value.

Canning. This preservation method allows us to enjoy low-cost fruits in any season of the year. Almost every variety of fruit is now canned commercially, but home canning has enjoyed a resurgence in recent years. When canning at home, it's extremely critical to heat a sealed jar of fruit enough to kill any present bacteria; otherwise, the bacteria will multiply and can cause serious FOOD POISONING. The more acidic fruits, such as apricots and plums, are less likely to spoil than pears, peaches, and other fruits that are low in acid.

Unfortunately, canning considerably reduces the vitamin content of most fruits; one analysis of eight canned fruits (apples, apricots, blueberries, cherries, oranges, peaches, raspberries, and strawberries) found that the content of thiamine, riboflavin, niacin, and vitamins A and C was reduced by 39 to 57 percent, compared to the fresh fruits. In addition, many canned fruits are packed in a heavy sweet syrup, adding empty calories in the form of sugar. Fruits packed in their own natural juice, rather than syrup, are a more healthful alternative.

Drying. This preserves fruits by removing most of the moisture that is needed to support the growth of bacteria and molds. Traditionally, fruits have been dried in the sun, and this method is still used in many areas. But sun drying also exposes the fruits to contamination or destruction by insects and birds; hence, many food processors now use indoor dehydrating equipment.

During drying, some vitamin C and beta carotene may be lost, especially if the fruits are dried in the sun. Adding sulfur compounds helps preserve these nutrients, but in turn destroys thiamine; sulfur can also provoke allergic reactions and asthma attacks in some susceptible people. Freeze drying minimizes nutrient loss without making it necessary to add sulfur.

Ounce for ounce, dried fruits are a more concentrated source of calories, fiber, natural sugars, and some nutrients than their fresh counterparts. Because they are lightweight, ready-to-eat, and nonperishable, they are ideal foods to pack for camping trips or a day outdoors. Figs and prunes contain natural laxative compounds in addition to large amounts of fiber. Although they are a popular home remedy for constipation, overindulgence can trigger a bout of diarrhea. Dried fruits tend to be sticky, and if bits are allowed to adhere to the teeth, they promote tooth decay. This can be prevented by brushing the teeth carefully, or at least rinsing the mouth, after eating dried fruits.

Fermentation. This process—used mainly to make wine—destroys most vitamins, but it also increases the availability of iron and certain other minerals. In fact, alcoholic iron tonics are a long-standing folk remedy for anemia.

Freezing. This method of preservation retains more of the fruit's vitamin content than canning; for example, only about 18 percent of vitamin C is lost by freezing compared to 56 percent lost during the canning process. Commercial bakers rely heavily upon frozen fruits, especially for pies. Home freezing is becoming a popular method of preserving garden or locally grown produce; it is easier and safer than home canning and more economical than purchasing commercial frozen foods.

Unless the frozen fruits have been packed in sugar or syrup, it's a good idea to thaw them quickly in a microwave to prevent the growth of bacteria and other microorganisms. The frozen fruits can also be heated by stewing or baking before serving.

Jams and jellies. The natural acidity of fruits combined with large amounts of sugar serve to preserve jams and jellies. Pectin is needed in order for the cooked fruits to gel; some fruits have enough natural pectin, but others need to have it added. Similarly, lemon juice or citric acid can be added to a low-acid fruit to help retard spoilage.

Juicing. An inexpensive and convenient way of getting the nutrients from fruits, JUICING has become popular in recent years as people have increased their consumption of fruit juices while lowering their intake of whole fruits. This trend is attributed to the increased availability and low cost of fruit juices, as well as awareness that they are more healthful than sugary soft drinks.

EXOTIC FRUITS

Nowadays, supermarket produce sections offer a wide choice of fruits from around the world, thanks to modern shipping and storage techniques. Many of these are tropical fruits with unique flavors and textures; others are from China and other temperate areas. Whatever their origin, most are good sources of valuable nutrients.

CAPE GOOSEBERRIES

One of the prettiest fruits, cape gooseberries contain reasonable amounts of beta carotene and vitamin C, which are important antioxidant nutrients, as well as potassium, which is vital for proper muscle function and is needed to maintain healthy blood pressure.

CUSTARD APPLES

This is the generic name given to a South American family (Annonacedae) of some 60 fruits. All are heart-shaped, with scaly skins. They are a good source of potassium as well as vitamin C.

KUMQUATS

These smallest of all citrus fruits originated in China. Unlike other citrus fruits, kumquats have a sweet edible rind. They are a good source of vitamin C and potassium; they also have fair amounts of calcium and vitamin A.

LONGANS

These Asian fruits, related to lychees, are also known as dragon's eyes. Their hard shell is easily cracked. Longans are a good source of iron, but not vitamin C.

LOQUATS

Also called Japanese plums, loquats have a tender, juicy flesh that is reminiscent of plums or cherries. They taste like a mixture of apple and apricot. Loquats are an excellent source of potassium and vitamin A.

LYCHEES

Originally from China and related to longans, canned lychees are popular in Asian cooking. Fresh lychees, available from November to January, have a sweetly perfumed aroma that is reminiscent of elder flowers; they are an excellent source of vitamin C and potassium.

PASSION FRUITS

One of the most fragrant and distinctive tasting of all tropical fruits, the passion fruit is also called *granadilla*, which means "little pomegranate." This delicacy originally came from Brazil; it is high in potassium and is also a good source of iron.

PERSIMMONS

This national fruit of Japan is also known as Sharon fruit. Persimmons supply useful amounts of vitamin A and potassium; the American variety is also high in vitamin C.

POMEGRANATES

A worldwide folkloric symbol of fertility, the pomegranate is a good source of potassium, but low in vitamin C; its seeds are high in fiber.

POMELOS

The largest citrus fruit, this ancestor of the grapefruit originated in Southeast Asia. Like most citrus fruits, pomelos are an excellent source of vitamin C.

GALLSTONES

CONSUME
- *Small meals at regular intervals.*
- *Breakfast daily.*

AVOID
- *Weight gain.*
- *Excessive alcohol.*

The gallbladder seems to serve no purpose other than to store and concentrate bile, a substance produced by the liver to digest fats in the small intestine. Removal of the organ appears to have no effect on digestion. Bile fluid contains high levels of cholesterol and the pigment bilirubin, both of which precipitate as crystals to form stones; these may be as fine as beach sand or as coarse as river gravel. Most gallstones are hardened cholesterol; the rest are made up of bilirubin plus calcium.

Gallstones can develop in both sexes, but they are most common in overweight middle-aged women. They also tend to run in families. Women, especially those who have borne children, are thought to be particularly vulnerable because of the high levels of blood cholesterol and bile that develop late in pregnancy and in the weeks following childbirth. It is believed, too, that the female hormones progesterone and estrogen, whether occurring naturally or taken in oral contraceptives, may play a role in gallstone formation. Crash diets are believed to be another precipitating factor; many people appear to develop gallstones after a period of yo-yo dieting, with repeated cycles of weight loss and gain, or after a single drastic weight loss.

Many people never know they have gallstones because they have no symptoms. For some individuals, however, the presence of gallstones can cause pain in the upper right abdomen when the gallbladder contracts to release bile after a meal, and inflammation of the gallbladder (cholecystitis) that brings on sudden, severe pain extending to the back and under the right shoulder blade, with fever, chills, and vomiting. If stones obstruct the flow of bile, the skin and the whites of the eyes become jaundiced. Left untreated, stones can lodge in the bile duct and cause inflammation of the liver or pancreas.

For frequent painful attacks, the usual treatment is surgical removal of the gallbladder, called cholecystectomy; the procedure can be performed by conventional surgery or by laparoscopy, involving only a tiny incision and a brief hospital stay. Medications have been used with mixed success to dissolve gallstones, but the stones often recur if the person stops taking the drug. Another option is a procedure called lithotripsy, which uses shock waves to break up the gallstones.

For years, people with gallstones have been warned to eliminate fats and cholesterol from their diets. This advice was based on the observation that most stones are formed of cholesterol. In actuality, there's little evidence that a low-cholesterol diet will lower the risk of gallstones. Some clinicians even claim that the occasional fatty meal causes the gallbladder to empty itself, which may be beneficial.

Although a diet high in fiber and low in fats is recommended for general health, there are no scientific grounds for believing that high fiber intake can favorably influence cholesterol metabolism, at least as far as gallstones are concerned. It's known, however, that the bile is more likely to form stones after the long period of fasting that occurs overnight, while we sleep. On this basis, some physicians recommend that people with gallbladder problems eat a substantial breakfast, which will cause the bladder to empty itself and flush out the stones and stagnant bile. Others go further, and advise patients to eat frequent small meals to maintain the filling and emptying cycle.

People with gallstones should avoid foods that cause discomfort. The diet should emphasize starchy foods, with lots of fruits and vegetables, moderate servings of protein, and small amounts of fat. Alcohol should be used in moderation, if at all, especially if the gallbladder disease also affects the liver and pancreas.

GARLIC

BENEFITS
- *May help lower high blood pressure and elevated blood cholesterol.*
- *May prevent or fight certain cancers.*
- *Antiviral and antibacterial properties help prevent or fight infection.*
- *May alleviate nasal congestion.*

DRAWBACKS
- *Causes bad breath.*
- *Can cause indigestion, especially if eaten raw.*
- *Direct contact irritates the skin and mucous membranes.*

Herbalists and folk healers have used garlic to treat myriad diseases for thousands of years. It is known that ancient Egyptian healers prescribed it to build physical strength, the Greeks used it as a laxative, and the Chinese traditionally used it to lower blood pressure. In the Middle Ages, eating liberal quantities of garlic was credited with providing immunity to the plague.

In more modern times, Louis Pasteur, the great 19th-century French chemist, demonstrated garlic's antiseptic properties, information that was put to use during World Wars I and II by the British, German, and Russian armies. Since then, numerous studies have confirmed that garlic can be effective against bacteria, fungi, viruses, and parasites. Today, naturopaths and other proponents of herbal medicine prescribe garlic to help prevent colds, flu, and other infectious diseases.

Scientists have begun studying garlic more intensely in recent years, with more than 500 papers having been published in medical journals on the protective effects of garlic since the mid-1980s. Much of this research has focused on the effects of garlic on blood cholesterol and blood pressure. Studies indicate that allicin, a chemical that forms when garlic is crushed, reduces cholesterol levels and lowers high blood pressure. Ajoene, one of garlic's many active compounds, also appears to reduce the ability of blood platelets to form blood clots, thus possibly reducing the risk of heart attacks and strokes. To date, however, these studies have not proved that garlic prevents heart attacks and other cardiovascular disorders.

Ongoing research is indicating that garlic has an anticancer potential. So far, it appears that eating garlic lowers the risk of stomach and colon cancers in humans. In addition, studies using laboratory animals have shown that garlic can help shrink cancers of the breast, skin, and lungs, as well as help prevent cancers of the colon and esophagus.

It is not yet known which of the active substances in garlic contribute to its health effects. Both allicin and SAC (S-allyl-cystein), another compound that has been shown to be effective against tumors in laboratory animals,

are found in fresh garlic, garlic powder, and garlic pills. The main drawback of garlic pills is that the products available vary greatly in the amount of active compounds they contain.

Just how much garlic must be consumed to achieve any health benefits is unknown. Many German doctors prescribe 4g (about two small cloves) to treat high blood pressure and elevated cholesterol. It takes much more—at least 10 cloves—to inhibit blood clotting to the same degree as a daily aspirin. Also, practitioners disagree as to whether cooked or dried garlic confers the same benefits imparted by eating it raw.

While there is no guarantee that garlic will prevent heart disease or cancer, at the very least it will add flavor to meals. Its major drawback is that it causes bad breath. Recently, "deodorized" garlic bulbs have appeared on the market, as well as Breath-Asure, a pill based on parsley oil that is effective in reducing garlic breath. Garlic may cause indigestion, especially if eaten raw. Handling raw garlic can irritate the skin and mucous membranes.

GASTRITIS

CONSUME
- *Regular meals with a balance of starchy foods, fruits, vegetables, and low-fat protein.*

AVOID
- *Fatty foods, tomato-based products, chocolate, alcohol, caffeine, and peppermint, which can cause acid reflux.*
- *Spicy foods if they irritate you.*
- *Frequent use of aspirin or other arthritis pain relievers.*

An inflammation of the stomach lining, gastritis is usually signaled by INDIGESTION, either with or without bleeding in the digestive tract. Acute gastritis often develops when people are subjected to sudden stress, such as from extensive burns or other severe injury or illness; it may also develop after surgery, leading to stress ulcers and severe intestinal bleeding.

Chronic inflammation can occur with long-term use of certain medications (such as aspirin and other arthritis drugs), gastrointestinal disorders (for example, CROHN'S DISEASE), ALCOHOLISM, or viral infections. It has recently been discovered that many cases of gastritis are caused by a bacterium, *Helicobacter pylori*. This organism has also been linked to peptic ULCERS and is the only germ currently known to be able to survive in the acidic environment of the human stomach.

Gastritis is more common with age, probably because the older we get, the more often we have been exposed to causative factors. Most people with gastritis complain of INDIGESTION AND HEARTBURN, nausea, and belching. Others have no symptoms, which can be dangerous if gastritis is caused by erosion of the stomach lining with bleeding—normally a result of aspirin or other medication.

Usually, people with acute gastritis caused by illness or injury have already been hospitalized for treatment of their overlying condition; therefore, symptoms of gastritis are managed in the course of their intensive care.

Although foods are not the cause of gastritis, people with pain and intestinal inflammation should avoid spicy or highly acidic foods, which can irritate the stomach lining. They should also avoid fatty foods, tomato-based products, chocolate, beverages containing caffeine, decaffeinated tea and coffee, peppermint, and alcohol. These foods and substances relax the valve between the stomach and esophagus and make it easier for the acid stomach contents to back up into the esophagus, causing further irritation.

If you need a pain reliever, such as for arthritis, ask your doctor to prescribe a nonirritating alternative to your usual aspirin or other nonsteroidal anti-inflammatory drug (NSAID). For gastritis caused by *H. pylori*, the doctor may prescribe antibiotics. Antacids, if your doctor recommends them, can soothe the irritation until the inflammation subsides on its own.

GASTROENTERITIS

CONSUME

- *Fluids, such as chicken broth or soup, for rehydration.*
- *Bananas, rice, applesauce, toast (the BRAT diet) to maintain nutrition.*
- *As symptoms subside, gradually reintroduce solid foods.*

AVOID

- *Alcohol and caffeine, which stimulate the lower bowel.*
- *High-fiber foods, which may irritate an inflamed bowel.*
- *If traveling abroad: unpeeled fruits and vegetables, uncooked foods, unboiled tap water, and ice cubes in drinks.*

An inflammation of the lower digestive tract, gastroenteritis has many causes: infection with a virus, bacterium, or parasite; ingestion of toxic substances; ALLERGY or INTOLERANCE to food; and medications, often antibiotics that alter the normal bacterial population of the lower tract. Also, people with eating disorders, such as ANOREXIA and BULIMIA, may develop gastroenteritis as a result of laxative abuse.

Thanks to clean water supplies and the enforcement of sanitation laws, gastroenteritis due to cholera and typhoid fever is now rare in the industrialized nations. These diseases are still a serious threat in underdeveloped nations, however, where the water supply may be unreliable and sanitary facilities rudimentary. Outbreaks of cholera in South America during the 1990s underscored the importance of vigilance for TRAVELERS, who should pay strict attention to what they eat and drink, especially when venturing off the beaten track in underdeveloped countries.

By contrast, gastroenteritis caused by parasites, such as giardia and amoebas, can strike in any country. Parasites can be transmitted in a variety of ways, such as through unsanitary food handling, contamination of drinking water, and close physical contact with an infected person.

Gastroenteritis caused by common bacteria or viruses is often referred to as "stomach flu." Provided the infecting organism is a bacterium or virus and not a parasite, symptoms—like those of DIARRHEA and FOOD POISONING—usually clear up within a few days, without any special treatment. Nausea and vomiting are not much more than a temporary inconvenience to otherwise healthy adults and older children. On the other hand, in vulnerable groups—babies, the frail elderly, the infirm, and individuals with a suppressed immune system—gastroenteritis can be severely debilitating and requires a doctor's immediate attention.

When vomiting and diarrhea persist longer than 48 hours, your doctor may prescribe a medication to quell nausea, as well as an antibiotic if it seems advisable. Tests may be warranted to identify and isolate the cause of gastroenteritis, such as food sensitivity or exposure to toxic substances. If diarrhea is bloody, your doctor may investigate the possibility of a parasitic infection or bacillary dysentery.

If you have stomach flu, give your digestive system a rest from solid food, but drink plenty of liquids to make up for fluid lost with diarrhea. Sipping ginger ale or chewing candied ginger can help to calm any surges of nausea. Chicken broth with rice is a palatable home rehydration remedy; the broth replaces fluid, as well as sodium and potassium to restore the balance of electrolytes, and the rice has a binding effect on the bowel. Don't drink alcohol or beverages containing caffeine; they stimulate the digestive tract and can worsen diarrhea.

As your bowel settles down, reintroduce solid foods gradually with small portions of the BRAT diet (see p.123): bananas, rice, applesauce, and toast. The bananas provide potassium and carbohydrates; rice in the form of boiled grain or cream of rice cereal is easily digested and provides energy; unsweetened poached apples and applesauce contain pectin, a soluble fiber that helps add bulk to the stool; and dry toast provides energy in the form of carbohydrates but doesn't overtax the digestive system with fiber that could be irritating to an inflamed bowel. After about 48 hours you should be able to tolerate other simple solid foods, such as steamed or boiled potatoes, cooked vegetables, and a boiled or poached egg. Leave dairy foods until last; the fat in cheese is difficult to digest and stays in the stomach longer than other foods, and some infections can temporarily interfere with your ability to digest lactose, the sugar found in milk and dairy products. Many people find they can tolerate low-fat yogurt even when other dairy foods provoke digestive problems. Keep up your fluid intake with water and juices, and resume a normal diet as soon as you feel up to it.

Because some drugs can cause severe gastroenteritis, it's important that you contact your doctor if any digestive upset occurs while you are taking an antibiotic or other medication. The doctor may decide to switch you to another medication or therapy.

GENETICALLY ALTERED FOODS

Insect- and spoilage-resistant tomatoes, leaner beef and pork, bigger ears of corn—these are just a few advances from plant geneticists. But at what price?

For centuries, food growers have tampered with plant and animal genetics by crossbreeding to bring out desirable traits while suppressing less desirable ones. Refinement of such techniques has enabled farmers to produce increasingly abundant crops.

But in recent years modern agriculture has added a new dimension, thanks to genetic engineering. Using space-age techniques, scientists can now alter cell DNA by means of cloning and other techniques to create a growing number of new strains of plants and animals.

The implications of this type of genetic engineering are almost limitless. Scientists say, for example, that it will make possible the development of animals that are genetically compatible with humans in order to supply transplant organs. Gene splicing and cloning techniques have already made it possible to harness colonies of bacteria to produce insulin, human growth hormone, and other substances that once could be obtained only from slaughtered animals or human donors.

IMPROVING ON NATURE

Genetic engineering enables research botanists to add desirable hereditary traits to almost any plant. These advances are already producing more nutritious foods; for example, a variety of CORN with increased high-quality protein; a type of rapeseed that synthesizes more of the unsaturated fatty acids of canola oil; and a TOMATO that ripens without becoming soft.

Agricultural scientists are also trying to alter plants to make them more productive or more able to withstand adverse growing conditions, such as drought or other weather extremes. This type of genetic engineering has tremendous potential in overcoming world food shortages; conceivably, arid desert areas may one day produce drought-resistant grains.

Another approach involves engineering plants to be resistant to disease and pests. One modification alters a plant's taste to make it less attractive to insects, allowing farmers to reduce pesticide use. Another is aimed at developing a plant resistant to new kinds of herbicides that do not harm the crops and beneficial insects.

THE DOWN SIDE

Despite the benefits of genetic modification, some people remain concerned that this type of manipulation may create unpredictable adverse consequences. One such worry revolves around the production of antibiotic-resistant bacteria. In order to measure their success, scientists will often incorporate an antibiotic-resistant gene (or tracer) into the genetic material that is being introduced into a plant. If the modified cell is able to survive the antibiotic treatment, it means that it has become resistant to that antibiotic and has probably taken on other characteristics carried in the newly added genetic material. So far, evidence that antibiotic-resistant tracers can be transferred to disease-causing microorganisms is sketchy, but theoretically, it could happen, with disastrous results.

Comparatively, animals subjected to genetic engineering do not fare nearly as well as plants. For example, sheep injected with genetically engineered hormones to increase wool growth become more vulnerable to the heat. Pigs and chickens treated with special growth hormones develop painful bone and joint problems. Experiments are under way to use human genetic material to modify dairy cows, enabling them to produce milk with the same composition of human breast milk. At this stage, it is not known what, if any, effect this will have on genetically modified cattle. Still, the adverse consequences experienced by other species have prompted a number of concerned people to question the ethical issue of tampering with animal genes.

AIMING FOR PERFECTION. *This genetically altered tomato is vine ripened but not overly soft.*

165

GINGER

BENEFITS
- *May prevent motion sickness.*
- *Can help to quell nausea.*
- *Ginger wine may help to relieve menstrual cramps.*

DRAWBACKS
- *Raw or candied ginger may irritate oral tissue and other mucous membranes.*

The use of ginger for flavoring foods dates back to the earliest civilizations. The Chinese were using ginger as long ago as the 6th century BC, and Arab traders introduced the spice to the Mediterranean before the 1st century AD. Transported from the Middle East to Europe by the Crusaders, ginger was an ingredient in almost every recipe found in a 1390 cookbook that was compiled at the English royal court. Spanish settlers brought ginger to the New World in the 1500s.

The Zingiberaceae family includes ginger and two other popular SPICES—cardamom and turmeric—as well as the banana, an unlikely distant cousin. Cardamom is widely used in tropical cuisines; in addition, it lends fragrance to Scandinavian breads and pastries. Turmeric, a major ingredient in commercial curry powders, is also used in Asia to dye fabrics yellow and in Western countries to improve the color of some margarines and dairy products.

A versatile flavoring, ginger is as appetizing in the piquant dishes of Asia as it is in Western confectionery, desserts, and drinks. Ginger's spicy character varies according to the form in which it is used. The fresh root, or rhizome, is relatively mild, while the flavor of the candied root is more concentrated. Dishes flavored with powdered ginger can range from mildly tangy to searingly hot, depending on the recipe.

Ginger has a long and honored tradition in folk medicine. Recent experience suggests that further investigation may be warranted to explore the scientific basis for ginger's effect.

In the meantime, for a comforting way to relieve the chills and congestion of a cold, you can make ginger tea by simmering one or two slices of fresh ginger root in water for 10 minutes; add a pinch of cinnamon for piquancy.

In England, before the introduction of modern painkillers and muscle relaxants, ginger wine was the traditional remedy for menstrual cramps. However, the wine's benefit may have been due not to the ginger but, instead, to the alcohol in which it was macerated. Alcohol is known to relax smooth muscles, including the muscle of the uterus. It may be that ginger also has an as yet undetected effect on smooth muscle, which could account for its reputation as a calming influence on the uterus as well as the intestinal muscles.

Recent studies have shown that beta ionone, a terpenoid found in ginger, has decided anticancer properties. Tumors induced in laboratory animals grow much more slowly if the animals are pretreated with beta ionone.

POPULAR ANTINAUSEANT

Various forms of ginger—nonalcoholic ginger ale or beer, pills, and candied ginger root—have been used to counter the nausea and vomiting of motion sickness. This practice is particularly well established in Germany, where it is a government-approved treatment for motion sickness and heartburn. A recent study found that ginger was as effective as Dramamine in preventing motion sickness, without causing the drowsiness the drug sometimes does.

Sipping flat ginger ale or sucking candied ginger may help to quell surges of nausea due to morning sickness, FOOD POISONING, GASTROENTERITIS, or cancer chemotherapy. Ginger is available in capsule form for those who find that the candy irritates the mouth.

GOOSEBERRIES

BENEFITS
- *A good source of vitamin C, potassium, and bioflavonoids.*
- *Fair amounts of iron and vitamin A.*
- *High in fiber, low in calories.*

DRAWBACKS
- *Their tartness is usually offset with large amounts of added sugar.*
- *Gooseberry bushes harbor a fungus that kills some types of pine trees.*

Gooseberries are prized for their acidic tartness in Europe—and to a lesser degree in Canada—where they are made

DID YOU KNOW?

- The origin of the name "gooseberries" has nothing to do with geese, even though their acidic flavor goes well with roast goose. Instead, the term comes from the Old English words for the berries— groser, grosier, and grozer. Gooseberries have been cultivated in Europe, and especially in England, since the 15th century.

- There are some 50 different species and more than 700 varieties of gooseberries. Although the gooseberry originated in Europe and western Asia, Canada and the United States now have the most species.

- Gooseberry bushes can attract a fungus that is devastating to white pine forests. For this reason, gooseberries are not cultivated near these forests, also, the berries are regularly inspected to prevent the spread of the fungus.

A BERRY OF MANY HUES. *Although green gooseberries are the most familiar, some of the more than 700 varieties are red and different shades of blue.*

into pies, jams, jellies, and sauces for poultry. New, sweeter-tasting varieties have been developed, which are more palatable for eating raw.

Gooseberries have many nutritional benefits. They are high in fiber (about 3g in a cup of raw berries), vitamin C (50mg per fresh cup), and potassium (230mg per cup). They are also rich in BIOFLAVONOIDS—plant pigments that help prevent cancer and other diseases. Some of these nutrients are lost in processing; a cup of canned gooseberries loses more than half of its vitamin C, as well as some potassium and vitamin A

(in the form of beta carotene). The canned berries are also high in calories, yielding 180 calories per cup, compared to 60 for the fresh fruit.

Folk healers in the past recommended gooseberry juice to treat liver and intestinal disorders. They also believed that a tea brewed from the plant's leaves was a remedy for urinary tract and menstrual disorders. Old herbal medicine books refer to the fruit as feverberries and recommend it for inflammatory disorders. However, there is no scientific evidence that gooseberries or their leaves have any special medicinal qualities.

Gooseberries carry fungi that are transmitted to pine trees and other types of fruit bushes. As a result, efforts are now under way to develop more disease-resistant strains of gooseberries through genetic engineering techniques.

GOUT

CONSUME PLENTY OF
- *Fluids to dilute the urine and prevent the formation of kidney stones.*
- *Fresh fruits and vegetables (except those high in purines) for vitamins, minerals, and dietary fiber.*
- *Cereals, pasta, and rice for energy.*

CUT DOWN ON
- *Vegetables high in purines, such as cauliflower, asparagus, and mushrooms.*
- *Fish, seafood, poultry, and meat to reduce protein intake.*

AVOID
- *Legumes, liver, cured or smoked fish and meat, and other high-purine foods.*
- *Alcohol, especially red wine and beer.*
- *Diuretics and aspirin-based drugs.*
- *Skipping meals and crash diets.*

A disease that is marked by swelling, inflammation, and excruciating tenderness in the joints, gout most commonly affects the joints at the base of the big toe, other foot joints, knees, ankles, wrists, and fingers. The slightest touch—even of a bedsheet—may prove to be unbearable during an attack.

In Canada, gout afflicts about 5 out of every 1,000 people, about half of whom are overweight. It is uncommon in women, especially before menopause.

Mistakenly, gout has had a persistent reputation for being the penalty to be paid for high living and overindulgence. In fact, gout is actually a type of ARTHRITIS that is caused by an inherited defect in the kidney's ability to excrete uric acid. This waste product of

167

Case Study

A swollen and excruciatingly painful big toe was Herbert's first indication that he, like his father and grandfather, had gout. The pain drove Herbert to his physician's office early the next morning. The doctor prescribed colchicine to alleviate the attack, to be followed by a daily dose of a drug to curtail the production of uric acid. At the time, Herbert expected that his doctor would also advise him to curtail his favorite activity—hiking. Instead, the doctor advised Herbert to lose 15 pounds and referred him to a dietitian to work out a low-purine diet.

The dietitian gave Herbert a list of high-purine foods to avoid: sardines, smoked fish, organ meats of all kinds, processed meats, lentils and other legumes, dried fruits, and alcoholic beverages, especially beer and wine. She also urged him to limit asparagus, cauliflower, spinach, dry cereals, foods made with baking powder, and a number of other foods to an occasional small serving. After 6 months without another flare-up of symptoms, the dietitian said that Herbert could experiment a bit and try an occasional cocktail and small amounts of other foods on his list.

protein metabolism comes both from the digestive process and from the normal turnover of cells.

When deposits of uric acid crystals build up in the synovial fluid that surrounds the joints, the human body's immune system attempts to eliminate them through the process of inflammation; unfortunately, this causes attacks of intense pain that can continue for days or even weeks if not treated. Over time, uric acid crystals also accumulate in the form of lumpy deposits under the skin of the ears, the elbows, and near the affected joints.

Gout attacks usually occur suddenly and unpredictably; however, several drugs are now available to stop pain and prevent future attacks. Colchicine, a drug derived from the autumn crocus flower, is one of the fastest acting and most effective, but it also causes severe nausea and diarrhea, which mandate stopping the drug immediately. Before these side effects develop, however, the attack has usually abated, and the patient is no longer taking the drug. Other, less toxic drugs are given on a long-term basis to prevent attacks; a flare-up is likely if these drugs are stopped. To reinforce the beneficial effect of drug treatment, dietary changes should be made to help reduce the production of uric acid.

MANAGING GOUT WITH DIET

Many people who have gout are obese; losing weight—especially fat around the abdomen—often prevents future attacks. Weight loss should be gradual, however, because a rapid reduction can raise blood levels of uric acid and provoke gout. Fasting increases the blood levels of uric acid, therefore, people with gout should avoid skipping meals.

In some cases, gout is brought on by the use of aspirin or certain diuretics taken for high blood pressure. These medicines may interfere with normal kidney function and, therefore, the elimination of uric acid. You should ask your doctor for a change in treatment

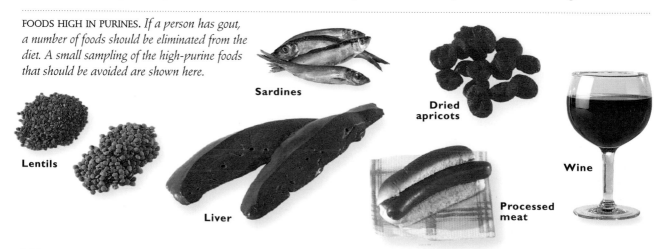

FOODS HIGH IN PURINES. *If a person has gout, a number of foods should be eliminated from the diet. A small sampling of the high-purine foods that should be avoided are shown here.*

Lentils

Sardines

Dried apricots

Liver

Processed meat

Wine

if you experience severe joint pain while on a drug therapy.

Foods with a high content of chemicals called purines promote the overproduction of uric acid in people with a tendency to gout. Foods very high in purines include organ meats, game, meat broths and extracts, smoked or pickled meat or fish (especially anchovies and sardines), canned fish, caviar, shellfish, lentils and other legumes, chocolate, beer, and red wine; these should be avoided completely. Those with moderately high purine content, such as dry cereals, asparagus, cauliflower, green leafy vegetables, mushrooms, and food made with baking powder, should be limited to one small serving a day. Always drink plenty of fluids—at least 2 quarts a day—to dilute the urine and prevent the formation of kidney stones. Although beer and wine, as products of fermentation, are the only alcoholic drinks known to be high in purines, any alcohol can interfere with the elimination of uric acid. Gout sufferers should drink only distilled alcohols in very small amounts.

The omega-3 fatty acids in fish have been found to reduce pain and inflammation in people with rheumatoid arthritis and may have a similar benefit in gout. However, gout sufferers should avoid purine-rich oily fish or any food that provokes attacks. Fish oil supplements are not recommended.

Many people with gout may have other conditions that influence their dietary choices at the same time, such as hypertension, heart disease, diabetes, and high blood cholesterol; these individuals may have to further modify their diets. In such situations, nutritional counseling by a registered dietitian may help in designing appetizing but healthful meals that strike a balance between these pressing health concerns on the one hand and the enjoyment of food on the other.

GRAINS

BENEFITS
- *An excellent source of starchy carbohydrate and dietary fiber.*
- *A good source of niacin, riboflavin, other B vitamins, iron, and calcium.*
- *More economical than meat, fish, and other diet staples.*

DRAWBACKS
- *An incomplete source of protein.*
- *Lack some of the essential vitamins and minerals.*
- *Gluten in some grain products provokes malabsorption symptoms in people who have celiac disease.*

Since prehistoric times, grain products have been one of the basic foodstuffs of agrarian societies. Almost every culture has a staple grain around which its cuisine is centered. Today, thanks to modern agricultural techniques and efficient transportation, we can sample a huge variety of grain products. Even in isolated areas, it's not unusual to find the basmati rice that is popular in Bangladesh, Moroccan couscous, Italian polenta, QUINOA from South America, and many other products once considered exotic to most Canadians.

Despite this proliferation of grains from around the world, Canadians still tend to make the greatest use of our native wheat, which is ground into flour and made into BREAD and other baked goods. To a lesser extent, we also consume corn, rice, oats, barley, and millet, and many exotic grains.

HEALTH BENEFITS

Grain products are inexpensive, easy to prepare, and highly nutritious. Whole grains, for example, are rich in complex carbohydrates, fiber, and many vitamins and minerals. They are also very low in fat, and when used in combination with beans and other legumes, grains are a good source of complete protein.

COOKING GRAINS

- Lightly roast grains in a dry skillet before cooking. This gives them a lighter texture and a nuttier taste.
- Most grains become sticky if stirred, so leave them alone while they cook. The result will be fluffier and tastier.
- Some grain dishes, such as bulgur and couscous, are actually fluffier if you do not cook them. Just pour boiling water over the grains, let stand for 15 to 20 minutes, then toss them with a fork before adding other ingredients or serving.

In the past, such grain products as bread and pasta were considered heavy, fattening foods. Today, nutrition experts urge Canadians to eat more grain products as a healthy substitute for the meat and other high-fat foods that so many people consume in abundance. Nutritionists recommend that 55 to 60 percent of total daily calories should come from CARBOHYDRATES, mostly grain-based starches, such as breads, cereals, pasta, and rice, along with potatoes and dried beans, peas, and other legumes. A person of normal weight should have 5 to 12 servings of starchy foods a day, with at least 4 to 6 of these servings coming from a grain product; for example, a slice of bread, a bowl of cereal, and a serving of rice or pasta.

WHOLE VS. REFINED

Many of the valuable nutrients in wheat and other grains are contained in the germ and outer covering that are removed during milling, or refining. In contrast, products made from whole grains retain most of their nutritive value; their high fiber content also adds texture and is filling. Refined grain products, including FLOURS, breads, and breakfast CEREALS, are fortified with calcium, iron, thiamine, riboflavin, and niacin. Some of these replace

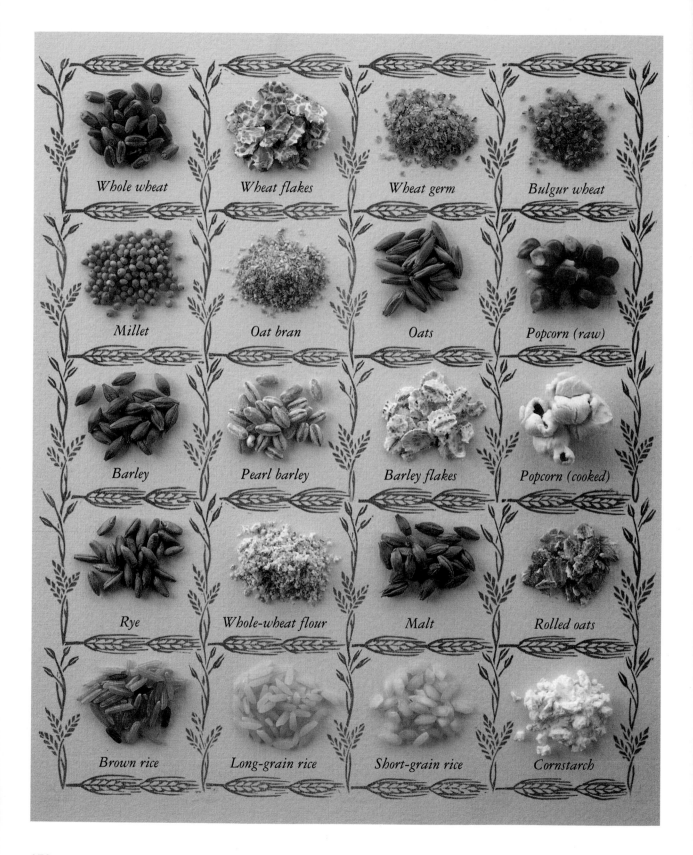

Whole wheat

Wheat flakes

Wheat germ

Bulgur wheat

Millet

Oat bran

Oats

Popcorn (raw)

Barley

Pearl barley

Barley flakes

Popcorn (cooked)

Rye

Whole-wheat flour

Malt

Rolled oats

Brown rice

Long-grain rice

Short-grain rice

Cornstarch

the nutrients lost in refining; others are added to prevent deficiency diseases. Despite the additions, refined products still have less vitamins, minerals, and dietary fiber than whole-grain products.

Labels on many grain products can be deceptive; look for the words "whole-wheat flour." A product labeled "wheat flour" is actually white flour.

COMMON GRAIN PRODUCTS

Barley, a staple food in the Middle East, is known to Canadians mainly as a soup ingredient. It has a somewhat sweet taste that makes it an interesting addition to casseroles and salads.

Corn, or maize, is gluten-free; hence, people with CELIAC DISEASE can eat products made from it. In addition to being served as fresh sweet CORN, it forms the basis of a wide range of foods, including popcorn, breakfast cereals, corn syrup, polenta, tortillas, corn bread, and hominy grits. Cornstarch is a gluten-free thickening agent.

Millet, an ancient grain of Asia and North Africa, is gluten-free; it is made into tasty flat breads and can also be used in pilaf or as a stuffing for vegetables. Toasting millet in a dry skillet before cooking helps it retain its shape and adds a nutty flavor.

Oats are used in breakfast cereals and baked goods. Oat bran is high in soluble fiber, which can help lower blood cholesterol levels, thus possibly reducing the risk of heart attacks. It also helps the body utilize insulin more efficiently, an important asset in controlling DIABETES. Products made with oats contain little or no gluten and can usually be tolerated by people with celiac disease. (Note, however, that oat flour is often combined with wheat in commercial baked goods.) Rolled oats can be added to many dishes, including meat loaf and fish cakes; they can also be used to thicken soups and sauces.

Rice is the staple food for about half the world's population. Among its many varieties, brown RICE is preferable to the polished grain, because it is unrefined and retains all its minerals, vitamins, and fiber. Long-grain brown rice is light and fluffy, and it is closer in taste to the refined white rice that most Canadians customarily eat. Short-grain brown rice has a heartier texture and a nuttier flavor; it takes longer to cook than white rice but requires little attention. Brown rice is high in B vitamins; it also provides some calcium and phosphorus. White rice, which is stripped of its outer layers, is mostly starch with a little protein; some types of white rice are fortified with thiamine.

Rye contains some gluten, but it has less than wheat flour, which is the reason rye bread and pumpernickel breads tend to be heavy and moist. Rye is also used in some crackers and crisp breads, and is the key ingredient in rye whiskey.

Wheat is one of the most widely consumed grains in the world. During milling, the bran (outer husk) and germ (located at the base of the grain) are removed, making the end product less nutritious than whole-wheat flour.

In addition to being the staple grain in cereals, pasta, breads, pastries, and other baked goods, wheat in its various forms can be made into a flavorful starchy side dish. Bulgur, for example, is cracked and roasted whole-wheat kernels; it has a nutty flavor and can be used to make pilaf or stuffing, or it can be combined with chickpeas, raisins, or nuts to make a high-protein salad. Couscous is made from durum wheat, the hardest type, which contains the most gluten. The wheat is ground, steamed, and dried into small pieces. It cooks fast and is light and fluffy, making it a good choice for quick meals.

HOW GRAINS ARE PROCESSED

The methods in which grains are processed vary according to the specific grain and geographic area. The following techniques are used in industrialized countries.

Cracking. The grains are put through machines that crack or break them into smaller pieces, which cook more quickly than whole seeds.

Extracting oils. The oil-bearing germ of the grain is pressed or heated to extract the oil.

Extracting starches. The grain is first soaked in a solution containing sulfur dioxide or sodium hydroxide, ground to remove the bran, and then spun in a centrifuge machine to separate out the starch.

Flaking. The grains are cooked, dried, and rolled through machines to produce flakes of the desired shape and size. Sugar and flavorings may be added to make cereals.

Milling. The grains are sent into grinders or rollers to remove the hulls, bran, and seed germ; at this time, they may also be cracked or crushed into meal or flour.

Parboiling. The grains (usually rice but sometimes wheat) are boiled in water before milling.

Polishing and pearling. After the hulls are removed, an abrasive is used to shape the kernels.

Puffing. The grains are placed in hot rotating cylinders, or puffing guns. Alternatively, the grains are milled and made into a dough that is puffed in an oven.

Rolling. The grains are compressed between large rollers to flatten them, as in rolled oats, or to convert them into flakes.

Shredding. The grains (usually wheat) are cooked, dried, and then squeezed through a grooved cylinder to form long strands.

KING OF THE CROP. *The pomelo grapefruit, the largest member of the citrus family, is grown in subtropical climates worldwide.*

GRAPEFRUITS

BENEFITS
- *High in vitamin C and potassium.*
- *A good source of folate, iron, calcium, and other minerals.*
- *Pink and red varieties are high in beta carotene, a precursor of vitamin A.*
- *High in fiber, low in calories.*
- *Contain bioflavonoids and other plant chemicals that protect against cancer and heart disease.*

DRAWBACKS
- *May provoke an allergic reaction in people sensitive to citrus fruits.*

Filling, flavorful, and nutritious—it's easy to understand why grapefruits are no longer just an option for breakfast.

Half a grapefruit provides more than 75 percent of the adult Recommended Nutrient Intake (RNI) of vitamin C; it also has 325mg of potassium, 25mcg (micrograms) of folate, 40mg of calcium, and 1mg of iron. The pink and red varieties are high in beta carotene which the body converts to vitamin A.

A cup of unsweetened grapefruit juice has 95mg of vitamin C, more than 200 percent of the RNI, and most of the other nutrients found in the fresh fruit. In the past, many people shunned unsweetened grapefruit juice because of its tartness, but a naturally sweet juice can be made by using red or pink fruits, or by blending their juice with that of white grapefruits. Mixing orange and grapefruit juices also makes a refreshing drink that doesn't need sweetening.

Over the years a number of FAD DIETS have promoted the grapefruit as possessing a unique ability to burn away fat. There is no truth to these claims; no food can do this. People following grapefruit diets lose weight because they eat little else—a practice that can lead to nutritional deficiencies and yo-yo dieting. Even so, grapefruits are a good food to include in a sensible weight-loss diet; a serving contains less than 100 calories, and its high-fiber content satisfies hunger.

Grapefruits are especially high in pectin, a soluble fiber that helps lower blood cholesterol. In addition, recent studies indicate that grapefruits contain other substances that prevent disease. Pink and red grapefruits, for example, are high in lycopene, an ANTIOXIDANT that appears to lower the risk of prostate cancer. Researchers have not yet

172

identified lycopene's mechanism of action, but a 6-year Harvard study involving 48,000 doctors and other health professionals has linked 10 servings of lycopene-rich foods a week with a 50 percent reduction in prostate cancer.

Other protective plant chemicals found in grapefruits include phenolic acid, which inhibits the formation of cancer-causing nitrosamines; limonoids, terpenes, and monoterpenes, which induce the production of enzymes that help prevent cancer; and BIOFLAVONOIDS, which inhibit the action of hormones that promote tumor growth. Some people with rheumatoid arthritis, lupus, and other inflammatory disorders find that eating grapefruit daily seems to alleviate their symptoms. This is thought to stem from plant chemicals that block prostaglandins, substances that cause inflammation.

People who are allergic to other citrus FRUITS are likely to react to grapefruits, too. The sensitivity may be to the fruit itself or to an oil in the peel.

Grapefruit juice should not be used to take certain medications, such as the blood-pressure lowering drug felodipine. Compounds in the juice make the active ingredient in the medication more bioavailable, possibly resulting in adverse effects.

GRAPES

BENEFITS
- *High in pectin and bioflavonoids.*
- *A fair source of iron, potassium, and vitamin C.*
- *A low-calorie sweet snack and dessert.*

DRAWBACKS
- *May contain pesticides.*
- *Often treated with sulfur dioxide to retard spoiling.*
- *Natural salicylates may provoke an allergic response.*

One of the oldest and most abundant of the world's fruit crops, grapes are cultivated on six of the seven continents. Most of the 60 million metric tons grown worldwide annually are fermented to produce wine. Grapes are also made into JAMS AND SPREADS, used in cooking, and eaten raw as a snack food.

Grapes are divided into two general categories: European, which encompasses most of the varieties used for table food and wine, and American, which have skins that slip off easily and are used mostly to make jams, jellies, and juice. The European type is the more nutritious of the two, but neither ranks high on the nutritional scale when compared to other fruits. A cup of European table grapes provides about 45 percent of the Recommended Nutrient Intake (RNI) for vitamin C, about five times that found in the American varieties. Most types provide fair amounts of potassium and iron.

Low in calories, grapes are favored for their sweet, juicy flavor. Another reason for eating grapes may be found in research on the disease-prevention role of BIOFLAVONOIDS and other plant chemicals. Grapes contain quercetin, a plant pigment that is thought to regulate the levels of blood cholesterol and also reduce the action of platelets, blood cells that are instrumental in forming clots. Some researchers theorize that it is quercetin that lowers the risk of heart attack among moderate wine drinkers.

Commercially grown grapes are usually sprayed with pesticides and are treated with sulfur dioxide to preserve their color and extend shelf life; they should always be washed

- Grapes originated in Asia Minor and were first cultivated about 7,000 years ago by the Egyptians. New varieties that could withstand colder climates were developed by the Greeks and Romans and eventually introduced into Europe.
- Worldwide, more than 25 million acres are devoted to cultivating more than 60 varieties of grapes.
- *Vitis vinifera*, a species of European grape, gave rise to some 10,000 different cultivars, including almost all of those used to make wine and our most popular types of table grapes—emperor, muscat, Thompson seedless, Ribier, and Tokay.
- When a grape blight threatened to wipe out the European wine industry in the early 1800s, the vines were revived with grafts of disease-free American varieties.
- California is now the world's leading producer of raisins; Turkey and Italy are other top producers.

before being eaten. People with asthma should either avoid grapes or look for those that have not been treated with sulfur. Grapes naturally contain salicylates, compounds similar to the major ingredient in aspirin. Salicylates have an anticlotting effect and may account for the benefits of wine with respect to heart disease. People who are allergic to aspirin may react to grapes and grape products.

RAISINS

It takes about 4½ pounds of fresh grapes to produce a pound of raisins. Raisins are a highly concentrated source of nutrients and calories; a cup contains a whopping 440 calories while providing 3g of iron, 1,090mg of potassium, and 10g of fiber.

Like other dried fruits, raisins are a concentrated source of sugar, and if bits adhere to the teeth, they promote dental decay.

GRILLED FOODS

Grilling has been a popular method of cooking for thousands of years. To preserve flavor and nutrients and to keep food safe, however, a few simple rules should be followed.

Involving direct exposure of food to the source of heat, grilling or broiling is the modern and controlled version of man's oldest culinary technique—namely, roasting over an open fire. Grilled foods have an intense flavor as a result of the numerous chemical reactions that take place when a food surface is subjected to very high temperatures. Grilling—whether by gas flame, electric element, or charcoal—demands temperatures four to six times higher than can be reached in an oven; an electric broiler heats to about 2,000°F (1,093°C) and a gas flame to about 3,000°F (1,649°C), compared with a maximum of 500°F (260°C) for domestic ovens. Unfortunately, the high heat that causes the appealing caramelization of browning has a less desirable aspect: the outside of the food may become unpalatably charred before the inside is cooked through. Grilling is best reserved, therefore, for quick-cooking foods, such as fish and the thinner cuts of meat and poultry. It is an excellent method of preparing such vegetables as eggplant, zucchini, peppers, and mushrooms; apples, peaches, and other fruits are also tasty when grilled.

The nutritional value of foods is only slightly impaired by grilling. Meat retains most of its riboflavin and 60 to 80 percent of its thiamine; a minor loss of lysine, an amino acid, is offset by the enhanced visual and taste appeal. Vegetables cook quickly with little loss of moisture or vitamins.

GRILLING PREPARATION

Pre-grill preparation requires little more than a brush with oil to prevent food from drying out, followed by a dusting of herbs. Use the least amount of oil to avoid adding unnecessary calories. Delicate foods, such as fish and vegetables, are easier to handle if placed on a metal grill tray.

Marinades can add exotic flavors. A small amount of honey or other sugar in the marinade can hasten caramelization because simple sugars brown at lower temperatures than proteins and starchy foods do. But don't make the mistake of assuming that a marinated meat is cooked just because the outside is browned. And despite the instructions in many recipes, there's nothing to be gained from prolonged marination. The marinade cannot penetrate past the surface of the meat, no matter how long the soaking. In addition, the acid of the marinade tenderizes the surface of the meat by denaturing the surface proteins. Left too long, marination results in a flavorful but mushy outer layer that contrasts unpleasantly with the inner texture.

POTENTIAL TOXICITY

At grilling temperatures, the surface fat on meat quickly burns away, releasing acrid fumes and creating a risk of fire. There's a further hazard to

---

BENEFITS
- *Adds flavor to food and preserves its nutritional value.*
- *Allows fat to drain off food.*

DRAWBACKS
- *May generate compounds that are responsible for causing cancer.*

174

grilling. The smoke generated when fat drips into the fire contains potent carcinogens. Home cooks do not need to be concerned about the smoke from occasional grilling, but it must be done in a well-ventilated area. You can further minimize exposure to the fumes by partly baking or parboiling the food, then finishing it off with a few minutes on the grill to achieve a crusty exterior and succulent interior. Choose lean cuts, and trim all visible fat from meat. Whether you're using an oven broiler or an outdoor grill, place a broiling pan to catch melted fat under a spatterproof metal shield.

Other potentially toxic compounds are generated by chemical reactions that take place during the cooking or processing of food. Although these substances can form during any cooking process—and even in the body during digestion—eating broiled or fried meats exposes human cells to up to 50 times more DNA-damaging chemicals than eating boiled or baked meats. More than 30 years ago, researchers at the University of Chicago demonstrated that a single well-done charcoal-broiled steak contained as much benzopyrene, a cancer-causing soot, as the smoke from several hundred cigarettes. Since then Japanese scientists have found that several compounds formed when high-protein foods are browned have mutagenic activity comparable to the most powerful known carcinogens. Hydrocarbons (including benzene and its derivatives) form in broiled meat, and carcinogenic nitrosamines form both during cooking and in the digestive tract when bacon and other foods that contain nitrite are cooked or eaten.

Still, there's no direct evidence that chemicals that damage DNA in bacteria cause cancer in animals, nor have scientists shown that substances causing cancer in animals necessarily cause the disease in humans. The browned foods that people have favored since the dawn of cooking probably do not constitute a threat to the population as a whole, especially if they are consumed only occasionally.

PROTECTIVE FOODS

Vitamins C and E block the chemical reaction that generates nitrosamines in the digestive tract. As ANTIOXIDANTS, these vitamins, as well as beta carotene, remove the by-products of cell metabolism. Wheat bran binds with nitrite and makes it unavailable for nitrosamine formation. You can balance your grilled breakfast bacon with a glass of vitamin C-rich citrus juice and fortified whole-grain cereal or a bran muffin for vitamin E.

Other substances found in vegetables and fruits bind directly to carcinogens, such as hydrocarbons, and prevent them from reacting with DNA. BIOFLAVONOIDS, the pigments in many fruits and vegetables, appear to block many carcinogens. Fiber may bind with or dilute carcinogens and speed their elimination from the digestive tract. When you barbecue, serve lots of leafy greens and whole-grain salads and breads along with the meat or fish, to ensure a healthy mixture of fiber and vitamins. Or make a vegetarian barbecue with an assortment of vegetables and slices of low-fat goat cheese grilled on whole-wheat bread to satisfy a desire for protein. Fresh fruits end a meal with a colorful cocktail of vitamins, fiber, and flavor.

MEALS ON STICKS. *Shish kebabs made from a variety of fresh vegetables and chunks of lean meat, chicken, or fish make delicious low-fat entrées.*

Four ounces of guava provide 275mg, compared to 57mg in the same amount of fresh orange. Guavas are also a good source of potassium and iron (330mg and 1mg, respectively, in four ounces). An average-size guava also provides 6g of fiber; much of it is in the form of pectin, a soluble fiber that lowers high blood cholesterol as well as promoting digestive function.

About half of the guava fruit is filled with hard seeds; although these are edible, most people discard them. If the seeds are eaten, they contribute extra fiber and lesser amounts of the same nutrients found in the flesh.

A VERSATILE FRUIT

With only about 60 calories per fresh guava, the fruit makes an easy, interesting, nonfattening dessert. Simply cut the fruit in half, scoop out the seeds, then spoon out the flesh. A dash of lime juice or lemon juice contrasts nicely with the sweet flavor. Alternatively, you can peel, seed, and chop or slice guavas to add to a fruit salad. Puréed guava flesh in combination with orange or other citrus juice makes a refreshing drink or cold summer soup. Unripe guavas, which are slightly tart, can be blended and cooked with defatted meat juice to make a low-calorie sauce for roasts and poultry dishes.

Look for fresh guavas during the late fall and early winter. When selecting guavas, choose fruits that are firm but not hard. A guava is ripe when the skin yields slightly when pressed.

Gourmet sections in supermarkets carry increasing numbers of guava products—jams, jellies, dried sheets, nectar, and a type of fruit pasta called guava cheese. Canned guava is also available, but it is usually processed with large amounts of sugar. Dried guavas are often treated with sulfites, which may provoke asthma attacks or allergic reactions in susceptible persons.

EXOTIC FRUIT. *The acid-sweet taste and strong aroma of guavas evoke images of a tropical paradise. Although the entire fruit is edible, many people discard the seeds and skins.*

GUAVAS

BENEFITS

- *An excellent source of vitamin C.*
- *High in pectin and other types of soluble dietary fiber.*
- *Good amounts of potassium and iron.*

DRAWBACKS

- *Fresh fruit is expensive and not widely available.*
- *Sulfites in dried guavas may provoke an asthma attack or allergic reaction in susceptible persons.*

A tropical fruit that is native to the Caribbean and South America, the guava is now grown in Florida, California, southern Asia, and parts of Africa. The pear-shaped fruit ranges in size from 1 to 4 inches in diameter. The thin skins, which vary in color from pale yellow to yellow-green, have a slightly bitter taste, so the fruit is usually served peeled. Most varieties have meaty deep-pink flesh, although some are yellow, red, or white. Ripe guavas have a fragrant aroma and a sweet flavor, with hints of pineapple or banana.

By weight, guavas have almost five times as much vitamin C as an orange:

HAIR AND SCALP PROBLEMS

EAT PLENTY OF

- *Low-fat dairy products, dark green vegetables, and deep yellow vegetables and fruits for vitamin A.*
- *Whole-grain products for niacin.*
- *Such fruits as bananas, prunes, and watermelon for vitamin B6.*
- *Fresh fruits for vitamin C.*
- *Nuts and legumes for biotin and zinc.*
- *Lean meat, poultry, and fish for high-grade protein.*

AVOID

- *Preparations containing raw egg whites, which interfere with biotin absorption.*

Baldness and dandruff are among the most pervasive hair and scalp problems. Hair loss may be either the result of illness or, more commonly, a normal genetic response to testosterone, the major male sex hormone. Dandruff—scaling of the scalp—may be due to stress or a chronic or recurrent skin disorder, such as seborrheic dermatitis.

Hair is composed of keratin, a protein that is found in nails, feathers, and scales. Although hair is made from protein, other nutrients that contribute to hair and scalp health include niacin, biotin, zinc, and vitamins A, B6, and C. A varied diet based on the BASIC FOOD GROUPS should provide ample amounts of these nutrients. Because hair is inert material, shampoos and rinses enriched with protein or other nutrients cannot repair damage or make hair healthier. Protein-based shampoos can make a temporary difference in hair's appearance, however, by leaving a shiny coating on the hair shaft.

HAIR LOSS

A healthy human head has from 80,000 to 150,000 hairs, each of which passes through three phases independently of all the others. At any time, 90 percent of the hairs are in the growing stage (anagen), which lasts 4 to 5 years. Growth is followed by a resting phase (telogen); this ends after a few months as the hair is shed (catagen) to allow new growth. A daily loss of about 50 hairs is a normal part of the cycle.

Although baldness is mediated by hormonal factors, it tends to run in families; your risk may be deduced from the number of bald males among members of both parents' families.

Abnormal hair loss may be precipitated by metabolic disorders (including diabetes, thyroid disease, and crash diets); damage to hair shafts caused by harsh treatments or congenital factors; stress brought on by acute illness or the hormonal changes of pregnancy; medical treatment, including drugs used for cancer chemotherapy; and in rare cases, very severe scalp disorders.

Only very rarely in Canada is hair loss related to nutrition. When diet is involved, the cause may be a grossly excessive intake of vitamin A or a deficiency of iron, biotin, zinc, or protein. Such deficiencies are rare, although an excessive intake of raw egg whites can lead to a depletion of biotin.

Hair loss due to an acutely stressful situation or drug treatment is generally temporary. Hair that falls out during a crash diet soon regrows once nutrition returns to normal. Hair lost in patches usually grows back without treatment, but in some instances, corticosteroid injections may be needed.

At present, the only medical treatment for baldness is minoxidil (Rogaine), a topical form of a medicine that was originally developed to treat high blood pressure. Unfortunately, minoxidil works in fewer than half of those who try it, and regrown hair falls out when the drug is stopped.

DANDRUFF

Many people shed a few flakes of dandruff, especially during the winter, when the scalp and skin may be dry. Some people, however, have a hereditary tendency to develop skin problems that are triggered by a sensitivity to specific foods. Because the offending food varies from one person to the next, the only reasonable advice is to avoid foods that seem to make your dandruff worse. Some people improve when they shun foods that cause the face and scalp to flush; typical offenders are hot liquids, heavily spiced foods, and alcohol.

To control mild dandruff, doctors usually recommend shampooing daily until the dandruff is under control, followed by twice-weekly shampooing for maintenance. Dandruff shampoos and prescription treatments contain selenium or zinc, which work as exfoliants to hasten the shedding of the dead cell layer from the scalp.

THE VALUE OF HAIR ANALYSIS

Scientific analysis of hair can confirm the presence of certain toxic elements months or years after poisoning. (Hair analysis was used more than 150 years after Napoleon's death to confirm that he suffered chronic arsenic poisoning.) However, hair analysis, as touted by quack nutritionists for detecting such health problems as vitamin or mineral deficiencies, is completely worthless.

HAY FEVER

EAT PLENTY OF
- *Fatty fish and other foods high in omega-3 fatty acids for their anti-inflammatory effect.*

AVOID
- *Honey and bee pollen capsules.*
- *Any food in the same plant family as sunflowers (the Compositae family).*
- *Fermented foods or those with molds if fungi spores trigger symptoms.*

Hay fever is a seasonal allergy triggered by the inhalation of pollen or, less commonly, molds. Medically known as seasonal or allergic rhinitis, the popular name of hay fever is a misnomer: Although symptoms may occur during the haying season, hay itself is not the culprit, nor is there a fever.

Ragweed is one of the most common offenders, but in susceptible people, tree, grass, and flower pollens can also cause the sneezing, runny nose, tearing eyes, itchiness, and other hay fever symptoms. In general, these symptoms

THE SUNFLOWER PLANT FAMILY

People who suffer ragweed hay fever may be advised to avoid the following plant foods:
- Artichokes
- Chamomile (used in herbal teas and medicines)
- Chicory
- Dandelions
- Endives
- Escarole
- Jerusalem artichokes
- Oyster plants (salsify)
- Safflower (used in many vegetable oils and margarines)
- Sunflower seeds and oil
- Tansy (used in some herbal medicines and folk remedies)
- Tarragon

are more irritating than serious or threatening. This is not the case for people with asthma, however; for them, hay fever can provoke repeated, sometimes life-threatening attacks.

Although foods aren't ordinarily associated with hay fever, people with certain types of seasonal allergies may experience symptoms after eating particular foods. For example, plants in the sunflower, or Compositae, family have antigens that cross-react with members of the Ambrosiaceae family, which includes ragweed. Thus, a person whose hay fever symptoms are triggered by pollen from ragweed may react to ingestion of any of a broad variety of herbs and vegetables in the sunflower family (see below left).

Contaminants or pollens in some foods can also trigger the onset of hay fever symptoms. This is especially true of HONEY, which may harbor bits of pollen, and bee pollen capsules, a food supplement and natural remedy that is sold in health-food stores.

There is no special diet that will alleviate hay fever symptoms, although some recent reports suggest that eating fatty fish and other foods that are high in omega-3 fatty acids may reduce the inflammation that is part of an allergic reaction. More research is necessary to confirm this; in the meantime, consumption of fish is still an important part of a varied and balanced diet.

MOLD AS THE CULPRIT

In some people seasonal allergies are triggered by mold spores instead of (or in addition to) pollen. Typically, these individuals suffer a flare-up of hay fever symptoms when it is cool and damp: usually, beginning in the spring, improving somewhat during the summer, and then worsening during the damp fall season. Although most mold spores are outdoors, some also grow in dark, moist indoor areas, especially in basements, shower stalls, refrigerator drip

trays, air conditioners, and garbage cans. Symptoms generally occur after inhaling the spores, but in some people eating foods and beverages that harbor molds also provokes a flare-up. Items that should be avoided include:

Alcoholic beverages, especially beer, wine, and other drinks made by fermentation processes.

Breads made with lots of yeast or the sourdough varieties.

Cheeses, especially blue cheese and other aged varieties.

Dried fruits, including raisins and others that are allowed to dry outdoors.

Mushrooms of all kinds.

Processed meats and fish, including hot dogs, sausages, and smoked fish.

Sauerkraut and other fermented or pickled foods.

Soy sauce, which is fermented.

Vinegar and products made with it, including salad dressings, mayonnaise, ketchup, and pickles.

HEART DISEASE

EAT PLENTY OF
- *Fresh fruits and vegetables, foods with plenty of vitamin C, beta carotene, and other antioxidant nutrients.*
- *Poultry, seafood, wheat germ, and fortified cereals for vitamin E.*
- *Apples, oat bran, and other foods high in soluble fiber.*

CUT DOWN ON
- *Meat, especially fatty cuts.*
- *Eggs, whole milk, organ meats, and other high-cholesterol foods.*
- *Fats, especially those that are saturated.*
- *Iron-fortified foods (unless recommended by your doctor).*

AVOID
- *Excessive alcohol.*
- *Tobacco use in any form.*
- *Salty foods (if you have hypertension).*

Despite dramatic gains against heart and blood vessel diseases in recent decades, they remain leading causes of death in Canada, claiming about 75,000 lives a year. Heart attacks, with about 44,000 deaths annually, top the list; strokes, with about 14,000 fatalities, are third (exceeded by cancer); and cardiac arrhythmias, high blood pressure, congestive failure, congenital defects, and other heart disorders account for about 17,000 deaths. The Heart and Stroke Foundation of Canada estimates that more than 6 million Canadians have some form of cardiovascular disease. In addition to the risk for premature death, cardiovascular disease represents a tremendous financial burden to the health care system.

Numerous population studies since the early 1950s have confirmed that diet is a major force in both the cause and prevention of heart disease. One of the most extensive research projects is the Framingham Heart Study, which has followed more than 5,000 men and women in this Boston suburb for more than 40 years. Another large-scale study has compared the incidence of heart disease among men in seven countries and then correlated these statistics with diet, smoking habits, physical activity, and other lifestyle factors.

By carefully analyzing the results, researchers have identified certain risk factors that predispose people to heart disease: heredity, advancing age, and gender (premenopausal women have a lower risk than men and older women) are among those over which people have no control. Tobacco use tops the list of controllable risk factors. Poor diet is instrumental in most other factors: they include high blood CHOLESTEROL, which promotes the buildup of fatty deposits in the coronary arteries and leads to angina and heart attacks; OBESITY, which increases the risk of heart attack and contributes to other cardiovascular risk factors; high BLOOD PRESSURE,

DOES GARLIC REALLY HELP?

Garlic inhibits the tendency of the blood to clot, lowers blood cholesterol, and helps reduce high blood pressure. Allicin, the chemical that gives garlic its distinctive odor, is thought to produce these various effects.

Several pharmaceutical companies have developed powdered garlic pills that contain allicin without causing bad breath and body odor. Studies indicate that the pills reduce clot formation and lower cholesterol in a significant number of patients; some also experience lowered blood pressure. Garlic pills should not be taken, however, without first consulting a doctor—they may increase the effects of aspirin and other anti-clotting drugs, which can result in serious bleeding problems.

which can lead to a STROKE and heart attack; DIABETES, a disease that affects the heart, blood vessels, and other vital organs; and excessive ALCOHOL use, which harms the heart and blood vessels.

THE PRUDENT DIET

If diet can promote heart disease, so too can it improve one's odds against it, even in the presence of such unalterable risk factors as advancing age and a family history of early heart attacks. There is nothing radical about a heart-healthy diet; in fact, it's the same common-sense balanced regimen that protects against cancer, adult-onset diabetes,

and obesity. Carbohydrates, especially such starchy foods as pasta, rice, potatoes, beans and other legumes, breads, and cereals, along with ample fresh fruits and vegetables, form the foundation of a prudent diet. About 10 to 12 percent of daily calories should come from protein foods—meat, fish, poultry, egg whites, and a combination of grains and legumes. Fats, sugars, and salt should be used sparingly.

Ideally, prudent dietary habits should be instilled during childhood, which is when ATHEROSCLEROSIS—the clogging of arteries with fatty deposits— begins. This was proved during the Korean War, when autopsies performed on young men killed in combat found that many had early atherosclerosis. It takes 20 to 30 years or even longer for the vessels to become clogged enough to produce symptoms. By that time, however, it may be too late; in a distressing number of cases, the first indication of atherosclerosis is a fatal heart attack. Still, most atherosclerosis can be prevented by adopting a low-fat, low-cholesterol diet, maintaining a healthy weight, and exercising regularly.

In addition to fostering a low-fat diet, it's also a good idea to accustom children to the natural flavor of foods, rather than adding lots of salt. While there are some conflicting reports, numerous studies show that populations with a high intake of salty foods have an increased incidence of hypertension.

Recently, a group of Finnish researchers identified excessive iron as another dietary factor that may damage the heart and blood vessels. Their studies found that men with high levels of iron in their blood also had an increased incidence of heart attacks. It's well known that excessive iron damages the heart, liver, and other vital organs, but this was the first time that iron levels in the high-normal range were linked to a serious health risk. This is another reason to cut down on red

A JIGSAW OF CONTRIBUTING FACTORS

An intricate web of factors influences the long-term health of the human heart. Some factors we can control—such as the food we eat, the habits we adopt, and the exercise we engage in—others we cannot. For some people, high blood cholesterol levels are simply part of their genetic inheritance; there are also external stresses in the workplace and at home. The following are some of the pieces of the jigsaw puzzle that appear to determine an individual's risk of heart disease.

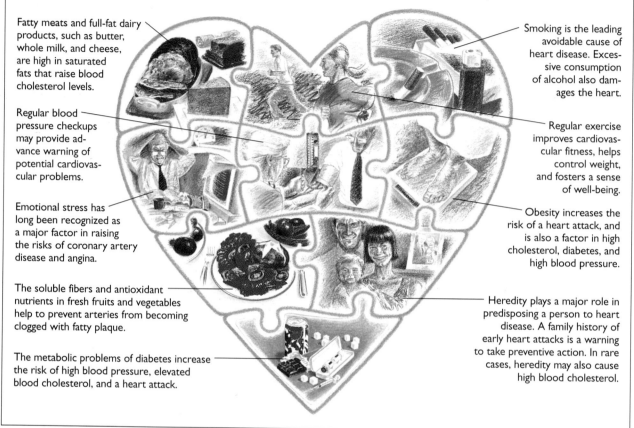

Fatty meats and full-fat dairy products, such as butter, whole milk, and cheese, are high in saturated fats that raise blood cholesterol levels.

Regular blood pressure checkups may provide advance warning of potential cardiovascular problems.

Emotional stress has long been recognized as a major factor in raising the risks of coronary artery disease and angina.

The soluble fibers and antioxidant nutrients in fresh fruits and vegetables help to prevent arteries from becoming clogged with fatty plaque.

The metabolic problems of diabetes increase the risk of high blood pressure, elevated blood cholesterol, and a heart attack.

Smoking is the leading avoidable cause of heart disease. Excessive consumption of alcohol also damages the heart.

Regular exercise improves cardiovascular fitness, helps control weight, and fosters a sense of well-being.

Obesity increases the risk of a heart attack, and is also a factor in high cholesterol, diabetes, and high blood pressure.

Heredity plays a major role in predisposing a person to heart disease. A family history of early heart attacks is a warning to take preventive action. In rare cases, heredity may also cause high blood cholesterol.

---

meat, one of our most abundant sources of iron. It also reinforces long-standing advice not to take any supplements without first consulting a doctor.

THE CHOLESTEROL FACTOR

Excessive cholesterol circulating in the blood is the major precipitating factor in atherosclerosis. In rare cases, an inherited disorder, familial hypercholesterolemia, causes high blood cholesterol. Without a stringent low-fat diet and cholesterol-lowering drugs, people with this disorder invariably suffer an early heart attack—sometimes during childhood. Far more often, high cholesterol is caused by an imprudent diet, lack of exercise, and other lifestyle habits.

For most people, moderately elevated cholesterol levels can be lowered by adopting a diet with less than 30 percent (but preferably 20 percent) of its calories coming from FATS, mostly the monounsaturated and polyunsaturated types found in plant oils and fish. Until recently doctors have advised using margarine, especially the kinds made with corn, safflower, and other unsaturated fats, instead of BUTTER. Then came reports that the trans fatty acids in hardened margarine may raise LDL cholesterol levels even more than but-ter's mostly saturated fat does. A closer look at the data shows that most margarines have low amounts of trans fatty acids, and soft or liquid margarines have even less. Therefore soft margarines are more heart-healthy than butter, but both should be used sparingly. Margarines labelled as nonhydrogenated contain no trans fatty acids.

HELPFUL FOODS

Numerous studies correlate a diet with at least three daily servings of fresh fruits and vegetables with a 25 percent or better reduction in both heart attacks and strokes. Researchers believe that it's the ample vitamin C, beta carotene, and other ANTIOXIDANTS in fruits and vegetables that account for the difference. Antioxidants protect cells against damage from the unstable molecules that are released when the body uses oxygen. Oxidation of LDL cholesterol—the type that forms fatty plaque—is thought to be instrumental in initiating atherosclerosis. Fruits and vegetables are also high in BIOFLAVONOIDS and other plant chemicals that act as antioxidants.

Vitamin E, too, seems to protect against heart disease; this may be due to its antioxidant properties, and also to the fact that it reduces the ability of blood platelets to form clots. Good sources include eggs (in moderation, as they are also high in cholesterol), wheat germ, fortified cereals, nuts, seeds, margarine, and vegetable oils.

Salmon, sardines, herring, trout, and other fatty cold-water FISH are high in omega-3 fatty acids, which reduce the tendency of blood to clot. This benefit can be had from two or three servings of fish a week. Although fish oil supplements are high in omega-3 fatty acids, they should not be taken without approval by a doctor, because they may increase the risk of a stroke.

Pectin, oat bran, and other types of soluble FIBER help lower cholesterol and improve glucose metabolism in people predisposed to develop diabetes. Apples, grapes, and other fruits are high in soluble fiber; so too are dried peas, beans, and other legumes. A combination of legumes and grains is a prudent low-fat meat alternative.

WINE AS MEDICINE

For years, researchers have tried to determine why the French have fewer heart attacks than their counterparts in other industrialized countries. It would seem that the French people's high-fat diet and pervasive tobacco use would predispose its citizens to more, not less

heart disease. Increasingly, researchers have settled on wine as the protective factor, although there is uncertainty over exactly what it is in wine that benefits the heart.

One theory centers on bioflavonoids, especially quercetin and resveratrol, found in GRAPES. Quercetin has been studied extensively since the 1970s; to date, it appears to have myriad beneficial effects. Not only does it protect against cancer, it also seems to prevent inflammation, allergic reactions, and a tendency for the blood to clot, which may explain the reduced risk of heart attack in wine drinkers.

A Niçoise salad (below) made with fresh vegetables and an olive oil dressing is typical of the Mediterranean diet, which is characteristically low in animal fat.

Vegetable and beef kabobs (left) with lentils make a nutritious low-fat, high-fiber dinner.

Risotto (below) made with defatted broth and dried fruits supplies vitamins, minerals, and fiber.

Grilled salmon (right) with a serving of broad beans and a watercress and walnut salad provides omega-3 fatty acids, vitamin E, and ample soluble fiber.

181

HERBS FOR HEALTH

Physicians and folk healers alike have relied on medicinal plants since ancient times. Today, researchers continue to scour the planet, looking for more healing herbs.

Many people regard herbal medicine as the province of alternative practitioners who shun orthodox medical practices. In fact, herbal medicine is a precursor of modern pharmacology; indeed, about one-fourth of all prescription medicines come from herbs and other plants. And a growing number of physicians and researchers are taking a new look at traditional herbal remedies.

Unfortunately, there are widespread misconceptions about the benefits and dangers of herbal medicines. Many people assume, for example, that because herbal remedies are made from natural ingredients, they are safer than synthetic drugs. In reality, herbal medicines—just like their pharmaceutical counterparts—can cause adverse side effects; some are even highly toxic. In addition, herbal remedies are not subject to the rigid testing and standards that Health Canada requires for synthetic drugs.

A LONG HISTORY

At one time or another, every society has relied upon the healing power of herbs to treat illness, and in some, herbal medicine still prevails. Traditional Chinese healers and ayurvedic practitioners, for example, continue to use ancient herbal remedies, although these may be combined with modern medical treatments. In Western societies most medicines are synthesized, including many that were originally derived from herbs. But there are exceptions: digitalis, the oldest effective heart medication, is still made from foxglove; morphine and codeine are derived from opium poppies; and vincristine, used to treat leukemia, comes from the Madagascar periwinkle.

THE HOME HERBALIST

Some people grow or gather their own herbs; more commonly, herbal preparations are bought from health-food stores or alternative practitioners. A number of pharmacies now sell herbal teas and other products, such as garlic pills, aloe vera skin preparations, and cough drops and syrups. Most products use dried herbs, which are more concentrated than the fresh plants.

Many medicinal herbs are taken as teas or infusions, which are generally more bitter than the herbal teas sold at the supermarket or health-food store. But herbal remedies take many other forms (see Herbal Medicine in Practice, p.184). Regardless of the form, caution is needed with any herbal product; while many are harmless, some that are safe for external use can be deadly if consumed. (A recent example is a rash of deaths that occurred when men ate a herbal impotence remedy that was intended only for external use.) Even some herbs intended for ingestion can be dangerous; for example, doctors advise against taking ma huang, or ephedra, if you have a heart disorder, because it can provoke cardiac arrhythmias. Fatal poisonings also occur among people who mistake a toxic herb for one that's safe or who use the wrong part of the plant. Another caution: never substitute a herbal drug for a prescribed medication, especially colchicine (a gout drug made from autumn crocus) and digitalis (a heart medication).

MULTIPURPOSE HERBS

In general, the herbs used in cooking are not potent enough to have medicinal effects, but many of them still confer some health benefits.

Basil. A mainstay in many dishes, basil is also used in larger quantities as a tonic and cold remedy. Basil oil is said to repel insects.

Bay. Used to season soups, casseroles, and stews, bay leaves in a tea or decoction form may also alleviate gas.

Chervil. This winter herb has a unique flavor that goes well with fish. It can also be used as a digestive aid; while some herbalists recommend it to lower blood pressure, there is no scientific proof to support that claim.

Chives. These tiny relatives to the onion complement potatoes and flavor soups and stews. Chives contain sulfur oil, which may lower blood pressure if eaten in large amounts.

Coriander. The pungent leaves enliv-

NATURAL HEALERS. *Many herbs not only lend flavor to recipes but confer health benefits as well.*

Basil

Thyme

Chervil

Chives

Coriander

Apple mint

Parsley

Oregano

Dill

Rosemary

Bay leaves

Sage

HERBAL MEDICINE IN PRACTICE

You can make your own herbal remedies at home following the methods described below. The amount of herb to be used varies according to whether it is dried or fresh; in general, dried or powdered herbs should be used more sparingly than fresh ones.

• **Decoctions.** Place the dried herb in a pan of cold water, heat, and simmer for up to 1 hour. Strain and consume in small amounts (usually ½ cup) two or three times a day.

• **Infusions or teas.** Place fresh or dried herbs in a cup or pot, cover with hot water, and let infuse for 10 minutes. Strain and drink as a medicinal tea.

• **Ointments and creams.** Blend crushed or powdered herbs with an appropriate oil, fat, or wax (water is used to make some creams) and cook in the top of a double boiler for 2 to 3 hours. Put the thickened mixture through a strainer or wine press and store in clean glass jars in a cool, dark place until you are ready to use.

• **Poultices and compresses.** To make a poultice, heat the herb or blend it with water to make a paste; apply directly to the skin and cover with gauze or a clean cloth. To make a compress, soak a clean cloth in a warm herbal tea or decoction.

• **Syrups.** Add honey or sugar to an infusion or decoction (see left), simmer until it reaches the desired consistency, and store in a clean glass bottle.

• **Tinctures.** Steep a dried or fresh herb in a mixture of one part vodka or other alcoholic beverage to three parts water. Place in a cool place for 2 weeks, then strain and pour the liquid into a clean glass jar. The alcohol preserves the mixture for up to a year.

en sauces and vegetable and poultry dishes; fresh coriander leaves or seeds may be chewed to ease indigestion.

Dill. Widely used in pickles, soups, salad dressings, and fish dishes, dill is also eaten to alleviate intestinal gas. Europeans often give their babies weak dill tea to relieve colic.

Mint. The leaves of many varieties add flavor to lamb, fruit, and ice cream. Chewing the leaves can freshen the breath; mint tea is a digestive aid.

Oregano. Used to flavor stuffings, salads, and tomato dishes, oregano used in a tea is said to aid digestion and alleviate the congestion of a cold.

Parsley. When consumed in portions of at least an ounce, this herb contains useful amounts of vitamin C (fresh parsley only), calcium, iron, and potassium. Parsley is also high in BIOFLAVONOIDS, monoterpenes, and other anticancer compounds.

Rosemary. This herb brings out the flavor of lamb and chicken; its leaves contain an oil that is used in liniments to relieve muscle aches. Rosemary tea is said to alleviate headaches.

Sage. This herb is used in bread stuffings for poultry and pork. Sage tea is used as a digestive aid and as a mouthwash or gargle to ease painful gums, mouth ulcers, and a sore throat. Some research indicates that sage oil can boost acetylcholine levels in the brain, improving memory.

Thyme. A favorite herb in Italian cooking, thyme is also used as a tea to quiet an irritable bowel, as a gargle for a sore throat, or as a syrup to treat a cough or chest congestion.

STRICTLY MEDICINAL

Many herbs that are not used for cooking are still cultivated or gathered for their medicinal properties.

Aloe vera. The leaves of this succulent plant exude a gel that is used externally to treat minor burns and cuts. Some herbal books recommend taking the juice as a tonic, but it can cause intestinal irritation.

Evening primrose. The oil extracted from the seeds of this plant contains gamma linolenic acid (GLA), a substance that is said to counter inflammation. Evening primrose is promoted to treat LUPUS and other types of inflammatory ARTHRITIS, premenstrual symptoms, breast pain, and numerous other disorders. A note of caution: because GLA reduces clot formation, its use can lead to bleeding problems, especially in people taking aspirin.

Ginkgo biloba. This herbal remedy is said to improve memory problems related to aging; recent studies show that it does improve circulation, including circulation to the brain, which may explain its benefits.

Ginseng. The Chinese use ginseng to strengthen the immune system, alleviate fever and pain, promote wound healing, overcome depression and fatigue, and treat impotence.

Saw palmetto. The berries of this plant may improve urinary flow and prevent benign prostate enlargement. Research indicates that it may alleviate symptoms related to an enlarged prostate, but more studies are needed to document this benefit.

HERPES

CONSUME PLENTY OF
- *Lamb, chicken, fish, milk, beans, fruits, and vegetables for lysine.*

CUT DOWN ON
- *Alcohol and caffeine.*

AVOID
- *Smoking.*
- *Excessive sun exposure.*

A very common and highly contagious infectious disease, herpes is caused by strains of the herpes simplex virus and is noted by painful and itchy blisters. Type 1 herpes, or oral herpes, typically causes cold sores or fever blisters around the mouth. In some cases, this type of herpes infects the eyes and can result in blindness or, even more seriously, can spread to the brain and result in life-threatening herpes encephalitis. Type 2, or genital herpes, is sexually transmitted and causes sores in the genital and anal areas. Engaging in oral sex with an infected person can cause mouth and throat blisters that are difficult to differentiate from type 1 herpes.

Regardless of the type or location, herpes blisters usually rupture into open weeping sores that crust over and eventually heal within a few days or weeks. Some people also experience a mild fever, swollen lymph nodes, and fatigue. Even after healing, the virus remains dormant in the body; some people never have another attack, while others have repeated but milder eruptions sporadically throughout life.

Recurrences may be triggered by hormonal changes, physical or emotional stress, fever, exposure to the sun, or other environmental factors. Certain foods and drugs precipitate recurrences in susceptible individuals. If you have frequent attacks, analyze your lifestyle and try to figure out what specific triggers may have precipitated them.

Although there is no known cure for herpes, some sufferers have reported relief when taking lysine, an amino acid supplement usually sold in health food stores in the U.S. (but not in Canada). To help reduce the frequency of herpes attacks, some advocates of natural medicine recommend taking 500mg to 1,000mg of L-lysine daily, on an empty stomach. This amino acid is also found in lamb, chicken, fish, milk, and beans.

In more severe herpes cases, physicians prescribe acyclovir, an antiviral medication that can be taken orally or used as a topical cream. Use of acyclovir can shorten the duration of an attack and help prevent a recurrence.

HELPFUL FOODS

Meats are naturally high in lysine; aim for three or four servings a week.

Fish are also high in lysine and can be alternated with lean meat.

Milk and other dairy products will provide lysine; cold milk compresses can be used to ease herpes sores.

Vegetables boost immunity, so they help protect against recurrences. Eat three to five servings daily.

Fruits protect against recurrences by boosting immunity; you should consume two to four servings daily.

Beans and other legumes provide lysine, starch, minerals, and B vitamins. Have one or more servings a day.

Warning: A pregnant woman who has had herpes should inform her obstetrician immediately. An active infection may be transmitted to the baby during delivery and can cause blindness, retardation, even death. A cesarean delivery can prevent transmission.

SELF-CARE
Most herpes treatment centers on self-care. If you have a warning symptom before an outbreak of oral herpes, prompt use of aspirin and ice packs sometimes forestalls the recurrence. Once the lesions appear, compresses of cold water or milk may ease the discomfort. To help protect others from infection, avoid kissing anyone or sharing dishes or utensils during outbreaks.

For genital outbreaks, warm baths or saltwater compresses can help ease inflammation. Keep the infected area clean and dry. Wash your hands after any contact with the sores to avoid spreading infection to other parts of your body. Because type 2 herpes is so contagious, those infected should never have sexual contact with noninfected persons during an attack. Always tell any prospective sexual partner that you are infected with herpes. Using a latex condom may lower, but cannot eliminate, the risk of sexual transmission.

To help prevent recurrences, try to stay in the best of health, strengthening your immune system to resist disease. This will mean eating a well-balanced, nutritious diet with plenty of whole grains, fresh fruits and vegetables, and high-quality protein. If you smoke, quit; also avoid excessive alcohol and caffeine. Balance your lifestyle with regular exercise and adequate rest to prevent exhaustion and alleviate stress. Avoid excessive sun exposure, and always wear a sunscreen with a high SPF when you are in the sun, regardless of the season. Do not take high doses of vitamin C; studies indicate these can actually provoke a recurrence of herpes.

HIATAL HERNIA

EAT PLENTY OF
- High-fiber foods, such as whole-grain cereals and breads, fresh fruits, salads, and raw or lightly cooked vegetables.

CUT DOWN ON
- Coffee and alcohol, including wine, especially before bedtime.

AVOID
- Gaining excess weight.
- Large meals and carbonated beverages.
- Fatty foods, chocolate, and peppermint.
- Smoking.
- Any food that produces symptoms.

Under normal circumstances, the hiatus is a small opening in the muscular diaphragm at the juncture where the esophagus meets the stomach. A hiatal hernia develops when the opening widens and allows the upper part of the stomach to protrude upward through the hiatus. Some hiatal hernias are present at birth. Most of them, however, develop during life as the opening of the hiatus becomes stretched, often as a result of pregnancy or excessive weight gain, both of which place upward pressure on the stomach. Severe coughing, vomiting, straining when moving the bowels, or sudden physical exertion may also stretch the hiatus.

Although hiatal hernias are quite common, occurring in about 40 percent of Canadians, most people are unaware of the condition because they don't experience symptoms or associated problems. A hiatal hernia is usually diagnosed after recurring bouts of INDIGESTION AND HEARTBURN, typically as a result of acid reflux into the esophagus and throat. Even when symptoms develop, the condition is usually not considered serious. There are, however, exceptions in which frequent exposure to stomach acids causes severe esophageal damage, including ulceration, bleeding, narrowing, and even obstruction or rupture. In such cases, surgical treatment is necessary. More often, however, self-care measures are all that's needed. These may entail losing excess weight to alleviate pressure on the stomach and not wearing constrictive clothing, tight belts or girdles.

DIETARY APPROACHES

Avoid large meals that overly distend the stomach; instead, eat four or five small meals spread over the course of a day. In addition, try to avoid drinking carbonated beverages, which may increase discomfort. After eating, do not lie down, stoop, or bend over for at least an hour, because this may promote reflux. Do not try to eat or drink anything for at least 2 hours before going to bed at night, when attacks are most likely to occur.

Avoid substances that relax the diaphragmatic muscle. Alcohol, including wine, is one such muscle relaxant; in particular, abstain from any alcoholic beverage in the evening.

Eliminate foods that tend to irritate your stomach or provoke a bout of indigestion. The culprits vary from one individual to another, but common offenders include spices, citrus fruits, tomato juice, pickles, and vinegar. Coffee in any form increases stomach acidity, as does tobacco. Chocolate and peppermint tend to relax the hiatal sphincter; fatty foods stay in the stomach longer than other foods and can also provoke indigestion. Small sips of water or a warm herbal tea may be useful when you feel a bout of regurgitation coming on, but avoid antacids that contain peppermint.

CONSTIPATION can worsen a hiatal hernia because straining distends the abdomen. Eat plenty of high-fiber foods, such as whole-grain cereals and breads, as well as fresh vegetables and fruits. Daily exercise and an adequate fluid intake are also important.

Case Study

The first time George, a 54-year-old contractor, was awakened by severe burning chest pains, he thought he was having a heart attack; a trip to the emergency room, however, revealed a severe case of heartburn instead. After several more attacks, his doctor referred him to a gastroenterologist for tests, which disclosed a hiatal hernia. Upon questioning, George revealed that he usually ate a large, late dinner, accompanied by two or three glasses of wine, and he often had a brandy and cheese before going to bed. The doctor suggested that George change his habits and eat three small meals during the day and a light, early dinner with no more than one glass of wine. He also urged him to forgo the brandy and cheese, and suggested that George elevate the head of his bed a few inches. These relatively simple measures paid off; at his next checkup, George reported that the nighttime heartburn had ceased.

People who experience frequent nighttime symptoms of a hiatal hernia can try raising the head of their bed 3 to 6 inches. This elevates the upper body and uses the force of gravity to keep the stomach in place and prevent a reflux of stomach acids.

If self-care measures fail to provide adequate relief, a doctor may recommend an antacid to neutralize stomach acid; a histamine blocker, such as cimetidine, to reduce stomach acid output; or an acid pump inhibitor, such as omeprazole. If lifestyle modification and conservative medical treatment do not alleviate symptoms, surgery may be recommended to reposition the stomach below the diaphragm and to narrow the hiatal opening.

HIVES

EAT PLENTY OF
- *Fortified cereals and breads, fish, poultry, and other niacin-rich foods to inhibit the release of histamines.*

AVOID
- *Foods that have previously caused hives or other allergic reactions.*
- *Foods and medications colored with Yellow No. 5 (tartrazine) if you are sensitive to this additive.*
- *Foods that contain salicylate if you are allergic to aspirin.*

Medically known as urticaria, hives are the itchy red welts that develop as a result of ALLERGIC REACTIONS TO FOODS and other provoking substances. For example, certain medications—aspirin, as well as penicillin and related antibiotics—can cause hives in some people. Even those without known allergies can develop hives after being stung by an insect or touching stinging plants, such as nettles, poison oak, or poison ivy. Hives may be accompanied by other symptoms of allergy, including swelling

of the eyes and other parts of the body. Many food allergies provoke swelling and itching of the lips and mouth.

Warning: If hives are accompanied by swelling of the throat and difficulty breathing, speaking, or swallowing, seek immediate medical help. These symptoms may signal anaphylaxis, a potentially fatal medical emergency.

The blotchy rash of hives can follow ingestion of almost any food, but among the most common causes are shellfish, nuts, and berries. A person who is allergic to aspirin (acetylsalicylic acid) should also be wary of foods that contain natural salicylates. These include apricots, berries, grapes, raisins and other dried fruits, tea, and foods processed with vinegar. Among the other well-known triggers of hives are emotional stress; exposure to sunshine, heat, or cold (including ice cubes in drinks); and viral infections.

Hives generally develop within hours after exposure to a trigger, but in unusual cases, they may appear several days later. This delayed reaction can make it difficult to identify the offending substance. Delayed reactions are most common with medications; if you develop a rash while taking any drug, report it to your doctor immediately. Medication-related rashes usually start around the head and spread progressively down to the feet. Sometimes a drug allergy develops abruptly after months or even years of taking a medication. In any event, make certain to mention your sensitivity to your pharmacist and to any doctor who may prescribe medications for you.

Although superfluous food additives are often blamed for causing allergic reactions, only tartrazine (Yellow No. 5), a common coloring agent, has been found to cause hives—and in fewer than 1 out of 10,000 people. Tartrazine is used to lend a brilliant yellow color to drinks, cheese-flavored snacks, artificial fruit drinks, and the

coatings on pills and candies. All food colorants must be listed on product labels; people who are sensitive to tartrazine should carefully read labels not only on commercial food products but also on medications and vitamin supplements.

DEALING WITH HIVES
An outbreak of hives may fade within minutes or persist for days or weeks. If you can link a particular food to hives, avoid it and consult a doctor. When hives persist for more than a few days, a doctor may prescribe an antihistamine medication, as well as a lotion to reduce itching and relieve inflammation. If you get hives repeatedly, the doctor may suggest that you keep a food diary; once you identify the suspect foods, eliminate them from your regular diet, then reintroduce them one at a time to pinpoint the problem.

Since hives and other allergy symptoms are triggered by the release of histamines, it may be useful to increase consumption of foods that are high in niacin (vitamin B$_3$), which is believed to inhibit histamine release. Good sources of niacin include poultry, seafood, seeds and nuts, and fortified cereals and breads. Choose these carefully, however, because some foods that are good sources of niacin are among those that tend to provoke an allergy.

Avoiding the culprit foods that trigger an allergic reaction is the safest way to prevent an outbreak of hives. Fortunately, most people are allergic to very few items, so avoidance doesn't mean being deprived of all the foods you enjoy. If you have had a severe allergic reaction to any substance, ask the doctor whether you need to carry special medication to be used if the reaction occurs again. It's also a good idea to have an identification tag or card that specifies your sensitivity so that emergency medical personnel can be alerted if you become incapacitated.

HONEY

BENEFITS
- *A source of quick energy.*
- *Adds flavor to foods and beverages and improves the shelf life of baked goods.*

DRAWBACKS
- *Contains more calories volume for volume than sugar.*
- *Contamination with* Clostridium botulinum *spores may be dangerous for babies under a year old.*

Our inborn taste for sweet foods led Stone Age humans to forage for the sweetness of honey. Although bees were first domesticated in artificial hives in Egypt and India about 4,500 years ago, it wasn't until about AD 1000 that bee-keepers began to understand the interplay between bees and flowers that is required to produce honey.

Honey remained the staple sweetener in Europe until the 1500s, when granulated sugar (more easily stored and transported) became available. But sugar could not entirely replace honey's more complex flavors, and honey remains a popular food.

Bees native to the Americas live only in tropical zones and lack stingers, although they do bite. They scavenge not only in flowers but also in fruits, dead flesh, and animal droppings to make honeys that taste strange and are often unsafe. A single Old World species, *Apis mellifera,* was brought to North America by colonists in the 1600s and now produces virtually all of our honey.

FROM FLOWERS TO HIVES

Plants and honeybees have a symbiotic relationship. As the bees gather nectar, they carry pollen with them from one

LIQUID GOLD. *Honey has been prized for its sweetness since ancient times. It takes the nectar of 1½ million flowers to make just a pint of honey.*

flower to another, thus ensuring cross-fertilization. The bees concentrate the flower nectar into honey, which is stored in their hives. Honeybees also collect and store pollen, which provides developing and young worker bees with protein and vitamins similar to the nutrients in dried beans and peas. While it is food for bees, pollen does nothing for humans that legumes can't do better, and it may trigger life-threatening allergic reactions in susceptible people.

As a bee gathers nectar, it's kept in a sac where enzymes begin a refining and filtering process. When the bee returns to its hive, a chain of workers greets it; each one pumps the nectar in and out of the honey sac until it becomes honey concentrated enough to resist bacteria and molds. It is then stored in a comb to ripen until it is needed for food.

Leguminous plants, especially clover, are widely cultivated for bee foraging. Other crops favored for the tang of the honey they produce include linden, sage, and thyme.

The liquid honey most popular in North America is removed from the comb by centrifugation, it is then pasteurized, strained, filtered, and bottled. Solid honeys are put through controlled crystallization before packaging.

HONEY AS FOOD

Despite the claims that honey is a wonder food, its nutritional value is very limited; all honeys are mostly sugars—fructose and glucose, with smaller amounts of sucrose. Some types provide minute amounts of the B complex and C vitamins, but eating honey can actually produce a negative vitamin balance. Here's how: Vitamins in the B group are used in the process that derives energy from carbohydrates and fats. Because honey contains only 3 percent of the thiamine and 6 percent of the niacin needed to release energy from its sugars, each serving of honey uses up more B vitamins than it provides.

ROYAL JELLY

Worker bees produce a substance called royal jelly to nurture the larvae selected to become queens. Although extravagant claims for royal jelly's health benefits have been made, they have not been borne out by studies; so far, there is no evidence that it provides worthwhile nutrients for humans. On the contrary, several scientific journals have reported grave asthma attacks, including fatalities, in adults and children taking royal jelly supplements.

Volume for volume, honey is higher in calories than sugar; a tablespoon of honey contains 64 calories, compared to 46 in a tablespoon of sugar. This is partly because a tablespoon of honey weighs more than the same volume of sugar. Honey can be substituted for sugar at the ratio of 1 measure of honey for every 1¼ units of sugar; the liquid in the recipe may need to be decreased to compensate for the water in honey. Breads and cakes sweetened with honey, however, stay moister than those made with sugar, thanks to honey's water-attracting (hygroscopic) properties.

RISK FOR BABIES

Spores of *Clostridium botulinum* have been found in about 10 percent of honeys sampled by the Centers for Disease Control and Prevention (CDC) in the U.S. Although not dangerous to adults and older children, infants should not be fed honey because *C. botulinum* can cause serious illness in the first year of life.

HOSPITAL DIETS: MEALS FOR CONVALESCENTS

*Many illnesses and medical treatments can cause
nutrition and feeding problems. Meanwhile, good nutrition
is essential for getting better and staying healthy.*

Balanced nutrition is especially important during periods of illness and convalescence. Many illnesses can result in nutrient deficiency, increasing the need for nourishment at a time when it is hard for patients to consume adequate amounts of food. A balanced diet can enhance the sense of well-being as well as prospects for recovery in people with cancer, those undergoing surgery, victims of severe burns, alcoholics, and patients with other conditions.

Another problem is that periods of prolonged bed rest weaken the muscles and bones, and contribute to the risk of blood clots in the deep veins. Exercise programs should be designed (even for bedridden patients) to maintain muscle tone, bone strength, and a brisk flow of circulation.

Attitudes to convalescence have undergone radical revision. Now, even after extensive surgery or an acute crisis, a prolonged period of enforced rest is rarely recommended. Rather, doctors encourage patients to resume normal activities, with realistic lifestyle changes that can be maintained for a lifetime of renewed good health.

EATING TO GET WELL

Diets for hospitalized patients, as well as for those being cared for at home, should complement medical and surgical treatment. For most patients, no special measures are necessary; they can recover on the hospital or family diet with only minor changes, where appropriate, in a few nutrients (such as sodium) or calorie content.

Good nutrition is especially important for people who are likely to remain in the hospital for extended periods. Studies have shown that patients can incur nutritional problems in the course of hospitalization, regardless of their status on admission. Malnutrition can develop during prolonged (5 to 7 days) administration of intravenous fluids without nutrient supplementation. Also, patients may suffer a loss of nutrients as a result of medical procedures, such as kidney dialysis, or specific symptoms, such as diarrhea. Extra energy is needed for healing and for fighting infection or fever. Finally, medications and treatments (typically, steroids, chemotherapy, and radiation) can interfere with the intake or metabolism of nutrients.

When a patient has special needs, hospital dietitians will devise an eating plan to include one or more of the following goals: to correct a nutritional deficiency; to compensate for the body's inability to handle certain nutrients; or to spare a specific organ by changing the form of nutrients or the timing of meals. Hospital diets can be further adjusted for patients with religious or personal preferences. Make your needs known at the time of hospital admission; include allergies and food intolerances and any vitamins or nonprescription drugs you may be taking. If the meals served are unsatisfactory, ask if alternative choices are available or if food may be brought in from outside the hospital.

When the nutrition plan represents a permanent change of eating habits or one that should be maintained for an extended period, the hospital should provide printed guidelines for preparing meals at home. Before leaving the hospital, make an appointment with a dietitian. In this way, you can find out if substitutions are allowed and how far you can bend the rules in order to increase variety in the diet.

As a caregiver, you can ask for the nutritionist's advice, too; you may have difficulty in weaning a patient from hospital liquids to solid foods, or you may need help in adjusting to a new form of feeding for special needs.

Planning for those continuing treatment should take MEDICINE-FOOD INTERACTIONS into consideration. Certain drugs can influence the absorption of nutrients, and a variety of nutrients affect the absorption of medications or alter the metabolism of drugs in the liver.

NUTRITION ALTERNATIVES

When patients cannot eat enough to meet their needs, doctors may order supplemental nutrition or feeding by an alternative route. At the basic level, a doctor may suggest larger portions or the use of nutrient-enriched drinks. Easy to eat and digest, these relatively high-calorie liquids may be fortified with protein, vitamins, and minerals. For those who haven't the time or resources to prepare supplemental foods at home, commercial formulas are available. It's important to keep supplements in their proper place, however; most will provide only selected nutrients and are not meant to take the place of solid food or a balanced diet. When a patient is restricted to liquid feeding alone, the doctor will specify a formula to cover complete nutritional requirements.

For patients who can absorb and digest food but cannot take enough nourishment by mouth, tube feeding—called enteral feeding—may be necessary. Most people need enteral feeding for only a limited time, but some must continue it indefinitely. A tube is usually threaded through the nose and into the digestive tract; this is called a nasogastric tube. In some cases, the tube may be inserted directly into the stomach (gastrostomy) or into the small intestine.

When enteral feeding is inadequate or impossible, parenteral (meaning outside the digestive tract) nutrition is given through a catheter directly into the bloodstream. Parenteral nutrition is sometimes used to spare the digestive tract after surgery, but it may also be needed permanently if large sections of the intestine have been removed. When a patient is dependent on the catheter for delivery of all nutrients, the procedure is termed total parenteral nutrition (TPN).

Managing feeding by tube or by catheter at home demands rigorous standards of care and cleanliness. Because patients with nasogastric tubes usually breathe through the mouth, they may need help in the form of wet swabs or frozen fruit juice cubes to moisten dried-out lips and mucous membranes. Chewing sugarless gum may stimulate the flow of saliva and provide some oral satisfaction.

Although many technical improvements have made procedures easier and more tolerable than in the past, patients on long-term tube feeding often experience a sense of withdrawal and depression. Counseling may help to smooth the initial adjustment, but most people eventually adapt well, focusing on the return to health instead of the relative inconvenience of tube feeding.

FEEDING SICK CHILDREN

Children's needs are more complicated than those of adults during illness. A diet has to provide sufficient nutrients and calories to maintain a healthy growth rate while also supplying the energy needed to fight the illness.

A sick child may need special help with feeding; finger foods and covered drinks with straws are much easier to manage than a tray laden with cutlery and spillable glassware. When the appetite is poor, parents or hospital caregivers may find it necessary to take the initiative by offering tempting foods and urging a listless young patient to take fluids and nourishment. However, it doesn't help to insist on a clean plate; most children will take as much as they can when they're ready. What is key is that an appealing, healthful selection of foods and beverages be available. Hospitals will frequently allow parents to bring a child's favorite foods from home.

FOOD PRESENTATION

It's important to take care in the presentation of food to an invalid. A weak appetite may be stimulated by the visual appeal of small, colorful portions attractively garnished and served at the correct temperature. Prepare textures that offer a pleasing contrast without taxing the patient's physical limitations (an elderly person, for example, may have difficulty chewing). Cut foods into manageable portions. A flower in a bud vase or juice served in a pretty glass may do more than any medication to lift the spirits and put the patient back on the road to health.

ATTRACTIVE AND NOURISHING. *A hearty tomato-pasta soup served with a cheese soufflé makes a nutritious meal for convalescents.*

HYPERACTIVITY

CONSUME
- *A variety of foods to provide a nutritionally complete diet.*

CUT DOWN ON
- *Caffeinated beverages.*
- *Hot dogs and other foods that contain large amounts of food additives and preservatives.*

AVOID
- *Self-treatment with high-dose vitamins and minerals.*
- *Diets that eliminate entire food groups.*

About 2 to 4 percent of all children suffer from hyperactivity (or attention deficit disorder), with boys outnumbering girls about fivefold. Parents often describe the hyperactive child as being in perpetual motion—always on the move, disruptive, impulsive, and unable to concentrate. Many researchers theorize that an imbalance in brain chemistry is responsible for the abnormal behavior, but a precise cause has not been identified.

In recent years, diet has been suggested as a possible cause of hyperactivity—a claim discounted by many experts. Although some nutritional deficiencies can affect behavior, these almost never occur in industrialized countries, where malnutrition is seldom a problem. Also, dozens of studies have failed to prove that diet plays any role in hyperactivity. Still, many parents and even some physicians believe that, at least for some children, there is a link. The diet hypothesis was first proposed in 1973 by Benjamin Feingold, a California allergist, who blamed hyperactivity on sensitivity to certain food additives and salicylates, compounds found in fruits, some vegetables, and in aspirin. Dr. Feingold recommended eliminating all foods that contain certain preservatives and artificial flavors and colors, as well as any natural sources of salicylates. Half of his hyperactive patients improved on this diet, and soon many doctors and parent groups were supporting the Feingold diet.

Although some reports suggest that an additive-free diet helps a few children, Dr. Feingold's finding of marked improvement in a significant percentage of cases has not been duplicated in scientific studies. Some pediatricians advise parents to try eliminating foods that are especially high in preservatives, dyes, and other additives—for example, hot dogs and other processed meats and some commercial baked goods—to see if there is an improvement. But avoiding all foods that contain natural salicylates is more problematic; there is no evidence that this actually helps, and it can lead to deficiencies of vitamin C, beta carotene, and other nutrients.

CAFFEINE has been linked to hyperactivity. Experts doubt that it actually causes the problem, but it may add to the restlessness of a hyperactive child. In any event, eliminating caffeine from a child's diet won't hurt.

Some proponents of orthomolecular therapy—the use of markedly high doses of vitamins and minerals to treat behavioral and other problems—advocate them as a treatment for hyperactivity. There is no evidence that this helps, but self-treating with megadose vitamins and minerals can cause serious nutritional imbalances and toxicity.

SUGAR CLEARED

Hyperactivity has often been blamed on a high intake of sugar. Again, there is no scientific proof of this. In fact, one study conducted by the National Institute of Mental Health in the U.S. found that children given a sugary drink were less active than a control group who had sugar-free drinks. Some researchers theorize that this calming effect is related to the fact that sugar prompts the brain to increase the production of serotonin, a chemical that reduces the brain's electrical activity. Even so, this is not a good reason to consume lots of sweets—sugar provides calories but is devoid of other nutrients; it also promotes DENTAL DISORDERS.

HYPOGLYCEMIA

CONSUME
- *Small meals that provide a balance of protein, carbohydrates, and fats.*

CUT DOWN ON
- *Carbohydrate-only (especially sugary) meals and snacks.*

AVOID
- *Consuming alcohol without food.*

Glucose, or blood sugar, is the body's major source of energy; it's also the only form of energy that the brain can use effectively. During digestion and metabolism, the liver converts all of the carbohydrates and about half of the protein in a meal into glucose, which is released into the bloodstream. In response to rising blood glucose levels, the pancreas secretes extra insulin, the hormone that enables cells to use the sugar to produce energy.

Low blood sugar, or hypoglycemia, occurs when the amount of insulin in the blood exceeds what is needed to metabolize the available glucose. It is seen often when a person with DIABETES takes too much insulin, but it can also develop in other circumstances, such as an overconsumption of alcohol; taking large amounts of aspirin or acetaminophen, beta blockers, and some antipsychotic drugs; or when tumors develop that secrete insulin.

REACTIVE HYPOGLYCEMIA

An unusual condition known as reactive hypoglycemia occurs when the body secretes more insulin than it needs, causing a drop in blood glucose levels. Stress, missed meals, and a low-calorie diet of mostly carbohydrates can cause this type of hypoglycemia. Symptoms include dizziness, headache, hunger, trembling, palpitations, irritability, and mood swings. (A diabetic who takes an overdose of insulin has similar but more pronounced symptoms.)

Many people who experience vague, unexplained symptoms assume that they have reactive hypoglycemia, but the condition is rare and exists under very unusual circumstances. This is because the human body has a very sensitive feedback system that controls insulin secretion. Reactive hypoglycemia can only be diagnosed by monitoring blood glucose levels after ingestion of a known dose of glucose.

A low-calorie diet that is made up mostly of carbohydrates may produce mild symptoms of hypoglycemia even though the blood sugar levels are usually in the low-normal range. Here's what happens: The person may skip breakfast or have only simple carbohydrates—for example, a glass of orange juice and a sweet roll. The pancreas will secrete a fair amount of insulin to process the glucose in this meal, but since it contains no protein or fat, which are metabolized more slowly than carbohydrates, the body will burn the glucose in 2 or 3 hours. Sensing a need for more energy, the brain sends out powerful hunger signals; the person may also have a headache or feel dizzy. A sweet snack will satisfy this hunger and provide a quick burst of energy, but again, the pancreas will pump out enough insulin to quickly metabolize the glucose. If the scenario is repeated throughout the day, a pattern is established in which a person experiences symptoms that are temporarily alleviated by taking in more carbohydrates. The cycle can be broken by consuming regular meals that include small amounts of protein and fats along with starches. These take longer than sugars to be digested and converted into glucose, and allow for a steady release of energy.

INSULIN OVERDOSE

A much more serious type of hypoglycemia occurs when a diabetic takes more insulin than is needed to metabolize the available glucose. Many circumstances can affect the amount of insulin a diabetic requires: exercise, stress, infection, a skipped or late meal, even the weather. The onset of symptoms of an insulin reaction—hunger, tingling sensations, sweating, faintness, impaired vision, mood changes, palpitations, and a cold, clammy sensation—can be reversed by immediately eating a tablespoonful of sugar or honey, sucking on a hard candy, or drinking a glass of orange juice or sugary drink. If ignored, an insulin reaction can lead to coma and even death.

Case Study

Almost daily, Sally, a 39-year-old editor and vegetarian, experienced strange symptoms, which began with a nagging headache accompanied by dizziness, difficulty concentrating, a racing pulse, and severe hunger pangs. Taking a couple of aspirins and eating a candy bar alleviated her symptoms for a while, but in an hour or two, they'd return worse than before. At first Sally attributed her symptoms to job-related stress, but she worried that they reflected a disease.

A checkup failed to find abnormalities. Sally consulted still another doctor, who also found nothing wrong. Then she read an article that described her symptoms and provided a diagnosis: hypoglycemia.

Sally returned to her doctor and requested an oral glucose tolerance test—an examination that measures blood sugar levels after sugar consumption. The doctor, who had a number of patients with similar symptoms, assured Sally that she did not have true hypoglycemia.

Suspecting diet as the culprit, the doctor asked Sally to keep a diary of all the food she ate and any symptoms. The diary showed a familiar pattern—orange juice and coffee for breakfast, frequent snacks of candy or other sweets, a light lunch of a salad and an apple, and a low-fat vegetarian dinner with a glass or two of wine. The doctor explained that Sally's symptoms were brought on by an unbalanced diet. She urged Sally to start the day with more protein—perhaps a boiled egg and a glass of milk—and to have some yogurt or a sandwich for her mid-morning snack. Lunch could be a cup of lentil soup and a whole-grain pita filled with fresh vegetables and sprouts, and dinner a combination of grains and legumes for protein and starch. After a few weeks on this diet, Sally reported that her troubling symptoms had ceased.

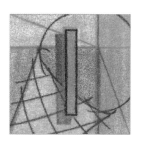

ICE CREAM

BENEFITS
- *A good source of calcium.*
- *Provides protein and digestible, high-calorie nutrition during an illness.*

DRAWBACKS
- *High in saturated fat and sugar.*

Federal standards decree that ice cream must be made with a minimum of 10 percent cream, or milk fat, and 36 percent solids (fat with protein, minerals, and lactose). Manufacturers may add various other ingredients, as well as enough air to double its volume. In general, the least expensive ice creams contain the minimum 10 percent fat and the maximum air, while the premium commercial brands have double the fat and half the air.

It is fat that gives ice cream its smooth texture; manufacturers of non-fat and low-fat ices and frozen yogurts compensate for the lack of fat by increasing the sugar—by up to twice the amount—and beating in less air. Therefore, although these products contain less fat, in the end they are not necessarily lower in calories.

Both soft ice cream and ice milk are 3 to 6 percent fat and 30 to 50 percent air. Sherbets are usually made with a small amount of milk fat and milk solids or, sometimes, egg white. Fruit ices, on the other hand, tend to be made with fruit pulp or juice, sugar, and water, with the possible addition

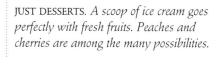

JUST DESSERTS. *A scoop of ice cream goes perfectly with fresh fruits. Peaches and cherries are among the many possibilities.*

of pectin or ascorbic acid. Most of these products contain about 200 calories per cup. Even a half cup of fat-free frozen yogurt with artificial sweetener has about 80 calories.

Ice cream has substantial amounts of calcium and protein, as well as some vitamin A and riboflavin. The price for these useful nutrients, however, is a large helping of saturated fat, with its adverse implications for heart disease, certain cancers, and other conditions. Fruit sorbets—which are high in sugar but fat-free—are a better choice when you want to end a meal with a frozen dessert. Fat-free frozen yogurt is a good substitute for ice cream; a half cup topped with fresh fruit and toasted wheat germ can satisfy cravings for a frosty treat and supply useful amounts of calcium, vitamins, and fiber.

WHAT'S IN A ½-CUP SERVING OF FROZEN DESSERT

TYPE	ENERGY (CALORIES)	FAT (g)	PROTEIN (g)	CARBOHYDRATE (g)	CALCIUM (mg)
Ice cream, vanilla	180	12	2	16	76
Ice cream, flavored	125–150*	6–8	2–3	16	73–93*
Ice milk, vanilla	90	3	2	15	88
Ice milk, chocolate	100	3	3	16	112
Fruit ice, sorbet	123	0	Tr	30	0
Frozen yogurt, fat-free	80	0	4	16	79
Sherbet, orange, made with milk fat and solids	135	2	1	29	52

* Varies according to flavor.

THE IMMUNE SYSTEM

The immune system defends the body from invasion and remembers every enemy it meets. Vitamins, minerals, and proteins help keep this defense system on the alert.

The immune system defends us against threats from both outside and inside the body. Most often, the external threats are infections caused by invading bacteria, viruses, and fungi, while abnormal or cancerous cells pose the major internal threats. In addition, this complex system oversees the repair of tissues that are injured by wounds or disease.

Once in a while the immune system mistakes a harmless foreign substance for an enemy, resulting in an allergic reaction, such as HIVES, HAY FEVER, and ASTHMA. Less commonly the immune system—mistaking an internal signal—attacks normal body tissue, leading to an autoimmune disease, such as DIABETES, some types of ARTHRITIS, and LUPUS.

The most remarkable characteristic of the immune system is its "memory" for every foreign protein it encounters. Confronted with a virus or other invading organism, the system creates an antibody that will recognize it and mount an attack against it at any future encounter. This mechanism, called acquired immunity, is what makes vaccinations work.

SYSTEM FAILURE

Infection, cancer, and other illnesses develop when the immune system is overwhelmed or weakened by any number of stressors, including viruses and other invading organisms, malnutrition, and the consequences of

---

EAT PLENTY OF

- *Fruits and leafy vegetables for vitamins A and C; wheat germ and fortified cereals for vitamin E.*
- *Fatty fish and vegetable oils for omega-3 and omega-6 fatty acids.*
- *Shellfish, low-fat red meat, fortified whole-wheat breads and cereals, and legumes for protein, zinc, and iron.*

AVOID

- *Immune-power diets, which have no proven benefits.*

---

aging. Fortunately, antibiotics and sulfa drugs can wipe out most bacterial infections in otherwise healthy people; progress is also being made in the development of antiviral drugs. At times doctors purposely lower immunity to treat an autoimmune disease or prevent rejection of a donor organ.

DIETARY INFLUENCES

Proteins are central to the proper functioning of the immune system; antibodies are formed from various amino acids, especially arginine and glutamine. These amino acids are found in meat and other high-protein foods; the body can also manufacture them.

Omega-3 and omega-6 fatty acids, known to be beneficial in heart disease and other conditions, also seem to fight infection, although it's not clear how they work. Omega-3 fatty acids

are especially beneficial in controlling inflammation and the harmful effects of rheumatoid arthritis and other autoimmune disorders.

ANTIOXIDANTS are also important to immune function: Vitamin A aids in warding off infection; vitamin E helps to preserve fatty acids; and vitamin C assists in bonding cells and strengthening the blood vessel walls.

Zinc and iron are among the minerals thought to boost immunity. A deficiency of zinc has been associated with slow wound healing, while adequate iron ensures that cells get the oxygen they need to function properly and resist disease. Both minerals are found in lean meat, poultry, shellfish, fortified whole-grain breads and cereals, and legumes.

FAD DIETS

Some unscrupulous practitioners, including opportunistic physicians, exploit the importance of the immune system and the difficulty of understanding its complexity by publicizing methods to boost your "immune power." These practitioners recommend a two-part remedial program, starting with an elimination diet, supposedly to "cleanse" the body, followed by megadoses of vitamins, minerals, and amino acids, supposedly to restore immune power. In reality, there is no evidence that such regimens boost immunity, and the high-dose supplements can be dangerous.

IMPOTENCE

EAT PLENTY OF
- Foods rich in zinc, such as yogurt, fortified cereals, wheat germ, vegetables, shellfish, and poultry.

CUT DOWN ON
- Alcohol and saturated fats.

AVOID
- Nicotine and all drugs except those prescribed for you.

Although psychological factors certainly affect male sexual function, recent studies show that most cases of impotence are due to an underlying disease or lifestyle factors. Diabetes, atherosclerosis, paralysis, or, less commonly, hormonal imbalances are among the organic causes of impotence. The use of a number of drugs—including alcohol, nicotine, and illegal substances, as well as prescription medications—can lead to impotence. Nicotine impedes the blood flow by constricting the small arteries, including those that bring blood to the penis. Medications that commonly cause impotence include antihypertensives, acid-suppressants for ulcers, antidepressants, sleeping pills, and antianxiety agents. In most cases, an alternative drug can be prescribed.

DIETARY FACTORS

Zinc is among the minerals thought to be essential to good reproductive health. While zinc intake may not have a direct effect on potency, it may be important for male sexual health, since very high levels are found in the seminal fluid. Good sources of zinc include shellfish and poultry, vegetables, wheat germ, whole grains, and yogurt. Zinc supplements are not recommended; in high doses they can interfere with the absorption of calcium and copper.

It's important to maintain a normal weight; obesity predisposes a person to diabetes, which is one of the leading causes of impotence. Also, a diet low in saturated fats helps prevent atherosclerosis, the buildup of fatty plaque that clogs not only the large vessels around the heart but also the penile artery.

Alcohol should be consumed in moderation. A high blood level of alcohol interrupts the relay of messages along the nervous system; heavy alcohol consumption over an extended period modifies the normal pattern of hormone production, which may affect sexual function.

There is no evidence that a high intake of vitamin E has any effect on potency or male sexual health. Nevertheless, a diet rich in vitamin E is certainly not harmful.

INDIGESTION AND HEARTBURN

TAKE
- Small meals at regular intervals.

CUT DOWN ON
- Alcohol, caffeine, and coffee in all forms.
- Tomato-based and other acidic foods.

AVOID
- Fatty foods.
- Eating within 2 hours of bedtime.
- Tobacco use of any kind.

Almost half of all adult Canadians have indigestion occasionally, but for some, it is a daily trial. The most common symptom is heartburn, a burning chest pain that occurs when stomach acid and other contents flow backward, or reflux, into the esophagus. Unlike the stomach, the lining of the esophagus has no protective lining of mucus-producing tissue, so the acid produces irritation and even ulcerations. OBESITY and PREGNANCY may lead to heartburn because of increased intra-abdominal pressure, which tends to force the stomach fluids up into the esophagus. A HIATAL HERNIA is another possible cause.

Heartburn caused by reflux can usually be controlled with a few lifestyle changes, starting with adopting a low-fat diet that includes a balance of protein, starches, and fiber-rich vegetables and fruits. (Fatty foods take longer to digest and thus slow down the rate of food emptying from the stomach.) Coffee, including decaffeinated brands, promotes high acid production; so does tea, cola drinks, and other sources of caffeine. There is no evidence that spicy foods—except possibly, red and black pepper—cause indigestion, but people who find that a highly spiced meal is followed by discomfort would be better off shunning such seasonings.

Avoid large meals, especially late in

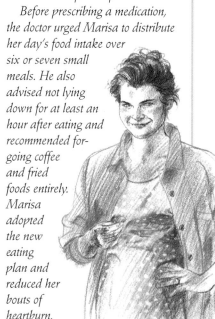

Case Study

During her pregnancy, Marisa began to suffer heartburn almost daily. She had been warned by her doctor not to take any drugs, but the frequent pain finally prompted her to ask her doctor for relief.

Before prescribing a medication, the doctor urged Marisa to distribute her day's food intake over six or seven small meals. He also advised not lying down for at least an hour after eating and recommended forgoing coffee and fried foods entirely. Marisa adopted the new eating plan and reduced her bouts of heartburn.

the day, and try not to eat in the 2 hours before bedtime. Sit up straight after meals; bending over, slouching, or lying down increases pressure on the stomach and promotes reflux. Stop cigarette smoking; nicotine relaxes the muscular sphincter between the esophagus and stomach. Limit alcohol intake to an occasional glass of wine or beer.

The use of nonprescription antacids to treat heartburn by neutralizing or suppressing stomach acid is questionable; the problem is not too much acid, but instead, acid in the wrong place. If you find that they do help, however, follow the instructions and never take them for longer than recommended.

INFERTILITY

EAT PLENTY OF
- *Fish, shellfish, lean meat, legumes, and fortified breads and cereals for the B vitamins, iron, and zinc.*
- *Fresh fruits and vegetables for vitamin C and beta carotene.*
- *Dairy products for calcium.*
- *Wheat germ, seeds, eggs, poultry, and seafood for vitamin E.*

CUT DOWN ON
- *Coffee and other sources of caffeine.*

AVOID
- *Alcohol and smoking.*
- *Becoming overweight or underweight.*

Defined as the inability to achieve a PREGNANCY after at least a year of trying, infertility affects more than 20 percent of North American couples. Experts cannot explain why the infertility rate has almost doubled in the last 25 years, but at least three factors stand out: the growing trend for couples to delay marriage and parenthood until their most fertile years are past, the rise in sexually transmitted diseases, and a puzzling drop in sperm production.

Many couples assume that infertility rests with the woman; in fact, men are just as likely to be infertile. In 40 percent of cases, the problem lies with the male, and in 40 percent of cases, it lies with the female. The cause can't be identified in the remaining 20 percent, or both partners may be contributing to the situation. While nutrition is not among the leading causes of infertility, consuming a balanced, healthful diet can enhance the chance of conceiving and delivering a healthy baby.

FEMALE INFERTILITY

The leading cause of female infertility is the failure to ovulate, which may be influenced by the diet, hormonal imbalances, and a variety of other factors. Women who are very thin or markedly overweight often do not ovulate because the amount of body fat is closely associated with estrogen levels. Women who have very little body fat—professional athletes, dancers, models, and chronic dieters—often stop menstruating, and their ovulation may also cease. At the other extreme, women who are obese may have abnormally elevated levels of estrogen, which can also result in a failure to ovulate.

Any woman who is considering becoming pregnant should try to achieve her ideal weight before trying to conceive. This should be done by eating a balanced diet; a woman who is underweight when she conceives is likely to have such problems as anemia during pregnancy and a more difficult labor. The baby may be smaller than normal and is more likely to have health problems. Conversely, dieting during pregnancy could be dangerous to the fetus. An overweight woman should diet before trying to conceive; this also lowers her risk of developing high blood pressure or diabetes during pregnancy.

Women who take oral contraceptives are likely to experience temporary infertility until their hormonal levels return to normal and they again start to ovulate. Long-term use can result in reduced reserves of folate (a B vitamin that is especially important in normal fetal development); vitamins B_6, B_{12}, C, and E; and calcium, zinc, and other minerals. Therefore, the woman's diet should emphasize foods that are rich in these nutrients—fruits and vegetables for vitamin C; milk products for calcium; and fortified breads and cereals, lean meat, poultry, and seafood for the B vitamins as well as iron, zinc, and other minerals.

Alcohol and smoking are known to reduce fertility in both women and men; a recent study indicated that coffee may have a similar effect on female fertility. Researchers at Johns Hopkins University found that women who drank more than three cups of coffee a day reduced their chances of conceiving in any given month by 25 percent.

MALE INFERTILITY

A low sperm count is the major cause of male infertility, and for unknown reasons, men worldwide are producing fewer sperm than a few decades ago. Some scientists believe certain pesticides, which have estrogenlike effects, may be linked to the declining sperm count. Alcohol and tobacco use both lower sperm production and should be avoided if there is difficulty conceiving.

Inadequate zinc may also lower male fertility; a recent study found that men who consumed 1.4mg of zinc daily produced fewer sperm and had lower levels of the male hormone testosterone than men whose daily zinc intake was 10.4mg—the male Recommended Nutrient Intake (RNI) of zinc is 12mg.

In addition, inadequate intake of vitamin C may impair male fertility. One study correlated low levels of vitamin C with an increased tendency of sperm to clump together, a problem that all but disappeared after 3 weeks of taking vitamin C supplements.

INTOLERANCE TO MILK AND OTHER FOODS

USE

- *Lactose-reduced milk or lactase enzyme drops and lactase enzyme tablets if you are unable to digest milk.*
- *Cheese (especially hard types) and yogurt, which contain little lactose.*

AVOID

- *Foods that cause any discomfort.*
- *Shrimp, dried fruits, sauerkraut, and other sulfite-preserved items if you are asthmatic or sensitive to sulfites.*
- *Medications containing lactose filler if you are lactose intolerant, provided substitutes are available.*
- *Foods containing MSG, especially on an empty stomach.*

A food intolerance may cause only mild discomfort, or it may be so severe that it is life threatening. Because it does not enlist the immune system in the production of antibodies, an intolerance is not a true allergy. Even so, the symptoms often mimic those produced by the immune system and may be hard to distinguish from allergies.

METABOLIC INTOLERANCE

People with metabolic intolerance lack the ability to digest specific nutrients. Lactose intolerance, the inability to digest milk sugar, is very common. Symptoms include gas, bloating, cramps, and diarrhea after consuming milk or milk products. The condition can be diagnosed by measuring the amount of hydrogen exhaled before and after ingesting lactose. An excessive amount of hydrogen confirms lactose intolerance.

Except for a few inedible shrubs, milk is the only source of lactose. Once prehistoric humans were weaned, they never had lactose again; hence, they no longer needed lactase, the enzyme that breaks down milk sugar in the digestive tract. With evolutionary thrift, lactase was programmed to disappear as milk was phased out of a child's diet.

Adults who can digest milk are a minority in the world population; 70 percent of people of African descent are partly or entirely lactose-intolerant after 3 to 4 years of age. By contrast, 90 percent of people of Northern European descent continue to produce lactase. This genetic trait probably enabled their forebears to absorb extra calcium in a dark, cold habitat where there was little sunlight available to develop vitamin D in the skin (vitamin D helps the body absorb calcium). Transient or permanent lactose intolerance may follow a gastrointestinal illness or treatment with antibiotics or anti-inflammatory drugs.

Most lactose-intolerant people can consume up to a pint of milk or 6 ounces of ice cream a day without much discomfort. They can also safely eat cultured dairy products because the bacteria used in fermentation use up most of the lactose for fuel. For people with more severe intolerance who still want milk and other dairy products, grocery stores sell lactose-reduced dairy products, and pharmacies carry enzyme drops that can be added to milk and enzyme tablets that can be taken before eating dishes that contain dairy products. Mixing milk with another food dilutes the concentration of lactose. Some people heat milk, which makes it more digestible.

Words of warning: Don't confuse lactose intolerance with milk allergy, which is hypersensitivity to the proteins in milk and dairy products. If you are allergic to milk, consuming a lactose-reduced product will not prevent a reaction. And if you're lactose intolerant, look for the milk sugar in a variety of products, including many medications. Always read labels carefully; milk solids are used as a filler in numerous foods.

Another metabolic intolerance is the inability to digest gluten that is the mark of CELIAC DISEASE. Treatment requires a diet that excludes grains and any products containing gluten.

ANAPHYLACTOID REACTIONS

Severe symptoms of hypersensitivity upon exposure to a certain food are termed an anaphylactoid reaction

Case Study

The doctor advised Vivienne, a 48-year-old clerk, that she needed more calcium to lower her risk of osteoporosis. Beginning the next morning, Vivienne switched from her regular toast and black coffee to an instant breakfast drink made with skim milk; she had another glass of skim milk that night at bedtime. After several days on the new regimen, she experienced bloating, cramping, and flatulence. Vivienne's doctor told her that she was probably among the majority of adults who cannot digest lactose. On his advice, she switched to lactose-free milk for her breakfast drink and fat-free yogurt for her late-night snack, and she no longer has gassy discomfort.

if laboratory tests fail to show evidence of allergy involving immunoglobulin E (IgE), the hallmark of true anaphylaxis. The entire body can be involved, with pain in the chest and abdomen, nausea and vomiting, diarrhea, rash, swelling, and a drastic drop in blood pressure.

Some people may suffer adverse effects from histamine released directly from unprocessed scombroid (spiny-finned) fish. Potentially dangerous species include mackerel, tuna, and mahi-mahi. High levels of histamine form if the fish are contaminated with certain bacteria or stored at temperatures above refrigeration range. Symptoms—including facial flushing, rash, vomiting, diarrhea, and headache—may last as long as 24 hours but generally disappear without further ill effect. Histamine intoxication is a form of FOOD POISONING.

FOOD ADDITIVES

Sulfites can cause severe, allergylike reactions. Sulfites are widely used to preserve such foods as shrimp, sauerkraut, processed potatoes, dried fruits, wines, and beer. Labels on packaged items must inform purchasers that sulfites are present, but shrimp and raw vegetables carry no such warning.

Read food labels carefully and avoid dried fruits or other sulfite-preserved foods if you believe you may be sensitive to sulfites. People with asthma are at special risk from sulfites and should shun questionable restaurant and convenience foods.

MIGRAINE TRIGGERS

While true food allergies are rarely a cause of MIGRAINE headaches, food often triggers these headaches in sensitive people by dilating the blood vessels in the head. The result is a pounding, usually one-sided headache.

Specific triggers vary with individuals, but tyramine is often the root cause. Tyramine is found in aged cheeses,

cured and preserved meats, pickled fish, fava beans, and figs. Nitrites, preservatives in meats, can also trigger headaches. This effect is independent of tyramine sensitivity. Phenylethylamine in chocolate is another common offender.

If you suffer from migraines, keep a diary for a month or two, noting your daily food intake as well as any migraine symptoms. In this way, you will be able to avoid trigger foods and possibly forestall many attacks.

OTHER POSSIBILITIES

Methylxanthine compounds—which occur naturally in coffee, tea, cola drinks, and chocolate—can cause very

distressing symptoms, including headaches, palpitations, panic and anxiety attacks, and vomiting. People who experience any of these symptoms should avoid problem foods and all beverages that contain CAFFEINE.

Individuals receiving medical treatment may experience symptoms, ranging from trivial to life threatening, as a result of MEDICATION-FOOD INTERACTIONS. A common and dangerous interaction occurs between monoamine oxidase (MAO) inhibitors and foods containing tyramine. Before taking any drug, ask your doctor or pharmacist to give you a list of foods you must avoid while taking the medication.

NONALLERGIC FOOD REACTIONS

Many reactions to foods mimic those of allergies, but they actually stem from faulty metabolism or other problems that are unrelated to antibodies and other components of the immune system. The following are among the most common examples.

CAUSES	DANGER FOODS	
METABOLIC ABNORMALITIES		
Gluten intolerance (Celiac disease)	Baked goods, pasta, gravies, salad dressings, ice cream, beer, and products that contain flour, wheat, barley, and rye.	
Lactose intolerance	Milk and other dairy products; medications and other products with lactose as an additive.	
ANAPHYLACTOID REACTIONS (THAT DON'T INVOLVE IgE)		
Histamine intolerance	Fish, such as tuna and mackerel.	
REACTION TO FOOD ADDITIVES		
Sulfites	Shrimp, processed potatoes, dried fruits, wines, beer, champagne, and some restaurant and salad bar foods.	
VASCULAR RESPONSES		
Methylxanthine toxicity	Coffee, tea, colas, chocolate, cocoa, and any other product containing caffeine or theobromine.	
Migraine headaches	Alcohol, MSG, strong or aged cheeses (especially Cheddar), cured meats (ham, bacon, and hot dogs), chicken livers, pickled herring and mackerel, fava beans, and canned figs.	

IRON OVERLOAD

CUT DOWN ON
- *Red meat, fish, and iron-fortified foods.*

AVOID
- *Liver and iron supplements.*
- *High doses of vitamin C.*

The human body needs a steady supply of iron, but only in tiny amounts—about 10mg to 15mg a day for healthy adults. In fact, excessive iron can cause irreversible heart and liver damage.

The body can utilize two types of iron—heme, which comes from animal sources, and nonheme, which comes mostly from plants. At any time, the body absorbs 20 to 30 percent of heme iron, compared with 5 to 10 percent of the nonheme type. When the body's iron reserves are low, however, the absorption of nonheme iron increases. Consuming iron-rich plant foods with some meat or with good sources of vitamin C also boosts nonheme iron absorption. By the same token, a number of substances—for example, calcium phosphate, tea, bran, and the oxalates found in spinach and kale—decrease the body's absorption of nonheme iron.

Genetic factors also influence iron absorption; about 10 percent of whites and up to 30 percent of people of African descent carry a gene that predisposes them to store extra iron. The presence of a single gene does not cause problems, but if a person inherits the gene from both parents, he is likely to develop iron overload, or hemochromatosis. Men and postmenopausal women are especially vulnerable.

An iron overload does not produce symptoms until a damaging amount of the mineral has accumulated in muscle tissue (including the heart), the liver, bone marrow, the spleen, and other organs; this usually occurs during middle age. One of the first indications is an unusually ruddy complexion; the person may also suffer chronic fatigue, joint and intestinal pain, and an irregular heartbeat. As the liver becomes increasingly damaged, JAUNDICE may develop.

A blood test can be used to diagnose an iron overload; in some cases, a liver biopsy may also be ordered. Treatment involves periodic removal of a pint or so of blood, which reduces iron levels by forcing the body to use some of its stores to make new red blood cells.

Even moderately elevated iron levels may set the stage for heart disease. In 1992 a group of Finnish researchers reported that men whose blood iron levels were in the high-normal range were more likely to develop coronary artery disease than those with low-to-normal levels. This supports the theory that excessive iron may injure the artery walls and promote the formation of fatty deposits, or plaque. This damage is probably due to iron's ability to catalyze oxidation processes. Some researchers now believe that the iron in our high-meat diet may be responsible for promoting heart disease, perhaps even more so than fat and dietary cholesterol are.

Some researchers also think that iron may contribute to the joint pain and damage that many women endure following menopause. Until now, most doctors assumed that the joint problems were due to ARTHRITIS.

Persons genetically predisposed to store extra iron should cut down on such iron-rich foods as meat, poultry, fish, seafood, dried apricots, and enriched breads and cereals. Foods high in vitamin C, which enhances iron absorption, should not be consumed along with iron-rich plant foods. Also, do not cook acidic foods in iron pots because they leach the metal from the cookware, increasing their iron content.

Unless prescribed by a doctor, nutritional supplements containing iron and large amounts of vitamin C should not be taken. Some experts now advise that anyone who is contemplating taking a vitamin C supplement should first have a blood test to measure iron levels.

Case Study

*A*lthough Russell had been troubled by vague symptoms of iron overload for several years, the condition was not diagnosed until he was 46 and had developed jaundice. Before then, Russell had attributed his swollen, aching joints to arthritis and blamed stress for his recurrent palpitations. As a redhead he had a ruddy complexion, so he wasn't troubled by a deepening skin tone. His condition was diagnosed when a physical examination found an enlarged liver and spleen, and blood tests showed high levels of iron. A liver biopsy confirmed moderate damage from a buildup of iron.

Over the next month, Russell had a pint of blood withdrawn each week; after that, he went for a monthly blood removal. The condition was caught before Russell's heart was seriously damaged, and with the lowering of its iron stores, the liver would heal itself. In addition, Russell worked with a dietitian to change his diet to restrict meat and other iron-rich foods in favor of pasta and other low-iron vegetarian dishes.

Irradiated Foods: A Nuclear Age Controversy

*Food growers and sellers hail irradiation as a safe
means of extending the shelf life of fresh foods, yet many
consumer groups still harbor serious doubts about it.*

Producers and sellers of foods are always looking for new ways to preserve the quality of fresh produce and extend its shelf life. Irradiation—the exposure of fresh foods to low levels of radiation—appears to be one such method. Exposure of foods to X-rays and other forms of ionizing radiation kills the molds, bacteria, and insects that cause spoilage. It also delays the ripening of fruits and berries, thus extending their shelf life. In addition, irradiation inhibits the sprouting of potatoes, garlic, onions, and other foods, which means that they stay fresh longer. Until now, heat and the use of chemicals (formaldehyde, alcohol, or various pesticides) were the major methods of sterilization, but each had its drawbacks. Heat sterilization entails cooking foods, so they are no longer fresh; chemicals that kill bacteria and other microorganisms often make foods inedible. Therefore, irradiation would seem to be an ideal means of sterilization, but the public has been slow to accept it as such.

RADIOACTIVE FOODS?

Despite assurances that irradiation with X-rays or certain isotopes does not make foods radioactive, some consumer and environmental groups remain unconvinced. They worry that any radiation exposure poses a potential environmental hazard, even if the foods themselves are not made radioactive. They also fear the radiation

---

BENEFITS

- *Kills disease-causing organisms.*
- *Increases food safety for people with low immunity.*
- *Prevents vegetables from sprouting.*
- *Kills or sterilizes insects in grains.*
- *Delays the ripening of fruits.*

DRAWBACKS

- *May alter the taste or texture of some meats and seafood.*
- *May destroy some vitamins.*
- *May hasten spoilage of some fats.*

---

may foster the development of dangerous mutant organisms.

The government mandates that only certain forms of irradiation can be applied to foods to ensure that they don't absorb the radioactive material. X-rays, which pass through an object without leaving behind radioactive material, are one such technique that can be applied to food; exposure to certain cobalt and cesium isotopes are also acceptable methods of food irradiation. These methods of cold sterilization allow most irradiated foods to retain their fresh appearance and taste. Exceptions occur, however, when meat, fish, and seafood are exposed to the high doses of radiation needed to destroy parasites, salmonella bacteria, and other organisms. In such instances, the flesh of some meat may darken slightly, and fish and seafood may become mushy. Irradiation can

also oxidize the fats in whole grains, causing them to taste rancid.

In general, irradiation preserves more nutrients—particularly niacin, riboflavin, thiamine, and other B-group vitamins—than other sterilization methods do. But very high radiation doses, such as those needed to sterilize meat, will destroy some of the fat-soluble vitamins A, E, and K. The effects of irradiation on vitamin C remain unknown; some studies show no loss of this nutrient, while others indicate major losses.

SPECIAL BENEFITS

Irradiation adds an extra measure of food safety for AIDS patients and others with lowered immunity; these people are cautioned not to eat uncooked fruits and vegetables and to make sure that all meat, fish, eggs, and other foods that may harbor disease-causing bacteria or parasites are cooked until well-done. Even after these precautions are taken, food-borne diseases are a major hazard for people with compromised immunity. High-dose irradiation can eliminate such dangers.

Advocates of irradiation also emphasize that the technique can increase food supplies in many parts of the world, especially in underdeveloped tropical areas. In India, for example, spoilage destroys half the food that is produced. Irradiation could conceivably solve the chronic food shortages in such areas.

IRRITABLE BOWEL SYNDROME

TAKE PLENTY OF
- *Nonalcoholic, caffeine-free fluids.*
- *Smaller meals.*
- *High-fiber foods (if constipation is a problem).*
- *Binding foods (if diarrhea is a problem).*

CUT DOWN ON
- *Alcoholic beverages.*

AVOID
- *Fried and other fatty foods.*
- *All sources of caffeine.*
- *Gas-producing foods, such as beans.*
- *Products sweetened with sorbitol.*

Afflicting up to 20 percent of all adults, irritable bowel syndrome, or IBS, can be very uncomfortable and interfere with daily living, but it is not a life-threatening medical condition. IBS is often characterized by abnormal muscle contractions in the intestines, resulting in too little or too much fluid in the bowel, however this is not the basis for the diagnosis of the disease.

Symptoms vary markedly from one person to another. Some people experience urgent DIARRHEA, usually upon awakening in the morning or during or immediately after a meal. Others experience the type called spastic colon, with alternating bouts of diarrhea and CONSTIPATION, as well as abdominal pain, cramps, bloating, gas, and nausea, particularly after eating. Still other symptoms may include mucus in the stool and feelings of incomplete evacuation after moving the bowels. Some people may also complain of fatigue, anxiety, headache, and depression.

There are no tests for IBS, which is diagnosed by ruling out COLITIS, cancer, and other diseases that cause similar symptoms. Although it may be aggravated by food intolerances or ALLERGIES, no specific cause for IBS has been established. It may be worsened by STRESS and emotional conflict, but it is not a psychological disorder. Various dietary factors can play a major role in exacerbating or calming IBS.

A doctor may prescribe medications to quell abnormal muscle contractions and alleviate diarrhea. However, self-care, stress reduction, and dietary modification are the mainstays of therapy.

SELF-AWARENESS
The first step in learning to control IBS symptoms is recognizing the factors that may trigger symptoms. A daily diary that records any IBS symptoms along with all foods and beverages ingested and any stressful events can help pinpoint possible culprits. A woman should determine whether symptoms flare up during certain times of her menstrual cycle. When tracking IBS symptoms, jot down the nature and location of any pain or cramping, as well as the frequency and consistency of stools and any related problems, such as headaches, soreness, or urinary problems. Your diary should also note all medications taken, including vitamin supplements, over-the-counter remedies, and prescription drugs. A doctor should review this diary to help identify specific contributing factors.

DIETARY MODIFICATION
Because IBS differs from person to person, it's essential to develop an individualized regimen to best treat your own symptoms. To begin, avoid foods that your diary suggests are causing problems. Try to eat several small meals a day rather than two or three large ones; this can reduce the meal-stimulated increase in bowel contractions and diarrhea.

To maintain adequate fluid in the intestinal tract, drink at least eight glasses of water or other beverages daily, but avoid such potential bowel irritants as alcohol and caffeine.

Most doctors advise against eating fried and other fatty foods because fat is the most difficult nutrient to digest. Many people find that it helps to avoid beans and other gas-producing foods.

Whole-grain products and other high-fiber foods can pose problems for some IBS sufferers who have chronic diarrhea. On the other hand, if constipation is the predominant symptom, a diet that includes ample fresh fruits and vegetables, whole-grain breads and cereals, nuts and seeds, and other high-fiber foods is usually recommended. If constipation is persistent, ask your doctor about taking ground psyllium seeds or another high-fiber laxative. Avoid chronic laxative use, which can lead to problems with diarrhea, as well as vitamin and nutritional deficiencies.

The sugar substitute sorbitol, which is used in many foods and dental products, triggers IBS symptoms in some people. For others, INTOLERANCE TO MILK manifests itself with symptoms similar to those of IBS. Avoiding milk, switching to lactose-free products, or using lactase enzymes usually solves the digestive problems.

Peppermint is a time-honored remedy to calm the digestive tract. To alleviate IBS, many practitioners of natural medicine recommend taking one or two enteric-coated capsules of peppermint oil between meals.

MANAGING STRESS
It is common for stress to exacerbate IBS symptoms, so it is important to make an effort to develop effective relaxation techniques, such as meditation, yoga, and biofeedback. A psychotherapist or other counselor can help you identify the stressors in your home or business life and develop better methods of managing them. In general, exercise can be very therapeutic for people with IBS because it helps reduce stress; it can also normalize bowel function if constipation is a problem.

JAMS AND SPREADS

BENEFITS
- *Jams and jellies contain pectin, a soluble fiber that helps control blood cholesterol, and simple sugars for quick energy.*
- *Peanut butter provides useful amounts of protein, B vitamins, and minerals.*

DRAWBACKS
- *Jams are less nutritious than fresh fruit.*
- *Peanut butter is high in sodium and fat.*
- *Other types of commercial spreads are often low in nutritional value but high in sodium and fat, as well as price.*

Jams were developed in ancient times as a means of preserving fruits that would otherwise quickly spoil. When preserved in sugar syrups and gels, fruits resist spoilage because they lack the water that microorganisms need in order to grow. Surface molds can be prevented by sealing homemade preserves with an airtight layer of paraffin.

Fruits boiled in sugar will gel via the interaction of fruit acids and pectin, a soluble fiber that is drawn out of the fruit cell walls by cooking. Apples, grapes, and most berries contain enough natural pectin; other fruits, such as apricots and peaches, need to

BRING ON THE JAM. *Fruit spreads, lower in calories than butter, may include (clockwise from front) black currant, low-sugar strawberry, apricot, marmalade, blackberry, raspberry, and strawberry.*

have it added. Low-calorie, reduced-sugar jams are gelled with a special pectin that sets at lower acidity and with less sugar. These products are often sweetened with concentrated fruit juice and thickened with starches.

For nutritional value, there's no comparison between jams and fresh fruits, because most of the vitamin C and other nutrients in fruits are destroyed by intense cooking. While fruit preserves contain substantial amounts of pectin—a soluble fiber that helps control blood cholesterol levels—this benefit is offset by their high sugar content. Simple sugars, however, make jams a source of quick energy.

PEANUT BUTTER
The majority of the peanuts grown in North America are ground into peanut butter. The high fat content of peanuts makes them easy to grind into a paste, but the oil quickly turns rancid when exposed to oxygen and light. Many commercial peanut butters are made with preservatives, stabilizers, and added salt and sugar; you can avoid these ingredients by buying fresh-ground peanut butter

made solely from nuts. The oil that rises to the top of the jar can be poured off to reduce the fat content. It's best to store peanut butter in a glass container in the refrigerator, where the darkness prevents the loss of B vitamins and the cold retards oil separation. Some peanut butters contain hydrogenated vegetable oils to prevent separation, but this increases the saturated fat content.

Peanut butter can be a valuable nutritional resource for children, who need extra dietary fat for proper growth and development. One tablespoon contains about 95 calories, with 5g of protein, 8g of polyunsaturated fat, and significant amounts of B vitamins, calcium, potassium, and magnesium, along with 100mg of sodium and traces of iron and zinc.

OTHER SPREADS
The supermarket shelves are stocked with many types of spreads, ranging from soft processed cheese products to chocolate-flavored nut butters and whipped marshmallow. Most of the cheese-based products provide small amounts of vitamin A and calcium but are high in sodium, fat, and cholesterol. Chocolate and marshmallow spreads offer little more than calories.

JAUNDICE

A yellowing of the skin and the whites of the eyes is the hallmark of jaundice. This condition typically occurs when bilirubin, a pigmented component of bile, builds up in the blood. Bilirubin is a by-product produced by the liver as it breaks down red blood cells to recycle their iron. It is mixed with bile, a digestive juice that is made by the liver, and eventually excreted from the body in the urine or stool. Jaundice usually develops if the bilirubin is allowed to accumulate in the body.

There are three general types of jaundice: the most common is due to hepatitis or some other LIVER DISORDER; another, known as obstructive jaundice, usually results from GALLSTONES or another gallbladder disease; and the least common involves some sort of abnormality in bilirubin metabolism.

Each year more than 2.5 million Canadians are afflicted with liver and gallbladder disorders, but not all of these people develop jaundice. Among those who do, hepatitis—an inflammation of the liver—is the likely cause. Five major forms of viral hepatitis have been identified to date; the liver inflammation may also be due to alcohol or drug abuse, adverse reaction to a medication, as well as bacterial, parasitic, or fungal infections of the liver. Some strains of viral hepatitis are highly contagious and can enter the human body through water or food (especially shellfish) that has been contaminated by human waste. Hepatitis can also be spread through blood transfusions from an infected person or by direct contact with infected body fluids or the use of contaminated syringes.

In addition to jaundice, the symptoms of hepatitis—which may vary in severity—include fever, fatigue, nausea, vomiting, diarrhea, and loss of appetite. The urine may be dark in color due to increased bilirubin content, and the stools may be light, clay-colored, or whitish, an indication that bilirubin is not being excreted as usual from the intestinal tract. In a few cases, hepatitis may be serious enough to result in liver failure, coma, and death.

Jaundice may also be due to Gilbert's syndrome (a disorder of bilirubin metabolism), which affects 3 to 5 percent of the population and may be misdiagnosed as hepatitis. In Gilbert's syndrome, chronic jaundice is the only abnormality and does not signify liver disease. Several other rare forms of jaundice are inherited disorders.

INFANT JAUNDICE

It is not uncommon for a baby to develop jaundice during the first few days after birth, especially if the infant is premature. This is known as physiological jaundice, and is usually caused by a liver that is not fully functional. There are usually no other symptoms, and the condition typically clears up within a week after birth, as the liver matures. Exposing the baby to ultraviolet light hastens the process, as the light changes bilirubin to a form that is more readily excreted.

Feeding the infant soon after birth and continuing with frequent feedings helps to reduce the risk of jaundice by stimulating the intestinal tract to produce frequent stools, which increases the excretion of bilirubin. In a few cases the newborn may be reacting to the mother's milk, and breast-feeding must be discontinued for a day or two in favor of a formula. After this resolves the problem, the mother may resume breast-feeding safely.

DIETARY APPROACHES

Any modification of the diet depends on the underlying cause of the jaundice. With a nutritious, well-balanced diet and rest, viral hepatitis resolves itself—although it may take several weeks. Unfortunately, many people find it difficult to eat at the very time that they need extra calories to help the liver recuperate and regenerate its damaged cells. Many individuals report that their appetite decreases and nausea increases as the day progresses, suggesting that breakfast may be the best tolerated meal.

When recovering from hepatitis, a person should consume at least 60g of protein daily, from both animal and vegetable sources. The best sources are lean meat, poultry, fish, eggs, dairy products, and a combination of legumes and grain products. If the appetite is poor, intersperse several small meals a day with a nutritious snack (such as a milkshake or an enriched liquid drink). Fried and very fatty foods, which are difficult to digest, should be avoided; a small amount of fat is acceptable, however, to provide needed calories and add flavor. In general, the fats in dairy products and eggs are easier to digest than those in fatty meats and fried foods.

Because they squelch the appetite for more nutritious foods, it is best to avoid sweets and sweet snacks. Alcohol should not be consumed, because it places added stress on an already sick liver. A glass of wine or beer may be tolerated after recovery, but first check with your doctor; some liver disorders mandate total abstinence from alcohol for life.

Juicing: A Fad of the '90s

*Drinking lots of fruit and vegetable juices may not cure
diseases and foster enhanced well-being, as many proponents claim,
but it is an easy, low-calorie way to improve nutrition.*

By now just about everyone knows that FRUITS and VEGETABLES are loaded with vitamins, minerals, and hundreds of other substances that protect against cancer and other diseases. Mainstream physicians and alternative practitioners alike are urging their patients to eat more fruits and vegetables, preferably raw or with minimal processing in order to preserve their nutrients. There's no clear agreement, however, as to how much you should eat. The Food Guide Rainbow (see p.39) calls for 5 to 10 servings of fruits and vegetables each day—more than what most Canadians now consume. But naturopaths contend that this recommendation is inadequate—a view shared by a growing number of doctors.

Proponents of raw-food diets urge

> **BENEFITS**
> - *Provides a low-calorie concentrated form of fruits and vegetables.*
> - *Easier to digest than the raw whole foods used in juicing.*
>
> **DRAWBACKS**
> - *Juicing removes pulp and fiber.*

that 75 percent or more of the diet should come from raw foods, but for most people, consuming this much uncooked food is unrealistic. Juicing has been proposed as one way to boost the consumption of raw fruits and vegetables without provoking the digestive problems that may result from eating large quantities of uncooked high-fiber foods. In addition, many followers of juicing regimens, which

typically call for three or four glasses of different juice combinations a day, report that they have more energy and fewer colds and other infections.

THE BASICS OF JUICING

The method is simple: various combinations of raw fruits and vegetables are placed in a machine that extracts their juice and leaves behind most of the pulp and fiber. First, the foods should be washed and the large ones cut into smaller pieces. Citrus and melon peels, pits, and most seeds, as well as carrot tops and rhubarb leaves (which are toxic), should be

FLAVORFUL AND NUTRITIOUS. *Various combinations of fruits and vegetables can be transformed into refreshing and healthful beverages.*

A blend of mango and carrot juices (right) is rich in beta carotene; pineapple and passion fruit (below) provide iron, potassium, and other minerals.

Delicious drinks high in vitamin C, beta carotene, and bioflavonoids can be made from (left to right) oranges, raspberries, pink grapefruit, and cranberries and apples.

THERAPEUTIC JUICING REGIMENS

The following is a sample of juicing combinations that are often recommended for relieving specific ailments or for boosting certain nutrients. Their effectiveness, however, has not been confirmed by controlled scientific studies.

PURPOSE	JUICING COMBINATION	HOW TO MAKE IT
ANTINAUSEANT To prevent nausea from pregnancy or motion sickness.	½-in slice of fresh ginger 1 lemon 1 apple 2 cups flat ginger ale	Put ginger, lemon, and apple through a juicer, stir the mixture into the ginger ale, and sip as needed.
CALCIUM SHAKE A good drink for those who don't like milk or have difficulty drinking it.	1 cup broccoli florets 2–3 kale leaves 3–4 carrots ½ apple	Remove carrot tops; juice ingredients together and chill.
FOLATE TONIC A good booster of this B vitamin for women on birth control pills or during pregnancy.	1 orange 2–3 carrots 1 cup chopped kale Handful of parsley	Remove carrot tops; put ingredients through juicer. Chill and serve with a slice of lemon as a garnish.
POTASSIUM BOOSTER To restore potassium stores after diarrhea or when taking diuretics.	1 orange ½ cantaloupe 2 or 3 carrots 1 banana	Put first three ingredients through juicer; puree banana in a blender and mix with juice.
PUMPING IRON To build iron reserves; a good drink during pregnancy.	1 bunch parsley 1 red pepper 1 cup broccoli florets 3 raw carrots	Put ingredients through juicer in the same order as in the list; flavor with lemon or orange juice if desired.
VITAMIN C REFRESHER A good drink when you feel a cold coming on.	1 kiwi 1 mango (peeled) ½ cantaloupe ½ cup strawberries	Put ingredients through juicer and serve chilled.

removed; otherwise, the entire fruit or vegetable can be put through the juicer. Bananas and avocados, which contain little juice, should be put in a blender instead of a juicer; the puréed fruit can then be mixed with other juices.

Juicing therapists and manuals suggest various combinations of fruits and vegetables to treat specific problems. A high-zinc drink said to prevent infections, for example, is made from ginger root, parsley, potato, garlic, and carrot. A drink high in vitamin C and BIOFLAVONOIDS that may speed recovery from a cold is a combination of parsley, lemon, watercress, red pepper, and kale. Recent medical studies show that cabbage juice may be an effective ulcer treatment; the juicing remedy uses ½ head of green cabbage, a stalk of celery, and a seeded apple.

Some commercial juice bars add amino acids and other types of supplements to their drinks. It is better, however, to include juices as part of the overall diet and to get protein and starches from other foods rather than from supplements.

TO FAST OR NOT

Many juicing regimens call for periodic fasting to clear toxins from the body. During a fast only distilled water and juices are consumed. An occasional brief fast may not be harmful, but doctors caution that frequent or prolonged fasting deprives the body of energy and a balance of nutrients.

During an infection or other type of illness, many juicing manuals advocate adding enemas to the fasting regimen, supposedly to speed the removal of toxins from the body. The fact is, the body has its own highly efficient system of detoxification—fasting and enemas will not improve on nature, and they may even be harmful. When a person is ill, the body needs extra nutrition to recover; juices should not be a substitute for other foods.

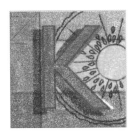

KALE

BENEFITS
- *An excellent source of beta carotene and vitamins C and E.*
- *A good source of folate, calcium, iron, and potassium.*
- *Contains bioflavonoids and other substances that protect against cancer.*

DRAWBACKS
- *May cause gas in some people.*

A member of the cabbage family, kale looks like collards but with curly leaves. It is a hardy autumn vegetable that grows best in a cool climate; in fact, exposure to frost actually improves its flavor. Although the types of kale that form leafy red, yellow, and purple heads are used more often for decorative purposes (both in the garden and on the table) than as a food, all varieties are edible and highly nutritious.

Kale—like its relatives in the cabbage family—is an excellent source of vitamin C and beta carotene, which the human body converts to vitamin A; in fact, a 1-cup serving provides more than twice the daily requirements for these nutrients. Other nutrients found in a cup of kale include 5mg of vitamin E, 30mcg (micrograms) of folate, 135mg of calcium, 2mg of iron, and 450mg of potassium. It also provides more than 1g of fiber and has only 50 calories; yet, it is filling, making kale an ideal, highly nutritious food for anyone who is weight-conscious.

In addition, kale contains more iron and calcium that almost any other vegetable; its high vitamin C content enhances the body's ability to absorb these minerals. Serving kale with a lemon dressing or in the same meal as another acidic citrus fruit further boosts absorption of the iron and calcium.

BIOFLAVONOIDS, carotenoids, and other cancer-fighting compounds are abundant in kale. It also contains indoles, compounds that can lessen the cancer-causing potential of estrogen and induce production of enzymes that protect against disease.

The typical way of preparing kale is to cook it. To preserve its rich stores of beta carotene and vitamin C, cook kale quickly in minimal water; it can be steamed, chopped, and stir-fried with other vegetables, or simmered until tender in broth to make a tasty soup. Kale shrinks considerably during cooking; it takes about 3 cups of raw greens to make a 1-cup serving. Even cooked, kale produces gas in some people.

KIDNEY DISEASES

CONSUME PLENTY OF
- *Liquids to replace lost fluids and maintain fluid balance.*

CUT DOWN ON
- *Foods high in oxalates (citrus fruits, berries, rhubarb, leafy green vegetables, beets, peppers, and chocolate), to prevent kidney stones.*
- *Protein from all sources to lessen the burden on the kidneys.*
- *Salt to reduce fluid retention and prevent high blood pressure.*

AVOID
- *Over-the-counter painkillers, vitamin pills, and calcium supplements, which have side effects and interactions that cause kidney damage.*

Kidney disease may be either a primary condition, such as kidney stones, or a consequence of other disorders, such as hypertension, atherosclerosis, or diabetes—all of which can severely damage the organs' blood vessels. Older men are susceptible to kidney infections stemming from enlargement of the prostate. Pregnant women and diabetics are vulnerable to infections of the urinary tract. Side effects from drugs are common and preventable causes of serious kidney disorders. For example, acetaminophen, aspirin, and other nonsteroidal anti-inflammatory drugs (NSAIDs) and calcium with vitamin D supplements are among the nonprescription drugs that can damage the kidneys. Combining aspirin and acetaminophen is especially damaging to the kidneys. Whenever you see your doctor, be sure to mention any over-the-counter medications or vitamin supplements you have been taking, even if occasionally.

Diet is crucial in treating kidney problems. If you

have a serious kidney disease, your doctor will probably refer you to a clinical dietitian for advice concerning dietary changes. The allowable types and portions of foods differ, depending upon the type and severity of the disorder.

Healthy people should not wait for problems to occur; rather, they should eat to prevent kidney disorders. Drink plenty of liquids to flush the urinary system and replace fluids lost through perspiration and excretion, and eat a low-fat diet that emphasizes starchy foods, vegetables, and fruits.

KIDNEY STONES

Approximately 1 in 1,000 Canadians is hospitalized each year for the treatment of kidney stones; men outnumber women about three to one. Some people suffer their first attack after taking up a steady exercise program, such as jogging, and failing to drink enough fluids to compensate for the amount lost in sweat. At least half of those who suffer one attack will have a recurrence.

Kidney stones form when crystalline minerals—normally flushed away in the urine—stick together to form clumps, ranging in size from a grain of sand to coarse gravel. The cause may be GOUT or another metabolic problem, or it may be a structural or metabolic abnormality within the kidney. When kidney stones block any part of the urinary system, especially the ureters or bladder, they cause intense colicky pain. Many stones pass through the system; others must be removed surgically or

by sound-wave treatment (lithotripsy).

In order to prevent recurrences, it is important to determine the cause of the kidney stones. Most are formed of calcium oxalate or calcium phosphate. Less commonly, stones may form from uric acid crystals, especially in people with gout. A fourth type, cystine stones, occurs in fairly rare metabolic diseases.

Regardless of the type of stone, however, it's essential to drink enough liquids to maintain fluid balance and flush away the minerals that accumulate to form stones. Other dietary changes may be necessary as well. Although most stones contain calcium, it's not a good idea to cut down on dietary calcium unless your doctor specifically orders it. If the human body fails to get enough calcium, it will rob the bones to get the mineral, thus increasing the danger of OSTEOPOROSIS. Sometimes, a high level of calcium in the urine may be raised even further by a high intake of salt. Doctors usually prescribe a diuretic for this type of problem and recommend a low-salt diet.

Phosphorus-rich foods contribute to the formation of calcium phosphate stones. The balance of phosphorus and calcium in the diet is very delicate, however, and restricting the intake of one may interfere with the other. A dietitian's or doctor's guidance is necessary when changing your intake of either essential mineral to maintain balanced nutrition.

Cutting down on foods that are high in oxalate helps prevent

calcium oxalate stones. Oxalate-rich foods include berries, grapes, and citrus fruits; most of the dark green leafy varieties of vegetables, the turnip family, beets, rhubarb, and green peppers; and beer and chocolate milk. It doesn't pay to take a drastic approach, however; eliminating all these foods depletes the diet of essential vitamins and minerals. A doctor or dietitian should provide a list of all the foods that can be eaten in moderation with little risk of causing a recurrence. Individuals with gout should keep to a low-purine diet (see p.169) to prevent attacks and reduce the risk of uric acid stones.

Kidney stones are rare in people who eat a strict vegetarian diet. While the connection between stones and protein is not fully understood, it is known that protein increases the acidity of urine, which probably plays a role.

Many individuals with kidney stones could reduce the risk of recurrence by increasing their fluid intake (plain water is best) in order to excrete about 2 quarts of urine a day and by cutting their daily protein intake to about 50g (1⅔ ounces) of pure protein. It's easier to reduce protein intake if you cut down on animal products. Combining complex carbohydrates, such as rice and beans, can supply the essential amino acids.

NEPHRITIS

Inflammation of the kidney—known medically as nephritis—may result from a bacterial infection or

FOODS TO AVOID. *The specific foods that should be eliminated from the diet vary according to the specific disorder. People with kidney stones may be advised to avoid the sources of oxalates, such as chocolate, citrus fruits, berries, green leafy vegetables, and certain sources of phosphates, such as colas. Milk may be contraindicated for a person with calcium stones. Salt and high-protein animal foods increase the kidneys' workload and can exacerbate kidney failure.*

Strawberries and raspberries

Citrus fruits

Chocolate

KIDNEY TRANSPLANT

Although an individual who has received a kidney transplant must follow dietary guidelines, the diet is usually less restrictive than the one followed during dialysis treatment. Because the diet is affected by medications taken to prevent rejection of the new kidney, however, the doctor and dietitian will continually make adjustments as recovery progresses.

In the weeks immediately after a transplant, most people are advised to eat more high-quality protein, such as eggs, low-fat meat, fish, poultry, skim milk, and low-fat cheese. Carbohydrates are generally limited to prevent interactions with the high doses of steroids that must be taken to prevent rejection. Complex carbohydrates from starchy foods are allowed, but simple sugars should be avoided. Salty foods, such as cured or smoked meats and fish, cold cuts, and most processed foods, should be eliminated, and no salt should be added to foods during preparation or at the table. The doctor or dietitian will provide guidelines regarding potassium-rich foods. Calcium, vitamin, or phosphorus supplements may be prescribed.

A sudden, moderate weight gain after receiving a kidney transplant is not unusual; however, if weight does become a problem, such high-fat foods as pastries should be avoided. Instead, between-meal snacks can include such foods as raw vegetables and fruits, low-fat crackers, and nonfat yogurt.

a number of other causes, including side effects of drugs. Infections sometimes arise elsewhere in the body and reach the kidneys through the bloodstream, or they enter the body through the urinary tract and travel up through the bladder to the kidneys. Kidney infections, like kidney stones, always require a doctor's intervention and must be treated with antibiotics. No special dietary measures are necessary, unless the physician recommends them; however, people with kidney infections should drink plenty of fluids to flush the system. A daily glass of cranberry juice helps to prevent the recurrence of many urinary tract infections in susceptible persons.

KIDNEY FAILURE

Kidney failure may be either a temporary response to acute shock or injury or a severe long-term state necessitating drastic treatment. Acute kidney failure may be caused by severe infection, burns, diarrhea or vomiting, poisoning (including drug effects or interactions), surgery, or injury to the kidneys. When the problem is resolved, function usually returns to normal. Chronic kidney failure may be caused by untreated hypertension, poorly controlled diabetes, or an inborn condition.

Severe chronic, or end-stage, kidney failure requires regular dialysis—in which a machine removes waste products from the blood—or where possible, kidney transplantation.

Diet is extremely important in the management of kidney failure; the general recommendations include restricting protein, salt, phosphorus, and potassium. Fluids must be carefully monitored. With too little fluid, the electrolytes are out of balance; with too much, fluid retention causes edema and electrolyte problems, and it also contributes to high blood pressure and perhaps congestive heart failure.

Studies show that if protein is limited to about half a gram per pound of body weight per day (i.e., just over 1 ounce a day for a 140-pound person), the patient on dialysis will receive the essential amino acids but reduce the risk of further kidney damage. Proteins from fish, egg whites, and combinations of legumes and grains are preferable to those in meat because they contain less saturated fat.

Kidney failure requires highly specialized medical care. No changes in diet should be made without a doctor's approval. Anyone receiving treatment for kidney failure should consult regularly with a specialist dietitian who will monitor the diet and make any necessary adjustments in the amounts of nutrients, including vitamin and mineral supplements.

Green leafy vegetables

Colas

Salt

Milk

Meat and eggs

Actinidia chinenesis

The kiwi vine bears the hairy brown-skinned fruit.

Inside the fruit, the bright green flesh is dotted with tiny edible black seeds.

MORE THAN A GARNISH. *Although kiwis are often used for decoration, they are also highly nutritious.*

KIWIFRUITS

BENEFITS
- *An excellent source of vitamin C.*
- *A good source of potassium and fiber.*
- *Can be used as a meat tenderizer.*

On the outside a kiwifruit looks like a fuzzy brown egg; on the inside its bright green flesh is sprinkled with a ring of small, black seeds. It has a distinctive, somewhat tart flavor with overtones of fruits and berries.

The kiwi originated in China and was known as the Chinese gooseberry until New Zealand fruit growers renamed it for their national bird and began exporting it. Kiwis were once considered an exotic fruit, but they are now grown in California and have become increasingly plentiful. Kiwis are harvested while green and can be kept in cold storage for 6 to 10 months, making them available for most of the year. Ripe kiwis are eaten raw; even the skin can be consumed if it is defuzzed.

Kiwis are very high in vitamin C; a large 4-ounce fruit contains more than 100mg. It also provides a good amount of potassium and pectin, a soluble fiber that helps control blood cholesterol levels. A 4-ounce serving has 70 calories.

An enzyme (actinidin) that is a natural meat tenderizer is found in kiwi. The fruit can be used as a marinade to tenderize tough meats. Rubbing the meat with a cut kiwi and waiting 30 to 60 minutes before cooking will tenderize the meat without imparting any flavor from the fruit. This enzyme also will keep gelatin from setting and will curdle milk and cream; these effects can be prevented by poaching the fruit beforehand. Don't overcook the fruit, however; it quickly turns to mush.

KOHLRABI

BENEFITS
- *High in vitamin C, potassium, and cancer-preventing antioxidants and bioflavonoids.*
- *High in dietary fiber.*

DRAWBACKS
- *May cause gas in some people.*

Similar to both cabbages and turnips, kohlrabi comes from the same cruciferous plant family. Because the bulb, which is the edible part of the plant, is not as rich in nutrients as the flowers or leaves, kohlrabi is not in the same nutritional league as broccoli, Brussels sprouts, and kale. Still, it is a good source of vitamin C; a ½-cup serving provides 75 percent of the adult Recommended Nutrient Intake (RNI). It also has about 200mg of potassium and a good amount of fiber.

This vegetable is high in BIOFLAVONOIDS, plant pigments that work with vitamin C and other ANTIOXIDANTS to prevent the cell damage that promotes cancer. Kohlrabi is also high in indoles, chemicals that reduce the effects of estrogen, and thus may reduce the risk of breast cancer. Isothiocyanates, another group of compounds in kohlrabi, promote the action of enzymes that may protect against colon cancer.

Kohlrabi should be harvested before it reaches full maturity; otherwise, it becomes woody. It can be sliced and eaten raw, but it is usually steamed until tender. People who get gas after eating other cruciferous vegetables may have the same response to kohlrabi.

LABELING OF FOODS

Most processed foods must carry labels that list all ingredients, but some manufacturers now voluntarily provide nutrition information too. This information can be useful in planning a balanced diet.

Because of a clause in the Canada-U.S. Free Trade Agreement which requires the two countries to work toward an equivalent labeling system, food labels in Canada are likely to change in the near future. At the present time, the only label requirement on processed foods is a list of ingredients in descending order by weight. The label also includes the name and address of the manufacturer, packager, or distributor; the packaging date or the last date on which it can be sold or consumed; plus storage information. Nutrition information, now optional, will probably be mandatory when the new policies and regulations are enacted. Health Canada and Consumer and Corporate Affairs Canada are currently reviewing these with the food industry, health interest groups, health professionals, and educators. The aim is to harmonize the two systems, rather than make them identical. Canada's plan is to show serving sizes, the number of servings in a package, and the calories per serving at the top of the label in much the same way as the United States currently does (see U.S. label at right).

The United States has established standard serving sizes for each type of food, regardless of brand. This is a departure from its practices in the past when one brand might specify a serving as half a cup, and another brand's serving would be one cup.

The new method is especially helpful to people who are watching their weight or who are on special diets. The Canadian plan is to match the American serving sizes in virtually all cases.

The new Canadian food label will simplify the breakdown of nutrients in a food, listing the grams contained in the five key categories: total fat and amount of saturated fat; cholesterol; sodium; carbohydrates, including sugars and fiber; and protein. Also, the percentage of Recommended Nutrient Intakes (RNIs) that these amounts represent will be shown. The label may also list the major vitamins and minerals along with the percentage of the RNI. Canada may follow the American lead which currently states the recommended daily amounts of carbohydrates, protein, and dietary fiber in diets that permit 2,000 and 2,500 calories a day.

INTERPRETING A NUTRITION LABEL. *Canada's proposed label will be similar to a typical U.S. label.*

SETTING A STANDARD

Proposed Canadian regulations aim to set standards for terms such as "light/lite" or "low-fat." For example, a food that normally derives more than 50 percent of its calories from fat can be marketed in a "light" version only if the fat content has been reduced by more than one-third. "Light" will also be allowed to describe characteristics such as flavor, texture or color, but the connection must be identified as in "light in flavor." Unlike the United States, Canada will not permit "light" in reference to nutrients such as sodium. Health claims are allowed as long as they are based on evidence accepted by qualified experts. Claims such as "calorie reduced," "low fat," and "low cholesterol" may be used as long as they conform to regulations. For example, calorie reduced means that a food has 50 percent fewer calories than the regular version. Low cholesterol means there can be no more than 3mg per serving, and the food must be low in saturated fat.

211

LAMB

BENEFITS
- *A rich source of minerals, including iron, phosphorus, and calcium.*
- *An excellent source of protein and B-complex vitamins.*

DRAWBACKS
- *Some cuts are high in saturated fat.*

Spring lamb has a uniquely delicate flavor and texture. Rarest of all is the meat of lambs raised in salt marshes, which has an unmistakably briny tang. Lambs born in the early spring are ready for market at about 6 weeks of age. Their meat is officially categorized as "lamb" up to 14 months of age; between 14 months and 2 years, it is yearling lamb (hogget in some sheep-raising regions); and after 2 years, the strong-flavored meat is called mutton, which is rarely eaten by North Americans.

Lamb has never enjoyed the same popularity as beef in Canada. In 1994, for example, per capita consumption of lamb was just under 2 pounds, compared to 50 pounds of beef.

RICH IN NUTRITION
Among red meats, lamb stands out for its high nutritional value. Although some cuts are high in fat, lamb is not marbled like beef. In addition, the meat is tender, because it is the relatively little-used muscle of young animals. Therefore, most of the fat can easily be removed from the lean meat before cooking. A 3-ounce portion of roasted lean lamb contains approximately 215 calories, with about 20g of protein and 15g of saturated fat, including about 80mg of cholesterol.

Lamb is a rich source of B-complex vitamins, as well as iron, phosphorus, calcium, and potassium. Because it is easily digestible and almost never associated with food allergies, lamb is a good protein food for people of all ages.

A NATURAL SANDTRAP. *Leeks must be thoroughly cleaned before they are cooked, because their layered structure retains a great deal of gritty sand or garden soil.*

LEEKS

BENEFITS
- *A good source of vitamin C, with lesser amounts of niacin and calcium.*

DRAWBACKS
- *Like other members of the onion family, may cause bad breath and gas.*

Leeks are closely related to onions—as the similarity in flavor shows—and are distant cousins of asparagus. All three are members of the lily family. Although the entire leek is edible, most people prefer to eat the white, fleshy base and tender inner leaves and to discard the bitter dark green leaf tops.

Although leeks probably originated in warm regions of Asia or the Mediterranean, they are now intensively cultivated in temperate to cool climates, particularly in Northern Europe. In Wales, where leeks are a national symbol, men parade in the streets with leek-bedecked hats on a special holiday.

Low-calorie leeks provide an appreciable amount of minerals and fiber together with plenty of vitamin C. A half cup of chopped, boiled leeks, served plain, contains only 15 calories but 25mg of vitamin C, as well as 16mg of calcium and a small amount of niacin.

Vegetables in the onion group may have a protective effect against stomach cancer, and like onions, leeks may help to lower cholesterol. On a more negative note, they can cause bad breath and, in some people, gassiness.

Leeks are useful in a range of dishes where their mild oniony flavor is desired. You can boil and sieve them with potatoes for a chilled vichyssoise soup; braise them in fat-free stock to serve hot; and brush them lightly with olive oil and grill for a mixed vegetable barbecue. To make a reduced-fat quiche, steam chopped leeks and mix them with eggs and low-fat yogurt.

LEGUMES

BENEFITS
- *Contain more protein than any other plant-derived food.*
- *A good source of starch, B-complex vitamins, iron, potassium, zinc, and other essential minerals.*
- *Most are high in soluble fiber.*
- *A good crop for nitrogen-depleted soil.*

DRAWBACKS
- *May cause bloating and intestinal gas.*
- *Can trigger allergies in some people.*
- *Must be cooked to destroy numerous toxic substances.*

The 13,000 different varieties of legumes that are grown worldwide share two major characteristics—they all produce seed-bearing pods, and have nodules on their roots which harbor bacteria that can convert atmospheric nitrogen to nitrate, a form of nitrogen the plant uses for nutrition. Otherwise, these members of the Leguminosae plant family differ greatly: some are low-growing plants (bush beans, lentils, and soybeans) or vines (many peas and beans); others are trees (carob) or shrubs (mesquite). Although peanuts are often classified as nuts, they are actually legumes; so too are clover and alfalfa, two major hay crops, and fenugreek, whose ground seeds are among those used to make curry powder.

Archeologists have found evidence that beans and peas were cultivated in Southeast Asia some 11,000 years ago, which may mean that they were actually grown before grains. Chickpeas, fava (broad) beans, and lentils have been cultivated in the Middle East since about 8000 BC, and beans have been grown in the New World since 4000 BC. The European colonists noted that Native people grew beans between rows of corn. At the time, they believed that this was to reduce weed growth; we now know that beans (and other legumes) also replenish the soil with nitrogen, a nutrient depleted by corn and other grains.

Combining beans and corn to make the popular Indian dish succotash provides complete PROTEIN, as does any combination of legumes and grains. Soybeans, however, contain almost all of the essential amino acids that make complete protein; they are also high in calcium. Thus, strict vegetarians whose diets exclude all animal foods can rely on TOFU AND OTHER SOY PRODUCTS for protein and some of their calcium.

NUTRITIONAL WINNERS

Legumes are among our most nutritious plant foods—high in protein, B-complex vitamins, iron, potassium, and other minerals. They provide large amounts of fiber, including the soluble type that is important in controlling blood cholesterol levels. Legumes are

---

BEANS, BEANS, AND MORE BEANS

There are hundreds of different varieties of beans; the following are among the more popular.

Adzuki. These small red beans are lower in B vitamins but higher in minerals than their larger red cousins, the kidney beans.

Black (turtle) beans. A staple in Latin American dishes, these are somewhat lower in folate than kidney beans but otherwise comparable in nutritional value.

Cannellini. These large white kidney beans are used in minestrone and other Italian dishes; they are usually purchased canned.

Cranberry. These oval-shaped beans with mottled pink skins are used either fresh or dried. Their nutrient content is comparable to that of kidney beans.

Great Northern. The largest white beans, they have a mild flavor that is especially suitable for casseroles and soups. They are somewhat less nutritious than other varieties.

Kidney. These red beans derive their name from their shape and are among the most nutritious of the dried types. They are a favorite for chilies, stews, and soups.

Limas. Used fresh or dried, lima beans are highly nutritious and are one of the most widely available beans. They are often combined with corn to make succotash, a high-quality protein dish.

Navy beans. A small, white version of Great Northerns, these have a milder flavor and slightly more folate and iron than most types.

Pinto. This mottled, multicolored bean is one of the most nutritious types used in North America.

Red beans. Often combined with rice or used in chili, red beans are similar to kidney beans.

Soybeans. Among the most nutritious of all the legumes, soybeans give rise to many widely consumed products, including bean curd, soy milk, and flour.

also a good food for a diabetic diet because their balance of complex carbohydrates and protein provide a slow, steady source of glucose instead of the sudden surge that typically occurs after eating simple carbohydrates.

Most legumes are low in calories and fat; soybeans and peanuts, however, are high in mostly unsaturated oils.

THE DOWN SIDE

Legumes harbor a number of toxic substances or compounds that interfere with the action or absorption of vitamins. Soybeans, for example, contain substances that destroy beta carotene and vitamins B_{12} and D; beans and peas have an anti-vitamin E compound. Heating and cooking inactivates most of these substances, but to compensate for vitamin loss, balance legume consumption with ample fresh fruits and yellow or dark green vegetables (for beta

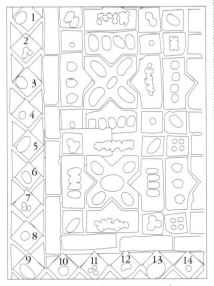

A FEAST OF BEANS. *Legumes are the most economical source of protein. Among the many varieties are pinto beans (1), puy lentils (2), red kidney beans (3), green lentils (4), borlotti beans (5), flageolet beans (6), mung beans (7), soybeans (8), cannellini beans (9), chickpeas (10), red lentils (11), black-eyed peas (12), broad beans (13), and adzuki beans (14).*

carotene), lean meat or other animal products (for vitamin B_{12}), and cooked greens, wheat germ, fortified cereals, seeds, nuts, and poultry (for vitamin E).

Other potentially harmful compounds in uncooked legumes bind with copper, iron, zinc, and other minerals; cause red blood cells to clump together; activate a form of cyanide; spur growth of a goiter by interfering with the thyroid's iodine metabolism; and bind with trypsin, a digestive enzyme. Adequate soaking and cooking renders these substances harmless.

People with GOUT are often advised to forgo dried peas and beans, lentils, and other legumes because of their high purine content. In susceptible people, purines increase levels of uric acid and can precipitate a gout attack. Some people of Mediterranean or Asian descent carry a gene that makes them susceptible to favism, a severe type of anemia contracted from eating fava beans. Anyone with a family history of this disease must not eat this type of bean.

Some legumes, especially peanuts, trigger an allergic reaction or migraine headaches in susceptible people. In such cases the offending foods should be eliminated from the diet.

Dried beans, lentils, and peas are notorious for causing intestinal gas and FLATULENCE. Individuals vary considerably in how much and what kinds of legumes they can tolerate; begin with small portions and experiment with different varieties. The method of preparation can help reduce gas production. Change the water several times during the soaking and cooking process. (Lentils don't need to be soaked, but rinsing them after cooking lowers their gas-forming potential.) Always rinse canned beans and chickpeas; combining cooked legumes with an acidic food may reduce gas production. Some herbs, especially lemon balm, fennel, and caraway, help prevent flatulence in some people. Beano tablets can often help reduce gas.

LEMONS

BENEFITS
- *An excellent source of vitamin C.*
- *A low-calorie alternative to oil dressings.*
- *May relieve dry mouth.*

DRAWBACKS
- *High acidity can erode tooth enamel.*
- *The peel contains an irritating oil.*
- *May be sprayed with a fungicide.*

Ideal for flavoring everything from fish and vegetables to tea, lemons are one of the most widely used of all citrus fruits. They are rarely consumed as is, however, because of their puckering tartness.

Sweetened, diluted, and chilled, fresh lemon juice is an old-fashioned summer thirst quencher. It's also an excellent source of vitamin C; the juice of a medium lemon has more than 30mg of vitamin C, or more than 75 percent of the Recommended Nutrient Intake (RNI). To get the most juice, place a lemon in warm water before squeezing.

Lemon juice improves the flavor of many vegetables, especially those that contain sulfur compounds, such as broccoli. It's also a nonfat alternative to butter, sauces, and oil dressings.

A tablespoon of lemon juice in a cup of honey-sweetened hot water is a popular sore throat remedy. Licking a lemon or sipping unsweetened diluted lemon juice can stimulate saliva flow in people who have a dry mouth. This remedy should be used in moderation, however, since the high acidity of plain lemon can damage tooth enamel.

Many recipes call for fresh lemon zest, which is the grated outer peel. But because lemons are often sprayed with fungicides to retard mold growth and pesticides to kill insects, wash them thoroughly before grating the peel. Select lemons that have not been waxed, (wax may seal in fungicides). Lemon peels contain limonene, an oil that can irritate the skin in susceptible persons.

LETTUCE AND OTHER SALAD GREENS

BENEFITS
- *Low in calories and high in fiber.*
- *Some varieties are high in beta carotene, folate, vitamin C, calcium, iron, and potassium.*

DRAWBACKS
- *Often eaten with large amounts of oily or high-fat creamy dressings.*

A green salad is often part of a healthy dinner, and although many vegetables may be used in it, lettuce is by far the most popular ingredient. According to government statistics, lettuce is the second most popular vegetable sold in supermarkets, topped only by potatoes. In fact, Canadians now consume an average of 20 pounds of lettuce a year. Two basic reasons account for its popularity: health-conscious people are consuming more fruits and vegetables; and low-cost lettuce and other fresh salad greens are now available year-round, thanks to modern refrigeration and food transportation.

Weight watchers are especially partial to salads—they are low in calories yet filling, since they are high in fiber. Unfortunately, a large green salad that contains only 50 calories can quickly become more fattening than a steak if it's drowned in a creamy high-fat dressing. There are, however, many tasty low-fat alternative dressings—herb vinegar mixed with a little olive oil, a sprinkling of herbs and lemon juice, or nonfat yogurt combined with garlic, chopped parsley, and lemon juice.

GOOD NUTRITION

Some types of lettuce and other salad greens contain high amounts of beta carotene, folate, vitamin C, calcium, iron, and potassium, but the amounts vary considerably from one variety to another. In general, those with dark green or other deeply colored leaves have more beta carotene and vitamin C than the paler varieties. Romaine and Boston lettuce, for example, have three times as much vitamin C and much more beta carotene than iceberg lettuce.

Such salad greens as arugula, chicory, escarole, mâche, and watercress are all more nutritious than lettuce; many people also find them more flavorful, and they are becoming readily available in restaurants and markets. Some, such as chicory, escarole, and WATERCRESS, are slightly bitter, yet they provide an interesting flavor and texture contrast when added to a salad of lettuce and other types of greens.

Arugula, a member of the same plant family as broccoli, cabbage, and other cruciferous vegetables, has a tangy, peppery flavor when grown during the cool spring and fall months, and a stronger, mustardlike taste if harvested during the summer. This is one of the most nutritious of all salad greens: 1 cup provides 2mg of beta carotene, 45mg of vitamin C, 150mg of calcium, and 0.5mg of iron—all in a serving that has only 12 calories! Watercress, another cruciferous vegetable, is also a nutritional winner: 1 cup contains a mere 5 calories, yet it provides 1.5mg of beta carotene, 15mg of vitamin C, 60mg of calcium, and 0.5mg of iron. Deeply colored lettuces and greens are also high in BIOFLAVONOIDS, plant pigments known to work with vitamin C and other ANTIOXIDANTS to prevent cancer-causing cell damage.

Lettuce and other greens can be mixed or combined with a broad spectrum of raw fruits or vegetables, cold pasta, or chunks of chicken or tuna to make a low-calorie, highly nutritious main dish. Raw SPINACH is often used as a salad green; although cooking makes some of its nutrients a bit easier to absorb, a spinach salad still provides good amounts of beta carotene, folate, vitamin C, calcium, and iron.

TYPES OF GREENS

There are dozens of different varieties of lettuce and salad greens; some of the more familiar are listed below.

Arugula, which resembles dandelion greens, is strongly flavored and tastes best when grown in cool temperatures.

Belgian endive, a slightly bitter relative of chicory, is grown under a soil cover to produce a small head of light yellow or white leaves. It adds an interesting texture and flavor to salads; it can be braised or steamed and served hot.

Butterhead, which includes Boston and bibb lettuces, forms loosely packed heads of tender, mildly flavored leaves.

Chicory and **escarole** are related greens with a somewhat bitter taste. They are nutritious but not widely used because of their assertive flavors.

Iceberg, a crisp, tightly packed head lettuce, is the most widely consumed salad ingredient in Canada, but it provides less nutrition than most other varieties of lettuce and greens.

Looseleaf includes green and red oak and green and red leaf lettuces, as well as other types that do not form heads.

Mâche, or lamb's lettuce, has small, delicate leaves. This expensive green is often sold in gourmet shops.

Romaine has long, crisp, dark green leaves that form a loose head. Also called cos lettuce, it is used to make Caesar and similar salads.

Watercress grows in cold streambeds in the late winter and early spring; it has a sharp flavor and is used mostly as a garnish or in soups.

MIXED SALAD. *The many varieties of lettuces and other salad greens include (clockwise from upper right) romaine, red leaf, watercress, curly endive, mâche, iceberg, radicchio, arugula, Belgian endive, escarole, and spinach.*

LIMES

BENEFITS
- *An excellent source of vitamin C.*
- *Can be used to flavor and tenderize meat, poultry, and fish.*

DRAWBACKS
- *Peels contain psoralens, which increase sun sensitivity.*

In the mid-1700s James Lind, a Scottish naval surgeon, discovered that drinking the juice of limes and lemons prevented scurvy, the scourge of sailors on long voyages. Soon British ships carried ample stores of the fruits, earning their sailors the nickname "limey." It was later learned that vitamin C deficiency causes scurvy, and that limes are very high in this essential nutrient.

Four ounces of lime juice has 30mg of vitamin C, or three-quarters of the Recommended Nutrient Intake (RNI). Limes are high in BIOFLAVONOIDS and other ANTIOXIDANTS, which help protect against cancer and other diseases.

Like lemons, their somewhat more sour cousins, limes are useful as flavoring agents. However, unlike lemons, limes do not impart a distinctive taste of their own when used as a cooking ingredient; instead, they tenderize and heighten the flavors of other foods, especially fish and poultry. Lime juice can also be used as a salt substitute for meat and fish dishes. A sprinkling of lime juice over a fruit salad prevents discoloration.

Lime peels contain psoralens, chemicals that make the skin sensitive to the sun; thus, care should be taken to minimize skin contact with lime peels. Cut away the peels before squeezing the fruit so that the citrus oil containing the psoralens doesn't get into the juice.

LIVER DISORDERS

EAT PLENTY OF
- *Fish, dark green vegetables, beans, and vegetable oils for omega-3 fatty acids.*
- *Fresh fruits and vegetables for vitamins and minerals.*
- *Small meals and snacks, if they are more appealing than large meals.*
- *Protein from plant sources, such as a combination of legumes and grains (but keep overall protein intake low).*

CUT DOWN ON
- *Proteins from animal sources.*

AVOID
- *Alcohol in all forms.*
- *Saturated fats.*

The liver, located in the upper right abdomen and protected by the ribs, performs thousands of vital chemical and metabolic functions—among them, the storage of fat-soluble vitamins, iron and other minerals, and glycogen for future needs. It manufactures cholesterol, amino acids, and other essential compounds, removes waste substances from the blood, detoxifies alcohol and environmental chemicals, and metabolizes most medications.

Amazingly, our bodies can continue to function when only one-quarter of the liver is healthy enough to operate. Unlike most other organs, even after severe damage, the liver can regenerate itself by growing new cells. When severely diseased or subjected to excessive abuse, however, the liver will fail—often with fatal results.

Liver diseases are common, but experts feel that many cases could be prevented by careful attention to diet and hygiene. The most common disorders are hepatitis (usually caused by a virus spread by sewage contamination or direct contact with infected body fluids), CIRRHOSIS, and liver cancer. The risk of liver cancer is higher in those who have cirrhosis or who have had certain types of viral hepatitis; but more often, the liver is the site of secondary (metastatic) cancers spread from other organs. Symptoms are often not felt until the disease is advanced. The most recognized symptom of liver disease is JAUNDICE, the yellowing of the skin and the whites of the eyes, caused by a buildup of bile pigments (bilirubin) in the skin.

People with liver disease are often deficient in the water-soluble vitamins, such as folate, niacin, and thiamine, as well as the fat-soluble vitamins A and D. In industrialized countries with abundant food, vitamin deficiencies are most common among alcoholics, who often substitute alcohol for food. Even when food intake is maintained, alcohol places undue demands on the liver, which must preempt detoxifying it over its other metabolic functions. Liver disease is also linked with problems in metabolizing carbohydrates.

FOOD FOR THE LIVER

The diet of a person recovering from a liver disorder should place the least burden on the organ. People with liver problems often have a poor appetite and find it easier to eat frequent, nutritious snacks rather than full meals.

Omega-3 fatty acids seem to facilitate the processing of fats in the liver; a diet rich in these nutrients lowers the rate at which the liver manufactures triglycerides, which is beneficial for people with circulatory and heart problems. These fatty acids are found in salmon and other oily fish, legumes, wheat germ, flaxseed and canola oils.

The total protein intake should be low: about 60g (2 ounces) a day for an average-size person. Proteins from legumes and grains are preferable to those from animal sources, which are high in saturated fat. Liver disease may cause a thinning of the bones (OSTEOPOROSIS) if stores of vitamin D, which helps to metabolize calcium, are depleted; such cases may require calcium and vitamin D supplements. For the most part, however, vitamins and minerals should be provided within the diet; supplements can upset the nutritional balance and, in the case of excessive iron, can cause severe liver damage.

The liver should not be taxed with fatty foods and snacks that are hard to digest. Alcohol should be avoided until complete recovery; in some cases, however, it must be eliminated for life.

LUNG DISORDERS

CONSUME PLENTY OF
- *Nonalcoholic fluids to help thin mucus.*
- *Fresh fruits and vegetables for beta carotene and vitamin C.*
- *Nuts, seeds, eggs, and vegetable oils for vitamin E.*
- *Oily fish for omega-3 fatty acids.*
- *Lean meat, oysters, yogurt, and whole-grain products for zinc.*

CUT DOWN ON
- *Foods that cause bloating and gas.*

AVOID
- *Smoking and exposure to secondhand smoke and other air pollutants.*
- *Alcohol.*

Among our leading causes of sickness, disability, and death, lung disorders range from usually minor infections, such as COLDS AND FLU, to chronic diseases, such as ASTHMA. Any condition that affects the passage of air to and from the lungs should always be taken seriously. The onset of respiratory symptoms is sufficient cause to see your doctor. The following are some of the more common lung disorders.

BRONCHITIS

Difficulty breathing, a relentless cough, and production of thick mucus, or phlegm, are the characteristic symptoms of bronchitis—an inflammation of the bronchi, or branching tubes, that carry air to and from the lungs. There may also be a low-grade fever and a burning sensation in the chest. Acute bronchitis, often a complication of a severe cold, flu, or other infection of the upper respiratory tract, may require antibiotic treatment, but it usually goes away in a week or two.

Chronic bronchitis is an extremely serious problem that develops when the bronchial tubes are irritated over a long period of time. Cigarette smoking is by far the most common cause, although exposure to air pollution and occupational dusts and chemicals may also be involved. Whatever the cause, the tubes become thickened, a mucus-producing cough is present almost all of the time, and air flow to the lungs is impaired. This creates an ideal breeding ground for infection and sets the stage for progressive lung damage.

EMPHYSEMA

Also known as chronic obstructive pulmonary disease, or COPD, emphysema afflicts about 2.1 million North Americans. It develops over a period of years, often as a consequence of smoking or chronic bronchitis. As the disease worsens, the air sacs, or alveoli, lose their elasticity and fill with stale air, leading to an increased shortness of breath and a distended, barrel-shaped chest.

PNEUMONIA

There are many different types of pneumonia, but the symptoms generally include a cough with a great deal of

AROMATHERAPY

A fragrant and soothing means of relieving lung problems is to inhale the steam from a bowl of hot water that contains a few drops of highly concentrated essential oils. A combination of eucalyptus, thyme, pine, and lavender oils is often recommended to ease bronchitis. Eucalyptus oil is particularly good for relieving the feeling of congestion and may be helpful to people with emphysema. Peppermint oil may also be added to hot water to relieve bronchial symptoms.

sputum, fever, chills, and chest pain. Pneumonia's causes include viruses, bacteria, fungi, parasites, and exposure of lung tissue to toxic substances. AIDS patients often develop *Pneumocystis carinii,* a rare type that strikes people with weakened immunity. One common bacterial type, pneumococcal pneumonia, can be prevented by a vaccine, which is recommended for everyone over 65 and for anyone over the age of 2 who has a chronic disease that increases their risk for pneumonia.

HELPFUL FOODS

A nutritious and well-balanced diet can help prevent or reduce the severity of bronchitis, pneumonia, and other lung infections because people who are in good health are more likely to fight off the underlying causes.

During any respiratory infection, adequate fluids are especially important because they help to thin mucus and make breathing easier. Physicians generally recommend that their patients drink at least six to eight glasses of non-alcoholic fluids a day. Although chicken broth and other warm fluids are particularly helpful in thinning mucus, cold fluids are also useful.

ANTIOXIDANTS help protect delicate lung tissue from the cellular damage caused by free radicals, unstable molecules that are released when the body uses oxygen. Important antioxidants are vitamins A, C, E, and beta carotene, which the human body converts to vitamin A. Vitamins A and C are also necessary to build and repair epithelial tissues, which line the lungs, bronchi, and other parts of the respiratory system; the tissues act as a barrier against bacteria. In addition, these vitamins are essential to building an immunity against lung disease. A healthful balanced diet that provides ample fresh fruits and vegetables, particularly those that are yellow, orange, and dark green, will provide reasonable amounts of vitamins A and C.

Vitamin E, along with omega-3 fatty acids, helps to reduce inflammation. Good sources of vitamin E include whole grains, vegetable oils, fortified cereals, poultry, seafood, and eggs. Salmon, sardines, and other oily fish are all rich sources of omega-3 fatty acids.

Zinc is important for boosting immunity, especially against upper respiratory infections. It is found in many foods, especially lean meat, oysters, yogurt, and whole-grain products.

People with emphysema generally feel better if they eat smaller, more frequent meals. Consuming too much at one time can increase the volume in

HOT AND STEAMY.
Chicken broth, herbal tea, and other warm liquids are just what the doctor ordered to help ease lung congestion.

the stomach and crowd the already distended lungs. Cut down on fried and other fatty foods. Fats remain in the stomach longer because they require more time to digest; thus, the stomach may crowd the lungs longer than when filled with other foods. Anything that causes gas and bloating should also be avoided; common offenders include beans and other legumes, cabbage, Brussels sprouts, broccoli, and onions. The volume of food in the stomach can be reduced by taking liquids an hour before eating and an hour afterward, rather than with your meals.

Some of the medications used to treat lung disorders can cause a loss of appetite. Ask your doctor about taking medicines right after eating. Make your meals enticing and don't rush; have small servings and eat slowly. Sharing a meal with a friend can also help improve your appetite. If you simply can't eat enough solid foods, JUICING or high-calorie liquids may be a solution.

LIFESTYLE HABITS

Smoking is by far the leading cause of chronic respiratory disorders, including chronic bronchitis, emphysema, and lung cancer. If you smoke, make every effort to stop. Also try to avoid second-hand smoke and air pollutants. If your job exposes you to harmful dusts or chemical gases, be sure to wear the proper protective masks.

Alcohol lowers immunity and should be avoided during any infection. Because chronic bronchitis and emphysema predispose a person to develop lung infections, it's a good idea to abstain from all alcoholic beverages.

LUPUS

CONSUME PLENTY OF
- *Grapefruit, broccoli, cabbage, and kale for antioxidants and bioflavonoids.*
- *Whole-grain products for vitamin E, zinc, and selenium.*
- *Plant seed oils, which are high in gamma linolenic acid.*

CUT DOWN ON
- *Protein, especially from meat sources.*

AVOID
- *Alfalfa in all forms.*
- *Fats, especially animal fats.*
- *Celery, parsnips, parsley, lemons, limes, and figs if you are sun sensitive.*

Also known as systemic lupus erythematosus (or SLE), lupus is a chronic autoimmune disease. Although arthritic joint pain, skin rashes, debilitating fatigue, and DRY MOUTH are the most common symptoms, it can also damage organs throughout the body, particularly the kidneys. Lupus strikes women about 10 times as often as men. While it is a mild disease for many people, with symptoms coming and going without any clear reason, lupus can be serious and even life threatening.

Lupus is believed to be caused by a genetic predisposition that is triggered by environmental factors, such as a virus; it may be worsened by other factors, such as sun exposure, infection, stress, and certain foods and drugs.

While lupus cannot be cured, it can usually be controlled with medical therapy and a careful lifestyle. But because lupus is such a variable disease, there is no one treatment regimen that helps everyone. The patient and physician may have to try different approaches over a period of months to find one that seems to work. Therapy often requires taking a nonsteroidal anti-inflammatory drug (NSAID) to suppress the inflammation that causes the pain of lupus, and hydroxychloroquine (a drug long used to fight malaria), which can increase resistance to sun exposure and help prevent lupus rashes and joint pain. For more severe problems, steroids or other immunosuppressive drugs may be prescribed.

HARMFUL FOODS

Alfalfa in any form, including sprouts, worsens lupus symptoms in many patients; other legumes may have a similar effect. Mushrooms and some smoked foods may also cause problems for lupus sufferers.

If you are one of the majority of lupus patients whose disease is worsened by exposure to the sun or unshielded fluorescent light, avoid or limit foods containing psoralens, such as celery, parsnips, parsley, lemons, and limes, which heighten photosensitivity.

Many lupus patients note an improvement after they decrease the consumption of fatty high-protein foods, especially animal products. Some experts recommend trying a modified vegetarian diet that allows eggs, skim milk, and other low-fat dairy products.

HELPFUL FOODS

Increase your intake of complex carbohydrates, such as whole grains and cereals, fruits, and vegetables. These foods are high in the ANTIOXIDANT vitamins and minerals—vitamins C and E, beta carotene, zinc, and selenium. These are beneficial not only for lupus itself but also protect against HEART DISEASE. People with lupus tend to have high blood cholesterol levels, which may be worsened by steroid medications. High-dose vitamin E supplements, up to 1,600 I.U. a day, have been shown to help reduce arthritic inflammation.

Broccoli and other cruciferous vegetables contain indoles that alter the metabolism of estrogen in a way that has a positive impact on lupus. Fresh citrus fruits, especially grapefruits, are

Case Study

When Linda, a 24-year-old university student, developed unremitting fatigue, swollen and painful joints, and a rash on her face, her doctor suspected rheumatoid arthritis or Lyme disease. After diagnostic tests ruled out these disorders, Linda was referred to a rheumatologist, who diagnosed lupus. This doctor advised Linda to alter her lifestyle by reducing stress as much as possible, making sure she got plenty of rest, and avoiding certain foods and exposure to the sun. He also prescribed a nonsteroidal anti-inflammatory drug to ease her joint pain and a low-dose steroid in hopes of achieving a remission.

Within 6 months Linda was feeling much better, so the doctor started weaning her off the steroids. Then one day she awakened with aching joints and felt so tired that she was unable to go to class. Careful questioning revealed that Linda had gone to a health-food restaurant the day before and had eaten a large salad that included alfalfa sprouts. She had forgotten that alfalfa was on her list of foods to avoid. Within a week, her symptoms had subsided, and Linda vowed to be more careful about her diet to prevent the recurrence of symptoms in the future.

high in BIOFLAVONOIDS that seem to help lupus patients. Because most lupus patients need to avoid exposure to the sun, they should make sure their diet provides adequate vitamin D. Good sources include fortified cereals, eggs, and moderate amounts of salmon and other fatty fish.

Increase your intake of gamma linolenic acid (GLA), which is found in such plant seeds as evening primrose, borage, black currants, flax, and hemp. These essential fatty acids replace the arachidonic acids found in animal fats as building blocks for prostaglandins, producing a less inflammatory environment in the human body.

DRUGS AND DIET

If you take aspirin or other NSAIDs, always take them with meals to help reduce the risk of stomach irritation. If you are taking corticosteroids, avoid salt; it will increase your water retention and contribute to steroid-induced high BLOOD PRESSURE. Because steroids increase your risk of OSTEOPOROSIS, consume plenty of calcium-rich dark green leafy vegetables, citrus fruits, and skim milk; you may still need supplements, however, to get adequate calcium and the vitamin D necessary to help your body use it properly. If you are taking cyclosporine, a powerful immune system suppressor, do not consume grapefruits or grapefruit juice; although these are generally recommended for most lupus patients, they can dramatically increase the body's ability to absorb cyclosporine, leading to severe toxicity. If you take methotrexate, ask your doctor about supplements of folate, a B vitamin that can reduce its side effects.

MALNUTRITION AND DIETARY DEFICIENCIES

*In a country where overeating and obesity are the
most common nutritional problems, it's easy to overlook
the fact that some people are actually malnourished.*

When it comes to malnutrition, most people envision famine-stricken regions in Africa, Asia, and other far-off underdeveloped areas. But even in affluent industrialized countries that have an unprecedented abundance of food, some people are malnourished. The most vulnerable groups are the elderly, the homeless and other economically disadvantaged people, alcoholics, and those suffering from CANCER, AIDS, and other diseases that interfere with nutrition.

In some cases, malnutrition occurs among otherwise healthy people who adopt a very restricted diet, typically to lose weight. Many FAD DIETS, if followed for any length of time, can lead to serious nutritional deficiencies. Strict VEGETARIAN DIETS that eliminate all animal products can still manage to provide complete protein from a combination of grains and legumes. However, getting enough vitamin B$_{12}$, calcium, iron, and zinc may be more difficult, because the best sources generally come from animal products. In such cases, supplements or fortified foods can be helpful.

Young children must depend upon others to provide them with adequate nutrition, which is especially critical during the early years. Undernourished babies simply do not thrive and grow at a normal rate. When offered an adequate amount of food, most babies and young children will set their own limits. But some misguided par-

ents put a baby on a low-fat diet to prevent obesity, not realizing that an infant needs extra fat and calories to grow and develop normally. Malnourished children also have difficulty concentrating and do poorly in school.

Many parents worry that adolescents who live mostly on fast foods and snacks will develop nutritional deficiencies. Although this usually does not happen, youngsters who eat a diet of high-fat salty or sugary foods risk malnutrition as well as later health

problems, including HEART DISEASE, high BLOOD PRESSURE, adult-onset DIABETES, and OBESITY.

USING THE RNIs

The Recommended Nutrient Intakes (RNIs) for most of the essential vitamins and minerals required by our bodies were established by the Nutrition Research Division of Health Canada. The RNIs take into account age and gender, and are based on the average height and weight for each group.

Case Study

Sarah began experimenting with vegetarian diets at the age of 13, first eliminating red meat, then poultry and fish, and finally, by the time she entered college, she had eliminated all animal products. She also prided herself on her athletic ability and had no difficulty making the college track team. So Sarah was shocked when a team physical examination found that she had mild iron-deficiency anemia. The doctor explained that her low-iron diet, vigorous exercise program, and heavy menstrual periods had worked in concert to reduce her iron reserves—a situation that was likely to get worse unless some changes were instituted.

A dietitian recommended a multivitamin that contained iron, and she advised her to eat more iron-fortified breads and cereals. The dietitian also

recommended that she invest in a cast-iron pot and use it when cooking tomatoes and other acidic foods. Luckily, Sarah had access to a kitchen, so she could follow this advice. In 2 months her iron levels were back to normal.

222

Establishing an RNI begins with a consideration of the minimal amount the body needs to absorb in order to prevent deficiency. Then the amount of a nutrient a person must eat to ensure that the minimum is absorbed is calculated and a safety margin is built in. In general, the RNIs provide several times what the body needs to prevent deficiencies, but there is conflicting opinion about whether current RNIs are sufficient to optimize health.

While the RNIs specify daily intake, they are actually based on an average intake over different periods of time. Many people mistakenly think that it's necessary to consume 100 percent of all the RNIs each day; what's really more important, however, is to eat a varied diet that, when averaged out over a week or so, will provide the recommended amounts.

VITAMIN DEFICIENCIES

Normally, the body builds the largest stores of the fat-soluble vitamins A, D, E, and K, which are not removed in appreciable amounts by the kidneys. There are smaller reserves of most of the water-soluble vitamins—C and the B-complex group—because excess amounts are excreted in the urine. Even so, depending upon the particular nutrient, it takes weeks or even months or years to develop a deficiency disorder. In one study, for example, it took more than 3 months of eliminating all sources of vitamin A and its beta carotene precursor from the diets of a group of volunteers for deficiency symptoms to develop.

Most of the vitamin deficiencies in Canada are actually due to problems of absorption rather than inadequate diets. People who are unable to digest fats may become deficient in the fat-soluble vitamins; less commonly, a person on a very low fat diet may not absorb adequate amounts of vitamins A, D, E, and K. Symptoms include night blindness and dry skin from vi-

tamin A deficiency; rickets and other bone abnormalities from insufficient vitamin D; and bleeding problems from too little vitamin K. Vitamin B_{12} is another example in which absorption problems are a greater factor in deficiency than diet. It may take 20 years or longer for a strict vegetarian who eats no animal products (the major source of B_{12}) to develop anemia and

other signs of deficiency. But those who lack intrinsic factor, a substance produced in the stomach, are unable to absorb the vitamin and develop pernicious anemia within a few months.

Many medications interfere with the absorption of vitamins; one of the most common examples involves birth control pills, which reduce the body's ability to use folate and vitamin B_6. A woman is unlikely to develop symptoms of deficiency herself, but low folate reserves should be replenished before she attempts to conceive.

ALCOHOL also interferes with the absorption of many vitamins, especially thiamine and others in the B group. In fact, ALCOHOLISM is one of the most common underlying causes of malnutrition in Canada.

MINERAL DEFICIENCIES

Dietary factors usually play more of a role in mineral deficiencies than they do in vitamin-related problems. OSTEOPOROSIS, for example, is perhaps the most common deficiency disease in industrialized countries. Although many factors, including aging and a genetic predisposition, contribute to this debilitating loss of bone minerals, calcium deficiency is a major cause. Adolescent girls and young women who avoid milk and milk products are setting themselves up for osteoporosis in their later years, because they are depriving themselves of calcium.

Most cases of iron-deficiency ANEMIA are a result of chronic blood loss; however, nutrition can play a role in some. Young women who follow a VEGETARIAN DIET are the most vulnerable. In addition to not getting enough iron from the diet, they lose some iron each month during menstruation. Excessive dietary FIBER also reduces the absorption of iron, zinc, and other important minerals. Antacids and high-dose supplements of calcium can lead to imbalances and possible deficiencies of other minerals.

SIGNS OF DIETARY DEFICIENCIES

Although uncommon, the following symptoms of nutritional deficiency can develop in some instances.

SYMPTOM	NUTRIENT LACKING
Anemia	Iron, vitamin B_{12}, folate
Bleeding gums	Vitamin C, folate
Cardiac arrhythmias	Potassium, magnesium
Clotting abnormalities	Vitamin K
Dental decay	Fluoride
Dry, rough skin	Vitamin A
Goiter	Iodine
Growth problems	Zinc
Healing abnormalities	Vitamin C, zinc
Light sensitivity	Riboflavin
Liver damage	Vitamin K
Mental confusion, mood disorders	B vitamins
Mouth sores, inflammation	Riboflavin, niacin, vitamin B_6
Muscle cramps, wasting	Thiamine
Muscle weakness	Magnesium, potassium
Nerve damage	Vitamin B_{12}
Night blindness	Vitamin A
Psychosis	Thiamine
Reduced immunity	Vitamins A and C, zinc
Rickets; bone deformities	Vitamin D, calcium

MALTED MILK, MALT EXTRACTS

BENEFITS
- *Good food for convalescents.*
- *Sugar provides quick energy.*
- *Malt extract is a good source of niacin, iron, and potassium.*
- *Warm malted milk promotes sleep.*

DRAWBACKS
- *Sugar content promotes cavities.*

Malt is a sweet powder made from barley that has been germinated and then dried after the sprouts are removed. Malt extract—a syrup made by mixing the powder with water—was once given to children as a "blood-fortifying tonic" because of its high iron content. The "tonic," which is also rich in niacin and other B vitamins, potassium, and magnesium, is still used in some European countries. In North America it is used mostly for flavoring food.

While malted milk has lost some of its popularity, it is still regarded as a good drink for convalescents because it is easy to digest. In addition, many malted milk powders are fortified with extra protein, iron, and other nutrients. When added to milk, the drink becomes a nearly complete food, rich in calcium, potassium, iron, and other minerals. It also contains some of the B vitamins that occur naturally in barley, and may be fortified with others.

Hot malted milk is a favorite sleep-inducing drink for insomniacs. Milk by itself is high in tryptophan, an amino acid that increases the production of serotonin, a brain chemical that promotes sleep. This effect is increased by the added sugar, in this case maltose, which also raises serotonin levels.

The high sugar content of malt extracts and malted milk can promote dental decay, so it's a good idea to brush your teeth after consuming either one.

FRUIT OF THE TROPICS. *A favorite fruit in India and other tropical countries, the mango is becoming increasingly popular in Canada for its unique flavor.*

MANGOES

BENEFITS
- *An excellent source of beta carotene and vitamin C.*
- *A good source of vitamin E and niacin.*
- *High in potassium and iron.*
- *Low in calories, high in fiber.*

DRAWBACKS
- *Can be messy to eat.*

Mangoes are regarded as a somewhat exotic fruit in Canada. This view is changing, however, as more of the fruit is being imported from the U.S., Hawaii, Mexico, and Central America. The soft, juicy flesh of a ripe mango makes it difficult to peel and messy to eat, but those who persevere say it's worth the effort (see How to Eat a Mango, facing page).

NUTRITIONAL VALUE

Like other orange or deep yellow fruits, mangoes are exceptionally high in beta carotene, which the body converts to vitamin A. One medium-size (8-ounce) mango has 135 calories and provides almost twice the adult Recommended Nutrient Intake (RNI) of vitamin A, and more than 100 percent of the RNI for vitamin C. Mangoes are a good source of vitamin E, potassium, and iron; they are also high in pectin, a soluble fiber that is important in controlling blood cholesterol.

There are hundreds of different varieties of mangoes, ranging in size from a few ounces to more than 4 pounds, but most of those sold in Canada are 8 to 12 ounces. Mangoes are usually picked and shipped while still somewhat green, but the skin should be turning yellow, becoming more orange or red as the fruit ripens.

When buying a mango, look for one with flesh that yields slightly when gently pressed and with an orange or reddish skin. Large dark spots may mean that the flesh is bruised. (If the skin is completely green, the fruit may not ripen; a fruit that is past its prime will have shriveled skin.) A flowery fragrance indicates that the mango is ripe and flavorful.

If you place an unripe mango in a paper bag in a cool location, it will ripen in 2 or 3 days. (Don't put it in a sunny spot; this can spoil the flavor.) Ripe mangoes should be eaten as soon as possible, but they will keep for 2 or 3 days in the refrigerator.

HOW TO EAT A MANGO

Some mango lovers advise eating the ripe fruit in the shower, where you can enjoy it without worrying about the juice running down your chin and onto your clothes. Here's a more practical approach. Make two vertical slices—one on each side of the pit—and use a sharp paring knife to remove one half of the fruit from the large seed. You can then cut the flesh into slices and remove the peel from each slice, one by one. Then cut around the pit of the remaining half, and again, slice and peel the fruit.

MAYONNAISE

BENEFITS
- *A good source of vitamin E, depending upon the type of oil used.*
- *Contains small amounts of vitamin A and some minerals.*

DRAWBACKS
- *Very high in fat and calories.*
- *May trigger an allergic reaction in people sensitive to eggs and molds.*
- *May contain gluten, which should be avoided by those with celiac disease.*
- *Raw eggs used in fresh mayonnaise may pose a risk of salmonella.*
- *Egg mayonnaise is high in cholesterol.*

The rich flavor and creamy texture of mayonnaise accounts for its wide popularity as a sandwich spread and salad dressing. There are several ways to make mayonnaise, but all involve the same basic ingredients—vegetable oil, eggs, and vinegar, lemon juice, or another acidic liquid—whipped together to form a semisolid spread. Egg yolks act as the emulsifying ingredient that allows the oil and vinegar or lemon juice to blend. Mustard, salt, sugar, and other seasonings may be added to supply extra flavor.

Most types of mayonnaise are high in vitamin E, yielding about 30 percent of the adult Recommended Nutrient Intake (RNI). The precise amount varies, however, according to the type of oil used; those made with sunflower, cottonseed, and safflower oils are highest in this ANTIOXIDANT nutrient. (In general, labels of commercial mayonnaise do not specify the type of oil used.) The eggs do contribute protein and some minerals, but the amounts are negligible considering the number of calories per serving. A tablespoon of mayonnaise provides about 100 calories, about the same amount found in a tablespoon of butter or margarine. The yolks add dietary CHOLESTEROL, which should be

minimized by anyone with high blood cholesterol, ATHEROSCLEROSIS, or HEART DISEASE.

If you're concerned about the type of oil used, you can make your own mayonnaise at home. Most recipes call for olive oil, which is largely monounsaturated fat, although polyunsaturated oils, such as corn or safflower, can be substituted for a lighter flavor. The raw eggs used in homemade mayonnaise are a potential source of salmonella; this risk can be avoided by using a pasteurized egg substitute. Fresh mayonnaise should be used within 2 or 3 days. Even then, it can become a source of food poisoning if allowed to stand at room temperature for more than an hour. Commercial mayonnaise is safer, because its high vinegar content and antioxidant preservatives discourage the growth of disease-causing organisms.

"LITE" VARIETIES

Mayonnaise-type salad dressings contain less fat and about one-third of the calories found in regular mayonnaise. Although similar in texture and appearance, the salad dressings have a more acidic flavor, which can be tempered by adding a small amount of yogurt or whipped nonfat cottage cheese.

Low-fat, cholesterol-free, and nonfat mayonnaise substitutes are available. The low-fat versions substitute air, water, starches, and other fillers for some of the oil; nonfat varieties may be made with tofu, yogurt, and other such ingredients. A homemade recipe calls for tofu, egg whites, lemon juice, salt, mustard, and a little bit of olive oil.

ALLERGY ALERT

Anyone allergic to eggs should avoid mayonnaise. The vinegar may trigger an allergic reaction in people sensitive to molds. Most commercial types of mayonnaise and salad dressing have fillers made of gluten, which should be avoided by anyone with CELIAC DISEASE.

MEDICINE-FOOD INTERACTIONS: HIDDEN DANGERS

Most people know that certain drugs don't mix with each other; but there are many foods that interact with medicines too—sometimes with deadly results.

Any medication that is taken by mouth travels through the digestive system in much the same way as food does. So it stands to reason that when a drug is mixed with a food, each can alter the way the body metabolizes the other. Some drugs interfere with the body's ability to absorb nutrients; similarly, foods can lessen or increase the impact of a drug. Medications may affect the digestive system itself; for example, aspirin and antibiotics are among the many that irritate the stomach and intestines. Others, such as insulin and similar protein-based hormones, are destroyed if they pass through the digestive system; therefore, they must be injected directly into the bloodstream. Still others are given by injection or absorbed into the bloodstream through a skin patch to bypass being metabolized by the liver, thereby reducing the risk of some side effects.

Mixing monoamine oxidase (MAO) inhibitors—a class of medications used to treat depression—with foods high in tyramine, an amino acid, produces one of the most dramatic and dangerous food-drug interactions. Symptoms, which can occur within minutes of ingesting such foods while taking an MAO inhibitor, include a rapid rise in blood pressure, a severe headache, and perhaps collapse and even death. (Foods high in tyramine include aged cheese, chicken liver, Chianti and certain other red wines, yeast extracts, bologna and other processed meats, dried or pickled fish, legumes, soy sauce, ale, and beer.)

While some drugs should be taken between meals when the stomach is empty, many others should be consumed with foods. The composition of the meal, however, may affect the speed with which the medication is absorbed into the body. Griseofulvin, a common antifungal medication, is better absorbed if it's consumed with fatty foods. In contrast, an antibiotic should not be taken with fat, which increases the time the drug is in the stomach and exposed to stomach acids that can reduce its efficacy. Most antibiotics should be taken between meals; for those that are ingested with food, lean meat and poultry are generally good food selections, because protein appears to speed up the metabolism of these medications.

Dietary fiber also affects drug absorption. Pectin and other soluble fibers slow down absorption of the painkiller acetaminophen; bran and other insoluble fibers have a similar effect on digoxin, a major heart medication. The effectiveness of antihypertensive drugs is reduced by eating large amounts of natural licorice or salty foods, both of which promote fluid retention, thereby raising blood pressure. Certain vitamins and minerals impact on medications too. Large amounts of broccoli, spinach, and other green leafy vegetables high in vitamin K, which promotes the formation of blood clots, can counteract the effects of heparin, warfarin, and other drugs given to prevent clotting.

Another situation to consider is that some dietary components increase the risk of side effects. Theophylline, a medication administered to treat asthma, contains xanthines, which are also found in tea, coffee, chocolate, and other sources of caffeine. Consuming large amounts of these substances while taking theophylline increases the risk of drug toxicity.

Alcohol is a drug that interacts with almost every medication, especially antidepressants and other drugs that affect the brain and nervous system. Doctors generally advise that patients abstain from alcohol while taking any medication; this recommendation includes over-the-counter (OTC) drugs.

BENEFICIAL FOODS

Some foods help prevent unwanted drug side effects. Many antihypertensive drugs, for example, deplete the body's reserves of potassium, an electrolyte that maintains the body's fluid balance and is also essential for nerve and muscle function. Thus, people taking diuretics to treat high blood pressure should eat extra bananas, citrus and dried fruits, tomatoes, and other potassium-rich foods to prevent the diuretic from depleting the body's reserves of this essential mineral.

FOODS AND DRUGS THAT DON'T MIX

Before taking any medication, always read the package instructions and ask your doctor or pharmacist about any dietary precautions. In some cases, drugs alter nutritional *needs; in other instances, foods can interfere with how a medication works. The table below details how particular foods can interact with some of the more commonly used drugs.*

DRUGS	EFFECTS AND PRECAUTIONS
ANTIBIOTICS	
Cephalosporins, penicillin	Take on an empty stomach to speed absorption of the drugs.
Erythromycin	Don't take with fruit juice or wine, which decrease the drug's effectiveness.
Sulfa drugs	Increase the risk of vitamin B_{12} deficiency.
Tetracycline	Dairy products reduce the drug's efficacy. Lowers vitamin C absorption.
ANTICONVULSANTS	
Dilantin, phenobarbital	Increase the risk of anemia and nerve problems due to a deficiency of folate and other B vitamins.
ANTIDEPRESSANTS	
Fluoxetine	Reduces appetite and can lead to excessive weight loss.
Lithium	A low-salt diet increases the risk of lithium toxicity; excessive salt reduces drug's efficacy.
MAO inhibitors	Foods high in tyramine (aged cheeses, processed meats, legumes, wine, beer, among others) can bring on a hypertensive crisis.
Tricyclics	Many foods, especially legumes, meat, fish, and foods high in vitamin C, reduce absorption of the drugs.
ANTIHYPERTENSIVES, HEART MEDICATIONS	
ACE inhibitors	Take on an empty stomach to improve the absorption of the drugs.
Alpha blockers	Take with liquid or food to avoid an excessive drop in blood pressure.
Antiarrhythmic drugs	Avoid caffeine, which increases the risk of an irregular heartbeat.
Beta blockers	Take on an empty stomach; food, especially meat, increases the drugs' effects and can cause dizziness and low blood pressure.
Digitalis	Avoid taking with milk and high-fiber foods, which reduce absorption. Increases potassium loss.
Diuretics	Increase the risk of potassium deficiency.
Potassium-sparing diuretics	Unless a doctor advises otherwise, don't take diuretics with potassium supplements or salt substitutes, which can cause potassium overload.
Thiazide diuretics	Increase the reaction to MSG.

DRUGS	EFFECTS AND PRECAUTIONS
ASTHMA DRUGS	
Pseudoephedrine	Avoid caffeine, which increases feelings of anxiety and nervousness.
Theophylline	Charbroiled foods and a high-protein diet reduce absorption. Caffeine increases the risk of drug toxicity.
CHOLESTEROL-LOWERING DRUGS	
Cholestyramine	Increases the excretion of folate and vitamins A, D, E, and K.
Gemfibrozil	Avoid fatty foods, which decrease the drug's efficacy in lowering cholesterol.
HEARTBURN AND ULCER MEDICATIONS	
Antacids	Interfere with the absorption of many minerals; for maximum benefit, take medication 1 hour after eating.
Cimetidine, famotidine, sucralfate	Avoid high-protein foods, caffeine, and other items that increase stomach acidity.
HORMONE PREPARATIONS	
Oral contraceptives	Salty foods increase fluid retention. Drugs reduce the absorption of folate, vitamin B_6, and other nutrients; increase intake of foods high in these nutrients to avoid deficiencies.
Steroids	Salty foods increase fluid retention. Increase intake of foods high in calcium, vitamin K, potassium, and protein to avoid deficiencies.
Thyroid drugs	Iodine-rich foods lower the drug's efficacy.
LAXATIVES	
Mineral oils	Overuse can cause a deficiency of vitamins A, D, E, and K.
PAINKILLERS	
Aspirin and stronger non-steroidal anti-inflammatory drugs	Always take with food to lower the risk of gastrointestinal irritation; avoid taking with alcohol, which increases the risk of bleeding. Frequent use of these drugs lowers the absorption of folate and vitamin C.
Codeine	Increase fiber and water intake to avoid constipation.
SLEEPING PILLS, TRANQUILIZERS	
Benzodiazepines	Never take with alcohol. Caffeine increases anxiety and reduces drugs' efficacy.

MELONS

BENEFITS
- *Sweet and flavorful, yet low in calories.*
- *Yellow varieties are high in vitamin A.*
- *Most are good sources of vitamin C and potassium.*
- *Some are high in pectin, a soluble fiber that helps control blood cholesterol levels.*

DRAWBACKS
- *Selecting a ripe melon is difficult.*

There are many types of melons; among them, cantaloupe, casaba, crenshaw, honeydew, Persian, and watermelon. Although mostly water, melons are very nutritious, providing vitamin A (in the form of beta carotene), vitamin C, potassium, and other minerals.

Cantaloupes and other yellow varieties are especially high in beta carotene, which the human body converts to vitamin A; a 4-ounce slice provides more than 65 percent of the adult Recommended Nutrient Intake (RNI) for this ANTIOXIDANT. Four ounces of cantaloupe also provide about 45mg of vitamin C, more than 100 percent of the RNI, and 320mg of potassium. Honeydews are also high in vitamin C, with about 75 percent of the RNI in a 4-ounce serving, as well as 275mg of potassium.

Many melon varieties are high in BIOFLAVONOIDS, carotenoids, and other plant pigments that help protect against cancer and other diseases. Watermelon, for example, contains lycopene, a carotenoid that is thought to lower the risk of prostate cancer.

Because melons are mostly water, they are very low in calories. A 4-ounce serving of any of the varieties contains only 30 to 35 calories. Although melon flesh is free of strings and other sources of insoluble fiber, it does contain pectin, a soluble fiber that helps keep blood cholesterol levels in check.

HOW TO BUY A MELON
Because melons do not contain starch that converts to sugar, they don't continue to ripen after they are picked from

COOL AND REFRESHING. *Popular varieties of melon include (from left to right): watermelon, honeydew, and small, sweet cantaloupe, gaylia, and charentais.*

the vine; therefore, melons that are harvested before they are fully ripe never achieve their peak flavor. In order to select a vine-ripened melon, check the stem area for a smooth, slightly sunken scar; this indicates that the melon was ripe and easily pulled from its vine. In contrast, if part of the stem still adheres to the scar, the melon was picked while it was still green and not fully ripe.

When purchasing melons, don't be shy about sniffing the fruit to see if it is fully ripe; a ripe melon will have a deep, intense fragrance.

A ripe watermelon should rattle when you shake it, because the seeds loosen as the fruit matures; thumping the melon should produce a slightly hollow sound. Watermelons come in several colors, but in all instances the rind should be firm and smooth, with a yellowish undertone.

228

MENOPAUSE

EAT PLENTY OF
- *Foods high in calcium and vitamin D, such as low-fat dairy products, dark green leafy vegetables, and legumes.*
- *Fiber-rich carbohydrates.*
- *Fresh fruits and vegetables for vitamins and minerals.*
- *Soy products, such as tofu.*

CUT DOWN ON
- *Alcohol and caffeine.*
- *Red meat, which increases calcium excretion.*

AVOID
- *Foods high in fat and sodium.*
- *Smoking.*

As a result of a progressive decline in levels of the hormone estrogen, menstrual periods cease and menopause begins. On average, this happens when a woman is between 45 and 50 years old and concludes by about age 55. Until recently, menopause was regarded not only as an end to a woman's reproductive years but as the beginning of old age. Fortunately, this has changed; today a majority of women in industrialized societies can expect to live more than a third of their lives after menopause with continued productivity.

Months or even years before menstruation stops, the ovaries begin to produce less estrogen, and periods become irregular. When a woman has not menstruated for a full year, she is considered postmenopausal.

Fluctuations in the levels of estrogen may cause hot flashes, night sweats, insomnia, vaginal dryness, leakage of urine, and rapid heartbeat. (Contrary to widespread belief, menopausal women are not more prone to mood swings.) Many women experience menopause with few symptoms, while others are confronted with extreme discomfort.

The important changes at menopause affect both life expectancy and the quality of life. Before menopause a woman's hormones protect her from the heart disease that is more common in men. With menopause that protection is lost, and by about 55 years of age, women die of heart disease at about the same rate as men. In addition, the gradual loss of bone mass that most women experience from 30 years of age onward is drastically accelerated at menopause. Bone loss results in part from the lack of estrogen as well as from inefficient absorption of calcium. A woman may lose 10 to 20 percent of her bone mass in the decade following menopause, with a slower but still significant loss thereafter. This bone thinning, or OSTEOPOROSIS, increases the risk of fractures, with the prospect of permanent disability and pain.

HORMONE REPLACEMENT

Many women choose to counteract some of the effects of estrogen loss with hormone replacement therapy, in which low doses of estrogen and progesterone, another female hormone, are administered. (Estrogen replacement alone raises the risk of uterine cancer; adding progesterone to the regimen prevents this. Progesterone is not needed, however, if a woman has had a hysterectomy to remove her uterus.)

Studies have shown that estrogen replacement can help in two vital areas: it helps to prevent heart disease, and it slows the rate of bone thinning. Recent research indicates that it may also protect against Alzheimer's disease and the increased inability to find the right words that many older women experience. Estrogen also stops early menopause symptoms and restores some of the elasticity to aging tissues.

Hormones can be taken in pill form or absorbed from an unobtrusive skin patch. The periodic bleeding that occurs in the first few months of the therapy disappears as treatment continues. If a woman stops taking the pills or wearing the patch, the effects of hormone replacement fade rapidly.

Postmenopausal osteoporosis can be slowed with a diet rich in calcium and vitamin D, hormone replacement, and weight-bearing exercises. Studies show, however, that hormone replacement doesn't improve bone loss unless treatment is continued for at least 7 years.

Women who have had breast cancer, or who have a very strong family history of breast cancer before menopause, may not be candidates for hormone replacement. Your gynecologist should present all the facts for and against hormone therapy so that you can make up your own mind about it.

EATING RIGHT

Although it is helpful in counteracting some of the effects of menopause, hormone replacement cannot stop aging. A healthy diet and exercise are the keys to enjoying good health at any age.

If you haven't already done so, adapt

HELPFUL FOODS

The foods below are especially useful for women going through menopause or who have completed it.

Dairy products, including milk and cheese, are the best sources of calcium to help prevent osteoporosis.

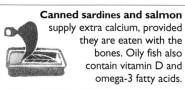

Canned sardines and salmon supply extra calcium, provided they are eaten with the bones. Oily fish also contain vitamin D and omega-3 fatty acids.

Green leafy vegetables, such as broccoli and cabbage, as well as legumes, have essential vitamins, minerals, and fiber needed to prevent weight gain.

Whole-grain products provide fiber as well as B vitamins and minerals.

your diet to follow the Food Guide Rainbow (see p.39), which emphasizes consuming more starchy foods, vegetables, and fruits, and smaller amounts of meat and dairy products. No more than 30 percent of calories should come from fat, with less than 10 percent from saturated animal fats. This type of diet not only makes it easier to fight middle-age spread, it helps protect against disease.

Try to get calcium from low-fat milk and other dairy products, dark green leafy vegetables, and such canned fish as sardines and salmon eaten with the bones. To absorb calcium, the body needs vitamin D, which can be made by the skin after exposure to the sun; dietary sources of this vitamin include fortified milk and margarine, eggs, and fish oils. Zinc and magnesium are also needed to make the best use of calcium and vitamin D; they can be found in whole grains, nuts, beans, fruits, and vegetables.

Estrogens occur naturally in certain plants; in fact, the hormones used to develop oral contraceptives were first ex-

tracted from yams. Not enough is yet known about the effects of dietary estrogen to make recommendations, but good sources are yams and soybeans. Some studies have, however, linked the "easier" menopause of Oriental women with a high consumption of soy products.

Caffeine and alcohol should be used only in moderation. Both of these compounds act as diuretics, which can cause unnecessary loss of calcium and zinc in the urine. Alcohol also dilates the small blood vessels and may trigger hot flashes and flushing of the face and neck.

GOOD HABITS

Women who smoke have lower estrogen levels at all ages than nonsmokers and may enter menopause as much as 5 years earlier. Among its bad effects, nicotine is directly toxic to the ovaries. Its effect on blood vessels may intensify hot flashes. Smoking also increases wrinkling of the skin and aggravates osteoporosis. If you smoke, make every effort to stop—no matter what your age.

Underweight women are at higher risk for osteoporosis because they lack the fat tissue that helps store estrogen and related hormones after menopause. Maintain your ideal weight and keep your shape with exercise. Participate in brisk walking or aerobic workouts to benefit the heart; these also stimulate the brain to release endorphins, chemicals that are natural painkillers and mood enhancers. Whenever possible, exercise outdoors to expose your skin to the ultraviolet sun rays needed to make vitamin D. Don't overdo the exposure, however; a sunscreen with an SPF of 15 or higher protects the skin but doesn't interfere with vitamin D production.

Although it's best to get vitamins and minerals from a healthy diet, many women—especially those with an INTOLERANCE TO MILK—may need to take calcium supplements. Check with your doctor first, and also ask if you should take vitamin D.

MENSTRUAL PROBLEMS

EAT PLENTY OF
- *Iron-rich foods, such as fish and shellfish, legumes, and lamb.*
- *Citrus fruits and vegetables rich in vitamin C to promote iron absorption.*
- *Whole grains, complex carbohydrates, vegetables, and fruits.*

CUT DOWN ON
- *Alcohol and caffeinated drinks.*

AVOID
- *Saturated fats and highly refined foods.*
- *Highly salted foods, which promote fluid retention and bloating.*

Most women in their reproductive years recognize the mild cramps or slight twinge in the lower back as the normal effects of menstruation, a complex physiological process. These effects, shared by women around the world, are not symptoms of any sickness and do not usually interfere with normal activities.

Many women, however, experience discomfort and even temporary disability from symptoms preceding their periods, such as severe cramps and nausea lasting several days. Others have irregular, sparse, or excessive bleeding that can make it difficult to plan activities and can seriously detract from the enjoyment of leisure time.

PREMENSTRUAL SYNDROME
More than 150 symptoms—notably, bloating, irritability, breast tenderness, food cravings, headache, and constipation—have been linked with premenstrual syndrome (PMS), which seems to be caused by hormonal changes during the latter half of the menstrual cycle. For 10 percent of the women who have PMS, the symptoms can cause serious social problems, disrupting work and family activities.

To prevent PMS and handle symptoms, doctors advise a balanced diet combined with exercise. Women should eat regular, moderate meals based on a combination of whole grains, legumes, vegetables, and fruits. Fats, highly refined foods, and caffeinated drinks should be avoided. Fresh fruits can provide a sweet finish, as well as fat-free, vitamin-rich snacks. Some researchers claim that vitamin B supplements are useful in alleviating symptoms of PMS.

Many women crave sweets—in particular, chocolate—in the days just before their periods start. An occasional piece of chocolate won't do much harm, but eating large amounts of sugary foods only adds empty calories and can actually worsen the craving for sweets by disrupting normal blood sugar levels. It's much better to satisfy such cravings with complex carbohydrates, such as low-fat whole-grain crackers or fresh vegetables, which are metabolized at a slower rate than sweets. These nutritious snacks are also low in calories, high in vitamins, and packed with fiber, which helps to prevent the constipation that some women experience as part of PMS.

According to a number of surveys, women who exercise regularly are less likely to suffer from PMS. The difference may be related to the levels of endorphins, which are released at an increased rate during exercise. Endorphins (chemicals in the brain that are natural mood elevators) can increase the sense of well-being and help the body to deal with stress.

PAINFUL PERIODS

Menstrual cramps (dysmenorrhea) are most common among young women who have never been pregnant. In most cases there is no underlying health problem, and symptoms often ease after pregnancy or with the use of oral contraceptives. Some women find sipping herbal tea beneficial. (Mint and raspberry teas are often recommended.) Relaxing in a warm bath or sitting with a heating pad over the abdomen can relieve muscle cramps and tension.

Research has found that prostaglandins, hormonelike substances that cause uterine contractions, play a part in causing menstrual cramps, but the precise mechanism is unknown. Aspirin, ibuprofen, and other nonsteroidal anti-inflammatory drugs (NSAIDs) block prostaglandin production and alleviate menstrual cramps in most women. Use these drugs with care, because they can cause stomach irritation and bleeding problems. Recent studies have found that evening primrose oil, a rich source of gamma linolenic acid (GLA), relieves PMS without adverse side effects.

In some instances, painful periods are related to other conditions, such as fibroid tumors (benign uterine growths) or endometriosis (the growth of uterine tissue outside the uterus). These conditions all require the attention of a gynecologist.

HEAVY PERIODS

Menstrual bleeding tends to be heavy and irregular at the beginning and end of a woman's reproductive years. Heavy periods, caused by hormonal fluctuations, often conclude anovulatory (i.e., no egg is released) cycles in the months following the first period (menarche) and in the year or two preceding MENOPAUSE. Although it can be inconvenient, heavy bleeding is rarely the signal of a more serious condition. However, excessive blood flow may result in a greater loss of iron, with a risk of ANEMIA. An adult woman needs 15mg of iron daily. Good sources are lean meat, poultry, fish and shellfish, legumes, fortified breads and cereals, and dried apricots. To help the body to better absorb iron, a food rich in vitamin C should be eaten at the same meal.

A woman who experiences persistently heavy or irregular periods should

Case Study

Beginning in her high school years, Judy had once-a-month crying spells, reacting to the slightest provocations. As the years went by, her mood swings and hypersensitivity to minor annoyances increased. She also had flare-ups of acne, along with nausea and vomiting at the start of her monthly period. By the time Judy was in her late twenties, she was severely depressed, got along badly with coworkers, and saw a bleak future for her recent marriage.

A doctor insensitively advised her to stop worrying and have a baby, but another doctor paid attention to her complaints and referred her to a dietitian. On the dietitian's advice, Judy switched from TV dinners and fast food to home-cooked meals that emphasized pasta and grains with fresh vegetables, low-fat poultry and fish, and plenty of fruit. It wasn't easy for Judy to make time for cooking instead of merely defrosting and microwaving, but she persevered and found that her premenstrual symptoms were much less troublesome. Today Judy has a much calmer marriage and an active toddler. She is also doing well in her job. She and her husband feel better on their healthy diet, and exercise helps Judy cope with any minor discomfort before her periods.

see a gynecologist to determine if she has a problem requiring treatment or, if she is approaching middle age, to obtain information about menopause.

MISSED PERIODS

The most likely reason for a missed period is PREGNANCY. However, the menstrual cycle may also be interrupted by hormonal imbalances related to OBESITY or DIABETES, THYROID DISEASE, a change in contraceptive pills, or an eating disorder such as ANOREXIA NERVOSA. Women involved in high-level athletic training are prone to menstrual problems, because they lack the critical amount of body fat to maintain adequate estrogen levels. A systematic meal plan can provide the nutrition essential to maintain top athletic performance while guarding against excess weight. A woman who is not having regular menstrual periods should see a doctor for a thorough checkup.

MIGRAINES AND OTHER HEADACHES

CUT DOWN ON

• *Coffee, tea, colas, and other beverages containing caffeine.*

AVOID

• *Alcohol, especially red wine, vermouth, champagne, and beer.*
• *Any food shown to trigger your attacks.*

Headaches afflict about 70 percent of adults at least occasionally and provoke millions of Canadians each year to seek medical relief. Most headaches are transient and due to tension or a temporary condition, such as a cold or the flu, but some reflect a serious underlying problem. Recurrent headaches warrant medical attention to diagnose the type and determine the best treatment.

When you see your doctor, bring a detailed written description of your headaches: their severity, ranging from mild to incapacitating; their frequency; their duration; the exact areas affected by the pain; and any related symptoms, such as nausea.

MIGRAINE HEADACHES

More than 3 million Canadians suffer from migraine, a one-sided, severe, throbbing or pulsating headache often accompanied by sensitivity to light and sound, as well as by nausea and vomiting. Migraines are also called vascular headaches, because they usually involve changes in the arteries of the head, resulting in a pulsating pain. The headaches may last from a few hours to several days or even longer.

About 10 percent of migraine sufferers experience a warning aura before the headache starts; this early symptom involves a visual disturbance, such as partial or temporary loss of sight or flashes of light and color. An aura may also cause tingling on one side of the face or body or a disturbance in the sense of smell. Even those who don't experience an aura may have warning signs in the few hours leading up to a migraine, such as feelings of cold, craving for a specific food, mood changes, a sudden burst of energy, or frequent yawning.

Migraines affect women about three times as often as men, and they most commonly start between the ages of 18 and 44. Doctors think that they begin when triggers—dietary, hormonal, environmental, emotional, and other factors—cause blood vessels in the brain to constrict and then relax. These distorted blood vessels prompt nerve endings to send out pain signals.

The triggers that can set off a migraine vary widely from one person to another, but some are more common than others. A number of the following triggers can be avoided entirely; others can at least be minimized.

THE FOOD-MIGRAINE LINK

Many foods, additives, and other dietary components can cause migraines, but the triggers vary greatly from one person to another. The following list covers the most common ones.

• Aged cheeses, sour cream, and certain other milk products.
• Fresh yeast, sourdough, and other yeasty breads.
• Fermented foods, including pickles, soy sauce, and miso.
• Some legumes, especially dried beans, lentils, and soy products.
• Nuts, seeds, and peanut butter.
• Chocolate and cocoa.
• Organ meats and meats that are salted, dried, cured, smoked, or contain nitrites.
• Sardines, anchovies, and pickled herring.
• Many fruits, including avocados, bananas, citrus fruits, figs, papayas, passion fruits, plantains, pineapples, raspberries, red plums, and raisins.
• Seasonings and flavor enhancers, especially artificial sweeteners, ginger, molasses, and MSG.

Environmental triggers include glare, bright lights, loud noises, strong odors, cigarette smoke, and changes in temperature, weather, or altitude.

Hormonal triggers are experienced by women and are usually related to the menstrual cycle; they can also be caused by the use of estrogen supplements or high-estrogen oral contraceptives.

Activity triggers include irregular or no exercise, inadequate or excessive sleep, eyestrain, and motion sickness.

Emotional triggers tend to be the negative ones, such as anger, resentment, depression, fatigue, anxiety, and stress.

Dietary triggers may be the easiest to control. Keep a food diary, note what foods seem to prompt symptoms (see The Food-Migraine Link, above), and then eliminate them. It's also important to eat regular meals, because excessive hunger can trigger a headache.

The caffeine in coffee and other beverages—as well as in many over-the-counter analgesic drugs—can play a dual role in migraines. Regular and excessive ingestion can contribute to the frequency of the headaches. On the other hand, once you are completely off caffeine, you may be able to use it to abort an impending attack, because it constricts dilated blood vessels. At the first sign of an aura or a pain, drink a cup of strong coffee or a cola, take two aspirin, and lie down in a dark, quiet room. The episode may pass within an hour or so.

In addition to using relaxation techniques to control stress, many doctors recommend taking a course in biofeedback to learn how to raise the temperature of your hands, thereby diverting some of the blood flow from the head to another part of the body. This technique can be used to abort a headache at the start of an attack.

Two different drugs can also abort a migraine if taken early enough. Sumatriptan (Imitrex) is a new medication that can be taken by self-injection, which typically gives relief within an hour, or as pills, which usually take up to 2 hours to work. Ergotamine drugs are older medications that are available as a pill placed under the tongue, a suppository, and a nasal spray.

CLUSTER HEADACHES

The most incapacitating of all vascular headaches, this type lasts from 15 minutes to 3 hours and typically occurs in clusters, coming and going repeatedly over several days or weeks and then disappearing for months or even years. Often starting during sleep, they cause excruciating, stabbing pain on one side of the head, usually behind or around one eye. Some people liken the pain to a hot poker stabbing the eye.

Cluster headaches are far more common in men than in women, especially among those who are heavy smokers and frequent alcohol users. Eliminating these habits may banish the headaches. In addition, keeping a diary of food and lifestyle factors may reveal that some of the factors known to trigger migraines can prompt clusters as well.

TENSION AND OTHER HEADACHES

Tension headaches are the most common type and are caused by muscle contractions or an imbalance of natural chemicals in the brain. The pain causes a bandlike pressure around the head and may be accompanied by a sense of tightness in the head and neck and shoulder muscles. They often begin in the afternoon or evening and produce a steady pain. Prevention is the best approach; relaxation techniques, such as biofeedback, massage, meditation, and visualization, work for many people. Another recommendation is to eliminate foods and drugs that contain caffeine, which can increase tension and anxiety, thus contributing to headaches.

Headaches also may be due to SINUSITIS, an inflammation of the lining of the sinus cavities. This causes a deep, dull ache around the eyes and sometimes in the forehead and ears. A good diagnostic clue is that the pain tends to worsen when you bend over.

So-called rebound headaches can result from overuse of over-the-counter analgesics, prescription pain medications and sedatives, and caffeine (which is a common ingredient in such drugs), resulting in a vicious cycle of growing tolerance and increasing dependence. These tend to be mild to moderate headaches. Although you may have to go through a painful, headachy period for a week or more to withdraw from dependence on these drugs, you will feel better in the long run.

Dental problems, too, can cause very severe one-sided headaches, which may feel like migraines or clusters, especially if a tooth is abscessed.

The many other factors that can cause headaches include squinting for hours in bright sun, eyestrain, hunger, excessive alcohol consumption, and too little or too much sleep.

HERBAL MIGRAINE RELIEF

Feverfew is the common name for *Tanacetum parthenium,* a member of the Chrysanthemum family. Its medicinal use dates from at least the Middle Ages, when the herb was believed to help reduce fever and other ailments, including headaches. Nibbling feverfew leaves continues to be a popular migraine remedy in some parts of the world. Recent research supports the practice, finding that regular feverfew dosing decreases the frequency and intensity of migraine headaches and their accompanying nausea. It cannot, however, stop an attack that has already started. Some doctors suggest taking one or two capsules of freeze-dried feverfew daily to reduce headache episodes. Start slowly, because feverfew can produce allergic reactions in some people, such as sores in the mouth or an inflammation of the mouth and tongue. If you have no side effects, you can continue this regimen indefinitely.

MILK AND MILK PRODUCTS

BENEFITS
- *Our best source of calcium.*
- *A good source of vitamins A and D, riboflavin, phosphorus, and magnesium.*
- *Low-fat dairy products are low in cholesterol and high in protein.*

DRAWBACKS
- *Whole milk and cream are high in saturated fat.*
- *Some people cannot digest milk sugar.*
- *Milk protein can trigger allergic reactions in susceptible people.*

Milk is an excellent source of dietary calcium, a mineral needed to build healthy bones and teeth and to maintain many of the basic functions of the human body. Calcium helps to prevent OSTEOPOROSIS, and recent studies indicate that it may also protect against high BLOOD PRESSURE and colon cancer. Milk also provides high-quality protein, vitamins, and other minerals. The Food Guide Rainbow (see p.39) recommends two to four servings a day of milk and other dairy foods. One serving is equal to an 8-ounce cup of milk or ¾ cup of yogurt or two slices (1¾ ounces) of cheese.

Milk has two major solid components: fat, including fat-soluble vitamins; and nonfat solids, which include proteins, carbohydrates, water-soluble vitamins, and minerals. Casein, a protein that is found only in milk, makes up 82 percent of the total protein.

The milk sold in Canadian markets is fortified with the fat-soluble vitamins A and D; it is also processed to accommodate preferences and nutritional needs (for example, to remove fat) as well as to improve its keeping qualities. Homogenized milk is pressure-treated to break up the fat globules and disperse them evenly in the liquid.

MORE THAN A DRINK. *Milk blended with fresh fruit makes a delicious and healthful shake; ice cream topped with strawberries is a high-calorie but nutritious dessert.*

Widely available milks include regular whole milk (3.6 percent fat), low-fat milk (1 or 2 percent fat), skim milk (almost fat-free, with 0.1 to 0.2 percent fat), and cultured buttermilk (less than 1 percent fat). Another type of milk known as UHT (ultra-high temperature) is processed at a high temperature so that it can be stored without refrigeration for extended periods.

Many Canadians have some degree of INTOLERANCE TO MILK because they lack the enzyme needed to digest milk sugar (lactose). The alternative is acidophilus milk, cultured with *Lactobacillus acidophilus,* a yogurt culture that absorbs the lactose and makes the milk digestible. The culturing process does not impair the nutrient quality, but it produces lactic acid, which gives a slightly sour taste to the milk.

Warm milk is a cold-weather treat, but children may be put off by the skin that forms on the surface when water evaporates and calcium and protein combine. If the skin is removed, valuable nutrients are lost. Instead, cover the pan to reduce evaporation or gently whisk the skin into the milk.

CREAM

Cream is milk with an extra-high concentration of fat. Light cream contains between 18 and 30 percent butterfat; heavy whipping cream is between 36 and 40 percent fat. Half-and-half is halfway between milk and cream, with a minimum of 10.5 percent fat. Gelatin or vegetable gums are often added to whipping cream to improve its foaming qualities.

PASTEURIZATION

Claims made for the superiority of raw milk should not be trusted. Disease-causing organisms often find their way into unpasteurized milk because of contamination from the cow, its human handlers, or from milking and processing equipment. In the pasteurization process milk is heated hot enough and long enough to kill most microorganisms without compromising the taste or the nutritional content. In Canada, the sale of unpasteurized milk is illegal and Health Canada urges Canadians who have weakened immune systems, as well as pregnant women, to avoid raw-milk cheese.

STORAGE

When buying milk, pay attention to the date on the carton, which indicates the last day on which the milk can be sold. Look for milk dated several days in the future. Even pasteurized milk contains bacteria and will quickly spoil unless refrigerated. (Putting milk in the microwave oven for 60 to 90 seconds before refrigerating extends its shelf life another 4 or 5 days.) Place milk toward the back of the refrigerator, where it is colder than on the door. A temperature just above freezing is ideal; however, milk should not be frozen. Milk is very sensitive to light, which rapidly breaks down the riboflavin and causes unpleasant changes in taste. Cardboard containers preserve their content better than clear glass bottles; milk stored in bottles should be kept in the dark.

GOAT'S MILK

Some people who are allergic to the proteins in cow's milk find that they can tolerate goat's milk and products made from it. Many supermarkets now carry a good selection of goat's milk products, including fresh milk, yogurt, and cheese. Goat's milk has a more pungent taste than bland cow's milk does, but it is a pleasant alternative to soy- or rice-based milk substitutes. It is similar in composition to cow's milk, but its fat is far more digestible. Vitamin supplements are not routinely added to goat's milk, so people using it exclusively should make sure that they get enough alternative sources of vitamins A and D, as well as folate.

THE MANY VARIETIES OF MILK

Milk is sold in many different forms. It is useful to be able to compare the benefits and drawbacks of different products, *especially their calorie and fat contents. Unless stated otherwise, the calorie figures in the following chart are for 8 ounces.*

TYPE	CALORIES	FAT (%)	DID YOU KNOW?
Whole milk	150	49	An 8-ounce cup of whole milk contains almost 20 percent of the body's daily needs for protein and calcium. It also provides riboflavin, phosphorus, and vitamin B_{12}. Most milk is fortified with vitamins A and D as well.
Low-fat milk (1%; 2%)	100; 120	23; 35	Low-fat milks are fortified with vitamins A and D. They provide nearly the same amounts of various nutrients as whole milk, but contain less fat and, therefore, fewer calories.
Skim milk	85	4	Skim milk has about 55 percent of the calories of whole milk but offers similar nutritional benefits. It has very little cholesterol.
Condensed, sweet (1 ounce)	125	23	Condensed milk is extremely nutritious, providing almost three times as much calcium as whole milk, but it is also high in calories and sugar and contains more than three times as much fat.
Heavy cream (1 tablespoon)	50	93	Cream is a good source of vitamin A but is high in fat and sodium. It is sometimes used in baked goods or certain soups.
Whipped topping (1 tablespoon)	10	65	Whipped creams and toppings appear to be light because, once whipped, half of their volume is air; however, they are actually very high in fat.
Dried skim milk (reconstituted)	100	1	Since fat becomes rancid when exposed to oxygen, dried milk is made from low-fat or skim milk. The absence of water makes it impossible for microbes to grow in it. Unlike liquid milks, it will remain fresh for several months if kept in a cool, dry place. It is used most often in baked goods.
Half-and-half (1 tablespoon)	20	76	Made up of half milk and half cream, 76 percent of the calories in half-and-half come from fat, most of which is saturated fat.

MINERALS

The human body needs numerous minerals to carry out its many vital functions. Luckily, most are required in tiny amounts that are easily obtained from a balanced diet.

Minerals are those elements that remain largely as ash when animal or plant tissues are burned. They constitute about 4 percent of our body weight and perform a variety of functions. To date, nutrition scientists have identified 16 minerals that are essential to maintain good health and promote proper metabolism and other bodily functions in humans. Calcium and a few others are present in relatively large amounts and are classified as macrominerals. However, most minerals are classified as trace, or micro, because they are needed in only minute amounts. The electrolytes generate electrical impulses to transport nerve messages; they also maintain the proper balances of fluids and body chemicals.

A varied and balanced diet provides all the essential minerals; supplements are generally not recommended, because many are highly toxic if consumed in large amounts. There are a few exceptions—for example, during pregnancy, when extra iron and calcium are needed. Also, the mineral content of foods varies according to the composition of the soil where the plants are grown or animals are grazed. Therefore, people may need dietary supplements in areas where the soil is deficient in a particular mineral.

A number of factors influence the body's ability to absorb and metabolize minerals. In general, the body is more efficient in absorbing a mineral during periods of increased need; thus,

---

BENEFITS

- *Build strong bones and teeth.*
- *Work with vitamins and enzymes to carry out many metabolic processes.*
- *Maintain the proper balance of body fluids and chemicals.*
- *Promote the proper function of most body systems.*

DRAWBACKS

- *Can be highly toxic if excessive amounts are consumed.*

---

a person who is anemic will absorb more iron from the diet than an individual who has a normal reserve of the mineral. Bran and other types of dietary FIBER bind with some minerals to reduce absorption; in contrast, vitamin C increases the uptake of iron, calcium, and some other minerals.

THE MACROMINERALS

Minerals make up about 3 to 5 percent of normal body weight; most of this comes from the macrominerals that are stored in the bones. But minerals also circulate in the blood.

Calcium. The most abundant mineral in the body, calcium weighs in at 980 to 1,260g in the typical adult male, compared to only 760 to 900g for women. Because calcium is essential for building and maintaining strong bones and teeth, it's not surprising that these structures hold 99 percent of the

---

body's calcium. This mineral also ensures proper nerve and muscle function as it moves in and out of bone tissue and circulates through the body.

Milk, cheese, yogurt, and other milk products are the best sources of calcium; the mineral is also found in canned sardines and salmon (if the bones are eaten), tofu (soybean curd), broccoli, and a variety of other vegetables and fruits. In general, the calcium in milk or soft bones is easier to absorb than that in plant foods.

Calcium deficiency can cause rickets in children and OSTEOMALACIA, a disorder characterized by soft, aching bones, in adults. In some cases, calcium deficiency is due to a lack of vitamin D, which the body requires to absorb the mineral. The deficiency may also be a result of physical inactivity, especially complete bed rest, which increases calcium loss. In addition, women need estrogen, the major female sex hormone, to metabolize calcium, which is why older women are so vulnerable to OSTEOPOROSIS.

Magnesium. The body contains only about 28g of magnesium, 60 percent of which is stored in the bones; the rest circulates in the blood or is stored in muscle tissue. Magnesium is essential to build bones and is needed for proper muscle function, energy metabolism, to transmit nerve impulses, and to make genetic material and protein.

Because magnesium is found in so many foods—green leafy vegetables, grains, legumes, meat, poultry, fish, and eggs—deficiency is rare. Reserves can be depleted, however, by alcoholism, prolonged diarrhea, liver or kidney disease, and severe diabetes.

Phosphorus. The second most plentiful mineral in the body, phosphorus works in conjunction with calcium and fluoride to give bones and teeth their strength and hardness. On average, it makes up 1 percent of normal body weight; 85 percent of this is in the bones, and the remainder is found in soft tissue. Phosphorus is essential for many metabolic processes and the storage and release of energy, as well as the activation of the B-complex vitamins and many enzymes.

Foods that are high in calcium (see facing page) also tend to be high in phosphorus; other good sources include meat, whole-grain products, and soft drinks.

THE TRACE MINERALS

Only very small, or trace, amounts of the following minerals are required to meet normal body requirements.

Chromium. Insulin and chromium appear to act together to metabolize glucose, the body's major fuel. Brewer's yeast is very high in chromium; other good sources include wheat germ, whole-grain products, liver, cheese, beer, and molasses.

Copper. A component of many enzymes, copper is essential for making red blood cells, skin pigment, connective tissue, and nerve fibers; it also stimulates absorption of iron. Excessive zinc appears to reduce the body's ability to absorb and store copper. Copper deficiency results in anemia, deterioration of the heart muscle, inelastic blood vessels, various skeletal defects, nerve degeneration, skin and hair abnormalities, and infertility.

Liver is the richest source of copper, but the mineral is also found in seafood, legumes, nuts and seeds, prunes, and barley. Using unlined copper pans can result in copper toxicity. Excessive copper can cause severe liver disease and mental deterioration; several metabolic disorders can cause a buildup of copper in the liver and other tissues. Patients suffering from Wilson's disease, for example, must take drugs to eliminate copper from their body.

Fluoride. Best known for preventing cavities and other DENTAL DISORDERS, fluoride is also needed to maintain strong bones. Fluoride occurs naturally in some areas; in fact, it was in these regions that the relationship between decreased incidence of tooth decay and fluoride was first noted. Some groups oppose adding fluoride to drinking

water, claiming it is a carcinogen. The prevailing scientific opinion, however, is that fluoridating drinking water is an appropriate health measure.

Iodine. This mineral has only one known function in humans: it is necessary to make thyroid hormones. An iodine deficiency can result in an overgrown thyroid gland, or goiter; in some severe cases, it can lead to hypo-

thyroidism. In addition, a baby borne by a woman with iodine deficiency may develop cretinism, a devastating type of mental retardation.

Seafood, kelp, and vegetables grown in iodine-rich soil are good sources of the mineral. Iodized salt is advisable in areas where the soil lacks iodine.

Iron. The body has only 3g to 5g of iron, 75 percent of which is in hemoglobin, the pigment in red blood cells that carries oxygen. Iron-deficiency ANEMIA is the most common nutritional deficiency in developed countries, but most cases are due to chronic blood loss, not an iron-poor diet. There are two types of iron: Heme is found in meat, poultry, fish, and eggs; nonheme is also found in animal products, as well as in vegetables, fruits, juices, grains, and fortified cereals. About 20 to 30 percent of heme iron is absorbed; lesser amounts of nonheme iron are absorbed, depending upon need and other dietary factors. Consuming nonheme iron with vitamin C or meat increases its absorption; bran, the tannins in tea, phytates in grains, and oxalates in many foods reduce its absorption.

As the body breaks down old red blood cells, it recycles most of their iron. A healthy adult man loses about 1mg of iron per day; compared to 1.5mg per day in a woman who is still menstruating. Except for pregnant women, the typical Canadian diet provides ample amounts of iron.

Manganese. A component of numerous enzymes, manganese plays an important role in metabolism; it is also needed to build bones and tendons. Manganese deficiency is unknown in humans, largely because most plant foods contain small amounts.

MINERAL	BEST FOOD SOURCES	ROLE IN HEALTH
MACROMINERALS		
Calcium	Milk and milk products; tofu; canned sardines and salmon (including bones); dark green vegetables.	Builds strong bones and teeth; vital to muscle and nerve function, blood clotting, and metabolism.
Magnesium	Leafy green vegetables; legumes and whole-grain cereals and breads; meats, poultry, fish, and eggs.	Stimulates bone growth; necessary for muscle function and metabolism.
Phosphorus	Meat, poultry, fish, egg yolks, legumes, dairy products, soft drinks.	Helps maintain strong bones and teeth; component of some enzymes; essential for proper metabolism.
MICROMINERALS		
Chromium	Brewer's yeast, whole-grain products, liver, cheese, beer.	Works with insulin to metabolize glucose.
Copper	Liver, shellfish, legumes, nuts, prunes.	Promotes iron absorption; essential to red blood cells, connective tissue, nerve fibers, and skin pigment. Component of several enzymes.
Fluoride	Fluoridated water; tea.	Helps maintain strong bones and teeth.
Iodine	Iodized salt, seafood, foods grown in iodine-rich soil.	Necessary to make thyroid hormones.
Iron	Liver, meat, seafood, legumes, fortified cereals.	Needed for transport and storage of oxygen.
Manganese	Coffee, tea, nuts, legumes, bran.	Component of many enzymes needed for metabolism; necessary for bone and tendon formation.
Molybdenum	Liver and other organ meats; dark green leafy vegetables; whole-grain products.	Component of enzymes needed for metabolism; instrumental in iron storage.
Selenium	Poultry, seafood, organ meats, whole-grain products, onions, garlic, mushrooms.	Antioxidant that works with vitamin E to protect cell membranes from oxidative damage.
Sulfur	Protein foods.	Component of two essential amino acids.
Zinc	Oysters, meat, yogurt, fortified cereals.	Instrumental in metabolic action of enzymes; essential for growth and reproduction.
ELECTROLYTES		
Chloride	Table salt, seafood, milk, eggs, meat.	Maintains proper body chemistry. Used to make digestive juices.
Potassium	Avocados, bananas, citrus and dried fruits; legumes and many vegetables; whole-grain products.	Along with sodium, helps to maintain fluid balance; promotes proper metabolism and muscle function.
Sodium	Table salt, dairy products, seafood, seasonings, most processed foods.	With potassium, regulates the body's fluid balance; promotes proper muscle function.

*Based on the Nutrition Research Division of Health and Welfare Canada Recommended Nutrient Intakes (RNIs).

**Many experts recommend 1,000 to 1,500mg following menopause.

RECOMMENDED NUTRIENT INTAKES* (FOR ADULTS OVER 24)		SYMPTOMS OF DEFICIENCY	SYMPTOMS OF EXCESS
MALES	FEMALES		
800mg	800mg**	Rickets in children; easy fractures, brittle bones, and osteoporosis in adults.	Calcium deposits in body tissues; abdominal pain. Inhibits iron absorption.
250mg	200mg	Lethargy, cramps, muscle weakness, cardiac arrhythmias.	Diarrhea.
1,000mg	850mg	Weakness and bone pain. Deficiency is rare.	Decreased blood calcium.
0.05–0.2mg***	0.05–0.2mg***	Diabeteslike symptoms.	Unknown for dietary chromium. Chromium salt is toxic.
2–3mg***	2–3mg***	Anemia marked by abnormal development of bones, nerves, lungs, and hair color.	Vomiting, diarrhea, and liver disease.
1.5–4mg***	1.5–4mg***	Tooth decay.	Mottling of tooth enamel.
160mcg	160mcg	Goiter; cretinism in babies.	Abnormal thyroid function.
9mg	9–13mg	Iron-deficiency anemia.	Organ damage, especially liver and heart.
2.5–5mg***	2.5–5mg***	Unknown.	Nerve damage.
75–250mcg***	75–250mcg***	Unknown.	Goutlike joint pain.
70mcg	55mcg	Heart disease and rare form of anemia.	Diarrhea, nausea, abdominal pain, tooth damage, fatigue, irritability, hair and nail loss.
Not established	Not established	Unknown.	None with dietary sulfur.
12mg	9mg	Low immunity; slow healing of wounds; retarded growth and sexual development.	Nausea, vomiting, heart muscle damage, kidney failure, muscle pain, atherosclerosis.
2–5g***	2–5g***	Deficiency is extremely rare; causes upset in acid-base balance when it occurs.	Disturbance in body chemistry.
2–6g***	2–6g***	Muscle weakness; cardiac arrhythmias.	Nausea and diarrhea; potentially fatal cardiac arrhythmias.
1–3g***	1–3g***	Muscle cramps, headaches, and weakness; rare, except as a result of injury or illness.	Exacerbates hypertension, heart failure, and kidney disease.

*** Recommended Nutrient Intakes (RNIs) have not been established; values for these minerals are based on current expert opinion.

Molybdenum. Another component of many enzymes, molybdenum helps regulate iron storage and is instrumental in the production of uric acid. A deficiency of this mineral almost never occurs. Overdoses, which cause goutlike joint symptoms, are also rare but have been reported in some parts of Armenia, where the soil is rich in this mineral.

Selenium. An important ANTIOXIDANT, selenium interacts with vitamin E to prevent the free radicals produced during oxygen metabolism from damaging body fat and other tissues. Human selenium deficiency is rare except in areas where the soil contains little of the mineral, where it causes a rare type of heart disease in children.

Foods that are high in selenium include seafood, organ meats, poultry, whole-grain products, mushrooms, onions, and garlic. Recent reports that selenium may help prevent cancer have not been proved, but they have led to increased sales of selenium supplements. Although selenium toxicity is uncommon, there have been a few cases among people taking high doses. Symptoms include nausea, diarrhea, fatigue, damage to the skin and nerves, and loss of hair and nails.

Sulfur. A component of several amino acids and B vitamins, sulfur is found in every cell of the body; it is particularly concentrated in the skin, nails, and hair. Humans cannot develop a sulfur deficiency, nor is it possible to overdose on dietary sulfur. However, some inorganic sulfur salts are toxic, and others, such as the sulfites used as food preservatives, can trigger asthma attacks and other allergic reactions in susceptible people.

Zinc. An essential component of many enzymes, zinc is necessary for some metabolic processes, normal growth and sexual development, and proper immune system function. It is also needed to make genetic materials (DNA and RNA) and for proper wound healing. A deficiency results in increased susceptibility to infection, fatigue, lethargy, loss of appetite, balding, and taste abnormalities.

Zinc is found in many foods; especially good sources include beef and other meats, eggs, oysters and other seafood, yogurt, wheat germ, and fortified cereals. The phytates in bran and some whole-grain products, however, bind with zinc and prevent the body from absorbing it. Even so, zinc deficiency is rare in North America.

In recent years zinc supplements have been promoted to increase immunity. These should be used only when specifically recommended by a doctor, however, because too much zinc can cause diarrhea, vomiting, degeneration of the heart muscle, accelerated development of atherosclerosis, kidney failure, and bleeding, among many other symptoms.

THE ELECTROLYTES

Three essential minerals are classified as electrolytes, substances that dissociate into ions when placed in water or other fluids. In the human body electrolytes conduct electrical charges and are instrumental in nerve and muscle function; they also help maintain the proper balance of body fluids.

Chloride. A component of table salt, chloride is essential to maintain the body's proper acid-base balance. Chloride is also a component of hydrochloric acid, one of the digestive juices produced in the stomach. A diet that includes a moderate amount of salt provides adequate chloride; deficiencies are rare but may occur during periods of excessive sweating or prolonged vomiting or diarrhea.

Potassium. Along with sodium, potassium helps regulate the body's balance of fluids. Potassium is essential for many metabolic processes; it is also instrumental in the transmission of nerve impulses, proper muscle function, and maintaining normal blood pressure. Most plant foods contribute varying amounts of potassium; especially rich sources include dried fruits, bananas, tomatoes, citrus fruits, avocados, potatoes, green vegetables, legumes, whole grains, and nuts.

Prolonged diarrhea or the use of diuretics to treat high blood pressure can lead to a potassium deficiency; typical symptoms include an irregular heartbeat, muscle weakness, and irritability. Caution is necessary when taking potassium supplements, however; an overdose can cause nausea, diarrhea, and serious cardiac arrhythmias that can result in sudden death.

Sodium. Table salt is composed of sodium and chloride, and the terms salt and sodium are often used interchangeably. Sodium is found in all body fluids and is largely responsible for determining the body's total water content. Like potassium, sodium ions carry positive electrical charges and help regulate nerve and muscle function. These two electrolytes also maintain the fluid balance inside and outside of body cells.

A sodium deficiency is very rare; overconsumption is a much more common problem, especially among those who liberally salt their food. In susceptible people excessive salt is linked to high BLOOD PRESSURE; it can also cause swollen ankles and fingers and other signs of a buildup of body fluids, or edema.

MONONUCLEOSIS

CONSUME PLENTY OF

- *Fruit and vegetable juices for vitamins and minerals.*
- *Milk shakes for calories, minerals, and vitamin D.*
- *Soups for energy and fiber.*
- *Soft foods to soothe a sore throat.*

AVOID

- *Alcohol.*

A common disease, mononucleosis is caused by the Epstein-Barr virus, which infects at least half of all Canadian children by the age of 5. The majority of these infections pass unrecognized, because the symptoms of mild fever and slight fatigue last only a short time and resolve spontaneously. The Epstein-Barr virus is transmitted in the saliva by coughing, sneezing, or kissing. Otherwise, most people who have only casual contact with an infected person do not get the disease.

Mononucleosis causes more debilitating illness in adolescents and adults, who generally have fatigue, fever, severe SORE THROAT, and swollen lymph nodes. Patients usually lose their appetite and complain of headaches and general achiness. Often, the fever and sore throat are misdiagnosed as tonsillitis. If the sore throat is treated with ampicillin, an antibiotic similar to penicillin, the patient with mononucleosis develops a rash. The spleen—and, less often, the liver—may become enlarged. In very severe cases the patient may develop JAUNDICE.

The symptoms typically last for a week or two, and most people are able to return to work at that time. In a few cases, however, recovery may take several months, as a low-grade fever, poor appetite, and fatigue persist for weeks after the other symptoms have disappeared. When this happens, mononucleosis may be mistaken for CHRONIC FATIGUE SYNDROME. In the past, chronic fatigue syndrome was at times referred to as chronic Epstein-Barr infection, but it is now known that they are unrelated.

THE ROLE OF DIET

A well-balanced diet can aid in recovery and boost the strength of the IMMUNE SYSTEM to fight mononucleosis. Stimulate a poor appetite with several light, appetizing meals rather than a few larger ones, which may be daunting. During the acute phase, when fever may be high, it's important to drink plenty of liquids in order to prevent dehydration. Drink at least eight glasses of water or juice daily. During recuperation, juices have the added benefit of providing vitamins and other immune-boosting nutrients.

Milk shakes and fruit nectars diluted with water soothe a sore throat and provide calories for energy, along with minerals and vitamins. Applesauce and other stewed fruits supply soluble fiber, which helps prevent constipation. Soups are nutritious and easy to eat. Soft foods, such as puddings, scrambled eggs, cottage cheese, and yogurt, are easily swallowed, even by someone with a sore throat. Fruits and vegetables can be pureed to make them easier to swallow; serve vegetables as a sauce over complex carbohydrates, such as rice or soft noodles. Herbal teas are soothing, and gargling with tepid salt water can relieve a sore throat. Avoid alcohol, which weakens the immune system and can further damage the liver.

TREATMENT

See a physician if you think you have mononucleosis, since blood tests are necessary for a definitive diagnosis. Rest is an important part of recovery. Take aspirin or some other nonsteroidal anti-inflammatory drug (NSAID) to ease symptoms. However, since the disease is a viral and not a bacterial infection, it should not be treated with antibiotics. People with mononucleosis just have to wait it out. Long-term complications are rare, but activity should be limited until you feel strength returning. Don't engage in vigorous activity until the doctor says the spleen has returned to its normal size; abrupt force can rupture an enlarged spleen and cause serious problems.

Case Study

When 16-year-old Todd became ill with severe fatigue and swollen glands, his mother feared that he might have leukemia. After a doctor's visit she was understandably relieved when blood tests found he had mononucleosis instead. But she became increasingly concerned when 6 weeks later, he still lacked energy and only picked at his meals.

A dietitian advised Todd's mother to try giving him smaller, frequent snacks of his favorite foods, such as milk shakes, scrambled eggs, puddings, pizza topped with cheese and vegetables, hearty soups, and ample fruit juices and nectars. This approach seemed to work, and before long Todd made a full recovery.

MOOD DISORDERS

EAT PLENTY OF
- *A variety of complex carbohydrates to supply the brain with amino acids.*
- *Seafood, dark green leafy vegetables, and whole-grain breads, cereals, and pasta for B-group vitamins.*

CUT DOWN ON
- *Caffeine and alcohol, which can cause sleeplessness and feelings of anxiety.*
- *Carbohydrates, especially sugar, at lunchtime to stay alert for the afternoon.*

Our thoughts, emotions, moods, and attitudes, as well as nerve and muscle functions, are all centered in the brain. While diet affects the health of all the organ systems, the links between diet and emotional health appear to be mostly negative ones. Deficiencies of some of the B vitamins, for example, can result in memory loss and various other mental and emotional changes. Now rare, thanks to the abundance of food and the fortification of grain products in the industrialized countries, these disorders are generally only experienced by people with special nutritional problems, such as alcoholics.

Positive links—foods that lift the mood—are harder to find. The brain's neurons communicate with one another by means of chemicals called neurotransmitters. These compounds are synthesized as needed from amino acids and other components of the diet.

The amino acid tryptophan, found in all complete proteins, such as meat, milk, and eggs, is used by the brain to produce serotonin. This neurotransmitter regulates sleep, pituitary hor-

mone secretion, and pain perception. Brain levels of serotonin are affected by the intake of tryptophan. After a high-protein meal, little tryptophan reaches the brain because of competition from other amino acids. Following a carbohydrate meal, on the other hand, insulin plays a greater role in the disposition of the amino acids; a larger amount of tryptophan is shunted to the brain, where it is converted to serotonin. A typical effect of serotonin is the drowsiness that follows a sugary snack or a high-carbohydrate lunch.

Choline and lecithin, which are present in eggs, liver, and soybeans, have been shown to favorably affect brain function in people with certain neurological diseases that involve mood changes. In large amounts, they may also benefit some movement disorders, such as tardive dyskinesia.

MOODS AND JUNK FOODS

There is no evidence that food allergies, including the disputed "yeast sensitivity," cause emotional or behavioral changes. Likewise, there is no evidence that food additives or junk foods influence mood or behavior, even though some courts have allowed defendants to enter the "Twinkie defense" as a justification for their misdeeds. Many parents maintain that

their children become hyperactive after eating sugary foods. A number of scientific studies have shown, however, that this is not the case. Sugar enhances serotonin formation and therefore tends to calm active children.

DIETARY MOOD CHANGERS

The best-known mood-altering dietary item is CAFFEINE, a stimulant found in coffee, tea, colas, and chocolate. While a cup of coffee may be a welcome eye-opener, too much caffeine causes palpitations, sleeplessness, and anxiety.

ALCOHOL is the next most often used mood-altering substance, and it sometimes has an effect opposite to the one intended. In reality, alcohol is a depressant that slows down certain physiological processes, including respiration, which decreases the supply of oxygen to the central nervous system. Alcohol can cause depression. People who awake depressed and short-tempered might benefit from taking a critical count of the previous evening's drinks. In addition, alcohol interferes with sleep, which can cause irritability, anxiety, and depression.

Because CARBOHYDRATES have a sedating effect, high-protein foods are better choices for lunch than foods that are heavy in starches and sugars.

A CALMING MEAL. *A pepper stuffed with rice and beans provides the amino acids and carbohydrates used to make soothing brain chemicals.*

MOUTH ULCERS

EAT PLENTY OF

- *Lean meat, legumes, dried fruits, fortified cereals, and other high-iron foods.*
- *Dark green leafy vegetables, wheat germ, and legumes for folate.*
- *Lean animal products for vitamin B_{12}.*
- *During an attack, soft, bland foods.*

AVOID

- *Salty, spicy, and acidic foods, or any other food that worsens symptoms.*
- *Alcohol and very hot beverages.*

Commonly referred to as canker sores, mouth ulcers (or aphthous stomatitis) appear as painful white or yellowish raised spots. Many people suffer recurrent episodes, which typically cause two or three isolated ulcers. In severe cases, however, a dozen or more may arise, either as single sores scattered through the mouth or as large clusters. They tend to be acutely painful for the first 3 to 4 days, last about 1 to 2 weeks, and then heal without consequence. Larger ulcers may last weeks or months and cause scarring; they may also be accompanied by fatigue, fever, and swollen lymph nodes.

Although the cause of these mouth ulcers is unknown, physicians believe that an abnormal immune response or a viral infection may be the underlying problem. Stress or local trauma, such as from ill-fitting dentures, may precipitate an attack. In unusual cases, mouth ulcers may be a symptom of a systemic disorder, for example ALLERGIC REACTIONS TO FOODS, ANEMIA, CELIAC DISEASE, CROHN'S DISEASE, or LUPUS. Deficiencies of iron, vitamin B_{12}, and folate have been associated with an increased risk of mouth ulcers; eating foods high in these nutrients may help to prevent occurrences.

During attacks, avoid any food or beverage that may irritate the sores. The most common offenders are hot beverages, alcohol, salty or spicy foods, and anything acidic. If painful ulcers interfere with eating, try sipping liquid or pureed foods through a straw. Bland foods that cause the least pain include gelatin, yogurt, custard, rice, and poached chicken.

For recurrent or severe ulcers, a dentist may prescribe a protective paste to cover the ulcerated areas, alleviate pain, and speed healing.

MULTIPLE SCLEROSIS

CONSUME PLENTY OF

- *Fiber-rich foods to prevent constipation.*
- *Cranberry juice to ward off cystitis.*
- *Pureed foods to ease swallowing.*

CUT DOWN ON

- *Caffeine to avoid bladder irritation.*

AVOID

- *Foods that can cause choking.*

An estimated 50,000 Canadians have multiple sclerosis (MS), a chronic, often disabling disease of the central nervous system that most often strikes people between the ages of 20 and 40. MS is characterized by the gradual destruction of the myelin sheaths that insulate the nerve fibers, thus robbing nerves of the ability to transmit impulses. Although the symptoms vary depending on the sites where myelin is destroyed in the brain and spinal cord, most people suffer abnormal fatigue, impaired vision, slurred speech, loss of balance and muscle coordination, difficulty chewing and swallowing, tremors, bladder and bowel problems, and, in severe cases, paralysis.

MS AND NUTRITION

Many different diets have been proposed to treat MS, but according to the Multiple Sclerosis Society of Canada, there is no scientific evidence of a nutritional cause, nor is there evidence that diet can contribute to a cure. Instead, the MS Society endorses the same dietary guidelines recommended for healthy Canadians, with the bulk of calories coming from carbohydrates—mostly starchy foods, fruits, and vegetables; moderate amounts of protein; and sparing use of fats and sugars. This diet—low in fat and high in fiber—benefits MS patients by providing energy and nutrients to maintain and repair tissues, to fight infections, and to keep the risk of constipation low.

Some physicians, as well as MS support groups, advocate the Swank diet (named for the professor who proposed it in 1950), which eliminates most animal fats. This diet was evaluated for many years in a large number of MS patients, with inconclusive results. While a low-fat diet carries no significant risks, and indeed is beneficial for healthy and infirm people alike, the Swank diet has not been shown effective in preventing the progression of MS. Other diets that have been proposed for treating MS are riskier, because they may lead to unbalanced or inadequate nutrition. Among them are liquid diets, crash diets that can lead to potassium deficiency, raw food diets, diets that restrict intake of pectin and fructose, and gluten-free regimens. None of these have been proved effective.

Vitamin therapy has also been promoted, but there is no evidence that MS is caused by a vitamin deficiency, and therefore no reason to supplement a healthy well-balanced diet with high doses of vitamins. Furthermore, megadoses of certain vitamins and minerals can cause health problems. Too much vitamin B_6, for example, causes nerve damage with symptoms that are similar to those seen in MS, such as numbness and tingling.

The main role of diet in MS is to help people control symptoms, such as

TIPS FOR EASIER EATING

- Call the stores and supermarkets in your area to find the ones that deliver telephone orders.
- When you're feeling energetic, cook double recipes and freeze meal-size portions for instant dinners for times when you're too tired to cook.
- When friends ask what they can do to help, ask them to prepare an extra portion that you can freeze at home.

- Find gadgets to make cooking and serving less tiring. Get longer utensils; use barbecue tongs; try a ladle instead of pouring food from a pot into a bowl; use a baster for small amounts; invest in a steamer basket with handles.
- Ask your pharmacist for the reaching and grasping aids designed for people with arthritis.

fatigue, constipation, urinary tract infections, and problems with chewing and swallowing. A balance between healthy diet, exercise, and rest can help to minimize fatigue. Eating more frequent but smaller meals also helps to provide a constant source of energy. Breakfast is particularly important; a low-fat, nutritious breakfast provides an energy boost to start the day.

MANAGING COMPLICATIONS

It is especially important to maintain an appropriate weight related to height. Excess weight can add to mobility problems and fatigue and strain the respiratory and circulatory systems. Skin becomes irritated and breaks down more easily in overweight, relatively inactive people. Being underweight is also undesirable, because it may decrease resistance to infection and increase the risk of developing pressure sores and other skin ulcers.

URINARY TRACT INFECTIONS are often a problem for people with MS, particularly when they have to undergo frequent catheterizations. Drinking CRANBERRY juice increases urinary acidity and creates an environment hostile to bacteria. If urinary incontinence is a problem, people with MS should avoid caffeinated drinks, such as coffee, tea, and colas, and they should save chocolate (it also contains caffeine) for an occasional treat. Caffeine has a diuretic effect and irritates the bladder.

Constipation is aggravated by an inadequate fluid intake. Plenty of water and fiber-rich foods, such as fruits, vegetables, and whole-grain products, encourage smooth bowel function. Prune juice and bran cereal are good breakfast choices. Cut down on refined foods that promote constipation. Cheese has a binding effect on the bowel; it's also high in saturated fat.

Some people with MS have problems with bowel incontinence, which may be worsened by diet. Try eliminating suspect items—for example, coffee, alcohol, and spicy foods—from the diet for a few days; then reintroduce them one at a time to see if the problem recurs. Because nicotine can (among many other health effects) stimulate the bowel, it is important not to smoke.

Difficulties with chewing and swallowing can be helped by modifying food preparation but adhering to the Food Guide Rainbow (see p.39). For example, substitute shakes, yogurt, fruit and vegetable purees, thick soups, and puddings for firm or dry dishes. Serve chopped spinach in place of salad, or diced, stewed fruit instead of a fresh apple or pear. Use a blender or food processor to achieve an acceptable texture, and serve smaller but more frequent meals. A speech pathologist may be recommended for suggestions about positioning food in the mouth or changing breathing patterns to relieve swallowing difficulties.

MUSCLE CRAMPS

CONSUME PLENTY OF
- *Low-fat dairy products for calcium to regulate muscle contractions.*
- *Potassium-rich foods, such as bananas, citrus fruits, dried fruits, tomato juice, deep yellow vegetables, pecans, walnuts, and sunflower seeds.*
- *Complex carbohydrates, such as rice, legumes, and pasta, for energy.*
- *Fortified whole-grain breads and cereals for iron and B-complex vitamins needed for energy conversion.*
- *Water to maintain the circulation and help flush lactic acid and other waste products from the muscles.*

CUT DOWN ON
- *Caffeine in coffee, tea, and cola, which can decrease the circulation to muscles.*

AVOID
- *Highly salted foods, which can cause fluid retention.*
- *Excessive protein, which can overload the kidneys.*
- *Smoking, which restricts the blood supply to the muscles.*

Cramps are painful spasms that mainly affect muscles in the legs and feet. A cramp generally lasts only a few minutes and then ends on its own, although massage and stretching can hasten the process, and certain foods may help to prevent its recurrence.

The human body is made up of about 600 groups of muscles, which constitute 40 percent of an average person's weight. Each muscle is made up of many thousands of long fibers bound together with connective tissue. The bundled fibers can shrink or lengthen, allowing muscles to contract or relax.

HOW MUSCLES GET ENERGY

Most of the fuel necessary for muscular activity comes from glucose, the end-product of carbohydrate metabolism, which is stored as glycogen in the liver and muscles. Vitamins, particularly those in the B group, are crucial to the process by which energy is derived from carbohydrates, proteins, and fats. In fact, our need for thiamine is directly related to the amount of energy we expend.

We need iron to form hemoglobin, the blood pigment that supplies muscles with oxygen for energy conversion. Also critically important to muscle function are sodium, potassium, and chloride; these minerals are called electrolytes, because their electrically charged particles (ions) relay nerve impulses from the brain to the muscles, instructing them when to contract and relax. Calcium is the trigger for muscle contraction. And to come full circle, potassium is stored in the muscles with glycogen and—like glycogen—it is rapidly depleted whenever the muscles undergo a vigorous workout.

When muscles burn glycogen for energy, lactic acid forms as a waste product and remains in the muscle tissue until circulating blood clears it away. During periods of intense exercise, a buildup of lactic acid can cause severe muscle pain and fatigue. The pain, which is similar to muscle cramps, dissipates with rest, which allows the blood to remove the extra lactic acid.

The spasms of true cramps may be caused by an inadequate supply of blood to the muscle, overstretching, or an injury. The correct fluid balance is important in muscle function. If the fluid volume is too low, the electrolyte balance is thrown off kilter, the kidneys respond by conserving sodium at a high rate, fluid is retained in the tissues, and there is not enough circulating fluid to flush out waste products and keep the muscle contraction mechanism working smoothly. There should be enough water to keep electrolytes in the proper concentration for relaying impulses from the nerves to the muscles, but not too much water, which dilutes the blood and lowers the electrolyte concentration.

Electrolyte depletion is not often a problem, because these minerals are amply supplied by a properly balanced diet. Although the electrolytes are excreted in sweat, the amounts lost are very small, even with profuse perspiration during vigorous activity. The exception is potassium, which is drawn out of body stores along with glycogen.

MANAGING MUSCLE CRAMPS

People who may suffer from leg cramps include athletes, who can deplete their glycogen reserves through very intense activity and lose potassium and salt in heavy perspiration; those being treated for hypertension with beta-blocking drugs or certain diuretics, which increase the amount of potassium excreted in the urine; and women in the later months of pregnancy, who also lose larger quantities of potassium in the urine.

A daily serving of a high-potassium food—for example, a handful of dried apricots, pecans, walnuts, or sunflower seeds; a glass of tomato juice or citrus juice; or a banana—can help to banish leg cramps and prevent their recurrence. CAFFEINE and nicotine constrict blood vessels, decreasing the circulation to the muscles and contributing to cramps. If cramps are a problem and you smoke, make every effort to quit; also switch to decaffeinated beverages if you haven't already done so.

People confined to bed rest or chair rest for extended periods often suffer leg cramps. Apart from dietary measures, the best remedy is regular exercise to tone the muscles and improve the circulation. Try curling and uncurling the toes a dozen times in quick succession; alternatively, straighten the leg, bend the foot upward, and then extend the foot and point the toes a dozen times in quick succession. Repeat these exercises throughout the day.

Occasional cramps that abate within a few minutes are no cause for concern. Frequent or prolonged cramps or spasms accompanied by other symptoms, particularly in older adults, should be evaluated by a doctor.

RESTLESS LEGS

Some people are awakened during the night by a jerking of their leg muscles; others suffer an aching, uneasy sensation that doctors call "restless legs syndrome." Certain medications that affect the nervous system may cause these conditions; often, they occur with no apparent cause. In some cases, drugs may help; getting out of bed and walking, or frequently changing positions, may give some relief.

CRAMP CONTROL.
Certain foods can help to reduce muscle cramps, including yogurt, pasta, bananas, tomato juice, milk, water, oranges, and whole-grain bread.

MUSHROOMS AND TRUFFLES

BENEFITS

- *Fat-free and very low in calories.*
- *Rich in minerals.*
- *High glutamic acid content may boost immune function.*

DRAWBACKS

- *Wild mushrooms may be poisonous.*
- *Truffles are expensive because they can't be cultivated as crops.*

All types of mushrooms, as well as truffles, are classified as fungi. They are primitive plants that cannot obtain energy through photosynthesis and therefore draw their nutrients from humus, the partially decomposed tissues of more complex vegetation. Many varieties of fungi live symbiotically with trees. The fungus draws sugars from the tree roots, while at the same time supplying the tree with minerals, such as phosphorus, which it gets from the soil more efficiently than the tree.

Mushrooms and truffles have another unique feature. Their cell walls are made of chitin, the same material that forms the external skeleton of insects. By contrast, higher plants' cell walls are composed of cellulose, which we value not as a nutrient (humans can't digest cellulose) but as fiber that promotes the elimination of digestive waste.

Used in every age and culture as food, mushrooms have also served as medicines and as stimulants or hallucinogens in religious ceremonies. Evidence that Stone Age humans used dried mushrooms as tinder was provided by the 5,000-year-old "Ice Man," whose body was discovered in the Tyrolean Alps a few years ago.

MANY VARIETIES

The common white mushroom, *Agaricus bispora*, was first cultivated by the French more than 300 years ago in abandoned gypsum quarries near Paris. Today, mushrooms are cultivated on beds of manure, straw, and soil in darkened buildings controlled for temperature and humidity. Only recently has it become possible to cultivate a number of other species on a commercial scale. Thanks to this development, a wide range of mushrooms is now offered by many supermarkets, including brown cremini, orange chanterelles, shiitake, and the ominously black but perfectly safe trumpets of death. The popular portobello mushroom, although cultivated, preserves much of the rich, earthy flavor of field mushrooms. With its firm, meaty texture, it is especially suitable for grilling and barbecuing. Many other varieties, including cèpes and tree-ears, are available dried.

Because of their high concentration of glutamic acid—the naturally occurring form of monosodium glutamate (MSG)—mushrooms are natural flavor enhancers in many dishes.

Warning: Many common species of wild mushrooms produce toxins that are quickly lethal whether eaten raw or cooked. Because there is no feature that distinguishes dangerous mushrooms, and poisonous varieties often closely resemble edible ones, never gather or eat wild mushrooms unless a mushroom expert has identified them as safe. Even then, caution is needed. Some safe wild mushrooms, for example, can be deadly when consumed with alcohol.

NUTRITIONAL VALUE

A good substitute for meat in many recipes, mushrooms can be combined with grains to make a meatless "meat" loaf. They are also appetizing and nutritious on their own. Extremely low in calories (a half cup contains only 10), mushrooms are fat-free. They provide moderate amounts of potassium, calcium, and selenium, along with modest amounts of niacin and vitamin C.

Mushrooms are a long-time staple of many Asian diets, and Japanese scientists have taken the lead in investigating their possible health benefits. Japanese studies have shown that mushrooms may favorably influence the immune system, with potential benefits in fighting cancer, infections, and such autoimmune diseases as rheumatoid arthritis and lupus. This effect may be related to the high content of glutamic acid, an amino acid that seems to be instrumental in fighting infections, among other immune functions. In addition, tree-ear mushrooms, used in many Chinese dishes, inhibit blood clotting. This may prove valuable in the treatment of certain heart diseases.

TRUFFLES: AN EXPENSIVE DELICACY

Truffles grow underground among the roots of certain oak, hazel, and linden trees. Their musky scent is due to androstenol—a sex attractant hormone identical to the one secreted in the saliva of male pigs. Because of this, trained sows are more efficient than dogs at rooting up the prized fungus in the truffle-growing regions of France and Italy. As a result of overharvesting and deforestation, truffles are now so rare and expensive that only minute shavings are used to flavor dishes. Truffles have been grown experimentally, but attempts to produce them on a commercial scale have been unsuccessful so far.

ALL SHAPES AND SIZES. *The many varieties of mushrooms include the giant portobello (center and far right) as well as (clockwise from upper right) the shiitake, morel, oyster, and button.*

NAIL PROBLEMS

CONSUME PLENTY OF

- *Lean meat, poultry, and fish for iron and high-quality protein.*
- *Citrus fruits for vitamin C.*
- *Dark green leafy vegetables, whole-grain products, legumes, and fruit juices for folate and other B vitamins.*

AVOID

- *Overuse of polish removers and other harsh chemicals.*

Most nail problems stem from abuse—everything from picking and biting to excessive manicuring and overuse of polish removers, glues, and other harmful chemicals. In some instances, however, unhealthy nails actually reflect a nutritional deficiency or an underlying medical problem.

Normally, nails grow about ⅛ inch a month, although illness, advancing age, and even cold weather slow the rate of growth. Nails are composed of keratin, the same hard protein that forms the outer layer of skin (the epidermis), hair, and animal hooves and horns. The visible portion, called the nail plate, rests over the tips of the fingers and toes and grows out of the lunula, the pale half-moon at its base. The cuticle acts as a protective seal between the skin and nail. Only the lunula is living tissue; the rest is made of dead cells that have been pushed up from the base.

Even though nails are mostly dead tissue, they are an important indicator of a person's state of health; this is the reason a doctor carefully examines them for clues to many diseases. Soft spoon-shaped nails that curve upward, for example, point to iron-deficiency ANEMIA. Rounded, club-shaped nails indicate impaired circulation or a serious lung disorder; thickened, discolored nails may be due to a fungal infection; psoriasis can cause pitting; and horizontal ridges may indicate a systemic infection or debilitating illness.

Healthy nails are strong and smooth, with a pinkish cast. Like hair, they need moisture for flexibility; without it, they become yellowish and break or chip easily. In order to maintain healthy growth and strength, nails require a steady supply of oxygen and other nutrients. But because the body is very efficient in delivering nutrients to its areas of greatest need, and the nails are not vital organs, they are one of the first to be short-circuited if there is greater demand elsewhere in the body.

Many of the nail problems that reflect diseases and nutritional deficiencies disappear when the underlying condition is corrected. In order to make keratin, the body needs high-quality protein from lean meat, poultry, fish, seafood, and other animal products; a combination of grain products and legumes will also supply complete protein. Most North American diets provide more than enough high-quality protein for strong, healthy nails.

A more common nutrition-related problem involves iron-deficiency or other anemias, in which the blood does not deliver adequate nutrients to the nails. Increasing the consumption of iron-rich foods—lean meat, poultry, fish, seafood, dried apricots, and enriched cereals and breads—may be enough to cure mild iron-deficiency anemia. A doctor should be consulted, however, to determine whether the anemia is due to other nutritional deficiencies or to chronic hidden bleeding. (Never self-treat with iron supplements; they can lead to toxicity and many other serious problems.) Vitamin C helps the human body absorb iron from plant sources; thus, a balanced diet should include citrus fruits and a variety of other fresh fruits and vegetables.

Some types of anemia that affect the nails are caused by a deficiency of folate, an essential B vitamin. Whole grains, legumes, dark green leafy vegetables, and fruit juices are good sources of folate and other important B vitamins.

COMMON MYTHS

Many of the numerous nutritional supplements that are promoted as nail builders actually have little if anything to do with nails. Gelatin is a prominent example; because it is made from animal hooves, many people assume that it contains the protein needed to build strong nails. In reality, however, gelatin

---

NAIL CONDITIONERS

Brittle and splitting nails are usually caused by excessive dryness, which increases with aging and is exacerbated by exposure to detergents and chemicals. Rubbing the nails with a moisturizing hand cream or a conditioner formulated for the nails may restore some of the lost water. Applications of nail hardeners may also help seal in moisture and provide a protective hard surface over the nails. Dermatologists generally recommend protein hardeners or products that contain nylon rather than ones made with formaldehyde, which causes severe reactions in some people. Contrary to some promotional claims, however, protein and other substances applied to the surfaces do not sink into or "feed" the nails.

is an incomplete protein and lacks the sulfurous amino acids that give nails their strength.

Another misleading notion is that calcium supplements will harden nails. Because nails contain very little calcium, taking supplements will not enhance their growth or strength. The same is also true of zinc; in the past, the white spots that sometimes develop in nails have been attributed to a deficiency of this mineral. Those spots, however, are usually caused by an injury to the nails, and taking extra zinc—which plays little or no role in nail health—will not get rid of them.

NECTARINES

BENEFITS
- *A fairly rich source of beta carotene and potassium.*
- *Provide moderate amounts of vitamin C.*
- *High in pectin, a soluble fiber.*

DRAWBACKS
- *The flesh darkens when exposed to air.*
- *The pits contain cyanide.*

Sweeter and more nutritious than peaches, their genetic cousin, nectarines were named after the Greek god Nekter; their juice was later called the drink of the gods. This juicy fruit, which is often described as being like a peach without the fuzz, is especially high in beta carotene, an ANTIOXIDANT that the body converts to vitamin A. One medium-size nectarine has 50 calories and provides more than 800 I.U. of vitamin A, about 20 percent of the adult Recommended Nutrient Intake (RNI). It is also high in potassium, contributing about 150mg. With 7mg of vitamin C, or 15 percent of the RNI, a nectarine is not as high in this nutrient as many other fruits.

The yellow flesh of nectarines is rich in BIOFLAVONOIDS, especially carotenoids; these plant pigments are antioxidants that help protect against cancer and other diseases by reducing

SUCCULENT SWEETNESS. *Nectarines harvested at their peak are brightly colored; their moderately firm flesh continues to soften until the fruits are fully ripe.*

the cellular damage that occurs when the body burns carbohydrates, fats, or proteins. Nectarines are also high in pectin, a soluble fiber that helps control blood cholesterol levels. The skins contribute insoluble fiber, which helps prevent constipation.

Cutting or peeling a nectarine releases an enzyme that causes a darkening of the flesh. The fruit may look less appetizing, but the browning doesn't alter its flavor or nutritional value. The discoloring can be slowed by immediately dipping the fruit in an acidic solution (for example, a teaspoon of vinegar diluted in a cup of water) or tossing sliced nectarines with a little lemon juice or lime juice.

Warning: Nectarine pits contain amygdalin, a compound that is converted to cyanide in the stomach. Although accidentally swallowing an occasional pit is not harmful, consuming several of them at a time can cause cyanide poisoning.

SELECTING THE BEST

Purchase fruit that is moderately firm but brightly colored. The fruit is ready to eat when the flesh yields to gentle pressure and has a sweet, fruity fragrance. To ripen firm nectarines, place them in a paper bag at room temperature; they should achieve full ripeness

in 2 or 3 days. Reject nectarines that are hard or have a greenish skin. These were harvested too early; even though they will soften, they will never achieve peak sweetness and flavor.

NEURALGIA

EAT PLENTY OF

• *Lean meat, poultry, eggs, and low-fat dairy products for vitamin B_{12}, and fortified breads and cereals for thiamine; eat all these foods plus spinach, potatoes, and melons for vitamin B_6.*

• *Eggs, poultry, seafood, nuts, seeds, wheat germ, and whole-grain foods for vitamin E.*

AVOID

• *Alcohol in all forms.*

Specialized nerves in the body carry pain messages to the brain, where they are interpreted and responses are transmitted over other sets of nerves. Neuralgia is an umbrella term for any type of throbbing, or paroxysmal, pain that extends along the course of one or more of the peripheral nerves. Neuralgia is classified by both the part of the body affected and the cause. In some cases, doctors can't find a cause for the pain; in many others, the neuralgia is due to an infection or underlying disease, such as arthritis, diabetes, malaria, or syphilis. Tumors, both cancerous and benign, can cause neuralgia. So too do structural problems in which nerves become compressed or pinched; sciatica, the throbbing pain that can extend from the lower back and buttocks to the feet, is one of the most common examples. Various medications, as well as arsenic and other toxins, can also produce neuralgia.

Deficiencies of the B-complex vitamins can result in neuralgia involving numerous nerves throughout the body, a condition known as polyneuralgia or

polyneuropathy. These nutritional deficiencies are rare in affluent industrialized countries, where there is an abundance of food. They do occur, however, among longtime alcoholics, whose diets are generally poor. A deficiency of thiamine—a B-complex vitamin found in various animal products and fortified cereals, breads, and other grain products—is especially common among chronic alcoholics, who typically suffer from nerve pain as well as muscle weakness. Their treatment starts with detoxification, to rid the body of ALCOHOL, and high-dose thiamine supplements. As recovery progresses and the diet improves, the supplements can gradually be decreased.

Long-term use of hydralazine (a powerful antihypertensive medication) or isoniazid (a drug used to treat tuberculosis) can result in vitamin B_6 deficiency, manifested by sensory loss and neuralgia. Anyone taking these medications should make sure that their diet provides extra vitamin B_6; good sources include lean meat, poultry, fish, spinach, sweet and white potatoes, watermelon, bananas, and prunes. A doctor may prescribe B_6 supplements; self-treating with high doses, however, can also damage sensory nerves.

A deficiency of vitamin B_{12}, which is found in all animal products, can lead to degeneration of the spinal cord and widespread neuralgia, as well as pernicious anemia. Most B_{12} deficiencies are due to a lack of intrinsic factor, a substance made by the stomach that is necessary to absorb the vitamin. Less often, a strict vegetarian diet can result in vitamin B_{12} deficiency.

In rare cases, malabsorption problems can result in low levels of vitamin E and cause a type of neuralgia. In such instances, doctors usually prescribe supplements of 30mg to 100mg a day; good dietary sources include nuts and seeds, wheat germ, fortified cereals, vegetable oils, eggs, poultry, and seafood.

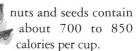

NUTS AND SEEDS

BENEFITS

- *Rich in vitamin E and potassium.*
- *Most are high in minerals, including calcium, iron, magnesium, and zinc.*
- *Some are good sources of folate, niacin, and other B vitamins.*
- *A good source of protein, especially when combined with legumes.*
- *Some are high in fiber.*

DRAWBACKS

- *High in fat and calories.*
- *Oils quickly turn rancid when exposed to oxygen.*
- *Common allergy triggers.*
- *May cause choking in children and people with swallowing problems.*
- *The molds in peanuts and other nuts may produce cancer-causing aflatoxins.*
- *Raw cashews contain an irritating oil.*

The embryos of various trees, bushes, and other plants, nuts and seeds are packed with all the nutrients that are needed to grow an entire new plant. Various nuts and seeds have been valued for their high nutritional content since prehistoric times, and as early as 10,000 BC humans began to cultivate nut- and seed-bearing plants.

Today, even though GRAINS and LEGUMES are more widely produced, nuts and seeds remain important food crops. COCONUTS are the world's leading nut crop, followed by peanuts, which are actually legumes but are often classified and consumed as nuts.

NUTRITIONAL VALUE

Nuts and seeds are the richest source of vitamin E, which is needed to make red blood cells and muscle tissue; it is also an important ANTIOXIDANT, which may be a source of protection against HEART DISEASE. A half cup of almonds provides more than twice the Recommended Nutrient Intake (RNI) of vitamin E.

Most nuts and seeds are a rich source of potassium; about 4 ounces of almonds, Brazil nuts, peanuts, pine nuts, pistachios, or sunflower seeds provide more than 500mg of this electrolyte. Almonds and pistachios, as well as flax, pumpkin, and sesame seeds, are very high in iron. A cup of almonds, Brazil nuts, hazelnuts, or pistachios, or an ounce of sesame seeds, contain as much calcium as a cup of milk. Other minerals found in most nuts and seeds include magnesium, phosphorus, and zinc. They are also rich in the B vitamins. Almonds and peanuts, for example, are especially high in folate. Most nuts are high in niacin; sunflower seeds and Brazil nuts are high in thiamine.

Although most nuts and seeds are high in fats, many of them provide good amounts of protein. With the exception of peanuts, however, they lack lysine, an essential amino acid necessary to make a complete protein. This amino acid can easily be obtained by combining them with legumes.

Finally, most nuts and seeds are a good source of dietary fiber. A cup of almonds, for example, provides 20g—more than any other nut.

THE ISSUE OF FATS

Nuts have two major drawbacks: they are high in calories and fats. But with the exception of coconuts and palm nuts, their oil is mostly mono- or polyunsaturated; hence, they are not as likely to promote ATHEROSCLEROSIS as saturated animal fats.

Still, nuts should be consumed sparingly. Macadamia nuts, with more than 1,000 calories per cup, are the highest in calories; Brazil nuts are a close second. Other nuts and seeds contain about 700 to 850 calories per cup.

Refrigerate or freeze shelled nuts; their oil quickly turns rancid. Never use nuts that are moldy or have an "off" taste; molds that grow on nuts (especially peanuts) create aflatoxins, substances that cause liver cancer.

OTHER PROBLEMS

Some nuts, especially peanuts, provoke ALLERGIC REACTIONS in many people. Symptoms range from a tingling sensation in the mouth to HIVES and, in extreme cases, to anaphylaxis, a life-threatening emergency. But because the different varieties are not closely related, a person who is allergic to walnuts, for example, may be able to eat another type of nut or seed.

Warning: Choking deaths are often traced to nuts. Young children and those who have difficulty chewing or swallowing should not be given nuts unless they have been finely chopped.

DID YOU KNOW?

- Gathered from trees in the Amazon basin, Brazil nuts are the only variety that is not cultivated.

- There are two varieties of almonds—the edible type is sweet; the inedible, or bitter, almond contains a form of cyanide.

- All pistachios are tan, but imported ones are usually dyed red, and some domestic varieties are bleached white.

- By weight, both pumpkin and sesame seeds have more iron than liver does.

- Cashew shells contain urushiol, the same irritating oil that is in poison ivy. Heating inactivates urushiol, so toasted cashews are safe to eat; the raw nuts, however, should never be eaten.

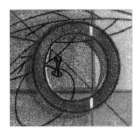

OBESITY

CONSUME PLENTY OF

- *Liquids, such as water and juice, to wash away metabolic wastes.*

EAT MODERATE AMOUNTS OF

- *Complex carbohydrates, such as pasta, potatoes, rice, legumes, and whole-grain products, for energy, vitamins, and fiber.*
- *Fresh vegetables and fruits for vitamins and minerals.*
- *Fish and skinless poultry for high-quality protein and minerals.*
- *Low-fat dairy products for vitamins and calcium.*

AVOID

- *High-fat items, such as candy, pastries, fatty meats, alcohol, and potato chips.*

Being overweight is the most common nutrition-related health problem in Canada, affecting more than 40 percent of all adults. Of these, some 28 percent are considered obese and, consequently, at increased risk for an early death.

While obesity is defined as a weight of 20 percent or more above the ideal for a person's height, age, and build, some experts believe that it is not just the amount of fat but also its distribution that is a key to the health risk. For example, excess abdominal fat has been linked to more serious health problems, including high blood cholesterol levels, than fat in the hips and thighs. The reason is that the liver converts more ab-dominal fat into forms that circulate in the bloodstream.

Few people are truly "fat and happy"; obesity can have devastating effects on health and happiness. Because thinness is highly valued in our culture, people who are overweight often have a poor self-image and are subjected to job and social discrimination. Obesity can also cause shortness of breath, skin chafing, and difficulty moving around, making it hard to enjoy a normal life. Obese people have an increased risk of coronary heart disease, high blood pressure, stroke, diabetes, and certain types of cancer. Other health consequences include damage to weight-bearing joints, leading to osteoarthritis and disability, which perpetuate the vicious circle by restricting movement and leading to further weight gain.

Obesity is difficult and frustrating to overcome. Yet newspaper and magazine articles attest to the constant demand for safe, sure, and rapid weight loss. It is estimated that Canadians spend more than $300 million a year on commercial weight-loss programs.

CAUSES OF OBESITY

If we eat more than we need, the surplus calories are stored as fat. For reasons that are not understood but may have a genetic basis, some people gain weight more readily than others. In fact, researchers have recently discovered a gene that appears to promote obesity. Hormones may also play a role.

Invariably, eating too much food and exercising too little are the key factors. One theory holds that each person has a biological set point for his or her "ideal" weight, and that the body adjusts its metabolism to maintain this set point whenever the person eats more or less than is expended. This set-point theory may be valid; nevertheless, research shows that we can reset our set point through gradual weight loss and increased physical activity.

Case Study

Elisa, a 32-year-old paralegal, was determined to shed 20 pounds in a month to fit into her wedding dress. She tried a high-protein low-carbohydrate crash diet; after a week she had lost 11 pounds. But then she started having dizzy spells and palpitations and felt drained of energy.

After fainting at work, Elisa was taken to an emergency room, where a doctor found that her potassium levels were dangerously low due to excessive urination brought on by her diet. Supplements quickly restored her potassium levels, and the doctor referred Elisa to a dietitian for a sensible weight-loss regimen.

While obesity often seems to run in families, the truth may be that parents who overeat encourage overeating in their children. It is a fact that fat cells are laid down in childhood and remain with us for a lifetime. They may grow larger or smaller to accommodate fat stores, but the number remains the same. That's why a person who was obese during childhood may always store fat more readily than a person who started life thin.

Because metabolism slows with age, some people put on weight as they approach middle age. Older people also may be less active; in either case, calorie needs decline with age, and a person's food intake should be scaled back accordingly.

CONTROLLING OBESITY

The biggest challenge is not losing weight but keeping it off. Most dieters regain all the weight they've lost within 1 to 5 years. The only successful route to permanent weight loss is a combination of EXERCISE AND DIET. However, anyone who is 20 percent or more above their ideal weight should see a doctor before embarking on any exercise program or restrictive diet.

Very low calorie diets tend to lead to the yo-yo phenomenon, in which people lose weight, then quickly regain all they've lost and more. The additional pounds are even harder to shed.

A balanced diet providing about 1,500 calories a day for a woman and 2,000 for a man is a reasonable approach. Combined with a moderate exercise program, it should allow a loss of 1 to 2 pounds a week. Since the aim is to find a diet you can live with in order to keep weight off permanently, it's better to shed pounds gradually by eating moderate amounts of lean meat and other high-protein foods, pasta and other starchy foods, and ample vegetables and fruits. Skim milk and other low-fat dairy products supply needed calcium and other nutrients.

No foods need to be totally forbidden, but the empty calories in alcohol, sugary desserts, and high-fat, high-salt snack foods should be avoided. Weight loss is its own reward. As pounds drop off, the urge to lose more will grow as the desire for fatty, sugary foods fades away. A dietitian can help you to get started on a sensible weight-loss diet and monitor your progress as you gain control of your weight.

OILS

BENEFITS
- *Provide essential fatty acids needed for hormone production.*
- *Make possible the absorption of fat-soluble vitamins A, D, E, and K.*
- *Improve the texture and flavor of food.*

DRAWBACKS
- *High in calories.*
- *Saturated types may raise blood cholesterol levels.*

Throughout history, various plant oils have served as an essential source of concentrated energy and nutrients during times of need. Before refrigeration, preserving foods with oil was critical to survival. Today, even with a limitless supply of healthy foods, oils are an important dietary component. They add an appetizing flavor, aroma, and texture to foods, and because they take longer to digest than the other main food groups, they satisfy hunger.

Oils and FATS belong to the lipid family and differ only in their melting points. Oils are liquid at room temperature; fats are solid. The two kinds of lipids are otherwise interchangeable and are needed in moderate amounts for several essential body functions. All fats and oils have a practically identical calorie content: 9 calories per gram, or 240 to 250 per ounce. They provide a concentrated source of energy and fatty acids that are essential to build and maintain cell walls. Fats are also necessary to make growth and sex hormones and prostaglandins (the hormonelike substances that regulate many body processes), as well as to absorb and use fat-soluble vitamins A, D, E, and K. Vegetable oils contain no cholesterol, it is found only in animal products.

Among the oldest crops for oil are OLIVES—which have been cultivated for both oil and fruit in the Mediterranean region of Europe for at least 6,000 years—and sesame, grown from Africa to India. Coconut palms and oil palms flourished untended in the tropics, where foragers gathered the nuts to extract oils. As techniques for extracting and preserving oils have improved, many more plants have been introduced to cultivation. Currently, the main oil crops are coconut, corn, cottonseed, olive, palm, peanut, rapeseed (marketed as canola), soybean, and sunflower. Recently, much research has been focused on methods of modifying cholesterol-free vegetable oils to take the place of saturated animal fats.

Most vegetable oils are concentrated in seeds or fruits, which are broken down by pressing or grinding. For some

---

TOXIC OILS

Many plant oils (especially from herbs and spices) contain toxic compounds that are often the source of the flavor. Myristicin, the compound that flavors nutmeg and mace, is also found in black pepper and carrot, parsley, and celery seeds. Used in culinary quantities, myristicin is only a flavoring. In massive doses (about two whole nutmegs) myristicin causes hallucinations, headaches, nausea, and cramps.

Thujone, the anise-flavored compound in wormwood, caused an epidemic of brain disease in drinkers addicted to the now-banned liquor absinthe. Sassafras contains the toxic compound safrole, similar to thujone, which is why it is no longer used to make root beer. Very high doses of menthol, from peppermint, may cause dangerous irregularities in the heart's rhythm.

shortenings are hydrogenated to give them a solid consistency and increase their shelf life. The hydrogenation process in effect turns polyunsaturates into saturates and raises levels of trans fatty acids, which increase levels of the detrimental LDL cholesterol. Nevertheless, margarine (fortified with vitamins A and D to match the value of dairy products) is better for cholesterol watchers than butter. About 20 percent of the fat in hard margarine and 13 percent of the fat in soft margarine is saturated; both of these products have much less than the 68 percent saturated fat content of butter, which is also high in cholesterol.

USING OILS

Monitor your oil consumption by buying single-source oils, such as pure canola or pure olive, rather than blended oils. Read labels: A blended oil often has an overwhelming proportion of the cheapest and probably least healthful oil mentioned, with only a token amount of the more expensive, better-quality oil. Check labels, too, for the oil content of processed commercial foods, especially baked goods. If a label states "Contains one or more of the following oils: corn, safflower, or coconut," the product is probably made only with coconut oil because it's the least expensive of the three listed oils.

Oils add a distinctive flavor and texture to salads and sauces. Along with margarines, they can replace dairy fats in most baking recipes. Oils are almost indispensable in the preparation of foods for grilling, broiling, and roasting. When frying, keep oil absorption low by making sure that the oil is at the correct temperature before you add raw foods. Use an oil thermometer if you find it hard to judge the temperature.

FLAVORED OILS. *The range of oils now available include, from left to right: toasted sesame, olive, olive and garlic, virgin olive, cold-pressed extra virgin olive, peanut, walnut, hot sesame, extra virgin olive, sunflower, hazelnut, garlic, and chili oil.*

oils the tissues that remain after pressing are further treated with solvents and heat to remove the last of the oil. "Virgin" oils are those extracted by pressing alone. Most oils are refined by lye treatment, centrifugation and filtration to remove undesirable solids, and steam deodorization; some go through "winterization" to remove substances that crystallize and make the oil cloudy when it is chilled.

HEALTH PROFILE

Oils contain varying amounts of saturated, monounsaturated, and polyunsaturated fatty acids. It's not understood why highly saturated fats interfere with the removal of artery-clogging LDL (low-density lipoprotein) cholesterol from the blood. What is known is that polyunsaturated and monounsaturated fats tend to lower LDL cholesterol. This is the reason people concerned about cholesterol are encouraged to avoid most saturated fats and replace them with mono- and polyunsaturates. The saturated fatty acids mostly responsible for raising cholesterol are lauric, myristic, and palmitic acids. Coconut, cottonseed, palm, and palm kernel oils all contain high levels of these damaging fatty acids. Palm, palm kernel, and coconut oils, like animal fats, are solid at room temperature and are highly saturated. The best all-purpose dietary oils are canola, corn, olive, peanut, safflower, soybean, flax, and sunflower oils, which have low levels of saturated fats.

Oils used to make margarines and

Before serving fried foods, drain off any excess oil on paper towels or bags.

OMEGA-3 FATTY ACIDS

FISH oils contain omega-3 fatty acids, which protect against heart disease and may help people with certain autoimmune diseases as well. The full benefit of the oils can be obtained from eating fish two or three times a week. However, some fish oils are high in cholesterol, which is undesirable for people on low-cholesterol diets. The protective fatty acids are also found in several plant oils, and many experts believe that these sources are preferable to fish. Good omega-3 sources are oils from evening primrose, rapeseed (canola), flax, and walnuts. The use of fish oil supplements is not recommended, because they are high in cholesterol, and when taken in large amounts, they inhibit clotting and can result in bleeding problems.

MINERAL OILS

Oils that have been extracted from petroleum and other forms of nondigestible hydrocarbons are sometimes used as laxatives, particularly by people who are trying to lose weight rapidly by purging. This is a dangerous practice that interferes with the absorption of many nutrients, especially fat-soluble vitamins. It may also cause embarrassing bowel leakage.

OKRA

BENEFITS
- *A good source of vitamins A and C, folate, and potassium.*
- *High in dietary fiber and low in fat and calories.*
- *A thickener of soups and stews.*

DRAWBACKS
- *Glutinous consistency is displeasing to some people.*

A relative of the hibiscus, okra was brought to the Americas from Africa in the 1600s. The dark green pods are the main ingredient in spicy Creole stews or gumbos. In fact, okra is nicknamed gumbo in many parts of the world.

This low-calorie, starchy vegetable is high in folate; a half-cup serving contains about 45 percent of the Recommended Nutrient Intake (RNI). It is also a rich source of the ANTIOXIDANT vitamins A and C and of potassium, an electrolyte that maintains proper fluid balance, helps to transmit nerve impulses, and is needed for proper muscle function and metabolism.

Okra's unique flavor and thickening properties make it a wonderful addition to stews and soups. As it cooks, it releases sticky juices that thicken any liquid to which it is added. This is due in part to the high content of pectin and other soluble fibers. Pectin helps lower blood cholesterol levels by interfering with bile absorption in the intestines and forcing the liver to use circulating cholesterol to make more bile. The large amount of soluble fibers also helps prevent constipation by absorbing water and adding bulk to the stool.

For many people, especially those who are put off by its gummy consistency, okra is an acquired taste. Nevertheless, there are a few ways to decrease this somewhat unappetizing attribute. Rather than boil okra, steam or blanch the pods until they are just tender; the longer okra cooks, the softer it becomes, and with either of these methods, there is less liquid to become glutinous. Don't slice the okra before cooking—less juice will be released if the inner capsule remains intact. Prepare okra along with an acidic vegetable, such as tomatoes, to reduce its gelatinous consistency. Some people prefer eating okra raw; it can be served with dips, as part of a fresh vegetable tray, or sliced into a salad.

OLIVES

BENEFITS
- *High in monounsaturated fats, which benefit blood cholesterol levels.*
- *A modest, low-calorie source of vitamin A, calcium, and iron.*

DRAWBACKS
- *Some varieties are high in sodium.*

The all-purpose crop of the Mediterranean area, olives are indispensable in this region in the preparation of traditional dishes, such as braised duck and lamb stew. In contrast, North Americans tend to use them as a relish or garnish for salads and pizzas. Once a staple for cooking, lighting, cosmetics, and high-quality soap, olive oil is now used mainly in salad dressings, as a cooking oil, and for canning fish.

A medium-size olive contains approximately 5 calories if green and 9 calories if ripe. High in monounsaturated fats, which may raise levels of the beneficial high-density lipoprotein (HDL) cholesterol, and very low in saturates, olives and their oil are thought to contribute to the low rate of heart disease in the Mediterranean countries. Olives provide fair amounts of calcium, iron, and vitamin A (in the form of beta carotene). Those pickled in brine or dry salt cured, however, are high in sodium, which may raise blood pressure in some people.

The method of processing olives varies by region, but the three main commercial processes are the Spanish method, which ferments unripe green olives; the American method, which soaks half-ripe olives in an iron solution to achieve a black color; and the Greek method, which preserves the fully ripe, almost black fruit. Most methods involve soaking the olives in a lye solution to neutralize their natural bitterness.

ONIONS

BENEFITS
- *The green tops are a good source of vitamin C and beta carotene.*
- *May lower elevated blood cholesterol.*
- *Reduce the ability of the blood to clot.*
- *May help lower blood pressure.*
- *Mild antibacterial effect may help prevent superficial infections.*
- *Can be used to flavor many dishes.*

DRAWBACKS
- *Low in most nutrients.*
- *Can cause bloating and gassiness.*
- *Raw onions produce unpleasant breath and skin odors.*

Folklore is filled with fascinating facts about the onion—among them that Alexander the Great fed huge quantities to his troops to strengthen them for battle. The Egyptian tomb paintings abound with onions; in fact, they are depicted more often than any other plant. Early Hebrew writings reveal that it was one of the foods that the Jews longed for after their flight from Egypt. And throughout history, healers have accorded onions near-magical powers to cure everything from baldness to infections.

Onions are members of the allium plant family, which also includes GAR-LIC, LEEKS, and shallots. Worldwide, the onion ranks number six as a vegetable crop; in Canada, it's number five. There are scores of different varieties of onions, with new ones constantly emerging. In general, however, onions are divided into two categories: spring

PUNGENT OR SWEET. *Onions come in many sizes, colors, and flavors. Common varieties include (hanging, left to right) small yellow onions, shallots, yellow field onions, and (on board, left to right) banana shallots, more small yellow onions, red onions, white onions, large sweet onions, and scallions.*

onions, which have a mild flavor and whose green tops and bulbs are eaten; and globe onions, which have a more pungent flavor and dry outer skins that are discarded. Shallots possess features of onions and garlic, but are milder.

With so many sizes, shapes, and flavors, and so many varieties of spring and globe onions available year-round, choosing an onion can be somewhat tricky. Scallions should have crisp, dark green tops and firm white bottoms. Although they will keep for a few days in the refrigerator, scallions should be used before they begin to soften. Globe onions should be firm, with crackly, dry skin. Reject any that feel soft, have black spots (indicating mold), or have green sprouts showing at the top (these are well past their prime). They should have a mild odor—a strong, oniony smell points to decay. Globe onions should be stored in a cool, dry place away from direct light, which can give them a bitter taste. They should not be stored near potatoes, which give off moisture and a gas that causes onions to spoil more quickly.

Red onions have a mild, somewhat sweet flavor, which makes them a favorite for salads and sandwiches. The stronger white and yellow varieties are ideal for cooking, because they become milder and sweeter upon heating and they also impart a pleasant flavor to other foods. There are a number of new sweet varieties of yellow onions, which are often named for the areas where they were originally developed.

THE MANY USES OF ONIONS
The versatility of onions is evidenced by the numerous ways they are used: sliced raw in salads and sandwiches; cooked into stews, soups, and omelets; and baked, boiled, sautéed, or creamed and served as a side dish. Spring onions can be included in a raw vegetable tray, chopped into salads or dressings, or braised and served hot. Build a light

meal around a bowl of French onion soup. To reduce the calorie content, use a defatted broth stock and just a sprinkling of low-fat cheese.

HEALTH BENEFITS
Cooks value onions more for the flavor they impart to other foods than for their nutritional content. Although onions are not high on the nutritional scale, the green tops of spring onions are a good source of vitamin C and beta carotene. A cup of boiled onions provides about 225mg of potassium.

Recent research has verified some of the centuries-old beliefs about onions. For example, folk healers have long recommended onions as a heart tonic; researchers have now documented that adenosine, a substance in onions, hinders clot formation, which may help prevent heart attacks. Studies also indicate that onions may protect against the artery-clogging damage of CHO-LESTEROL by raising the levels of the protective high-density lipoproteins (HDLs). Still other studies suggest that eating ample amounts of onions may help prevent high blood pressure.

Sulfur compounds in onions can cause bad breath and an unpleasant skin odor; however, they also block the cancer-causing potential of some carcinogens. In addition, onions contain substances that have a mild antibacterial effect, which may validate the old folk remedy of rubbing a raw onion on a cut to prevent infection.

Cutting an onion allows its sulfur compounds to combine with enzymes and release volatile molecules which react with moisture in the eyes to form sulfuric acid. Tearing is a natural reaction of the eyes to eliminate the irritant. This effect may help clear congested nasal passages during a cold. A syrup made from onions and honey is an old cough remedy. But consuming raw onions can cause bloating and gas in some people.

ORAL THRUSH

EAT PLENTY OF
- *Lean meats, fish and shellfish, fortified breads and cereals, and dried fruits for iron and zinc.*
- *Soft foods that are easy to swallow.*
- *Raw garlic for its antifungal properties.*

AVOID
- *Candy and sugary foods.*

Candida albicans, a yeastlike fungus that lives in the skin and the mucous membranes of the mouth, digestive tract, and vagina, is normally kept in check by beneficial bacteria. Given an upset in normal body chemistry, however, the fungus can overgrow and cause VAGINITIS, DIARRHEA and other intestinal problems, respiratory problems, an eczemalike skin rash, or oral thrush.

Thrush is signaled by clusters of raised, white, curdlike patches on the tongue, roof of the mouth, and cheeks. If the white layer is scraped off, as when the teeth are brushed, the inflamed underlying mucous membrane may bleed slightly. Left untreated, candida plaques may completely coat the mouth and throat and extend down the esophagus to the stomach or the lungs. MOUTH ULCERS and BAD BREATH are associated symptoms.

Yeast overgrowth may occur when antibiotic therapy kills beneficial bacteria along with infecting microorganisms. Oral thrush is common in people with iron-deficiency ANEMIA. At high risk are individuals with immune systems that have been compromised, perhaps through an inborn defect, HIV infection, or long-term treatment with corticosteroids. In addition, oral thrush may afflict people who are OBESE, have DIABETES or other hormone-related disorders, or suffer DRY MOUTH. It is occasionally a complication of a debilitating disease or severe stress, and it can occur during cancer chemotherapy.

Infants are especially vulnerable to oral thrush because they lack protective bacteria, which develop with time and exposure to the environment.

TREATING THRUSH

For normally healthy people, oral thrush is inconvenient and uncomfortable, but for those with immune deficiencies, it can be very serious. In either instance, a doctor should be consulted. Doctors usually prescribe nystatin, an antifungal medication that is first used as a mouthwash and then swallowed.

Case Study

When Gloria, a 32-year-old teacher, was put on steroids to treat her lupus, she was given a list of possible side effects, including a dry mouth. Her doctor had not mentioned oral thrush, however, so when Gloria developed white patches throughout her mouth, she rushed to see him. He diagnosed oral thrush, a common complication of steroid therapy, and prescribed an antifungal mouthwash. To prevent a recurrence, the doctor instructed Gloria to see her dental hygienist every 3 months. He also suggested an artificial saliva product to alleviate the dry mouth, which can lead to a candida overgrowth.

Severe thrush may make eating food difficult. Drink plenty of liquids, especially enriched milk drinks for vitamins, minerals, and energy. Soft, moist, easy-to-swallow foods will make eating more comfortable until severe symptoms improve. If iron-deficiency anemia is contributing to thrush, try soft preparations of iron-rich foods, such as scalloped fish and shellfish, soups made with milled legumes, and pureed dried apricots mixed with fortified cereals.

Preventive measures may be called for in people at high risk. They should practice good oral hygiene by brushing the teeth frequently and using an antiseptic mouthwash if this is recommended by the doctor or dentist.

Recent studies appear to substantiate previous claims that eating cultured dairy products helps prevent thrush or bacterial overgrowth caused by antibiotic treatment. This benefit stems from *Lactobacillus acidophilus,* a bacterium in the yogurt culture that keeps yeast in check. Yogurt is also a good source of zinc, a mineral that is important in maintaining immunity. Other foods high in zinc include beef, shellfish, and fortified grains and cereals.

Herbalists believe that garlic has antifungal properties. Eating one or two raw cloves daily—either peeled and swallowed whole like a pill or chopped fine and mixed with foods—may help prevent fungal overgrowth. You can take garlic capsules or dried preparations as an alternative, but they are less effective than the fresh bulb.

High blood sugar levels can promote fungal growth, which is why people with diabetes are particularly vulnerable to yeast infections. They can usually be prevented by normalizing blood sugar levels. Although candy and other sugary foods do not directly cause oral thrush, they should be avoided by people with diabetes, because they can contribute to elevated blood sugar.

GOLDEN FRUITS. *Once native to Southeast Asia, Jaffa oranges are now grown in sunny climates worldwide. The smaller blood orange is grown mainly in Italy and Florida.*

ORANGES

BENEFITS
- *An excellent source of vitamin C.*
- *A good source of beta carotene, folate, thiamine, and potassium.*

DRAWBACKS
- *May produce allergic reactions in some susceptible people.*

One of our most popular fruits, oranges are usually associated with vitamin C, and with good reason. One medium-size orange provides about 70mg, more than the adult Recommended Nutrient Intake (RNI). As an ANTIOXIDANT, vitamin C protects against cell damage by the free radicals produced when oxygen is used by the human body, and it may reduce the risk of certain cancers, heart attacks, strokes, and other diseases. Oranges also contain rutin, hesperidin, and other BIOFLAVONOIDS, plant pigments that may help prevent or retard tumor growth. They also have smaller amounts of other vitamins and minerals; these include beta carotene, thiamine, folate, and potassium.

Oranges are low in calories (one orange contains approximately 60). An additional benefit is that the membranes between the segments of the fresh fruit provide a good amount of pectin, a soluble dietary fiber that helps control blood cholesterol levels.

Fresh oranges are not only a delicious snack or dessert, they are also a flavorful ingredient in salads and some meat dishes. A half cup of freshly squeezed orange juice has roughly the same amount of nutrients found in the fresh fruit; much of the pulp and membranes are strained out of most commercial brands. Canned oranges lose most of their vitamin C and some minerals during processing, and they are usually packed in high-sugar syrups.

The peel of the orange is sometimes dried to make candied orange peel or flavorings. Caution is needed, however, because the peel may be treated with sulfites, which can trigger serious allergic reactions in susceptible people. Also, orange peels contain limonene, an oil that is a common allergen. Many people who are allergic to commercial orange juice, which becomes infused with limonene during processing, find they can tolerate peeled oranges.

TYPES OF ORANGES

There are many varieties of oranges; the following are some of the commonest.
Hamlins are grown mostly in Florida. These oranges are seedless and pulpy; they are used mainly for juicing.
Jaffas are imported from Israel and other sunny regions. They are slightly sweeter than Valencias.
Maltese, or blood, oranges are sweet, deep red oranges originating in Italy.
Navel oranges are sweet and seedless and are the second most common type in North America.
Sevilles are sour oranges that are used mostly for marmalades.
Temples are very sweet, juicy, and full of seeds, and are a cross between tangerines and oranges.
Valencias, the most common variety in North America, are used for eating and juicing.

ORGAN MEATS

BENEFITS
- *An inexpensive source of protein.*
- *Liver and kidneys are excellent sources of vitamins A and B$_{12}$, folate, niacin, iron, and other minerals.*
- *Most are good sources of potassium.*

DRAWBACKS
- *Most are very high in cholesterol.*
- *The liver may harbor toxins.*
- *Excessive liver consumption can cause a buildup of vitamin A.*

Despite their high nutritional value, organ meats have never achieved in North America the popularity that they enjoy in France and some other European countries. In recent years they have fallen even further out of favor because some, especially liver and brains, are very high in cholesterol. The furor over mad cow disease (bovine spongiform encephalitis) in England has added to the wariness over consuming brains for fear of contracting a similar fatal brain disease in humans. Still, dishes like calf's liver, kidneys, sweetbreads (calf thymus and pancreas), and tripe (stomach) regularly appear on the menus of ethnic and gourmet restaurants. Many patés and popular luncheon meats, such as liverwurst, are made from organ meats and perhaps other variety cuts, such as the feet.

LIVER

Because the liver is a storehouse for vitamin A, iron, and many other nutrients, it follows that it is also a highly nutritious meat source. A 4-ounce serving of beef liver provides more than 10 times the Recommended Nutrient Intake (RNI) of vitamin A, 50 to 100 times (depending upon how it's prepared) the RNI of vitamin B$_{12}$, 100 percent or more of the RNIs for folate and niacin, and more than 50 percent of the RNIs for iron and zinc.

The 200 calories in a 4-ounce serving of liver is less than in most other cuts of beef, but liver's major drawback is its high cholesterol content, which ranges from 400mg in 4 ounces of braised beef liver to 500mg when it's pan fried. The Heart and Stroke Foundation of Canada recommends that dietary cholesterol should not exceed an average of 300mg a day; however, an occasional serving of liver in an otherwise low-fat, low-cholesterol diet probably is not harmful unless you have heart disease or high blood cholesterol, in which case it may be advisable to forgo this meat.

One of the liver's main functions is to metabolize and detoxify various chemical compounds. Thus, the liver may harbor residues of antibiotics and other drugs fed to meat animals, as well as environmental toxins. For this reason, some doctors advise against eating liver on a regular basis.

Liver is one of the richest dietary sources of vitamin A. When a person consumes more vitamin A than is needed, the excess is stored in the body. Over time a buildup of vitamin A can result in liver damage, fatigue, and other problems. Studies show, for example, that consuming 5 to 10 times the RNI of vitamin A before and during early pregnancy can increase the risk of birth defects. Normally, it's difficult if not impossible to consume toxic amounts of vitamin A from an ordinary diet. But because liver is so high in this nutrient, an individual who consumes it several times a week may develop a toxicity.

OTHER ORGAN MEATS

Brains are higher in cholesterol than any other food; a 4-ounce serving of beef brains has more than 2,000mg, and pork brains contain an even larger amount. On the plus side, they are an excellent source of vitamin B$_{12}$.
Heart is also high in vitamin B$_{12}$, iron, and potassium; in addition, it provides high-quality protein and less fat and cholesterol than other organ meats.
Kidneys are low in fat and high in protein. They provide large amounts of vitamin B$_{12}$, riboflavin, and iron, and they supply useful amounts of B$_6$, folate, and niacin.
Sweetbreads are high in fat, but they provide useful amounts of potassium.
Tongue, also high in fat, contains useful amounts of most of the B vitamins, especially B$_{12}$.
Tripe provides high-quality protein, a fair amount of potassium, and small amounts of minerals.

ORGANIC AND HEALTH FOODS

*If you are skeptical of the many additives found
in foods today, you can always turn to organic products—
but don't expect them to be nutritionally superior.*

The notion of nutritious food produced by natural methods understandably appeals to consumers who are worried about the health effects of pesticides, growth hormones, antibiotics, and other chemicals often used by today's farmers. Defenders of modern agriculture counter that their methods are safe and are responsible for the unprecedented abundance of foods enjoyed by Canadians.

Despite the continuing controversy, there is little doubt that the health-food movement is growing. Only a few years ago, organic products were typically found solely in health-food stores or farmers' markets; but today everything from free-range meat, poultry, and eggs to organic vegetables, fruits, and wines are marketed alongside their conventionally

---

BENEFITS
- *Less likely to contain traces of pesticides, dyes, and other chemicals.*
- *Natural farming methods restore nutrients to the soil.*
- *Animals are raised in a more natural and humane environment.*
- *Animal products are free of antibiotic and hormone residues.*

DRAWBACKS
- *Usually are much more costly.*
- *Spoil faster and may contain harmful organisms.*
- *Fresh produce is less attractive.*
- *Crop yields are generally lower.*
- *Promotional messages are often confusing and misleading.*

---

produced counterparts in supermarkets and other commercial food outlets. Two major differences stand out, however: the natural, or organic, foods are usually more expensive, and they often lack the visual appeal of their competitors. As far as nutrition goes, food experts contend that there's virtually no difference.

WHAT THE TERMS MEAN
The terms "organic," "natural," and "health foods" are often used interchangeably to identify foods grown with organic fertilizers and natural weed and insect control. This is frequently not the case, however; many foods produced conventionally are marketed as natural or organic products. In an effort to prevent fraud and clarify definitions, the organic food industry has created their own standards, but there are no national guidelines to define organic products.

NUTRITIONAL CONTENT
Purveyors of natural foods often promote their products as being both safer and more nutritious than those produced with artificial aids. Many people mistakenly assume that manure and natural compost produce plant foods that are more nutritious

A WIDER CHOICE. *Consumer demand has led to a great variety of organic products—everything from fruits and vegetables to meat, fish, and even organic wine and chocolates.*

than those grown with commercial fertilizers. This simply is not the case. A plant's genetics, the weather, availability of water, and the time of harvest all have a greater impact on the nutritional content than the type of fertilizer. As it grows, a plant extracts various minerals and other substances from the soil and converts them into new organic material. Without adequate nutrition, the plant won't grow, but ultimately it makes no difference whether the nutrients it needs come from natural or artificial fertilizers.

Numerous laboratory tests to compare the nutrients in organically and conventionally grown produce have not found any substantial nutritional differences. Indeed, artificial fertilizers can actually improve nutritional value if they contribute nutrients, such as iodine, that are lacking in some soils.

Modern farming methods do yield larger crops than natural or organic methods. A study comparing per-acre yields found using commercial fertilizers and pesticides more than doubled the number of bushels of corn, soybeans, and wheat produced by organic farm methods. The lower yield is one reason organic foods are so costly.

A MATTER OF TASTE

While there may not be significant nutritional differences between organic and conventionally grown foods, there are some marked differences in taste and appearance. Organic fruits and vegetables tend to be smaller and more flavorful; at the same time, some may also have blemished skins from insect attacks and lack the even or intense color that is often achieved by spraying the foods with dyes or waxes.

Meat from chickens that are allowed to forage outdoors also has a different flavor in comparison to their factory-reared counterparts. The meat tends to be leaner, somewhat tougher, and more flavorful. Some people also claim that meat from pigs and cattle

GROWING YOUR OWN

One way to guarantee that your food is truly natural, or organic, is to grow it yourself. If you plan to engage in organic gardening, the following tips may prove useful.

• Instead of using artificial fertilizers, turn organic garbage into compost.

• If you do opt for commercial fertilizer, try a natural product, such as sterilized manure, fish meal or bone meal, or dried blood. These replenish the soil, are easily absorbed, and encourage the growth of soil bacteria and worms, which in turn promote healthy plant growth.

• Mulching with bark chips adds nutrients to the soil, discourages weeds, and retains moisture.

• Some weeds are actually beneficial. A nettle plant, for example, attracts ladybugs, which feed on aphids.

• Instead of using pesticides, intersperse rows of vegetables with bright, scented flowers to attract insects that attack garden pests.

• Learn to distinguish the good bugs from those that eat your plants. Good bugs include bees, fireflies, lacewings, ladybugs, and spiders. Frogs, garter snakes, and toads have an appetite for insects too.

• Put up feeders or plant thick bushes to attract birds, which also prey on insects.

• If your garden is infested with destructive worms, try natural parasites, such as nematodes, microorganisms that feed on cutworms, or *Bacillus thuringiensis* (BT), a bacterium that feeds on cabbageworms.

• Try companion planting to control pests. Plant rosemary with cruciferous vegetables to discourage cabbage moths. Marigolds help fend off carrot rust flies, and summer savory protects beans from whiteflies.

that are not treated with growth hormones tends to be more flavorful.

THE SAFETY ISSUE

There's no question that many commercial pesticides are toxic, but when used properly, they are not considered a major health hazard for consumers. (In contrast, they can be very dangerous for the farm workers who apply them without taking proper precautions or who go into recently treated fields unprotected.) Some pesticides actually lower potential health risks; for example, fungicides retard the growth of molds that give off cancer-causing toxins.

When it comes to pesticides, consumers should be more wary of imported foods than of domestic produce, because some of the more dangerous products that are banned in Canada are used abroad. In any case, it's a good idea to wash all fruits and vegetables before eating, and in some cases the foods should be peeled.

There are some natural foods that are major health hazards and should be avoided. For example, unpasteurized milk and products made from it can harbor organisms that cause tuberculosis and other serious diseases.

A PRUDENT APPROACH

In general, Canadians enjoy an abundant and safe food supply. It is not, however, problem free. Scientists worry that modern agricultural methods and our liberal use of pesticides will eventually upset the ecological balance and create major problems. We have seen indications of this in the past—for example, the decimation of bird populations that led to the banning of DDT.

Consumers who are concerned about chemical residues do have other choices; they can patronize farmers' markets or buy organic foods. Or they can join the growing number of people who are rediscovering the rewards of growing foods in their own gardens.

OSTEOMALACIA

TAKE IN MODERATION

- *Low-fat milk and dairy products for calcium and phosphorus.*
- *Oily fish for vitamin D, and canned salmon and sardines for calcium.*
- *Liver, egg yolks, fortified milk, margarine, and cereals for vitamin D.*
- *Sensible exposure to sunlight.*

CUT DOWN ON

- *Wheat bran, rhubarb, spinach, tea, coffee, and other foods that can interfere with the absorption of calcium.*

The adult form of rickets, osteomalacia, involves a loss of minerals and bone density that causes the bones to soften, become deformed and painful, and fracture easily. As with OSTEOPOROSIS, the bones most often affected are those in the spine, the pelvis, and the legs.

Both osteomalacia and rickets are now rare in industrialized countries, thanks to the abundance of foods high in vitamins and minerals. For healthy bone growth, we depend on a balance of calcium, phosphorus, and vitamin D, among other nutrients. Osteomalacia may be caused by a lack of vitamin D in the diet; however, this is an unlikely cause because industrialized countries routinely fortify milk with vitamin D, and most people have at least moderate exposure to sunlight. More likely causes are gastrointestinal conditions, such as CELIAC DISEASE or CYSTIC FIBROSIS, which prevent the absorption of fats needed to absorb vitamin D; stomach and intestinal surgery, which may prevent calcium and vitamin D from being absorbed; or LIVER DISORDERS or KIDNEY DISEASES that interfere with the metabolism of vitamin D.

DIET FOR HEALTHY BONES

While general dietary guidelines may be given for people with primary osteomalacia due to lack of calcium and vitamin D, they may not be appropriate for those with bone disease that is secondary to other diseases. These conditions require a meticulous balance of proteins and other essential nutrients to prevent further damage to the organs involved. In these cases, patients should carefully follow the diets prescribed by their doctors and dietitians.

The management of osteomalacia always involves medical treatment of the underlying disorder. If vitamin and mineral supplements are needed, the doctor will prescribe them; they should not be taken without a doctor's recommendation. Eating foods that are rich in vitamin D and calcium may help, but patients should adhere strictly to the doctor's and dietitian's recommendations. Excessive intake of vitamin D can be toxic, leading to kidney damage, and calcium deposits in the heart, kidneys, and blood vessels.

Exposure to just 10 to 15 minutes of bright sunlight two or three times a week gives the body enough resources to synthesize vitamin D. Elderly people may need somewhat longer exposure, however, because the normal metabolic changes of age reduce their ability to synthesize vitamin D in the skin. In northern areas, where the winters are long and the hours of daylight few, the sunlight may be too weak to stimulate vitamin D production between November and March. People living in these areas, as well as shut-ins, may need extra portions of D-rich foods in winter, but again, they should not take vitamin D supplements without consulting a doctor.

Vitamin D and calcium are absorbed together; that's the reason calcium-rich foods, such as milk and other dairy products, are fortified with vitamin D. Other good sources of calcium are canned fish with bones, such as salmon and sardines, BROCCOLI, and TOFU.

In people with underlying health problems, osteomalacia may develop when they eat too much of foods that hinder calcium absorption. These include foods with oxalic acid (found in cocoa, chard, SPINACH, and RHUBARB); phytic acid (found in bran, soybeans, and other LEGUMES); and a very high intake of dietary FIBER. For healthy people eating a balanced diet, normal quantities of any of these foods will not hinder calcium absorption enough to adversely affect their bones.

People following a strict VEGETARIAN DIET may be at risk for osteomalacia because they eliminate milk and other dairy products, our best sources of calcium, and rely on plant foods, which contain little vitamin D. Further, some plant foods high in calcium contain other substances that interfere with its absorption. To ensure that calcium intake is adequate, vegans should consume plenty of fortified soybean milk and tofu processed with calcium sulfate.

OSTEOPOROSIS

TAKE PLENTY OF

- *Low-fat milk, yogurt, canned fish with bones, and other foods rich in calcium.*
- *Foods rich in vitamin D, such as oily fish and fortified dairy products.*
- *Legumes for phosphorus.*
- *Weight-bearing exercise.*

CUT DOWN ON

- *Alcohol.*
- *Coffee, tea, colas, and other beverages containing caffeine.*

AVOID

- *Smoking.*

Throughout life, our bones are in a state of constant renewal, called remodeling. While some bone cells are breaking down and being resorbed, others are forming to take their place. When resorption occurs faster than formation, the bones become weak and extremely porous. Fractures can occur with little or no pressure. This condition is called osteoporosis. Lack of estrogen appears to be its key contributing factor, but a falling off of androgens—the male hormones—is also involved, coupled with an inadequate intake of calcium and vitamin D.

Osteoporosis is often not detected until the bones have suffered extensive damage and have spontaneously fractured. The "dowager's hump" that makes many women in midlife appear round-shouldered is caused by compression fractures of the spinal vertebrae. As the vertebrae compress, the spine curves and the woman loses height. Her internal organs are displaced and the abdomen protrudes, with severe discomfort as a result of pressure on the digestive tract.

After their bones reach a peak density at about age 30, both men and women begin to lose some bone mass with increasing age. In women, however, the loss is greatly accelerated with the decline in estrogen production at MENOPAUSE. Osteoporosis affects all women, but those of Northern European and Asian ancestry have the highest risk. Women of Mediterranean and African descent are less severely affected, perhaps because they tend to have more bone mass and typically get the sun needed to make vitamin D.

Moderate weight-bearing exercise can protect the bones at any age, and in fact, exercise is one factor that is known to improve bone strength in later life. However, a very high level of athletic training in adolescent girls robs their bodies of the fat they need to produce and store estrogen. Highly trained teenage athletes and ballet dancers, who often have menstrual irregularities, may be at increased risk for developing early, severe osteoporosis. Anorectic girls who starve themselves in order to get rid of the normal subcutaneous layer of fat are at high risk as well.

HELPFUL FOODS

Dairy products, such as low-fat or skim milk, nonfat yogurt, and reduced-fat cheese, are high in calcium. Eat 3 or more servings daily.

Sardines and canned salmon, eaten bones and all, provide extra calcium; have a serving once or twice a week.

Mackerel and other oily fish, as well as fortified milk and margarine, provide vitamin D, which is needed by the body to absorb calcium. Consume at least 1 serving daily (or spend a few minutes in the sun each day).

Smoking cigarettes greatly increases the risk of severe osteoporosis. For instance, women who smoke have lower levels of estrogen at all ages, and they may enter menopause up to 5 years earlier than their nonsmoking counterparts. In addition, nicotine is known to interfere with the ability of the body to use calcium.

Women whose ovaries are surgically removed experience an abrupt withdrawal of estrogen production rather than a gradual decline. They may suffer more severe osteoporosis than those who have normal menopause. Other medical conditions may add to the risk of osteoporosis, including KIDNEY DISEASES and the use of steroid drugs.

PREVENTION

Osteoporosis prevention should begin in childhood, with a healthy diet and regular exercise to build bone density. Adults and children should consume plenty of calcium, the building block of bone; they also need vitamin D to ensure that the body uses the calcium to its best advantage. Experts usually suggest that older adults aim for a daily calcium intake of 1,000 to 1,500mg. Phosphorus, also essential to bone formation, is found in most of the foods that contain calcium.

Foods that are especially rich in calcium and phosphorus include milk and dairy products, dried beans and peas, tofu, canned fish eaten with the bones, and dark green leafy vegetables. The darker the greens, the more calcium they contain; the one exception is spinach because it is high in oxalic acid, which inhibits calcium absorption.

Those who shun whole milk because of its fat content can drink skim milk, which has even more calcium ounce for ounce. Low-fat cheese, yogurt, and lactose-free milk are excellent dairy sources of calcium for people who have an INTOLERANCE TO MILK. Strict vegetarians can get calcium from enriched soy milk and tofu, as well as from green vegetables. Seaweed, now available at many ethnic markets and in Japanese restaurants, has more calcium than some cheeses and is very low in calories.

If the doctor recommends a calcium supplement, read the label carefully to find out how much elemental calcium is in each pill and what form it's in. Calcium citrate and calcium carbonate are the most easily absorbed forms; calcium carbonate and calcium chloride may cause intestinal discomfort, including constipation, bloating, and gas; and calcium gluconate sometimes causes diarrhea. Taking supplements along with meals helps absorption. Some physicians suggest that women obtain extra calcium from over-the-counter indigestion remedies. However, these antacids are designed to neutralize stomach acid and may have an adverse effect on the digestion if used for long periods of time. Bone meal and dolomite supplements are not recommended because they may be contaminated with heavy metals, such as arsenic, lead, mercury, and cadmium.

Just as important as calcium is vitamin D, which the body needs in order to absorb calcium. Adults need at least 2.5mcg (micrograms) of vitamin D daily. The main source of this vitamin is sunlight, but it can also be obtained from dietary sources, including oily fish and egg yolks. Some calcium sources, such as milk, are fortified with vitamin D, as are many breakfast cereals.

Regular weight-bearing exercise is essential to maintain bones. Walking, jogging, aerobics, tennis, and dancing are all excellent activities for this purpose. This type of activity stimulates the remodeling process and improves the circulation, which brings vitamins and minerals to the bones.

WHAT TO AVOID

High protein intake can increase the excretion of calcium. It's wise to limit protein to the Recommended Nutrient Intake (RNI) of 64g a day for men and 51g a day for women.

Caffeine and alcohol both promote urination and hasten calcium loss. In addition, alcohol prevents the body from absorbing calcium properly and is toxic to bone cells.

Medications can affect the levels of calcium in the body. Antacids containing aluminum can promote calcium excretion. Calcium is also lost during long-term use of other drugs, including certain antibiotics, diuretics, and steroids.

BEYOND DIET

Although diet and exercise are without a doubt beneficial, they may not be enough to stave off osteoporosis. Many doctors typically recommend that women have a baseline bone density scan, similar to an X-ray, when menstrual periods become irregular. Depending on the results, the doctor may recommend calcium and vitamin D supplements or other therapy.

ESTROGEN REPLACEMENT

For women, the most effective preventive treatment for osteoporosis is hormone replacement therapy (HRT) to replace the estrogen lost at menopause. Estrogen can dramatically cut the rate of vertebral and hip fractures. Progesterone is normally added to decrease the risk of endometrial cancer from estrogen replacement therapy; however, HRT is not advised for women with a family history of estrogen-linked cancer, including certain types of breast cancer. Taking estrogen in the form of a skin patch prevents the nausea—similar to morning sickness—that some women experience at the beginning of hormone replacement therapy.

Although prevention is still important, new medications are available that are designed to treat osteoporosis. These include bisphosphonates, such as etidronate (Didronel), pamidronate (Aredia), and alendronate (Fosamax). These medications all decrease bone resorption and shift the balance toward the formation of healthy tissue. Calcitonin (Miacalcin), a hormonal preparation that can be taken by injection or as a nasal spray, works in a similar fashion to increase bone density and reduce the rate of vertebral fractures. In addition, slow-release fluoride preparations, which have been available in Europe for a number of years and are now sold in North America, appear to increase bone formation and thereby reduce vertebral fractures.

Yet another new medication is raloxifene (Evista), which helps prevent osteoporosis by modulating the body's estrogen receptors. This drug, while not a hormone, offers many of the same benefits as estrogen without increasing the risk of breast and uterine cancers.

Case Study

When 48-year-old Suzanne stopped having menstrual periods, she was anxious to avoid the problems her mother had experienced in later life. Suzanne's mother, a lifelong smoker, developed severe osteoporosis in her mid-sixties, which eventually kept her housebound. By the time she died at the age of 78, she had suffered many fractures and had lost several inches in height; complications from a hip fracture precipitated her death. The doctor said that her low-calcium diet, smoking, sedentary lifestyle, and lack of sun exposure were all factors that had contributed to her osteoporosis.

Suzanne, by contrast, was a non-smoker who enjoyed a varied diet with plenty of low-fat dairy products, legumes, and green vegetables. A tennis enthusiast, she kept active year-round. A baseline scan showed Suzanne's bone density to be only slightly below the ideal for a woman her age. Because of her family history of osteoporosis, she followed her doctor's recommendation to start hormone replacement therapy. With adequate estrogen replacement, vigorous activity, and a diet rich in calcium and vitamin D, it's much less likely that Suzanne will become a shut-in as her mother was.

PALPITATIONS

EAT PLENTY OF
- *Foods high in potassium and magnesium (if you are taking diuretics).*

CUT DOWN ON
- *Coffee, tea, colas, and other sources of caffeine, as well as alcohol.*

AVOID
- *Smoking and the use of cocaine and other illegal or recreational drugs.*

Most people experience occasional palpitations when the pulse races or the heart seems to thump or skip a beat. Typically, these irregular heartbeats occur during exercise or when a person is under emotional stress. The sensation of the heart thumping in the chest can be alarming, but it is usually short-lived and harmless. A doctor should be consulted, however, if the palpitations recur frequently, are prolonged, or are accompanied by shortness of breath or dizziness. In such cases, possible causes that should be ruled out include HEART DISEASE, an overactive THYROID gland (hyperthyroidism), ANEMIA, or a metabolic disorder.

ALCOHOL and such stimulants as CAFFEINE and nicotine are among the many substances that can affect the heartbeat. Long-term heavy use of alcohol can damage the heart and result in cardiac arrhythmias. Some people who are overly sensitive to caffeine develop palpitations after drinking only a cup or two of coffee, but more often it takes six or more cups a day to have this effect. Nicotine also speeds up the heartbeat. The best approach is to use alcohol and caffeine only in moderation and, if you smoke, make every effort to stop immediately.

Street drugs, especially amphetamines (uppers) and cocaine, can cause palpitations and more serious cardiac arrhythmias. Obviously, no one should indulge in the use of these illegal substances, and anyone who is addicted should seek professional help. Some ASTHMA drugs can have a similar effect. In such cases, an alternative drug can usually be prescribed.

Potassium helps regulate the heartbeat, and both too much or too little can result in cardiac arrhythmias. People taking diuretics or other drugs that increase potassium excretion should make sure that their diet provides ample citrus fruits, bananas, dried fruits, legumes, and fresh vegetables.

Magnesium deficiency, which may occur in alcoholics or people with kidney disease or severe prolonged diarrhea, can also upset the normal heart rhythm. Foods high in magnesium include green leafy vegetables, legumes, fortified grain products, and seafood.

PAPAYAS

BENEFITS
- *An excellent source of vitamins A and C and potassium.*
- *An extract is used to tenderize meat.*

DRAWBACKS
- *Can cause dermatitis in some people.*

Native to Central America, papayas are now grown in tropical climates around the world. They should not be confused with the North American pawpaw—although often called by the same name, the two are unrelated.

Like most yellow-orange fruits, papayas are high in vitamin C and beta carotene, the plant form of vitamin A. A medium-size papaya supplies more than four times the adult Recommended Nutrient Intake (RNI) of vitamin C, 75 percent of the RNI of vitamin A, and 800mg of potassium.

Papayas contain papain, an enzyme that is similar to the digestive juice pepsin. Because this enzyme breaks down protein, papain extract from papayas is marketed as a meat tenderizer. It has also been used medically to treat ruptured spinal disks, but this treatment has fallen out of favor in most places. Topical ointments containing papain are sometimes applied to promote the shedding of dead tissue. Papain causes the dermatitis that some people experience when handling papayas; this irritation is not necessarily an allergic reaction.

Usually eaten raw, the fruit should be washed, split open, and the black seeds scooped out. These seeds are normally thrown away, but they can be dried and used like peppercorns.

You can also use papayas in cooking; they impart a sweet Caribbean flavor to chicken or fish dishes. A few pieces of papaya added to a stew tenderizes the meat, while its pectin serves as a natural thickener.

Papaya nectar is a popular beverage, but many bottled varieties are mostly water and sugar. A product that contains only 33 percent papaya juice can still be sold as papaya nectar.

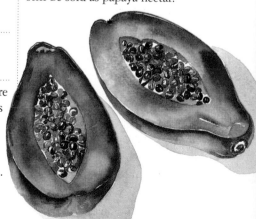

PARKINSON'S DISEASE

CONSUME PLENTY OF
- *Fresh vegetables, fruits, and whole-grain products to prevent constipation.*
- *Fluids to promote good digestion.*
- *Soft or pureed foods to ease swallowing.*

CUT BACK ON
- *High-protein foods if taking levodopa.*

AVOID
- *Excessive weight gain.*

About 100,000 Canadians are afflicted with Parkinson's disease, a chronic and progressive nerve disorder that causes uncontrollable shaking or trembling (tremors), a fixed staring expression, muscle rigidity, stooped posture, and an abnormal gait. The disease varies from one person to another; some people develop speech problems and difficulty swallowing, while others suffer progressive dementia. Parkinson's affects men and women equally and generally develops after the age of 50.

The symptoms of Parkinson's disease are due to progressive destruction of a part of the brain, the substantia nigra, where cells make dopamine, a chemical necessary for proper neuromuscular function. The underlying cause of the disease is usually unknown. In some cases, however, cocaine use and head injuries, such as those suffered by boxers, have resulted in a type of parkinsonism. In a few cases, the use of a street "designer drug" (an altered version of demerol) induced parkinsonism in drug addicts.

There is no cure for Parkinson's, but various medications, especially levodopa, can reduce symptoms and slow the progression of the disease. There are also surgical treatments, but these are usually reserved for severe advanced disease.

THE ROLE OF DIET

Although there are no nutritional treatments for Parkinson's disease, diet helps to increase the effectiveness of treatment with levodopa and manage such problems as constipation and difficulty in chewing and swallowing.

To be its most effective, levodopa should be absorbed from the small intestine as soon as possible after it is taken. Some physicians advise taking the drug 20 to 30 minutes before meals, but if this provokes nausea, it can be taken with a carbohydrate snack, such as crackers or bread. Protein delays absorption of levodopa, so the medicine should not be taken with animal products. There have been some reports that a reduced intake of protein may be beneficial. Some doctors advise consuming the day's protein allowance in the evening, when it's less likely to create problems for patients on levodopa.

Constipation can be minimized by consuming ample fresh fruits and vegetables, whole-grain cereals and breads, and other high-fiber foods, as well as drinking six to eight glasses of water or other fluids daily. Exercise promotes healthy bowel function and is advised for anyone with Parkinson's disease, because it preserves muscle tone and strength. It is also important to avoid becoming overweight, as this makes mobility even harder.

PROBLEM SOLVING

Patients with advanced Parkinson's often have trouble chewing food and swallowing it normally, because the disease affects the tongue and facial muscles. Excessive drooling and shaky hands are also common problems. Medications can help reduce drooling, and meals should emphasize foods that are easy to chew and swallow. These include cooked cereals or well-moistened dry cereals, poached or scrambled eggs, soups, mashed potatoes, rice, soft-cooked pasta, tender chicken or turkey, well-cooked boneless fish, pureed or mashed vegetables and fruits, custard, yogurt, and juices. If eating is tiring, try smaller but more frequent meals.

To avoid choking, sit up straight and tilt your head slightly forward when swallowing. Take small bites, chew thoroughly, and swallow everything before taking another bite. Concentrate on moving food backward in your mouth with your tongue, and swallow again if you feel that food did not go down completely. Sip a liquid between bites to help wash food down. If you do cough or choke, lean forward and tuck your chin down while coughing.

PARSNIPS

BENEFITS
- *Low in calories and high in fiber and carbohydrates.*
- *A flavorful alternative to potatoes.*
- *A useful source of vitamin C, folate, and potassium.*

Parsnips have a sweet, nutty flavor that goes well with other vegetables in soups or stews. They can also be served as a side dish or instead of potatoes or other starchy foods. This winter root vegetable tastes best after the first frost; exposure to cold begins to convert its starch into sugar. Because parsnips are too fibrous to eat raw, they are served cooked.

Parsnips are a low-calorie, nutritious starchy food. A half-cup serving has only 60 calories and is high in fiber; it also provides 300mg of potassium and between 10 and 20 percent of the daily requirements of vitamin C and folate.

When buying parsnips, select ones about the size of a medium carrot; reject any that are covered with roots or are soft and shrunken. If the tops are still attached, cut them off before storing them so they don't draw moisture from the roots. They can be kept for a few weeks in the refrigerator.

PASTA

BENEFITS

- *An excellent source of starches.*
- *A useful source of protein, B vitamins, iron, and other minerals.*
- *Low in fat and sodium.*
- *Can be served in many different ways.*

DRAWBACKS

- *Often topped with high-fat sauces.*

Long a staple food of Mediterranean diets, pasta has now become a passion for Canadians as well. As a nation, we prepare about 130 million pounds of pasta at home each year, and this does not include what's served in restaurants. Although pasta was first introduced to North Americans by Thomas Jefferson, our preference for pasta is relatively recent; until the 1980s this food was often dismissed as boring and fattening.

Pasta comes in hundreds of different shapes, sizes, textures, and flavors, but the Italian, or Western, style prevails as our favorite. This is changing, however, with the increasing popularity of Asian noodles and dumplings made from wheat, rice, mung bean, and buckwheat flours.

Most dry Italian-style pasta is made with semolina, a very fine-textured flour derived from durum wheat. A growing number of supermarkets also carry pastas made from corn, quinoa, Jerusalem artichokes, and other types of flours, as well as varieties flavored with garlic and other herbs, spinach and other vegetables, and squid ink.

NUTRITIONAL VALUE

Provided that it is not served with a high-fat, high-calorie sauce, pasta is a

A MEDLEY OF PASTA. *Although spaghetti is the most recognized pasta, Canadians are now choosing pasta from among hundreds of varieties from around the world.*

filling, low-calorie food. For example, 2 ounces of spaghetti, when cooked, becomes a 1-cup serving with 200 calories. Most of these calories come from complex carbohydrates, but a 1-cup serving also provides about 5 to 7g of protein. Although this protein lacks some essential amino acids, these can easily be obtained from a sprinkling of Parmesan cheese as a low-calorie (25 per tablespoon) topping. Egg noodles provide complete protein, but they also contain a modest amount of fat and about 50mg of cholesterol per serving. There are also high-protein pastas that are enriched with soy flour and milk solids.

Pastas are a good source of iron (with about 2mg in a 1-cup serving), potassium, and dietary fiber; many are also enriched with thiamine, niacin, and other B vitamins.

All too often pasta is turned into a fattening dish with butter, cheese, and rich sauces. But there are many ways to avoid these extra calories. The 400 to 500 calories in a 6-ounce serving of a traditional meat-and-cheese lasagna, for example, can be cut almost in half by substituting vegetables for the ground meat and using low-fat or skim ricotta and mozzarella cheeses.

A VERSATILE FOOD

Pasta can find a place in nearly every meal. For breakfast, make an omelette with leftover cooked pasta mixed with an egg (just the white if cholesterol is a concern). Another hearty breakfast choice is a cup of pasta tossed with a small amount of Parmesan or Romano cheese and heated in a microwave oven. Like other complex carbohydrates, pasta is filling and will provide the energy needed to start the day.

For lunch, add some leftover cooked pasta to a soup or toss it with raw vegetables, tuna, or thinly sliced chicken. For dinner, make a side dish of orzo, couscous, or other small pasta as a substitute for rice or potatoes. Sauté or

HEALTHY PASTA SAUCES

Pasta dishes can be transformed by the addition of sauces. Traditional ingredients include olive oil, garlic, onions, mushrooms, tomatoes, and fresh basil. Many classic sauces, such as cheese, pesto, and bolognese, are high in fat and calories. The following are ideas for creating tasty low-calorie dishes.

- Toss pasta with fresh tomatoes or a broth for a simple sauce.
- Use half of the oil, cheese, and nuts in a pesto recipe, while increasing the basil and garlic. Add white wine if the sauce is too dry.
- Puree vegetables in a blender or food processor, simmer them with herbs and spices, and toss with spaghetti or another pasta.
- When making a cream sauce, substitute low-fat milk or evaporated skim milk for the cream.
- Toss a pasta salad with a dressing made from nonfat yogurt or mock sour cream instead of regular sour cream or mayonnaise.
- Combine pasta with beans, lentils, or other legumes to create a high-protein vegetarian meal.
- Instead of a buttery cheese sauce, toss pasta with a broth and sprinkle it lightly with grated Parmesan or Romano cheese.
- Add vegetables instead of meat to a light tomato sauce.

stir-fry fresh vegetables and toss them with pasta to make a primavera dish, which can be an appetizer, a side dish, or an entrée. For a special occasion, top linguine or angel hair pasta with a seafood medley of clams, mussels, shrimp, and scallops.

Pasta can also be a healthy snack—for example, a pita pocket stuffed with orzo pasta salad. Tortellini, bow-shaped farfalle, and ziti are a few of the interestingly shaped pastas that are ideal as BEGINNER FOODS for toddlers.

PEACHES

BENEFITS
- *A good source of vitamin A, with useful amounts of vitamin C and potassium.*
- *A good source of dietary fiber.*

DRAWBACKS
- *May provoke allergic reactions in susceptible people.*

Nutritious and versatile, peaches can be enjoyed fresh, added to fruit salads, or cooked with meat and poultry dishes. They can also be baked, grilled, broiled, or poached to create pies, cobblers, and other desserts.

While there are hundreds of varieties, peaches are usually classified into one of two categories: freestone, with a loose, easily removed pit, or cling, in which the stone is enmeshed in the fruit's flesh. Freestones are mostly sold fresh, while clingstones are reserved for canning, freezing, and preserves.

Fresh peaches are a low-calorie source of ANTIOXIDANT vitamins; a medium-size fruit contains only 35 calories, approximately 535 I.U. of vitamin A (in the form of beta carotene), and 7mg of vitamin C (just slightly more than 15 percent of their respective Recommended Nutrient Intakes, or RNIs). They are high in fiber, especially pectin, a soluble fiber that is instrumental in lowering high blood cholesterol. Canned and frozen peaches contain lower levels of vitamins A and C and are higher in calories than the fresh; a cup of sweetened frozen peaches contains 235 calories, compared to 190 in those canned in heavy syrup, and 110 in juice-packed brands.

Ounce for ounce, dried peaches contain the most calories, because it takes 6 to 7 pounds to produce just 1 pound of the dried. Ten dried peach halves provide 310 calories; on the plus side, they are also a more concentrated source of various essential nutrients. Those 10 halves provide 2,810 I.U. of vitamin A, 1,295mg of potassium, and 5mg of iron. After eating dried peaches, brush your teeth to remove their sticky residue; it can create dental problems. Dried peaches often contain sulfites, a preservative that produces an allergic reaction in susceptible people.

Peaches may produce an allergic reaction in people with allergies to such related fruits as apricots, plums, and cherries, as well as almonds. They also contain salicylates, which may provoke a reaction in aspirin-sensitive people.

In North America, the season for peaches runs from April through mid-October, peaking in July and August. Peaches do not increase in sweetness after picking, so when choosing fruits avoid those that are rock hard. A peach should feel heavy, indicating that it is juicy, and it should have a sweet odor. The skin should be smooth and have a warm yellow or reddish color. Avoid any peaches that are bruised.

In terms of texture, it is best to choose relatively soft peaches if they are to be eaten right away. If you buy firm peaches, placing them in a paper bag at room temperature will hasten the ripening process. Unless they are going to be eaten within the day, store ripe peaches in the refrigerator; they will keep for 3 to 5 days.

PEARS

BENEFITS
- *A good source of vitamin C and folate.*
- *A good source of dietary fiber.*

DRAWBACKS
- *Dried pears often contain sulfites, which provoke asthma attacks or allergic reactions in susceptible people.*

Called the "butter fruit" by many Europeans in reference to its smooth texture, a pear makes an ideal snack, dessert, or even a sweet or spicy side dish. Pears are a delicious treat when served fresh, but they can also be baked, poached, or sautéed.

One medium-size (6-ounce) pear has less than 100 calories and provides about 7mg of vitamin C (more than 15 percent of the adult Recommended Nutrient Intake, or RNI). Most of the vitamin C is concentrated in the skin of the fruit, so pears should be eaten unpeeled. Pears also have useful amounts of folate, potassium, and iron, as well as pectin (a soluble fiber that helps control blood cholesterol levels) and cellulose (an insoluble fiber that promotes normal bowel function).

Dried pears provide a more concentrated form of calories and nutrients than fresh pears; however, their high sugar content and sticky texture may promote tooth decay, so be sure to brush your teeth after consuming them. Most dried pears also contain sulfites, which can provoke asthma or an allergic response in susceptible individuals.

Canned pears lose most of their vitamin C due to the combined effect of peeling and heating. They are also usually high in calories, especially if they are packed in heavy syrup.

TYPES OF PEARS
While there are hundreds of varieties of pears in North America, four types predominate: Anjou, a juicy, oval-shaped winter pear that has a yellowish green skin; Bartlett, a summer pear that is eaten fresh or canned; Bosc, which has a slender neck and a firm, crunchy texture that makes it ideal for baking and poaching; and Comice, a green-skinned variety that is considered the sweetest and tastiest winter pear.

POPULAR PEARS. *Among the numerous varieties are (clockwise from lower left) Bosc, Comice, red and regular Bartletts (the three at the top), and Anjou.*

PEAS AND PEA PODS

BENEFITS

- *A good source of vitamins A and C, thiamine, riboflavin, and potassium.*
- *High in pectin and other types of fiber.*
- *Provide complete protein when served with grain products.*

DRAWBACKS

- *High in purines, which can precipitate a flare-up of gout symptoms in people with this disorder.*

Throughout history the pea has been a plant of significance. It is mentioned in the Bible, and dried peas have even been found in Egyptian tombs. In more recent times pea plants provided data for Gregor Johann Mendel, the founder of modern genetics. Peas are classified as LEGUMES, and as such, they form a complete protein when combined with grains. Fresh green peas are more convenient than dried legumes, because they do not require a long cooking time and can even be eaten raw.

Besides being high in protein, fresh green peas are a good source of pectin

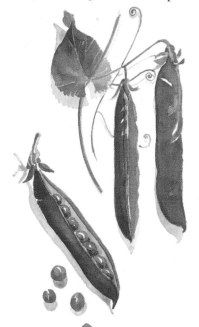

and other soluble fibers, which help control blood cholesterol levels. The pods are high in insoluble fiber, which helps prevent constipation. Green peas are lower in calories and fat than other high-protein foods; a half-cup serving contains about 60 calories and 4g of protein. A half-cup serving of cooked green peas also provides about 15 percent of the Recommended Nutrient Intake (RNI) of vitamin C and 10 to 20 percent of the RNIs of vitamin A, thiamine, and riboflavin, as well as 1mg of iron and 215mg of potassium.

The younger green peas are, the sweeter and tenderer they are. In fact, very young peas can be eaten in their pods. Once picked, peas should be eaten or refrigerated, because their sugar quickly converts to starch. After shelling, green peas can be eaten raw or cooked. To minimize the loss of vitamins, peas should be cooked in as little water as possible until just tender. Cooking some of the pods with the peas or with soup stock adds flavor and nutrition; discard them before serving.

Peas are also sold frozen or canned. Of the two, frozen peas are a better choice than canned, which have fewer nutrients, added salt and sugar, and less color and flavor than their fresh or frozen counterparts.

Snow, or sugar, peas are often used in Chinese stir-fried dishes and are available either fresh or frozen. They are always eaten in their flat pod, because they are harvested while still immature; consequently, they contain less protein than green peas do. However, they are higher in vitamin C (a half cup supplies about 40mg, or 100 percent of the RNI) and have slightly more iron. Since they are eaten in their fibrous pods, a serving of snow peas is lower in calories (about 35 per cup).

Like other legumes, peas are high in purines, which can precipitate an attack of gout in people with this disease.

PEPPERS

BENEFITS

- *An excellent low-calorie source of vitamins A and C.*

Sweet peppers are related to CHILIES, or hot peppers. Both are native to the Western Hemisphere and were named by Spanish explorers who confused them with the unrelated peppercorn.

The four-lobed bell peppers are the most common of the sweet varieties in Canada. Depending on the degree of ripeness, bell peppers range in color from green to yellow to red. Those picked while green will not become red, because peppers ripen only on the vine. Peppers grow sweeter as they ripen, which is the reason red ones are sweeter than yellow ones, which are sweeter than green ones. Other varieties of peppers include banana peppers, which derive their name from their yellow color and elongated shape; cubanelles, which are tapered, about 4 inches long, and range from green to red in color; and orange-red pimientos, which are heart shaped.

A half-cup serving of peppers contains only 12 calories, but the vitamin content varies according to color. Ounce for ounce, peppers are a better source of vitamin C than citrus fruits. One serving of green peppers provides more than 100 percent of the adult Recommended Nutrient Intake (RNI) for vitamin C, whereas red peppers provide 50 percent more of this ANTIOXIDANT. In contrast, a half-cup serving of green peppers supplies only about 5 percent of the RNI of vitamin A in the form of beta carotene, compared to 55 percent of the RNI of vitamin A in red peppers. In addition, peppers supply smaller amounts of vitamin B_6 and folate.

Deeply colored peppers are high in BIOFLAVONOIDS, plant pigments that help prevent cancer; phenolic acids, which inhibit the formation of cancer-causing nitrosamines; and plant sterols, precursors of vitamin D that are believed to protect against cancer.

Peppers can be served in a salad or with a dip, steamed, roasted, or stuffed and baked. Steaming, stir-frying, and other fast cooking methods do not significantly lower their nutritional value.

PICKLES AND OTHER CONDIMENTS

BENEFITS
- *Sauerkraut is a good source of vitamin C, iron, potassium, and other nutrients.*
- *Pickles are low-calorie snacks.*

DRAWBACKS
- *Most pickles and condiments are extremely high in sodium.*
- *Sweet pickles, ketchups, and chutneys are high in sugar.*
- *In large amounts, pickled foods may increase the risk of cancer.*

Pickling was once essential for keeping sufficient food stores over the winter. Long before vitamin C and other essential nutrients were identified, sauerkraut—pickled CABBAGE—was used to prevent scurvy during extended sea voyages. Today, however, pickled foods are consumed mostly for their taste.

In pickling, food is preserved by saturating it with acid, which prevents most microorganisms from growing. Two basic methods are used: soaking in acid, usually a vinegar-based solution; and brining, a fermentation process that takes place through the action of acid-producing bacteria.

In the first method, vegetables are presoaked in brine to draw off moisture that would dilute the vinegar. They are then sealed in jars to mature in the vinegar, usually with pickling spices. This method is used for sweet and sour pickles. Chutney, ketchup, and piccalilli (a mustard mixture) are cooked, pulped variations on the basic vinegar pickle. Bacteria rarely grow in these mixtures, but molds and yeasts may flourish on imperfectly sealed surfaces.

Fermented pickles, such as dill pickles, are vegetables that are immersed in a brine that is strong enough to inhibit the growth of unwanted bacteria but mild enough to nourish several species that produce lactic acid. This and other compounds contribute to the characteristic flavor. (Dill pickles are also flavored with dill seeds and fronds.) No bacteria are inoculated into the brine; instead, they are attracted to the mixture from the surrounding air. Fermented pickles are more difficult to make than vinegar pickles because, given the wrong temperature or salt concentration, hostile bacteria will thrive and make the pickles soft and unpalatable.

SAUERKRAUT

One of the few pickled dishes served as a vegetable, sauerkraut has only 20 calories in a half-cup serving. It provides 17mg of vitamin C (almost 50 percent of the Recommended Nutrient Intake, or RNI), almost 2mg of iron, and useful amounts of the B vitamins,

IN A PICKLE.
Though often low in vitamins, pickles and other condiments add zest to foods.

calcium, potassium, and fiber. Sauerkraut is high in sodium (800mg per half cup), and the salt content may be increased by foods often served with it, such as frankfurters.

KETCHUP AND OTHER SAUCES

Most ketchup is made from tomatoes, although plums and other soft fruits, and even green walnuts, can be used. The huge variety of commercial barbecue sauces are variants on the basic ketchup recipe of tomatoes, brown sugar, vinegar, salt, pepper, and spices. These sauces are condiments, with negligible nutritional value. The large amount of salt in most may be harmful for people with high BLOOD PRESSURE and others who are on low-salt diets.

Soy sauce, basic to Asian cooking, is very high in sodium—1,000mg per tablespoon compared with 60mg in mustard and 55mg in ketchup. Even reduced-sodium soy sauce should be off-limits to people on restricted-salt diets.

Mustard is a spice obtained from the seeds of a plant in the cabbage family. Its pungent smell and flavor develop only after the seed is crushed and moistened, allowing enzymes to react with isothiocyanates to form mustard oils. Most mustards are sold premixed, and many specialty varieties, which are mixed with white wine or herb-flavored vinegars, are marketed both as fine pastes and as coarser blends that contain unground seeds. The addition of turmeric gives some types their brilliant yellow color and extra tanginess. In making prepared mustard, the dry powder is usually blended with wheat flour to improve its mixing qualities; people with CELIAC DISEASE, who are gluten sensitive, should look for mustards that don't contain wheat.

CANCER RISK

A diet that is high in pickled or other salt-cured foods and condiments has been linked to an increased risk of stomach and esophageal cancers. This is thought to stem from their high levels of nitrates, which are converted to cancer-causing nitrosamines during digestion. Nitrates are often used in the pickling solution to impart flavor and prevent the growth of undesirable microorganisms. Vitamins A and C, beta carotene, and other ANTIOXIDANTS are thought to inhibit the cancer-causing potential of nitrosamines; eating ample fresh vegetables and fruits may counteract any risk from pickled foods.

PINEAPPLES

BENEFITS
- *A good source of vitamin C, with useful amounts of vitamin B₆, folate, thiamine, iron, and magnesium.*

DRAWBACKS
- *May cause dermatitis in individuals sensitive to bromelain, an enzyme in pineapple juice.*

Native to South America, pineapples are now grown in tropical areas worldwide. They are available in frozen and dried forms, but the majority of the crop is reserved for canned varieties, juices, or fresh fruit. Although pineapples are available year-round, their peak season takes place during June and July.

The sweet and tangy flavor makes fresh pineapple a delicious snack or dessert choice; it can be added to fruit salads and grilled or baked with seafood, ham, poultry, or other meats. As pineapple is cooked, its texture softens due to the breakdown of cellulose, a type of fiber in its walls.

Fresh pineapple contains bromelain, an enzyme that is similar to the papain in papayas that dissolves proteins. Consequently, fresh pineapple is a natural meat and poultry tenderizer when it is added to stews or marinades. If pine-

apple is to be used in a gelatin mold, however, the fruit should be canned or boiled beforehand in order to deactivate the bromelain; otherwise, the gelatin (a form of protein) will not set properly and will become soupy. Bromelain may cause skin irritation or allergic dermatitis in susceptible people.

One cup of fresh pineapple chunks contains 75 calories and provides 25mg of vitamin C (60 percent of the Recommended Nutrient Intake, or RNI). It also offers useful amounts of other nutrients, including 0.1mg of thiamine, 16mcg (micrograms) of folate, 0.15mg of vitamin B₆, 0.6mg of iron, and 17mg of magnesium. Pineapple is high in soluble fiber, which may aid in controlling high blood cholesterol.

Canning does not significantly lower pineapple's vitamin C; a cup of juice-packed fruit retains all of its vitamin C, while a cup packed in heavy syrup provides about 20mg. However, canning heats the fruit enough to destroy its bromelain. It also adds extra calories if syrup is used—a cup of juice-packed chunks contains 150 calories, compared to 200 in a cup packed in heavy syrup.

After picking, a pineapple will not ripen further. When buying a pineapple, look for one that exudes a fragrant odor and has light yellow or white flesh. Brown patches indicate spoilage. If you are buying the fruit whole, make sure that it seems dense and heavy for its size and that the leaves are green.

PLUMS

BENEFITS
- *A useful source of vitamin C, riboflavin and other B vitamins, and potassium.*

DRAWBACKS
- *May cause allergic reactions in susceptible people.*

Whether they are eaten whole, added to fruit salads, baked goods, compotes, puddings, or meat dishes, or made into butters, jams, purees, or sauces, plums are a nutritious low-calorie food. One medium-size fresh plum contains only 36 calories and is a good source of such dietary fibers as cellulose and pectin. It also supplies useful amounts of several nutrients, including 6mg of vitamin C, 0.06mg of riboflavin, and 113mg of potassium. Canned plums contain comparable amounts of riboflavin and potassium but are significantly lower in vitamin C (one canned plum provides only 1mg). Fruits canned in heavy syrup are higher in calories than fresh—for example, one canned plum packed in a sugary syrup yields 60 calories. In their dried form some plums become PRUNES, which are a more concentrated source of calories and nutrients.

In North America, the plum season extends from May to October, beginning with the Japanese varieties and ending with the European types. More than 140 varieties of plums are available in North America, so it's not surprising that they vary in shape, color, and flavor. Despite this wide array of choice, there are only five main types:

American plums include the DeSoto, Golden Beauty, and Pottawattomi varieties. These native plums are available locally, but they generally are not produced commercially.

Damson plums, which have dark flesh and skins, resemble European plums but are slightly smaller in size and

SWEET AND JUICY. *Tree-ripened plums are full of flavor and nutrients, yet they are low in calories.*

more tart in flavor. They are often used to make jams and preserves.

European plums, which are also referred to as common plums, have blue or purple skins and a golden yellow flesh. These plums are denser, smaller, and less juicy than the Japanese varieties. Some varieties are sold fresh, others are dried. The ones that are more tart in flavor are ideal for cooking or making preserves.

Japanese plums are consumed fresh, cooked, or canned, but they are never dried to make prunes. Most have a juicy reddish or yellow flesh and skin ranging from deep crimson to black-red.

Ornamental plums are used mostly for jellies and jams.

Fresh plums do not ripen after they have been picked; before buying one, look for brightly colored fruit that yields slightly to the touch. Color, which varies from one variety to another, may not be a good indicator of ripeness. Overripe plums tend to be soft, with a bruised or discolored skin, and they are sometimes leaky. Firm plums can be stored for a day or two at room temperature to soften them.

Plums may produce an allergic reaction in individuals with confirmed allergies to apricots, almonds, peaches, and cherries, which come from the same family. Similarly, people who are allergic to aspirin may also encounter problems after they have eaten plums. In addition, like peaches and apricots, the pits of plums contain amygdalin, a compound that breaks down into hydrogen cyanide in the stomach, and can cause cyanide poisoning if consumed in large amounts.

POLLUTANTS AND PESTICIDES

Pesticides and fertilizers assure an abundant food supply, but some people fear their health effects. Certain foods may bolster the body's mechanisms for detoxifying natural and added chemicals.

People who fear that all chemicals are bad for their health might stop to reflect on the fact that all living matter is made of chemicals, some of which may indeed be harmful or lethal in large doses. Some of these harmful chemicals occur naturally in foods; others are added, but in amounts that pose no danger to health when consumed with the nutrients found in a varied and balanced diet.

Potentially harmful chemicals can enter the food supply during growing, processing, and packing. These include pesticides that are applied to crops; antibiotics, hormones, and other substances included in animal feed; and environmental pollutants, such as heavy metals, asbestos, PCBs, and vinyl chloride. While many contaminants pose no threat with short exposure, accidental spills often carry severe risks, leaving residues that persist in the environment for a long time.

REGULATING PESTICIDES

Some chemical pesticides and fertilizers are needed to ensure that there is enough food at a reasonable cost; even with modern pesticides, one-third of the world's crops are lost to pests each year. Most crops retain traces of pesticides; animal products may contain even larger amounts. Because high doses of certain pesticides have been linked to health problems in animals, it's not surprising that Canadians are concerned that some chemicals in the food supply may cause birth defects, neurological diseases, and even cancer.

In Canada, the manufacture and use of pesticides are regulated by Agriculture Canada, Health Canada, and Fisheries and Oceans Canada. These agencies, along with their provincial counterparts, also monitor the presence of pesticides in animals, humans, and the environment, and set tolerance levels for pesticide residues in food. These tolerance levels are usually set at a fraction of the level that is still safe for laboratory animals.

CONSUME PLENTY OF
- *Broccoli and other cruciferous vegetables for cancer-fighting indoles.*
- *Vegetables and fruits for detoxifying bioflavonoids.*
- *Fresh fruits and vegetables for antioxidant nutrients.*
- *Fish and vegetable oils for omega-3 fatty acids.*
- *High-calcium foods to reduce intestinal tumor growth.*
- *Onions and garlic to reduce exposure to carcinogens.*

AVOID
- *Meat fat and the skin on fish and poultry.*
- *The outer leaves of leafy vegetables, such as cabbage and lettuce.*
- *The peels of vegetables or fruits that are waxed or heavily exposed to pesticides.*

Regulations in many foreign countries are less strict than in Canada. Consequently, some imported foods may have higher concentrations of pesticides than domestic foods do.

In Canada, total pesticide use is on the decline as farmers increasingly rely on integrated pest management. This refers to the appropriate use of insect traps, crop rotation, natural insect predators and more specific and powerful pesticides when needed to control pests.

Although foods are regularly tested, it is impossible to totally eliminate pollutants from the food supply. What's more, all fruits and vegetables produce natural pesticides; one example is nicotine, which protects tobacco plants from pests. Many of these pesticides are more potent cancer-causing agents than synthetic chemicals, at least in the doses that the government allows in foods. Luckily, the plants also have cancer-fighting substances that cancel out the potentially harmful effects of the others.

THE FOOD CHAIN

Whether a contaminant is harmful or not depends on how long it lingers in the body or the environment. A substance that resists chemical or biological breakdown accumulates as it is ingested by one species after another, steadily building up as the food chain progresses from small, weak species to the large and dominant. The highest levels of pollutants, therefore, are ingested by large animals and humans at the top of the food chain.

If the body rapidly excretes a substance or metabolizes it into a harmless compound, brief exposure may do no harm. But when a contaminant interacts with body systems, it may be dangerous. Most chemical carcinogens are relatively harmless in themselves. They become dangerous when the body transforms them into reactive compounds that can damage its DNA. Most of this transformation, called metabolic activation, takes place in the liver. Some toxins are stored in fatty tissues and remain out of harm's way until the fat is mobilized for energy. That's why trimming the fat from animal products can help to reduce the amount of pollutants you consume.

FIGHTING POLLUTANTS

To ensure sound nutrition while guarding against exposure to high levels of pollutants and pesticides, the wisest course is to eat a wide variety of foods and avoid consuming too much of a few items that may carry a heavy contaminant load. For contaminants we can't avoid, our bodies are remarkably well equipped with preventive mechanisms to detoxify them.

ANTIOXIDANTS, such as vitamins C and E, for example, prevent certain carcinogens (especially nitrosamines) from being produced in the digestive tract. These vitamins—as well as, possibly, beta carotene, which the body converts to vitamin A—also scavenge and quench the highly reactive byproducts of cells' normal metabolism. Wheat bran and an amino acid compound in codfish, dissimilar substances in most other respects, bind nitrites and keep them from forming nitrosamines. Phenolic compounds in plants bind directly to carcinogenic hydrocarbons and stop them from reacting with DNA.

Chlorophyll and fiber in the digestive tract may prevent cancer-causing substances from entering our cells; fiber, too, dilutes carcinogens and hastens their passage out of the digestive tract.

There are also backup mechanisms to arrest the carcinogens that may slip through our barricades. Many substances in foods suppress tumor promotion, the process that gradually transforms a single mutated cell into an actively growing tumor. Isothiocyanates (in vegetables of the cabbage family) and natural

NATURAL PESTICIDES. *Instead of chemical sprays, organic gardeners rely on beneficial insects to destroy pests.*

antioxidants including plant phenolics (in apples and other fruits) and BIOFLAVONOIDS (especially high in citrus fruits) induce the body to release enzymes that detoxify carcinogens before they can be activated. The same omega-3 fatty acids that help to prevent HEART DISEASE also suppress tumor development. Terpenes in citrus fruits and the sulfur compounds in garlic and other members of the onion

family bind carcinogens to neutralizing molecules before they can cause damage. Calcium, which is abundant in dairy products as well as in dark green leafy vegetables, binds to irritating free fatty acids and bile acids to reduce cell multiplication in the lining of the intestines.

LOWERING THE RISKS

The amount of pesticide residue in the diet depends on several factors: the type of foods eaten and how they are prepared; growing conditions that may require using extra pesticides; and the timing of the applications. Careful food preparation can reduce the risks associated with pesticides (see Removing Pesticides, above left).

A low-fat diet that provides ample vegetables and fruits is naturally rich in detoxifying compounds. But many other factors, such as heredity, lifestyle, and exposure to environmental pollutants and occupational hazards, affect susceptibility to diseases. For the time being, it's safest to rely on dietary sources for detoxifying compounds; supplements often contain untested and potentially toxic high doses.

ENVIRONMENTAL ESTROGENS

Some scientists warn that synthetic chemicals, such as bisphenol-A in certain plastics, mimic the effects of estrogen, the major female sex hormone. They claim that these estrogenlike substances have caused a dramatic drop in sperm counts worldwide, a view disputed by other experts, who contend that the amounts from chemicals are minute when compared to the amounts occurring naturally in our food. Until experts agree, it's difficult to know what course to take. If there is a risk in using pliable plastics, it will do no harm to recycle glass containers for storing leftovers, especially for fatty items, such as meat and butter, which may be more susceptible to contamination from plastic.

PORK

BENEFITS
- *Fresh, lean pork is a good source of high-quality protein and B vitamins.*
- *Ham and bacon have high levels of vitamin C, which is added as a preservative.*

DRAWBACKS
- *Nitrites in cured pork products form cancer-promoting nitrosamines.*
- *Ham, bacon, and other cured pork products are high in salt and may also be high in fat.*
- *Undercooked pork may carry parasites.*

Thrifty cooks used to boast that when it came to pigs, they could use everything but the squeal. A pig yields chops and other cuts of fresh meat; cured or processed products, such as ham and bacon; and skin for gelatin and leather.

Although some pork products are high in saturated fat, trimmed, lean pork is close to skinless poultry in its fat and calorie content. A 3-ounce serving of lean roast pork has 185 calories, with substantial amounts of protein; the B vitamins thiamine, riboflavin, and niacin; and a few minerals, such as calcium, potassium, and iron. The tenderloin, center-cut leg, and loin chops are the least fatty cuts. While pork has a higher proportion of unsaturated fats than other meats, its cholesterol content is also high: 80mg in a 3-ounce pork chop and 100mg in 3 ounces of spare ribs. Salt-cured pork products are extremely high in sodium and should be avoided by people on low-salt diets.

Pork cooked to an internal temperature of 150°F (65°C)—or medium doneness—will remain moist and tender. This temperature also ensures the destruction of the parasites that cause trichinosis. Freezing for a minimum of 3 weeks at 15°F (−9°C) will also kill these parasitic microorganisms.

The pink color of cured pork is due to nitrites, which are used to inhibit bacterial growth and preserve flavor. During cooking, and in the digestive tract, these chemicals combine with others to form nitrosamines, compounds that are known to promote cancer in animals. Cured meats, however, supply only about 20 percent of the nitrites that form nitrosamines; the rest come from related compounds in plants. Controversy over the safety of nitrites led to a sharp reduction in the use of these substances by food processors.

Ascorbic acid (vitamin C) and a related harmless compound, erythorbate, are often used to speed curing, stabilize color and flavor, and improve the antibacterial effect of nitrites in cured pork products. These compounds also reduce the formation of nitrosamines. In addition, nisin, an antibiotic substance produced naturally by the cultures that turn milk sour and make cheese resistant to spoilage, has a synergistic effect that makes it possible to use lower doses of nitrites in curing.

Nevertheless, some consumers continue to press for an outright ban on nitrites because, with modern curing processes, the chemicals are used mainly to enhance the meat's appearance.

Most of the pork produced in Canada is now grown factory-style in which the pigs are confined to cages or pens in large buildings. This agribusiness method has enabled farmers to raise many more pigs in a small space, but it is also highly controversial. The waste from these pig factories is usually piped into large open holding tanks or ponds, which creates pollution and odor problems. If the holding tanks leak, groundwater can become contaminated. Also, the large amounts of ammonia emitted by pig farms return to earth in rain and help create algal blooms. Some consumer groups have raised questions about the increased use of antibiotics and growth hormones to produce meat; others decry the factories as cruel to animals.

POTATOES

BENEFITS
- *A good source of vitamins C and B_6, and potassium and other minerals.*
- *An inexpensive, filling, and nutritious starchy food.*
- *Their flavor complements most foods.*

DRAWBACKS
- *Often prepared with fat and sodium.*
- *Green and sprouted potatoes may contain solanine, a poisonous substance.*

Although they are often associated with Ireland, potatoes are native to the Andes Mountains and were first cultivated by Peruvian Indians at least 4,000 years ago. Spanish explorers introduced potatoes to Europe in the 1500s, where they became a staple food source for the poor. Potatoes are now cultivated worldwide; in fact, they are the world's largest and most economically important vegetable crop. For most Canadians, potatoes are a major component of the diet—usually in processed forms that are high in fat and salt.

There are many varieties of potato, but YAMS AND SWEET POTATOES are not among them; the white potato is not even related to these. Instead, it's a member of the nightshade family, and is related to peppers and tomatoes.

Potatoes are surprisingly nutritious and low in calories. When eaten with the skin, they are high in complex carbohydrates and fiber; one medium-size baked potato (with the skin) provides 25mg of vitamin C, which is more than 45 percent of the adult Recommended Nutrient Intake (RNI), along with a good supply of vitamin B_6, and about 10 percent of the RNIs of niacin, iron, and magnesium, 800mg of potassium, and a moderate amount of zinc.

The flavor and nutritional content of a potato varies according to how it is prepared. Many people think potatoes are fattening, but this is true only when they are fried or served with butter and rich sauces. A medium-size baked or boiled potato has between 60 and 100 calories, a small amount of protein, and almost no fat. The same potato turned into potato chips has 450 to 500 calories and up to 35g of fat; 4 ounces of French fries contain about 300 calories and 15 to 20g of fat. A cup of mashed potatoes with milk provides about 130 calories, compared to 355 calories in a cup of scalloped and au gratin potatoes. French fries and other processed potatoes are almost always high in salt.

When preparing potatoes, it is best not to remove the skin because most of the nutrients are near the surface; instead, scrub them under water with a vegetable brush. If you do peel them, try to remove as thin a layer as possible. Once sliced or peeled, raw potatoes will discolor when exposed to oxygen, so cook them immediately or place them in water with vinegar or lemon juice added. Baking, steaming, or microwaving preserves the maximum amount of nutrients. Pierce a potato's skin with a fork before baking or microwaving to avoid having it explode. If you boil potatoes, leave the skin on, use as little water as possible, and cook in a covered pot. Some nutrients, particularly vitamin C, are lost in the water during boiling. To salvage some of the lost nutrients, you can add the potato water to soups or stews, or use it to make bagels.

When buying potatoes, look for firm ones with few eyes and no black spots. Avoid those with a green tint to the skin, and remove any sprouts; they will taste bitter and may contain solanine, a toxic substance that can cause diarrhea, cramps, and fatigue.

Store potatoes in a dark, cool place, but not in the refrigerator. Temperatures below 45°F (7°C) convert the starch to sugar, giving the potato a strange taste. Don't store potatoes and onions together; the acids in onions aid the decomposition of potatoes, and vice versa.

MANY SHAPES, SIZES, AND COLORS. *Just a few of the hundreds of varieties of potatoes grown worldwide are shown below.*

POULTRY

BENEFITS

- *An excellent source of protein.*
- *Lower in saturated fat than red meats.*
- *A good source of vitamin A, the B vitamins, and minerals.*

DRAWBACKS

- *Susceptible to bacterial contamination.*

Higher in protein and lower in saturated fat than red meats, poultry—including chicken, turkey, Rock Cornish game hen, duck, goose, guinea fowl, squab, pheasant, and quail—is an excellent source of high-quality protein, with all the essential amino acids, as well as calcium, copper, iron, phosphorus, potassium, and zinc.

All poultry has a similar range of nutrients; the main difference, apart from flavor, is in the fat content. A 3-ounce portion of roasted, skinless light turkey is the lowest in calories and fat, with 135 calories and 3g of fat, compared to 145 calories and 4g of fat in a comparable portion of chicken and 170 calories and 10g of fat in 3 ounces of skinless roasted duck.

Most poultry fat is under the skin; removing the skin before eating the meat greatly reduces the fat content.

The fattiness of duck can be reduced by pricking the skin all over before roasting it to allow the fat to drain off.

Poultry meat is a good source of vitamin A and a modest-to-moderate source of the B vitamins. Chicken and duck contain the same amounts of cholesterol—75mg in a 3-ounce portion of skinless roasted meat—whereas a similar serving of turkey contains 60mg.

Dark poultry meat comes from muscles that get more exercise. That's why drumsticks are darker than breast meat, and why game birds, which spend much of their life on the wing, often have breast meat that is dark, like their drumsticks. The extra oxygen these muscles need is stored in the purplish pigment, myoglobin.

BUYING POULTRY

You can be confident that a bird is young and tender if its legs and wings spring back after being pulled out. Youth and tenderness, however, may not be the prime considerations for long-cooking dishes; a mature boiling fowl has more flavor and firmer flesh that improves with simmering.

Skin color does not affect the taste, but don't buy poultry with rough, dry, or bruised skin, which may be a sign that the bird was harshly treated and that the texture and flavor of the meat are inferior. Contrary to advertising claims, the very yellow skin of some poultry brands is not a sign of better health; these birds are fed colorants, such as marigold flowers, which do not alter nutritional value but may inflate the price to consumers.

POULTRY SAFETY

Because most poultry is sold with its skin intact, it is susceptible to spoilage from bacteria that remain on the skin and in the cavity after processing. Kept at 40°F (4°C), the average refrigerator temperature, chicken skin will become slimy in only 6 days, indicating a 10,000-fold increase in bacteria. All poultry should be washed under running water before being prepared for cooking. You should wash your hands frequently during preparation, and scrub knives and cutting boards in hot, soapy water before reusing them.

Poultry is thoroughly cooked when the leg joints move easily, the juices run clear if the thigh is pierced with a knife, and the meat is soft to the touch. Chickens that come with plastic meat thermometers often require an additional 10 or 15 minutes of roasting after the thermometer pops up to get rid of bloody streaks around the joints.

Never refrigerate a stuffed bird before cooking it. Stuffed poultry should be cooked at 325°F (163°C); lower temperatures may allow bacteria in the stuffing to multiply, while higher temperatures may cook the meat but leave the stuffing undone. Use the leftovers within a day or two, or freeze them.

Packaged poultry is seldom wrapped appropriately for freezing. Wrap the meat tightly in plastic or freezer paper. Freezing promotes the oxidation of unsaturated fats, which causes a rancid taste and limits the freezer life of raw poultry to a few months. Poultry up to 4 pounds in weight thaws in the refrigerator in about 12 to 18 hours; a bird weighing from 4 to 12 pounds requires about 1 to 2 days; and a 12- to 20-pound turkey needs 2 to 3 days.

POULTRY FACTORIES

The industrialization of poultry farming has brought unquestionable economic benefits and accounts for the fact that Canadians now consume an average of 55 pounds of chicken a year, a 30 percent increase since 1985.

Chicken coops and barnyards have been replaced by giant automated processing plants, where chicks are hatched in incubators, and fattened on laboratory feed. All broiler poultry reared in Canada is free-run grown within a confined area, however, lighting schedules are used to prevent movement and promote tender meat and maximum weight gain. Most birds are now slaughtered between 5 weeks and 5 months of age, and many farms have a constant turnover of hundreds of thousands—even a million—chickens. The carcasses are scalded in huge vats of water, eviscerated, rinsed, and water or air chilled to keep the bacterial level to a minimum. All federally registered poultry plants are subject to government inspections.

Poultry flesh is monitored for traces of the antibiotics routinely given to prevent the infections common in animals confined in close quarters. Some experts warn that this wholesale use of powerful antibiotics may be contributing to the growing emergence of resistant bacteria, which may foster deadly infections.

PREGNANCY

CONSUME PLENTY OF
- *Lean meat, poultry, fish, dried beans, lentils, and eggs for protein and iron.*
- *Milk and dairy products, canned sardines and salmon (with bones included), and other high-calcium foods.*
- *Citrus fruits, dark green vegetables, legumes, whole grains, and fortified cereals for folate.*

CUT BACK ON
- *High-fat foods.*
- *Sugary desserts and candy.*
- *Coffee and other caffeinated drinks.*

AVOID
- *Alcohol use and smoking.*
- *All drugs unless prescribed by a doctor.*

At no other time in a woman's life is good nutrition more essential than during pregnancy. While the need for calories increases only about 15 percent, the requirements for some nutrients more than doubles, and a woman needs to plan her diet carefully to meet these needs. She should work with her doctor or other health professional providing prenatal care to design an eating program that supplies optimal nutrition for her and her baby. As a matter of fact, any woman planning a pregnancy should also evaluate her eating habits. Even before trying to conceive, she should achieve her ideal weight.

Women who are too thin often have low-birth-weight babies, while those who are overweight have a greater risk of gestational DIABETES and giving birth to an oversized baby. Infants who are either too small or too large at birth often suffer serious problems, including respiratory disorders and even death.

This is also the time to reduce alcohol consumption or, preferably, to abstain completely, because alcohol causes the most harm to a fetus during the first few weeks of a pregnancy, and the woman may not know that she has conceived. Studies show that women who have one to two drinks a day tend to have undersized babies. A greater danger is incurred by alcoholics and binge drinkers during early pregnancy; these women have a high risk of giving birth to a baby with fetal alcohol syndrome, a constellation of congenital defects that may include mental deficiency, facial and heart malformations, an undersized head, and retarded growth.

Any woman who smokes should make every effort to quit before becoming pregnant. Smoking not only reduces fertility, it is dangerous to the fetus, increasing the risk of miscarriage and low birth weight. Infants whose mothers smoke also have a higher incidence of crib death (sudden infant death syndrome), as well as asthma and other respiratory problems.

The use of any vitamin supplements also should be evaluated. In particular,

---

COPING WITH MORNING SICKNESS

Despite its name, morning sickness can occur at any time of the day, but it usually disappears after the first 3 months of pregnancy. In order to ease the nausea and vomiting, try these strategies:

- Eat dry cereal, crackers, or dry toast before you get out of bed.

- Avoid greasy, fried, and spicy foods.

- Instead of three big meals, eat several small meals during the day.

- To quell nausea, sip ginger ale or suck candied ginger.

- Try wearing an acupressure bracelet, such as those used to prevent motion sickness.

- Have someone else prepare food if cooking odors provoke nausea.

FOOD CRAVINGS

From pickles to ice cream, stories abound about the food CRAVINGS of pregnant women. The cravings are certainly real, but they rarely reflect any true nutritional problem. The one exception is craving ice, which may be a sign of iron-deficiency anemia. Some women, however, inexplicably develop pica, a craving for bizarre, inedible substances, such as clay, soil, paint, coffee grounds, and laundry starch. Some of these cravings are thought to be rooted in folk medicine, such as a mistaken belief that eating soil provides extra iron or will ease childbirth. In reality, eating soil, clay, or starch lowers iron absorption.

high doses of vitamin A should be stopped several months before attempting pregnancy, because large stores of this vitamin can cause severe birth defects. Women planning a pregnancy may be urged to forgo liver because of its high vitamin A content.

WEIGHT GAIN

During pregnancy, the recommended weight gain for a woman of average weight experiencing an average pregnancy is approximately 20 to 32 pounds. Women who are underweight at conception may need to gain as much as 40 pounds, however, and women who are overweight may be advised to gain no more than 15 to 25

pounds. But even an obese woman should not try to lose weight during pregnancy; to do so exposes her fetus to numerous hazards.

The pattern of weight gain is just as important as the number of pounds. It is normal for most women to gain no weight or even to lose a little during the first trimester of pregnancy. After that, a healthy woman who was at her ideal weight before conceiving should gain an average of 1 pound a week; underweight women should gain slightly more each week, while overweight women should gain more slowly.

Most women need to add approximately 300 calories to their daily diet to support normal fetal growth, especially during the last two trimesters. This is a relatively small amount, despite the saying about "eating for two." A woman who doubles what she normally eats will certainly gain excessive weight. Appropriate foods that add up to 300 extra calories include $2\frac{1}{2}$ cups of low-fat milk; a sandwich made with 3 ounces of lean chicken; or an egg and two slices of toast.

PROTEIN

A pregnant woman needs to consume approximately 60g of protein daily, or only 10g more than the amount recommended for women who are not pregnant. Ten grams is about the amount of protein that is contained in $1\frac{1}{2}$ ounces of meat or $1\frac{1}{4}$ cups of milk. Because Canadians tend to eat more protein than necessary, most women will not need to make a specific effort to increase their protein consumption during pregnancy. In fact, some studies suggest that excessive protein may be detrimental to the fetus, causing delayed growth or premature birth.

When selecting protein-rich foods, include lean meats, poultry, and fish, which are also good sources of B vitamins and iron and other trace minerals. Other foods high in protein include

eggs, cheese, and a combination of GRAINS and LEGUMES. Lacto-ovo VEGETARIANS can obtain protein from milk and eggs; vegans, who eat only plant foods, should consult a dietitian on how to plan an adequate diet.

VITAMIN SUPPLEMENTS

Experts agree that women should take folate and iron supplements during pregnancy, but there are differing views about whether other supplements are necessary. Many doctors believe that a balanced diet that includes a variety of foods in the recommended amounts will meet most needs, while others prescribe a multivitamin supplement as added insurance against deficiencies.

CALCIUM

A pregnant woman needs 1,200mg of calcium a day, about 50 percent more than normal. Because most Canadian women do not get enough calcium, it's a good idea to increase consumption of calcium-rich foods even before becoming pregnant. This is especially important for women under 30, whose bones are still increasing in density.

Low-fat or nonfat milk and other dairy products are the best dietary sources of calcium; other good sources include leafy green vegetables, tofu, canned sardines and salmon with the bones included, and calcium-fortified foods, such as some types of orange juice and cereals. Consume at least three to four servings of calcium-rich foods a day, or the equivalent of one quart of milk. If a doctor recommends calcium supplements, they should be consumed with other meals to increase absorption and reduce intestinal upsets.

IRON

A woman's iron requirement almost doubles during pregnancy, going from 13mg to 23mg daily. This increase is necessary because the woman's blood volume doubles and because the fetus must store enough iron to last through the first few months of life. Iron-rich foods include red meat, fish, poultry, enriched breads and cereals, legumes, eggs, dried fruits, and leafy green vegetables. However, the heme iron in animal products is absorbed more efficiently than the nonheme iron in plants and eggs. Absorption of nonheme iron can be increased by eating the iron-rich food together with one that is high in vitamin C, such as orange juice.

Even a well-balanced diet provides a maximum of only 12mg to 15mg of iron a day, and if a woman's iron stores are low when pregnancy begins, she risks developing anemia. Most women need to take a 25mg iron supplement daily during the last 6 months of pregnancy. These supplements are absorbed best if they are taken between meals with orange juice or liquids other than coffee, tea, and milk, which decrease the absorption of iron.

FOLATE

Adequate folate, or folic acid, can help prevent birth defects, especially those involving the brain and spinal cord, such as spina bifida—a condition in which the spine does not form normally. It is estimated that 50 to 70 percent of such defects could be prevented if all women of childbearing age consumed sufficient folate. The Recommended Nutrient Intakes (RNIs) call for at least 180mcg (micrograms) of folate for women who are not pregnant; this increases to 400mcg during pregnancy and then

EATING FOR TWO. *Being pregnant should not mean eating double portions; however, a healthful balance of nutritious food will help the baby get off to a good start.*

drops to 260mcg to 280mcg during breast-feeding. Many women, particularly those who have been taking birth control pills, have low levels of folate. Because the most critical period for folate consumption is during the first 4 to 6 weeks of pregnancy, when the fetal central nervous system is being formed, women planning to become pregnant may be advised by their physicians to take a supplement even before conceiving. Good dietary sources of folate include citrus fruits and juices, peanuts and other legumes, whole grains, fortified breakfast cereals, and dark green leafy vegetables.

SODIUM

In the past, pregnant women were routinely advised to cut down on salt, because it was once thought to increase the risk of toxemia, a potentially life-threatening condition. There is no evidence, however, that salt restriction prevents or alleviates toxemia; on the contrary, a woman's sodium requirement actually increases during pregnancy. In most cases, it is not necessary to consume additional sodium, since the typical Canadian diet already provides ample salt.

ARTIFICIAL SWEETENERS

Controversy has swirled around the use of artificial sweeteners in foods and beverages, especially during pregnancy. The low-calorie sweeteners allowed in Canada are aspartame, saccharin (as a table-top sweetener only), cyclamate, acesulfame-K, and sucralose. Extensive studies for aspartame suggest that it is safe to use during pregnancy, unless the woman has phenylketonuria (PKU). Saccharin can cross the placenta, but there is no proof that it harms the fetus. Acesulfame-K and sucralose pass through the digestive tract and are excreted unchanged, and no toxic effect has been shown. Most experts now believe that low-calorie sweeteners are not harmful during pregnancy.

CAFFEINE

A recent study found that women who are heavy coffee drinkers have a reduced fertility rate. But numerous studies have failed to find any association between caffeine consumption and birth defects or premature delivery. However, drinking more than two or three cups of coffee a day increases a woman's risk of having a low-birth-weight baby. Experts suggest that pregnant women limit their daily intake of caffeine to 300mg, or the equivalent of about two cups of brewed coffee, and that consumption be spread throughout the day.

PREPARATION AND STORAGE OF FOOD

The techniques used to clean, store, and prepare food not only affect its taste, texture, and nutritional value, but are also instrumental in preventing spoilage and food-borne illness.

By using the proper methods to prepare and store foods, you can keep them wholesome and nutritious; preserve their appetizing appearance, taste, and texture; and use them economically. Exposure to heat, light, moisture, and air can cause some foods to spoil or deteriorate, and many lose flavor, texture, and nutritional value if kept too long. Improper handling and storage also raise the possibility of FOOD POISONING.

FOOD STORAGE

Heat and humidity greatly increase the risk of food spoilage, so you should never store foods in warm places, such as near the stove or refrigerator or under the kitchen sink. To minimize the risk of contamination and accidental poisoning, always keep foodstuffs and cleaning products in separate areas.

Because even canned foods deteriorate with time, you should stack cans in the order of their date so that the oldest can is used first. Store them away from moisture in a 50°F to 70°F (10°C to 21°C) temperature range, preferably at the cooler end of the range. Dry goods should be kept in a cool, dark, dry pantry or cupboard and used before the expiration date.

GRAINS AND NUTS

GRAINS, FLOURS, and other foods packed in materials easily penetrated by moths and other insects—for example, unopened cardboard boxes, paper bags, and cellophane packages—should be transferred to plastic, metal, or glass containers with tight-fitting lids. (Even then, insect eggs in the flour or grains may hatch. To kill the eggs before storage, put the product in a microwave oven set on High for 2 to 3 minutes; or refrigerate it to help prevent the eggs from hatching.) Whole-grain flours and meals spoil within a few weeks, because their fats turn rancid. Storing them in a freezer extends their shelf life.

BREAD, CEREALS, and crackers are normally best kept in closed containers at room temperature. Cereals, like other foods made from grains, should be stored in a dark place, because they will lose riboflavin if left exposed to light. Yeast breads will keep for a few days if wrapped in plastic or foil and stored in a cool, dark place, such as a bread box. In hot weather, refrigeration may be required to prevent mold.

Unshelled NUTS can be kept at room temperature for 3 to 6 months; shelled nuts may become rancid unless refrigerated or frozen. Discard any that smell musty or are moldy.

PRODUCE

Raw FRUITS and VEGETABLES often slowly lose their vitamins when kept at room temperature, but tropical fruits deteriorate rapidly if stored in the cold. Most produce is best stored at about 50°F (10°C); if refrigerated, put it in the crisper section; the restricted space slows down moisture loss. Avoid storing fruits and vegetables for long periods in sealed plastic bags; they cut off the air supply, causing the produce to rot. Paper and cellophane are better storage materials, because they are permeable. Keep juice in a small container so that vitamins are not lost through exposure to oxygen.

In regions where winter temperatures average 30°F (–1°C) or less, fruits and vegetables bought in bulk can be stored in a cool basement or root cellar. CARROTS, CABBAGE, and LETTUCE keep well at about 32°F (0°C). Wash lettuce and other salad greens, spin dry, and store them in a plastic bag with a paper towel to absorb any excess moisture. To prevent rot caused by dampness during storage, wash other produce just before using them.

Leave the stems on berries until you're ready to use them, and refrigerate PEAS and beans in their pods. Cut the green tops off root vegetables, such as carrots, BEETS, PARSNIPS, and TURNIPS, or they will continue to draw nourishment from the roots.

When stored below 40°F (4°C), POTATOES develop a sweetish taste from the conversion of starch to sugar; the sweetness disappears when the tubers are returned to room temperature. Potatoes are often packaged in burlap bags or covered with mesh that protects them from light while still allowing air to circulate. Store potatoes in the dark, because exposure to light causes poisonous alkaloids, such as solanine and chaconine, to form.

Freezing raw fruits and vegetables causes the water they contain to form ice crystals that break down cell membranes and walls, resulting in a mushy texture and a loss of nutrients. Deterioration of fruits and vegetables can also be caused by enzymatic activity; blanching prevents this problem. Immerse vegetables for a few seconds in rapidly boiling water to deactivate their enzymes, then plunge them into cold water to stop the cooking process. Most fruits are not suitable for blanching, but you can prevent browning and deterioration by packing them in a solution of sugar, either with or without ascorbic acid.

All produce should be wrapped airtight to prevent freezer burn, which causes dry patches that have a rough texture and "off" taste. Frozen vegetables should be cooked straight from the freezer; thawing encourages the destructive activity of residual enzymes and microorganisms. Do not refreeze foods that have been thawed.

The home canning process preserves foods by rapid heating of hermetically sealed containers. The heat destroys microorganisms and stops enzyme ac-

AIRTIGHT. *Fill food storage containers close to the brim, and remove as much air as possible before sealing storage bags.*

tion, and the vacuum seal prevents contamination. An improperly canned food may cause serious food poisoning with the potentially lethal *Clostridium botulinum.* Long boiling after opening the container will destroy the botulin toxins but not the spores, which can survive boiling for as long as 5 hours. Cans and jars that show any sign of bacterial activity—bubbles, incomplete seals, or escape of gas on opening—must be discarded.

Surprisingly, some commercially processed foods may be more nutritious than fresh. Produce for freezing or canning is often harvested in peak condition and processed quickly to preserve its appearance and nutritional value. Many fresh fruits and vegetables, on the other hand, are picked before ripening and matured under refrigeration; they never reach peak flavor. Look for vine- and tree-ripened varieties, and buy produce in season for economy, flavor, and nutrition.

MEAT, POULTRY, AND FISH

Store meats and FISH in the coldest part of the refrigerator. Wrap meat for freezing in freezer paper. Avoid using gas-permeable plastic wrap; it allows moisture to evaporate and causes freezer burn. SHELLFISH cannot be kept more than a few hours at refrigerator temperature, but they last 2 or 3 days on ice or at a temperature below 32°F (0°C).

Hot dogs and cold cuts stay fresh until their expiration dates if they are refrigerated unopened in their original vacuum-sealed bags. Once opened, however, they should be rewrapped in an airtight bag and used within a few days. Cured and smoked meats are best stored in their original wrappings; make sure that cold cuts bought from the deli counter are wrapped well and used within a day or two. Meat with discoloration, an off smell, or any sign of mold must be discarded. The one exception to this rule is mold on dry salami; simply trim away the mold and the adjacent inch of meat. The unmoldy meat is still edible.

DAIRY PRODUCTS

Fresh MILK and cream should be tightly sealed to prevent tainting by odors from other foods. Milk retains its nutritional value better in cartons than in clear bottles or plastic jugs, because exposure to light destroys some of the vitamin A and riboflavin. Store nonfat powdered milk in a tightly closed container at room temperature in a place where it's not exposed to light.

Keep soft CHEESE and BUTTER tightly covered and refrigerated. Because of concerns about chemical contamination, some people keep plastic materials away from fatty foods, including cheese and butter (see POLLUTANTS). Foil is a good wrapper. Butter freezes well in its original wrap-

285

ping. It's not necessary to refrigerate hard cheese and other ripened cheeses, which keep well covered in a cool, dark cupboard. If mold develops, pare it off; the cheese remains safe to eat.

OILS AND SUGARS

Fats turn rancid on exposure to air and pick up odors from other foods. Store tightly sealed oils in a dark cupboard or in the refrigerator. Exposure to light and warm temperatures can rob oils of vitamins A, D, and E. The cloudiness that forms in some oils when refrigerated will clear at room temperature.

Margarine, like butter, should be well covered and refrigerated; stores for future use may be frozen. You can refrigerate commercial MAYONNAISE after opening it. Use homemade mayonnaise as soon as it's made, however; discard leftovers to reduce the risk of food poisoning by salmonella bacteria.

Corn syrup and molasses keep well at room temperature, because they are too sugary for bacteria to thrive. However, natural maple syrup and artificially flavored syrups are susceptible to molds; refrigerate them after opening. Crystallized maple syrup, like HONEY, will liquefy if the bottle is warmed in a pan of water. Refrigerate opened JAMS AND SPREADS.

FOOD PREPARATION

Cooking for too long or at too high a heat and using excessive liquids are common food preparation faults that detract from flavor and nutritional value. It is the water-soluble vitamins that are lost through poor preparation. Vitamin C is more easily destroyed than any other nutrient, so if vitamin C is conserved, others will be too.

MEATS AND FISH

Trim visible fat off red meat before cooking it to reduce calories, saturated fat, and traces of fat-soluble pollu-tants. Discard POULTRY skin; it is high in saturated fat and calories. Make up for lost flavor with herbs and spices.

You can wipe red meat with a damp cloth or wash it to remove animal hairs or other contaminants. Wash poultry under running water and pat it dry with paper towels before preparation. Some experts recommend washing with diluted vinegar to reduce the risk of food poisoning from bacterial cont-amination. Rinse fish and pat dry.

Dry cooking methods—roasting, baking, broiling, and grilling—are suitable for tender cuts of meat. Moist-heat methods—poaching, braising, and stewing in liquid, such as stock or wine—break down the connective tissue in leaner, tougher cuts. Strain and rapidly boil down the liquid to make a nutrient-rich sauce.

A meat thermometer is useful for indicating if dry-cooked meat is done. A thermometer in a rare-cooked roast or broiled steak should register 140°F (60°C), the temperature at which most food-borne bacteria are killed. Ground meat is handled often, so it is very susceptible to contamination and should not be eaten rare; hamburgers should be brownish-pink to brown in the center. Poultry is cooked when the leg joints move easily and the juices run clear. FISH should flake easily with a fork when thoroughly cooked. PORK should have no pink color. Most cured hams are sold fully cooked and can be eaten cold or reheated.

FRUITS, VEGETABLES, AND GRAINS

If left to soak in water, vegetables lose vitamins and minerals. Right before using them, wash vegetables and fruits under running water to remove soil, insects, and water-soluble pesticides. Scrub heavily soiled produce or wax-treated citrus peels with just a little dish detergent and rinse thoroughly.

Most nutrients in produce are concentrated in the skin or immediately below it. Unless fruits and vegetables were treated with wax coatings or pesticides, cook them in their skins and peel after boiling. The coarse outer leaves of many green vegetables have more concentrated nutrients than the hearts, but—unless organic or home-grown—they are also more exposed to pesticides and are better discarded.

Chopped and bruised fruits and vegetables rapidly lose vitamins A and C, because fluids drain out of broken tissues or deteriorate on exposure to the air. Cook fruits and vegetables whole or in large pieces, whenever possible, and do not chop, peel, or tear them until you're ready to cook them or prepare them for serving raw.

While most vegetables, including root vegetables, can be eaten raw, they are more often prepared by boiling, steaming, or frying. Steaming and stir-frying use little water, so they preserve nutritional content. When boiling vegetables, bring water to a boil first, then add the vegetables and cover with a tight-fitting lid. To add flavor and nutrients to soups and stews, re-cycle the drained cooking liquids.

Cooked vegetables should retain their crispness; overcooking makes them mushy and less nutritious. Some cooks add baking soda to preserve color, but this also destroys the nutritional content and breaks down the plant tissues, giving a slimy texture to green vegetables.

Commercially canned vegetables should be reheated but not recooked, which makes them soft. Home-canned vegetables, especially those low in acid, should be boiled for at least 10 minutes to destroy any bacteria.

Rice and pasta should never be washed, although rice (like other grains and legumes) should be picked over for pebbles and other contaminants. Measure the liquid for cooking rice and other grains; usually, twice the volume of liquid will be completely absorbed without the loss of nutrients.

How to Freeze and Thaw Foods Safely

FOOD	PREPARATION	PACKAGING	TIPS	USE WITHIN (MONTHS)	THAWING (HOURS PER LB.)	
					REFRIGERATOR	ROOM TEMPERATURE
Apples	Sprinkle with lemon juice or powdered ascorbic acid.	Use plastic container or freezer bags.	Alternatively, freeze in syrup containing ascorbic acid.	9	6	3–4
Berries	Freeze on baking sheet; then pack in plastic bags. Freeze soft berries in sugar and syrup.	Transfer to a closed container.	Strawberries and raspberries may be frozen without sugar.	9	6	2
Peaches and plums	Remove pits. Wash and peel peaches. Pack with syrup and ascorbic acid to preserve color.	Use plastic containers or waxed cartons.	A tablespoon of lemon juice per pint of syrup preserves color.	9	6	3–4
Vegetables, green	Wash, trim, blanch, and drain.	Use plastic freezer bags or cartons.	Squeeze air out of bags.	12	6	3
Butter	Freeze in its wrapper.	Overwrap if it is soft.	Unsalted butter stores longer than salted.	3–8	3	1–2
Beef and lamb; pork roasts	Cut into meal-size portions.	Cover protruding bones with foil and wrap tightly with extra layers so that holes are not poked through the wrappings.	Debone joints before freezing to save freezer space.	9–12 (pork roasts, 9)	5	2
Ground meat	Divide into meal-size portions.	Use plastic containers or sealed freezer bags.	Freeze only fresh-ground meat.	4	6	1–2
Pork and lamb chops	Separate with sheets of freezer paper.	Wrap tightly in foil, not plastic.	Thaw pork or lamb chops in refrigerator.	6	3–5	2
Sausages (commercial)	None necessary.	Freeze in commercial packaging. Use freezer bags or plastic wrap for fresh sausages.	Cured and sliced meats do not keep as well as solid cuts.	1	3–5	1–2
Fish steaks	Separate into meal-size portions; wrap in freezer paper.	Wrap in plastic wrap, freezer paper, or foil.	Dry with paper towels to absorb moisture before freezing.	2	8	4
Fish, whole (white and oily)	Scale and fillet.	Wrap in plastic wrap, freezer paper, or foil.	Cut into meal-size portions before wrapping.	2	8	4

PROSTATE PROBLEMS

CONSUME PLENTY OF
- *Tomatoes, red grapefruits, watermelons, and berries for lycopene.*
- *Vegetable oils, margarine, wheat germ, whole-grain products, and nuts and seeds for vitamin E.*
- *Fruits and vegetables for antioxidants.*
- *Fish, shellfish, lean meat, yogurt, legumes, and other zinc-rich foods.*
- *Fluids to flush the bladder.*

CUT DOWN ON
- *Fatty foods, especially animal products.*

AVOID
- *Alcohol, caffeine, spicy foods, and other substances that irritate the urinary tract.*
- *Excessive weight gain.*

The prostate, a walnut-size gland located just below the bladder, is the source of many male urinary problems, including cancer, benign enlargement, and inflammation (prostatitis). Sexually transmitted diseases, urinary tract infections, and such lifestyle habits as smoking, heavy alcohol consumption, and a high-fat diet seem to predispose a man to some of these problems. But often, factors that are beyond our control are more instrumental.

As a man ages, the prostate gland tends to enlarge, a condition called benign prostatic hypertrophy, or BPH. About one-third of all men over 50 experience noncancerous enlargement of the prostate gland, the result of a gradual process that can eventually cause severe obstruction of urinary flow.

Prostate cancer, with an estimated 18,000 new cases a year, is the most common male malignancy. If it is treated in an early stage, this type of cancer is highly curable. In many cases, however, it has already spread to other organs at the time of diagnosis. For this

reason, the Canadian Cancer Society recommends that all men over 50 undergo annual screening for prostate cancer, starting with a digital rectal examination. The same group also advocates that a blood test to measure prostate-specific antigen (PSA), a possible indicator of cancer, should be done annually in addition to the rectal exam, starting at age 50.

The treatment of prostate disorders varies, depending on the underlying condition. Prostatitis is usually treated with antibiotics, warm baths, and occasionally prostatic massage. Some men with BPH require no treatment; other cases may call for surgery to remove the enlarged part of the prostate or drugs to shrink the gland. Prostate cancer may be treated with surgery, radiation, hormone therapy, or a combination of these methods.

THE ROLE OF DIET

Diet cannot cure prostate problems, but it may play a role in maintaining the health of the gland, and it may also help prevent prostate cancer. A recent study of nearly 48,000 men found that lycopene, a pigment that is found in such foods as tomatoes, red grapefruits, watermelons, and berries, appears to reduce the risk of prostate cancer. These findings support earlier recommendations to increase consumption of fruits and vegetables, which are high in other ANTIOXIDANTS and BIOFLAVONOID pigments that protect against various cancers. Cooking appears to release more of the lycopene in tomatoes, so tomato-based pasta sauces and soups may be especially beneficial.

The human body needs zinc in order to use the lycopenes in foods. Zinc-rich foods include whole fish and shellfish (especially oysters), baked potatoes (if the skin is eaten), lean meat, calves' liver, yogurt, and legumes.

Vitamin E has also been associated with reducing inflammation and per-

HELPFUL FOODS

Tomatoes, watermelons, grapefruits, and berries for lycopene; have 10 servings a week.

Tofu and other soy products to help prevent prostate enlargement; consume 4 or 5 times a week.

Nuts, seeds, wheat germ, grains, and eggs for vitamin E; eat 1 or 2 servings daily.

Oysters, yogurt, and other foods high in zinc daily.

Fish and vegetable oils for daily allowance of polyunsaturated fats.

haps protecting against prostate cancer. Good sources include margarine, vegetable oils, egg yolks, nuts and seeds, wheat germ, and whole-grain products.

Tofu and other soy products appear to help prevent prostate enlargement. This effect is attributed to isoflavones, plant chemicals that help lower dihydrotestosterone (DHT), a male hormone that stimulates the overgrowth of prostate tissue. Some experts credit the large amount of soy products in the Japanese diet with their low incidence of prostate problems. The composition of fats in the diet also appears to play a role in prostate health. Fish and vegetable oils that are high in polyunsaturated fats seem to reduce the risk of prostate cancer. In contrast, a diet that is high in saturated animal fats, as well as obesity, has been linked to an increased incidence.

Anyone with an enlarged prostate should drink plenty of water and other nonalcoholic fluids. He should also eliminate from his diet caffeine and spicy foods that irritate the bladder.

PROTEIN: THE BODY-BUILDING NUTRIENT

*Every cell in the body needs protein for growth
and repair. Protein also plays an essential role in
digestion, immunity, and many other body functions.*

Protein is the quintessential nutrient that every cell in the human body requires for growth or repair. Also, the antibodies that protect us from disease, the enzymes needed for digestion and metabolism, and insulin and many other hormones are all made of protein. CHOLESTEROL travels through the bloodstream attached to a lipo- (fat-carrying) protein. A connective tissue made from protein forms the matrix of bones; chromoproteins are a combination of protein and pigments that form hemoglobin; keratin, still another type of protein, is used by the body to make hair and nails. Any dietary protein not needed for these and other functions is stored as fat; some may also be converted to glucose, or blood sugar, and burned for energy.

With so many essential functions allotted to protein, you might assume that it is the number-one nutrient in the diet, but this is not the case. In an ideal balanced diet, only 10 to 12 percent of daily calories should come from protein. Requirements for protein vary according to age, weight, and state of health; on average, a normal adult needs 0.36g of protein per pound of body weight. Thus, a person weighing 140 pounds requires 50g, or slightly less than 2 ounces, of protein per day.

AMINO ACIDS

Proteins are exceedingly complex and diverse structures built of amino acids

---

BENEFITS
- *Used to manufacture and repair all body cells.*
- *Necessary to make antibodies, enzymes, and hormones.*
- *When needed, protein is converted to glucose for energy.*

DRAWBACKS
- *Protein-rich meats and other animal products are often high in fat and cholesterol.*
- *Excessive intake strains the kidneys and liver.*
- *Excessive protein and amino acid supplements increase the excretion of calcium and other minerals.*

---

that are linked together into long chains by peptide bonds. There are many thousands of different proteins, but they all have a backbone of carbon atoms interlaced with nitrogen atoms. Various groupings of atoms can be attached to this backbone.

Human beings need 20 different amino acids; 11 of these can be made in the body, but the other 9, referred to as essential amino acids, must come from the diet. Just as the various letters in the alphabet are joined to make words, so too are amino acids arranged in an almost infinite number of different ways to form the more than 50,000 different proteins in the body. Proteins are made up of hundreds of amino acids. DNA (deoxyribonucleic

acid), the genetic material that is found in the nucleus of each body cell, provides the blueprint for how amino acids are arranged to form individual proteins.

DIETARY PROTEIN

The body is constantly building protein from amino acids, some of which are recycled from the body tissue that is being rebuilt. Even so, a certain amount of protein is lost through normal wear and tear and must be replaced from the diet. But to use this protein, the body must first break it down into its individual amino acids and then reassemble them according to its unique genetic code.

With the exception of oils and pure sugar, all foods contain at least some protein, but its quality varies according to the number of amino acids it provides. Animal protein (with the exception of gelatin) provides all nine essential amino acids in the proportions required by the human body; it is often referred to as complete, or high-quality, protein. In contrast, plant protein (with the exception of soy, which is almost as complete as animal food) lacks one or more of the essential proteins. Because not all plant foods lack the same amino acids, however, the body can build a complete protein if these foods are combined in such a way that they complement each other. For example, grains are high in the essential amino acid methionine, but

HIGH-PROTEIN WEIGHT-LOSS DIETS

High-protein, low-carbohydrate crash diets are ketogenic regimens that force the body to turn to protein and stored fat for energy. For the first few days, the body breaks down its lean muscle tissue and converts the protein to glucose. But if this process continues, death may occur within weeks. Instead, the body tries to conserve protein by burning fat. Ketones, a toxic by-product of excessive fat metabolism, build up in the blood, so the kidneys increase urination to get rid of them. Dieters mistake the drop in weight for a loss of fat.

In reality, most early weight loss is water, and weight quickly returns when carbohydrates are consumed again. Long-term weight loss can be achieved only by a common-sense diet.

Low-calorie liquid protein diets have a similar ketogenic effect, but they can have even more severe consequences than high-protein, low-carbohydrate regimens. Even with protein supplements, the body is forced to break down muscle tissue, including the heart, for energy. This can lead to sudden death from cardiac arrhythmias.

---

they lack lysine. This essential amino acid is plentiful in dried beans, peanuts, and other LEGUMES, which are deficient in methionine. So by combining a grain food with a legume, you can obtain the complete range of amino acids.

Interestingly, low-meat ethnic diets all have dishes that provide complementary proteins: the refried beans and corn tortillas of Mexico; the rice and dahl (split peas) of India; the tofu, rice, and vegetable combinations in Asian cuisine; and the chickpeas and bulgur wheat in Middle Eastern dishes. Even strict VEGETARIAN DIETS can supply ample protein by combining complementary grains and legumes. However, if an essential amino acid is missing from the diet, the body breaks down lean tissue to get it. This may be acceptable on a short-term basis, but over time, it leads to muscle wasting.

Moderate cooking makes protein easier to digest because heat breaks down some of the bonds that join amino acids together. Overcooking, however, can cement some amino acids together, making the protein more difficult to digest and to break down into individual amino acids. Al-

cohol, vinegar, lemon juice, and such enzymes as papain in papayas break some peptide bonds, making these substances good meat tenderizers.

In the stomach, long chains of amino acids are broken into shorter chains called polypeptides. Digestion continues in the small intestine, where pancreatic and other enzymes complete the process. The individual amino acids are absorbed into the bloodstream and transported to the liver, where some are used to make lipoproteins and new enzymes. Others are returned to the bloodstream, which carries them to cells.

Because amino acids are not stored as such, those that are not used in a relatively short time are returned to the liver, where the nitrogen is removed and sent on to the kidneys to be excreted as urea. The remaining protein molecules are stored as fat or converted to glucose for energy.

PROTEIN DEFICIENCY

People in affluent industrialized countries generally consume more than enough protein, but deficiencies are relatively common, especially among children, in rural Africa and other un-

derdeveloped areas where the dietary staples are protein-deficient foods, such as yams, cassava, and other starchy foods. Kwashiorkor, the medical term for severe protein deficiency, is marked by poor growth and mental impairment in children, edema, anemia, muscle wasting, decreased immunity, and metabolic abnormalities.

EXCESSIVE PROTEIN

The typical North American diet provides much more protein than the human body actually needs. This does not pose a serious threat for healthy persons, but too much protein adds to the workload of the kidneys and liver. Thus, people with diseases affecting these organs are generally put on a low-protein diet.

On the down side, meat and other high-protein animal foods come with large amounts of saturated fat and cholesterol—substances that promote ATHEROSCLEROSIS, HEART DISEASE, and OBESITY. Even well-trimmed lean beef derives half of its calories from fat.

SUPPLEMENTS

Purified protein and amino acid powders or pills are often promoted as high-energy, muscle-bulking supplements for athletes and bodybuilders, as well as weight-loss aids for dieters. None of these claims is valid; indeed, taking these supplements can have serious health consequences. In the early 1990s at least 20 deaths were traced to contaminated tryptophan supplements, prompting the Canadian government to ban the sale of individual amino acids. Studies have shown that amino acid supplements can upset normal protein synthesis, setting the stage for nutritional imbalances. Some researchers also maintain that taking amino acid supplements increases calcium excretion and may increase the risk of OSTEOPOROSIS. Excessive intake of dietary protein may also cause the same problem.

PRUNES

BENEFITS

- *A rich source of vitamin A.*
- *High in B vitamins, vitamin E, potassium, and iron.*
- *Help to relieve constipation.*

DRAWBACKS

- *High in calories.*
- *Leave a sticky residue on the teeth that can lead to cavities.*

Although all prunes are plums, not all plums are prunes. Prunes are the dried fruit from a few particular species of plum trees whose fruit has firm flesh and is naturally high in sugar and acidity. These traits allow the fruit to dry without fermenting if the pit is left in.

Like all dried fruits, prunes contain very little water and are a more concentrated source of energy and nutrients than their fresh fruit counterparts. They are also higher in calories and sugar (a half cup of the stewed fruit or five large pitted prunes contain approximately 115 calories), and they leave a sticky residue on the teeth that can cause cavities. On the plus side, prunes are rich in vitamin A; a 4-ounce serving provides about 50 percent of the Recommended Nutrient Intake (RNI) for adults (in the form of beta carotene), as well as 3mg (30 percent of the RNI) of vitamin E, 3mg of iron, and 750mg of potassium. They are also a good source of B vitamins, magnesium, and phosphorus.

Prunes are popular as a remedy for preventing or treating constipation. This effect can be attributed to prunes' high dietary fiber content; they also contain isatin, a natural laxative.

Unlike other types of juice, prune juice retains most of the fruits' nutrients because it is made by pulverizing the dried prunes and then dissolving them in hot water. One cup of prune juice contains between 20 and 30 percent of the adult RNI of iron and about 700mg of potassium. However, it is also very high in calories, about 200 per cup. Because prune juice is naturally high in sugar, it does not need any additional sweeteners. Although prune juice is not as good a source of fiber as whole prunes, it still helps to relieve constipation because it, too, contains isatin.

PUMPKINS

BENEFITS

- *A rich source of beta carotene.*
- *A good low-calorie source of vitamin C and potassium.*
- *High in fiber.*
- *The seeds are a good source of protein, iron, B vitamins, vitamin E, and fiber.*
- *Can be stored for long periods of time.*

To most Canadians, pumpkins (which are a type of winter squash) are a symbol of Halloween and Thanksgiving. In fact, they have more uses than just as traditional jack-o'-lanterns and pie filling—the strong-flavored flesh of pumpkins can be baked or roasted, used in soups or stews, and turned into a filling for ravioli-style pasta.

Pumpkins were an important food throughout the Americas long before Colonial times. They have been cultivated in Central America for at least 9,000 years, and remains of the fruit have been found in the United States in ancient Southwestern cliff dwell-

ings. Pumpkins are now grown around the world, providing edible flesh, seeds, and flowers; the baby fruit can be baked and consumed whole.

Like all orange-pigmented vegetables, pumpkins are rich in beta carotene, the plant form of vitamin A; a half cup of canned or baked pumpkin provides over 450 percent of the adult Recommended Nutrient Intake (RNI). Studies have shown that this ANTIOXIDANT may help prevent some forms of cancer. Pumpkins are also high in vitamin C; a half-cup serving supplies over 20 percent of the RNI, as well as 275mg of potassium. A half cup has only 40 calories and is very low in fat and high in fiber. Because pumpkins absorb water, they lose some nutrients and have fewer calories per ounce when they are boiled. Sugar pumpkins, which are smaller and sweeter than the large deep-orange pumpkins used for jack-o'-lanterns, are the best choice for cooking and baking.

Although the seeds are often thrown away when a jack-o'-lantern is carved, they are a rich source of protein. One ounce of pumpkin seeds provides 7g of protein—almost as much as an equal serving of peanuts—as well as 3mg of iron (20 to 30 percent of the adult RNI). They are high in unsaturated vegetable oil, a source of vitamin E, and rich in B vitamins. When the coverings are consumed too, the seeds are high in fiber. Pumpkin seeds are easy to prepare: scoop out the seeds, wash them and let dry, then bake them on an oiled baking sheet at 250°F (121°C) for an hour. Commercial varieties are often fried and salted.

Because pumpkins have hard shells, like other winter squashes, they are ideal for storing. Pumpkins last about a month in a cool, dry place. They should not be refrigerated or stored at temperatures below 50°F (10°C), which speeds deterioration.

QUINCES

BENEFITS
- *A good source of vitamin C, iron, and potassium.*
- *High in pectin, a soluble fiber.*

DRAWBACKS
- *Often cooked with large amounts of sugar to offset tartness.*
- *Seeds contain a cyanide compound.*

A member of the same rose family as apples and pears, the quince has an acidic tartness that most people find astringent; because of this, the fruit is rarely eaten raw. Cooking, however, cuts the acids, and the fruit takes on a mellow flavor similar to that of a slightly tart apple, with the texture of a pear.

Raw quinces are high in vitamin C; a medium-size fruit provides more than 20mg, or 50 percent of the adult Recommended Nutrient Intake (RNI). Much of this vitamin C is lost, however, when the fruit is cooked. The same-size quince also provides 1mg of iron, which the vitamin C helps the body to absorb, and 305mg of potassium.

The 90 calories in a medium-size quince is comparable to the energy content of apples and pears of the same size. Like these two cousins, quinces are high in pectin, a soluble fiber that helps control blood cholesterol levels and promotes smooth digestive function. Because pectin forms a semisolid gel when cooked, quinces are ideal for making jams and jellies.

Quinces may be round or somewhat pear-shaped. Look for fruit that is firm, with pale yellow skin covered with fuzz; reject any that are small, irregularly shaped, or bruised. The fuzz rubs off easily after the fruit is washed.

Poaching and baking are the most nutritious methods of preparing the fruit. Don't be misled by the tartness of raw quince and add too much sugar. The fruit becomes sweeter as it cooks, so wait until it's done to add a sweetener—you may find you don't need it. Cooking also changes the color of the flesh from pale yellow to pink or red.

Warning: Always remove the quince seeds before cooking. As with apples, apricots, and similar fruits, the seeds contain amygdalin, a compound that turns into hydrogen cyanide in the stomach. Eating a large amount of seeds can result in cyanide poisoning.

QUINOA

BENEFITS
- *An excellent source of iron, magnesium, potassium, phosphorus, zinc, and other minerals.*
- *A good source of B-complex vitamins.*
- *High in protein.*

DRAWBACKS
- *Not widely available and more expensive than most grains.*

Although it is often classified as a grain, quinoa is actually a member of the same plant family as spinach, whereas true grains come from grasses. While the green leafy quinoa (pronounced ki-NOH-wah) tops are edible, it's the seeds that are served most frequently.

For more than 5,000 years, quinoa has been the staple food of the Incas and other native peoples of the Andes, where it is one of the few crops that grows well in the dry mountainous climate and poor soil. It is relatively new

---

A BITTER COATING

Quinoa seeds taken directly from the plant are inedible because they are coated with a bitter oil containing compounds called saponins. After the seeds are harvested, they are soaked in an alkaline solution to remove the coating. Plant scientists theorize that saponins evolved to protect the seeds from the sun's strong ultraviolet rays at the high altitudes in which the plant grows; the bitter taste also repels birds and bugs.

---

in North America, however, and in many areas it is still considered an exotic luxury food that is more expensive than most grain products.

The tiny quinoa seeds are packed with important nutrients; a 1-cup serving (made from ¼ cup of dry quinoa) provides about 5mg of iron, more than any unfortified grain product. One cup also contributes large amounts of several other essential minerals, including 100mg of magnesium, 200mg of phosphorus, 370mg of potassium, and 1.5mg of zinc, as well as numerous B vitamins, especially B_6, folate, niacin, and thiamine.

Most of the 160 calories in 1 cup of cooked quinoa come from complex carbohydrates. However, it also provides 7g of protein, which is of a higher quality than similar products because it provides lysine, an amino acid missing in corn, wheat, and other grains.

A VERSATILE FOOD

Quinoa cooks quickly into a fluffy, delicately flavored grainlike dish that lends itself to many uses. It can be served as a substitute for rice, potatoes, and other starchy foods; combined with vegetables, poultry, or seafood to make a pilaf; and added to soups and stews.

RADISHES

BENEFITS
- *A useful source of vitamin C.*
- *Low in calories and high in fiber.*

DRAWBACKS
- *Can produce gas in some people.*
- *Salicylate content may provoke an allergic reaction in people sensitive to aspirin.*

A member of the cruciferous family, the radish is closely related to cabbage, kale, turnips, and cauliflower. While not especially high in most essential nutrients, radishes are low in calories, making them ideal for snacking and as a spicy addition to salads, soups, and vegetable side dishes.

A useful source of vitamin C, radishes also contain small amounts of iron, potassium, and folate. Four medium-size raw radishes provide 4mg of vitamin C, or 10 percent of the Recommended Nutrient Intake (RNI), and they yield only 5 calories. They also supply sulfurous compounds that may protect against cancer.

Like other cruciferous vegetables, radishes can cause bloating and gas in some people. Also, radishes contain salicylates—compounds similar to the active ingredient in aspirin; many people sensitive to aspirin may suffer an allergic reaction to radishes.

The peak season for radishes spans from April to July, but most varieties are available year-round. Summer radishes have a more intense peppery flavor than those cultivated during spring or fall. Although the bright red globe variety is the best-known in North America, other types include black radishes, daikons, and white icicles.

When selecting red globe radishes, avoid the larger ones if possible, as they may be pithy. A bright color indicates freshness. If there are leaves on the stems, make sure they are green and crisp. Regardless of which variety you are buying, the vegetables should feel solid and have an unblemished surface.

Unless the radishes are going to be served the same day, you should remove any leaves and tops; the radishes will stay fresh longer without the tops. If they are not already packaged, store radishes in plastic bags.

RASPBERRIES

BENEFITS
- *A rich source of vitamin C.*
- *Contain useful amounts of folate, iron, and potassium.*
- *Provide bioflavonoids, which may protect against cancer.*
- *High in fiber.*

DRAWBACKS
- *Contain a natural salicylate, which can cause an allergic reaction in aspirin-sensitive people.*
- *Contain oxalic acid, which can aggravate kidney and bladder stones in susceptible persons.*

There is no sweeter surprise on a summer day than to stumble across a wild raspberry patch. Raspberries—both wild and cultivated—are low in calories and a rich source of vitamin C.

A half-cup serving of raspberries contains 30 calories and 15mg of vitamin C (40 percent of the Recommended Nutrient Intake, or RNI). It also provides 3mcg (micrograms) of folate, 125mg of potassium, and some iron. The vitamin C content increases the iron's absorption, although this may be offset by the oxalic acid in raspberries, which binds with this mineral.

The seeds in raspberries provide an insoluble fiber that helps prevent constipation. The fruit is also high in pectin, a soluble fiber that helps control blood cholesterol levels. In addition, raspberries contain ellagic acid and other BIOFLAVONOIDS, ANTIOXIDANT plant pigments that may help prevent some types of cancer. Cooking does not destroy ellagic acid, so even raspberry jam may be beneficial.

Raspberries spoil faster than most berries do because of their delicate structure and hollow core. Once picked, they should be eaten as soon as possible. Freezing, however, will preserve them for up to a year.

Cultivated raspberries can be found year-round in gourmet and specialty stores, and when they are in season, at many supermarkets. Before buying raspberries, check that all of them, not just the ones on top, are in good condition; even then, they mold quickly and should be used within 24 hours.

Berries often produce allergic reactions, and raspberries are no exception. Those who are sensitive to aspirin may also react to raspberries, which contain a natural salicylate, similar to the major ingredient in aspirin. Oxalic acid can precipitate kidney and bladder stones in susceptible people; however, it would take a very large amount of raspberries to create problems.

RESTAURANTS AND EATING OUT

*Restaurant meals can be heavy on calories and light
on important nutrients. Plan ahead to avoid nutrition traps,
and patronize restaurants that offer healthy choices.*

For a growing number of Canadians, eating out is no longer just an occasional treat. According to a 1992 government survey, Canadians spent an average of $5,686 per household on meals away from home (this includes restaurants, school cafeterias, and other such establishments).

When dining in a restaurant, people who are following special diets for weight loss or other health needs have to pay attention to the language of menus to bypass nutritional pitfalls—such as excessive calories, fat, and sodium; too few vitamins and minerals; and insufficient fiber. These traps can be avoided by following the guidelines in What to Order for Healthy Eating (facing page). Thanks to consumers' insistence and the growing understanding of nutrition, it's becoming easier to order healthful meals at all types of establishments. Many restaurants now list low-fat dishes and "healthy choices" in a special section of the menu.

The restaurant's staff should be prepared to answer questions about how the food is prepared and to make simple adjustments, such as leaving off sauces and dressings. Restaurants that prepare food to order often cater to special requests, such as dry-broiling fish rather than sautéing it in butter.

DRINKING WITH MEALS

Many people mark special occasions with a restaurant dinner and a celebratory drink or bottle of WINE. Although low to moderate ALCOHOL intake (two drinks a day for men and one for women) reduces the risk of a heart attack, excessive drinking leads to serious health problems. It's a good idea, therefore, to quench your thirst with a glass of water before the alcohol and to drink water liberally during the meal. This rehydrates tissues dried out by alcohol and also reduces the temptation to overindulge.

AVOIDING DIET TRAPS

It makes sense to choose a restaurant whose style of food fits the diet that you're following. It's easier, for instance, to order a low-fat meal in a Japanese restaurant than it is in a steak house. The same Japanese meal, however, may supply two to three times the amount of salt that is normally found in Western-style dishes, making it an unwise choice for someone on a low-salt diet.

For many diners, especially when they're hungry, a complimentary basket of breads may be an irresistible temptation. Bread itself contains little fat and, depending on the type, can be a good source of fiber. However, a thick spread of butter or margarine can increase the fat and calories dramatically. Eat the bread plain or ask for a fruit spread instead of butter or margarine. Another good habit is to read the menu as soon as you sit down and order your food right away, thus limiting the time exposed to tempting bread or other fattening appetizers while waiting for your entrée. Or call ahead to ask about the day's specials so you can decide on your entrée in advance; you'll be less tempted to overindulge if you've already made up your mind about what you want.

To avoid overeating, pass up the fixed-price menu and select two or three items from the à la carte menu. Begin with a filling, low-calorie first course—for example, salad, broth-based soup, or shrimp with cocktail

BENEFITS
- *Convenient, especially when you are away from home.*
- *Provide a relaxing relief from routine kitchen tasks.*
- *Offer opportunities to sample exotic cuisines.*

DRAWBACKS
- *Expensive, if they take the place of home cooking.*
- *Many dishes are high in calories, fat, and sodium.*
- *May not be appropriate for people on special diets.*

sauce. Many restaurants serve large portions. Don't feel compelled to clean your plate; instead, take the leftovers home. There's no need to pass up dessert, but if you select a high-fat item, share it with your companions.

If you are on a restricted diet, call ahead and ask that a special dish be prepared for you. Most restaurants will accommodate such requests, especially if they have advance notice.

SALAD BARS

Many restaurants have SALAD BARS, which make choices easier for nutrition- and calorie-conscious consumers. Lettuce, spinach, tomatoes, and other fresh vegetables are high in fiber and vitamins and low in calories. It's all too easy, however, to undermine your dietary efforts by overloading the meal with high-calorie toppings and SALAD DRESSINGS, or selecting deli-style potato salad, macaroni salad, and cole-slaw, which are made with large quantities of commercial MAYONNAISE.

FOOD-BORNE ILLNESS

Despite strict laws governing the way food is handled in restaurants, there are still health risks associated with eating out. Managers may follow the letter of the law with regard to cleanliness, but they—like their patrons—are at the mercy of employees who may not always maintain the required standards for hygiene and food handling. You can get a good idea of a restaurant's attention to good hygiene from the general appearance of the dining area. (In some restaurants the kitchen is visible to diners, although it will be partitioned off from the dining area, as required by law.) The staff should appear neatly groomed in clean uniforms and with hair tied back or covered. Soiled table linens, smeared glasses, stale odors, and chipped or discolored plates and utensils are all signs telling the customer to seek out another restaurant.

WHAT TO ORDER FOR HEALTHY EATING

Dining out does not have to be at the expense of balance, moderation, and variety—the tenets of good nutrition. The following suggestions are healthy, tasty alternatives to fatty, unhealthful meals in several popular types of restaurants.

ORDER	INSTEAD OF
NORTH AMERICAN FOOD	
Broth-based soup	Cream soup
An entrée of grilled, broiled, or flame-cooked meat, fish, or poultry	Breaded or batter-dipped meat, fish, or poultry
Sandwiches on whole-wheat or rye bread or a pita	Sandwiches on croissants or biscuits
Baked potato with herbs or margarine	Home-fried or deep-fried potatoes; sour cream or butter
Steamed or baked vegetables	Sautéed or deep-fried vegetables; cream sauces
Salads from the salad bar	Salads made with mayonnaise (coleslaw, pasta, potato, or tuna)
Fresh fruit or frozen yogurt	Pies, cakes, ice cream, or pastries
CHINESE	
Hot and sour soup	Egg rolls
Wonton soup	Fried wontons
Beef with broccoli	Sweet and sour pork or shrimp
Chicken, scallops, or shrimp with vegetables	Peking duck
Steamed rice	Fried rice
ITALIAN	
Minestrone soup	Antipasto platter
Dry breadsticks	Buttered garlic bread
Chicken or fish	Sausage dishes
Pasta with red sauce or clam sauce	Pasta with creamy white or butter sauce
Oil and vinegar dressing	Creamy Italian dressing
Espresso	Cappuccino
Italian ice	Cream-based desserts or pastries
MEXICAN	
Black bean soup	Guacamole dip with taco chips
Burritos, soft tacos, enchiladas, tamales	Tacos, taco salad, tostadas, chili relleños, quesadillas
Soft, plain tortillas	Crispy fried tortillas
Salsa	Sour cream and cheese

Never hesitate to send a dish back if it is undercooked or stale, or if you suspect that it may not have been kept in hygienic conditions. Mistakes can happen in even the best-run establishments, and most restaurant proprietors will be grateful if you bring potential problems to their attention.

RHUBARB

BENEFITS
- *High in vitamin C and potassium.*

DRAWBACKS
- *Usually prepared with substantial amounts of sugar or other sweeteners.*
- *Contains oxalic acid, which inhibits calcium and iron absorption.*
- *Leaves are highly poisonous.*

Although rhubarb is generally regarded as a fruit, botanically it is a vegetable. It is available in frozen and canned forms, but most people prefer to cook the fresh stalks themselves. One cup of fresh diced rhubarb yields a mere 26 calories and provides 10mg of vitamin C (25 percent of the adult Recommended Nutrient Intake, or RNI), as well as 350mg of potassium. This same serving size also contains more than 100mg of calcium; however, rhubarb is not considered a good source of this mineral, since it also contains oxalic acid, which not only blocks the absorption of its calcium but also that from any other dietary sources. Because it has a high oxalic acid content, large amounts of rhubarb should be avoided by anyone with a tendency to develop oxalate-containing kidney stones or bladder stones.

Only the rhubarb stalks are eaten—the leaves are highly poisonous. Because raw rhubarb stalks are stringy in texture and tart in flavor, most people will consume them only when cooked with large amounts of sugar or honey, thus inflating the calorie count.

One cup of cooked sweetened rhubarb yields 280 calories. To avoid extra calories, try cooking the stalks with sweet fruits, such as strawberries or apples.

A favorite springtime pie filling, rhubarb can also be made into preserves, or it can be stewed to make a compote or sauces to complement poultry, other meat dishes, and desserts.

When cooked and sweetened, rhubarb will turn brownish in color. It should not be prepared in aluminum or cast iron pots, which will interact with the acid in the vegetable and darken both the pot and the rhubarb.

RICE

BENEFITS
- *Enriched varieties provide B vitamins and iron.*
- *Makes a complete protein when combined with beans and other legumes.*
- *Gluten-free and suitable for people with celiac disease.*
- *Easy to digest and useful in restoring bowel function after a bout of diarrhea.*
- *Rarely, if ever, causes food allergies.*

DRAWBACKS
- *Diets high in white rice may be deficient in thiamine.*
- *Brown rice is more nutritious but takes longer to cook than white rice.*
- *A substance in brown rice can inhibit absorption of iron and calcium.*

For thousands of years, rice has been the staple food for more than half the world's population. In some Asian countries per capita consumption exceeds 300 pounds a year, and survival still depends on the rice crop. In contrast, the average Canadian eats only about 27 pounds of rice a year, which includes all types of rice, as well as breakfast cereals.

Like barley and oats, rice grows in a protective husk that has to be re-moved if the grain is to be used as food. (Wheat, rye, and corn, by contrast, are bare seeds that require less processing.) Many nutrients are lost with the bran and germ that are removed in milling to make white rice. Brown rice—intact kernels that retain their bran layers—is somewhat more nutritious than white rice, but it also contains phytic acid, a substance that interferes with the absorption of iron and calcium.

Although not grown in Canada, most of the white rice that is grown and processed in the United States is fortified with iron, niacin, and thiamine, which are applied in a solution to the outside of the grain, coated with a protein powder, and dried. Rinsing the grain before cooking washes away these important nutrients. Rice should be cooked in just twice its volume of water, which will be completely absorbed by the grain and will preserve the nutritional content.

Converted rice is processed by a 2,000-year-old method; this involves parboiling the whole grain, which makes milling easier by loosening the husk. Conversion improves the nutritional quality of the grain by causing the B vitamins in the bran and germ to permeate the endosperm. It also gelatinizes the fat- and nutrient-bearing aleurone layer, which then adheres to the grain instead of being lost with the bran. Thanks to this technique, the thiamine deficiency known as beriberi was never a serious threat to people in India and Pakistan, although it ravaged Asian people who subsisted on unconverted white rice. Instant rice should

THE LONG AND THE SHORT OF IT.
Varieties of rice include: (left row, from top) instant long-grain white, long-grain brown, instant basmati, and risotto; (middle row, from top) long-grain white, instant long-grain brown, and glutinous brown; (right row, from top) long-grain white, wild, soft pudding, brown basmati, and basmati.

not be confused with converted rice, which takes at least as long to cook as other types. Much of the rice sold in Canada is also polished in special machines to make it shiny. An extra sheen is achieved by coating the grains with talc and glucose. This is a cosmetic process with no nutritional impact.

NUTRITIONAL VALUE

Ninety percent of the calories in rice come from carbohydrates. A half cup of cooked rice constitutes one of the 5 to 12 daily servings of carbohydrates recommended in the Food Guide Rainbow (see p.39). A half cup of white rice contains about 100 calories, while brown rice may have 105 to 110. Brown rice is significantly higher in fiber, with 1.6g per half cup compared to 0.03g in the same volume of white rice.

The protein content of rice, ranging from 2.0 to 2.5mg per half cup, is less than that of other cereals, but the amino acid balance is superior to that of other grains. Processed rice contains only a trace of fat and no sodium.

Macrobiotic regimens were FAD DIETS in the 1960s; the most restrictive seventh level of the diets provides little else but brown rice. It fell out of favor when people became aware of the serious nutritional deficiencies created when some individuals adopted this strict level. Like other carbohydrates, rice must be counterbalanced with foods from the other compartments of the Food Guide Rainbow to provide a complete range of vitamins, minerals, and protein.

HEALTH BENEFITS

Rice has a binding effect in DIARRHEA, and as such, is part of the BRAT (for banana, rice, applesauce, and toast) diet. It helps restore normal bowel function and provides needed energy for someone recovering from diarrhea. Rice pudding made with low-fat milk and flavored with cinnamon is a soothing, easy-to-digest dish for convalescents.

Several studies have shown that rice bran helps to reduce cholesterol and may reduce the risk of bowel cancer. Some studies also show that rice helps regulate glucose metabolism in people with diabetes. As a complex carbohydrate, it provides a slow, steady supply of glucose, and not the rapid rise that occurs after eating sugars.

Along with lamb and a few other foods, rice rarely if ever provokes an allergic reaction. This quality makes rice ideal as the basis of the strict elimination diet that is sometimes used to identify food allergens.

A VERSATILE STAPLE

Rice is a true staple in menu planning. Risotto, made with fat-free broth and vegetables, and pilaf, based on fat-free broth, chopped nuts, and dried fruits, are economical, nutritious, low-fat entrées. Rice is an ingredient of hot and cold breakfast cereals, an excellent base for salads, and a natural companion to vegetables, fish, meats, and cheese. Rice bran also adds bulk to baked goods.

RICE VARIETIES

Rice is classified by size and shape (long, medium, and short grain). Long-grain rice remains dry and separate when cooked; short-grain rice, which is wetter and stickier, is more often used in Asian and Caribbean cooking.

Arborio rice is a creamy-textured, medium-grain Italian rice used in making risotto because it remains firm at the center through long cooking.

Basmati is an aromatic rice native to Pakistan and India. When cooked, the grain swells only lengthwise. Basmati grains stay dry and separate and are especially suitable for pilafs.

Jasmine is an aromatic rice with origins in Thailand. It has a soft, moist texture and grains that cling together.

Wild rice, a very distant relative of common rice, is a grass native to the lakes and marshes of the Great Lakes region. Once gathered by hand in the wild by Chippewa Indians, wild rice is now cultivated commercially and harvested by machine. Wild rice contains more protein than common rice does and is richer in lysine, the amino acid lacking in most grains.

DID YOU KNOW?

- We commemorate an ancient Asian fertility symbol when we shower bridal couples with rice.

- Wild rice grows in marshlands and waterways from Manitoba to the Atlantic Ocean. It is one of the few wild plant foods harvested and marketed in Canada.

- Rice is an important component of many commercially produced baby foods, because it is easy to digest and hypoallergenic.

- According to legend, rice was accidentally introduced to the Americas when a storm-stricken ship docked in Charleston, South Carolina, and the captain gave some seeds to a local planter.

- The outer, most nutritious parts of the rice kernel are removed and fed to livestock when rice is milled.

- Broken grains of rice are used for brewing beer.

SALAD BARS—THE MANY PROS AND CONS

*Although typical salad bar offerings are perceived
as healthy alternatives to fast foods,
a number of them are loaded with fat and salt.*

Once considered a trendy fad in family restaurants, the salad bar is now as ubiquitous as fast-food eateries. Even chic high-priced restaurants have set up salad bars; they're also found in fast-food establishments, delicatessens, and a variety of institutional settings. Many salad bars provide complete meals, with everything from soups and relishes, raw and cooked vegetables and fruits, to hot and cold entrées, and even desserts.

There are advantages to such a set-up. It allows diners to put together their own meals without having to wait, and it enables restaurants to cut staffing costs. But there are also some drawbacks, especially for those watching their fat intake and weight. Although most people regard salads as low-calorie dishes that can be eaten with impunity, the fact is, many salad bar meals have more fat and calories than a hamburger and French fries. It's all a matter of what you pick and which dressings and toppings you use.

PRACTICING RESTRAINT

Salad bar devotees say there's an art to creating a healthful meal from the 50 or more selections at a typical setup. Many people make the mistake of going to a salad bar when they're hungry, and then starting at one end and dishing up whatever looks appealing until their plate or takeout container is overflowing. A better approach is to survey the offerings and plan your

---

BENEFITS

- *Many offer a wide choice of greens, fresh vegetables, and fruits.*
- *Consumers can create their own salad or entrée, usually for less than it costs to order from the restaurant's regular menu.*

DRAWBACKS

- *Many choices are high in fat and sodium.*
- *The temptation to sample many offerings can result in overeating.*
- *Foods may be exposed to flies and other disease-carrying pests.*
- *There's a risk of food poisoning from items allowed to stand at room temperature for more than an hour or two.*

---

meal. If you're creating a salad to complement a restaurant meal, concentrate on a modest beginning—perhaps some raw vegetables or an assortment of greens with a low-calorie dressing. Remember, your main dish will probably be served with vegetables or other side dishes, so you don't need to fill up before it arrives.

Even if you're making an entire meal from the salad bar, you should still survey the choices and plan your menu before you start loading your plate. Decide on a single main dish—for example, a helping of lasagna, chili, broiled fish, or sliced turkey (all common salad bar offerings). Then

plan what you want to accompany it: perhaps a green salad or slice of melon as a first course; steamed or raw vegetables, a baked potato, or a serving of rice as side dishes; and sorbet or fresh fruit for dessert. Only after you've planned your meal should you start putting food on your plate. Begin with small helpings; many salad bars allow repeat trips, so you can always go back for more if you're still hungry.

You should use the same approach if you're assembling a take-out meal. Even though you won't be able to go back for seconds, you should still limit yourself to those selections that will form a balanced meal. Emphasize complex carbohydrates and add plenty of raw or lightly cooked vegetables, fresh fruit, and a modest serving of lean meat, poultry, seafood, or other high-protein selection.

TOPPINGS AND DRESSINGS

A 100-calorie plate of greens, vegetables, and, perhaps, fruits can be transformed into an 880-calorie meal (with very little added nutrition but extra calories and fat) by topping it with an ounce of croutons (120 calories), 2 tablespoons of blue cheese (180 calories), an ounce of sunflower seeds (160 calories), and ¼ cup of regular Italian dressing (320 calories). Instead, you can achieve a similar taste by adding 1 tablespoon of Parmesan cheese (23 calories), 2 tablespoons of sliced mushrooms (2 calories), 2 tablespoons of raw onions (7 calories), and 2 table-spoons of low-calorie Italian dressing (14 calories), for only 146 calories. Of course, many salad bar offerings have already been mixed, often with high-fat ingredients and dressings. Reject vegetables and other foods surrounded by oil, butter, or other fat. The high sheen on steamed or sautéed vegetables usually comes from oil, which is added to keep the foods from looking dry and withered. It's also a good bet that too much mayonnaise has been used to make egg, tuna, chicken, and seafood salads; avoid these items unless they're labeled as having been made with a low-fat dressing.

SALAD BAR SAFETY

In the past a number of severe ASTHMA attacks were traced to salad bar foods sprayed with sulfites to preserve their color and freshness. Sulfites are no longer used for this purpose, but people with severe food allergies, CELIAC DISEASE, and other food sensitivities still need to approach salad bars and cafeteria-type setups with caution; their offerings may be made with hidden offending ingredients, such as flour, wheat, and cornstarch.

Each year millions of North Americans suffer bouts of food poisoning, and many of these are linked to open salad bars. Fortunately, most such incidents are short-lived, but some people—the very young, the elderly, and anyone with a chronic debilitating disease or lowered immunity—can suffer more serious consequences and may be well-advised to forgo salad bars or to select products in sealed containers.

When inspecting a salad bar, look for clues, such as withered greens and dried-out pasta, that might indicate if the food has been standing too long. Does the bar's surface feel cold (a sign that it's refrigerated or filled with ice)? Are there flies or evidence of other insects? If in doubt, go elsewhere or order freshly prepared food.

WISE SALAD BAR CHOICES

Most salad bars offer a few low-calorie choices and a wide range of tempting, high-fat alternatives. Use the following guide to create a healthful, interesting meal that's not overweighted with high-fat foods.

LOW-CALORIE OPTION	CALORIES	HIGH-CALORIE ALTERNATIVE	CALORIES
CONDIMENTS/TOPPINGS (2 tbsp)			
Alfalfa sprouts	2	Sunflower seeds	160
Anchovies (3)*	20	Bacon bits*	55
Chopped egg	25	Croutons* (1 oz)	120
Dill pickles (1 medium)*	5	Green olives* (8)	30
Parmesan cheese*	45	Blue cheese*	180
Raw chopped onion	7	Shredded Cheddar cheese*	55
DRESSINGS (1 tbsp)			
Garlic yogurt*	25	Cheese garlic*	90
Low-fat blue cheese*	11	Regular blue cheese*	75
Low-fat French*	22	Regular French*	65
Low-fat herb*	20	Caesar*	75
Low-fat Italian*	7	Regular Italian*	80
Low-fat vinaigrette*	8	Classic vinaigrette*	45
Nonfat mayonnaise*	20	Regular mayonnaise*	100
FRUITS, DESSERTS			
Applesauce (½ cup)	75	Apple pie	280
Chocolate chip cookie	50	Chocolate pudding (½ cup)	175
Fruit ice (½ cup)	80	Strawberry ice cream	270
SALADS (½ CUP)			
Carrot-raisin	45	Pasta (with mayonnaise)*	165
Fresh fruit	30	Waldorf (fruit, nut)	185
Mixed greens	10	Greek (with olives)*	95
Pickled beets	70	Potato (with mayonnaise)*	180
Red cabbage	30	Coleslaw	125
Tofu with chopped peppers	60	Lentil (with oil)*	140
Tomato-cucumber	25	Chickpeas (with oil)	160
Water-packed tuna*	120	Oil-packed tuna*	190
SOUPS (1 CUP)			
Beef barley*	60	Cream of mushroom*	315
Chicken noodle*	75	Cream of chicken*	200
Vegetable*	85	Split pea with ham*	250
SPECIALTY ITEMS			
Baked potato with herbs	140	Baked potato with cheese	520
Calamari (marinated)	140	Calamari (deep fried)	250
Fish fillet (baked)	90	Fish (breaded, deep fried)	200
Sushi (rice, vegetable)	40	Fried Chinese dumpling	150

Note: Calorie values vary from place to place; those quoted here are an average.
* High in sodium unless labeled low-salt.

Salad Dressings

BENEFITS
- *Add flavor and interest to lettuce and other salad greens.*
- *A good source of vitamin E.*

DRAWBACKS
- *Cheese, creamy, and oil dressings, as well as mayonnaise, are high in fat.*
- *Those made from raw eggs may harbor salmonella bacteria.*
- *Additives can cause allergies or adverse reactions in susceptible people.*

Various dressings give flavor and zip to lettuce and other greens; they are even more important in potato, egg, chicken, tuna, seafood, and similar salads because they help hold the ingredients together. The olive, corn, canola, and other vegetable oils used in most salad dressings provide vitamin E; because their fats are unsaturated, they do not tend to raise blood cholesterol levels. But traditional salad dressings also add lots of calories, and those made with eggs, cheese, or sour cream contain saturated fats and cholesterol. Fortunately, there is an increasing number of low-fat alternatives.

The classic vinaigrette dressing, a mixture of vinegar and oil, is the simplest to make and one of the easiest to modify. The standard recipe calls for 3 to 4 parts oil to 1 part vinegar, but you can reduce the amount of oil in several ways. For instance, you don't need as much oil if you mix it with a mild balsamic, wine, or rice vinegar. Another option is to dilute a stronger vinegar with water, defatted broth, wine, or juice, depending upon the desired taste. You can also reduce the amount of oil by selecting one with an assertive flavor, such as walnut or olive oil. A blend of oils adds extra flavor and also cuts the amount needed.

DON'T OVERDRESS

A salad that's drenched in dressing is not only high in unnecessary calories but becomes soggy quickly, because the vinegar wilts lettuce and other greens. Use a very light sprinkling of oil to coat the greens, and mix the other ingredients—for example, raw vegetables or artichoke hearts—with a small amount of vinegar. Then toss the two together just before serving.

As a general rule, 1 to 2 tablespoons of dressing should be ample for 4 cups of salad greens, and ¼ cup of a mayonnaise-type dressing should be enough for 4 cups of potato, tuna, or chicken salad.

Also go easy on the toppings; extras like shredded cheese, bacon bits, seeds, and croutons are usually very high in fat. (See Wise Salad Bar Choices, facing page.)

For a creamy texture and appearance without the saturated fat, add nonfat yogurt to the vinaigrette dressing. Or replace some of the oil with buttermilk. Experiment with HERBS and SPICES. To make your own low-fat Italian dressing, start with equal parts of olive oil and wine vinegar, add oregano and other herbs, and top with a sprinkling of Parmesan or Romano cheese. Create low-fat variations of Russian or Thousand Island dressings by blending ketchup or tomato paste with chopped pickles, yogurt, and vinegar to taste. For a tangier dressing, add cumin or chili pepper.

When eating at a RESTAURANT or from a SALAD BAR, mix your own low-fat dressing by asking for oil and vinegar or a fresh lemon. If you elect a house dressing, ask that it be served on the side.

Blue cheese dressings rank near the top in fat and calories, and their distinctive flavor is hard to duplicate with low-fat alternatives. Try blending equal

amounts of nonfat cottage cheese and yogurt with a little vinegar to make a creamy dressing; then crumble in a small amount of blue cheese for flavor.

If a recipe calls for a MAYONNAISE dressing, start with a low-fat type. You can reduce the amount needed by first splashing the ingredients with a little vinegar. Then blend the mayonnaise with an equal part of nonfat yogurt and add mustard or horseradish for zip.

SAFETY ISSUES

Although some dressing recipes, such as homemade mayonnaise and Caesar salad dressing, call for raw eggs, they should not be used because they may harbor salmonella bacteria. Instead, use imitation egg products; these contain egg whites that have been treated to kill bacteria. Commercial salad dressings are pasteurized to kill any microorganisms, and their high vinegar content discourages the growth of new ones. Commercial dressings often contain wheat or corn starches, soy, and perhaps eggs. Anyone with food allergies, CELIAC DISEASE, and other food intolerances should check the labels carefully. Products made according to a standard recipe do not list all the ingredients. In such cases, call the manufacturer for a list of ingredients.

SALT AND SODIUM

BENEFITS
- *Sodium helps to maintain fluid balance, regulate blood pressure, and transmit nerve impulses.*
- *Salt improves the flavor of many foods.*
- *Salt is a useful food preservative.*

DRAWBACKS
- *Sodium promotes fluid retention and may contribute to high blood pressure.*

While the terms are often used interchangeably, salt and sodium are not the same. Sodium is an element that joins with chlorine to form sodium chloride, or table salt. Sodium occurs naturally in most foods, and salt is the most common source of sodium in the diet. Most Canadians consume far more salt than they need, which may lead to or worsen high BLOOD PRESSURE, STROKE, and KIDNEY DISEASES.

The human body needs only about 500mg of sodium a day to maintain health. This amount is easily found in balanced meals prepared without any added salt. Although the recommended daily intake for a healthy person is no more than 2,400mg—the equivalent of a teaspoon of salt—the average Canadian consumes about 3,100mg a day. The major sources of this excess sodium are processed and preserved foods. Salty foods, such as potato chips and salted nuts, are easy to identify, but hidden sodium has to be tracked down on package labels. Cereals, cold cuts, canned and frozen vegetables, prepackaged meals, and commercial baked goods are usually high in sodium.

BLOOD PRESSURE

People with high blood pressure are typically advised to cut back on salt, because sodium influences the circulatory system and affects the kidneys' ability to rid the body of wastes and fluid. This is a sound recommendation, although salt is only one of many factors that raise blood pressure.

When the body's sodium level is low, the kidneys retrieve the chemical from the urine and return it to the circulating blood. Some individuals, however, have a genetic tendency to conserve sodium, which may predispose them to develop high blood pressure. As the kidneys retain more salt than they need to, they excrete less urine so that fluid is available to maintain the sodium at the correct concentration. As a result, the heart is forced to pump harder to keep this extra fluid in circulation, and the blood pressure increases to maintain the blood flow.

Restricting salt intake may correct this form of high blood pressure. Although opinions differ, many hypertension specialists believe it's a good preventive measure to keep sodium intake low from an early age. This is especially important for people of African descent, who often have an inherited tendency to salt sensitivity that increases the risk of high blood pressure.

The increase in blood volume that occurs during PREGNANCY temporarily increases the body's need for salt, but the amount required is normally supplied in a varied, balanced diet. Pregnant women should prepare meals with a normal amount of salt and not add salt to food at the table, nor should they indulge in salty snacks.

REDUCING SALT INTAKE

Preparing most dishes from scratch and avoiding processed foods helps to cut down on salt intake. Supermarkets and food stores now stock a growing variety of salt-free or low-salt versions of processed foods, including the canned broths that home cooks use in making fresh soups and stews. All food labels now list the amount of sodium in a serving; however, the serving specified on the label—and therefore the sodium content—may be much less than the amount you typically eat. It's also important to understand what food labeling terms mean.

- **Sodium free** has less than 5mg of sodium per 100g serving.
- **Low-sodium** products must have at least 50 percent less sodium than comparable products and cannot have more than 40mg per 100g serving except for Cheddar cheese, which can have up to 50mg. Meat, fish, and poultry products can have up to 80mg per 100g serving.
- **Light in sodium** is an alternate term for low sodium.

SODIUM IN EVERYDAY FOODS

A teaspoon of salt supplies over 2,000mg of sodium. The level in some common foods is surprisingly high, as shown below.

Bacon (3 slices):
Grilled, 300mg

Breads (1 slice):
Rye, 175mg
White, 125mg
Whole wheat, 160–180mg

Cereals (1 oz):
Cornflakes, 350mg
Puffed rice, 340mg

Cheese (1 oz):
American cheese, 400mg
Blue cheese, 395mg
Swiss, processed, 390mg

Snacks (1 oz):
Olives, green, 925mg
Peanuts, salted, 120mg
Pickles, dill, 440mg
Potato chips, 135mg
Pretzels, 475mg

Soups (1 cup, canned):
Chicken noodle, 1,105mg
Tomato, 870–930mg

• **Unsalted** products can have no added salt.

Also check the label for code terms, such as brine, broth, cured, corned, pickled, soy sauce, and teriyaki sauce, that indicate other high-sodium ingredients have been added.

For many people, adding salt to food at the table is a reflex response to seeing the salt shaker; if you remove the shaker from the table, you may not miss the salt. You can also reduce salt intake by cutting down or eliminating salt in cooking. The amount of salt and other sodium-containing seasonings in most recipes can be cut by half or even more without a noticeable change in taste or texture. Herbs and spices, unsalted garlic or onion powder, and lemon juice are healthful alternatives to salt. Adding these ingredients shortly before serving keeps their flavors from being lost during prolonged cooking.

Warning: Most commercial salt substitutes contain potassium. These may be dangerous for people with kidney disorders or those taking potassium-sparing diuretics or supplements. Before using a salt substitute, especially if you're taking a diuretic or potassium supplements, first check with a doctor.

PICKLES AND OTHER CONDIMENTS, such as mustard, ketchup, salad dressings, and barbecue sauces, are high in sodium. When eating in restaurants, ask for dressings and sauces to be served on the side. In restaurants where the food is cooked to order, some selections can usually be prepared without salt.

The use of a home water softener may add a substantial amount of sodium to your drinking water. The company that installed the water softener should tell you how much sodium is in the system; you may prefer to drink bottled water instead.

Many over-the-counter medications contain sodium. If you are on a sodium-restricted diet, check with your physician or pharmacist before using antacids, painkillers, or laxatives.

Contrary to what you may read, sea salt is not a healthier product than table salt. There are no documented health advantages to sea salt, and the sodium content is similar.

SAUCES AND GRAVIES

BENEFITS

- *Used sparingly, sauces complement flavors and enhance appearance.*
- *Salsa-style garnishes supply fiber and antioxidant vitamins, provided they are carefully prepared.*
- *Pasta sauces based on fresh vegetables and olive oil are good sources of vitamins, fiber, complex carbohydrates, and unsaturated fat.*

DRAWBACKS

- *Traditional sauces made from butter, flour, cream, and egg yolks are very high in cholesterol.*
- *Asian-style sauces are high in salt and should be avoided by people on low-sodium diets.*

An 18th-century Italian unfavorably compared England and France: "England has 60 religions," he wrote, "and one sauce, whereas France has 60 sauces and one religion." Like so many exaggerations, this one had a grain of truth. French cuisine is still renowned for its sauces, while Anglo-Saxon culinary preferences tend toward little more than a dollop of butter, commercial ketchup, or brown gravy. In contrast, Italian cooks tend to favor vegetable-based mixtures that are often enlivened with a dusting of fresh or dried herbs or a sprinkling of grated cheese.

The North American sauce style is still evolving, but it is moving away from the calorie-laden French mode and the overpowering flavors of ketchup toward the lighter Italian pasta sauces and the invigorating fruits, vegetables, and spices of Latin American salsa.

The word *sauce,* like *salsa,* comes from the root meaning "salty." Early sauces were heavily salted spice mixtures. The salt helped to preserve the food, and the spices helped to mask the flavors of tainted meats. No longer needed as a cover-up, sauces today are added to enhance or complement the flavors of other foods.

THANKSGIVING TURKEY GRAVY

Nobody expects you to do without the gravy that glazes the Thanksgiving turkey. By using a stock-based method, however, you can reduce the fat and calorie content and improve the nutritional quality.

Brown the turkey giblets and trimmings in a hot oven or under the broiler, drain off the fat, and simmer the browned scraps with vegetables and herbs (an unpeeled onion stuck with a clove, a celery stalk, carrot, leek, and turnip; thyme, parsley stems, peppercorns, and a bay leaf) to make a rich stock. Drain the stock, discard the vegetables, then chill the stock, which will make it easier to remove the congealed fat from the surface. Next, concentrate the skimmed stock by boiling it down to a half or third of its volume. When the turkey is done, drain the fat from the roasting pan and pour in the hot stock to dissolve the clinging browned bits of meat. Boil the liquid to blend the flavors together, season, and serve hot with the turkey.

There is a major difference between sauces that are made fresh and commercial preparations. Fresh-made sauces are limitless in range, from a world-renowned chef's classic concoctions to the home cook's on-the-spot invention of a fresh salsa from vegetables and handy herbs. In contrast, commercially prepared sauces, such as ketchups, barbecue sauces, and hot pepper sauces and spicy blends are made to patented formulas of ingredients.

Traditional sauce-making techniques are based on four main methods: the reduction of stock or vegetable pulp; the roux (pronounced *roo*), in which similar quantities of fat and flour are cooked together, blended with milk or another liquid to a velvety consistency, and flavored; hot egg-based sauces (such as Hollandaise), in which egg yolks and butter are blended to make an emulsion with concentrated wine or vinegar and seasonings; and cold egg sauces (such as MAYONNAISE), where oil is blended into an emulsion with egg yolks and vinegar or lemon juice.

These traditional sauces generally contain only moderate amounts of vitamins A and D from their milk, cream, butter, and egg yolk components. Considering the small portions in which they are meant to be served, however, the vitamin quotient is negligible and is far outweighed by the negative impact of saturated fats and calories. Two tablespoons of a homemade white sauce contain about 50 calories; the addition of grated cheese to make a Mornay sauce typically increases the calorie count to 125.

Sauces made from commercial mixes are somewhat lower in calories than homemade ones. For example, Hollandaise sauce from a packet contains about 30 calories in 2 tablespoons, and a dry-mix cheese sauce, approximately 40 calories. Packet sauces are extremely high in sodium, however, and offer few useful nutrients.

The trend away from flour-based sauces got its first big push from the calorie-conscious nouvelle and spa cuisines that emerged in the 1970s. Professional chefs and home cooks alike began to spurn flour thickeners and egg yolk, cream, or butter enrichment in favor of the pure, intense flavors obtained by concentrating fat-free stocks and vegetable purees. While traditional sauces were typically laden with saturated fat and cholesterol, the new garnishes manage to add piquancy in a low-fat, low-calorie form.

SALSA

A welcome recent arrival, salsa is a more healthful approach to garnishing than butter- and cream-based sauces.

While commercial salsas are usually modified vinegar pickles cooked and thickened with starch, fresh salsas are mixtures of fine-chopped vegetables or fruits, highly seasoned with garlic, scallions, citrus juice, and fresh herbs, such as cilantro and basil. In contrast to the traditional sauces, salsa homemade from fresh fruits or vegetables is fat-free if made without oil, high in fiber, very low in calories, and rich in such ANTIOXIDANTS as vitamin C and beta carotene (provided the mixture is not left exposed to the air for any length of time before serving).

PASTA SAUCES

Pasta sauces, such as Alfredo, that are made with cream, butter, egg yolk, and cheese, are very high in fat and cholesterol. They should be used only sparingly to coat pasta, and people with high cholesterol levels should avoid them altogether. The variety of low-fat pasta sauces is limited only by a cook's imagination and the ingredients available. Excellent sauces can be made with fresh tomatoes chopped with basil and garlic and blended with a few drops of olive oil; sun-dried tomatoes blended with a little low-fat goat cheese and chopped parsley; or black olives, anchovies, fennel, and tomatoes quickly sautéed in a little olive oil and enlivened with a sprinkling of garlic and red pepper flakes. All of these garnishes provide generous amounts of fiber, beta carotene, vitamins C and E, calcium and iron, and a small amount of unsaturated fat.

GRAVIES

Practically unknown outside North American and British kitchens, gravies are variations on the roux. Flour is cooked in fat drippings from dry-cooked meat, then blended with water or another liquid to make a smooth sauce. Red-eye gravy, a specialty in the American South, is con-

HEALTHY TOPPINGS. *Updated versions of traditional sauces add flavor without lots of fat and calories.*

cocted from ham or bacon drippings and black coffee; cream gravies are enriched with either cream or milk.

Commercially canned gravies are also available. Two tablespoons of canned beef or mushroom gravy contain approximately 15 calories, compared to 25 in the same amount of canned chicken gravy. Individuals on low-sodium diets should avoid commercial gravies, which are extremely high in salt. These gravies have fairly substantial amounts of fat and trivial amounts of other nutrients. No matter if the gravy is homemade or commercial, it contributes only a negligible amount of nutrition.

ASIAN SALT SAUCES

The sauces used in Asian cooking are generally fat-free, but they are extremely high in sodium. Those most familiar to Westerners are soy, fish or oyster sauce (*nuoc mamh* or *nam pla*), hoisin and other bean-based sauces, and stir-fry sauce (a mixture of other sauces). Some of these may be thickened with wheat gluten and should be avoided by people with CELIAC DISEASE. Even the reduced-salt versions are high in sodium and should be avoided by people on low-sodium diets or those at risk of developing high blood pressure.

DESSERT SAUCES

Dessert sauces, such as hot fudge and caramel, elevate the fat and calorie content of an ice cream sundae to dizzying heights. Fat-free versions of many of the classic soda-fountain sauces, including hot fudge and butterscotch, are available at many grocery stores, but the calorie content is still high, and the nutritional value is low or nonexistent. More healthful alternatives include nonfat frozen yogurt topped with chopped fresh fruit and nuts, sieved poached apricots and toasted almond flakes, or frozen berries blended and sweetened to taste.

SCHIZOPHRENIA

EAT PLENTY OF
- *A combination of animal protein and starchy foods to increase brain levels of tryptophan, a calming amino acid.*

CUT DOWN ON
- *Beverages high in caffeine.*

AVOID
- *Alcohol, which can interact with antipsychotic medications.*
- *Nicotine, which acts as a stimulant.*

About 1 percent of any population worldwide (about 270,000 Canadians) suffers from schizophrenia, a devastating mental illness characterized by hallucinations, delusions, and bizarre thoughts and behavior. Mental health professionals classify it as a psychotic disorder, defined as being out of touch with reality. The disease generally manifests itself during adolescence, but it can also develop earlier and later in life. The cause remains unknown, but because it appears to run in some families, researchers theorize that a genetic susceptibility may be involved. Recent studies suggest that excessive dopamine, a brain chemical that transmits messages within the brain, is also a factor. In fact, drugs used to treat schizophrenia appear to work because they prevent some of the brain's nerve receptors from taking up dopamine.

There is no cure for schizophrenia, although powerful antipsychotic drugs can often control the more severe symptoms, which vary considerably from one person to another. In some cases, symptoms appear to come and go; in others, there are long remissions, while a few people require constant care.

THE ROLE OF DIET

There is no clear link between diet and schizophrenia, and although some alternative practitioners advocate high-dose (orthomolecular) vitamin therapy, there is no evidence that it is of any benefit. Some doctors advise against consuming large amounts of coffee, tea, colas, and other caffeinated beverages because caffeine is a stimulant, and as such, it may exacerbate symptoms. Nicotine may have a similar effect, so tobacco use should be avoided as well. Unquestionably, anyone with schizophrenia should abstain from alcohol, which is not only toxic to the brain but also interacts with the drugs used to treat the disorder.

In theory, at least, some dietary strategies may alleviate symptoms by altering the levels of certain brain chemicals. Serotonin, another chemical that transmits messages within the brain, has a calming effect. Tryptophan, an amino acid found in meat, milk, eggs, and other animal products, is a precursor of serotonin. Blood levels of tryptophan increase after eating a meal that includes high-quality protein, but this does not necessarily mean that more of it reaches the brain. The tryptophan must compete with other amino acids to pass from the bloodstream into the brain, so a high-protein meal may actually decrease the amount that reaches the cells that make serotonin. Also, a high-protein meal increases levels of tyrosine, another amino acid, which the brain makes into dopamine, the chemical implicated in schizophrenia.

Eating a high-carbohydrate meal with a small portion of a food high in tryptophan (for example, 2 ounces of turkey or $1/2$ cup of milk) may actually increase the amount of tryptophan that reaches the brain. After eating a meal high in carbohydrates, blood levels of insulin rise, and this hormone prompts the competing amino acids to enter the muscles, clearing the way for more tryptophan to get into the brain. While this approach to meal planning is unlikely to alleviate all the symptoms, it may well calm the feelings of agitation.

Seaweed

BENEFITS
- *An excellent source of iodine.*
- *Provides a wide spectrum of minerals, including calcium, copper, iron, magnesium, and potassium.*
- *Some types are rich in the B vitamins, vitamin C, and beta carotene.*
- *Some are a good source of protein.*

DRAWBACKS
- *Some are very high in sodium.*

There are more than 2,500 varieties of seaweed, which include everything from the algae that forms on ponds to kelp and other marine plants with long stems and leaves. In general, seaweed is classified according to its color—brown, red, green, and blue-green.

A remarkably versatile and tasty vegetable, seaweed can be used in a broad spectrum of ways. In Japan, for example, seaweed makes up 25 percent of all food in the diet; it is also used to enhance flavors in a variety of dishes, from salads and soups to meat and seafood dishes. Kombu, a type of kelp (a brown plant that is one of the most common seaweeds), is used to flavor soup stocks. Wakame, another type of kelp, is used in Japan in soups and stir-fries.

Seaweeds are found in the diets of other cultures. For example, laver, a red algae called nori by the Japanese, is used by the Irish and Welsh to make flat cakes. The Scots use a seaweed called dulse to make soup. Irish moss, a red algae that is a major source of carrageenan, is used in the industrialized world as a thickening agent in such products as salad dressings. Seaweed is also part of some macrobiotic diets.

An excellent source of many essential nutrients, including protein, most seaweeds are a rich source of iodine. The thyroid gland needs iodine to make the hormones that regulate body metabolism; a goiter, marked by an enlarged thyroid, is a sign of iodine deficiency.

The mineral content of the various types of seaweed differ, but most provide calcium, copper, iron, potassium, and magnesium. Some supply beta carotene, a precursor of vitamin A; the levels vary with the cooking method.

Seaweed also tends to be low in calories; a ½-cup serving of kelp, for example, contains about 50 calories. The same serving also provides 2g of protein, almost 200mcg (micrograms) of folate (45 percent of the adult Recommended Nutrient Intake, or RNI), 120mg of magnesium (about 50 percent of the RNI), and useful amounts

A SUSHI FEAST.
Nori strips form edible wrappers for sushi and rice cakes, staples of the Japanese diet.

> ### SEAWEED SEASONING
> Dried sheets or strips of seaweed, or nori, impart a distinctive salty flavor due to their high sodium content. Sold at Asian groceries and health food stores, nori is used to season salads, soups, and noodles and is soaked to use as wrappers for rice cakes and sushi.

of iron and calcium. In comparison, a ½-cup serving of raw laver contains only 40 calories, and it provides 6g of protein as well as 5,200 I.U. of vitamin A as beta carotene (more than 100 percent of the RNI) and 2mg of iron (more than 10 percent of the RNI). This type, however, contains smaller amounts of magnesium and calcium than kelp does.

The major drawback to seaweed is that many types are high in sodium. A ½-cup portion of raw wakame contains approximately 900mg of sodium; an equivalent amount of dried spirulina yields more than 1,100mg. (The recommended daily sodium intake for a healthy person should not exceed 2,400mg.) The same amounts of kelp and laver are lower in sodium, containing 250mg and 60mg, respectively. However, anyone who has high BLOOD PRESSURE or is on a low-salt diet should avoid foods containing seaweed.

SUPPLEMENTS

Kelp tablets, spirulina, chlorella, and other seaweed supplements are often promoted as energy boosters. Some alternative practitioners also claim that such supplements boost the immune system. None of these claims has been proven however. Some seaweed supplements can even cause health problems. High doses of kelp tablets can set off an outbreak of ACNE. The high iodine content can cause THYROID DISORDERS; varieties containing iron can provoke IRON OVERLOAD.

SEX DRIVE

EAT PLENTY OF
- *Legumes, fortified grains and cereals, poultry, wheat germ, and dark green leafy vegetables for B-group vitamins.*
- *Fruits and vegetables for vitamin C.*
- *Poultry, seafood, and wheat germ for a good supply of vitamin E.*
- *Lean meat, fish, shellfish, legumes, and fortified cereals for iron.*
- *Yogurt, grains, and oysters for zinc.*

CUT DOWN ON
- *Saturated fats and alcohol.*

AVOID
- *Smoking.*

Some people vouch for the effect of foods on their sex drive, but extravagant claims for aphrodisiacs are not borne out by scientific studies. While sexual function may be our physical response to a cascade of hormones, sexual drive is basically maintained by an active mind in a healthy body.

Good nerve function, healthy hormone levels, and an unobstructed blood flow to the pelvic area are essential to both mental and sexual performance. To keep these systems in good working order, a diet should be based on legumes, grain products, and other complex carbohydrates, with plenty of fruits and vegetables and modest levels of protein; this type of diet will provide plenty of vitamins—especially those in the B group. Particularly important are citrus fruits for vitamin C to strengthen blood vessel walls, and low-fat dairy products, fortified grains, and dark green leafy vegetables for riboflavin to maintain the mucous membranes that line the female reproductive tract.

Vitamin B5, also called pantothenic acid, is essential for production of the adrenal hormones that influence nerve function. While pantothenic acid is found in almost all foods, it is also manufactured by the normal intestinal bacteria, which ensures that a supply is maintained even when the diet is lacking in other essential nutrients.

No confirmed connection has been shown between vitamin E and sexual function. However, many experts believe that without a good supply of this vitamin from eggs, poultry, seafood, grains, wheat germ, and fortified cereals, sexual function is likely to suffer.

Fatigue and depression are common culprits in sexual complaints. These conditions are often linked, and both may be helped by a program of regular exercise, which stimulates the production of endorphins (mood-elevating brain chemicals). In some cases, iron-deficiency ANEMIA may be responsible for fatigue. A diet that includes lean meat, fish and shellfish, legumes, fortified cereals, and dried apricots helps to replenish iron stores.

It is known that zinc is tied to sexual function, although its importance to the sex drive has yet to be explained. Without enough zinc, sexual development in children is delayed, and men, too, need zinc to make sperm. Zinc is found abundantly in fortified cereals, low-fat yogurt, oysters, and beef.

People readily accept the link between a high intake of saturated fats, elevated blood cholesterol levels, and a buildup of atherosclerotic fatty plaques on the blood vessels around the heart. It's less well understood, however, that similar plaques develop on the myriad tiny vessels in the penis. Without free-flowing circulation, the penis cannot respond to messages from the sex drive. Men and women alike should consume a diet low in saturated fats; for men, however, it's doubly important.

Alcohol's effect on sexual function was neatly captured by William Shakespeare, who noted that wine "provokes the desire, but robs the performance." Excessive alcohol lifts behavioral inhibitions, but this liberating effect may be canceled out by its depressant effect. Alcohol also has an action similar to the female hormone estrogen. This can have a devastating effect on masculinity, causing impotence and shrinking of the testes in men who drink heavily.

Like saturated fats, nicotine is an enemy of the arteries. Nicotine not only promotes the formation of atherosclerotic plaque in the penile blood vessels but also constricts them.

APHRODISIACS

The power of aphrodisiacs is no more than the power of suggestion. For example, their suggestive shape has lent an aphrodisiac aura to such vegetables as asparagus and the carrot. While both are low in calories and rich in nutrients, neither improves sexual performance.

Herbalists recommend saffron as a sexual stimulant, but there is no evidence of its aphrodisiac effect. Some also recommend summer savory as a sexual stimulant and tonic, and winter savory to dampen sexual desire. Neither claim has been proved.

Health Canada classifies the herb ginseng as safe but does not allow claims for aphrodisiac or medicinal qualities. Studies show that ginseng boosts stamina and mating behavior in mice and rats. It's not a safe bet, however, that effects in mice and men are similar.

Yohimbe, a tropical tree, is valued as an aphrodisiac in some countries; although extracts dilate the blood vessels in the skin and mucous membranes, they also lower blood pressure and can cause temporary impotence. Yohimbe is unsafe and may be dangerous if taken with tyramine-containing foods, such as aged cheese or red wine.

Spanish fly, an extract of dried cantharides beetles, causes intense irritation in the urinary tract and genital organs, which some people misinterpret as sexual stimulus. In reality, Spanish fly is a potentially fatal drug.

SHELLFISH

BENEFITS
- *A low-fat source of high-quality protein.*
- *A rich source of minerals, including calcium, fluoride, iodine, iron, and zinc.*
- *A good source of B-group vitamins.*

DRAWBACKS
- *Some are high in cholesterol.*
- *Susceptible to spoilage and environmental contamination.*
- *Can provoke allergies in some people.*

Shellfish is the catchall term applied to mollusks and crustaceans—water-dwelling creatures that wear their skeletons on the outside. Mollusks, such as oysters and mussels, lead a sedentary life inside rigid shells, which they affix with threadlike excretions to rocks or pilings. But octopus and squid, which are free swimming and have no shells (squid have a transparent internal quill, or beak), are also mollusks. Another exception is snails, which are mollusks that live on dry land or in the water and move about, carrying their shells.

The soft bodies of crustaceans, such as lobster, shrimp, and crab, are covered by hinged plates of chitin, like suits of armor, that allow mobility but shield them from predators. Soft-shell crabs are taken in the molting season, when they have discarded their old shells but before the new shells have hardened.

NUTRITIONAL VALUE
Shellfish are among our most valuable sources of high-quality protein. In contrast to protein from warm-blooded animals, shellfish protein is very low in actual fat. Most varieties, however, contain fairly high levels of CHOLESTEROL, which is not a fat, although it is in the same lipid family. The harsh warnings about the cholesterol content of shellfish have been tempered recently with the realization that it appears to have relatively little effect on the actual lev-els circulating in the bloodstream. This is probably because shellfish are very low in saturated fat, the lipid most likely to raise blood cholesterol levels. Shellfish also contain fewer calories, weight for weight, than other sources of animal protein do.

A 4-ounce serving of shellfish provides a fine array of B vitamins, with 10 percent of the thiamine, 15 percent of the riboflavin, and 50 percent of the niacin we need daily. Shellfish are especially rich in minerals, including calcium, phosphorus, and fluoride needed for healthy bones and teeth; copper to help in the production of blood cells, connective tissue, and nerve fibers; iodine for thyroid gland function; iron for healthy red blood cells; magnesium for metabolism, bone growth, and production of genetic material; potassium for nerve and muscle function and general metabolism; and zinc for the immune system and reproductive health.

POTENTIAL DANGERS
If grown in polluted waters, shellfish may be contaminated with bacteria and carry a particular risk for hepatitis. Don't gather shellfish at the seashore or near wharf pilings or built-up areas. Instead, buy them from fish markets and food stores that keep shellfish well covered with ice or, in the case of lobsters, in tanks with circulating water aerated with oxygen. Shallow-water shellfish, such as clams and mussels, are the most susceptible to pollution; sea scallops and other deep-water varieties are less likely to be exposed to waste. Fresh shellfish may be covered with ice chips and stored for several hours at 32°F (0°C). Eat them on the day they are purchased.

Oysters are available year-round, but the old rule of eating them only in the months with the letter "R" remains a sound one. During the non-R summer months, warmer water temperatures may promote bacterial growth.

From time to time, swarming plankton cause the phenomenon known as "red tide" in coastal waters. Shellfish exposed to the red tide ingest the microorganisms, which produce a toxin that can survive cooking. The symptoms of red tide poisoning usually appear within 30 minutes of consuming contaminated fish; they include facial numbness, breathing difficulty, muscle weakness, and partial paralysis. Never take shellfish from red-tide areas. In Quebec in 1987 more than 100 people became ill after eating mussels tainted with domoic acid, a compound produced by certain algae which mussels ingest. Some of the victims suffered permanent damage to their nervous systems, others experienced memory loss. Four people died. Mussels tainted with domoic acid are undetectable by consumers; however, government authorities monitor for its presence.

Because of their susceptibility to spoilage, shellfish should be kept alive until they are ready to be cooked or served raw. Buy clams, mussels, and oysters only if the shells close tightly when tapped. An open shell indicates that the shellfish has died and is therefore unsafe to eat. Conversely, when steaming or boiling mollusks in the shell, discard any that fail to open at the end of the specified cooking time.

Fresh shellfish, whether in the shell or shucked, should smell briny, without any hint of iodine or fishiness. Oysters and clams show their freshness by "flinching" when you squeeze lemon juice on them.

Shrimp and crabmeat are exceptions to the live-shellfish rule. Most shrimp are trimmed and frozen in bulk at sea, then thawed for sale at onshore retail

SEAFOOD PLATTER. *Choose from a tasty selection of nutritious, low-calorie shellfish, including (clockwise from top left) shrimps, Amande clams, Venus clams, mussels, scallops, oysters, crab, whelks, prawns, and lobster.*

markets. Shrimp processed in this way should be labeled "previously frozen." Most crabmeat is cooked in the shell, or extracted and pasteurized, then frozen. Shellfish that is frozen or canned is usually ready to eat as purchased. Because crabmeat is separated from the shell by being passed through rubber rollers, however, it should be picked over to remove shell fragments.

Don't eat lobster tomalley or crab mustard, soft organs that filter impurities and may have high levels of toxins.

PREPARING SHELLFISH

Like finned fish, shellfish have fragile flesh that should be cooked just to the point where its protein coagulates. Cooked too long, the tissues toughen or dry out and fall apart.

Commercially prepared shellfish are often needlessly high in calories and fat because they are coated with batter or bread crumbs and intended for frying.

The butter dips and sauces frequently served with shellfish add calories and saturated fat. Cocktail sauce is lower in calories and fats than tartar and other MAYONNAISE-based dips. Minced shallots blended with lemon juice and herbs complement clams, lobsters, and other shellfish. To make a calcium-rich sauce, you can pound the shells of shrimp and lobster smooth, then boil them down with clam juice, lemon juice, white wine, and herbs.

A COMMON ALLERGEN

Many people are allergic to shellfish, and an allergic reaction to one type often means that the others should be avoided too. A severe reaction, with widespread hives, swelling, and difficulty breathing, indicates possible anaphylaxis, a life-threatening emergency. People allergic to shellfish may react to the iodine used in many of the dyes administered for contrast X-rays. Tell your doctor if you have ever experienced an allergic reaction to shellfish.

NUTRIENTS FOUND IN DIFFERENT SHELLFISH

Low in saturated fat and high in protein, shellfish have many of the qualities health-conscious people are looking for. They are rich in B vitamins (all are excellent sources of B_{12}) and are useful sources of trace minerals. However, they are prone to contamination, so extra care should be taken when buying, preparing, and cooking shellfish. All values below are for 100g (3½ oz) except where noted.

SHELL-FISH	PROTEIN (g)	FAT (g)	SODIUM (mg)	VITAMINS	MINERALS
Abalone (canned)	16	0.3	250	Good source of thiamine. Contains some riboflavin and niacin.	Good source of iron and magnesium.
Clams (raw)	12.6	1.6	60	Useful source of riboflavin and vitamins A and C.	Excellent source of iron, potassium, and zinc. Contain some calcium.
Crabs, Alaskan king (steamed)	19.3	1.5	180	Good source of vitamin A. Useful source of folate and pantothenic acid. Some vitamin B_6.	Good source of zinc. Contain some iron and magnesium.
Crabs, blue, Dungeness, (steamed)	17.3	1.9	250	Useful source of pantothenic acid, niacin, and vitamins A and B_6.	Good source of zinc. Contain some iron, potassium, magnesium, and calcium.
Crabs, soft-shell (1 medium)	12	1.3	300	Fair source of niacin. Contain some vitamin B_6, riboflavin, and thiamine.	Good source of iron. Contain some calcium and magnesium.
Lobster (boiled)	18.7	1.5	350	Excellent source of vitamin B_{12}. Contains some folate.	Good source of zinc. Some magnesium, potassium, and calcium.
Mussels, blue (steamed)	22	4.2	570	Good source of vitamins A and E. Contain some riboflavin, thiamine, and niacin.	Good source of iron. Contain zinc and magnesium.
Oysters (meat only, raw)	14	5.1	205	Contain some thiamine, riboflavin, and vitamins A and C.	Rich in zinc. Excellent source of iron. Contain some magnesium.
Scallops, bay, sea (steamed)	23.2	1.4	160	Good source of vitamin B_{12}.	Contain some magnesium and zinc.
Shrimps (boiled)	20.8	1.1	222	Contain some niacin, vitamin B_6, and folate.	Fair source of iron. Some zinc and magnesium.
Squid (raw)	16.1	0.7	310	Contains some riboflavin.	Good source of iron. Contains some zinc.

SHINGLES

CONSUME PLENTY OF
- *Olive and other vegetable oils, nuts, seeds, and wheat germ for vitamin E.*
- *Fresh fruits and vegetables for antioxidants and bioflavonoids.*

Herpes zoster, the medical term for shingles, is a reactivation of the varicella-zoster virus that causes chicken pox. It usually develops in older adults who have had chicken pox years earlier. What causes a reactivation of the virus is unknown, but shingles often develop when the immune system is suppressed due to excessive STRESS, the use of steroids or other immunosuppressive drugs, or lymphoma or other illnesses.

An attack typically starts with a localized tingling and burning sensation of the skin. A few days later blisters similar to those of chicken pox, only more painful, develop. These blisters follow the path of a nerve, most often on a shoulder, the chest, near the waist, or on one side of the face. Serious complications can develop if the virus infects an eye or migrates to the brain.

The severity of an attack may be lessened if acyclovir (Zovirax) or another antiviral drug is taken at the onset of symptoms. Some doctors believe that good nutrition may help prevent postherpetic neuralgia, a long-term complication marked by nerve pain even after the rash and other symptoms of shingles disappear. Beneficial nutrients include vitamin E, an ANTIOXIDANT found in nuts, seeds, wheat germ, and vegetable oils, and the BIOFLAVONOIDS found in fruits and vegetables that are high in vitamin C. These nutrients may also help prevent the inflammation associated with postherpetic neuralgia. If neuralgia does develop, however, the pain may be eased with applications of an ointment that contains capsaicin (Zostrix), the volatile oil that gives CHILIES their distinctive spicy bite.

SINUSITIS

CONSUME PLENTY OF
- *Fresh fruits and vegetables for vitamin C and bioflavonoids.*
- *Whole-grain products, legumes, nuts, and other foods high in B vitamins.*
- *Sunflower seeds, vegetable oils, and avocados for vitamin E.*
- *Garlic, onions, and chilies to alleviate sinus congestion.*

AVOID
- *Milk and milk products.*
- *Smoking.*
- *Dry, overheated rooms.*

Sinusitis is a painful inflammation of the lining of the sinus cavities in the skull. A very common problem, it occurs most often after a cold or in people who suffer from hay fever or other allergies involving the nasal passages.

The sinuses, which help warm and moisten the air before it travels to the windpipe and lungs, are lined with membranes similar to those lining the nasal passages. Normally, mucus produced by these membranes drains through narrow ducts into the nasal cavity. Acute sinusitis is usually the result of a viral, bacterial, or fungal infection. Chronic sinusitis is more apt to be caused by allergic reactions or dental infections.

Regardless of the cause, the sinus lining swells and blocks the passages, resulting in a stuffed-up feeling, facial tenderness and possibly swelling, and a deep, dull headache. A good clue in the diagnosis of sinusitis is that the pain tends to worsen whenever you bend over. There may also be a thick yellow or green nasal discharge.

For fast relief, cover the face with hot, wet towels to promote sinus drainage and increase blood flow to the area. Steam inhalation also promotes sinus drainage. Depending upon the cause, a doctor may prescribe antihistamines, decongestants, antibiotics, or steroids.

DIETARY APPROACHES

Although nutrition does not play a direct role in sinusitis, some dietary measures may help. In one study, patients with chronic sinusitis reported improvement after eliminating milk products from their diets. Persons trying this approach should ask their doctor about supplements or increase their consumption of nondairy calcium.

Case Study

Maria suffered from chronic headaches that caused a dull aching pressure on her forehead and often spread down her face and to her ears. Because the pain worsened when she bent over, gardening and certain other tasks had become difficult.

When she finally sought her doctor's advice, Maria was told that the problem was chronic sinusitis. Since there was no evidence of infection, her doctor suggested that she use a humidifier in her bedroom, eliminate dairy products from her diet, and have an occasional dish made with garlic, chilies, horseradish, or other hot, spicy ingredients. After a few weeks of following these measures, Maria's symptoms began to disappear.

To boost your immunity against colds and other infections, eat plenty of whole-grain products, legumes, and nuts for B vitamins, and fresh fruits and vegetables to ensure a good intake of vitamin C. Citrus fruits (rather than just the juice), grapes, and blackberries are useful because they also contain BIO-FLAVONOIDS, plant pigments that have anti-inflammatory properties. Vitamin E, too, has anti-inflammatory benefits and supports the immune system.

Some foods are natural decongestants; these include GARLIC, ONIONS, CHILIES, and horseradish. Decongestant HERBS and SPICES include ginger, thyme, cumin, cloves, and cinnamon.

Smoking causes nasal and sinus inflammation; if you smoke, make every effort to stop and also avoid secondhand smoke. Heat and dry air can produce swollen, dry nasal membranes that are predisposed to sinusitis; a humidifier may be a solution.

Skin Problems

CONSUME PLENTY OF

- *Yellow fruits and vegetables and dark green vegetables for vitamins A and C.*
- *Legumes, whole-grain or fortified breads and cereals, eggs, and dark green vegetables for the B vitamins.*
- *Seafood, poultry, and grains for zinc.*
- *Oily fish and evening primrose oil for omega-3 fatty acids.*

CUT DOWN ON

- *Animal protein (if you have rosacea or psoriasis).*
- *Alcohol, hot spices, and any other foods that aggravate the skin problem.*

The skin reflects a person's state of health in many ways, including nutritional status. A deficiency of vitamin A, for example, leads to rough, dry, scaly skin. A lack of riboflavin causes scaly, greasy red skin around the nose and mouth and on the ears and eyelids. A vitamin B_{12} deficiency causes skin on the face, hands, and feet to turn brown or, if anemia occurs, pale yellow. Zinc deficiency causes peeling skin lesions. While most of these deficiencies are uncommon in developed countries, some may develop in strict VEGETARIANS or people on FAD DIETS, as well as in those with DIGESTIVE AND MALABSORPTION DISORDERS.

DRY SKIN

In its most common form, dry skin, or xeroderma, does not reflect any underlying illness; instead, the skin loses some of the moisture that confers a smooth, pliable feel and appearance. Aging causes some drying of the skin, which may worsen in cold weather; other contributing factors include frequent bathing and exposure to the sun, wind, chemicals, or other environmental factors that leach natural oils from the skin. The use of mild, high-fat soaps and a daily moisturizer can help alleviate symptoms. Some people experience improvements in dry skin by boosting their intake of vitamins A and C, the B-group vitamins, and zinc.

A more severe type of dry skin, ichthyosis, is often inherited and tends to be linked to other conditions, such as THYROID disorders and lymphoma. Ichthyosis is characterized by roughness, scaling, and wrinkling of the skin, as well as dryness and itching. It should be evaluated by a doctor.

ROSACEA

An inflammatory skin disorder, rosacea causes redness, pimples, pustules, and tiny red streaks due to dilated blood vessels, or telangiectasia. Although the symptoms occur mostly on the nose (giving it a bulbous appearance) and the center face, they also may arise on the neck, chest, back, arms, and legs. Rosacea resembles ACNE, but it does not produce the blackheads characteristic of true acne. This condition tends to arise between the ages of 30 and 50, and is then a lifelong, chronic disorder.

Depending on its severity, rosacea may be treated with topical applications as well as oral drugs. Although diet does not appear to play any role in causing rosacea, some dietary factors worsen symptoms. Alcohol and foods that cause facial flushing should be avoided. A diet low in fat and animal protein may lessen symptoms. Omega-3 fatty acids, which are found in oily fish and evening primrose oil, help to reduce inflammation.

Because STRESS can provoke a flare-up of rosacea, practicing stress reduction techniques may be helpful.

PSORIASIS

Although the inflammation and scaly rash of psoriasis can occur anywhere on the body, it is most common on the knees, elbows, lower back, and scalp. The condition often recurs unpredictably, may be worse in the winter, and is frequently aggravated by physical or emotional stress or infections. The disease seems to run in families, but the cause remains unknown.

Psoriasis cannot be cured, but it can usually be kept in check by medication, judicious exposure to the sun's ultraviolet rays, and in severe cases, methotrexate, an anticancer drug that slows down cell reproduction. Folate supplements appear to lessen the side effects of methotrexate.

Some researchers report that reducing consumption of animal protein can help some patients. Again, the omega-3 fatty acids may help reduce inflammation. Etretinate (Tegison), a drug derived from vitamin A, has been approved to treat psoriasis. Another new psoriasis drug, calcipotriene (Dovonex), is related to vitamin D. Self-treatment with these vitamins should be avoided, however, because they can accumulate to toxic levels in the body.

SLEEP AND DIET

*Diet plays an important role in getting a
good night's sleep that not only refreshes the mind
but also allows the body to repair itself.*

The quality of sleep has an enormous impact on daily life, since poor or disordered sleep can affect your work, concentration, and ability to interact with others. During sleep, both physical and mental restoration take place, allowing you to feel fresh and alert in the morning.

Although sleep needs vary from one person to another, the optimal average is 7 to 9 hours. You can judge whether or not you're getting the right amount by how you feel the next day—both too much and too little sleep leaves a person feeling tired and irritable. Because growth hormones are released during sleep, babies, young children, and adolescents require more sleep than adults do.

Sleep researchers discount the common myth that older people require less sleep; instead, the amount of sleep that an adult needs remains fairly constant. With advancing age, however, the nature of sleep changes and the incidence of sleep disorders rises. The degree of time spent in the deeper stages of sleep often lessens with age, and an older person is likely to awaken more frequently during the night.

CONSUME
- *Light bedtime snacks.*
- *Carbohydrates along with milk or other foods high in tryptophan.*
- *Decaffeinated herbal teas.*

CUT DOWN ON
- *Alcoholic beverages.*

AVOID
- *Coffee, tea, colas, and other sources of caffeine.*
- *Heavy late-night meals, especially foods that are fatty and spicy.*

SLEEP WELL. *Starchy foods, such as bread and pasta, sweetened malted milk drinks, and honey-sweetened herbal teas can promote drowsiness and restful sleep.*

What makes us sleep is still not fully understood, but scientists know that a person's circadian rhythm is established shortly after birth and is apparently maintained by two internal oscillators that act as a body clock. Some natural chemicals in the body enhance sleep, and diet also plays a part. Because hunger tends to disrupt sleep, a light snack at bedtime can promote sleep—but too much food can cause digestive discomfort that leads to wakefulness. Small amounts of alcohol can promote the onset of sleep. However, as the body metabolizes the alcohol, sleep may become fragmented. Any food or beverage that contains caffeine can disturb sleep, although this is not true for everyone; some people can drink a cup of strong coffee before bed and promptly fall asleep.

Tryptophan, an essential amino acid, is among the natural dietary sleep inducers. It works by increasing the amount of serotonin, a natural sedative, in the brain. This is why so many folk remedies for sleeplessness include warm milk, which contains tryptophan, with a teaspoonful of honey, a simple sugar. (Carbohydrates facilitate the entry of tryptophan into the brain.) A turkey sandwich will provide another sleep-inducing combination of tryptophan and carbohydrates. On the other hand, consuming a high-fat evening meal or eating foods that promote INDIGESTION AND HEARTBURN can cause restless sleep.

313

GOOD HABITS FOR A GOOD NIGHT'S SLEEP

• Keep a sleep log for several weeks to help identify activities and behavior that may interfere with your sleep. Each day, write down when you wake up and go to bed, and when you drink caffeinated beverages, exercise, and take naps.

• Exercise regularly, preferably in the late afternoon. Do not exercise strenuously within 2 or 3 hours of bedtime, as it may impair your ability to fall asleep.

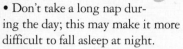

• Don't take a long nap during the day; this may make it more difficult to fall asleep at night.

• Eat at regular times during the day, and avoid a heavy meal close to bedtime.

• After lunch, stay away from anything that contains caffeine.

• Don't smoke; if you can't quit, at least try not to smoke for an hour or two before bedtime.

• Avoid excessive mental stimulation before bedtime.

• Establish a schedule to help regulate your body's inner clock. Go to bed and get up at about the same times every day, and follow the same bedtime preparations each night to create a sleep ritual.

• A warm bath or a few minutes of reading in bed, listening to soothing music, or meditating are all useful sleep rituals. Try each one to see what works for you.

• Keep your bedroom dark and quiet. If you can't block outside noise, mask it with an inside noise, such as the hum of a fan.

• Use your bedroom only for sleeping, not for working or watching TV.

• Wear nightclothes that are loose-fitting and comfortable.

• If your worries keep you awake at night, deal with them some other time. Devote 30 minutes after dinner to writing down problems and possible solutions, and then try to set them aside.

• If you can't sleep, don't stay in bed fretting for more than 15 minutes or so. Get up, go to another room, and read or watch TV until you are sleepy. Be sure to get up at your regular time the next day.

Many herbs are said to be useful for inducing sleep; one of the most popular and reliable of these is valerian. Its qualifications as a sedative have been supported by research demonstrating that active ingredients in the valerian root depress the central nervous system and relax smooth muscle tissue. Valerian that is brewed into a tea or taken as a capsule or tincture can lessen the time it takes to fall asleep and produce a deep, satisfying rest. It does not result in dependency or cause a "hung-over" feeling, as some sleeping pills do. Other herbal remedies include teas made of chamomile, hops, lemon balm, and peppermint.

ROLE OF MELATONIN

A hormone produced by the brain, melatonin is instrumental in regulating the body's sleep-wake cycle. Researchers think that it may control the onset of puberty, a woman's menstrual cycle, mood, and the release of growth hormones. In the U.S., melatonin supplements have emerged as one of the health-food fads of the mid-1990s, but they are not allowed in Canada. Melatonin can alleviate insomnia, although in some cases it has caused disturbed sleep. When taken correctly, it can prevent jet lag, but the many other claims for melatonin—for example, that it can prevent cancer, boost immunity, and forestall aging—are unproved.

Melatonin appears to be safe when it's taken in small amounts to overcome a temporary bout of insomnia or jet lag. But experts caution against taking large doses or long-term use because of melatonin's potential side effects, which include grogginess, depression, and sexual dysfunction. Melatonin should not be taken by women who are attempting to conceive, pregnant, or breast-feeding; nor should it be administered to children or used by anyone with severe allergies, mental illness, rheumatoid arthritis or other autoimmune diseases, and lymphoma and certain other types of cancers.

SLEEP DISORDERS

Insomnia can be one of the symptoms of anxiety, DEPRESSION, or STRESS, or it can be caused by a medical problem. Overcoming the underlying cause of these disorders is essential to improving the quality of sleep, but attention to nutrition and other aspects of sleep hygiene can also help.

OBESITY may interfere with sleep if it affects breathing. Sleep apnea is a potentially serious sleep disorder in which a pattern of loud snoring builds to a crescendo, after which the person stops breathing and awakens briefly. It is more common among overweight people, especially middle-aged men. People with obstructive apnea can stop breathing for 10 seconds or longer a hundred or more times a night.

MUSCLE CRAMPS and restless legs, a vague discomfort that is relieved only by moving the legs, can also interfere with sleep.

SMOKED, CURED, AND PICKLED MEATS

BENEFITS
- *Preserved meats have more concentrated minerals (but generally lower vitamin content) than fresh meats.*
- *Used sparingly, add flavor without excessive fat or calories.*

DRAWBACKS
- *Cured meats have more concentrated fat than fresh meats.*
- *Nitrites in preserved meats may form cancer-causing nitrosamines.*
- *High sodium content makes most unsuitable for people on low-salt diets.*
- *Preserved meats must be carefully handled to prevent food poisoning.*
- *Sausages made with corn solids or syrup or cereal fillers may cause symptoms in people sensitive to these grains.*
- *Cured meats may contain high levels of tyramine, which triggers migraine in susceptible people and causes serious reactions in those taking certain drugs.*

Before the development of refrigeration, people the world over used similar methods for preserving meat by salting, smoking, and air drying. Although curing is no longer essential to preserve meats in industrialized countries, our taste for salty, smoky flavors persists.

Cancers of the esophagus and stomach are common in countries where people eat large quantities of smoked and salt-cured foods. In Canada, however, deaths due to stomach cancer have decreased in recent decades, even though the consumption of smoked and processed meat increased. In part, the reason for this difference may be that foods cured for consumption in Canada are less heavily treated with preservatives than in countries where refrigeration is not so widely available. In addition, most foods sold as "smoked" are not smoke-cured but flavored with a compound called liquid smoke, which does not appear to cause cancer.

Warning: Tyramine, a metabolic product of the amino acid tyrosine, is found at high concentrations in cured meats. This substance can trigger MIGRAINE attacks in susceptible people. More seriously, it can cause a severe reaction involving an abrupt rise in blood pressure, headache, and even fatal collapse in persons taking monoamine oxidase (MAO) inhibitors to treat DEPRESSION.

SMOKE CURING
Smoking preserves meat and fish both by slow cooking at a low temperature and by treatment with chemicals in the smoke. More than 200 components have so far been identified in smoke, including alcohols, acids, phenols, and several toxic—and possibly cancer-causing—substances. These chemicals inhibit the growth of microorganisms that cause meat spoilage, and the phenolic compounds slow the oxidation of fat and prevent it from becoming rancid. Smoking is now used primarily for flavor—for example, the distinctive hickory or oak aroma associated with smoked bacon, and mesquite and other aromatic wood chips that are used to enhance the taste of GRILLED FOODS.

AIR CURING
Air curing, or preserving by dehydration, has been used for thousands of years. Drying generally concentrates some nutrients, especially minerals, but the vitamin content of dried meat is much less than that of fresh. Native peoples dried venison, buffalo meat, and fish—sometimes mixing them with fat and dried berries—to make a nutritious and long-keeping food. Chipped beef is an air-dried throwback to pioneer preserving methods. Prosciutto is air-cured ham. As with other preservation techniques, air curing has been superseded by refrigeration and is now used mainly to give flavor and texture, although dried meats keep well.

SALT CURING
Whether in a brine solution or a dry salt bed, salt curing draws water from the meat and from bacteria and molds. While the meat remains wholesome, the microorganisms shrivel and die. (The coarse grains of salt used in curing used to be called corns, thus the origin of the term "corned beef.") We no longer need to salt meat to store it over the winter, but the method is still used because people like the taste of salty meats, such as ham and bacon.

The more salt used in curing, the better the meat's keeping qualities but the greater the loss of nutrients. Heavily salted meat must be soaked to make it palatable; this causes even more vitamins and minerals to drain off. Today's curing solutions, however, are much weaker than those formerly used, and salted meat—with a few exceptions, such as cured Smithfield ham—seldom needs to be soaked before cooking.

SAUSAGES
Link sausages are usually made from pork with cereal fillers, herbs and spices for flavoring, and preservatives. People with CELIAC DISEASE or who suffer ALLERGIC REACTIONS to corn or wheat should avoid sausages made with corn syrup or solids or cereal fillers.

Because sausages, like ground meat, go through several stages of handling, they are more susceptible to contamination than fresh meat and should be cooked thoroughly before eating.

Sausages in the wurst family vary in their meat, filler, and additive content. Those sold as all-beef kosher frankfurters and bologna contain the fewest added ingredients. In addition, kosher products must be made only with approved cuts of meat; they do not contain scraps and certain organ meats.

All pork and beef sausages are high in salt and saturated fat. Reduced-fat franks, knockwurst, and other sausages are available, but the benefits of lower fat may be offset by higher salt.

Liverwurst varies in ingredients according to the brand. While high in minerals, vitamins A and C, and the B vitamins, liverwurst is also high in saturated fat; several brands are flavored with bacon, which substantially raises the sodium content. Because the liver filters out toxic substances, products made from it, including liverwurst, may contain residues of drugs, feed additives, and environmental pollutants.

Dry salami and other sausages made by traditional methods are air cured, and sometimes smoked as well. Salami is the single exception to rules about discarding moldy meat; salami with a small amount of mold, or "bloom," may be eaten, provided that an inch surrounding the mold is cut away. Salami and other dried sausages contain high levels of saturated fat and sodium.

POTTED MEATS

Rarely eaten in Canada, potted meats are popular in Europe. They are made by cooking pork, duck, or goose very slowly to render the fat. The well-cooked meat is then shredded (although small joints of poultry may be left whole), mixed with some of the fat, packed in earthenware or glass jars, and sealed with the remaining fat to keep out air. The shredded meats are spread on bread; the whole joints are used in hearty, long-baked legume dishes. Potted meats conserve most of the nutrients of fresh meat but are extremely high in saturated fat and should be consumed only occasionally and in small amounts.

NITRITES AND NITRATES

The reddish-pink color of cured meats is due to the presence of nitrites, chemical compounds that enhance the effect of salt by inhibiting bacterial growth and slowing fat oxidation.

Critics claim that nitrite should be banned because it combines with amino acids during cooking and digestion to form cancer-causing nitrosamines. What's more, nitrite itself can cause tumors in laboratory animals that consume it in very high doses. But the meat industry and the government insist that nitrite should be retained because it is extremely effective against *Clostridium botulinum,* the microorganism that causes botulin poisoning, or botulism. They also point out that only about a fifth of the nitrites that form nitrosamines come from meats—the rest are formed in the body from nitrates in various plant foods.

C. botulinum thrives in oxygen-free surroundings (such as sealed cans, jars, and plastic packaging), and its spores survive long boiling. If vacuum-packed or canned meats are allowed to reach 50°F (10°C), any spores present may develop into active bacteria and produce the lethal toxin. Botulin toxin is destroyed at temperatures of about 160°F (71°C), but cold cuts are not usually cooked before eating, and even a baked or boiled ham may not be cooked long enough to reach a high enough temperature in the center.

Not only does nitrite suppress active bacteria, but it also weakens the heat-resistant *C. botulinum* spores. This means that the spores can be destroyed without the need for pressure cooking and reduces the risk that spores will develop if the meat is carelessly handled.

The risk of cancer from nitrites in the doses currently used is much less than the risk of botulism from tainted meat. However, these hazards are less likely than the damage to the arteries, heart, and brain from excessive consumption of saturated fats in animal products. If you enjoy smoked and salted meats, make sure you eat them only in moderation.

SIMPLY SAUSAGES. *This ancient method of meat preservation has found its way into the cuisines of many countries. Traditionally, most sausages are high in fat and sodium, but some markets offer low-fat varieties made from turkey and fish.*

SMOKING AND DIET

Diet can't keep people from smoking or prevent all of its many consequences. But healthy eating may help the body to ward off some of the harmful effects.

Tobacco smokers face a greatly increased risk of heart attacks, respiratory disease, and cancer. The evidence that tobacco use is dangerous to health is overwhelming, with more than 40,000 Canadians dying each year from diseases caused by smoking; worldwide, the annual toll exceeds 3 million. According to the Canadian Cancer Society, smokers lose an average of 15 years of life, with about one in four dying of heart disease. Smoking accounts for more than 30 percent of all cancer mortality, about 17,000 deaths a year. Of these, 14,000 are from lung cancer—the most common fatal malignancy in both men and women. Smoking is also the leading cause of emphysema and chronic bronchitis.

Smoking is particularly risky during PREGNANCY because of its dangerous effects on the fetus. Smoking is directly related to low birth weight, and babies who weigh less than 5½ pounds at birth have a greater risk of health and developmental problems. Women who smoke are also more likely to have a miscarriage, a premature birth, or a baby who is born dead or dies shortly after birth. In addition, babies whose mothers smoke are more vulnerable to crib death, asthma, and other respiratory disorders.

Faced with these facts, the best decision a smoker can make is to quit. But for those who cannot seem to overcome their dependence on tobacco, a healthy diet may at least boost

CONSUME PLENTY OF
- *Citrus fruits and fresh vegetables for vitamin C and bioflavonoids.*
- *Orange fruits and vegetables and green leafy vegetables for beta carotene; liver, oily fish, fortified milk, and eggs for vitamin A.*
- *Broccoli and other cruciferous vegetables for sulforaphane and other protective plant chemicals.*
- *Vegetable oils, wheat germ, nuts and seeds, and green leafy vegetables for vitamin E.*
- *Milk, low-fat cheese, tofu, and fortified orange juice for calcium.*

CUT DOWN ON
- *Fatty foods to discourage weight gain when trying to quit.*
- *Alcohol to avoid consuming "empty" calories.*

the body's ability to defend itself against some of smoking's detrimental effects. There is no diet, however, that can prevent entirely the many health-related problems of smoking.

LIMITING THE DAMAGE

There is evidence that cigarette smoking affects nutritional status and metabolism. In a number of studies, smokers have been found to have lower levels of vitamin C in their blood than nonsmokers, as well as reduced levels of calcium, vitamin A, and beta carotene. Because vitamin C is an impor-

tant ANTIOXIDANT that may slow tumor growth, the diet should include at least one daily serving of a citrus fruit, along with other fresh fruits and vegetables. While it may seem logical for smokers to take a vitamin C supplement, this can actually do more harm than good. Large doses of vitamin C cause nicotine—the addictive substance in tobacco—to be excreted in the urine. As the amount of nicotine in the body is reduced, the urge to smoke a cigarette increases.

Lower levels of vitamin A and its precursor, beta carotene, may have implications with regard to cancer, since these ANTIOXIDANTS help to protect against it. Smokers may be able to reverse this deficiency to some degree by increasing their consumption of foods rich in vitamin A, beta carotene, and vitamin E, another antioxidant. However, the beta carotene connection has been called into question by two recent studies that have demonstrated an increase in lung cancer among smokers taking beta carotene supplements. Based upon this it is recommended that smokers refrain from taking beta carotene supplements.

Some research studies have found that smokers who eat several helpings of BROCCOLI a week have a reduced incidence of lung cancer. This protective effect is attributed to sulforaphane, an anticancer chemical that is especially abundant in broccoli and is found, to a slightly lesser degree, in BRUSSELS

SPROUTS, CABBAGE, and other cruciferous vegetables.

Scientists do not know exactly why calcium levels are lower in smokers, nor is it fully understood why women who smoke reach menopause earlier, although it may be related to their reduced production of estrogen. This earlier menopause, combined with already decreased calcium levels, may help to explain why women smokers have an increased risk of OSTEOPOROSIS. It may be helpful for women who smoke to increase their calcium intake, although there is no direct proof that this will counteract the effect of smoking and reduce the likelihood of developing osteoporosis.

Concerning heart disease, it appears that smoking tends to increase the buildup of fatty deposits on the lining of blood vessels, a condition known as ATHEROSCLEROSIS, which causes chest pains and heart attacks. Nicotine also increases the risk of cardiac arrhythmias and spasms of the coronary arteries, both of which can decrease the flow of blood to the heart muscle—and result in chest pain. It has also been found that smoking lowers the level of HDL (high-density lipoprotein) cholesterol, the type that lowers overall blood cholesterol levels and protects against atherosclerosis. Some researchers have found that even following a low-fat diet, which normally raises HDL levels, does not produce this benefit in smokers. However, it is still advisable to follow a low-fat diet.

BENEFITS OF QUITTING

It is almost never too late to obtain some health benefits from quitting smoking. A person's breathing improves as soon as he quits, which is particularly important for anyone with bronchitis or emphysema. The smoking-related risk of cancer of the esophagus and pancreas falls almost immediately. After about a year of not smoking, the risk of heart disease be-

---

HELPFUL FOODS

Although foods cannot totally erase the harmful effects of smoking, the following may help reduce the risk.

Citrus fruits for their high vitamin C content to help make up for what is lost by smoking. Have at least 1 serving daily.

Cruciferous vegetables, such as broccoli and related vegetables, provide sulforaphane, which may cut the risk of smoking-related cancers. Consume 3–4 servings per week.

Vegetable oils, wheat germ, nuts, seeds, and green leafy vegetables provide vitamin E. Have at least 1 serving daily.

Dairy products to increase calcium intake. Consume 2–3 servings a day of low-fat milk, yogurt, or cheese.

---

gins to diminish; after 10 years, it's about the same as for nonsmokers. Seven years after quitting, the risk of bladder cancer decreases to that of a nonsmoker. And after 10 years, life expectancy begins to approach that of a person who has never smoked, as does the risk of contracting cancers of the lungs, larynx, and mouth.

WEIGHT GAIN

After stopping, the typical ex-smoker gains an average of 10 to 15 pounds, apparently for varied reasons: food tastes and smells better, and appetite improves after stopping. It is easy to trade one habit for another and substitute snacking for smoking. Nicotine also affects metabolism; smokers use up to 10 percent more energy than nonsmokers. Thus, less food is needed to maintain the same weight.

There are ways to counteract this problem, mainly through careful attention to diet and exercise. While substituting a snack for a cigarette can help you stop smoking, make sure it's low in calories—for example, air-popped popcorn, raw vegetables, nonfat yogurt, and low-calorie cereals.

EXERCISE is a good way to control weight and fosters a sense of well-being that helps overcome the craving for nicotine. Moreover, many former smokers find that as breathing improves, exercise becomes easier and increasingly enjoyable. Because a history of smoking heightens the risk of a heart attack, a doctor should always be consulted before starting an exercise program.

Another helpful strategy is to cut back on alcoholic beverages. WINE confers some health benefits, but only when it is consumed in moderation. ALCOHOL is basically high in calories, which contributes to weight gain. And drinking is often associated with smoking, thereby fostering a situation in which a person is tempted to have a cigarette. Try doing something else at the time you might be having a drink and a cigarette: go for a brisk walk after work instead of a visit to a bar; go out to a movie instead of sitting in front of the TV with a beer and a cigarette.

There is evidence that the nicotine gum that is sometimes used to help a smoker quit can also help reduce the amount of weight an ex-smoker may gain. This gum, now available without a prescription, should be used only as a temporary aid to minimize withdrawal symptoms. Nicotine is also available in a prescription form—a skin patch that allows a slow, steady release of the substance into the bloodstream. Both the nicotine skin patch and nicotine gum should be used temporarily and gradually tapered off as the craving and withdrawal symptoms lessen.

SNACKS AND DIPS

BENEFITS

- *Snacks can help meet recommendations in the Food Guide Rainbow.*
- *Fruit and vegetable snacks are fat-free and high in vitamins and minerals.*
- *Well-timed low-calorie snacks can take the edge off hunger and help to prevent overeating at mealtimes.*

DRAWBACKS

- *Snacking on candy bars and high-fat foods adds empty calories and fats.*
- *Many commercially prepared snacks and dips are high in sodium.*

The human body is programmed to send out hunger signals whenever it needs an energy boost, which is usually between meals. The carbohydrate (glycogen) stores in the liver and muscles, which help maintain a normal level of blood sugar, are used up in 4 to 6 hours. Food replenishes them, and snacks help to fill this need.

Properly handled, snacking can be a healthy response to hunger and even prevent overeating. But many people snack even when they're not hungry—such as while watching a movie or TV, attending a ball game, or simply out of boredom. Others fall into the trap of reaching for a candy bar, potato chips, or other convenient high-fat snack simply out of habit. These types of snacks can result in serious weight gain and even eating disorders.

Snacks don't have to be fattening. On the contrary, eating a low-calorie snack during a long stretch between meals can take the edge off hunger and prevent overeating at the next meal. If snacks are well timed, they won't spoil the appetite for meals and may help to boost flagging energy, especially in children. Some people intentionally blunt their appetites with a filling low-calorie snack before going to an event where calorie-laden foods are served.

For many people, snacking or having frequent small meals is an alternative to the usual three large ones. This is a good solution for young children whose small stomachs can't consume

QUICK NUTRITION. *Low-fat snacks, such as raw fruits and vegetables, nonfat yogurt, and rice cakes, are not only a quick energy source but also help supply needed vitamins and minerals.*

enough at one sitting to sustain their need for energy. Older adults often can eat only small portions; supplemental snacks can help them to maintain a balanced diet. The same is true for people who are convalescing. While a plateful of food can be daunting, smaller portions and snacks may be appealing and help them to regain strength.

Fast-growing adolescents should snack to fuel their growth and compensate for lapses in their eating patterns. Athletes of all ages typically have an increased demand for energy, especially from carbohydrates, which the body converts to glucose, its major fuel. Pregnant women often suffer bouts of nausea during the early months, and heartburn or a feeling of constant fullness toward the end of pregnancy. Many are more comfortable snacking than eating a large amount at one time.

RAINBOW SNACKING

If you are among those who snack regularly, it is important to include snacks in your overall nutrition plan. Using the Food Guide Rainbow (see p.39), choose snacks that will provide balanced nutrition as well as meet energy needs.

Snacks can provide several of the 5 to 12 recommended daily servings of starchy foods or the 5 to 10 servings of fruits and vegetables. For example, half a bagel with an apple, or a small pita pocket filled with chopped raw vegetables, makes a filling, nutritious snack that can be incorporated into the day's meal plan. Other quick, fat-free foods, such as bags of fresh vegetables—carrot and celery sticks, bell pepper slices, broccoli, snow peas, or cherry tomatoes—and dips made of nonfat yogurt or cottage cheese blended with herbs, can be kept on hand for snacking after school or while watching TV.

The Food Guide Rainbow calls for two to four servings of milk and other dairy products a day. A glass of skim milk or 2 ounces of low-fat cheese are satisfying snacks that supply valuable calcium and vitamins A and D. Low-fat or skim milk also goes well with whole-grain cereal or crackers.

SNACK TRAPS

Everybody knows that a raw carrot is healthier than a frosted doughnut, but some snack foods that sound nutritious are not much better than a doughnut. Read labels carefully to find hidden sugar and fats. Beware of granola bars; they are often loaded with sugar and fat. Fruit drinks may contain very little fruit juice but have large amounts of added sugar, such as high-fructose corn syrup. Microwave popcorn is often high in fat, as are trail mixes and other packaged combinations of nuts and seeds. Most commercial fruit rolls and pastes contain very little fruit and provide large amounts of added sugar and starch thickeners. Unsweetened apricot and other fruit leathers sold in ethnic food markets are usually made from pure fruit, but snackers should be careful to brush their teeth to remove clinging remnants that can promote cavities.

COPING WITH HUNGER

If you try to find a snack when hunger pangs are overwhelming, you're likely to find yourself at the mercy of a vending machine. Instead, anticipate snack attacks with nutritious, low-calorie foods that require little preparation.

Any number of simple and speedy solutions can fill in the gaps after school, work, or play. Canned, juice-packed mandarin orange slices, for example, mixed with a sliced banana, chopped apple, and a few frozen blueberries or other fruit make an instant fruit salad. For a quick dessert, cut a banana lengthwise, add nonfat frozen yogurt, and top with berries.

On cold days a cup of soup is a warming snack. Many canned and dried soups contain high levels of sodium, however, and may not be suitable for people on low-salt diets. Another hearty cold-weather snack is half a baked potato topped with low-fat cottage cheese and a sprinkling of chives.

Add several healthy snacking foods to your weekly shopping list. When you have the right foods on hand, it's easy to prepare snacks to take on trips, to school, or to work. Stay away from prepackaged high-fat items, such as potato chips and tortilla chips. If you can't resist cookies, you can sample the low-fat ones now on the market, but it's better to control the fat and sugar content by making them at home. Try air-popped popcorn, baked tortilla chips without added salt, or fat-free pretzels.

When you snack, don't forget dental hygiene. It's important to remind children to brush after snacking or, if they can't brush, to rinse their mouths vigorously with plain water.

REDUCING THE FAT IN SNACKS AND DIPS

TRY:	INSTEAD OF:
Angel food cake	Pound cake
Bagel with fat-free ricotta cheese or fruit preserves	Doughnut
Baked tortilla chips	Corn chips
Fat-free cookie	Butter cookie
Frozen juice bar	Ice cream bar
Fruit smoothie or nonfat yogurt shake	Milk shake
Low-fat string cheese	Cheddar cheese
Nonfat frozen yogurt	Ice cream
Nonfat yogurt/garlic blend	Mayonnaise dip
Pretzels	Potato chips
Salsa	Sour cream–based dip
Soft pretzel	Croissant
Spiced applesauce	Apple pie

SOFT DRINKS

BENEFITS

- *Carbonated drinks are refreshing and may provide a quick energy boost from their sugar or caffeine.*
- *Sipping ginger ale or cola can help to quell nausea and provide energy for people unable to take solid food.*

DRAWBACKS

- *Soda pop contains large amounts of sugar and acids that can lead to weight gain and dental decay.*
- *High phosphorus content may interfere with calcium absorption.*
- *Caffeine may cause health problems in adults or behavior and development problems in children.*

Carbonated waters were originally invented to cash in on an 18th-century fad for naturally sparkling mineral water. The taste for carbonated drinks (originally hangover cures) has never faltered; indeed, the average Canadian consumes about 29 gallons a year.

Soft drinks are broadly defined as nonalcoholic beverages, and carbonated soft drinks are classified as soda pop, or in some areas simply sodas or pop. They consist mostly of carbonated water mixed with sugar or an artificial sweetener, plus various patented natural or artificial flavorings, and coloring agents. Many contain CAFFEINE.

Apart from a quick energy boost from the caffeine or sugar, most soft drinks and soda pop offer little or no nutritional value. An 8-ounce cola contains about 100 calories; a diet soft drink, because it is artificially sweetened, is virtually devoid of calories, although it may have caffeine.

HEALTH IMPLICATIONS

A high intake of sugary drinks adds empty calories that can add to weight problems. These drinks also cause DENTAL DISORDERS, because their sugar encourages the growth of cavity-causing bacteria; in addition, many contain acids that can erode tooth enamel.

Consumers should read labels carefully to determine what's actually in various soft drinks and mineral waters. Colas and pepper-flavored soda pop, for example, contain large amounts of phosphates, which interfere with the absorption of calcium and may impair bone and tooth development in youngsters who regularly consume them in large amounts. In addition, some soft drinks and mineral waters may contain high levels of sodium. Also consider that when a 60-pound child drinks a 12-ounce cola containing 50mg of caffeine, he's getting the equivalent of 4 cups of coffee in a 175-pound man. A child who is restless or sleepless may be experiencing the effects of too much soda pop. In adults, excessive caffeine may raise blood pressure and cause irregular heartbeats. People who react to caffeine should choose one of the decaffeinated soft drinks that are available.

When patients can't take other foods and liquids, soft drinks can provide energy during illness. Some people find that sipping flat ginger ale or cola quells the nausea associated with MIGRAINE and morning sickness.

Marketers claim that so-called sports drinks rapidly replenish the water and electrolytes lost by athletes. In fact, experts recommend that athletes should rehydrate with plain water or diluted fruit juice; only in grueling endurance training during extremely hot weather is an athlete likely to lose a significant amount of electrolytes.

Don't be misled by the names of fruit-flavored drinks. On close reading, labels will disclose that noncarbonated fruit drinks often contain less than 10 percent fruit juice while harboring large amounts of sweeteners and dyes.

Soft drinks and soda pop need not be harmful if consumed in moderation. The danger is that if taken regularly in large amounts, they may satisfy hunger and take the place of essential nutrients in the diet. Children who fill up on sugary drinks shortly before and during meals may spoil their appetites for healthful foods.

HEALTHY DRINKS

You can make refreshing and economical drinks at home by mixing sodium-free seltzer or fruit-flavored sparkling waters with fruit juice, a mixture of chopped fresh fruit, or any of the wide variety of fruit nectars and syrups now sold in food stores and supermarkets.

COOL AND REFRESHING. *You can satisfy your thirst with plain tap water, or you can choose bottled mineral water, a carbonated cola or citrus drink, orangeade, or sparkling fruit punch.*

SORE THROAT

CONSUME PLENTY OF
- *Citrus and other fruits and fresh vegetables for vitamin C.*
- *Yellow and orange fruits and vegetables and green vegetables for beta carotene.*
- *Seafood, lean meat, yogurt, and fortified grain products for zinc.*
- *Nonalcoholic and caffeine-free fluids.*

AVOID
- *Alcohol and tobacco smoke.*

A raw, stinging throat can often be the first sign of a viral upper respiratory infection, such as a cold or flu, or less commonly, a bacterial infection, such as a strep throat. In children, swollen and infected tonsils can cause a sore throat; among adults, smoking is a common cause of mild, chronic throat pain. Respiratory viruses and strep organisms spread easily from one person to another, but careful attention to hygiene and good nutrition can help prevent many episodes.

DIETARY FACTORS

Although scientific evidence is lacking, many people are convinced that high doses of vitamin C help to reduce the duration and severity of a sore throat and other symptoms of viral respiratory infections. Like other ANTIOXIDANTS, vitamin C is instrumental in immune function, so adequate amounts can protect against viruses, bacteria, and other infectious agents. What constitutes "adequate," however, remains unresolved. A recent study indicates that 200mg of vitamin C a day may be a more optimal amount than the present Recommended Nutrient Intake (RNI) of 40mg. This same study found that doses above 200mg are of no added benefit, because the body tissues are unable to absorb more than that amount per day. Indeed, for many people, the higher amounts may be detrimental be-cause they can lead to IRON OVERLOAD and other problems.

A diet that follows the Food Guide Rainbow's (see p.39) recommended 5 to 10 servings of fruits and vegetables a day can easily provide 200mg of vitamin C, as well as other essential vitamins and minerals. Especially rich sources of vitamin C include citrus and other fruits, berries, and dark green vegetables. These foods are also high in beta carotene, which the body converts to vitamin A, another antioxidant that is instrumental in building immunity.

Several studies have demonstrated that zinc lozenges can shorten the duration of a sore throat. A diet that provides adequate zinc strengthens the body's immune defenses. Good sources include yogurt, oysters and other seafood, lean meat, eggs, grains, and fortified cereals.

Alcohol, which reduces immunity and irritates inflamed mucous membranes, should be avoided until the sore throat clears up. It's also a good idea to cut down on or eliminate caffeine; its diuretic effect increases the loss of body fluids and results in a drying of the membranes and thickening of mucus. Make every effort to stop smoking, and avoid secondhand smoke.

EASING SYMPTOMS

Increased intake of nonalcoholic fluids, both hot and cold, can alleviate painful swallowing. Some doctors even advise temporarily switching to a liquid diet to maintain nutrition without exacerbating throat pain. Good choices include milk shakes, fruit juices, broths and soups, and semiliquid foods like custards and gelatin.

Home sore throat remedies abound, and many are useful in alleviating symptoms. Gargling with salty warm water is a time-honored favorite; you can make an alternative gargle by adding 2 teaspoons of cider vinegar to a half cup of warm water.

SOUPS

BENEFITS
- *Can be highly nourishing.*
- *An ideal food for convalescents.*
- *Easy to make and economical.*

DRAWBACKS
- *Commercial varieties are often high in salt and fat.*

Nourishing, comforting, and inexpensive, soup is a staple food worldwide. A simple soup can be made in minutes with a few vegetables, broth, and seasonings, while more elaborate concoctions may be based on long-simmered stocks and exotic ingredients.

HOMEMADE SOUPS

Even a novice cook can make a delicious soup with a few basic ingredients: diced carrots, potatoes, and other vegetables simmered in a broth with herbs. Leftover meat or seafood can be added for more flavor and nutrition. Cooks who have the inclination can simmer leftover bones with vegetables to make a soup stock; reduced-sodium canned broths are also acceptable. Bouillon cubes can be used, but they are high in monosodium glutamate (MSG), sodium, and other additives; taste the soup before adding salt or seasonings.

Although some vitamins may be lost during the slow cooking of vegetables, soups made with fresh ingredients still provide an excellent variety of nutrients, including vitamins, minerals, and protein. Vitamin loss can be minimized by adding the vegetables toward the end of the cooking process, bringing the soup to a boil, and cooking only until the vegetables are barely tender.

Making your own soup allows you to control the salt content, an important consideration for people with high BLOOD PRESSURE or those who are on a sodium-restricted diet. Use herbs and natural vegetable flavors to replace salt.

Chilling the stock forces the fat to congeal on the surface and makes it easy to remove for fat-free soups. Or remove the fat by pouring the stock through a defatting cup. Cream soups and New England-style chowders contain high amounts of saturated fat; this can be reduced without losing flavor or texture by substituting evaporated skim milk for cream and whole milk.

COMMERCIAL SOUPS

Canned and instant soups come in many flavors; the quality and nutritional value are equally variable. Read labels and choose soups low in fat and sodium. Although canned soups are not as nutritious as

STOCK IDEAS. *Suitable for any occasion, soups can be as humble or extravagant as you want to make them.*

Pasta, vegetables, and beans combine to make minestrone.

Soup made with carrots, apples, and tomatoes is economical and highly nourishing.

Thai prawn soup is made with broth and prawns.

their homemade counterparts, they are better than instant soups, which are so highly processed that food authorities have described them as little more than a mixture of MSG, artificial flavors, sodium, dyes, and other additives.

TYPES OF SOUP

Whether made from scratch or canned, soup falls into one of six types. Cooking methods and ingredients frequently overlap.

Chowders, such as bouillabaisse, combine coarsely chopped vegetables and fish, shellfish, or meat with stock for a stewlike consistency.

Clear broths, such as consommé or bouillon, are strained concentrated stocks made from a mixture of aromatic vegetables, either cooked in water or beef or chicken broth. Noodles, vegetables, and diced meat may be added to the strained broth. Some broths are thickened with a beaten egg just before serving. When a concentrated beef or chicken consommé is chilled, its natural aspic forms a solid jelly, which is a digestible food for convalescents.

Cold soups, such as the Spanish gazpacho and Scandinavian-style fruit soups, are always served chilled. Others, such as the leek-and-potato vichyssoise, are equally flavorful and nourishing whether served hot or cold.

Cream soups, based on vegetables, meat, or seafood, are often thickened either with the same roux that is used for SAUCES or with cream. The fat and calorie content of cream soups can be drastically reduced by replacing milk and cream with evaporated skim milk or double-strength reconstituted skim milk. (Nonfat yogurt can be used instead of sour cream in some soups, but it will curdle if the soup is cooked after it is added.)

Vegetable purees (potage) are smooth-textured soups made from vegetables that are simmered in stock or another liquid and then blended or sieved.

Vegetable soups, including minestrone, are made with chopped vegetables boiled quickly in water and are thickened with rice or pasta.

323

Spices: More Than Flavorings

*Centuries ago, the taste for spices kindled international
trade and sparked voyages of discovery. Today,
spices are still prized for the variety they lend to the diet.*

For thousands of years, spices have been used as flavorings, medicines, perfumes, dyes, and even weapons of war. They can stimulate the appetite and add flavor to humdrum dishes.

Characterized by pungent aromas and flavor, spices are the fruits, flowerbuds, roots, or bark of plants. While rich in minerals, spices are used in minute amounts, so they have little nutritional value. Because spices lose their pungency on exposure to light, heat, and air, keep them in a dark, dry cupboard and replace them annually.

SPICY REMEDIES

Through the ages, spices have been used as remedies for almost every ailment. Although most specific health claims have not been borne out by scientific studies, several traditional uses appear to be grounded in fact.

Allspice, so called because its flavor seems to blend the aromas of cinnamon, nutmeg, and cloves, is believed to aid digestion.

Black pepper, like white pepper, is the fruit of a tropical vine; it accounts for 25 percent of the world's spice trade. Sniffing ground pepper may help prevent fainting attacks.

Caraway is a member of the carrot family. Caraway seeds are especially popular as a flavoring for breads, cakes, cheese, and red cabbage and other vegetable dishes. Drinking an infusion of caraway may stimulate milk flow in nursing mothers.

Cardamom is used to flavor coffee in Arab countries, sweet breads in Scandinavia, and to enhance the flavor of cooked fruit. Cardamon is also recommended to relieve indigestion.

Cayenne (also called chili pepper) and related spices are used to flavor the hot dishes of Mexico and many other countries. Capsaicin, a volatile oil, gives CHILIES their "bite" and is used as a topical painkiller. Consumption of cayenne and other fiery substances is thought to stimulate the production of endorphins, the brain's natural mood enhancers, which may explain the euphoria people feel after eating spicy food.

Cinnamon, an ancient spice obtained from the dried bark of two Asian evergreens, is a highly versatile flavoring as well as a carminative that relieves bloating and gas.

Clove oil, long used as a home remedy for toothaches, is no longer recommended for this purpose because it can burn mucous membranes. However, eugenol, a mild derivative, is a popular flavoring ingredient in some brands of mouthwash and toothpaste.

Coriander has been used as a digestive tonic since ancient times. Freshly chopped greens in large amounts are a good source of vitamin C.

Cumin, a hot spice, blends well in chili, curries, and such Middle Eastern specialties as hummus.

Ginger, popular in Asian dishes as well as in Western desserts and soft drinks, is a common motion sickness remedy; sipping flat ginger ale may help to ease nausea.

Juniper berries are used in pâtés and sauerkraut; the pungent berries also give gin its flavor. In large doses, juniper acts as a diuretic that may also cause uterine contractions.

Mustard has been used in poultices and smelling salts to relieve pain and congestion since Roman times.

Nutmeg and mace come from the same plant; nutmeg is the shelled seed, mace its hull. Very high doses of myristicin, a component of nutmeg oil, cause hallucinations.

Saffron, the most expensive of all spices, is obtained from the stamens of a single variety of crocus. It is used to flavor vegetable soups, rice dishes, fish, and sweet rolls. It is sometimes touted as an aphrodisiac.

Star anise gets its licorice flavor from an oil containing anethole. Anethole-based flavorings have long been used in cough syrups and digestive preparations, as well as in ouzo, arak, and anisette liquors.

Turmeric, an essential ingredient of Indian curries, gives mustard its yellow color. It is a natural antibiotic that Ayurvedic practitioners use to treat inflammation and digestive disorders.

A SAMPLING OF SPICES. *Just a small amount of a spice can perk up even the most mundane foods.*

Cloves

Nutmeg and mace

Cardamom

Cinnamon

Juniper berries

Cumin seeds

Caraway seeds

Star anise

Coriander seeds

Ginger

Mustard seeds

Saffron

SPINACH

BENEFITS
- *A rich source of vitamin A and folate.*
- *High in vitamin C and potassium.*
- *A vegetarian source of protein.*

DRAWBACKS
- *Oxalic acid reduces iron and calcium absorption, and can accelerate the formation of kidney and bladder stones.*

Contrary to popular belief, spinach is not an especially good source of iron. The myth about its high iron content arose from an analytical procedure in which a decimal point was erroneously displaced. But the vegetable's dark green leaves do contain many other valuable nutrients, especially the ANTIOXIDANTS and BIOFLAVONOIDS that help block cancer-causing substances and processes. For example, spinach is rich in carotenoids, plant pigments that are responsible for its dark green color. Among these carotenoids are beta carotene, the plant source of vitamin A, and lutein, both of which may help prevent cancers of the lungs and prostate. One cup of raw spinach or a $\frac{1}{2}$-cup serving of cooked spinach provides a full day's supply of vitamin A. One cup of fresh spinach also supplies 190mcg (micrograms) of folate, a nutrient that is especially important for women who are pregnant or are planning a pregnancy, because it helps prevent congenital neurological defects. Folate deficiency can also cause a severe type of anemia.

Rich in vitamin C, one cup of raw spinach supplies over 100 percent of the Recommended Nutrient Intake (RNI) of this vitamin, and 500mg of potassium, plus some riboflavin and vitamin B$_6$. Spinach is a good vegetarian source of protein; it contains more than most green vegetables do. Although this protein lacks the amino acid methionine, this can be obtained by eating rice or another grain dish at the same meal.

VERSATILE VEGETABLE. *Young spinach leaves are delicious raw or lightly cooked. Either way, you should wash them thoroughly and discard damaged leaves and tough stalks.*

On the negative side, the nutritional benefits of spinach are somewhat offset by its high concentration of oxalic acid. Although spinach contains iron, calcium, and other minerals, their absorption is hindered by the oxalic acid. Absorption can be increased by eating spinach with other foods that are rich in vitamin C.

Oxalic acid can also pose a problem for people susceptible to kidney and bladder stones that form from oxalates.

SERVING SPINACH

Spinach can be served either raw or cooked. To avoid overcooking, try steaming or stir-frying it. These cooking methods preserve texture and flavor, and they minimize the loss of many water-soluble vitamins. Although some of these nutrients are lost in cooking, a $\frac{1}{2}$-cup serving of the cooked vegetable actually provides more nutritional value than 1 cup served raw because it contains 2 cups of leaves. In addition, heating makes the protein in spinach easier to break down. The nutritional value of raw spinach can be enhanced by serving it with orange or grapefruit slices for added vitamin C.

Before serving spinach, be careful to remove all the sand and dirt. One effective method is to submerge the spinach in a bowl of cold water and let the sand fall to the bottom, then remove and rinse the leaves.

Sports Nutrition: Fueling Up for Fitness

Athletes perform best when they have high energy reserves that they can tap as needed. Along with diligent training, balanced nutrition is the key to achieving one's personal best.

Our understanding of sports medicine and nutrition has grown immensely as we have become more aware of the importance of exercise. At the same time, a number of popular beliefs about an athlete's nutritional needs have been proved false. In reality, athletes need the same balance of nutrients as their more sedentary counterparts, although the special demands of intensive sports training require extra energy. Thus, athletes can rely on the same Food Guide Rainbow (see p.39) that is recommended for all healthy people, but they may need the maximum number of servings in each group to fulfill their higher energy requirements.

CARBOHYDRATES

Because starches and other CARBOHYDRATES supply the body's major source of energy (in the form of glucose, or blood sugar), it follows that an athlete's diet should be built around these nutrients. At least 55 to 60 percent of daily calories should come from carbohydrates; during periods of intense training, this may be increased to 65 or even 70 percent. At least 80 percent of the carbohydrates should come from starchy foods—pasta, rice and other grains, breads, cereals, legumes, and ample fruits and vegetables. The complex carbohydrates are metabolized more slowly than sugars, which provide fast bursts of energy that are quickly depleted.

CONSUME PLENTY OF

- *Starches and whole grains, legumes, and pasta for energy.*
- *Lean meat, poultry, fish, and eggs for protein; these foods plus fortified cereals and dried fruits for iron; and citrus juice to improve iron absorption.*
- *Dark green leafy vegetables and lean poultry for folate.*
- *Grains, potatoes, lean meats, and seafood for B vitamins; fresh fruits and vegetables for beta carotene and vitamins A and C.*
- *Low-fat dairy products, canned fish with bones, and tofu for calcium and vitamin D.*
- *Lean meat, seafood, yogurt, and fortified cereals for zinc.*
- *Bananas, oranges, tomatoes, and other fruits and vegetables for potassium.*
- *Water and other nonalcoholic beverages to replace body fluids that are lost in sweat.*

AVOID

- *Fatty foods.*
- *Excessive sugar.*
- *High-dose vitamin and amino acid supplements.*

The body can convert some glucose into glycogen and store it in the liver and muscles. On average, 2,000 calories of reserve energy are stored as glycogen, enough to carry a 150-pound person through a day of moderate physical activity. An athlete can double this reserve by consuming a high-carbohydrate diet and by engaging in weight training, which increases large-muscle mass to store more glycogen.

Although all athletes benefit from a high-carbohydrate diet, the practice of carbohydrate loading—eating almost nothing but starches and sugars before competition—is now recommended only for people who engage in prolonged activities, such as marathons or long-distance cycling, or those who engage in several hours of intensive training every day. It should be noted, however, that the additional glycogen can cause some bloating, because almost 3g of extra body fluid is added for each gram of stored glycogen. (On a positive note, the extra fluid helps protect against dehydration during prolonged competition, especially if water is not readily available during the event.)

Eating a large pregame meal is not advisable. Exercising on a full stomach can result in painful cramps and indigestion, since blood that is needed for digestion is diverted from the stomach to the muscles. As a general rule, the pregame meal should be at least 3 hours before the start of competition to allow enough time for the stomach and upper intestine to empty. The meal should be large enough to prevent hunger during competition, but not large enough to cause drowsi-

327

ness. Many trainers recommend pasta along with low-fat milk and fruit, or a sandwich of lean meat without MAYONNAISE or other fatty spreads.

Some athletes find that when they begin hard training they have an increased appetite and tend to crave sweets. As they become fitter, this craving disappears, especially if their diet provides ample complex carbohydrates, which take longer to digest than sugary foods.

PROTEIN

Many athletes take amino acid supplements or adopt a high-meat diet based on the mistaken notion that they need huge amounts of PROTEIN to build powerful muscles. Recent research indicates that some athletes need a bit more protein than sedentary persons do, but because the typical Canadian diet already provides about twice the Recommended Nutrient Intake (RNI) of protein (.36g per pound of body weight), athletes are likely to get the recommended .45 per pound

without having to make any changes. (It's not necessary to calculate grams of protein; instead, strive to have 12 to 15 percent of your daily calories come from high-protein, low-fat foods. Good sources include lean meat, poultry, fish, egg whites, and a combination of legumes and grains.)

Although the body converts some excess dietary protein into glucose, eating a high-protein diet contributes little to energy needs. Even during prolonged exercise when carbohydrate stores are depleted, the body derives only 5 to 15 percent of its energy by turning protein into glucose. The liver converts other excess protein to fat.

FATS

While FAT is the body's most concentrated form of energy, it is not an efficient source of fuel during exercise, because it takes longer to metabolize than carbohydrates and protein. In addition, too much dietary fat promotes weight gain in athletes, just as it does in sedentary people. No more than 30 percent of daily calories should come from fat, and many nutritionists advise that 20 to 25 percent is preferable. Most of these fats should come from vegetable oils and other plant sources, with no more than 10 percent from saturated animal fats or tropical oils.

VITAMINS FOR ATHLETES

Contrary to popular belief, VITAMINS are not a source of energy, and supplements cannot make athletes run faster or lift heavier weights. Vitamins are, however, essential for metabolizing other nutrients and converting food into energy. In this regard, thiamine, niacin, and other B-group vitamins are especially important. Good sources include fortified cereals and whole grains, lean meats, seafood, and potatoes. It is best to obtain vitamins from the diet rather than from supplements. If supplements are used, they should not provide more than 100 percent of

the RNI—more can often be detrimental. High doses of niacin, for example, increase the rate at which glycogen is used and may sap endurance in long events.

The diet should also include citrus fruits and juices and a variety of other fruits and vegetables to provide ample vitamin C, beta carotene, and other ANTIOXIDANTS. Exercise produces high levels of free radicals, the unstable molecules that are by-products of oxygen metabolism. Antioxidants help minimize cell damage caused by these free radicals.

PROTECTING IMMUNITY

Researchers have found that athletes who persistently overtrain or work out to exhaustion are more susceptible to viral infections, especially of the upper respiratory tract. In the past this was wrongly attributed to the drying of the mucous membranes in the air passages. It is now known that the increased susceptibility occurs because extreme muscular effort depresses some of the processes involved in the immune response. (Moderate exercise, on the other hand, improves resistance to infections.)

To increase immunity, athletes should eat plenty of fruits and vegetables for vitamins A and C. Zinc also boosts immunity; good sources include lean meat, oysters and other shellfish, yogurt, wheat germ, and fortified grain products. Two to three servings of fish each week provide omega-3 fatty acids, which also appear to boost immune defenses.

HEALTHY BLOOD

Athletes training hard lose and need more iron than people who exercise moderately, and endurance athletes have the highest iron needs of all. Young women are at special risk, because they lose iron during menstruation and often eat little meat. A lack of iron affects athletic performance and

Case Study

Bob competes in long-distance cycle races on weekends. As a journalist, he works erratic hours, with little time for training, but he manages a daily workout at a health club and trains longer on weekends.

Over the years, Bob has developed an eating pattern that works well for him and might serve as a model for other athletes. On the whole, his diet is high in starchy carbohydrates, low in fat and sugar, and somewhat higher in calories than is typical. He has a daily serving of meat or other high-protein food, and he rarely drinks alcohol, except for an occasional beer. After a long training session or a race, Bob has a banana or two and an orange to provide an energy boost and restore potassium. He also drinks plenty of plain water and diluted fruit juice before, during, and after training sessions and competitions. Finally, he carries granola bars with him for energy boosts on long rides.

overall health, and has marked effects on immune function, concentration, and temperature regulation.

Excellent sources of iron are lean meat, fish and shellfish, legumes, and fortified breads and cereals. Dried fruits, especially apricots, are also rich in iron. Avoid tea and coffee, which impair iron absorption, as do many whole grains. The heme iron in meat and other animal products is more readily absorbed than the nonheme iron in plant foods. Having orange juice or other sources of vitamin C at the same meal can greatly increase absorption of nonheme iron; so too does a small amount of a food high in heme iron, such as beef or chicken.

Studies have shown that women athletes with low levels of iron in their red blood cells also have low blood levels of folate. Women should consume plenty of dark green leafy vegetables, fortified cereals and breads, citrus juice, and lean poultry for folate to help form healthy red cells.

BONE STRENGTH

Regular weight-bearing exercise helps to prevent OSTEOPOROSIS, provided athletes consume plenty of calcium and vitamin D from dark green vegetables, low-fat dairy products, and such foods as canned sardines and salmon (with bones), tofu, and oysters.

Women athletes, and dancers who undergo very vigorous training, may lack the body fat they need to produce estrogen and maintain their menstrual cycles. Often overly concerned with body image, women in these groups also run a high risk of eating disorders, such as ANOREXIA and BULIMIA, which disrupt hormone production and predispose women to developing osteoporosis long before MENOPAUSE. Active women should safeguard their bodies by eating a well-balanced diet to maintain their hormonal cycles, taking special care to include foods high in calcium and vitamin D. Exer-

cising outdoors can help the body to make vitamin D from sunlight.

ELECTROLYTE BALANCE

One of the most persistent myths holds that athletes need salt to make up for sodium lost in sweat. The 2,000 to 6,000mg of sodium, or 1 to 3 teaspoons of salt, in the average Western diet is far more than the 500mg the body needs each day. Even with strenuous, prolonged daily exercise, the salt requirement increases very little and is more than compensated for by the excess salt in many foods. Muscle and heat cramps are more likely to be caused by lack of water, not sodium depletion. Athletes can help to prevent cramps by drinking plenty of water before, during, and after long events, and by avoiding vigorous exercise in extreme heat and humidity.

Potassium is another story. This mineral is stored in the muscles with glycogen and released into the bloodstream when the body draws on the stored carbohydrate for energy. An athlete should consume bananas, oranges, tomatoes, and other fresh fruits and vegetables rich in potassium.

WATER

Experienced athletes know that they should have frequent drinks of water or diluted fruit juice when they exercise. If they wait to drink until they feel thirsty, they may already be suffering from DEHYDRATION. However, athletes in long events, such as marathons, should take care not to drink too much water all at once, which can dilute the amount of sodium available to conduct nerve impulses, causing muscle cramps.

Male runners develop kidney stones more often than other men. Sports medicine specialists recommend that runners avoid dehydration and dilute the stone-forming chemicals in their urine by drinking plenty of water and exercising at cooler times of the day.

SQUASH

BENEFITS

- *Summer varieties provide some folate and vitamins A and C.*
- *Winter varieties are extremely rich in vitamin A and are a good source of vitamin C, folate, and potassium.*

Members of the same family as MELONS and CUCUMBERS, all types of squash are gourds—fleshy fruits protected by a rind. Squash is divided into two categories: summer, which includes the chayote, patty pan, yellow crook- and straightnecks, and ZUCCHINI varieties; and winter, which includes the acorn, banana, buttercup, delicata, dumpling, hubbard, spaghetti, and turban varieties. The flowers, immature and mature fruits, and seeds are all edible.

SUMMER SQUASH

Eaten while immature, summer squash has a soft shell and tender flesh. Because it has a high water content, it is low in calories (20 per cup). A ½-cup serving provides 15 percent of the Recommended Nutrient Intake (RNI) of vitamin C, 15mcg (micrograms) of folate, and small amounts of beta carotene, which the body converts to vitamin A. Intensely colored squashes have more beta carotene than paler ones.

Summer squash can be eaten raw. If it is cooked, stir-frying or steaming minimizes nutrient loss. The mild flavor complements stews, soups, and mixed vegetables, but squash can make some dishes watery. To avoid this problem, lightly salt the squash and place it on absorbent paper towels; rinse it before adding it to the recipe.

WINTER SQUASH

Harvested when fully mature, winter squash has a hard shell and large seeds. It is larger, darker in coloring, and richer in nutrients than summer squash. Like their PUMPKIN cousins, winter squash is rich in beta carotene, but the amount varies with the color of the flesh. Half a cup of butternut squash contains enough beta carotene to equal more than 80 percent of the RNI of vitamin A; 1 cup of light-colored spaghetti squash provides only 5 percent. A ½-cup serving of baked winter squash has at least 15 percent of the RNIs of vitamin C and folate, 450mg of potassium, and 40 calories. Winter squash also has more fiber than summer squash, 1g per ½-cup serving. The strings and squash seeds are high in insoluble fiber, which helps prevent constipation; the flesh contains soluble fiber, which helps lower cholesterol.

Unlike summer squash, which spoils quickly, winter squash can be stored for several months in a cool, dark place. Do not refrigerate it, because temperatures below 40°F (4°C) speed its deterioration.

Bake or steam winter squash; boiling is not recommended, because it destroys vitamin C and other nutrients. You can serve it with herbs and a little butter or margarine, stuffed and baked, or add it to breads, soups, and stews. It can be substituted for pumpkin in pies.

The seeds can be dried or baked for a snack; they are an excellent source of iron, potassium, zinc, and other minerals. They also provide some protein, beta carotene, and B vitamins.

STRAWBERRIES

BENEFITS

- *An excellent source of vitamin C.*
- *A good source of folate and potassium.*
- *Low in calories and high in fiber.*
- *Provide anticancer bioflavonoids.*

DRAWBACKS

- *Provoke allergies in many people.*
- *Contain oxalic acid, which reduces mineral absorption and may aggravate kidney and bladder stones.*

Strawberries are delicious, low in calories (about 40 per cup), and very high in vitamin C. In fact, ounce for ounce, they are a better source for this vitamin than oranges are. One cup contains about 85mg, or 200 percent of the Recommended Nutrient Intake (RNI). Strawberries are also a good source of folate; 1 cup provides 25mcg (micrograms), or roughly 10 percent of the RNI, as well as 250mg of potassium and useful amounts of riboflavin and iron.

The seeds in strawberries provide insoluble fiber, which helps prevent constipation; however, they can be irritating to people with such intestinal disorders as inflammatory bowel disease, or diverticulosis, a condition in which small pouches bulge outward along the intestinal wall.

Strawberries are a good source of pectin and other soluble fibers that help lower cholesterol. They also contain BIOFLAVONOIDS, including red anthocyanin and ellagic acid, substances that may help prevent some cancers. Cooking does not destroy ellagic acid, so even strawberry pie and jam may be beneficial.

Shop for medium-size, bright red berries with healthy green tops. Strawberries can be stored whole in the refrigerator for a few days (sliced berries gradually lose their vitamin C). Unwashed strawberries have been linked to outbreaks of infectious diarrhea, but to avoid molding, wash the fruit just before serving it.

Because strawberries contain a common allergen as well as a natural salicylate, an aspirinlike compound, many people are allergic to them. They also contain oxalic acid, which can aggravate kidney and bladder stones in susceptible people, and reduce the body's ability to absorb iron and calcium.

SWEET AND JUICY. *More than 70 varieties of strawberries are grown in North America, and all are naturally sweet.*

STRESS: STRATEGIES FOR COPING

Prolonged stress, whether psychological or physical, plays havoc with digestion and nutritional needs. Certain foods can provide the extra energy or comfort needed to get through a stressful period.

When people talk about stress, they are usually referring to tension or emotional distress. Medically, however, stress is defined as any condition or situation that places undue strain on the body. The sources can be a physical illness or injury, as well as numerous psychological factors—including fear, feelings of anger or frustration, and even unusual happiness. What constitutes almost un-bearable stress to one person may be the spice of life to someone else. In either case, a stressor (a stimulus that causes stress) can trigger the body's automatic stress-response system. This sets the stage for decreased immune resistance and increased vulnerability to illnesses, ranging from the common cold to heart attacks and cancer.

While physical stress is often episodic, emotional stress is part of daily life. This is not a modern phenomenon. Our early ancestors experienced much more stress than we do—from the constant quest for food to dangers from hostile neighbors and wild animals. While we don't usually encounter such situations, our bodies will still respond to any stress much as they would have in prehistoric times. This stress-coping mechanism, called the fight-or-flight response, floods the body with adrenaline and other hormones that raise blood pressure, speed up the heartbeat, tense muscles, and put other systems on alert. Metabolism quickens to provide extra energy; digestion stops as blood is diverted from the intestines to the muscles.

NUTRITIONAL NEEDS

Diet plays a critical role in helping the body deal with stress. In fact, stress quickly exhausts the body's supply of glucose, its major fuel. Once this happens, the body starts to break down the protein in muscles, a quicker source of energy than body fat. Consequently, extra CARBOHYDRATES, both sugars and starches, are required to provide fast energy. In addition, extra dietary PROTEIN, preferably from lean meat, fish, low-fat milk, and egg whites, is needed to help prevent muscle wasting. (Vegetarians can get protein from tofu and combinations of grains and lentils, dried beans and peas, and other legumes.) Unfortunately, prolonged stress can diminish

---

ARE YOU STRESSED?

Because stress can cause many different symptoms, both physical and mental, it's often difficult to determine their true source. A doctor may order medical tests, even if he suspects that stress is the real problem. The following are common manifestations of stress:

Physical symptoms
• Palpitations, shortness of breath, chest pain, and other signs of heart disease (which must be ruled out).
• High blood pressure.
• Unusual rapid breathing, dizziness, or light-headedness.
• Tingling sensations in the hands and/or feet.
• Chronic or recurring backache and neck pain.
• Frequent headaches.
• Diarrhea or constipation.
• Heartburn and other types of digestive problems.

• An increased vulnerability to colds and other illnesses.

Psychological symptoms
• Unexplained irritability or feelings of sadness.
• Difficulty in concentrating and in making decisions.
• Sleep problems.
• Chronic fatigue, even after adequate rest.
• Prolonged anxiety.
• Changes in appetite and an increased reliance on alcohol, nicotine, or other drugs.
• Difficulty coping with what are normally minor setbacks.
• Needless worrying over even trivial problems.
• Decreased enjoyment of pleasurable activities and events.
• A diminished interest in sex.
• An increased likelihood of being in accidents.

STRESS RELIEVERS

- Eat regular and healthful meals, starting with breakfast.
- For a few minutes each day, sit quietly with your eyes closed.
- Exercise regularly to increase the production of endorphins, brain chemicals that lift mood.
- Listen to your favorite music; it, too, increases endorphin levels.
- Learn a relaxation technique, such as yoga, meditation, or deep-breathing exercises.
- Make a things-to-do list for the day; arrange the items by importance. Do an item at a time; move undone ones to the next day's list.
- Consider having a pet; stroking an animal can help you relax.
- Share your problems with a family member, friend, or counselor.

appetite, further compounding the problem of muscle loss.

A balanced diet that provides ample fruits, vegetables, and whole-grain products compensates for any nutrients that were lost because of stress and meets the body's increased need for vitamins A and C and for thiamine, riboflavin, and other B vitamins. Stress also prompts the kidneys

to increase the secretion of important minerals, in particular calcium, zinc, and magnesium. Contrary to advertising claims, taking high doses of so-called antistress vitamins will not calm jittery nerves.

When under stress, some people are always hungry and binge on food; others have to force themselves to eat. Because stress interferes with digestion, it's better to eat four to six small meals spaced throughout the day instead of the traditional three large ones. A varied diet of mostly complex carbohydrates and protein provides essential energy and nutrients and is easier to digest than a high-fat one.

COMFORT FOODS

Almost everyone has a favorite food that provides comfort during stressful times; the choices vary from one person to the next. For some people, it's a food that harks back to childhood, such as milk. Others crave chocolate or sweets, which increase the production of serotonin, a brain chemical that

has a calming effect. Soups are also favorite choices, as are bland, easy-to-digest foods like rice pudding, custards, yogurt, and omelets. Experiment and go with whatever works best for you.

BETTER OFF WITHOUT

Because stress can play havoc with normal digestion, foods that normally are well tolerated may trigger IN-DIGESTION AND HEARTBURN. Fatty foods, which are difficult to digest at any time, should be avoided. Many people also find that hot or spicy foods cause problems during times of stress.

Avoid ALCOHOL, CAFFEINE drinks, and cigarettes. These substances are stimulants that can add to jittery feelings. Instead, try a herbal tea, low-fat milk, fruit juice, or a noncaffeinated soft drink.

COMFORT FOODS. *Quietly relaxing with a cup of herbal tea is a time-honored stress beater. A carbohydrate snack of toast or a similar food helps restore depleted glucose supplies.*

STROKE

EAT PLENTY OF

- *Fresh fruits and vegetables for vitamin C and other antioxidants.*
- *Nuts, seeds, green leafy vegetables, wheat germ, and fortified cereals for vitamin E; these foods plus bananas and other fruits for potassium.*
- *Oily fish for omega-3 fatty acids.*
- *Oat bran, legumes, and fruits for pectin and other soluble fibers.*
- *Onions and garlic, which may help to prevent blood clots.*

CUT DOWN ON

- *Animal and dairy products that are high in saturated fats and cholesterol.*
- *Salt, which may raise blood pressure.*
- *Alcohol use.*

AVOID

- *Smoking.*
- *Excessive weight gain.*

Each year more than 500,000 North Americans suffer strokes, roughly one every minute. In Canada, strokes claim over 14,000 lives annually, making stroke our third leading cause of death (exceeded only by heart attacks and cancer). Approximately 80 percent of all strokes occur when a clot blocks blood flow to a part of the brain. Most of these clots form in an artery that is already narrowed by ATHEROSCLE-ROSIS, either in the brain itself or, more commonly, in the carotid artery in the neck. The remaining 20 percent are hemorrhagic strokes, in which there is bleeding in the brain, such as from a burst blood vessel or severe head injury. Hemorrhagic strokes, which are more likely to be fatal than those caused by clots, are more common in people with high BLOOD PRESSURE.

The warning signs of a stroke include sudden weakness or numbness of the face, arm, and leg on one side of the body; difficulty speaking or understanding others; dimness or impaired vision in one eye; and unexplained dizziness, unsteadiness, or a sudden fall. Immediate treatment is critical, even if the symptoms disappear, as in the case of a ministroke (transient ischemic attack), a common prelude to a full-blown stroke. Prompt treatment may be lifesaving, and it may also minimize permanent damage, which can include impaired movement, speech, vision, and mental function.

PREVENTIVE MEASURES

The death rate for stroke has been cut to less than half of what it was in 1950, thanks largely to a better understanding of the underlying causes, especially the key risk factors, such as high blood pressure, HEART DISEASE, arteriosclerosis, and DIABETES. A number of unhealthy lifestyle habits also increase the risk of a stroke; these include SMOKING, excessive use of ALCOHOL, OBESITY, and a sedentary lifestyle.

Diet plays an important role in reducing or eliminating these risk factors. In fact, many of the same nutritional recommendations made for people who have heart disease, high blood pressure, and elevated blood CHOLESTEROL levels apply to people at risk for, or who have had, a stroke. A good starting point is to adopt a diet that is low in fats, especially saturated animal fats and tropical (palm and coconut) oils. About 60 percent of calories should come from carbohydrates, with emphasis on such starchy foods as pasta, grains, and legumes, along with five to ten daily servings of fruits and vegetables. These foods are high in the soluble fibers that help control cholesterol levels and reduce the risk of atherosclerosis, which narrows the arteries and sets the stage

REDUCING THE RISKS. *The key to avoiding stroke is a diet low in salt and saturated fat and high in fiber and the omega-3 fatty acids found in some oils and oily fish.*

Blackberry sorbet (above) is a delicious low-salt, fat-free dessert.

Broccoli and salmon pasta (left) is rich in flavor, vitamin C, and omega-3 fatty acids but low in saturated fat.

for developing the blood clots that block the flow of blood to the brain.

A number of foods appear to lower the risk of a stroke. Some fish, for example, are rich in omega-3 fatty acids, which help to prevent blood clots by reducing the stickiness of blood platelets. Doctors recommend eating salmon, trout, mackerel, sardines, or other oily cold-water fish two or three times a week. Other good sources of omega-3 fatty acids include wheat germ, walnuts and walnut oil, canola (rapeseed) oil, soybeans, and purslane (a popular salad green in a number of Mediterranean countries).

GARLIC and ONIONS appear to decrease the tendency of the blood to clot, and they also boost the body's natural clot-dissolving mechanism. A Chinese mushroom called the tree ear may have similar beneficial effects. This mushroom is available dried in Chinese markets and gourmet shops, and when rehydrated with a little boiling water, it makes a tasty addition to soups, stews, and casseroles. A recent study found that a tablespoon of the soaked mushroom consumed three or four times a week may be as effective in preventing strokes and heart attacks as a daily aspirin—but without the risk of gastrointestinal irritation.

A growing body of scientific evidence shows that vitamin E, too, reduces the tendency to form blood clots. Foods high in this ANTIOXIDANT include nuts, seeds, wheat germ, fortified grain products, and green leafy vegetables. Other antioxidants include vitamin C, which strengthens blood vessel walls and thus may protect against brain hemorrhages; most fruits (especially citrus) and vegetables are good sources. Many of these foods, as well as grains and legumes, are high in potassium, an electrolyte instrumental in maintaining normal blood pressure.

Anyone who has high blood pressure, or a family history of this disease

or of strokes, should limit salt intake; excessive sodium—a main component of salt—increases the body's fluid volume and may raise blood pressure.

Numerous studies link excessive alcohol use, defined as more than two drinks a day for men and one for women, to an increased incidence of stroke; the risk is compounded if the person also smokes. The best approach is to abstain completely from smoking and to use alcohol only in moderation, if at all. Regular exercise not only reduces the risk of a stroke and heart attack by helping control weight and blood cholesterol levels, but it also fosters an enhanced sense of well-being.

SUGAR AND OTHER SWEETENERS

BENEFITS
- *Sugar satisfies an inborn taste for sweets.*
- *Artificial sweeteners satisfy our sweet tooth without adding calories.*

DRAWBACKS
- *Excess sugar may be consumed instead of useful nutrients and lead to obesity.*
- *Sugar fosters the growth of cavity-causing bacteria.*

Refined sugar is a relatively new food in the human diet, becoming widely available only since the 1500s. It didn't take long for this sweetener to become a major commodity, and for tooth decay to reach epidemic proportions.

Sugars have been described as a "standard currency" for living organisms, because all plants and animals store energy chemically as sugar. The sugars adapted for our diet are natural substances produced by photosynthesis in plants. Nutrition experts distinguish two main types of sugar: intrinsic sugar,

which gives an appealing taste to such foods as fruits and sweet vegetables, and extrinsic sugar, which is added to food during preparation or processing or at the time of consumption.

Sugarcane and sugar beets are our main sources of sugar; some liquid sweeteners, such as molasses, are by-products of sugar refining. Manufacturers favor liquid sweeteners made from corn or potatoes because their sweetness and thickness can be regulated. They add a chewy texture to foods, and they prevent moisture loss and extend the shelf life of products.

The main sugar in our diet is sucrose, familiar to us as white sugar. But contrary to popular belief, Canadians on average do not consume too much sugar. In fact, sugar consumption has changed little since the 1920s. The average Canadian consumes about 10 to 15 percent of total calories from added sugars, an amount consistent with generally recommended guidelines. Consumption is highest in younger age groups, contributing about 13 to 15 percent of calories, and declining to approximately 9 percent of calories after age 50.

FOOD VALUE

At 99.9 percent sucrose, white sugar is an extremely pure food. Sucrose is a disaccharide (double sugar) made up of two monosaccharides (single sugars): glucose (known as blood sugar, dextrose, or grape sugar) and fructose (the sugar in fruits and maple sap).

The intrinsic sugars in fruits, vegetables, and starches are bound up with essential vitamins, minerals, fiber, and oils. Extrinsic sugar, however, contains empty calories that can supply energy, but it provides no valuable nutrients, although it satisfies our taste for sweetness and can enhance the flavor of many foods. And while many of the evils blamed on sugar—hyperactivity, acne, high blood pressure, obesity—have

ARTIFICIAL SWEETENERS

Although sugar substitutes are considered safe for adults, children should not use them, because it's difficult for their smaller bodies to eliminate substances that may possibly be harmful.

• **Acesulfame-K** passes through the body unchanged, and is therefore noncaloric. Two hundred times sweeter than sugar, it withstands heat and can be used for baking.

• **Aspartame** contains the same calories, weight for weight, as sugar, but since it is 200 times sweeter, it can provide a teaspoon's worth of sweetness with only one-tenth of a calorie. Aspartame loses its sweetness when cooked or exposed to certain acids. Aspartame is unsafe for people with phenylketonuria (PKU), and it should be avoided by people with epilepsy.

• **Cyclamates** are allowed in Canada, but not in the United States. Studies associating them with an increased risk of bladder cancer led to their removal from the U.S. market. But many researchers, and the Canadian government, believe that these studies were flawed and that the compounds are safer than saccharin.

• **Saccharin.** The body cannot absorb saccharin; instead, it is excreted by the kidneys. Although very high doses have been associated with bladder cancer in rats, saccharin has been in use for so long that most experts consider the risk to be low for adults using normal amounts. In Canada, saccharin is allowed as a tabletop sweetener only.

• **Sucralose** is 600 times sweeter than sugar. Since it is not absorbed by the body, it is calorie-free. It is allowed in Canada both as an additive in beverages and processed foods, and as a tabletop sweetener.

been found to be unrelated or only indirectly linked through overconsumption, it is true that sugar is a major cause of DENTAL DISORDERS and that people who turn to sugary fast foods for a quick energy boost may neglect less convenient but much more nutritious foods.

All forms of sugar provide about the same energy value: 4 calories per gram. In everyday terms, a cup of white sugar contains 770 calories, compared to 820 in a cup of densely packed brown sugar. A tablespoon of white sugar has 45 calories, and an individual serving packet, 25. Although sugar itself is not especially high in calories, many sweet foods, such as chocolates and pastries, are also high in fat, which contains 9 calories per gram.

Confectioners' sugar has about 385 calories in a cup. Although the sugar is pure sucrose, the product is packaged with cornstarch to prevent clumping. Because of this, people with ALLERGIES to corn may suffer adverse reactions

from the powdered sugar in frostings and desserts. Raw sugar—the first crystals obtained during the refining process—is not sold in Canada because it is contaminated with soil, plant refuse, and insect droppings and parts. Turbinado sugar, available in health-food stores, is raw sugar that has been purified.

Contrary to the claims of natural-food enthusiasts, neither brown sugar nor HONEY is more nutritious than white sugar, but consumers who find the taste more appealing can substitute brown for white sugar in any recipe. Brown sugar is made by coating white sugar crystals with molasses. While molasses contains iron and other minerals, the amount in brown sugar is too small to be of nutritional value.

MAPLE SUGAR

Maple sugar and syrup are made by boiling down maple sap—a technique developed by North America's native people long before the arrival of white explorers. Pure maple products are expensive because production is limited. A tablespoon of maple syrup contains 50 calories, and 1 ounce of maple sugar has 100. Pure maple products contain traces of potassium, calcium, and other minerals, but not in amounts sufficient to be of much nutritional value.

DENTAL PROBLEMS

All types of sugar—white table sugar, brown sugar, honey, molasses—encourage the growth of the oral bacteria that are responsible for causing dental caries. And when starchy foods are broken down by the enzymes in saliva, they, too, form cavity-causing sugars. More dangerous than the amount of sugar is the length of time the sugar remains in contact with the teeth. Thus, much of the damage can be prevented by brushing soon after eating a sweet.

Sugar alcohols, such as sorbitol, that are used as sweeteners in commercial products do not cause cavities, but do contribute calories. Xylitol—not available by itself but used in sugar-free products, including gum—seems to protect against tooth decay. Other sugar substitutes were thought to be beneficial only because they are not broken down into acids in the mouth, but studies in laboratory animals show that saccharin, like xylitol, may actually protect against cavities.

A UNIQUE SWEETENER

Artichokes contain cynarin, a unique organic acid that stimulates sweetness receptors in the taste buds. After eating artichokes, some people find that everything—including plain water—tastes sweet for a short time. However, efforts to convert this natural substance into a commercial sugar substitute have not yet been successful.

SUPPLEMENTS—WHO NEEDS THEM?

Nutritionists maintain that vitamin and mineral pills are unnecessary for most people. So why do so many Canadians persist in taking them, often in very high doses?

Millions of Canadians take nutritional supplements, usually without the advice of a doctor. Some take supplements because they fear their diets may be lacking; others believe that if a little of something is good, a lot must be even better. What many people don't know is that a varied diet based on the Food Guide Rainbow (see p.39) provides all the nutrients a healthy person needs. In fact, if someone consumes more nutrients than his body can use or store, the excess is usually excreted in the urine and feces. And when taken in large amounts, some supplements—for example, iron and vitamins A and D—are highly toxic.

Nutritionists stress that the diet is the best source of the necessary vitamins, minerals, fatty acids, amino acids, and fiber, because, as components of food, they come packaged with a host of other chemicals. Some of these substances promote the absorption of a nutrient; others delay it. In any case, the natural form of the food is usually the one best adapted to the human digestive system. In contrast, supplements contain only one form of a nutrient and lack the other chemicals, energy, fiber, and dietary components that provide a proper nutritional balance.

People who depend on vitamin and mineral supplements to compensate for gaps in their daily dietary intake may not understand the principles of sound nutrition. The recommended daily servings in the Food Guide Rainbow are actually based on the desirable average of food consumption over the course of about 2 weeks. The liver, which stores vitamins and minerals, can make up for any occasional dietary lapses by releasing stored nutrients as they are needed. Well-nourished people typically have enough stored vitamins and minerals for at least 3 months of deprivation before they begin to develop symptoms of deficiency diseases.

In the early years of this century, such diseases as pellagra (caused by a lack of niacin) and beriberi (a thiamine deficiency disease) were widespread in some regions and income groups. After these essential B vitamins and other nutrients were added to refined grain products and other common foods, such deficiency diseases all but disappeared except in special situations, such as alcoholism or other diseases that foster malnutrition.

One exception is iron-deficiency ANEMIA, which is relatively common in young women worldwide because of their monthly blood loss through menstruation. Most of these women do not need iron supplements, however; a diet that includes such iron-rich foods as lean meat, poultry, fish, enriched breads and cereals, and legumes can prevent anemia.

USEFUL SUPPLEMENTS

Even though most people do not need supplements, there are a few exceptions. Sometimes doctors advise individuals on low-calorie weight-loss diets to take daily multivitamin supplements that provide no more than 100 percent of the Recommended Nutrient Intakes (RNIs) for any nutrient. Similarly, supplements may be recommended for elderly people, who may have poor appetites or metabolic problems, or for convalescents, who

---

BENEFITS
- *May hasten recovery in people whose severe illness or injuries interfere with nutrition.*
- *Can improve the health of expectant mothers and their babies.*
- *Compensate for nutritional deficiencies in the treatment of alcoholism and eating disorders, and in the elderly and convalescents.*

DRAWBACKS
- *Not a substitute for sound nutrition from a varied diet.*
- *Several vitamins and minerals are hazardous in high doses.*
- *Wasteful and expensive if they provide more nutrients than the body can absorb.*

may need extra nutrients to promote their recovery.

Occasionally, healthy people also require supplements. During PREGNANCY, for example, doctors usually prescribe extra iron and folate, because most women have low stores of these nutrients. Many physicians also recommend extra calcium and a daily multivitamin pill. However, a pregnant woman should never take any supplements except those prescribed by her physician; excesses of some vitamins and minerals can be dangerous for both the mother and her developing baby.

Certain medications can interfere with the absorption of vitamins or minerals. Common offenders include blood pressure drugs, oral contraceptives, antibiotics, and over-the-counter painkillers and laxatives. People taking any of these medications may benefit from supplements if increasing dietary intake doesn't compensate for the nutritional drain. For example, doctors sometimes prescribe a potassium supplement when patients on diuretic or digitalis treatment can't get enough extra potassium from tomatoes, oranges, bananas, and other fruits and vegetables. Individuals on steroid medications may be advised to take calcium pills to help minimize the drugs' effects on the bones. If you are taking a medication, ask your doctor whether you need supplements.

Alcoholics usually need supplements to overcome their severe nutritional deficiencies. These have often resulted from an inadequate diet over a prolonged period of time and by overindulgence in alcohol, which interferes with the absorption of many nutrients. The latter problem may be compounded by LIVER DISORDERS related to ALCOHOL USE.

When taken in high doses, vitamins and minerals assume pharmacologic properties and may be prescribed as drugs. High doses of niacin, for instance, may lower blood cholesterol, and vitamin E may be prescribed as an alternative to low-dose aspirin to protect against a heart attack.

COMMON MYTHS

Most theories about the benefits of megavitamin supplements haven't stood up to scientific scrutiny. Contrary to media reports, megadose vitamins have no proven value in treating SCHIZOPHRENIA, HYPERACTIVITY, and other brain or neurological disorders. Efforts to change criminal behavior with megavitamins have not been successful. And although deficiencies of vitamins B6 and B12 can lead to depression and other mental disorders, B-complex supplements sold as "stress vitamins" do not help people cope with emotional tension.

While ANTIOXIDANTS such as beta carotene and vitamins A, C, and E have been associated with a reduced risk of cancer and other diseases, the evidence to date indicates that they have this effect only when consumed in foods—not as supplements.

Although smoking interferes with vitamin C metabolism, taking vitamin C supplements seems only to hasten the excretion of nicotine and thus increases the urge to smoke.

DANGEROUS DOSES

Taking high doses of certain vitamins and minerals can be harmful. A recent study involving healthy men found that about 200mg of vitamin C a day was an optimal amount. This is well above the 40mg RNI, but it is still a fraction of the megadoses often touted—without scientific proof—as preventing colds, cancer, and a host of other ailments. Many people mistakenly believe that even if high doses don't fulfill such promises, at least they're not harmful. In reality, vitamin C doses above 1,000mg a day can increase the risk of kidney stones and cause bladder irritation. In addition, about 10 percent of the population is genetically predisposed to conserve iron, a condition known as hemochromatosis. High doses of vitamin C increase iron absorption and can lead to IRON OVERLOAD in these susceptible people.

In high doses vitamin A causes liver damage, skin problems, fatigue, and other symptoms; taken before and during pregnancy, it can cause serious birth defects. High doses of vitamin D can result in calcium deposits in the heart and blood vessels; they also upset calcium metabolism and can lead to bone loss. Taken over an extended period of time, very large amounts of both vitamins can be fatal. Excessive zinc and several trace minerals have effects ranging from nausea and diarrhea to death if taken in doses that allow buildup in body tissues.

RISKY OR WORTHLESS

Although many supplements sold in health-food stores are promoted as having special health benefits, they are not subjected to the rigorous testing required for drugs. Most of these are of dubious benefit, and a few are even deadly. Ephedra, or ma huang, a herbal preparation marketed as a stimulant and weight-loss aid, has caused several deaths, even among people using it as directed. Millions of Americans take melatonin, a hormonal preparation that is touted as a remedy for insomnia and jet lag, and is said to delay the ravages of aging. The evidence for a positive risk-benefit ratio is so weak that the Canadian government does not allow the sale of melatonin supplements. Fish oil supplements contain high levels of cholesterol, as well as vitamins A, D, and K, which can accumulate to toxic levels when high doses are taken for a long time. Amino acid supplements have no proven dietary value and can lead to nutritional imbalances. Some may contain tyramine, which interacts with monoamine oxidase (MAO) inhibitor drugs, prescribed for depression.

TANGERINES

BENEFITS
- *A good source of vitamin C, beta carotene, and potassium.*
- *Contain pectin, a soluble fiber that helps control blood cholesterol.*

DRAWBACKS
- *Oils in peels may irritate the skin of some people.*

Although we often use the terms *tangerines* and *mandarins* interchangeably, tangerines—along with clementines and satsumas—are actually types of mandarin oranges. These sweet citrus fruits with loose-fitting skins originated in China, but they are now grown in many parts of the world. As they moved into other tropical and subtropical areas, the original mandarin oranges were crossed with other citrus fruits to produce a variety of hybrids, including tangelos and tangors.

Ounce for ounce, oranges have about twice as much vitamin C as tangerines, but even so, tangerines contribute a good amount of this ANTIOXIDANT; a medium-size fruit fulfills about 75 percent of the adult Recommended Nutrient Intake (RNI). In addition, tangerines are richer in vitamin A (in the form of beta carotene) than any other citrus fruit. A medium-size tangerine contains 775 I.U. (or 77 R.E.) of vitamin A, as well as 130mg of potassium. It is also high in pectin, a soluble fiber that helps lower blood cholesterol.

Citrus reticulata

The membranes and pith contain pectin and fiber.

Choose fruit with deep orange skin and that feels heavy for its size, an indication of a high juice content.

FRUIT FOR CHRISTMAS.
Native to the Far East, tangerines are now available in Canada year-round, but they are at their most flavorful in the winter.

Like other citrus fruits, tangerine peels contain oils that can cause an itchy rash. Because tangerines are easy to peel, this can usually be avoided.

TYPES OF TANGERINES
While most varieties are available from November to March, tangerines are an especially popular Christmas fruit. The following are among the most common types sold in Canada.

Clementine. This fruit is seedless, and smaller and sweeter than most other varieties. It is sometimes called an Algerian tangerine, but most clementines sold in Canada are actually imported from Morocco and Spain.

Honey tangerine. Also known as a murcott, this variety has a greener skin than other tangerines, but the flesh is more orange and the flavor is sweeter.

Satsuma. Any of several varieties of tangerine, satsumas are a little larger than clementines, nearly seedless, and very thin-skinned. Japan is the leading producer of satsumas.

Tangelo. A cross between a tangerine and a grapefruit, the tangelo looks like an orange, is tangier than a tangerine, and is sweeter than a grapefruit.

Tangor. This hybrid, also known as temple orange, looks like a tangerine but tastes like an orange; it is juicy and contains many seeds.

TEA

BENEFITS

- *A refreshing stimulant that is almost calorie-free if drunk plain.*
- *Contains antioxidants and bioflavonoids, which may lower the risk of cancer, heart disease, and stroke.*
- *Green tea is high in vitamin K.*
- *Tannins may provide protection against dental decay.*
- *Herbal teas are caffeine-free.*

DRAWBACKS

- *Tannins decrease iron absorption if tea is consumed with meals.*
- *Has a diuretic effect that increases urination.*
- *May cause insomnia in caffeine-sensitive people.*

Refreshing and stimulating, tea is the world's most popular nonalcoholic beverage. While most tea is produced in Asia, the Irish are the leading tea-drinkers, with an annual per capita consumption of 1,456 cups, compared to Canada's annual per capita consumption of 275 cups. About 90 percent of all tea in Canada (excluding iced tea) is sold in tea bags, which were inadvertently invented in 1904 by a New York merchant when he sent out tea samples enclosed in silk.

Most tea is grown in India, Sri Lanka, China, Japan, Taiwan, and Indonesia from a shrub in the camellia family. Like coffees, the best-quality teas are grown in the shade at high altitudes, and the finest leaves are plucked from the youngest shoots and unopened leaf buds, which also contain the highest levels of phenols, enzymes, and caffeine.

Processing produces three main types of tea leaves: black (Indian), green (Japanese and Chinese), and oolong (Chinese black). Black tea is produced by drying and fermenting the leaves to convert the flavorless, colorless phenols into pigmented, astringent tannins.

Green tea, favored in Asian nations, is steamed, not fermented. Oolong tea emerges from a process that combines the black and green types. Brand-name teas are mixtures of as many as 20 different varieties of leaves, blended to ensure a consistent flavor.

During the 18th and 19th centuries, the adoption of tea as the staple beverage in the British Isles coincided with a wave of malnutrition, which social commentators blamed on the loss of nutrients formerly provided by ale and beer. (More likely explanations are the inadequate diet adopted by poor workers who were flocking to the cities to work in the factories of the Industrial Revolution as well as the growing preference for refined white bread.) Today, however, researchers are discovering evidence that tea may offer not only soothing warmth and mild stimulation, but health benefits as well.

A cup of hot brewed tea has only 2 calories and—with one exception in green tea—no appreciable vitamins or minerals, except for fluoride. Green tea is high in vitamin K, a nutrient needed for normal blood clotting. Flavoring with milk and sugar adds calories and some nutrients; lemon lends a refreshing flavor and vitamin C. A cup of instant sweetened tea provides 85 calories.

HEALTH BENEFITS

A recent study found that the risk of stroke was reduced by about 70 percent in men who drank five or more cups of black tea a day. Researchers believed the effect was due to BIOFLAVONOIDS, plant pigments that studies have linked to protection against heart attacks, cancer, and other diseases. There are many types of bioflavonoids, but researchers believe that their protective effect comes from their ANTIOXIDANT properties. These substances may protect against stroke in two ways. They reduce the ability of blood platelets to form clots, the cause of most strokes. They also block some of the damage caused to arteries by free radicals, the unstable molecules that are released when the body consumes oxygen. While green tea is also high in bioflavonoids (the men in the study drank black tea), its high vitamin K content may offset their anticlotting properties.

Naturally occurring theophyllines in tea dilate the airways in the lungs and have been found to help some people with ASTHMA and other respiratory disorders to breathe more freely. In fact, theophyllines have been developed as drugs to treat asthma and other constrictive lung disorders.

Tannins, which are found in WINE as well as tea, are chemicals that bind surface proteins in the mouth, producing a tightening sensation together with the impression of a full-bodied liquid. They also bind and incapacitate plaque-forming bacteria in the mouth and thus may have a beneficial antiseptic effect in people who are susceptible to DENTAL DISORDERS. The fluoride in tea—particularly green tea—also protects against tooth decay.

DRAWBACKS

Tea leaves contain twice as much caffeine, weight for weight, as coffee beans do. But when measured by volume, tea has only half as much caffeine as coffee because tea is drunk weaker and coffee is more completely extracted from the grounds. With its low level of caffeine, tea is a mild stimulant, but drinking strong tea or many cups throughout the day may cause restlessness or difficulty in falling asleep and can cause INDIGESTION AND HEARTBURN. Even decaffeinated tea is not entirely caffeine-free. Tea may trigger a MIGRAINE headache in hypersensitive people; for others, it may alleviate headaches when

HEALING TEAS. *Leaves, seeds, and flowers are all used by herbalists in their quest for the most effective natural remedies.*

Raspberry leaf

Fennel seed

Chamomile

Thyme

Dandelion

Nettle leaf

Peppermint leaf

Rose hip

Lavender flower

Lemon balm

Rosemary leaf

Elder flower

taken with aspirin or similar pain-killers. Theobromine, which is also found in tea, has effects similar to those of caffeine but milder.

The tannins in tea can cut iron absorption by more than 80 percent when tea is drunk with an iron-rich meal. Tea-drinking vegetarians are especially susceptible. Individuals with a tendency to ANEMIA can drink citrus juice at mealtimes to promote iron absorption; squeezing a wedge of lemon or adding milk to tea also binds the tannins and partly blocks their effect on iron. Tea drinking between meals does not affect iron absorption. Young children should not drink tea, which can increase their risk of iron-deficiency anemia. In addition, tannins can stain natural teeth and dental work, and some mouthwashes may intensify the staining.

Tea, like coffee, has a diuretic effect, which increases the kidneys' output of urine. Excessive urination can upset the body's fluid and chemical balance by washing potassium from the body.

HERBAL TEAS

Many plants, especially herbs, can be brewed into teas, also called infusions or tisanes. These teas are sometimes flavored with spices and essential oils. Because most of them do not contain caffeine, they offer a pleasant alternative for people who prefer to avoid this stimulant. Some herbal teas aid the digestion, and their soothing warmth can promote relaxation at bedtime.

Always choose herbs carefully. Although the herbs and spices used in herbal teas have been approved by Health Canada for use as seasonings, they have not been proved safe as teas, and some may be harmful. Nutmeg, for example, is harmless when used to flavor foods but can cause severe symptoms, including hallucinations, when brewed into a strong tea. Other herbs, such as oregano, have a stimulating effect and cause wakefulness.

ICED TEA

On the whole, most Canadians prefer hot tea—it accounts for about 80 percent of all the tea we drink. Still, sales of ready-to-drink iced tea amount to about $39 million annually.

Iced tea becomes cloudy because caffeine and pigment molecules crystallize at low temperatures. Sun tea, which is made by steeping several tea bags in lukewarm water for several hours (in or out of the sun), is less likely to become cloudy than tea brewed with hot water.

Commercial iced teas, flavored with fruit syrups and sweetened with sugar, contain about as many calories as soft drinks. Iced teas sweetened with aspartame contain only 2 to 4 calories per cup. Because aspartame contains phenylalanine, these diet teas are unsafe for people who have phenylketonuria (PKU).

Folk healers have long used herbal teas for medicinal purposes, but few teas have been tested scientifically. Care is needed when self-treating with herbal teas, especially if the herbs have been gathered in the wild. Many plants are poisonous, and these may be mistaken for safe herbs. The following are among the more popular herbal teas.

Chamomile. A mild sedative, chamomile tea is said to aid digestion and relieve menstrual cramps. Small amounts of pollen residue in the tea may cause dermatitis or other allergic symptoms in people sensitive to ragweed, chrysanthemums, and other members of the daisy family.

Dandelion. Tea made from this common weed is mildly diuretic. Some women use it to reduce problems of premenstrual bloating.

Elder flower. Extracts of elder are sometimes used in over-the-counter cold remedies, and elder-flower tea may alleviate COLD AND FLU symptoms. The flowers and ripe berries of the elder are safe, but avoid the roots, stems, and leaves. The tea is a mild stimulant.

Fennel. With a flavor similar to licorice, fennel tea is used to soothe an upset stomach. Traditional herbalists often recommend it as an appetite-suppressant and slimming aid.

Lavender flower. Tea brewed from dried lavender flowers is said to be mildly sedative.

Lemon balm. This minty tea may help soothe jittery nerves.

Nettle. Made from the same plant that causes stinging skin irritation, nettle tea is rich in vitamin C and several minerals. Herbalists recommend it to treat arthritis and gout and to increase milk production in nursing mothers.

Peppermint. Tea from this mint plant is refreshing and may stimulate digestion. It should be avoided by anyone with a HIATAL HERNIA, because peppermint promotes reflux of the stomach contents into the esophagus.

Raspberry leaf. Herbalists recommend raspberry tea to ease discomfort from menstrual cramps.

Rose hip. Rich in vitamin C, rose hip tea can substitute for orange juice when citrus fruits are not readily available.

Rosemary. Tea from this popular garden herb is said to relieve gas and colic, but drinking more than two or three cups a day may irritate the stomach.

Thyme. Herbalists recommend thyme tea for gastrointestinal complaints and to alleviate lung congestion.

INSTANT TEA

Instant tea is made by brewing strong tea, then evaporating the water to leave a powder. The tea is reconstituted by adding water. Fruit juice can be used instead of water to make a flavored iced tea.

Thyroid Disorders

EAT PLENTY OF
- *Seafood, dark green leafy vegetables, deep yellow or orange fruits and vegetables, fortified cereals, and low-fat dairy products for iodine and vitamin A.*

CUT DOWN ON
- *Alcohol and caffeine, if the thyroid gland is overactive.*
- *Raw vegetables in the cabbage family, if the thyroid gland is underactive.*

AVOID
- *Smoking.*
- *High-dose kelp supplements.*

The thyroid, a butterfly-shaped gland that lies over the windpipe (trachea) and just below the Adam's apple (larynx), produces triiodothyronine (T_3) and thyroxine (T_4), hormones that influence almost every function of the body. These hormones regulate metabolism, physical and mental development, nerve and muscle function, and circulation. Thyroid hormones also affect the actions of other hormones; for example, they intensify the action of insulin and the body's response to the adrenal hormones (catecholamines) that are instrumental in reacting to stress.

Unlike other hormone-producing glands, the thyroid needs a specific nutrient—iodine—to produce its hormones. Both too much and too little iodine can cause the thyroid to malfunction. Goiter, an overgrown thyroid that is marked by a swelling in the lower neck, usually signals a thyroid disorder. It is common in regions where people are dependent on crops raised in iodine-poor soil and do not receive iodine supplements in the diet. Goiter is also common among Japanese people, who often consume very large amounts of iodine-rich seaweed.

People who lack iodine also appear to be more susceptible to the toxic effects of radioactive iodine, a contaminant released into the atmosphere during aboveground testing of nuclear weapons. Iodine deficiency, although still a common cause of thyroid disorders in developing nations, has been almost wiped out in the industrialized countries by the introduction of iodized salt. Because seawater contains high levels of iodine, food crops grown on coastal farmlands generally have sufficient levels of the mineral. Iodine deficiency more commonly occurs in mountainous regions, such as the Alps, or in inland areas, such as China and parts of the Midwestern United States.

Although they affect both sexes, thyroid disorders tend to occur more frequently in women. Cretinism, a type of mental retardation and growth deficiency, is a birth defect caused by a lack of iodine in the mother. Cretinism still prevails in parts of China but is rare in the United States, where babies are tested at birth for thyroid deficiency.

Thyroid problems usually involve either overactivity or underactivity of the gland. Although there is some overlap, the symptoms of one disorder present almost a mirror image of the other. The usual causes of thyroid problems are an infection, autoimmune disorder, hormonal imbalance, tumor, exposure to high levels of ionizing radiation, or congenital or hereditary problems.

HYPERTHYROIDISM

People with overactive thyroids (hyperthyroidism, or Graves' disease) tend to be nervous and jittery. Their metabolism speeds up, and they experience unusual hunger, weight loss, muscle weakness, and rapid heartbeat, among other symptoms. They find heat hard to bear and sweat excessively. Whether or not a goiter distorts the neck, a person with an overactive thyroid develops protuberant eyes.

Case Study

Sandra, a 52-year-old speechwriter, suffered a number of symptoms that were beginning to worry her. Apart from mood swings, for which her doctor prescribed an antidepressant, she was gaining weight, her skin was dry, and her hair was falling out. She also noticed that her eyelids were somewhat puffy. Her joints were stiff and sore, especially in the morning—symptoms she attributed to arthritis. Sandra often felt cold when others found the temperature comfortable. Perhaps her most troubling symptom, however, was persistent fatigue. Walking up a flight of stairs left her exhausted, and she usually felt sleepy even after a full night's sleep.

When blood tests showed a low level of thyroid hormone, Sandra's doctor prescribed thyroid pills. After only a few weeks of daily thyroid replacement pills, Sandra regained her energy, she no longer needed the antidepressant, her skin and hair gradually returned to their original state, and her other symptoms progressively disappeared.

343

Treatment is aimed at the cause and involves reducing hormone production either by giving radioactive iodine or antithyroid drugs or by surgery to remove all or parts of the thyroid.

HYPOTHYROIDISM

An underactive thyroid, or hypothyroidism, slows down the metabolism, causing weight gain and lethargy. The early symptoms are subtle and easily overlooked. Progressive fatigue, sleepiness, and muscle weakness are common. People with hypothyroidism often complain of memory and concentration problems. They feel cold, even on hot days, and develop dry skin and thinning hair. Their nails grow slowly and become brittle. They often lose the outer third of their eyebrows, and the skin on their eyelids becomes darker and puffy. Because metabolism slows down, weight gain is common, even though the person may be eating less than normal. Women will often develop menstrual irregularities; constipation is another common problem.

Hypothyroidism is frequently caused by chronic inflammation due to an autoimmune disorder. Treatment usually requires lifelong hormone replacement with thyroxine pills.

DIETARY APPROACHES

An adult needs 50 to 75mcg (micrograms) of iodine a day to prevent goiter. Even people on low-salt diets get plenty of iodine from seafood, green leafy vegetables, and dairy products. To provide an extra safety margin, government scientists recommend a daily intake of 160mcg for adolescents and adults and additional allowances of 25mcg and 50mcg for pregnant women and nursing mothers. The use of iodized salt in the typical Canadian diet, which provides 2g to 6g of salt each day, easily supplies much more than these recommended amounts of iodine. However, iodine intake of up to 1,000mcg a day has no adverse effects on the thyroid.

Certain vegetables, mainly CABBAGE, BROCCOLI, and other cruciferous vegetables, contain substances known as goitrogens, which block the effects of thyroid hormones and may lead to goiter. Cooking these foods inactivates the goitrogens; consumption of sufficient iodine also prevents their adverse effects on the thyroid.

Thyroid problems are more severe when both iodine and vitamin A are lacking at the same time. People with thyroid disorders should use small amounts of iodized salt and eat plenty of seafood, beans and other legumes, and fresh spinach and other vegetables for iodine. Low-fat dairy products, fortified cereals, deep yellow or orange fruits and vegetables, and dark green vegetables provide vitamin A.

CAFFEINE may worsen the jittery feeling in someone with an overactive thyroid. Decaffeinated coffee, tea, and soda pop may refresh without adding to nervousness. The nicotine in tobacco also adds to feelings of nervousness. ALCOHOL may aggravate the sleepiness and fatigue in a person with an underactive thyroid gland.

ABUSE OF HORMONES

Some people, usually women who are overly weight-conscious, take thyroid hormones as a diet aid. This can have dangerous results, including drug-induced hyperthyroidism, metabolic abnormalities, and irregular heartbeats. Thyroid pills should be taken only under careful medical supervision—never for weight control.

ASIAN FLAVOR. *Triangles of tofu stir-fried with thin slices of pork and vegetables make a satisfying main dish.*

TOFU AND OTHER SOY PRODUCTS

BENEFITS
- *A vegetarian source of high-quality protein and iron.*
- *A good source of B vitamins, calcium, potassium, zinc, and other minerals.*
- *May protect against heart disease and some forms of cancer.*
- *Low in calories and fat.*

DRAWBACKS
- *Fermented soy products are high in sodium and may provoke allergies.*
- *Soy protein may hinder iron absorption.*

Members of the pea family, soybeans are the leading legume crop around the world; they are also one of the most nutritious and versatile plant foods. Ounce for ounce, soybeans contain more protein than beef, more calcium than milk, more lecithin than eggs, and more iron than beef. Soybean protein contains good amounts of all the essential amino acids, making it the only plant protein that approaches or equals animal products in this essential nutrient. Soybeans are also good sources of

B vitamins and potassium, zinc, and other minerals. Soybean oil is mostly polyunsaturated fatty acids, which do not raise blood cholesterol levels.

Flours and meals made from dried soybeans are more nutritious than grain flours. A cup of defatted soy meal, for example, provides 60g of protein, 44g of carbohydrate, good amounts of all the B vitamins except B_{12} (which is found strictly in animal products), 3,040mg of potassium, 300mg of calcium, and 17mg of iron. Defatted soy flour has a similar range of nutrients, but in lesser amounts.

Although many soy products are high in iron, it is not well absorbed; absorption can be improved by adding foods high in vitamin C to the meal.

A VERSATILE LEGUME

Soybeans can be prepared like other dry beans; ground into flour or meal; or processed into oil, milk, curds, and protein concentrates. Tofu, a cheeselike curd made by pressing a mixture of soaked and ground soybeans, is a staple in Asian cuisine. It is also substituted for cheese and other high-fat ingredients in such North American favorites as ice cream, cheesecake, and "veggie" burgers.

Soy milk is an alternative for strict VEGETARIANS, who shun all animal products. Because it is hypoallergenic, it is given to babies who cannot tolerate formulas made from cow's milk.

Textured soybean protein and concentrates are vegetarian alternatives to meat that can be used to make "veggie" burgers, meatless "meatloaf," and other dishes. These products can be flavored to taste like meat and are economical, low in fat, and cholesterol-free.

Some soy products are fermented with molds—these include tempeh, a type of soy curd; miso, a paste used to flavor soups and vegetables; and the familiar soy sauce. Tempeh is more nutritious than tofu, providing good amounts of vitamin A, larger amounts of B vitamins, and some minerals. Miso and soy sauce are very high in sodium and should be avoided by anyone on a salt-restricted diet. Tempeh and other soy products, however, are naturally low in sodium, although salt is often added for flavor. People who are sensitive to molds should avoid fermented soy products, which may provoke an allergic reaction.

Dried soybeans can be soaked and prepared like other dried beans. Relatively new to the North American marketplace are sweet soybeans, which are about the size of baby lima beans but a brighter green, sweeter, and firmer. Sweet soybeans are sold frozen in health-food stores and Asian markets and can be served like fresh lima beans.

HEALTH BENEFITS

Recent research indicates that replacing some animal products with soy protein can reduce the risk of a heart attack. This is because soy lowers levels of the artery-clogging LDL (low-density lipoprotein) cholesterol without reducing levels of the beneficial HDL (high-density lipoprotein) cholesterol. In one study of men whose total blood CHOLESTEROL levels exceeded 250mg/100ml (6.5mmol/L) (200mg/100ml [5.2mmol/L] or lower is desirable), LDL cholesterol dropped an average of 13 percent when about 1 ounce of soy protein was added to the daily diet.

Throughout Asia, where soy has long been a dietary staple, the rates of breast and prostate cancer are much lower than in Western countries. Some researchers attribute the low incidence of these cancers to the fact that soy is high in isoflavones, plant chemicals that reduce the effects of estrogen on breast and prostate tissue. Estrogen is thought to stimulate tumor growth in genetically susceptible people. Recent research also indicates that soy isoflavones may slow the loss of bone minerals after menopause, thereby protecting against OSTEOPOROSIS.

TOMATOES

BENEFITS
- *A useful source of vitamins A and C, folate, and potassium.*
- *A good source of lycopene, an antioxidant that protects against some cancers.*

DRAWBACKS
- *Raw or cooked, may cause indigestion and heartburn.*
- *A common cause of allergies.*

Equally delicious raw or cooked, tomatoes are low in calories and rich in vitamins and other healthful substances. Tomatoes, like potatoes, sweet peppers, and eggplants, belong to the nightshade family. Brought to Europe from Central America by the Spanish during the 16th century, tomatoes were grown as decorative plants in northern Europe,

where it was feared that poisons in the leaves might be present in the fruit as well. Colonists emigrating from this area brought this misconception to the New World. Meanwhile, the Spanish and Italians discovered that tomatoes were indeed edible, and as they immigrated to North America, they brought their taste for tomatoes with them. Today, the tomato ranks third as a vegetable sold in Canada.

SPECIAL BENEFITS

Recent good health news for men is that eating tomatoes regularly may reduce the risk of prostate cancer. Harvard researchers found that men who consumed tomatoes or tomato-based foods—including pizza—at least four times a week had a 20 percent lower risk of prostate cancer than those who avoided tomatoes. Men who ate tomatoes 10 times a week reduced their risk by almost half. It didn't matter what form the tomatoes were in, although cooked tomatoes appeared to be more protective than fresh.

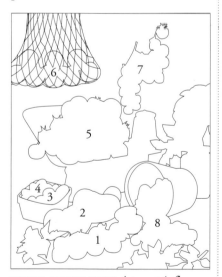

BETTER ON THE VINE? *A tomato's flavor depends more on the type and how ripe it is than on where it has ripened. The varieties include vine (1), beefsteak (2), yellow cherry (3), baby cherry (4), vine (5), plum (6), cherry (7), and baby plum (8).*

The researchers theorize that lycopenes—carotenoids that are closely related to beta carotene—are the natural cancer-fighting agents in tomatoes. (Lycopenes are also found in pink GRAPEFRUITS and watermelons.) They also speculate that cooking releases the fat-soluble lycopenes from the fruits' cells, and that a small amount of oil, such as that in pizza or tomato sauce, intensifies the protective effect.

Although no single food can prevent cancer altogether, nutrition experts advise us to hedge our bets by consuming plenty of fruits and vegetables, such as tomatoes, that are rich in ANTIOXIDANT nutrients, which protect against the cancer-causing cell damage that occurs when the body uses oxygen.

NUTRITIONAL VALUE

One medium-size ripe tomato contains only 25 calories, together with about 20mg of vitamin C and 1,400 I.U. of vitamin A, in the form of its precursor, beta carotene. Most of the vitamin C is concentrated in the jellylike substance that encases the seeds. Many recipes advise removing the seeds to prevent the development of a bitter taste during cooking; cooks who prefer to conserve all possible nutrients may use plum tomatoes, which have smaller seeds that impart less bitterness than larger ones.

Commercially prepared tomato sauces vary in calorie content, depending on added ingredients. Some tomato products may have high levels of added salt; people on low-sodium diets should look for those with no extra salt. On average, a half cup of canned tomato sauce contains about 85 calories, which may increase substantially with the addition of oil. A half cup of canned tomatoes contains only 25 calories. Tomato paste is a concentrated source of nutrients—a 3½-ounce can contains about 80 calories, with 2,100 I.U. of vitamin A and 50mg of vitamin C, together with good amounts of the

B-group vitamins and 970mg of potassium. Canned tomato juice, like fresh tomatoes, is a good source of vitamin A. Some vitamin C is lost in the processing, but some brands are fortified to raise the vitamin C content to the same level as found in fresh tomatoes.

Red tomatoes contain up to four times as much beta carotene as green, but ripe and unripe tomatoes are otherwise nutritionally similar. Ripe tomatoes should be stored at room temperature; at 40°F (4°C) or below, the flesh becomes mealy. The green tomatoes left on the vine at the end of the season should be harvested and cooked, frozen, or pickled. Sun-dried tomatoes are a flavorful addition to many dishes, but those packed in oil are high in calories.

DRAWBACKS

Solanines are toxic substances present in minute quantities in all members of the nightshade family; they may trigger headaches in susceptible people. Tomatoes are also a relatively common cause of ALLERGIES. An unidentified substance in tomatoes and tomato-based products can cause acid reflux, leading to INDIGESTION AND HEARTBURN. People who often have digestive upsets should try eliminating tomatoes for 2 or 3 weeks to see if there's an improvement.

TOMATO CONDIMENTS

Many commercially prepared PICKLES AND OTHER CONDIMENTS are based on tomatoes, including ketchup and chili sauce, pasta sauces, chutneys, and the Latin-American salsa that has overtaken ketchup as North America's most popular condiment. While these preparations add zest to food, they add little nutrition in the quantities used. In addition, their calorie content is often boosted with generous quantities of sugar and oil. And because many are high in salt, they should not be eaten by people who need to restrict their sodium intake.

Traveler's Health: Being Prudent Pays Off

*By following a few simple guidelines, a smart traveler
can get the most out of a trip and not let
digestive upsets, jet lag, or other medical problems spoil it.*

Travel to far-flung destinations has become commonplace for both business and pleasure. But as enriching as travel can be, it is also stressful. Travelers are exposed to new strains of common bacteria and viruses as well as unfamiliar microorganisms to which they lack immunity. Changes in climate, altitude, time zones, and diet require the body to adapt at a rate nature never intended. With a little forethought, however, travelers can cope with stress, avoid hazards, and reduce the risk of illness.

TRAVELER'S DIARRHEA

Most people experience a change in bowel habits (usually diarrhea but sometimes constipation) during their first few days in a foreign place. These changes are not necessarily illness; they simply show that the body is adapting to foreign strains of *Escherichia coli,* the common bacterium that is part of our normal intestinal fauna. Strains that the body hasn't encountered before produce mild toxins that require getting used to. In the meantime, they can interfere with the intestines' ability to absorb water. The digestive tract usually settles down in 2 or 3 days without any need for treatment other than avoiding CAFFEINE, ALCOHOL, and foods that might irritate the intestines, and drinking plenty of fluids to prevent DEHYDRATION.

When a trip involves several short stays in different places, the body no

---

CONSUME
- *Ample fluids to prevent dehydration and constipation.*
- *The BRAT (bananas, rice, applesauce, and toast) diet if traveler's diarrhea develops.*

CUT DOWN ON
- *Alcohol to prevent dehydration and ensure restful sleep.*
- *Caffeine to prevent wakefulness.*

AVOID
- *Salads and unpeeled fruits and vegetables.*
- *Tap water for drinking or brushing teeth in underdeveloped areas.*
- *Antidiarrheal drugs or other medications except as prescribed.*

---

sooner adapts to one new strain than it's confronted with another. But adaptation can be eased by following guidelines for avoiding diarrhea during the first few days: drink bottled water; don't accept ice cubes in drinks; and don't eat salads, raw vegetables, or fruits that you haven't peeled yourself. If upsets occur, emphasize the binding foods in the BRAT diet for treating DIARRHEA: bananas, rice, applesauce, and dry toast.

It's safe to brush your teeth with tap water in places with reasonable sanitation, but use bottled water for gargling and swallowing. In places with poor sanitation, use bottled water for brushing your teeth too.

INFECTIOUS DIARRHEA

Travelers everywhere—especially in the developing regions of Africa, the Middle East, and Latin America—are at risk of contracting infectious diarrhea, usually through fecal contamination

of food and water. Perhaps because they are less cautious in choosing food and drink, young adults are more likely to contract diarrhea than older people are. However, they are less likely to suffer serious effects.

Infectious diarrhea usually clears up in 3 to 7 days. While uncomfortable, it is rarely serious in healthy adults. Symptoms, apart from diarrhea, include nausea, bloating, and urgency (a sudden need to use the toilet), as well as general discomfort and fatigue.

Travelers with diarrhea should drink plenty of bottled water, diluted soda pop, and other fluids to ward off dehydration. Children and older adults are at high risk for severe symptoms and should be given extra fluids, including a commercial oral rehydration solution (available at pharmacies overseas), if necessary. Hot soups, stews, and puddings provide safe nourishment. For severe diarrhea, experts recommend fluids and salted crackers only. Sufferers should avoid dairy products, fruit juices, and beverages likely to contain unsafe water. Travelers should seek medical help if diarrhea doesn't resolve within a few days or if diarrhea is severe, bloody, or accompanied by a fever and chills.

Antibiotics should not be taken for prevention because they can create additional problems, but doctors may prescribe them to stop diarrhea. Nonprescription antidiarrheal drugs are not advised; while they decrease the number of stools, they may prolong the infection and cause complications.

FOOD FOR TRAVEL

The best way to avoid health problems while traveling is to choose foods and drinks carefully, but this doesn't mean depriving yourself of the opportunity to sample local specialties altogether. Although unpeeled fruits and vegetables or raw foods may be contaminated, cooked food that is still hot can usually be safely eaten. Some FISH may be unsafe even after cooking, however, because of toxins in their flesh. High-risk areas for fish are the islands of the West Indies and the tropical areas of the Pacific and Indian oceans.

PURE WATER

In places with poor sanitation, travelers should be sure to drink only boiled water, beverages that are made with boiled water, canned or bottled soda pop and juices, beer, or wine (avoid ice cubes). It is usually better to drink directly from the container than risk a dirty cup. Wipe cans and bottles clean and dry to prevent infection from drops of contaminated water or ice.

Travelers venturing into out-of-the-way places should carry chemical disinfectant tablets, which are sold at pharmacies and sporting goods stores. These are important for campers, who may have to depend on natural water sources. Even in countries with excellent standards of sanitation, streams and lakes may be polluted with giardia and other microorganisms. Travelers in these areas should disinfect water for toothbrushing or use bottled water. Some freshwater, especially warm springs, harbors organisms that can cause meningitis and other serious diseases. Swimmers at certain Mediterranean beaches have developed infections from the polluted seawater. Government tourist or health offices can indicate where it's safe to swim.

RISKY BUSINESS. *When shopping for food while on vacation, you take your health in your hands. It is better to avoid sliced fruits and ready-cooked dishes from outdoor kiosks and roadside stands.*

JET LAG

Researchers studying natural biorhythms, or chronobiology, have discovered that an internal clock governs the human body, influencing every event, from internal surges of hormones to the results of medical treatment and surgery. Two factors play key roles in setting the body's clock: bright light and melatonin, a hormone produced by the pineal gland in the brain. The clock can be reset by shift work or when you move to different time zones, but you suffer the discomfort of jet lag until the new timing is fully synchronized. Jet lag disrupts sleep, memory, and concentration. It causes irritability and saps physical strength.

Studies indicate that melatonin may have potential as a drug to help overcome jet lag for such people as international flight crews, whose bodies are under constant stress. But, although health-food marketers in the U.S. are promoting melatonin as a miracle drug, doctors warn that not enough is known about its long-term effects. Some physicians who specialize in travel medicine, however, feel that it is safe if taken in small, well-timed doses. Rather than self-treating with

FOODS TO AVOID OR TREAT WITH CAUTION

- FISH and SHELLFISH unless in a reputable hotel or restaurant; avoid raw shellfish altogether.
- Undercooked food or any food that has either been kept warm or is served lukewarm.
- Food exposed to flies.
- ICE CREAM from potentially unreliable sources, including street vendors or market stalls.
- Unpasteurized milk.
- Salad, unless it has been washed in boiled or bottled water.
- Soft drinks that may have been diluted with tap water.

melatonin, it's a good idea to consult such a specialist. The Canadian government does not allow the sale of melatonin supplements.

There are also nondrug approaches to minimize jet lag. Immediately reset your watch to the time zone of your destination. Eat lightly during the flight, and drink plenty of water or juice to compensate for the drying effects of airplane air. Avoid caffeine, which causes sleeplessness, and alcohol, which causes interrupted sleep.

On arrival, follow the local schedule for sleep and meals immediately. Staying up with lights on has an effect like that of melatonin and helps to reset the body's clock. Daytime naps should be short—they should refresh but shouldn't cut into overnight rest.

MOTION SICKNESS

Some people suffer nausea, vomiting, and headaches when traveling because of a discrepancy between what they see and what they sense with the balance mechanism of the inner ear.

Anyone who tends to get motion sickness should eat a light starchy meal—for example, a few crackers—before setting out. Nausea is more likely to develop if the stomach is empty or overly full. Avoid alcohol, caffeine, and fatty foods. Many people find focusing on a distant point can help to quell the nausea. Over-the-counter remedies usually help, but they may cause drowsiness. Chewing a few pieces of candied GINGER can help to prevent motion sickness without drowsiness. Wearing an acupressure bracelet also helps many people.

RISKS FROM AIRCRAFT AIR

Airplanes recirculate air with highly efficient systems that can filter out particles as small as a single bacterium. To reduce the risk of transmitting airborne diseases, the air is filtered even more often than in hospital isolation rooms. But despite these mea-

sures, flu and other infectious diseases are sometimes transmitted, especially in flights lasting longer than 8 hours.

DISINFECTION

Some aircraft may be sprayed with approved insecticides before passengers disembark, and people with ALLERGIES may experience symptoms. They should ask their travel agent or airline for details before going to Latin America, the Caribbean, Australia, New Zealand, or the South Pacific islands.

IMMUNIZATION

All travelers should make sure their tetanus shots are up to date. For travelers to Europe, the Pacific, and major cities of Asia, no special immunizations are needed. Diphtheria, mumps, and rubella (German measles) still cause serious illness, however, and those who lack immunity should be vaccinated whether or not they travel.

In developing countries, the risk of serious viral infection increases with the length of stay and the type of accommodation. It's highest for those who spend time in rural areas, trek in the countryside, or eat and drink in areas with poor sanitation. People who plan to travel to these regions should consult a doctor at least 2 months before the departure date. Vaccination may be recommended against hepatitis A or B, and a poliomyelitis booster may be required. Children should have all the immunizations appropriate for their ages. Young children and the elderly should receive flu shots.

Travelers to Asia, the Middle East, Africa, and Central and South America may need vaccinations against yellow fever, cholera, and typhoid fever. Those heading for tropical regions, including northern Australia, may need antimalaria drugs before departure and throughout the journey.

People allergic to eggs may not be able to receive certain vaccinations; ask about other methods of protection.

TUBERCULOSIS

CONSUME PLENTY OF

- *Lean meat, poultry, eggs, and fish for high-quality protein.*
- *Legumes, pasta, grains, and other starchy foods for energy.*
- *Fresh fruits and vegetables for vitamin C and beta carotene.*
- *Fortified milk, eggs, and fatty fish for vitamin D.*
- *Animal products, grains, spinach, and potatoes for vitamin B6 (especially if taking isoniazid).*
- *Lean meat, shellfish, and fortified cereals and breads for zinc.*

AVOID

- *Alcohol, smoking, and exposure to secondhand smoke.*
- *Sharing eating utensils and other personal objects.*
- *Low-calorie diet foods.*

With about 2,000 new cases a year, tuberculosis (TB) is relatively uncommon in Canada, but worldwide it's a leading cause of death, claiming 3 million lives annually. Further, it is estimated that one-third of the world's population is infected with one of several strains of *Mycobacterium,* the bacillus that causes TB. Although the disease is inactive in most of these people, at any given time there are some 30 million active cases of TB.

The TB bacillus is spread when an infected person coughs or sneezes, releasing the microorganism into the air. Infection occurs when the bacillus is inhaled and enters the lungs, where it can silently multiply. The immune system usually eradicates the infection at this early stage, but in some people the bacillus remains dormant in the body. Even so, most infected people never develop symptoms, although they will still have a positive TB skin test, indicating the presence of antibodies against the disease-causing organism.

A latent infection can develop into full-blown TB if the immune system becomes weakened by malnutrition, age, or a serious disease, such as AIDS or cancer. The initial symptoms—loss of appetite and weight, night sweats, fever and chills, and general malaise—may resemble a lingering bout of flu. But as the disease progresses, more severe manifestations appear: typically, a chronic cough, profuse sputum that may be blood-tinged and malodorous, increasing weakness, and eventually, muscle wasting. Although the lungs are TB's most common target organ, the disease can attack almost any part of the body, including the brain, kidneys, spine, bones, and skin.

For most of this century, the number of TB cases in Canada declined steadily. In 1985, however, a sharp increase was reported, mostly among AIDS patients and the homeless. In addition, a number of persons who had been treated for (and presumably cured of) TB in the 1940s and 1950s suffered recurrences. Often, the reactivated TB was resistant to some of the more effective medications, so the patients required longer and more intensive multidrug treatment. Since 1987, the number of TB cases in Canada has remained constant.

ROLE OF DIET

The typical TB treatment regimen calls for 6 to 18 months of daily administration of several powerful antibiotics: usually isoniazid, rifampin, pyrazimadide, and either ethambutol or streptomycin. While undergoing treatment, patients must abstain from alcohol, which interacts with the drugs and also increases the risk of liver and nerve damage—common side effects of the TB regimen. Both the disease and the medications cause loss of appetite, but it is critical to maintain good nutrition to minimize weight loss, bolster immunity, and rebuild damaged tissue.

The diet should provide ample high-quality protein, preferably from lean meat, poultry, fish, eggs, milk, and other animal products. (Although the results are inconclusive, some studies suggest that vegetarians are more vulnerable to TB and its complications than are people whose diets include some animal protein.) Citrus fruits and other fresh fruits and vegetables provide vitamin C and beta carotene, ANTIOXIDANTS that the body needs to boost immunity. Zinc is also important to foster healing and a strong immune system; good sources include oysters and other shellfish, lean meat, yogurt, and fortified cereals and breads.

Doctors have long observed that TB patients who spend time in the sunshine and fresh air often improve faster. Researchers have now found an expla-

---

HELPFUL FOODS

Fresh fruits and vegetables for vitamins A and C and other antioxidants. Strive to have five to nine servings each day.

Salmon and other fatty fish for vitamin D. Other good sources are eggs, fortified milk, and margarine. Eat three servings weekly.

Lean meats, poultry, fish, and eggs for protein, which is needed to heal damaged tissue. The diet should provide at least two servings daily.

Spinach, potatoes, and grain products for vitamin B6 to help prevent nerve damage while taking isoniazid. Meat and other animal products are also high in B6. Have one serving daily.

Pasta, legumes, grains, and other starchy foods for energy. TB patients need the maximum of 12 (or more) servings stipulated in the Food Guide Rainbow (see p.39).

nation. White blood cells that are armed with high concentrations of vitamin D appear to be more effective in destroying the bacillus. The body makes vitamin D when the skin is exposed to the sun; good dietary sources include fortified milk and margarine, eggs, and fatty fish.

Isoniazid is especially destructive to the nerves. To reduce this risk, some doctors prescribe vitamin B6 supplements. Foods that are high in this nutrient include most animal products, grains, spinach, and potatoes.

It is critical to consume more calories than usual to counter the weight loss that is characteristic of TB. The diet should emphasize foods that are dense in calories and easy to digest. In addition to the foods already mentioned, good choices include legumes, pasta, grains, and other starchy foods; milk shakes or perhaps enriched milk-based drinks; and rich soups, custards, eggs, puddings, and ice cream.

OTHER MEASURES

Because TB usually damages the lungs, it's important to avoid exposure to tobacco smoke and other pollutants that are harmful to the lungs. It's imperative that smokers give up the habit; secondhand smoke should also be avoided as much as possible.

Although TB is highly contagious, the risk of spreading it can be minimized by practicing good hygiene and not sharing eating utensils and other personal items. When coughing or sneezing, the patient should always cover his mouth with a tissue and then promptly dispose of it. Because sun and fresh air help destroy airborne bacilli, air the house frequently and let in as much sunshine as possible. Anyone who lives in close contact with a TB patient should undergo testing for the disease; in some cases, preventive antibiotic treatment may be warranted.

TURNIPS

BENEFITS
- *A useful source of vitamin C, as well as some calcium and potassium.*
- *A low-calorie source of fiber.*
- *May protect against certain cancers.*

DRAWBACKS
- *May cause flatulence.*
- *Contain substances that interfere with the production of thyroid hormones.*

Although less nutritious than their rutabaga cousins, turnips are nevertheless economical, healthful, and easy to prepare and cultivate (even in soil of poor quality). One cup of boiled turnips yields only 30 calories while providing 18mg of vitamin C (almost one-half of the daily needs), 35mg of calcium, and 210mg of potassium. They are also a useful source of fiber, including soluble dietary fibers that help control blood cholesterol levels.

The turnip tops, or greens, which many cooks discard, are even more nutritious than the roots themselves. One cup of boiled greens provides 40mg of vitamin C, about 200mg of calcium, and nearly 300mg of potassium. In addition, unlike the roots, the greens are an excellent source of beta carotene, an important

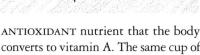

ANTIOXIDANT nutrient that the body converts to vitamin A. The same cup of boiled greens yields nearly 4,000 I.U. of vitamin A, which is 80 percent of the adult Recommended Nutrient Intake (RNI).

As a member of the cruciferous family, which includes CABBAGE, BROCCOLI, and RADISHES, turnips contain sulfurous compounds that may protect against certain forms of cancer. However, like other cruciferous vegetables, turnips can cause bloating and gas.

Turnips contain two goitrogenic substances, progoitrin and gluconasturtin, which can interfere with the thyroid gland's ability to make its hormones. Although moderate consumption of goitrogens is not a hazard for healthy people, they can promote development of a goiter (an enlarged thyroid) in persons with THYROID disease.

Most people serve turnips fresh or boiled, but they can also be baked, braised, steamed, or stir-fried. Their versatility and sweet, peppery flavor make turnips a tasty addition to salads, stews, soups, or vegetable dishes.

Some herbal practitioners recommend turnips, either fresh, as a juice, syrup, or even as a pack placed over the chest, to treat bronchitis and sore throats. These benefits, however, have not been proven.

ULCERS

EAT PLENTY OF
- *Lean meat, poultry, fortified breads and cereals, seafood, legumes, and dried fruits for iron lost through bleeding.*
- *Citrus fruits—if they don't cause symptoms—to promote iron absorption.*

CUT DOWN ON
- *Coffee, including decaffeinated, and other sources of caffeine.*
- *Alcohol.*

AVOID
- *Smoking.*
- *Fatty foods.*
- *Late-night snacks.*

All sores that erode mucous membranes or the skin and penetrate the underlying muscle are referred to as ulcers. Those that occur in the lower part of the esophagus, the stomach, or the duodenum are known more specifically as "peptic ulcers," because they form in areas exposed to stomach acids and the digestive enzyme, pepsin. When the erosion occurs in the duodenum, the upper part of the small intestine, the term duodenal ulcer is used to describe the lesion; an ulcer in the stomach is called a gastric ulcer.

A person with an ulcer may describe the pain as gnawing or burning and can often pinpoint the exact spot. The pain usually occurs 2 to 3 hours after eating, is worse when the stomach is empty, and can be relieved by eating a small amount of food or taking an antacid.

Some people never have ulcer pain; however, they may develop intestinal bleeding, heartburn, bloating, and gas, possibly together with nausea and vomiting.

CAUSES OF ULCERS

The antacid industry is based on the notion that oversecretion of stomach acid causes ulcers as well as INDIGESTION AND HEARTBURN. The cause is more likely to be a weakness in the tissue, which allows acid to wash over layers where it does not belong.

Doctors have recently found that most ulcers develop when a common bacterium, called *Helicobacter pylori,* infects the intestinal tract. Smoking, emotional stress, and heavy drinking can also contribute to a person's risk of ulcers, and some people may have a hereditary predisposition. Ulcers frequently occur in people subjected to extreme physical stress, such as serious burns or surgery.

The other major cause of ulcers is the heavy use of drugs like aspirin, ibuprofen, naproxen, and other nonsteroidal anti-inflammatory drugs (NSAIDs), which erode the mucous membranes. Aspirin's effects are particularly serious, because it also inhibits blood clotting and promotes bleeding.

MEDICAL TREATMENT

Better understanding of the causes of ulcers has enabled doctors to devise new treatments. If tests confirm the presence of *H. pylori,* "triple therapy" is initiated. This includes an antibiotic to eradicate the bacteria, bismuth subsalicylate (Pepto-Bismol) to protect the intestinal lining, and an acid secretion inhibitor to prevent secretion of acids by the cells of the stomach. The bacteria are usually eradicated in a couple of weeks.

Smoking is one factor closely linked to poor healing and ulcer recurrence. Cigarette smokers often continue to suffer from ulcers until they quit.

People with ulcers caused by NSAID use must discontinue the offending drug. Individuals who need ongoing pain relief for other conditions, such as arthritis, should ask their doctor to prescribe a safer alternative.

Mindful that "it's not what you're eating, it's what's eating you," people with ulcers may benefit from relaxation techniques and biofeedback to cope with stress. Regular exercise promotes the release of endorphins, brain chemicals that dull pain and elevate mood.

RISKY HOME REMEDIES

Many people self-treat pain due to ulcers, heartburn, and indigestion with over-the-counter drugs or with home remedies concocted from baking soda (sodium bicarbonate) to neutralize stomach acid. This approach is risky.

Long-term use of antacids containing aluminum hydroxide can prevent the body from absorbing phosphorus and result in the loss of bone minerals. Prolonged ingestion of baking soda or antacids containing calcium carbonate may lead to a buildup of calcium and alkali, resulting in nausea, headache, and weakness, with a risk of kidney damage. Check with a doctor before using acid-suppressant drugs, as they can interfere with proper digestion.

DIET AND ULCERS

A bland diet was once the mainstay of treatment, but it is no longer necessary, although it may still be prescribed for some patients. People with ulcers need a balanced, varied diet to promote healing. There is no proof that high-fiber foods irritate ulcers, and spices—except for black pepper and chili powder—do not cause pain or slow healing.

People with ulcers should avoid certain foods and seasonings that cause pain. Triggers vary for individuals, but common offenders are coffee (including decaffeinated), CAFFEINE in beverages and CHOCOLATE, ALCOHOL, peppermint, and TOMATOES and tomato-based products. Fatty foods can slow down stomach emptying and stimulate acid release. Milk and dairy products temporarily relieve pain but can cause a rebound increase in acid secretion.

Bleeding from untreated ulcers can lead to iron-deficiency ANEMIA. People with ulcers should eat plenty of lean meat, poultry, seafood, fortified breads and cereals, and dried beans and other legumes. Dried fruits, especially apricots, are also rich in iron. Unless they cause pain, citrus fruits and other good sources of vitamin C should be included to promote iron absorption.

Patients with complicated chronic ulcers may need surgical treatment that can have permanent effects on digestion and the absorption of nutrients. They should consult a dietitian for nutritional advice after surgery.

EATING PATTERNS

When and how people eat may be more important than what they eat. Doctors no longer recommend frequent small meals, which can provoke rebound symptoms. Rather, they suggest several moderate-size meals spaced at regular intervals. Late-evening snacks should be avoided, because they stimulate acid secretion during sleep.

UNDERWEIGHT

EAT PLENTY OF
- *Larger portions and high-calorie choices from the Food Guide Rainbow.*
- *Nutritious between-meal snacks.*

CUT DOWN ON
- *Alcohol and caffeine, which can suppress the appetite.*

AVOID
- *Smoking.*
- *Sugary snacks that quench the appetite for nutritious meals.*
- *Eating on the run.*

In a society that prizes leanness and spends millions on weight-loss products, people find it hard to accept that excessive thinness (unrelated to ANOREXIA NERVOSA) is unhealthy. But while OBESITY is dangerous, surveys show that people who are of average weight at age 50 live longer than those who are markedly underweight.

There's no such thing as a perfect weight; however, for every height and build there is a desirable range in which the rates of disease and death are lowest. Underweight is defined as 15 percent or more under the low end of the range (your doctor can advise you what your range should be). Mild underweight is not associated with serious health hazards, but people who are very thin lack energy reserves, are vulnerable to infections, and often feel the cold because they lack insulating fat. Patients weighing less than 80 percent of their desirable weight on admission to a hospital are at high risk for complications. Severely underweight people who are confined to bed rest easily develop pressure sores over bony areas.

Thinness also is a problem if it's a result of poor nutrition, such as chronic dieting, which can lead to infertility in some women. For those who conceive, being underweight during PREGNANCY may cause anemia, heart and lung complications, and a high risk of toxemia. Their babies are often premature, have a low birth weight, and may experience slow growth and development.

Adolescents with erratic schedules are frequently prone to slip below their ideal weight—especially if they exercise a lot—unless they take time out to eat. Overly thin teenagers and adults alike sometimes feel too busy to eat.

A CORRECTIVE DIET

Gaining a pound a week can require 500 to 750 extra calories a day. For some, dietary adjustments can be as taxing as a weight-loss regimen. The aim should be to build up muscle tissue and increase the level of energy to sustain the weight gain. Unless extremely weak, underweight people should exercise regularly to help build lean tissue as well as store some fat.

A plan for increasing weight focuses, first, on increasing food intake and, second, on consuming foods that provide lots of calories in a compact volume. Raw vegetables, for example, are nutritious but satisfy hunger long before they've provided significant calories. And although a low-fat diet is important, an underweight person may need to relax the rules about fat consumption until the desired weight goal has been reached. Increasing dietary fat can rapidly make a difference, because fat contains more than twice as many calories (9 per gram) as protein and carbohydrates do (4 per gram).

Nutrition experts advise adhering to the Food Guide Rainbow (see p.39), but increasing portions and choosing the highest-calorie foods within each group: peanut butter or cheese instead of lean meat, avocados instead of cucumbers, pancakes instead of toast, a milk shake instead of skim milk. They recommend dressing cooked vegetables with melted butter, adding cream and sugar to coffee, using creamy dressings on salads, and sour cream on baked potatoes. Because CAFFEINE suppresses the urge to eat, replace tea or coffee with juices and caffeine-free sodas.

People who have lost weight due to illness may benefit from a concentrated liquid formula, which is easy to swallow. Doctors and dietitians can recommend liquid supplements.

Many underweight people feel uncomfortably full when they begin eating larger, more frequent portions to gain weight. This feeling eventually passes. People trying to gain weight, like those trying to lose it, occasionally reach a plateau. Increasing calorie intake is necessary to restart the process.

URINARY TRACT INFECTIONS

CONSUME PLENTY OF

- *Nonalcoholic and caffeine-free fluids to flush out the urinary system.*
- *Cranberry juice and blueberries to acidify the urine.*
- *Citrus fruits and fresh fruits and vegetables for vitamin C.*
- *High-calcium foods and low-fat dairy products to reduce bladder irritability.*

AVOID

- *Bladder irritants, such as coffee, tea, and alcoholic beverages.*

Also known as cystitis, most urinary tract infections (UTIs) affect the bladder, but some may involve the kidneys, the ureters (the tubes that carry urine to the bladder), and the urethra (the tube through which urine exits the body). The most common symptom is an urgent need to urinate, even when the bladder is not full. Urination may

PREVENTIVE TACTICS

Hygiene measures can help women avoid recurrent UTIs; many doctors recommend the following.

- Wear loose-fitting white cotton underwear and panty hose that have cotton crotches.

- Avoid douching and using vaginal deodorants, which can cause bladder irritation.

- If you use a diaphragm, ask your doctor to check the size; one that is even slightly too large can irritate the urethra and bladder.

- Urinate and drink a glass of water before sexual intercourse and urinate within an hour afterward to flush out the urinary tract.

- After a bowel movement, wipe from the front to the back to reduce the risk of carrying intestinal bacteria to the urethra.

be accompanied by pain or burning and, in severe cases, small amounts of blood. There may also be a low-grade fever and an ache in the lower back.

Most urinary infections are caused by *E. coli* bacteria, organisms that live in the intestinal tract but that can travel to the bladder. Chlamydia, a sexually transmitted organism, is another cause of UTIs. Women are more vulnerable to urinary infections because the female urethra is shorter than that of males, and its location provides a convenient entryway for bacteria. Many women develop so-called honeymoon cystitis, inflammation caused by sexual activity or an oversize diaphragm.

ROLE OF DIET

Antibiotics are needed to cure bacterial urinary infections, but dietary approaches can speed healing and help prevent recurrences. Doctors advise drinking at least eight glasses a day of fluids to increase the flow of urine and to flush out infectious material. Avoid coffee, tea, colas, and alcoholic drinks, however; these increase bladder irritation. Naturopaths recommend drinking bearberry or celery seed herbal teas, which may be natural diuretics with anti-inflammatory properties.

CRANBERRY juice is a favorite home remedy, and one that is supported by research. Cranberries (and BLUEBERRIES) contain a substance that speeds the elimination of bacteria by preventing them from sticking to the bladder wall. Most commercial cranberry juice is too diluted and overly sweetened, however, to be of much help. Health-food stores sell pure unsweetened cranberry juice, which can be made less tart by mixing it with apple juice. You can also use a juicer to create your own cranberry-apple juice.

Vitamin C helps strengthen the immune system, fight infection, and acidify the urine. And calcium may help reduce bladder irritability.

Case Study

After suffering three bouts of cystitis in less than a year, Jennifer, a 29-year-old loan officer, was referred to a specialist. Various tests failed to find any urinary tract abnormalities, but the urologist discovered a number of lifestyle factors that can contribute to recurrent bladder infections. Jennifer had been fitted with a diaphragm that was too large; she also used superabsorbent tampons as well as a vaginal deodorant.

For starters, the urologist suggested another method of birth control. He also recommended using pads instead of tampons and forgoing the deodorant, explaining that a daily shower was all she really needed. Finally, he suggested drinking 6 ounces of natural cranberry juice sweetened with an equal part of apple juice every morning and evening. Six months after making these changes, Jennifer was happy to report that she had not experienced any further symptoms of cystitis.

VAGINITIS

EAT PLENTY OF
- *Dairy products, eggs, green and yellow vegetables, yellow and orange fruits, and fish for vitamins A and D.*
- *Fortified grains and cereals, poultry and seafood, bananas, dark green leafy vegetables, nuts, and seeds for B vitamins.*
- *Shellfish, beans, and legumes for magnesium and zinc.*

CUT DOWN ON
- *Foods high in refined sugar.*

AVOID
- *Fad diets for yeast hypersensitivity.*
- *Tight-fitting clothing.*
- *Irritating soaps and hygiene products.*

If the acid-alkaline balance of the vagina is upset, yeasts and other microorganisms that are normally held in check by beneficial bacteria may proliferate. The result is vaginitis, a condition marked by itching, irritation, and inflammation. The usual causes are various species of yeast, most commonly *Candida albicans,* the protozoal organism *Trichomonas vaginalis,* and the bacterium *Gardnerella vaginalis,* which grows in oxygen-free conditions. Yeast infections can be identified by a cheesy discharge (unlike bacterial and protozoal infections, which are usually signaled by characteristic odors). In addition to itching and burning, symptoms may include an abnormal discharge, chafing, painful intercourse, and perhaps an urge to urinate more frequently than usual. However, some infections, such as chlamydiosis or trichomoniasis, may be present for years without symptoms.

Among the various conditions that may lead to vaginitis are lowered resistance due to fatigue, poor diet, or an infection elsewhere. Douching can upset the acid-alkaline balance, as can oral contraceptives. Hormonal changes that are brought about by PREGNANCY, DIABETES, or MENOPAUSE also increase vulnerability to vaginitis.

High blood sugar levels promote the growth of yeasts and other organisms, which is why diabetic women often develop vaginitis. Undiagnosed diabetes should be considered if a woman suffers unexplained bouts of vaginitis.

Women are particularly vulnerable to vaginitis when taking antibiotics for infections in other parts of the body. Certain antibiotics have side effects, including diarrhea and the overgrowth of natural yeasts, which can spread infecting organisms to the vagina. In menopausal women, low estrogen levels cause the vaginal walls to become thin, dry, and susceptible to abrasions that allow germs to enter.

DRUG TREATMENT

Doctors typically prescribe antifungal creams or pills to treat yeast infections; bacterial infections can usually be eradicated with antibiotics. While sexual partners often require treatment to prevent reinfection with bacteria or trichomonas, yeast infections may recur. Women taking certain antifungal pills should avoid alcohol; an interaction can cause a sudden rise in blood pressure.

Some topical antifungal medications are now available without a prescription. If you know the symptoms of yeast infection and your doctor agrees, you can try self-treatment. Follow the directions exactly; if you stop using the medication too soon, symptoms may recur and the yeast could become resistant to treatment. See a doctor if over-the-counter medication doesn't relieve symptoms within a day or two.

Menopausal women often find that vaginitis clears up after they begin estrogen replacement therapy. Using a vaginal lubricant during sexual intercourse protects tissues from abrasion and reduces the risk of infection.

HYGIENIC MEASURES

Changing the form of contraception may reduce the risk of vaginitis. Oral contraceptives change the vagina's acid-alkaline balance, which can foster the growth of yeasts and bacteria.

Women should avoid tight-fitting clothing that allows heat and moisture to build up in the vaginal area, encouraging yeast and bacterial growth. They should wear white cotton underwear and panty hose with cotton crotches. After vigorous exercise or swimming, they should change into dry clothing.

Feminine hygiene sprays and douches can irritate the vaginal mucous membranes. Some women douche with vinegar, but most doctors advise against this, because vinegar can harbor organisms that colonize the vaginal tissues.

HEALTHY FOODS

Although a link between diet and vaginal infections has not been proved, many doctors advise patients with recurrent infections to cut down on sugary foods. Many women claim that eating a daily portion of YOGURT with active cultures prevents vaginitis, and recent studies seem to support this.

It's also claimed that allicin, an antibiotic in GARLIC, helps to stop yeast infections by blocking growth of the organisms. The protective effect may be obtained by eating raw garlic or taking garlic pills, however there is no way of knowing how much allicin garlic pills actually contain.

CRANBERRY juice protects against URINARY TRACT INFECTIONS; drinking it may prevent bacterial vaginitis from spreading to the bladder.

Research has linked low levels of vitamin A, the B vitamins, magnesium, and zinc with recurrent vaginal infections. Vitamin A, in particular, is necessary to keep mucous membranes and skin healthy and resistant to infections. Green and deep yellow vegetables and deep yellow and orange fruits are high in vitamin A. The omega-3 fatty acids in fish oils may reduce inflammation due to vaginitis; two or three servings of fish a week provide ample omega-3 fatty acids. Fortified grains and cereals, poultry and seafood, dark green leafy vegetables, potatoes, bananas, nuts, and seeds all provide the B vitamins. Good levels of magnesium and zinc can be obtained from frequent helpings of shellfish, beans, and legumes.

FAD YEAST-FREE DIETS

Several books have promoted strict yeast-free diets as a cure for yeast infections. There is no evidence that these fad diets are of any value. On the contrary, candida lives in the mouth, skin, and intestines of most healthy people, and eliminating these organisms with diet or drugs can be harmful.

HELPFUL FOODS

Deep green and yellow vegetables for vitamin A to maintain healthy mucous membranes that are resistant to infection. Have at least one serving daily.

Peas, beans, and lentils provide magnesium and zinc. Include a serving of legumes in your daily allotment of starchy foods.

Yogurt and garlic are thought to protect against yeast infections. Eat low-fat yogurt daily; use garlic as a food flavoring or take in an odorless pill form daily.

VEGETABLES

BENEFITS

- *Many are rich in vitamins A, C, and E, folate and other B vitamins, and potassium and other minerals.*
- *High fiber content promotes regular bowel function.*
- *Rich in bioflavonoids and other chemical compounds that help prevent disease.*

DRAWBACKS

- *Eating large amounts may satisfy hunger without meeting energy needs.*
- *Goitrogens in cruciferous vegetables may interfere with thyroid function.*
- *Some are fairly common allergens.*

Because plants are capable of synthesizing energy from sunlight and air and combining it with minerals from the soil, they are the source of the nutrients essential to animal life.

Many of the plant foods that we call vegetables are, botanically speaking, fruits—these include green BEANS, CUCUMBERS, EGGPLANTS, TOMATOES, and even CORN kernels.

Root vegetables, such as BEETS, CARROTS, PARSNIPS, and TURNIPS, are food storage organs and valuable sources of CARBOHYDRATES. Stems, such as CELERY and FENNEL, conduct nutrients between roots and leaves, and in some plants, such as POTATOES and water CHESTNUTS, underground stems have evolved into storehouses for starch. Vegetables with dark green leaves, including members of the cabbage family (such as BROCCOLI, CAULIFLOWER, collard greens, KALE, and mustard greens) and SPINACH, are rich in ANTIOXIDANTS, BIOFLAVONOIDS, and the B vitamins, whether or not you eat the leaves. The leaves of all vegetables are factories for the production of high-energy sugars through photosynthesis. They are the most fragile parts of the plant, which is the reason they shrink more than other parts when cooked.

The leaves of plants in the ONION family have grown into fleshy bulbs that store carbohydrates and water to nourish the plant during its next year of growth. The flowers of some plants are also eaten; broccoli stems are eaten with their unopened flower buds and the flowers of ZUCCHINI are a delicacy.

HOW MUCH? OR HOW MANY?

The Food Guide Rainbow (see p.39) recommends 5 to 10 servings of fruits and vegetables daily. A serving is a half cup of raw or cooked vegetables, a cup of leafy salad vegetables, or a half cup of juice. Nutritionists recommend choosing from the cabbage family several times a week. In addition to antioxidants and bioflavonoids, these plants are teeming with the disease-fighting compounds known as phytochemicals and are rich in vitamins and minerals.

NUTRITIONAL VALUE

Green vegetables get their bright color from chlorophyll, the pigment that traps the energy from sunlight and makes it available for the production of sugars from water and carbon dioxide. Although chlorophyll is soluble only in fats, cooking vegetables in water liberates the enzyme chlorophyllase, which breaks chlorophyll down into water-soluble components. This has no nutritional consequence, but the green color of the vegetable is diminished. Some vitamins are also water-soluble, and are leached out into the cooking water.

Color is a useful guide to the vitamin content of vegetables. Plants produce vitamin C from sugars formed by photosynthesis in their leaves. The larger and darker the leaves are, the more vitamin C and beta carotene they contain; the pale inner leaves of lettuce and cabbage, for instance, have only about 3 percent of the carotene found in the dark outer leaves. Unfortunately, outer leaves are often discarded because they

are damaged or have been exposed to POLLUTANTS AND PESTICIDES.

Deep yellow, orange, or dark green vegetables derive their color from carotenoid pigments; these include beta carotene, an antioxidant that is converted to vitamin A in the intestinal wall. Because these pigments are stable in cooking and soluble in fat, the nutritional content is well preserved during baking or boiling.

Soluble and insoluble FIBER in vegetables keeps bowel function regular and thereby reduces the colon's exposure to potentially toxic by-products of digestion. In some people, however, fiber can cause gas and bloating.

ANTICANCER FOODS

Cancer develops when mutant cells escape the body's protective immune system, allowing the growth of tumors made up of abnormal cells. Plants are also susceptible to cancer and have developed their own protective mechanisms. Vitamins A, C, and E are natural antioxidants that hinder cancer-causing cell damage by scavenging and inactivating free radicals, the unstable molecules that are released when the body uses oxygen. Some phytochemicals block the growth of blood vessels that feed tumors, others inactivate the enzyme systems that allow cancer cells to spread, and still others suppress the hormones that promote cancer growth. Studies have found that people who eat ample raw vegetables and FRUITS enjoy a reduced incidence of many cancers. By contrast, researchers have found that people who eat few vegetables are more prone to develop colon cancer.

Vegetables have a protective effect that is lacking in vitamin pills. Whole

VEGETABLES GALORE. *Packed with vitamins, minerals, and phytochemicals that maintain health and help prevent cancer and other diseases, vegetables are the nutrition stars of the 1990s.*

plants contain a balance of vitamins, minerals, fiber, phytochemicals, and as-yet-unidentified compounds. It is this blend that's important in blocking the effects of cancer-causing compounds.

PRESERVING NUTRIENTS

While vegetables provide starches, sugars, and proteins, their main contributions are vitamins, minerals, and fiber. Their nutrient content, color, and texture are affected by the method of preparation, the length of cooking time, and the volume of water used.

The yellow carotene pigments are not water soluble and are well preserved in cooking, but vitamin C and the B vitamins leach into the cooking liquid. Vitamin C is also quickly destroyed on exposure to oxygen. In addition, up to 20 percent of the vitamin C in a vegetable may be lost during each minute that it takes the water to heat from cold to boiling. This is because an enzyme that destroys vitamin C becomes more active as temperature rises; however, it stops its destructive action at the boiling point. For this reason, vegetables should be added to water that is already boiling. Steaming or cooking in a small amount of water retains more than twice the vitamin C that boiling does.

The yellow and orange carotenoid pigments are changed only by the high temperatures reached with pressure cooking. The brilliant green of chlorophyll in plant tissues is dulled, however, when heat causes chemical changes. The old-fashioned practice of adding a pinch of baking soda is not recommended—it produces a bright green color that breaks down the plant tissues, making the texture mushy and destroying many of the vitamins.

Color can be preserved by cutting vegetables into small, uniform pieces and cooking them rapidly; leafy vegetables needn't be cut. Using a large volume of water protects color, as it dilutes the color-destroying enzymes that

seep out of the plant tissues, but it may leach out vitamins. Some cooks blanch such vegetables as beans and broccoli in boiling water for a minute or two, then plunge them into cold water to hold the color. This is satisfactory for vegetables that are served cold, but if they are served hot, they require rapid reheating, with further loss of nutrients.

STORAGE

Because harvested vegetables lose flavor, sweetness, and texture as they use their own food stores, the least amount of time stored, the better. Corn and peas can lose up to 40 percent of their sugar if kept at room temperature for just 6 hours after picking. Beans and stem vegetables, such as broccoli and ASPARAGUS, become tough.

Vegetables that originated in warm climates (such as beans, eggplants, PEPPERS, OKRA, SQUASH, and tomatoes) keep best at 50°F (10°C). Potatoes convert their starch to sugar below 40°F (4°C); keep them cool and out of the light to prevent the development of poisonous alkaloids. Most other vegetables keep best at 32°F (0°C). The salts and sugars in their sap prevent them from freezing until several degrees colder.

POSSIBLE HAZARDS

Most vegetables are safe to eat either raw or cooked. The exceptions are lima and kidney beans and other LEGUMES, which contain toxic substances that are inactivated through cooking. Broccoli, kale, and other cruciferous vegetables harbor goitrogenic compounds that can interfere with iodine metabolism. Cooking inactivates these compounds, but eating large amounts of these vegetables raw may worsen a pre-existing thyroid condition.

Most vegetables do not provoke ALLERGIES, but some people react to members of the nightshade family which includes eggplants and tomatoes. Corn is another common allergen.

VEGETARIAN DIETS: HEALTHY, ECONOMICAL, HUMANE

A balanced vegetarian diet provides essential nutrients while keeping weight down naturally. Also, vegetarians have few ills linked to fat consumption.

Until the most recent times, grains were the staple diet, while meat was a luxury reserved for the wealthy few. Today, in our affluent society with its huge surpluses of plant foods, we use grain to fatten stock animals. Critics contend that this is a wasteful use of resources, because it takes less grain to feed a person directly than it takes to fatten animals to feed that person.

On the whole, Canadians obtain about twice as much protein as is needed, and experts in medicine and nutrition warn that we are paying for our high consumption of meat and animal products with record rates of heart disease, stroke, certain cancers, and other disorders. A recent report by the Physicians Committee for Responsible Medicine, a group that advocates vegetarianism, claimed that Americans spend some $50 billion a year to treat illnesses related to a high-meat diet. However, many health experts have loudly criticized the report's findings as an overstatement.

Vegetarianism today has many adherents among people concerned with ecological issues, such as environmental pollution and population growth, as well as those who have age-old religious and philosophical concerns.

HEALTH BENEFITS

Although there is no scientific proof that vegetarians necessarily live longer than meat eaters, as a group they clear-

---

BENEFITS

- *Vegetarians are less likely to be obese or have heart disease; they also have lower blood pressure and fewer intestinal problems than meat eaters.*
- *A vegetarian diet is an economical use of the earth's resources.*

DRAWBACKS

- *Strict vegetarian diets may lack some vital nutrients.*
- *Diets restricted to plants may not be adequate for children.*

---

ly enjoy certain health advantages. For example, OBESITY is rare among vegetarians, probably because their diet is bulky and filling, high in fiber, low in fat, and relatively low in calories. They also tend to have lower blood cholesterol levels than meat eaters. Studies show that a cholesterol-free plant-based diet that is also low in saturated fats can reduce the risk of ATHEROSCLEROSIS, HEART DISEASE, and STROKE.

Vegetarians have lower BLOOD PRESSURE than meat eaters do and are less likely to develop hypertension, possibly because they have lower body weight and their diet is high in potassium. Intestinal disorders, such as CONSTIPATION and diverticulosis, are rare among people who consume a high-fiber plant-based diet.

Several other disorders—including OSTEOPOROSIS, kidney stones, GALL-

STONES, and adult-onset DIABETES—afflict vegetarians less often, although heredity, exercise, and environment are contributing factors as well.

ENSURING BALANCE

The nutritional needs of vegetarians are the same as those of omnivores and can just as easily be met by following the Food Guide Rainbow (see p.39). Adjustments must be made in a few areas, however, to make up for the lack of animal sources of several nutrients, namely protein, calcium, zinc, iron, vitamins D and B_{12}, and riboflavin.

Vegetarians must combine GRAINS, seeds, and LEGUMES to obtain PROTEINS with all the essential amino acids. Adults can achieve their amino acid balance by eating different plant proteins at separate meals in the course of a day, but children should be given both types of protein at the same meal. The Recommended Nutrient Intake (RNI) for protein is based on a diet including foods of both animal and vegetable origin. The daily needs for strict vegetarians are increased by 25 percent. For example, a 150-pound vegan should eat 68g of plant protein to match the 54g from mixed sources needed by an omnivore or ovolactovegetarian (a vegetarian who includes dairy products and eggs in his diet). Soy products are useful, because soy is the only plant source of complete protein.

Lactovegetarians (vegetarians who supplement plant foods only with

COMPLEMENTARY PROTEINS

Combining plant foods to make a complete protein can be as simple as eating a legume (peanut butter) with a grain (whole-wheat bread). Alternatively, nuts and seeds can be combined with dairy products or grains. Examples of complete-protein combinations are:

- Rice and beans.
- Bean-vegetable chili served with tortillas.

- Baked beans and corn bread.
- Hummus (made with chickpeas and sesame seeds).
- Cheese rolled in chopped nuts.
- Breadsticks with sesame seeds.
- Multigrain bread made with sunflower seeds.
- Macaroni and cheese.
- Split-pea soup sprinkled with cheese and served with a whole-wheat roll.

dairy products), ovolactovegetarians, and pescatarians (they include fish, dairy products, and eggs in their diet) can easily obtain most of the essential minerals from their diet. Tofu, dark green vegetables, seeds, nuts, fortified cereals, and whole grains are rich sources of calcium, zinc, and riboflavin and other B vitamins. Dairy products, egg yolks, and fish supply vitamin B$_{12}$.

A vegetarian diet may not provide enough iron, because people absorb only a fourth as much nonheme iron, which comes from plants, as the heme iron in meat, fish, and poultry. Every vegetarian meal should

include foods high in vitamin C to promote iron absorption. In addition to citrus fruits, good sources include potatoes, cruciferous vegetables, peppers, melons, and strawberries.

Vitamin D is needed for calcium absorption; good dietary sources are egg yolks, fortified milk, and fatty fish. Exposure to sunlight enables the body to manufacture vitamin D.

It is more difficult for vegans and fruitarians (who eat only raw and dried fruits, nuts, honey, olive oil, and, perhaps, grains and legumes) to consume enough calories for energy and to achieve nutritional balance

without supplements. Large helpings of nut butters, dried fruits, and breads can help maintain weight. Calcium-fortified soy milk or orange juice can help ensure adequate intake of this mineral. Nutritionists recommend iron and vitamin B$_{12}$ supplements.

CHILDREN'S NEEDS

Strict vegetarians should plan for PREGNANCY and nursing by modifying their diets and taking supplements as advised by their obstetricians.

Parents should consult a dietitian for advice about a child's nutrition. While a balanced ovolactovegetarian diet can easily meet the demands of infancy, as well as CHILDHOOD AND ADOLESCENT NUTRITION, strict vegetarian diets are not recommended for babies and young children. Restricted vegan diets can hamper growth and development; undernourished children risk lifelong ill-health from rickets, iron-deficiency anemia, and other disorders. Vegan parents should plan meals with the advice of a registered dietitian who has special understanding of the child's needs. A pediatrician should monitor the child's growth.

VEGAN VARIETY. *Balance can be achieved by eating ample legumes, nuts, seeds, grains, fruits, and vegetables and by substituting soy milk for dairy products.*

VERTIGO

EAT PLENTY OF
- *Low-fat high-fiber foods to prevent atherosclerosis.*

CUT DOWN ON
- *Salty and fatty foods.*

AVOID
- *Alcohol.*

Although many people use the terms *vertigo* and *dizziness* interchangeably, there are important differences between the two. Vertigo is characterized by an unpleasant illusion that you or your surroundings are spinning out of control, and it is often accompanied by severe nausea. In contrast, dizziness is less severe: light-headedness and an unsteady gait are the major features.

Vertigo usually stems from an imbalance of fluid in the inner ear, which affects one's sense of balance. It is a common complication of Ménière's disease, and it also occurs in older people with ATHEROSCLEROSIS.

Dizziness can originate in the ears too, but a more likely cause is hypotension, a temporary fall in the pressure of blood flowing to the brain. Other conditions that can cause dizziness include ANEMIA, fatigue, FEVER, HEART DISEASE, HYPOGLYCEMIA, various infections, STRESS, and motion sickness. Overindulgence in ALCOHOL can also produce dizziness.

ROLE OF DIET

People who suffer frequent attacks of vertigo are often advised to reduce their salt intake to help prevent a buildup of body fluids. A doctor may also prescribe a diuretic to reduce the body's fluid volume. To maintain good circulation and to prevent atherosclerosis, the diet should emphasize high-fiber, low-fat foods—fruits, vegetables, and legumes, grains, and other starches.

Other dietary approaches depend upon the underlying cause of the vertigo or dizziness. Those who experience attacks of dizziness when they are overly hungry may find that eating frequent small meals alleviates the problem. Although a low-salt diet may be indicated for vertigo, this is not the case for dizziness stemming from hypotension; some people actually need extra salt to maintain normal blood pressure. Attacks of dizziness can also be minimized simply by avoiding any abrupt movements of the head and by slowly assuming an upright position.

VINEGAR

BENEFITS
- *Basis for a low-calorie salad dressing.*
- *Can be used to preserve other foods.*

DRAWBACKS
- *May trigger an allergic reaction in people sensitive to molds.*

For centuries, vinegar was a by-product of wine and beer making; in fact, the name comes from the French word *vinaigre,* which means sour wine. Apple cider and wine remain the most popular basic ingredients, but almost any product that produces alcoholic fermentation can be used to make vinegar, as evidenced by the dozens of varieties available today. Although vinegar probably lacks the healing power accorded to it by naturopaths, it provides a low-sodium, low-calorie flavoring.

THE PRICEY BALSAMICS

Rich, dark, and mild-flavored balsamic vinegar, which is produced from a type of red wine, originated in Modena, Italy. The most prized—and expensive—varieties are aged 15 to 50 years.

All vinegars are 4 to 14 percent acetic acid. They are made in two stages. First, yeasts or other molds are added to turn the natural sugars in the basic ingredient into alcohol. Then, bacteria are introduced to convert the alcohol into acetic acid.

VARIETIES OF VINEGAR

Plain white (clear) distilled vinegar is the type used for making pickles and other condiments. It can be transformed into a flavored or gourmet vinegar simply by adding various herbs, spices, or fruits—for example, dill, tarragon, lemon balm, mint, GARLIC, green peppercorns, CHILIES, citrus, or RASPBERRIES. These and many other varieties are widely available, or you can make your own by adding fresh herbs or fruit to distilled, cider, or wine vinegars. Cover tightly and store in a dark cupboard. The acetic acid keeps the herbs or fruits from spoiling.

HEALTH BENEFITS

Herbalists and naturopaths often recommend various vinegars to treat arthritis, indigestion, and other ailments. Such claims have never been proved scientifically, but some arthritis sufferers insist that a tonic of cider vinegar and honey alleviates joint pain.

Vinegar is virtually devoid of calories, so it's an ideal alternative to fatty salad dressings. To reduce its acid bite, the vinegar can be mixed with orange juice or fruit syrup and a little oil.

A note of caution: People who are allergic to molds may react to vinegar as well as to foods preserved with it. Symptoms include a tingling or itching sensation around the mouth, and possibly hives.

SHARP FLAVORS. *As a preserving liquid, vinegar has no equal—once sealed, it can last indefinitely. Enliven salads with (from left to right) balsamic, tarragon, citrus, wine, and sherry vinegars.*

VITAMINS

*Although the body can manufacture some vitamins,
most of them must come from the diet. A deficiency of any
of 13 essential vitamins can result in serious disease.*

For more than 2,000 years folk healers and physicians have known that eating certain foods prevents or cures diseases. In 400 BC, for example, Hippocrates found that eating liver cured night blindness. In 1747 James Lind, a British naval surgeon, advocated eating lemons and limes to prevent or cure scurvy, a disease rampant among sailors who subsisted on biscuits and salt pork on long voyages.

In 1912 Dr. Casimir Funk, a Polish biochemist, put forth the theory that foods contained essential chemical substances, which we now know as vitamins (see What's in a Name?, facing page). In 1913 vitamin A became the first vitamin to be identified by two separate American research teams.

To date, 13 vitamins essential to maintain health and prevent deficiency diseases have been discovered. Other vitaminlike substances—BIO-FLAVONOIDS, choline, carnitine, and taurine, among others—have also been identified. Some appear to be essential to health, but Recommended Nutrient Intakes (RNIs) for them have not been established. Researchers believe there are probably many more unknown vitamins, which is why they recommend eating a wide variety of foods to gain complete nutrition.

Only very small amounts—typically a few milligrams or even fractions of milligrams—of vitamins are needed to maintain good health. The Nutrition Research Division of Health

---

BENEFITS
- *Cure or prevent deficiency diseases, such as scurvy and rickets.*
- *Essential for energy conversion and many other metabolic processes.*
- *Antioxidant properties may help prevent cancer, heart disease, and other disorders.*

DRAWBACKS
- *High doses of some can be toxic.*

Canada has established RNIs for nine vitamins. The RNI is the amount needed to prevent deficiency diseases; however, it is not necessarily the optimum amount in terms of health. In general, eating a variety of foods in keeping with the Food Guide Rainbow (see p.39) will meet all the RNIs.

CLASSIFICATION

Vitamins are classified according to how they are absorbed and stored in the body. Vitamins A, D, E, and K are soluble only in fats, whereas vitamin C and the B vitamins are soluble in water. The body can store fat-soluble vitamins in the liver and fatty tissue. Since most excess water-soluble vitamins are excreted in the urine, they need to be consumed more often.

Provitamins are substances that the body can convert into vitamins; examples include beta carotene, a precursor of vitamin A, and a type of steroid in the skin that, after exposure

to the sun's ultraviolet rays, is used by the body to make vitamin D.

Antivitamins, or vitamin antagonists, are compounds in foods that can interfere with the action of real vitamins, to which they are chemically related. Though the body may recognize these substances as true vitamins and incorporate them into tissue, they are unable to carry out any functions.

FAT-SOLUBLE VITAMINS

These vitamins require the presence of fat in order to be absorbed from the intestinal tract. Thus, a person who has a fat-malabsorption disorder can develop deficiency symptoms even though the diet supplies adequate amounts of a vitamin. On the other hand, toxic amounts may build up if a person takes high-dose supplements or consumes an extraordinary amount of certain foods (for example, the huge amounts of polar bear and seal livers consumed by early Arctic explorers resulted in vitamin A toxicity).

Vitamin A. There are several forms of this vitamin—the preformed, or active, ones are retinol, retinoic acid, and retinyl esters. Beta carotene is a precursor form. Vitamin A, as the name *retinol* implies, is essential to normal vision and to prevent night blindness. But it is also necessary for normal cell division and growth, the development of bones and teeth, and for the health of skin, mucous membranes, and the epithelial tissue that lines the intestines, airways, and other organs. Its ANTIOXIDANT properties help prevent the cancer-causing cell damage of free radicals, unstable molecules that are released when the body uses oxygen. The body also needs Vitamin A to

synthesize amino acids as well as thyroxine and other hormones.

Excessive vitamin A can cause toxicity, which can lead to death in extreme cases. A woman contemplating PREGNANCY should never take high-dose vitamin A supplements or isotretinoin (Accutane), a powerful acne drug derived from vitamin A. Because vitamin A is stored in the body, these should be stopped at least 3 months before attempting to conceive.

The amount of vitamin A may be listed in international units (I.U.) or retinal equivalents (R.E.). One R.E. is equal to 1mcg (microgram) of the retinol form of vitamin A, or 6mcg of beta carotene; 1 R.E. is equal to 3.5 I.U. from plant sources and about 10 I.U. of beta carotene.

Vitamin D. There are two forms of this vitamin: D_2, which comes from plants, and D_3, which the body synthesizes when the skin is exposed to ultraviolet (UV) rays from the sun.

The body must have vitamin D in order to absorb calcium. It also promotes absorption of phosphorus and

prevents the kidneys from excreting protein in the urine. Because of its role in mineral absorption, vitamin D promotes the growth of strong bones and teeth; deficiency causes rickets in children and OSTEOMALACIA in adults. Other deficiency symptoms include convulsions and muscle twitching.

Vitamin E. The tocopherols in vitamin E prevent the oxidation of vitamin A and fats, especially unsaturated fatty acids, in the intestinal tract and body tissues. They also help to maintain healthy red blood cells and muscle tissue, protect the lungs from pollutants, and regulate the synthesis of vitamin C and DNA. Recent studies indicate that when taken in high doses of 200 to 400mg a day, vitamin E may protect against heart attacks, stroke, and some aspects of aging. Unlike other fat-soluble vitamins, tocopherols do not accumulate to toxic levels in the body; instead, any excess is excreted in the stools.

Vitamin K. The liver requires vitamin K to manufacture blood proteins (Factors II, VII, IX, and X) that are es-

sential for blood clotting. Intestinal bacteria make half the needed vitamin K; the rest comes from the diet.

Deficiency is characterized by excessive bleeding from even minor cuts. Some newborn infants are especially vulnerable to vitamin K deficiency, because they lack the intestinal bacteria needed to make it.

WATER-SOLUBLE VITAMINS

As water-soluble vitamins, the B vitamins and vitamin C are more easily absorbed than the fat-soluble vitamins are, because there is always fluid in the intestines. At the same time, deficiencies may develop more quickly because the body stores water-soluble vitamins in only small amounts.

Biotin. Closely related to folate, pantothenic acid, and vitamin B_{12}, biotin is essential for the proper metabolism of carbohydrates, especially glucose, as well as proteins and fats. Some biotin is made by intestinal bacteria; it is also found in many foods. Deficiency occurs mostly in infants; in adults, it can be induced by eating lots of raw egg whites, which contain avidin, a substance that binds with biotin.

Folate. Also referred to as folic acid or folacin, this B vitamin is converted into enzymes that the body needs to

make DNA, RNA, and red blood cells, and to carry out other important metabolic functions. During pregnancy, folate helps prevent neurological defects, particularly a malformed spinal column, in the developing fetus. Recent research indicates that mild folate deficiency is common, especially among infants, adolescents, and pregnant women. Alcohol and oral

VITAMIN	BEST FOOD SOURCES	ROLE IN HEALTH
FAT-SOLUBLE VITAMINS		
Vitamin A (from retinols in animal products or beta carotene in plant foods)	**Retinols:** Liver, salmon and other cold-water fish, egg yolks, and fortified milk and dairy products. **Beta carotene:** Orange and yellow fruits and vegetables, such as carrots, squash, and cantaloupes; leafy green vegetables.	Prevents night blindness; needed for growth and cell development; maintains healthy skin, hair, and nails, as well as gums, glands, bones, and teeth; may help prevent lung cancer.
Vitamin D (calciterol)	Fortified milk and butter; egg yolks; fatty fish; fish-liver oils. (Also made by the body when exposed to the sun.)	Necessary for calcium absorption; helps build and maintain strong bones and teeth.
Vitamin E (tocopherols)	Eggs, vegetable oils, margarine, and mayonnaise; nuts and seeds; fortified cereals; green leafy vegetables.	Protects fatty acids; maintains muscles and red blood cells; important antioxidant.
Vitamin K	Spinach, cabbage, and other green leafy vegetables; pork, liver, and green tea.	Essential for proper blood clotting.
WATER-SOLUBLE VITAMINS		
Biotin	Egg yolks, soybeans, cereals, and yeast.	Energy metabolism.
Folate (folic acid, folacin)	Liver; yeast; broccoli and other cruciferous vegetables; avocados; legumes; many raw vegetables.	Needed to make DNA, RNA, and red blood cells, and to synthesize certain amino acids.
Niacin (vitamin B_3, nicotinic acid, nicotinamide)	Lean meats, poultry, and seafood; milk; eggs; legumes; fortified breads and cereals.	Needed to metabolize energy; promotes normal growth. Large doses lower cholesterol.
Pantothenic acid (vitamin B_5)	Almost all foods.	Aids in energy metabolism; normalizing blood sugar levels; and synthesizing antibodies, cholesterol, hemoglobin, and some hormones.
Riboflavin (vitamin B_2)	Fortified cereals and grains; lean meat and poultry; milk and other dairy products; raw mushrooms.	Essential for energy metabolism; aids adrenal function.
Thiamine (vitamin B_1)	Pork; legumes; nuts and seeds; fortified cereals; and grains.	Energy metabolism; helps maintain normal digestion, appetite, and proper nerve function.
Vitamin B_6 (pyridoxine, pyridoxamine, pyridoxal)	Meat, fish, and poultry; grains and cereals; green leafy vegetables, potatoes, and soybeans.	Promotes protein metabolism; metabolism of carbohydrates and release of energy; proper nerve function; synthesis of red blood cells.
Vitamin B_{12} (cobalamins)	All animal products.	Needed to make red blood cells, DNA, RNA, and myelin (for nerve fibers).
Vitamin C (ascorbic acid)	Citrus fruits and juices; melons, berries, and other fruits; peppers, broccoli, potatoes; and many other fruits and vegetables.	Strengthens blood vessel walls; promotes wound healing; promotes iron absorption; helps control blood cholesterol and prevent atherosclerosis.

RECOMMENDED NUTRIENT INTAKES* (FOR ADULTS OVER 24)		SYMPTOMS OF DEFICIENCY	SYMPTOMS OF EXCESS
MALES	FEMALES		
1,000mcg R.E.	800mcg R.E.	Night blindness; stunted growth in children; dry skin and eyes; increased susceptibility to infection.	Headaches and blurred vision; fatigue; bone and joint pain; appetite loss and diarrhea; dry, cracked skin, rashes, and itchiness; hair loss. Can cause birth defects if taken in high doses before and during early pregnancy.
2.5mcg	2.5mcg	Weak bones, leading to rickets in children and osteomalacia in adults.	Headaches, loss of appetite, diarrhea, and possible calcium deposits in heart, blood vessels, and kidneys.
9mg	6mg	Unknown in humans.	Excessive bleeding, especially when taken with aspirin and other anticlotting drugs.
80mcg†	65mcg†	Excessive bleeding; easy bruising.	May interfere with anticlotting drugs; possible jaundice.
30–100mcg†	30–100mcg†	Scaly skin; hair loss; depression; elevated blood cholesterol levels.	Apparently none.
230mcg	185mcg	Abnormal red blood cells and impaired cell division; anemia; weight loss and intestinal upsets; deficiency may cause birth defects.	May inhibit absorption of phenytoin, causing seizures in epileptics taking this drug; large doses may inhibit zinc absorption.
19mg	14mg	Diarrhea and mouth sores; pellagra (in extreme cases).	Hot flashes; liver damage; elevated blood sugar and uric acid.
4–7mg†	4–7mg†	Unknown except in medical experiments; then fatigue, low blood sugar, numbness, digestive problems, and lowered immunity.	Very high doses may cause diarrhea and edema.
1.4mg	1mg	Vision problems and light sensitivity; mouth and nose sores; swallowing problems.	Generally none, but may interfere with cancer chemotherapy.
1.1mg	0.8mg	Depression and mood swings; loss of appetite and nausea; muscle cramps. In extreme cases, muscle wasting and beriberi.	Deficiency of other B vitamins.
2mg†	1.6mg†	Depression and confusion; itchy, scaling skin; smooth, red tongue; weight loss.	Sensory nerve deterioration.
1mcg	1mcg	Pernicious anemia; nerve problems and weakness; smooth or sore tongue.	Apparently none.
40mg	40mg	Loose teeth and bleeding gums; bruises; loss of appetite; dry skin; poor healing. In extreme cases, scurvy and internal hemorrhages.	Diarrhea; kidney stones; urinary-tract irritation; iron buildup; bone loss.

* Based on the Nutrition Research Division of Health Canada Recommended Nutrient Intakes (RNIs).

† No RNI has been established; this range is estimated to be safe and adequate.

contraceptives interfere with absorption, increasing the risk of deficiency.

Niacin. Also known as vitamin B_3, nicotinic acid, and nicotinamide, niacin is important in energy metabolism, normal growth, and the synthesis of fatty acids, DNA, and protein. Mild niacin deficiency causes mouth sores and diarrhea; if unchecked, it can lead to pellagra, a disease characterized by chronic diarrhea, dermatitis, dementia, and if untreated, death.

When consumed in high doses (1,000mg or more per day), niacin may lower blood cholesterol levels. But such high doses should be taken only under careful medical supervi-

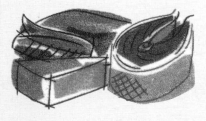

sion, with frequent blood checks for liver damage and high blood sugar.

Pantothenic acid. As implied by its name, which comes from the Greek term for widespread, pantothenic acid is found in almost all plant and animal foods; it is also manufactured by intestinal bacteria. Deficiency is unknown except in medical experiments.

Riboflavin. Essential for the release of energy, riboflavin is needed to metabolize carbohydrates, proteins, and fats. It is also necessary to utilize niacin and vitamin B_6, and it may play a role in the production of corticosteroid hormones. Riboflavin deficiency does not cause any specific diseases, but it can contribute to other B vitamin deficiency disorders.

Thiamine. Also known as vitamin

B_1, thiamine is instrumental in turning carbohydrates, proteins, and fats into energy; it is also needed to convert glucose into fatty acids. Still other important functions include promotion of normal nerve function, muscle tone, appetite, and digestion. A mild deficiency causes fatigue, listlessness, irritability, mood swings, numbness in the legs, digestive problems, and retarded growth in children. Severe deficiency leads to beriberi, a disease that now occurs mostly in alcoholics.

Vitamin B_6. Made up of three interchangeable and related compounds (pyridoxine, pyridoxamine, and pyridoxal), vitamin B_6 is a coenzyme that is essential for protein metabolism. It is needed to release energy in forms that the cells can use, and it is instrumental in the functioning of the nervous and immune systems and the manufacture of red blood cells. Deficiency is noted by oily, scaling skin, especially around the eyes, nose, and mouth; weight loss; muscle weakness; a smooth, red tongue; irritability; and depression. High-dose supplements can cause drowsiness and a loss of sensation in the fingers and legs.

Vitamin B_{12}. Like other B vitamins, B_{12} functions as a coenzyme with many roles. It is essential for the growth and division of cells, as well as for making red blood cells, genetic material, and myelin, the fatty sheath that surrounds nerve fibers. A deficiency can cause pernicious anemia, neurologic symptoms, and weakness.

The majority of cases of vitamin B_{12} deficiency in Canada is not due to

a poor diet; instead, it is almost always caused by an inability to absorb the vi-

tamin from the intestinal tract due to a lack of intrinsic factor. The stomach's production of intrinsic factor declines with age. Many intestinal disorders also result in inadequate intrinsic factor. In such cases, B_{12} must be injected; oral forms will not be absorbed.

Vitamin C. Also called ascorbic acid, vitamin C is necessary to make and maintain collagen, the connective tissue that holds body cells together. It promotes healing of wounds and burns, helps to build teeth and bones,

and strengthens the walls of capillaries and other blood vessels. Vitamin C increases iron absorption and is instrumental in the metabolism of folate, protein, and fats. In addition, it helps prevent atherosclerosis.

Vitamin C has not been proved to prevent colds, but deficiency does increase the risk of infection. More obvious deficiency symptoms are fatigue, joint pain, sore and bleeding gums, easy bruising, weakened bones that fracture easily, and slow healing of wounds. As these symptoms worsen into scurvy, gum ulcers form, the teeth loosen, and hemorrhages can develop.

A recent report found that 200mg a day may be closer to an optimal dose than the current RNI of 40mg. But many people persist in taking higher doses. Doctors warn that even a 200mg daily supplement can cause serious problems for anyone with a genetic tendency to store excessive iron. Very high doses (8g or more a day) can cause diarrhea, kidney and bladder stones, destruction of red blood cells, and loss of bone minerals.

WATER: VITAL FOR ALL LIFE

*Most people don't equate water with good nutrition;
yet it is second only to oxygen as a substance
that is essential to maintain human life.*

Composed of two parts hydrogen and one part oxygen (H_2O), water is by far the most abundant substance in the human body, comprising up to 70 percent of the weight of a reasonably lean adult. Although water contains no calories or other nutrients, the human body can go for only a few days without it. (In contrast, a healthy person can survive for 6 to 8 weeks without food.) A loss of only 5 to 10 percent of body water results in serious dehydration, while a 15 to 20 percent loss is usually fatal.

On average, an adult body contains about 45 liters of water, 30 of which circulate within the cells and are referred to as intracellular fluid. Of the remaining 15 liters, about 3 circulate as blood plasma, which carries protein and other nutrients that can penetrate the capillary walls, and 12 liters comprise the interstitial fluid, which surrounds the cells and makes up lymph and various secretions. With the exception of bone tissue, in which water is tightly held, there is a constant exchange of intra- and extra-cellular fluids through the cell membranes.

VITAL FUNCTIONS

Water is essential to virtually every body function. It is used for the digestion, absorption, and transport of nutrients; it serves as the medium for various chemical processes; it is a solvent for body wastes and also dilutes them to reduce their toxicity and aid in their excretion from the body; and it helps regulate body temperature. In addition, water provides a protective cushion for body cells, and in the form of amniotic fluid, protects the developing fetus. Water is needed to build all body tissues and is the base of all blood and fluid secretions (tears, saliva, gastric juices, synovial fluid, among others) that lubricate the various organs and joints. It also keeps the skin soft and smooth.

As the body ages, it naturally dries out somewhat; for example, the body of a newborn infant is 75 to 80 percent

---

BENEFITS
- *The most abundant and least expensive of all thirst quenchers.*
- *Needed by the body to carry out virtually all of its functions, including chemical processes.*
- *Essential nutrients are transported to body cells via the watery component of blood.*
- *Cushions all body cells.*
- *In the form of perspiration, helps maintain normal body temperature, especially during hot and humid weather.*
- *An essential body lubricant.*
- *Drinking extra water can help prevent kidney stones.*

DRAWBACKS
- *Can easily be contaminated with microorganisms and pollutants.*

---

water, compared to 50 percent after age 65 or 70. This drying out is reflected in the wrinkled skin, reduced flow of saliva, and stiffened joints that occur naturally with aging.

DAILY NEEDS

On average, an adult needs to take in 6 to 8 glasses of water a day. Most of this comes from beverages—plain water, coffee, tea, juices, soft drinks—but a substantial amount is contained in foods. Fruits and vegetables, for example, are 70 to 95 percent water, compared to 75 percent of an egg, 40 to 60 percent of meat, poultry, and fish, and 35 percent of bread. Metabolism of carbohydrates, proteins, and fats also adds a small amount of water.

Daily needs vary considerably; you need to consume more water when the weather is hot, during exercise, or when you have a fever, cold, or other illness. Extra water is also necessary during pregnancy to provide for the amniotic fluid and the expanded volume of blood, as well as to meet the needs of the developing fetus. Nursing mothers need to increase their fluid intake in order to produce milk, which is 87 percent water.

As a general rule, the amount of water consumed should be equal to what is excreted in the urine or stool, vapor from the lungs, or perspiration from the skin. Some dietary components increase the need for water to maintain this balance. Taking diuretics or other drugs that increase urination requires drinking extra fluids; consuming large amounts of tea or coffee has a similar diuretic effect, which can offset the fluids in these beverages. Eating salty foods also increases the body's need for extra water to maintain a proper balance of fluids.

Any drop in the body's water content results in a decrease in the volume of blood, a slight rise in its salt content, and a drop in saliva production. These changes set in motion a chemical and hormonal process resulting in the sensation of thirst, which can be quickly quenched by drinking water or another fluid. In the meantime, the kidneys will conserve water by returning more of it to the bloodstream, resulting in a more concentrated urine. (In this regard, it should be noted that chronic underconsumption of water increases the risk of developing kidney and bladder stones.)

Thirst naturally lessens with age, so older people should make it a point to drink water periodically, even if they don't feel thirsty. Similarly, thirst may lag behind the body's need for water during intense exercise or when it is extremely hot and humid; by the time you feel thirsty, you may already be somewhat dehydrated. To prevent dehydration under these circumstances, drink water or other fluids regularly.

If you drink more fluid than you need, the kidneys get rid of the excess by increasing the volume of urine. If a person drinks vastly more water than the kidneys can handle, the excess is taken up by the cells. In extreme cases, this can lead to water intoxication and a serious imbalance of body chemistry that can result in convulsions and even coma and death. Such extreme overconsumption often reflects a serious psychiatric disorder (psychogenic polydipsia), but it has also occurred in

people who have had severe head injuries or who have lung tumors. It has also been reported among people on fad weight-loss diets that require drinking vast amounts of fluids.

WATER SAFETY

On the whole, Canadians enjoy one of the world's safest and most reliable water supplies; however, thousands of people each year incur a waterborne illness and many episodes of diarrhea and intestinal upset attributed to food poisoning or other causes may actually stem from contaminated water. In addition, a growing number of public health officials are warning that surface water supplies are becoming increasingly polluted by industrial wastes, fertilizer runoff, pesticides, and chemical and nuclear wastes.

Under the Guidelines for Canadian Drinking Water Quality, Health Canada makes recommendations about the conditions which affect the quality of drinking water and specifies maximum acceptable concentrations for certain substances that are known or suspected to cause adverse effects on health. These include levels of coliform bacteria, as well as concentrations of over 40 chemical species ranging from specific pesticide residues to heavy metals. The Guidelines have no legal strength, but are voluntarily adhered to by local authorities. Water that continually contains substances at levels greater than the maximum acceptable concentrations may be deleterious to health, but short-term elevations above these levels are not believed to constitute a risk.

Several recent outbreaks of waterborne cryptosporidiosis, an intestinal disorder caused by the cryptosporidium parasite, have fueled public distrust of tap water. Actually, cryptosporidium, which is shed in the feces of infected people and animals, exists in almost all surface water. The number of organisms is usually too small

TYPES OF BOTTLED WATER

Once consumed mostly by travelers abroad, bottled water has become a fashionable alternative to alcoholic beverages and soft drinks. Still, misconceptions abound about the sources and contents of various bottled waters. The following are the most common types.

• **Club soda** is tap water that has been filtered, carbonated, and flavored with bicarbonates, citrates, phosphates, or other types of mineral salts.

• **Distilled water** is purified by evaporation, which removes its minerals; the vapors are then recondensed into its liquid form—water.

• **Drinking water** is marketed in containers in a wide variety of sizes and brands. It can be drawn from any approved source: municipal tap water, springs, rivers, reservoirs, or wells. It is then filtered and disinfected, and the mineral content may be adjusted.

• **Mineral water** contains at least 500mg of minerals per liter. Products sold as natural water have no added or subtracted minerals; in other products the manufacturer may adjust the mineral content.

• **Purified water** has been sterilized and filtered to remove its natural minerals.

• **Seltzer** is usually tap water that is filtered and carbonated. Artificial flavors are added to some brands, but seltzer does not contain any added minerals or salts.

• **Sparkling water** contains dissolved carbon dioxide gas to make it bubbly. Natural sparkling waters come that way from a spring or other source; otherwise, the carbonation is added.

• **Spring water** is taken from a natural spring; it may be plain or contain gas bubbles, either from natural or added carbonation. The mineral content is usually natural.

to cause disease. Municipal water treatment does not eradicate cryptosporidium, but some commercially available home water filters can remove the organism from drinking water. Most people who develop cryptosporidiosis contract it through poor hygienic practices, such as not washing up after going to the toilet and then handling food. Even when it comes from drinking water, most healthy people shake off the infection in a week or two. However, the disease can be life-threatening among persons with lowered immunity—the very young, the old, people with AIDS, or those taking drugs that suppress the immune system. Using boiled water removes the danger of waterborne infections, but generally does not eliminate chemical contaminants.

LEAD CONTAMINATION

The presence of lead in drinking water has become another major health concern, since high levels of lead can damage the nerves, brain, kidneys, and other organs. A common source of contamination is corrosion of old water pipes and plumbing. Anyone whose home was built before about 1930, when lead pipes and plumbing solder were used, should test their water. The Guidelines for Canadian Drinking Water Quality suggest a maximum acceptable level of 0.01mg of lead per liter.

Some towns and cities still deliver municipal water through lead connector pipes, which were used until the 1970s. Ask your utility company whether it still has such pipes; if so, request that your water be tested and, if necessary, the pipes changed.

Use the cold tap for all drinking and cooking water (hot water leaches more lead than cold). After more than a few hours of disuse, let the water run until it's cold. Because soft water leaches more lead than hard water, use softeners only on the hot-water line. Also, consider using a water filtering system.

WATER IN EVERYDAY FOODS

About one third of our daily intake of water comes from solid foods, and it is surprising just how much water some contain. Fruits and vegetables supply the most, but meat, fish, bread, and dairy products also provide fair amounts.

FOOD	AMOUNT OF WATER
BREADS AND BAKED GOODS	

Most breads are around 35 percent water. Dry crackers are 3–7 percent water; cookies, 3–6 percent; donuts, 21 percent; and cakes, 20–35 percent.

DAIRY PRODUCTS

Soft cheeses are about 60 percent water; hard cheeses, 35–40 percent; and soft, rinded cheeses, 50 percent. Butter and margarines are 16 percent water, while low-fat spreads are about 50 percent water. Milk is about 90 percent water, and cream is 48–80 percent water.

FISH AND SHELLFISH

The water content of various fish is similar, with cod, haddock, lemon sole, salmon, and trout having around 75 percent. Most shellfish contain a similar amount of water, but some, such as oysters, are higher, at 85 percent water.

FRUITS

The edible parts of most fruits and berries generally comprise around 80 percent water. Dried fruits are much lower; dried apricots, for example, are 30 percent water; raisins and currants, 15–18 percent.

JAMS AND SPREADS

Honey is 18 percent water, while fruit jams and jellies are typically 20–30 percent water. Reduced-sugar jam has a greater water content, around 65 percent. Marmalade is 29 percent water, and maple syrup is 32 percent.

POULTRY, MEAT, AND EGGS

Most well-done meats are 40–50 percent water; rare to medium, 50–70 percent. Bologna and other luncheon meats are about 50 percent water; hot dogs, 55 percent. Eggs are 74 percent water.

VEGETABLES

Some vegetables, such as celery and cucumbers, have as much as 95 percent water. Broccoli and cabbage are 90–92 percent water; carrots, 88 percent; and tomatoes, 93 percent. Even a baked potato is 71 percent water.

COOL AND FRESH. *Watercress, which grows in streambeds, is at its best in the early spring. It should be well washed to remove any harmful microorganisms.*

ecules that are produced when the body uses oxygen. A single cup of chopped watercress provides 1,600 I.U. of vitamin A, approximately 15mg of vitamin C, and useful amounts of calcium, iron, and potassium, yet it contains less than 5 calories.

Alternative practitioners suggest watercress to alleviate gastrointestinal upsets, respiratory problems, and urinary tract infections. Some claim that it also acts as a mild antidepressant, an appetite stimulant, and a diuretic. Application of its juice is recommended to clear up ACNE. These health benefits have not been proved, however.

BUYING AND SERVING WATERCRESS

Watercress is only available fresh and is usually sold in bunches. When purchasing the vegetable, look for crisp leaves and a bright green color; bypass any with yellow or wilted leaves. Although watercress may be found in small streambeds, it's not a good idea to pick it in the wild. Streams often contain parasites and bacteria that may cause intestinal infections. Even watercress bought in a supermarket, which has usually been grown in a controlled environment, should be washed thoroughly before it is served.

The pungency of watercress is complemented by citrus flavors. Use a light citrus dressing on a green salad containing watercress, or toss orange or grapefruit slices with watercress for a refreshing fruit salad.

Watercress can also be added to a variety of cooked dishes. However, to preserve its vitamins and to prevent the leaves from turning brown, it should be cooked rapidly (microwaving works well) and served right away.

WATERCRESS

BENEFITS

- *A good source of beta carotene, a precursor of vitamin A, and vitamin C.*
- *A useful source of calcium, iron, and potassium.*
- *Rich in antioxidants, which help prevent cancer and other diseases.*

DRAWBACKS

- *May be contaminated by parasites and bacteria, depending on where it's grown.*

Whether it's eaten raw, used as a garnish, or added to salads, sandwiches, and soups, the dark green, peppery leaves of watercress are among the more nutritious salad greens.

Watercress is a cruciferous vegetable that is rich in ANTIOXIDANTS, BIOFLAVONOIDS, and other substances that may protect against certain types of cancer, particularly those of the digestive system. This green vegetable is also a good source of vitamins A (in the form of beta carotene, its precursor) and C, antioxidants that protect against cell damage by free radicals, unstable mol-

WILD FOODS: NATURE'S BOUNTY

The woods and seashores still harbor the nutrient-rich ancestors of cultivated plants. Hikers and other nature lovers can live off the land if they can identify edible varieties.

Spoiled by the variety and abundance of foods available in supermarkets year-round, in only a few generations we have lost our knowledge of the wild foods our forebears gathered for subsistence as well as seasonal treats. In earlier times, when the food supply was limited by the seasons, people foraged to enrich their diet and treat their ailments.

In spring, fiddlehead ferns gave a vital boost of vitamin C and other nutrients after a long winter with few vegetables available. Today many people living in rural areas—and even city dwellers pining for their country roots—still seek out dandelions and wild asparagus in the early part of spring. These flavorful plants happen to be good sources of vitamins and minerals, as well as the all-important ANTIOXIDANTS and BIOFLAVONOIDS, plant chemicals that can help protect against disease.

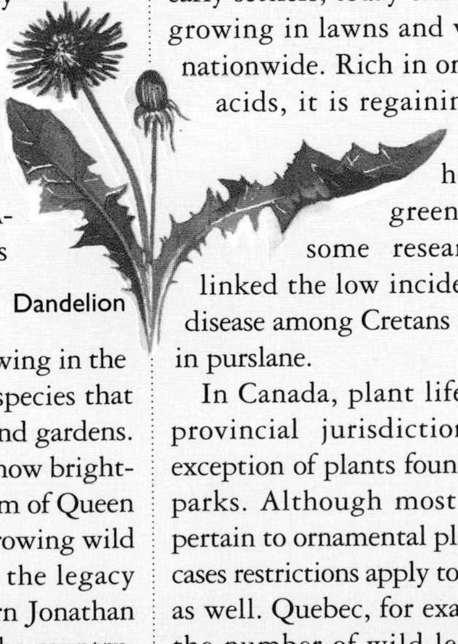

Dandelion

Many edible plants growing in the wild are the offspring of species that were cultivated in farms and gardens. Wind-blown carrot seeds now brighten the roadsides in the form of Queen Anne's lace. Apple trees growing wild in the United States are the legacy of Johnny Appleseed (born Jonathan Chapman), who roamed the countryside for half a century, leaving a

---

> **BENEFITS**
> - *An inexpensive source of vitamins and minerals.*
> - *Unusual flavors contrast with cultivated varieties.*
>
> **DRAWBACKS**
> - *Some edible species have poisonous look-alikes.*
> - *May contain high levels of environmental pollutants.*
> - *Many wild foods require lengthy preparation to ensure safety and palatability.*

---

trail of seeds from cider presses. Purslane, which was brought by the early settlers, today can be found growing in lawns and vacant lots nationwide. Rich in omega-3 fatty acids, it is regaining its status as a chic and healthy salad green. In fact, some researchers have linked the low incidence of heart disease among Cretans to a diet rich in purslane.

In Canada, plant life falls under provincial jurisdiction with the exception of plants found in national parks. Although most regulations pertain to ornamental plants, in some cases restrictions apply to edible plants as well. Quebec, for example, limits the number of wild leeks that can be harvested annually to no more

than 50 bulbs. Check with local authorities before you seek out wild plants, and ask the owner's permission, too, before you forage on private property, no matter how remote the spot.

SAFETY FIRST

Never gather wild plants for food unless you are absolutely certain that you have identified them correctly. Some plants have poisonous look-alikes. Water hemlock, for example, looks like wild ginseng. A few bites, however, can harbor enough toxin (cicutoxin) to kill an adult. Plants can be identified by their leaves, bark, flowers, fruit, and in many cases, scent. Those within a group share a characteristic stem, such as the square stem of the mint family. Often, it's the characteristic underground part of the plant—whether root, bulb, tuber, or rhizome—that is edible, but uprooting it can be destructive unless you definitely recognize it and intend to use the plant.

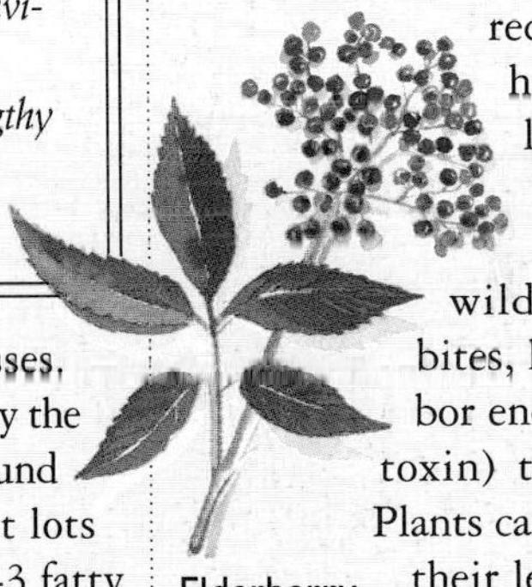

Elderberry

Names don't necessarily help. Edible and poisonous species are sometimes known by similar common names, and names for a single species may change from one region to another. If you have any doubts about a plant, leave it alone.

Learn to recognize the poisonous plants that are common where you live, and familiarize yourself with species you're likely to encounter on hikes or camping trips, or when participating in other outdoor activities.

Many plants have parts that are safe and others that are toxic, such as the elderberry, which has edible flowers and ripe berries but poisonous leaves and stems. Some are edible only in certain seasons, such as the tightly curled fiddleheads in early spring.

MUSHROOMS and fungi are in a class by themselves. It's foolhardy to pick mushrooms in the wild unless you are thoroughly experienced in distinguishing edible varieties from toxic ones.

Edible plants, such as dandelions, sorrel, and purslane, often grow on cultivated lawns. The fertilizers and herbicides approved for lawn cultivation are not safe for food crops, however, so don't forage on a lawn unless you know its history. Because areas alongside railroad tracks are often sprayed with dangerous herbicides, and some homeowners use pesticides to keep ticks away from children and pets, avoid taking plants from these areas.

Golf courses often have wilderness areas, but their surrounding manicured grass is the result of heavy applications of fertilizers and herbicides, which can infiltrate the groundwater as well. Don't be misled by reassurances that only organic chemicals are used. All this means is that the compounds contain carbon; it doesn't mean that they're not toxic. Never eat plants grown on or near a golf course.

Don't forage for edible plants in areas popular with dog walkers, and avoid pastures and woodlands with animal droppings. Plants from these areas are likely to be contaminated with WORMS AND OTHER PARASITES.

Stay off the beaten path: Even though lead is no longer permitted in gasoline in Canada, the soil near well-traveled roads is still contaminated with this heavy metal. Most of the lead from exhaust fumes settles within 50 feet of the sides of the road, but contamination spreads well beyond that limit. Generally speaking, faster-growing plants, such as herbs and grasses, will have less heavy metal contamination than slower-growing species, such as trees. However, certain plants, including fast-growing wild onions, have a greater tendency to accumulate heavy metals than others. Leaves, roots, and stems often contain the highest concentrations of lead; fruits, berries, and nuts generally contain the lowest amounts.

You should collect water plants only after you've had the water source tested. Many water plants—especially those eaten raw, like WATERCRESS—carry parasites and microorganisms that can cause FOOD POISONING. Consult Health Canada for recommendations on local water-testing laboratories.

While many seaweeds are edible, don't be tempted by freshwater algae. As a rule, they contain dangerous nerve toxins and are one important reason why it's not safe to drink from stagnant ponds.

Wild legumes—all plants that look like beans or peas—should be avoided unless foragers are guided by an expert botanist. Plants in this family contain high levels of toxic cyanogens (only trace amounts are found in cultivated varieties) that can lead to cyanide poisoning.

Carefully wash wild plants at home under running water and store them in the refrigerator. Dry

them well before storage, because molds will grow quickly in moisture.

Store seeds, nuts, and grains in sealed paper bags.

Wild leek

CONSIDER ECOLOGY

Take only the parts of a plant you can use. Don't pull up a plant by the roots if you intend to eat only the leaves or stem. When collecting root vegetables, take only as much as you need, since each root means an entire plant is destroyed.

Never take endangered or legally protected plants, and don't harvest even common plants in areas where few grow. Take no more than 10 percent of the usable part of any wild plant. Avoid trampling nearby vegetation, and leave enough mature plants to reproduce and continue the supply.

WOODLANDS

The rich woodland harvest begins when fiddlehead ferns and wild leeks push through the ground cover before the trees sprout enough leaves to shade the forest floor. You can be certain that wild leeks and wild onions are safe to eat because, botanists claim, no plant that smells like an onion is poisonous.

Fiddleheads, the young shoots of ferns, may be eaten only as long as the heads are tightly furled. They should be cooked to destroy thiaminase, an enzyme that breaks down thiamine. Raw fiddleheads can deplete the body of this B vitamin. The below-ground rhizomes can be toxic, and eating the mature fronds can cause hemorrhages.

Sorrel

Dandelions and goose grass contain large amounts of vitamin C. Dandelion greens are edible, either in a salad or cooked;

the cooked shoots and young plants of goose grass make a nourishing dish. Chicory, a bitter green related to the dandelion, can be used as a cooked green or salad vegetable. The taproot, too tough and bitter to eat, may be roasted and ground as a coffee substitute or additive.

Sorrel and its cousins in the goosefoot family are high in

Wild or dog rose

vitamin C, but they contain high levels of oxalates, which can interfere with the absorption of iron and calcium and lead to kidney stones in susceptible individuals.

Chickweed can be eaten raw in salads or steamed; it's a good source of vitamin C and beta carotene, among other nutrients. Chickweed lotions and salves have been used by herbalists to soothe rashes and dry skin.

Rose hips, a rich source of vitamin C, can be gathered in the woods or at the shore in the fall and made into tea, jelly, or syrup. Rose petals add a delicate touch to jelly. Crab

Blueberries

apples are generally too sour to be eaten raw, but they may be pickled or used for a sauce or jelly.

Blackberries and wild raspberries provide vitamins A and C and the B vitamins, as well as calcium, phosphorus, and iron. Wild strawberries are sweeter and more flavorful than most cultivated varieties.

Blueberries, huckleberries, and related berries all share an important feature that distinguishes them from poisonous blue-black berries, such as

deadly nightshade. The edible varieties all wear a crown on the end opposite the stem; in contrast, all the poisonous berries are smooth and rounded. Berries in this family contain

Hazelnut

high levels of anthocyanins, which are believed to improve night vision.

Elderberries may be made into a jam containing high levels of beta carotene, bioflavonoids, and vitamin C. The flowers and berries are safe, but the stalks and leaves are toxic.

WILD HERBS FOR HEALTH

Accustomed to effective painkillers and other medications that relieve symptoms, many people are disappointed when wild plants and herbs fail to provide the same quick fix.

Responsible herbalists recommend the use of herbs to maintain health and promote healing, not to replace the medicines and surgery that doctors use to treat illness.

Even when a herb is known to be therapeutic, it's impossible for most people to judge the amount of active ingredients in a dose. For example, a measured dose of the heart drug digitalis is safe under a physician's supervision; in contrast, taking a handful of foxglove (the plant from which digitalis is derived) may be lethal.

By all means, forage for herbs and wild plants, but don't use them to treat major disorders. Although the plant may do no harm, an untreated disease could be fatal.

Hazelnuts (filberts) are found in the woods as well as on old dwelling sites. Lucky is the forager who finds the tasty hazelnuts before the squirrels and other rodents do. Hazelnuts are a good source of potassium, vitamin A, and the B vitamins. The nuts should be dried well before storage to prevent them from becoming moldy.

Horseradish is especially prolific near old dwelling sites. The huge taproot can be grated into vinegar or a small amount of whipped or sour cream to make a fiery condiment. Diehards use the leaves in salads. Horseradish should always be scrubbed and scraped under running water; its volatile oils can burn the eyes and blister the skin.

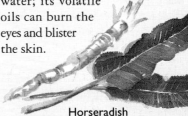

Horseradish

SHORE PLANTS

All plants growing at or near the shore have high levels of sodium and iodine. Therefore, people who are on low-sodium diets should not eat large amounts of plants foraged from these areas.

Seaside sorrel has levels of vitamin C and oxalates similar to its inland cousin. Laver—which is familiar to sushi eaters as nori—is rarely seen on Eastern beaches but is plentiful on the Pacific Coast. Like most seaweeds, laver provides moderate amounts of protein, minerals, and B-group vitamins, as well as some beta carotene in the spring and vitamin C in the fall.

Glasswort, also known as beach asparagus, abounds on salt marshes and is often available at fish markets. It's best cooked; raw glasswort tends to irritate the throat.

WINE

BENEFITS

- *Moderate consumption may decrease the risk of heart disease and certain cancers.*
- *Increases the absorption of calcium, magnesium, phosphorus, and zinc.*
- *Pigments, such as anthocyanins and tannins, may protect against viruses and inhibit the formation of dental plaque.*
- *Promotes relaxation.*

DRAWBACKS

- *May trigger allergies and migraine headaches in some people and increase the risk of stroke.*
- *Excessive consumption can cause liver disease and birth defects.*

A GLASS OR TWO. *Wine in moderation can benefit health, but some people may suffer adverse effects.*

Although the art of wine making is some 7,000 years old, the process of fermentation was not understood until the discoveries of Louis Pasteur in the 19th century. Wine is palatable and resistant to deterioration only after it has undergone fermentation, which is a type of controlled spoilage. Alcohol, a waste product of fermentation, is toxic to all living beings; even the yeasts that excrete it cannot tolerate an environment of more than 15 percent alcohol, which is why fermentation stops at about this concentration. Most French and Canadian wines are about 12 percent alcohol, and American wines, 13 to 14 percent. Extra alcohol is added to fortified wines, such as sherry and port.

THE COMPONENTS OF WINE

Red wine is made from purple grapes, but white wine is not necessarily made from white grapes. Many white wines are made from purple grapes, but the skins are removed before they color the fermenting juice, called must. The skins contain most of the bioflavonoids, phenols, tannins, and other compounds that give wine its flavor and possibly healthful properties. The longer the must stays in contact with the skins,

the deeper the color will be. Some dessert wines are made with specially overripened grapes to achieve a prized sweetness and a rich consistency.

A 4-ounce glass of red wine has about 80 calories, compared to 75 in white wine and 175 in dessert wine. Many wines have trivial amounts of minerals; red wine has a trace of iron.

WINE AND THE HEART

Numerous studies show that moderate consumption of alcohol—two 4-ounce glasses of wine a day, preferably with a meal—is associated with a lower risk of heart disease. Often referred to as the French paradox, a large study that was first reported in 1991 showed that

despite consuming as much or more fat than Canadians or Americans, the French had a heart attack rate only one-third as high as that of North Americans. Annual wine consumption in Canada is about 2 gallons per person, compared to about 17 gallons per person in France.

Researchers have not determined what it is in wine that may prevent heart attacks, but some theorize that compounds such as quercetin and resveratrol in grape skins, as well as other BIOFLAVONOIDS may be responsible. Others speculate that the French habit of drinking wine with meals may provide the small but regular intake of alcohol needed to reduce clot formation, a cause of most heart attacks. Still other research suggests that moderate amounts of wine may raise the levels of the protective HDL (high-density lipoprotein) CHOLESTEROL.

OTHER HEALTH BENEFITS

Laboratory studies indicate that the anthocyanin pigments and tannins in wine can fight viruses, but this effect has not been proved in humans. Tannins can inhibit the growth of plaque-forming bacteria on the teeth and may protect against cavity formation.

Wine appears to contain substances (still to be identified) that slow the rate of alcohol absorption; studies show that a moderate amount of wine has a less intoxicating effect than the same volume of distilled liquor. Still, some claim that wine makes them more sleepy than other alcoholic beverages do; this effect may be due to ingredients other than alcohol.

Compounds in wine promote absorption of calcium, phosphorus, magnesium, and zinc. In older people, an occasional glass of wine may help to ward off OSTEOPOROSIS; excessive alcohol, however, has an opposite effect by promoting calcium loss.

THE NEGATIVE EFFECTS

The benefits of moderate wine drinking, which may extend to reducing the risk of some cancers, are lost when consumption exceeds 8 ounces a day. Overconsumption can lead to alcoholism and cirrhosis and other liver disorders; even moderate alcohol consumption may raise the risk of stroke. In addition, heavy use of alcohol in early pregnancy can cause birth defects.

Most wines contain sulfites and other preservatives that can trigger allergic reactions in susceptible people. Wine, especially red wine, is also a common trigger of migraine headaches.

WORMS AND OTHER PARASITES

EAT PLENTY OF
- *Lean meat, poultry, seafood, legumes, and other iron-rich foods.*
- *Citrus fruits and green vegetables for vitamin C to promote iron absorption.*
- *Animal products for vitamin B12.*

AVOID
- *Undercooked pork and raw fish and shellfish unless prepared professionally.*

With improvements in sanitation and living conditions, many once-common intestinal parasites have almost disappeared from countries with clean water and reliable food supplies. A few parasitic organisms have proved to be unshakable, however, and several have become prevalent as more Canadians travel to remote destinations. Occasionally, a new parasite emerges, such as the cyclospora microbe, which causes recurring diarrhea.

Intestinal parasites come in many shapes and sizes, but the main divisions are single-celled protozoa, or amoebas, and multicellular flatworms and roundworms. While the single-celled organisms can multiply inside the digestive tract, few parasitic worms can reproduce inside the human body, although they may grow in a host for years.

Some worms hardly even make their presence felt, while others cause symptoms that come and go, including fever, coughs and wheezing, diarrhea, and weight loss. No matter how mild or severe the symptoms, all worms drain the host's resources, and most rob the body's stores of iron and vitamin B12.

PINWORMS

These universal parasites typically infest school-age children, causing intense itching around the anus when worms emerge to lay their eggs. A doctor can prescribe a safe, rapidly effective medication; if there are several young children in the family, all may have to be treated. Children should be told to wash their hands every time they use the bathroom and before eating. They may trap worm eggs under their fingernails when they scratch and should be shown how to use a nail brush.

Pinworms seldom cause serious illness, but a longstanding infection may cause ANEMIA. The diet should include low-fat meat, poultry, fortified cereals, and other iron-rich foods; a citrus drink or other source of vitamin C at every meal can help increase iron absorption.

WORMS IN MEAT

Tapeworms from BEEF and PORK are now rare, but pork still must be well cooked to prevent trichinosis, another type of parasite. However, tapeworms and roundworms have been reported more often with the growing popularity of raw fish dishes, such as sashimi and ceviche. Experienced chefs are skilled in preparing raw fish safely, and there is little risk in restaurants. Infections are more likely when smoked or raw fish is served by home cooks.

The common fish tapeworm robs the body of vitamin B12. Symptoms, if present, include fever and fatigue. A doctor will prescribe medication, and recovery may be hastened by consuming foods rich in iron and vitamin B12.

PARASITES FROM PETS

Toxocara canis—a dog worm— and its feline cousin, *Toxocara cati,* are parasites passed in dog and cat feces. Children easily pick up their eggs from contaminated soil in parks and playgrounds. Pet owners should be meticulous about keeping dogs leashed and cleaning up after their pets.

YAMS AND SWEET POTATOES

BENEFITS
- *A rich source of beta carotene.*
- *A good source of vitamins C and B₆, folate, and potassium.*
- *Naturally sweet and high in fiber.*

DRAWBACKS
- *Spoil quickly.*

Although the two vegetables are unrelated, sweet potatoes are often called yams in this country. Sweet potatoes are also not related to the common white POTATO. In their own right, however, these sweet tubers are highly nutritious, and their rich, sweet flavor belies their humble origins as a New World plant that was introduced to Europeans by Columbus and other explorers.

Sweet potatoes derive their flavor from an enzyme that converts starches to sugar. As the tuber matures and is cooked, it becomes sweeter. Immediately after harvesting, sweet potatoes are cured—stored at about 85°F (29°C) for 4 to 6 days—to increase their sweetness and decrease the danger of spoiling.

Like other orange-yellow colored vegetables, sweet potatoes are an excellent source of beta carotene, an ANTIOXIDANT precursor to vitamin A. On average,

a ½-cup serving provides three to four times the Recommended Nutrient Intake (RNI) for vitamin A, about 60 percent of the RNI for vitamin C, 10 percent of the folate RNI, along with a good supply of vitamin B₆. High in dietary fiber, half a cup of sweet potatoes also contains 400mg of potassium and some iron.

Sweet potatoes spoil quickly, and any that have moldy spots or are shriveled should be thrown away. Cutting away the bad spots does not always help, because an unpleasant flavor may have already spread to the rest of the potato. Store sweet potatoes in a cool place but not in the refrigerator; temperatures below 50°F (10°C) will give them a hard core and an off taste.

Since their skins are very thin, sweet potatoes should be treated gently. If peeling is necessary, it is easily done after they are cooked.

Traditional recipes for candied sweet potatoes, a Thanksgiving basic, often call for a lot of unnecessary sugar and fat. A lighter alternative is to use thickened apple juice as a glaze and to substitute pineapples for marshmallows. Sweet potatoes can replace white potatoes and PUMPKINS in a number of recipes, and mashed sweet potatoes with defatted broth or grated orange peel is a vitamin-packed side dish.

YAMS

Deriving their name from the Senegalese word *ñam* ("to eat"), yams are often confused with the sweet potato. Although many varieties of sweet potato are marketed as yams in Canada, true yams are native to Africa and are seldom seen in this country. Growing up to 100 pounds, they are much larger than sweet potatoes and not as rich in vitamins. They are, however, a good source of potassium and starch and are a carbohydrate staple in parts of Africa and Asia.

YOGURT

BENEFITS
- *An excellent source of calcium and phosphorus.*
- *Provides useful amounts of vitamin A, several B vitamins, and zinc.*
- *More digestible than milk for people with lactose intolerance.*

DRAWBACKS
- *Flavored, sweetened commercial yogurt may be high in calories.*

To make yogurt, pure cultures of bacteria are added to pasteurized milk. Fermentation is allowed to proceed until the desired acidity is reached, then it is stopped by cooling the yogurt to refrigerator temperature. A mixed culture of *Lactobacillus bulgaricus* and *Streptococcus thermophilus* consumes the milk sugar, or lactose, for energy and excretes lactic acid, which curdles the milk. (This is similar to the acid that builds up in muscles during intense exercise and blocks energy production, making the limbs feel heavy and weak.) Dried milk solids, gelatin, and other ingredients may be added for body.

The finished product reflects the fat, mineral, and vitamin content of the raw material, whether it be whole or skim milk. Following fermentation, yogurt has only one-third to two-thirds the amount of lactose found in milk, and therefore is more easily digested by people with INTOLERANCE TO MILK.

YOGURT AND HEALTH

Yogurt is a healthful food and a useful source of minerals and vitamins. But claims that the yogurt cultures themselves are curative or healthful are based on the assumption that these bacteria can suppress the growth of harmful microorganisms in the human body. Scientists disagree about the validity of this assumption. Some studies indicate that *L. bulgaricus* does not survive human

SWEET AND SOUR. *Fruit and honey complement the tart taste of plain yogurt.*

with pectin, gelatin, cornstarch, or alginate (seaweed) thickeners. These ingredients do not make a substantial difference to the nutritional content, but people hypersensitive to corn and other additives should check labels carefully.

Goat's milk yogurts are made with whole goat's milk, which adds a sharp flavor. These yogurts are lower in saturated fat and somewhat lower in calories than cow's milk products.

Yogurt can be made at home by mixing a few spoonfuls of commercial yogurt that is made with live cultures into low-fat milk and leaving the covered culture overnight at lukewarm or room temperature.

digestion. More recent research disputes these findings and backs the age-old observation that yogurt is useful in restoring normal intestinal flora. Regardless of who's right, eating yogurt when taking antibiotics (which can upset intestinal flora) does no harm and may well be helpful. Not all yogurts contain live cultures, however; if they do, it will be listed on the label.

An excellent quick snack and a versatile dessert, yogurt can be served chilled or frozen, plain or flavored. Nonfat frozen yogurt contains only 110 calories in a $\frac{1}{2}$-cup serving and gives almost the same pleasure as ice cream, with fewer calories and without the harmful saturated fats.

Because it contains the same amount of fat as the milk it was made with, nonfat or low-fat yogurt is the best choice for those on a low-fat diet. An 8-ounce serving of plain yogurt made with whole milk contains 140 calories, compared to 150 calories for the same-size glass of whole milk. A serving of yogurt contains 415mg of calcium, about 530mg of potassium, and 1.5mg of zinc, with 14mg of cholesterol. Vitamins include 150 I.U. of vitamin A, 1.2mcg (micrograms) of vitamin B_{12}, 23mcg of folate, and 0.5mg of riboflavin.

Calorie content rises considerably with the addition of sweeteners and fruit purees: 8 ounces of low-fat yogurt flavored with fruit and sugar contains about 230 calories, and whole-milk yogurt flavored with coffee, vanilla, or lemon essence and sugar contains 270 calories. Nonfat yogurt sweetened with aspartame is the least calorie-laden, but this sweetener is not recommended for children and is unsafe for people with phenylketonuria (PKU; see Glossary).

Custard-type yogurts are thickened

YOGURT GOES WITH EVERYTHING

• **Fruit smoothie:** Combine $\frac{1}{2}$ cup plain yogurt with $\frac{1}{2}$ cup diced ripe fruit, add one or two ice cubes, and puree in a blender.

• **Yogurt shake:** Blend $\frac{1}{2}$ cup fruit-flavored, frozen nonfat yogurt with $\frac{1}{2}$ cup low-fat milk until creamy.

• **Cucumber dip:** Peel, seed, and dice a large cucumber and combine with 1 cup plain yogurt, salt, pepper, and chopped fresh herbs. Serve as a dip for vegetables, a dressing for salad, or a sauce for fish.

• **Mild salsa:** Mix $\frac{1}{2}$ cup plain yogurt with 1 mashed ripe avocado, 1 diced tomato, and chili powder to taste. Serve as a dip with tortilla chips or a sauce for enchiladas or hamburgers.

• **Vegetable sauce:** Mix plain yogurt with minced fresh dill and chopped cashews.

• **Garnish:** Top cold cucumber soup or vichyssoise with plain yogurt and minced chives.

ZUCCHINI

BENEFITS

• *Low in calories.*
• *A good source of vitamins A, C, and folate.*

Elongated, dark green zucchini are sometimes mistaken for CUCUMBERS. (There is also a golden variety of zucchini, as well as some that have dark green stripes.) Although both zucchini and cucumbers are members of the gourd family, zucchini are closer cousins to PUMPKINS than to cucumbers. Zucchini are by far the most popular summer squash in Canada. (Other varieties include the yellow crookneck squash and the yellow straightneck, which looks like a golden zucchini.) Picked and eaten while still immature, zucchini have a soft shell and tender light-colored flesh.

Zucchini, like other summer squash, are about 94 percent water, making them one of the lowest calorie vegetables. One cup of raw sliced zucchini has less than 20 calories and provides 12mg of vitamin C, 30 percent of the adult Recommended Nutrient Intake (RNI); 28mcg (micrograms) of folate, about 16 percent of the adult RNI; and 250mg of potassium. One cup of unpeeled zucchini also contains enough beta carotene, which the body converts to vitamin A, to make up 10 percent of the RNI for that nutrient. (This important ANTIOXIDANT is lost, however, if the skin is discarded.)

The unobtrusive flavor of zucchini complements other ingredients in a variety of dishes. They are an especially suitable companion to tomatoes and are a splendid addition to vegetable lasagna, marinara sauce, and ratatouille. As zucchini cook, they release water, and this may cause some dishes to become too watery. To avoid this problem, lightly salt the sliced zucchini and set it on paper towels. When enough water has seeped out, rinse to remove the salt and add the zucchini to your recipe.

Squash is an adaptation from several Native American words meaning "something eaten raw"; in fact, all summer squash are tender enough to eat uncooked. Raw zucchini is a pleasant addition to a vegetable platter or salad, and dieters sometimes keep bags of sliced zucchini in the refrigerator for easy snacking.

Orange-colored squash blossoms are edible and contain some of the same nutrients present in the squash. Of these, zucchini blossoms are the most often consumed and are considered a delicacy. However, the blossoms are usually served battered and deep-fried, which adds unnecessary fat and calories. Try sautéing or steaming them instead.

Zucchini can grow very large, and summer gardeners will often find them

---

DID YOU KNOW?

• Zucchini, like other varieties of squash, are New World plants that were cultivated by North America's native people long before the arrival of European explorers and settlers.

• The world record for the largest zucchini is an impressive 64 pounds 8 ounces.

• A single plant can produce more than a bushel of zucchini, explaining why home gardeners who plant a whole row are eager to give away bags of the vegetable.

A DIFFERENCE OF COLOR. *Yellow and green varieties of zucchini are equally nutritious; the flowers are edible too.*

in gigantic proportions lurking under the dense plants. However, zucchini taste best when eaten small—ideally, 6 to 9 inches long. As they grow larger, they tend to become stringy and less flavorful. When buying zucchini, look for ones that feel firm and heavy. Although they can be refrigerated for a few days, zucchini spoil quickly.

ZWIEBACK

BENEFITS

• *An ideal finger food for teething babies.*
• *A nonperishable alternative to bread.*
• *Provides some of the same nutrients found in bread.*

Also known as rusks, zwieback is a crisp bread that is often sold as baby food. The German name means "twice baked" and describes how it is made.

Zwieback was originally developed as an alternative to fresh bread for sailing voyages. It's ideal for camping trips or outings where it is impractical to take bread. It also can be served as an alternative to crackers. But the most popular use is as a teething aid for babies; chewing on zwieback seems to alleviate the gum soreness that accompanies the eruption of teeth.

Because zwieback is dehydrated, ounce for ounce it has more calories than fresh bread; 1 ounce contains 120 calories, compared with 60 calories in 1 ounce of bread. Most of these calories come from carbohydrates, but zwieback also contains some protein and fat; the amounts vary according to the type of bread used to make it.

To retain its crispness, zwieback should be stored in an airtight container. Crisp it in a warm oven for a few minutes if it becomes soggy.

GLOSSARY

The following are important terms that do not appear as separate entries in the book.

ACUTE. Describes a condition that comes on quickly, produces marked symptoms, and rapidly reaches a peak.

ADIPOCYTE. A fat cell.

AFLATOXIN. A poison produced by molds that grow mainly on peanuts, cottonseed, and corn.

ALBUMIN. A protein found in most animal and many plant tissues that coagulates on heating.

ALKALOIDS. Nitrogen-containing compounds produced mainly by plants. Some (codeine, morphine, quinine) are used for medicinal purposes; others (nicotine, solanine in potatoes exposed to light) are poisonous.

ALLERGEN. A substance foreign to the body that causes an allergic reaction (see *Anaphylaxis*).

AMINO ACIDS. Organic (carbon-containing) acids that the body links to make proteins. Nine amino acids are termed essential, because they must be provided in the diet; the body produces the remaining 11 as they are needed.

ANAPHYLAXIS. An extremely severe allergic reaction that can be fatal; it occurs after repeated exposure to an antigen.

ANTIBODIES. Circulating proteins (immunoglobulins) formed by the body to resist future invasion by spe-cific microorganisms or foreign sub-stances (see *Antigen*).

ANTICARCINOGENS. Compounds that are thought to counteract certain cancer-causing substances.

ANTIGEN. A foreign substance that stimulates the body to defend itself with an immune response.

ARRHYTHMIA. An irregularity in the normal heartbeat.

ARTERIOSCLEROSIS. The stiffening and hardening of the arterial walls.

ASPARTAME. An artificial sweetener that is 200 times sweeter than sugar.

BACTERIA. Single-celled microorgan-isms that are found in air, food, water, soil, and in other living creatures, including humans. "Friendly" bacteria prevent infections and synthesize cer-tain vitamins; others cause disease.

BASAL METABOLIC RATE. The energy required by the human body to main-tain vital processes per 24-hour period.

B-GROUP VITAMINS. Although not chemically related to one another, many of the B vitamins occur in the same foods, and most perform closely linked tasks within the body. B vita-mins are known either by numbers or names, or both: B_1, thiamine; B_2, riboflavin; B_3, niacin; B_5, pantothenic acid; B_6, pyridoxine; B_{12}, cobalamin; biotin; and folate.

BIOTIN. One of the B vitamins.

BOTULISM. A serious, often fatal, form of food poisoning caused by *Clostridium botulinum*.

CALCIUM. The most plentiful mineral in the body; a major component of bones, teeth, and soft tissues. Calcium is needed for nerve and muscle func-tion, blood clotting, and metabolism.

CALORIE. The basic unit of measure-ment for the energy value of food and the energy needs of the body. Because 1 calorie is minuscule, values are usually expressed as units of 1,000 calories, properly written as kilocalo-ries (kcal), or simply calories.

CARCINOGEN. A substance that can cause cancer.

CARIES. A decay of tooth or bone.

CAROTENES. Yellow and red pigments that color yellow-orange fruits and vegetables and most dark green veg-etables. They are among the antioxi-dants that protect against the effects of aging and disease. The human body converts one such pigment—beta carotene—into vitamin A.

CELLULOSE. One of the main ingredi-ents of plant cell walls, this indigest-ible carbohydrate is an important source of insoluble fiber.

CHLORINE. A nonmetallic element that is a necessary component of body cells and fluids, such as hydrochloric acid; it is found in gastric juice and is important to digestion.

CHROMIUM. A trace mineral that ensures proper glucose metabolism.

CHRONIC. Describes a condition that develops slowly or lasts a long time.

COBALAMIN. One of the B vitamins, also known as B_{12}.

COENZYMES. Compounds that work with enzymes to promote biological processes. A coenzyme may be a vitamin, contain one, or be manufactured in the body from a vitamin.

COFACTORS. Nonprotein substances that must be present before certain enzymes can function.

COLLAGEN. The fibrous protein that helps hold cells and tissue together.

COMPLEMENTARY PROTEIN. Protein-containing plant foods that lack one or more of the essential amino acids but can be paired with another plant food to supply a complete protein.

COMPLETE PROTEIN. A protein that contains all the essential amino acids. It's found in single animal foods; it can be constructed by combining two or more complementary plant foods.

COMPLEX CARBOHYDRATES. Starches and fiber that have a more complicated chemical structure than simple carbohydrates (sugars).

CONGENITAL. Present at birth, or inborn.

COPPER. A trace mineral necessary for the production of red blood cells, connective tissue, and nerve fibers. It is a component of several enzymes.

DEOXYRIBONUCLEIC ACID (DNA). The basic genetic material of all cells; the "genetic blueprint" that causes characteristics to be passed on from one generation to the next.

DIURETIC. A drug that causes the body to excrete excess urine.

ELECTROLYTES. Substances that separate into ions that conduct electricity when fused or dissolved in fluids. In the human body, sodium, potassium, and chloride are electrolytes essential for nerve and muscle function and for maintaining the fluid balance as well as the acid-alkali balance of cells and tissues.

ENDORPHINS. Natural pain-killers made by the brain, with effects similar to those of opium-based drugs, such as morphine.

ENZYMES. Protein molecules that are catalysts for many of the chemical reactions that take place in the body.

EPINEPHRINE. Also called adrenaline, an adrenal hormone that prepares the body to react to stressful situations.

ESCHERICHIA COLI. Bacteria that occur naturally in the intestines of humans and other animals; one of the common causes of diarrhea and urinary tract infections.

ESTROGEN. A female sex hormone produced in both sexes, but in much greater quantities in females.

FETAL ALCOHOL SYNDROME (FAS). A constellation of mental and physical defects caused in the fetus by the mother's consumption of alcohol.

FOLATE. One of the B vitamins, also known as folic acid.

FREE RADICALS. Waste products of oxygen metabolism that can damage cell components.

FRUCTOSE. A naturally occurring, simple (monosaccharide) fruit sugar.

GASTROESOPHAGEAL REFLUX. When the lower esophageal sphincter opens at inappropriate times, food mixed with stomach acid flows back (refluxes) into the esophagus, causing indigestion and heartburn.

GLUCOSE. A simple sugar (monosaccharide) that the body converts directly into energy; blood levels of glucose are regulated by several hormones, including insulin.

GLYCOGEN. A form of glucose stored in the liver and muscles, which is converted back into glucose when needed.

GRAM (G). A metric unit of weight; one gram is equal to 1,000mg. There are 28.4g to an ounce.

HEME IRON. Iron that is found in hemoglobin in animal foods; the body absorbs about four times as much heme iron as nonheme iron, which is found in plants.

HEMOGLOBIN. The iron-containing pigment in red blood cells that carries oxygen.

HIGH-DENSITY LIPOPROTEINS (HDLS). The smallest and "heaviest" lipoproteins, they retrieve cholesterol from the tissues and transport it to the liver, which uses it to make bile; called "good cholesterol," because high blood levels of HDLs do not increase the risk of a heart attack.

HISTAMINE. A key chemical in the body's immune defense. Released during allergic reactions, histamine causes swelling, itching, rash, sneezing, and other symptoms.

HORMONES. Chemicals secreted by the endocrine glands or tissue; they control the functions of all the body's organs and processes, including growth, development, and reproduction.

HYDROGENATION. The process for transforming an oil (unsaturated liquid fat) into a hard fat by incorporating hydrogen. Hydrogenated fat is similar to saturated fat and linked to an increased risk of heart disease.

INCOMPLETE PROTEINS. Proteins, usually from plant sources, that lack one or more essential amino acids.

INDOLES. Nitrogen compounds found in vegetables and believed to protect against certain cancers by accelerating the elimination of estrogen.

INSOLUBLE FIBER. Fiber, such as cellulose, that passes undigested through the digestive tract.

INSULIN. A hormone that regulates carbohydrate metabolism.

IODINE. A mineral that is essential for the formation of thyroid hormones.

IRON. A mineral that is essential for the manufacture of hemoglobin and the transport of oxygen.

ISOTHIOCYANATES. Plant chemicals that are believed to strengthen the body's defenses against certain cancers (see *Phytochemicals*).

KETONES. Potentially toxic wastes produced from the body's partial burning of fatty acids for fuel.

LACTASE. An enzyme needed for the digestion of lactose.

LACTOSE. The natural sugar in milk.

LACTOVEGETARIAN. A vegetarian who consumes dairy products but no eggs, poultry, fish, meats, or other animal products.

LECITHIN. A phospholipid constituent of cell membranes and lipoproteins; a natural emulsifier that helps stabilize cholesterol in the bile. Lecithin is not an essential nutrient, because it is synthesized by the liver.

LINOLEIC ACID. One of the omega-6 essential fatty acids.

LINOLENIC ACID. One of the omega-3 essential fatty acids.

LIPID. A fatty compound made of hydrogen, carbon, and oxygen. Lipids are insoluble in water. The chemical family includes fats, fatty acids, carotenoid pigments, cholesterol, oils, and waxes.

LIPOPROTEIN. A combination of a lipid and a protein that can transport cholesterol in the bloodstream. The main types are high density (HDL), low density (LDL), and very low density (VLDL).

LOW-DENSITY LIPOPROTEINS (LDLS). These abundant, so-called "bad" lipoproteins carry most of the circulating cholesterol; high levels are associated with atherosclerosis and heart disease.

LOWER ESOPHAGEAL SPHINCTER. A muscular ring at the base of the esophagus; it opens to let food pass into the stomach and closes to prevent acidic stomach contents from flowing back (see *Gastroesophageal Reflux*).

MACRONUTRIENTS. Nutrients the body requires in large amounts for energy—specifically, carbohydrates, proteins, and fats.

MAGNESIUM. A trace mineral that is needed for healthy bones, the transmission of nerve signals, protein and DNA synthesis, and the conversion of glycogen stores into energy.

METABOLISM. The body's physical and chemical processes, including derivation of energy from food, that are needed to maintain life.

MICROGRAM (MCG). A unit of weight equivalent to 1/1000 milligram.

MICRONUTRIENTS. Essential nutrients that the body needs in only trace or very small amounts.

MICROORGANISM. An organism, such as a bacterium or virus, too small to be seen with the naked eye.

MILLIGRAM (MG). 1/1000 gram.

MONOUNSATURATED FATS. Fats that have one carbon-carbon double bond. They tend to be liquid at room temperature and semisolid or solid under refrigeration. They may help protect against heart disease.

MUCOUS MEMBRANE. The moist lining of the mouth, stomach, and many other cavities. It secretes a protective barrier of mucus, which serves as a lubricant as well as a medium for carrying enzymes.

NEUROTRANSMITTERS. Chemicals released from nerve endings that relay messages from one cell to another.

NITRATES. Nitrogen-containing compounds that occur naturally in certain foods. Used as preservatives in some meat products, as fertilizers, and in vasodilator drugs.

NITRITES. Compounds that are produced in the body by the action of bacteria on nitrates; also used as meat preservatives.

NITROSAMINES. Compounds that are formed in the body through the reaction of nitrites with amines in foods; regarded as carcinogenic, although no definite link has been established between nitrosamines and cancer in humans.

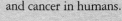

NONHEME IRON. Dietary iron obtained from plants; less well absorbed than iron from animal sources, although consumption with vitamin C (ascorbic acid) promotes absorption (see *Heme Iron*).

ONCOGENE. A gene for cancer; whether or not it is expressed (i.e., develops into cancer), and how fast, is affected by the diet.

OVOLACTOVEGETARIAN. A vegetarian who abstains from meat, poultry, and fish, but consumes eggs as well as milk and other dairy products.

OXALIC ACID. A potentially toxic chemical found in certain plants that inhibits the absorption of calcium, iron, zinc, and other minerals. Can promote the development of oxalate kidney stones.

OXIDATION. A chemical process in which food is burned with oxygen to release energy.

PANTOTHENIC ACID. One of the B vitamins.

PARENTERAL NUTRITION. Direct administration (through tubes inserted into the veins) of nutrient fluids into the bloodstream.

PASTEURIZATION. Heating of milk or other fluids to destroy microorganisms that might cause disease.

PECTIN. Soluble dietary fiber that regulates intestinal function and can help to lower blood cholesterol levels.

PERISTALSIS. Wavelike muscle contractions that help propel food and fluids through the digestive tract.

PHENYLKETONURIA (PKU). A genetic defect that prevents metabolism of the amino acid phenylalanine. People with PKU must follow a phenylalanine-free diet and avoid the artificial sweetener aspartame.

PHOSPHOLIPIDS. Waxy compounds, containing phosphoric acid, that are constituents of cell membranes.

PHOSPHORUS. A mineral needed for healthy bones and teeth, nerves, muscles, and for many bodily functions.

PHYTATES. Salts of phytic acid, found in grains and legumes, that hinder the absorption of minerals.

PHYTOCHEMICALS. Chemicals derived from plants; some have powerful effects, including both the prevention and the promotion of certain cancers, heart disease, and degenerative conditions linked to aging.

PHYTOESTROGENS. Plant chemicals with effects similar to those of the female hormone estrogen; found in yams, soybeans, and other legumes.

PLASMA. The clear yellow fluid that makes up about 55 percent of the blood and carries cells, platelets, and vital nutrients throughout the body.

PLATELETS. Disc-shaped cells, manufactured in the bone marrow, that are needed for blood coagulation.

POLYPHENOLS. Organic compounds, including tannins, that combine with iron and can hinder its absorption; found in a number of foods, tea, and red wines.

POLYPS. Small growths on mucous membranes; rarely malignant, although polyps in the lower bowel may become cancerous.

POLYUNSATURATED FAT. A fat containing a high percentage of fatty acids that lack hydrogen atoms and have two or more carbon-carbon double bonds. They tend to be liquid at room temperature.

POTASSIUM. A trace mineral that is needed to regulate fluid balance and many other functions (see *Electrolytes*).

PROSTAGLANDINS. Hormonelike chemicals involved in many body processes, including hypersensitivity (allergy) reactions, platelet aggregation (blood clotting), inflammation, pain sensitivity, and smooth muscle contraction.

PURINES. Compounds that form uric acid when metabolized; they are found in a number of foods, particularly high-protein foods, such as organ meats. Caffeine (in coffee and tea), theobromine (in chocolate), and theophylline (in tea) are related compounds. People prone to gout or kidney stones should avoid purines.

PYRIDOXINE. One of the B vitamins; more commonly called B_6.

RECOMMENDED DIETARY INTAKE (RDI). Standards established by the World Health Organization (WHO).

RECOMMENDED NUTRIENT INTAKES (RNIs). Defined by Health Canada as the level of intakes of essential nutrients that will meet the needs of healthy people. The RNIs are expressed on a daily basis, but should be regarded as the average recommended intake over a period of about a week.

RIBOFLAVIN. One of the B vitamins.

RIBONUCLEIC ACID (RNA). A substance in every cell that enables the body to develop according to the information contained in the DNA.

SACCHARIDES. A term for sugars.

SALICYLATES. Compounds related to salicylic acid, which are used for making aspirin and other painkillers and as a preservative. Naturally occurring salicylates in fruits or vegetables may produce allergic reactions in people who are sensitive to aspirin.

SALMONELLA. A bacterium that is a frequent cause of food poisoning.

SATURATED FAT. A fat that contains the maximum number of hydrogen atoms. Found mostly in animal products, they tend to be solids at room temperature. They are linked to an increased risk of heart disease, certain cancers, and other diseases.

SELENIUM. An essential trace mineral with antioxidant properties.

SEROTONIN. A neurotransmitter that helps promote sleep and regulates many body processes, including pain perception and the secretion of pituitary hormones.

SODIUM. A trace mineral essential for maintenance of fluid balance; it combines with chloride to form table salt.

SOLUBLE FIBER. A dietary fiber that becomes sticky when wet and dissolves in water.

STAPHYLOCOCCUS. A family of bacteria that can cause disease, including skin infections and food poisoning.

STARCH. A complex carbohydrate that is the principal storage molecule of plants and the major source of carbohydrate and energy in our diet.

STEROIDS. A general class of compounds that includes hormones such as estrogen and testosterone. Synthetic steroids are used as anti-inflammatory drugs.

SUCROSE. A sugar composed of glucose and fructose. The sugar obtained from cane and beets; it's also present in honey, fruits, and vegetables.

SULFITES. Sulfur compounds that are used in food preservation and brewing. They may trigger asthma attacks.

SYNTHESIS. The process by which new compounds are created from components, such as new proteins assembled from amino acids derived from the proteins in food.

SYSTEMIC. Describing a condition or drug affecting the entire body.

TESTOSTERONE. A hormone that is produced in both sexes but primarily by the male testes.

THIAMINE. One of the B vitamins.

TOXIN. Any substance that is introduced into the body in a sufficient amount to cause an adverse effect.

TRACE NUTRIENTS. Nutrients, such as minerals, that are essential, though needed in very small amounts, to maintain health.

TRANS FATTY ACIDS. Fats that have been artificially hardened to remain solid at room temperature (see *Hydrogenation*).

TRICHINOSIS. A parasitic disease; it is caused by consuming *Trichinella* larvae in undercooked pork.

TRIGLYCERIDES. The most common form of dietary and body fat; high blood levels have been linked to heart disease.

TRYPTOPHAN. An essential amino acid found in many animal foods; a precursor of serotonin. Its use as a dietary supplement has been linked with serious illness, most likely due to contamination during the manufacturing process.

UREA. A waste product of the breakdown of protein, which is excreted by the kidneys.

URIC ACID. A nitrogen-containing waste product of protein metabolism. Buildup in the body causes gout.

VEGAN. A strict vegetarian who consumes no animal products.

VERY LOW DENSITY LIPOPROTEINS. A fat-carrying protein that transports mostly triglycerides in the blood.

VIRUS. Infectious, disease-causing particles that reproduce by invading and taking over living cells.

WATER-SOLUBLE VITAMINS. Vitamins that dissolve in water, specifically vitamin C and the B-group vitamins.

XANTHINES. Alkaloid compounds that occur in many plants, including coffee (caffeine), cocoa (caffeine, theobromine), tea (caffeine, theobromine, theophylline), and cola nuts (caffeine); related to *Purines*.

ZINC. A trace mineral that is essential for many processes, including metabolism, the healing of wounds, and normal growth.

HELPFUL ORGANIZATIONS

*The following organizations may be helpful in obtaining
more information about diet and specific disorders.*

**Allergy/Asthma Information
Association**
30 Eglinton Avenue W, Suite 750
Mississauga, ON L5R 3E7
(905) 712-2242

Arthritis Society
250 Bloor Street E, Suite 901
Toronto, ON M4W 3P2
(416) 967-1414

**Bulimia Anorexia Nervosa
Association**
3640 Wells Avenue
Windsor, ON N9C 1T9
(519) 253-7421 (hotline)

**Canadian Association of Poison
Control Centres**
Children's Hospital
840 Sherbrooke Street
Winnipeg, MB R3A 1S1
(204) 787-2591

Canadian Cancer Society
10 Alcorn Avenue, Suite 200
Toronto, ON M4V 3B1
(416) 961-7223, ext. 330

**Canadian Council on Smoking
and Health**
170 Laurier Avenue W, Suite 1000
Ottawa, ON K1P 5V5
(613) 567-3050

Canadian Dental Association
1815 Alta Vista Drive
Ottawa, ON K1G 3Y6
(613) 523-1770

Canadian Diabetes Association
15 Toronto Street, Suite 800
Toronto, ON M5C 2E3
(416) 363-3373

Canadian Dietetic Association
480 University Avenue, Suite 604
Toronto, ON M5G 1V2
(416) 596-0857

Canadian Hemochromatosis Society
272-7000 Minoru Boulevard
Richmond, BC V6Y 3Z5
(604) 279-7135

**Canadian Institute for Health
Information**
377 Dalhousie Street, Suite 200
Ottawa, ON K1N 9N8
(613) 241-7860

Council for a Drug-Free Workplace
44 King Street W
12th floor
Toronto, ON M5W 1H1
(800) 563-5000

Epilepsy Canada
1470 Peel Street, Suite 745
Montreal, QC H3A 1T1
(514) 845-7855

Health Canada
(General Enquiries)
Tunney's Pasture
Ottawa, ON K1A 0K9
(613) 957-2991

Health Canada Food Directorate
Bureau of Chemical Safety
Room 309 B, Sir Frederick G. Banting
Building, Postal Locator 2203 G2
1 Ross Avenue
Ottawa, ON K1A 0L2
(613) 957-0973

Heart & Stroke Foundation of Canada
160 George Street, Suite 200
Ottawa, ON K1N 9M2
(613) 241-4361

**International Association for
Medical Assistance to Travelers**
1287 St. Clair Avenue W, Suite 1
Toronto, ON M6E 1B8
(416) 652-0137

Lupus Canada
Box 64034
5512 4th Street NW
Calgary, AB T2K 6J1
(800) 661-1468

**M.E. Association of Canada
(Myalgic Encephalomyelitis—
Chronic Fatigue Syndrome)**
246 Queen Street, Suite 400
Ottawa, ON K1P 5E4
(613) 563-1565

Ménière's Self-Help
c/o Toronto General Hospital
Room EN7-209
200 Elizabeth Street
Toronto, ON M5G 2C4
(416) 340-3666

The Migraine Foundation
120 Carlton Street, Suite 210
Toronto, ON M5A 4K2
(800) 663-3557
(416) 920-4916

Osteoporosis Society of Canada
33 Laird Drive
Toronto, ON M4G 3S9
(800) 463-6842

**Pediatric Epilepsy Center
at Johns Hopkins Hospital**
Meyer 2-147
600 North Wolfe Street
Baltimore, MD 21287
(410) 296-5386

INDEX

Page numbers in **bold type** refer to illustrations.

CREDITS AND ACKNOWLEDGMENTS

Demos Publications. *The Epilepsy Diet Treatment: An Introduction to the Ketogenic Diet,* by John M. Freeman, M.D., Millicent T. Kelly, R.D., Jennifer B. Freeman. 1994.

The following are among the many organizations that provided helpful materials and information for this book:

Addiction Research Foundation

Agriculture and Agri-Food Canada

Asthma Society of Canada

Canadian Cystic Fibrosis Foundation

Canadian Infectious Disease Society

Canadian Pediatrics Society

Centers for Disease Control and Prevention

La Leche League International

Pediatric Epilepsy Center of the Johns Hopkins Medical Institutions

Statistics Canada

PRODUCTION

BOOK PRODUCTION DIRECTOR
Robert G. Whitton, jr.

PREPRESS MANAGER
Ann Kennedy Harris

BOOK PRODUCTION MANAGER
Michael R. Kuzma

PRODUCTION SUPERVISOR
Joseph A. Fazzi

ASSISTANT
PRODUCTION SUPERVISOR
Tracey Grant

PREPRESS SYSTEMS ANALYST
Karen A. Goldsmith

SYSTEMS ANALYST
Rose Wong

ENGRAVER
Rodney Howe Ltd.

PRINTER
**R.R. Donnelley & Sons
Willard Manufacturing
Division**